Low-Code Application Development with Appian

The practitioner's guide to high-speed business automation at enterprise scale using Appian

Stefan Helzle

BIRMINGHAM—MUMBAI

Low-Code Application Development with Appian

Group Product Manager: Alok Dhuri
Publishing Product Manager: Harshal Gundetty
Senior Editor: Ruvika Rao
Content Development Editor: Urvi Shah
Technical Editor: Maran Fernandes
Copy Editor: Safis Editing
Language Support Editor: Safis Editing
Project Coordinator: Deeksha Thakkar
Proofreader: Safis Editing
Indexer: Sejal Dsilva
Production Designer: Prashant Ghare
Marketing Coordinator: Deepak Kumar

First published: April 2022
Production reference: 2120822

Published by Packt Publishing Ltd.
Livery Place
35 Livery Street
Birmingham
B3 2PB, UK.

978-1-80020-562-8

www.packt.com

To all the colleagues and customers from whom I have learned so much over the years on the winding path I now call my career.

– Stefan Helzle

Contributors

About the author

Stefan Helzle is a manager at PricewaterhouseCoopers WPG GmbH, Germany. He has dedicated his career to low-code enterprise software development and is an Appian Certified Solution Architect and Appian Certified Lead Developer with expertise in finance, insurance, healthcare, IT services, and pharmaceuticals. He has been working since 2009 as a business analyst, Appian Senior Developer, and Consultant Appian Solution Architect. Since 2015, Stefan has built a team of over 30 Appian designers, conducted foundation training for almost 100 colleagues and clients, mentored and coached all colleagues, and supported them in more than 30 projects. He has worked on Appian projects as diverse as re-insurance claims management and underwriting, a management suite for podiatry therapists, ITIL-based IT service management, procurement (requests, approvals, tendering, supplier management), end-to-end car financing and leasing processes, and a document intake OCR and data extraction platform.

I want to thank the people who have been close to me and supported me, especially my wife, Andreja, my son, Samuel, and my daughters, Lisa and Dana.

About the reviewer

Marcel Paradies is an Appian practioner with more than five years of experience in IT. He has worked in both the pharmaceutical and the insurance industries and is currently overseeing the Appian platform at a multinational corporation, where he is responsible for architecture and governance.

Andres Felipe Cortes Novoa is a husband and a systems analyst at Bison transport in Canada. He is a former business analyst and Appian developer at Citibank. He was a risk technology analyst at Scotiabank as well as a technology consultant at Tata Consultancy Services in Colombia. He has worked for more than 10 years in the IT field providing stakeholders with accurate solutions to their business. In 2017 he completed a post-graduate certificate in information security, which has enabled him to explore different areas in the IT field, and his education has provided many opportunities for him to give back to different companies.

Table of Contents

Preface

Section 1: No-Code with Appian Quick Apps

1

Creating an Appian Quick App

Login and first contact with Appian	4	Setting permissions and generating an app	15
Naming your Quick App	10	Testing your app	17
Defining case data	11	Summary	22
		Further reading	22

2

Features and Limitations of Appian Quick Apps

Managing record items in Quick Apps	24	Reporting in Quick Apps	32
Managing tasks in Quick Apps	25	Modifying a Quick App	33
Managing documents in Quick Apps	31	Summary	36

3

Building Blocks of Appian Quick Apps

The basic workings of the Appian Designer environment	38	Tempo	42
Introduction to Appian Records	40	List	42
		User filters	44
Source & Default Filters	42	Views	45

Related Actions   46
Performance   48

**Checking the Appian process
models**   48

Learning about Appian
interfaces   51

Understanding Appian
expression rules   56

Object dependencies in Appian   61

Summary   62

4
The Use Cases for Appian Quick Apps

Managing conference attendees   64
Advanced task management   67

The simple software
development process   70

Requirements management   71
Product backlog   71

Summary   75

Section 2: A Software Project with Appian

The meaning of software
development   77

Software development using
Appian   78

Starting a software project
using Appian   79

5
Understanding the Business Context

The people at Tarence Limited   82

Christine – Business Owner   82
Paul – Product Owner   83
Melanie – Key Stakeholder   83
Igor – IT Architect   84
Beth – Key User   84
You   85

Discovering the IT landscape   86

Business architecture   87
Information architecture   88

Technology architecture   89

Motivation for the project   90

Cost reduction   90
Scaling up   90
Team upskill   90

**Implementing low-code
Business Process Management
(BPM)**   90

The potential of Appian   91

The expectations of companies 92
Goals versus potential versus change 92

Summary 93

6

Understanding Business Data in Appian Projects

Learning objectives 96
Main business data entities 97
Adding relations 99
One-to-one 100
One-to-many 100
Many-to-many 100

Adding details 101
UID 102
External IDs 102
Name 103
Description 103

Created 103
Modified 103
Status 103

Adding application data 105
Process data 105
Audit trail 105
Monitoring 105
Reporting 106

Finding the right level 108
Summary 108

7

Understanding Business Processes in Appian Projects

Learning objectives 110
Useful methodologies 110
Business-Process-Modeling-Notation 110
Five-Whys 111
Ishikawa diagram 112
SIPOC 112

As-is process 114
Software-driven processes 116

Task-driven processes 116
Case management 117
Basic principles 117
Theses 117

To-be process 119
Summary 122

8

Understanding UX Discovery and the UI in Appian Projects

Understanding UX discovery 124
User experience 124
User interface 125

Supporting people doing their tasks 126
Scope 126

Information	127	The benefits of wireframes	130
Input	127		
Orientation	127	**Designing screens in an Appian context**	**131**
Understanding management needs	**127**	Record	131
		Task	132
A wireframing introduction and tools	**128**	Report	134
		Summary	**135**
Understanding wireframes	129		

Section 3: Implementing Software

9

Modeling Business Data with Appian Records

Creating the application object	**140**	**Records**	**156**
Custom data types	**144**	Creating records	157
Creating the CDT	145	**Relationships**	**162**
Creating more fields	148	Adding many-to-many relations	168
Creating more CDTs	150		
		Best practices	**171**
Data stores	**151**	**Summary**	**171**
Creating the data store	152		
Managing the database	155		

10

Modeling Business Processes in Appian

A first simple process	**174**	Cancel behavior	196
Creating the model	174	**Adding related actions and record actions**	**200**
Adding a process variable	178		
Adding the start form	179	Updating a record	200
Testing the model	183	Deleting a record	205
Persisting data	**185**	**Completing the process**	**207**
Adding the process to the record	**190**	Modifying the Create Invoice interface	208
		Setting up the case	210
Assigning the process	191	Assigning the first task	216

Best practices	219	Process data flow	219
Process modeling habits	219	Summary	220

11

Creating User Interfaces in Appian

Technical requirements	222	Creating reusable interface components	254
Creating interfaces from scratch	222	This happens next	254
Record views	222	Formatted amount field	255
Process start forms	236	**Best practices**	**256**
User Input Task	242	User experience	256
Sites	247	Expression mode versus design mode	257
Adding validation logic	249	Performance view	257
Date validation	249	Variable flow	258
Range check	250	Local variables	258
		Rule inputs	258
Creating dynamic interfaces	251	Reusable components	258
		Debugging	258
		Summary	259

12

Task Management with Appian

Technical requirements	262	Exceptions	278
Assigning tasks	262	Process reports	279
Reassignment behavior	263	Creating a process report	280
Re-assignment privileges	264	Display a process report	282
Process model security and reassignment	264	Completing the process	286
Dynamic task assignment	265	An interface for Clarify Invalid Invoice	287
Assigning tasks using process variables	266	Modify initial verification	291
Assigning tasks using decision tables	267	The task and interface for Assign Invoice	297
Escalations and exceptions	271	Logic to finalize the invoice and the case	298
Escalations	275		

Best practices	**300**	Task exceptions	300
Using groups	300	**Summary**	**301**
Task due date	300		

13
Reporting and Monitoring with Appian

Data sources and preparation	**304**	**Visualizing data**	**316**
Monitoring process activity	304	Status over timeline chart	317
Reporting	304	Case status donut chart	320
Periodic data measurement	305	Case grid	322
Storing measurements	306	Billboard cards	323
Preparing the case record	307		
Measuring data	308	**Adding interaction**	**330**
Completing the measuring process model	310	**Best practices**	**335**
		Stakeholder groups	335
Aggregating data	**313**	Historic reports	336
		Make reports interactive	336
Cases over time	313	Composing reports	336
Current case status	313	**Summary**	**337**

Section 4: The Code in Appian Low-Code

14
Expressing Logic with Appian

Decisions – simple logic in a visual designer	**342**	Documents	349
		Process models	349
Input configuration	344	Constants summary	349
Output configuration	345		
Decisions summary	347	**Expressions – constant logic expressed in text**	**349**
Constants – managing literals and application configuration	**347**	Programming paradigms	349
		Inputs, locals, and outputs	353
String literals	347	Data types	355
Groups	348	Dictionaries and maps	357
Data store entities	348	Working with lists	360

Best practices   371

15
Using Web Services with Appian Integrations

Technical requirements	374	OpenAPI summary	384
HTTPS, authentication, and JSON	374	**Connected systems and integrations**	**385**
HTTPS	374	Creating a web service	385
HTTP request	375	Integrating the web service	388
HTTP response	377		
Security	377	**Using integrations**	**396**
JSON	378	**Best practices**	**399**
OpenAPI basics	**382**	Validate incoming data	399
		Wrapping integrations	400
servers	383	Security	401
paths	384		
components	384	**Summary**	**401**

16
Useful Implementation Patterns in Appian

Technical requirements	404	Designing for reusability	412
Solution patterns	404	Expression rule patterns	414
Process versus case management	404	Managing collections of constants	414
Recording audit trails	405	Universal null check	416
Record security	405	Nested indexing	417
CDT first versus database first	407	Validating IBANs	419
Waiting for external triggers	407	Flexible looping predicate	421
		Additional Appian modules	423
Process patterns	**408**	IDP	424
Creating process chains	408	RPA	424
Using subprocesses	408	Process mining	425
Multiple Node Instances	409	Appian Portals	425
Building loops in processes	410		
		Summary	**426**
Interface patterns	**411**		
Building wizards	411		
Tabbed interfaces	412		

Summary   371

Index

Other Books You May Enjoy

Preface

The analysts at Venture Beat, Gartner, and others expect that by 2024, 80% of enterprise software development will be low-code. There are many flavors of low-code available on the market. **Robotic Process Automation (RPA)** tries to automate manual interaction with software and systems missing technical interfaces. Other systems allow the creation of workflows on documents.

Appian enables us to go a huge step further. Using Appian, we implement a whole end-to-end business process, not just a small step in it. We use technologies such as process automation, RPA, and Artificial Intelligence to transfer the business process into software. We relieve people from tedious and repetitive manual work and empower them to concentrate on their business challenges and decision-making.

This book enables you to be part of this movement.

This book is an exhaustive overview of how the Appian Low-Code BPM Suite enables tech-savvy professionals to rapidly automate business processes across their organization, integrating people, software bots, and data. This practical guide helps you master business application development with Appian as a beginner low-code developer. At first, you'll learn the power of no-code with Appian Quick Apps to solve some of your most crucial business challenges. You'll then get to grips with the building blocks of an Appian, starting with no-code and advancing to low-code, eventually transforming complex business requirements into a working enterprise-ready application.

By the end of this book, you'll be able to deploy Appian Quick Apps in minutes and successfully transform a complex business process into low-code process models, data, and UIs to deploy full-featured, enterprise-ready, process-driven, mobile-enabled apps.

Who this book is for

This book is for software developers and tech-savvy business users. *Low-Code Application Development with Appian* gives software developers a new tool with which to increase efficiency by a huge margin, and it speeds up the delivery of new features to the ever-demanding business departments. Business users with a maker's attitude finally have the chance to get closer to developing their own business applications, as low-code drastically reduces the complexity of traditional software development.

What this book covers

Chapter 1, Create an Appian Quick App, covers building a simple application using no code.

Chapter 2, Features and Limitations of Appian Quick Apps, contains a detailed view of Quick Apps features.

Chapter 3, Building Blocks of Appian Quick Apps, explains how Quick Apps work.

Chapter 4, The Use Cases for Appian Quick Apps, discusses how to make the most out of Quick Apps.

Chapter 5, Understanding the Business Context, explains the business background for the book's project.

Chapter 6, Understanding Business Data in Appian Projects, contains methodologies and patterns in data modeling.

Chapter 7, Understanding Business Processes in Appian Projects, explains how to analyze a business process and prepare it for automation.

Chapter 8, Understanding UX Discovery and UI in Appian Projects, shows you how to create an application experience users deserve.

Chapter 9, Modeling Business Data with Appian Records, covers converting the abstract data model into a real model.

Chapter 10, Modeling Business Processes in Appian, discusses creating automated workflows from process diagrams.

Chapter 11, Creating User Interfaces in Appian, explains how to turn wireframes into actionable forms.

Chapter 12, Task Management with Appian, covers task assignment and automated management.

Chapter 13, *Reporting and Monitoring with Appian*, explains designing visual dashboards using real-time data.

Chapter 14, *Expressing Logic with Appian*, dives deep into Appian business logic.

Chapter 15, *Using Web Services with Appian Integrations*, shows you how to integrate systems easily using low-code.

Chapter 16, *Useful Implementation Patterns in Appian*, explains how to speed up development and solve common challenges.

To get the most out of this book

You will need access to an Appian environment version 21.3 or higher. This can be your corporate development sandbox or the Appian Community Edition you can request from your Appian Community account.

While Appian is constantly evolving the platform in a quarterly release cycle, the code and concepts in this book will keep working in future versions.

If you are using the digital version of this book, we advise you to type the code yourself or access the code from the book's GitHub repository (a link is available in the next section). Doing so will help you avoid any potential errors related to the copying and pasting of code.

Download the example code files

You can download the example code files for this book from GitHub at `https://github.com/PacktPublishing/Low-Code-Application-Development-with-Appian`. If there's an update to the code, it will be updated in the GitHub repository.

We also have other code bundles from our rich catalog of books and videos available at `https://github.com/PacktPublishing/`. Check them out!

Download the color images

We also provide a PDF file that has color images of the screenshots and diagrams used in this book. You can download it here: `https://static.packt-cdn.com/downloads/9781800205628_ColorImages.pdf`

Conventions used

There are a number of text conventions used throughout this book.

1. `Code in text`: Indicates code words in text, database table names, folder names, filenames, file extensions, pathnames, dummy URLs, user input, and Twitter handles. Here is an example: "Remove some columns, but keep at least the following:

   - `ID`
   - `Created At`
   - `Owner`
   - `Status`
   - `Due At`
   - `Priority`

Bold: Indicates a new term, an important word, or words that you see onscreen. For instance, words in menus or dialog boxes appear in **bold**. Here is an example: "In **Case Record**, click **NEW CUSTOM RECORD FIELD**.

Select **Extract Partial Dates** and click **NEXT**.

Select **createdAt** as the field and **Date** for **Unit of Time**, and click **NEXT**."

> **Tips or important notes**
> Appear like this.

Get in touch

Feedback from our readers is always welcome.

General feedback: If you have questions about any aspect of this book, email us at customercare@packtpub.com and mention the book title in the subject of your message.

Errata: Although we have taken every care to ensure the accuracy of our content, mistakes do happen. If you have found a mistake in this book, we would be grateful if you would report this to us. Please visit www.packtpub.com/support/errata and fill in the form.

Piracy: If you come across any illegal copies of our works in any form on the internet, we would be grateful if you would provide us with the location address or website name. Please contact us at copyright@packt.com with a link to the material.

If you are interested in becoming an author: If there is a topic that you have expertise in and you are interested in either writing or contributing to a book, please visit authors.packtpub.com.

Share Your Thoughts

Once you've read *Low-Code Application Development with Appian*, we'd love to hear your thoughts! Scan the QR code below to go straight to the Amazon review page for this book and share your feedback.

https://packt.link/r/1-800-20562-7

Your review is important to us and the tech community and will help us make sure we're delivering excellent quality content.

Learn more on Discord

To join the Discord community for this book – where you can share feedback, ask questions to the author, and learn about new releases – follow the QR code below:

http://packt.link/lcncdserver

Section 1: No-Code with Appian Quick Apps

The classic program in software development is "Hello World". Its purpose is to get in touch with the tools required to write and run a program. You will need to download and install software packages, restart your computer, and go through a complex process. In the end, you will have written a program that prints "Hello World" in a console window.

Creating an Appian **Quick App** is a great way of getting in touch with the Appian environment. No download or installation is required. Open your browser, log in, and get familiar with the different parts of the environment. You'll get your first application up and running in no time.

You will learn how to build an application without any coding, in less than 30 minutes, and it will add real business value and not just print "Hello World" to the screen.

This section contains the following chapters:

- *Chapter 1, Create an Appian Quick App*
- *Chapter 2, Features and Limitations of Appian Quick Apps*
- *Chapter 3, Building Blocks of Appian Quick Apps*
- *Chapter 4, The Use Cases for Appian Quick Apps*

1
Creating an Appian Quick App

In this chapter, you will have your first contact with the Appian platform and create your first app. Creating an app will give you an impression of how the Appian **user interface (UI)** looks. You will define the data fields of a case as the foundation of that app. Appian will then automatically generate a framework of ready-made functionality around case management, task assignment, document management, and reporting.

The use case for this Quick App is the management of improvement requests by the **quality assurance (QA)** department. Typically, you will receive improvement requests by email, a phone call, or in a nice chat at the coffee machine. You enter and manage them in the Quick App to improve collaboration and transparency in your team.

We'll be covering the following topics in this chapter:

- Login and first contact with Appian
- Naming your Quick App
- Defining case data
- Setting permissions and generating an app
- Testing your app

Getting your own Appian Community Edition is simple. Create an account at `community.appian.com`, go to your profile page, and request and manage your own Appian environment.

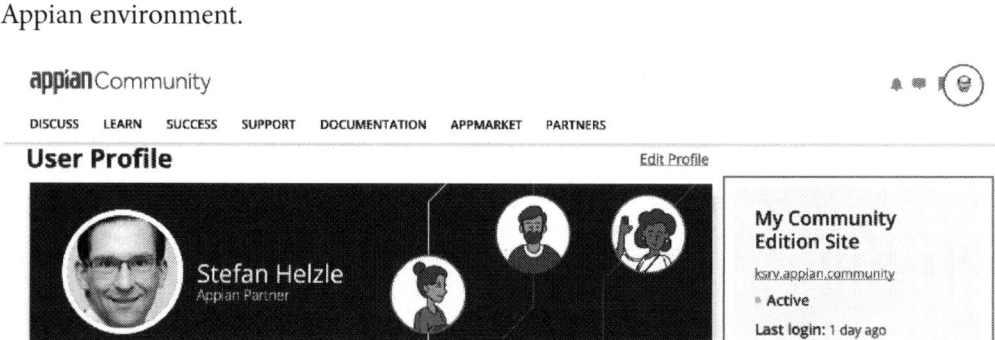

Figure 1.1 – Appian Community profile

Login and first contact with Appian

To get started, you will need to log in to your Appian environment (the Community Edition or a corporate one). If your company enabled **single sign-on** (**SSO**), you do not need to enter a username and password and you can skip *step 3*. The following steps will guide you to the **Quick Apps Designer**:

1. Enter the web address of your Appian environment. If you use the Community Edition, you will need to accept the license agreement.

2. Once you are done with that, you will get the login screen. There, you will need to enter your credentials and click **Sign In**.

3. Appian Community Edition greets you with a nice screen with information on how to learn more about the Appian platform, as illustrated in the following screenshot:

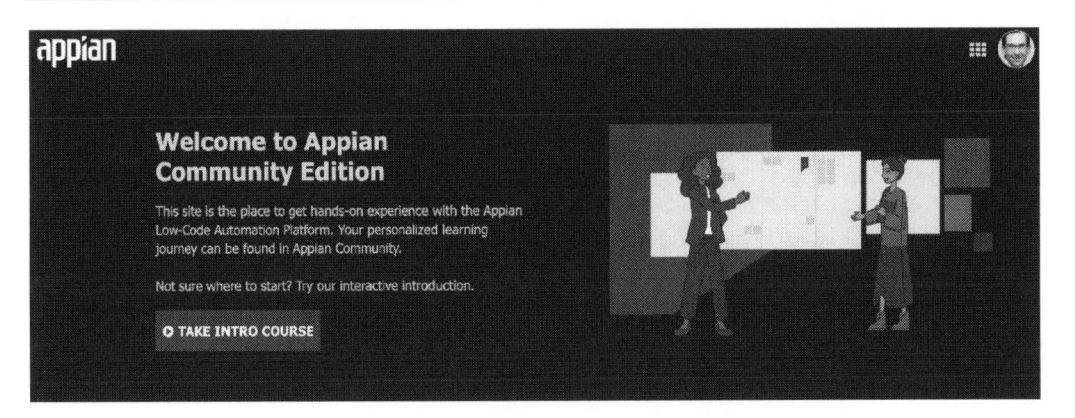

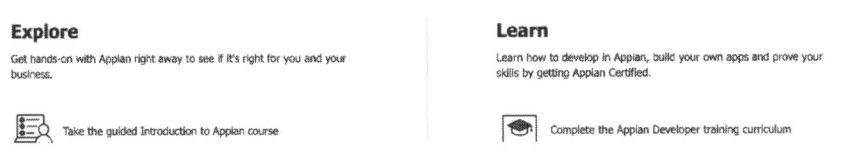

Figure 1.2 – Appian Community Edition after login

4. From the waffle menu at the top right of the screen, select **Quick Apps Designer**, as illustrated in the following screenshot:

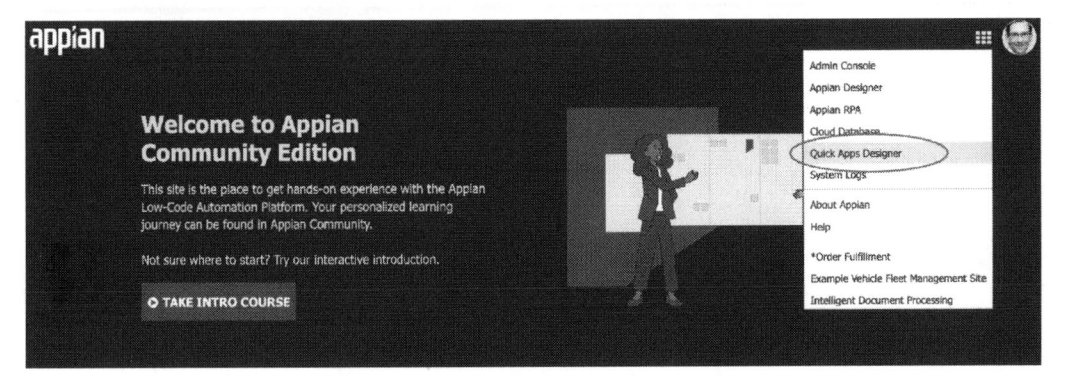

Figure 1.3 – The Appian waffle menu and its items

In case you do not see the **Quick Apps Designer** item in the waffle menu, please follow the next five simple steps:

> **Tip**
> This will only work if you are an administrator user in your environment. So, contact your system administrator if you are working in a corporate environment and do not see that menu item.

5. Open the **Appian Administration Console** by clicking the **Admin Console** item in the waffle menu, as illustrated in the following screenshot:

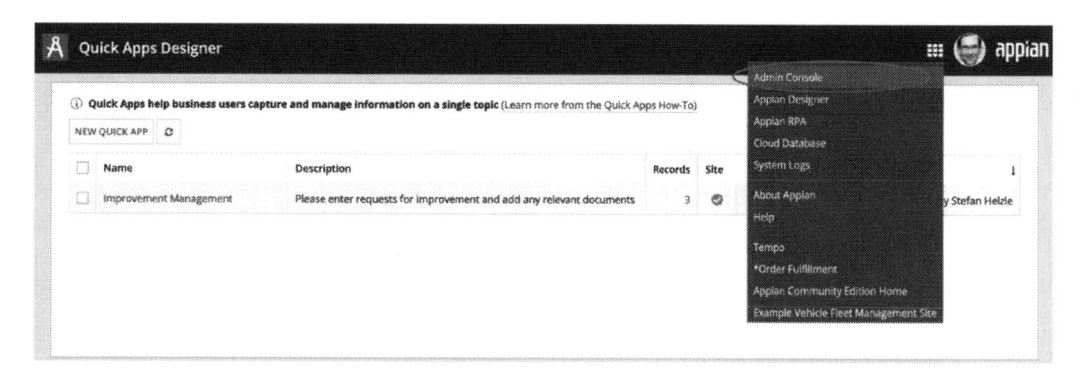

Figure 1.4 – Opening Admin Console

6. Navigate to the **Permissions** tab, as illustrated in the following screenshot:

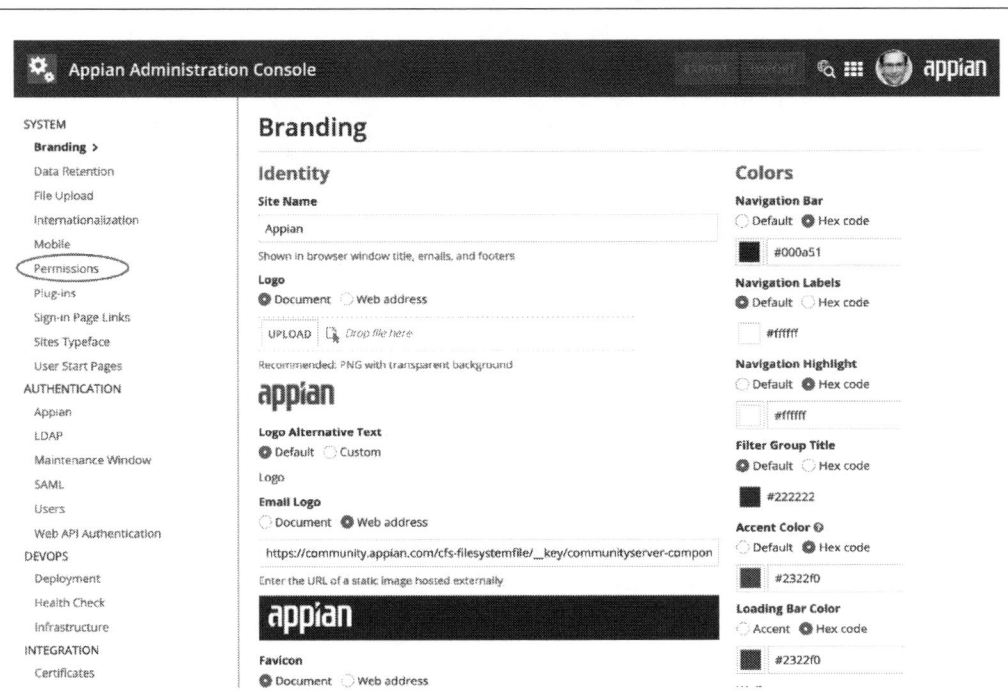

Figure 1.5 – The Appian Administration Console

7. Click the **Add Users to the Quick App Creators role** link, as illustrated in the following screenshot:

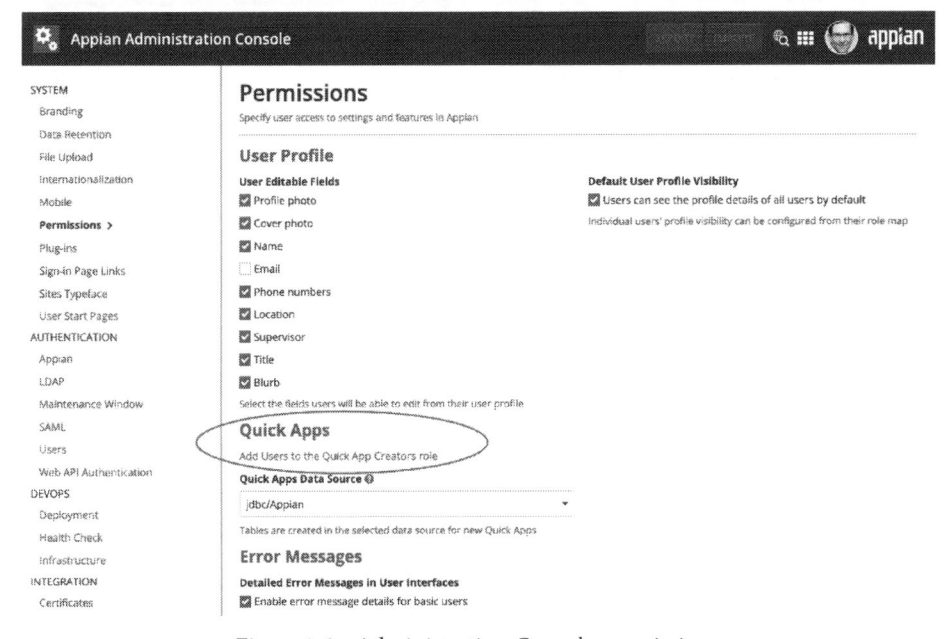

Figure 1.6 – Administration Console permissions

8. Click **ADD MEMBERS** in the membership list of the **Quick App Creators** group, as illustrated in the following screenshot:

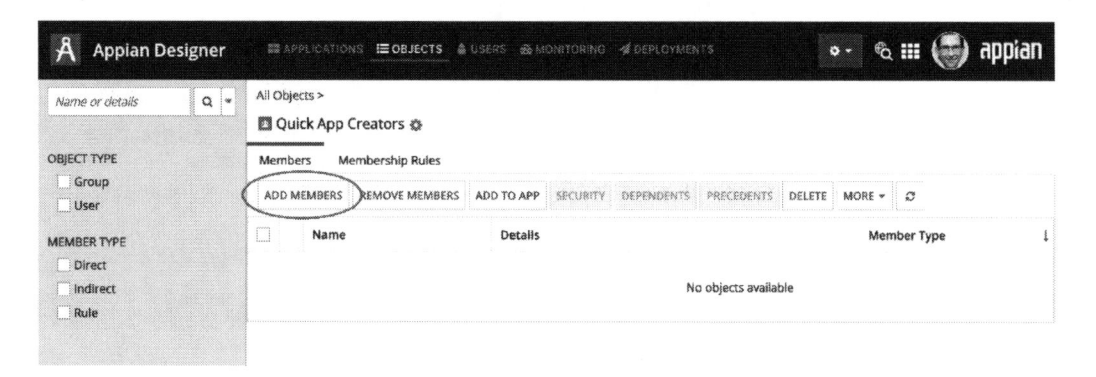

Figure 1.7 – Membership list

9. Enter **Designers** and click **ADD**, as illustrated in the following screenshot:

Figure 1.8 – The group to be added

10. Appian will reload the screen to reflect that change. Now, all users who have access to the Appian design environments also have access to the **Quick Apps Designer**, as reflected in the following screenshot:

Quick App Creators ⚙

| Members | Membership Rules |

| ADD MEMBERS | REMOVE MEMBERS | ADD TO APP | SECURITY | DEPENDENTS | PRECEDENTS | DELETE | MORE ▾ | ↻ |

	Name	Details	Member Type
☐	Designers	Members of this group will be able to design applications.	Direct
☐	Process Model Creators	Members of this group will be able to create new process models	Indirect
☐	CEH Designers	Users who have access to design objects	Indirect
☐	Appian Administrator	Administrator	Indirect
☐	AppianRPA.sa Service Account	AppianRPA.sa	Indirect
☐	community admin	community.admin	Indirect
☐	Stefan Helzle	stefan.helzle@pwc.com community.admin	Indirect

Figure 1.9 – Group added

You have now modified the permissions in the Appian environment and made the **Designers** group a member of **Quick App Creators**. As you are a member of **Designers**, you now have permission to access the **Quick Apps Designer** as well. If you want to allow everybody to create **Quick Apps**, add the **All Users** group instead. You might need to reload the browser window or log out and log in for the permission changes to take effect.

Click the **NEW QUICK APP** button in the top left of the screen, as illustrated in the following screenshot, to initiate a simple four-step wizard:

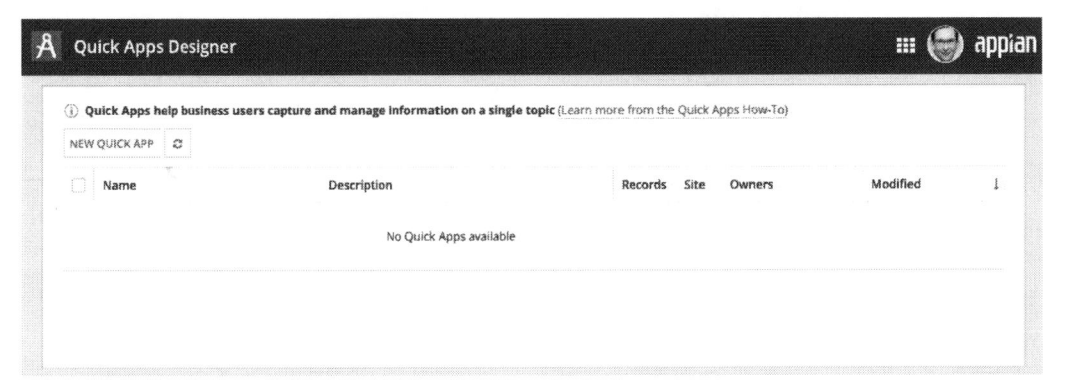

Figure 1.10 – The Quick Apps Designer

Naming your Quick App

To get started, think about a proper name and description for your new **Quick App**. Then, give the entries a name that implies what to enter. This helps your team to understand what the new app is about. Next, proceed as follows:

1. Appian asks for some basic information, as shown in the following screenshot, which you enter according to the use case idea of improvement management:

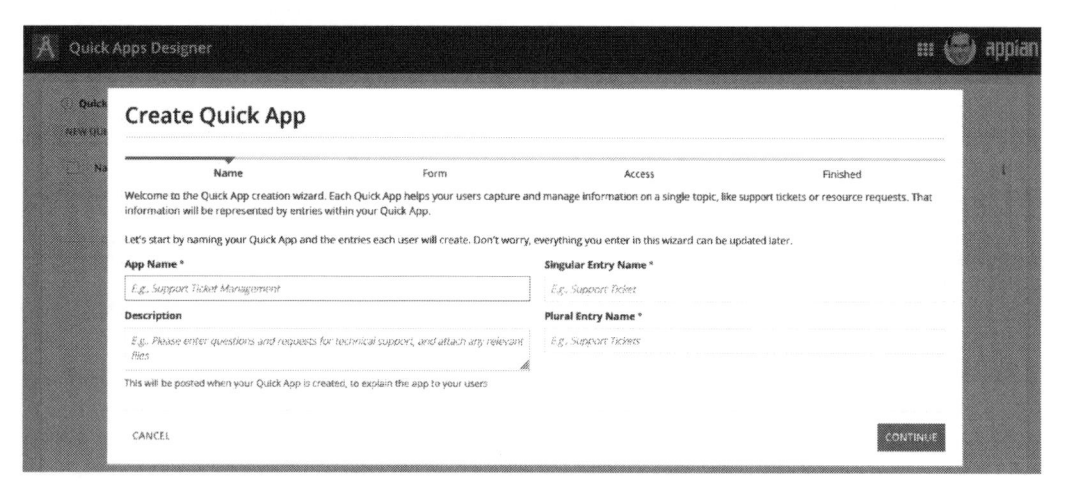

Figure 1.11 – Quick App and entry naming

2. Click the **CONTINUE** button shown in the following screenshot to get to the next step:

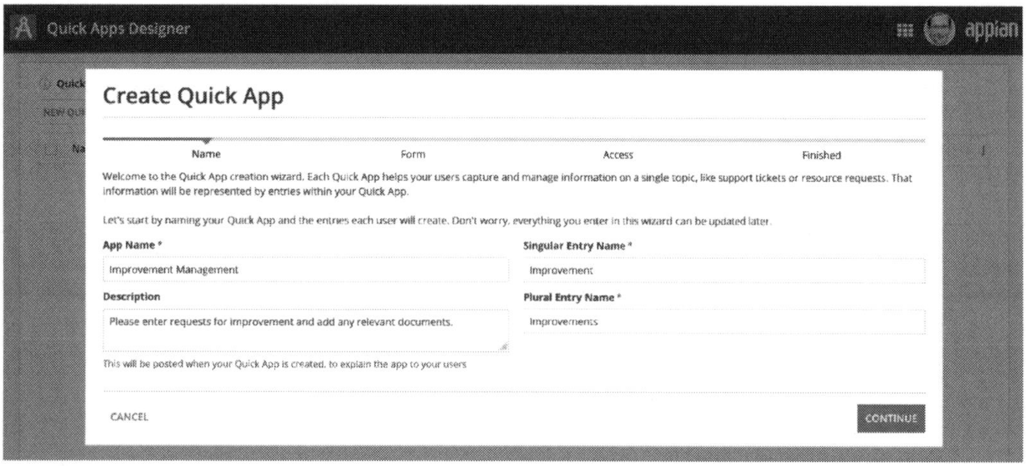

Figure 1.12 – Filled-out form for improvement management use case

Defining case data

The default fields are a good starting point. Leave them as they are. I will explain how to add the following fields to enable proper data management:

- **Description**: A paragraph to describe the improvement

- **Department Manager**: The manager responsible for the implementation

- **Department**: The name of the department in which the improvement would need to be implemented

The default fields are shown in the following screenshot:

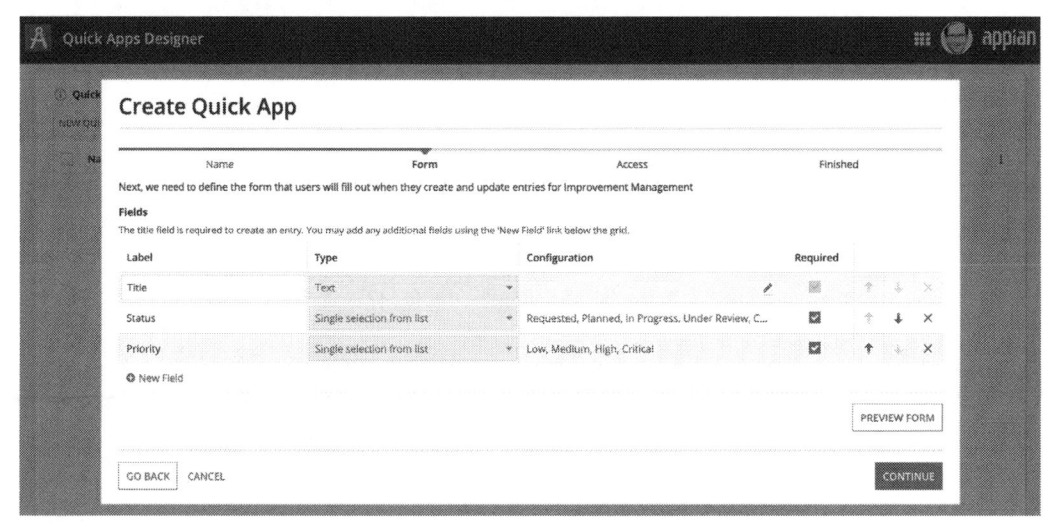

Figure 1.13 – Predefined default fields

For each field, you define the name, a data type, and whether it is required or not. Some fields have additional options, which we will have a look at later.

Let's follow the next series of screenshots to add these three fields, as follows:

1. Click the **New Field** button, as indicated in the following screenshot:

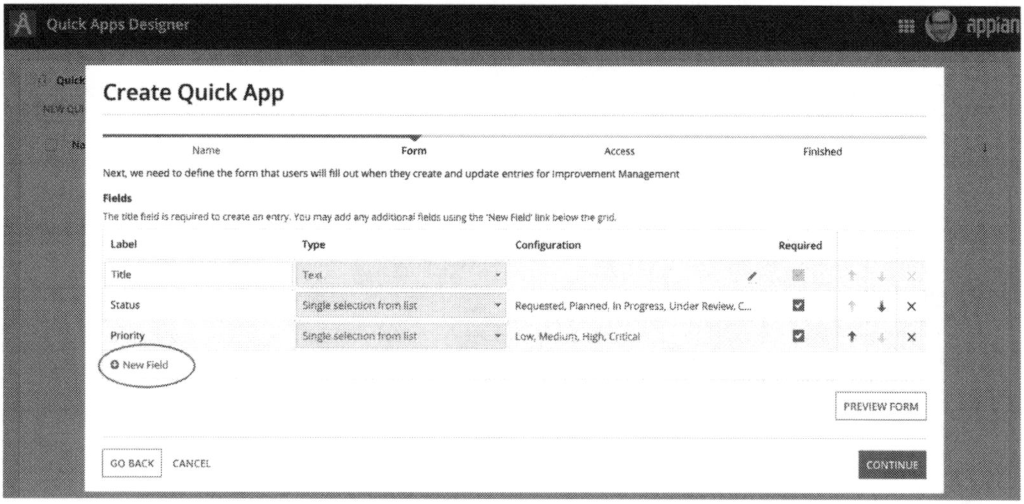

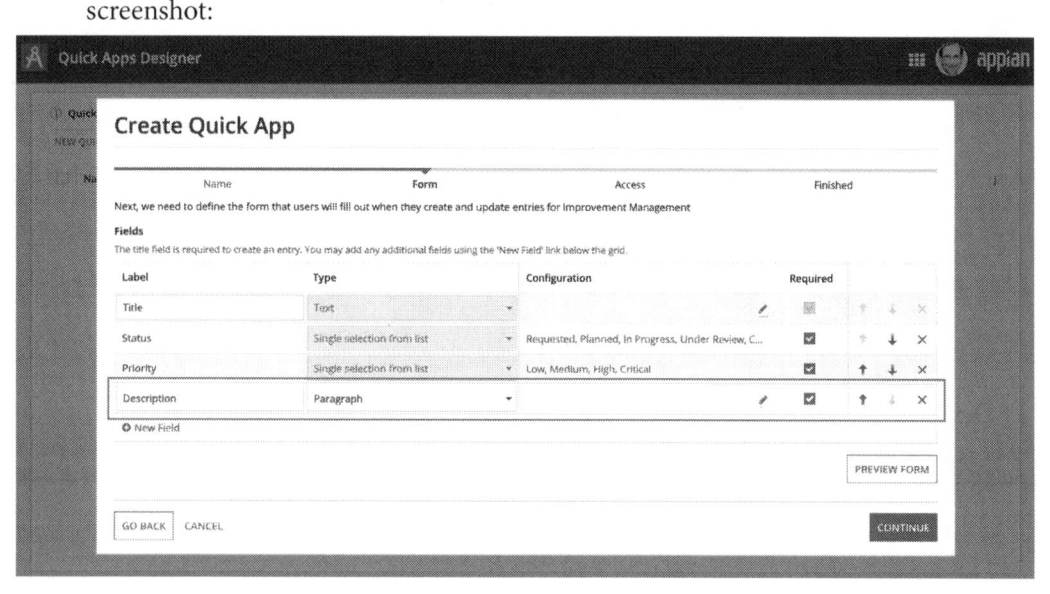

Figure 1.14 – Adding a new field

2. Enter and select **Paragraph** for the data type, as highlighted in the following screenshot:

Figure 1.15 – Paragraph type

3. Add another field and enter **Department Manager** for the label and select **User** as the type, as highlighted in the following screenshot:

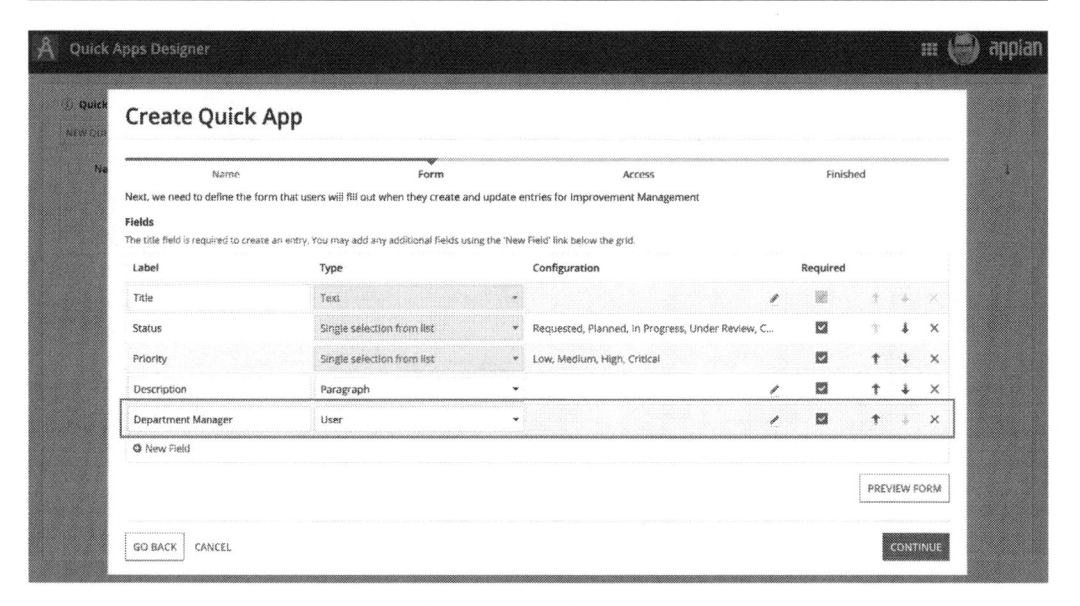

Figure 1.16 – User type

4. Name the last field **Department** and give it the type of **Text**.

5. After adding the three fields, let's look at how the form and the dashboard will look. Click the **PREVIEW FORM** button to do so, as illustrated in the following screenshot:

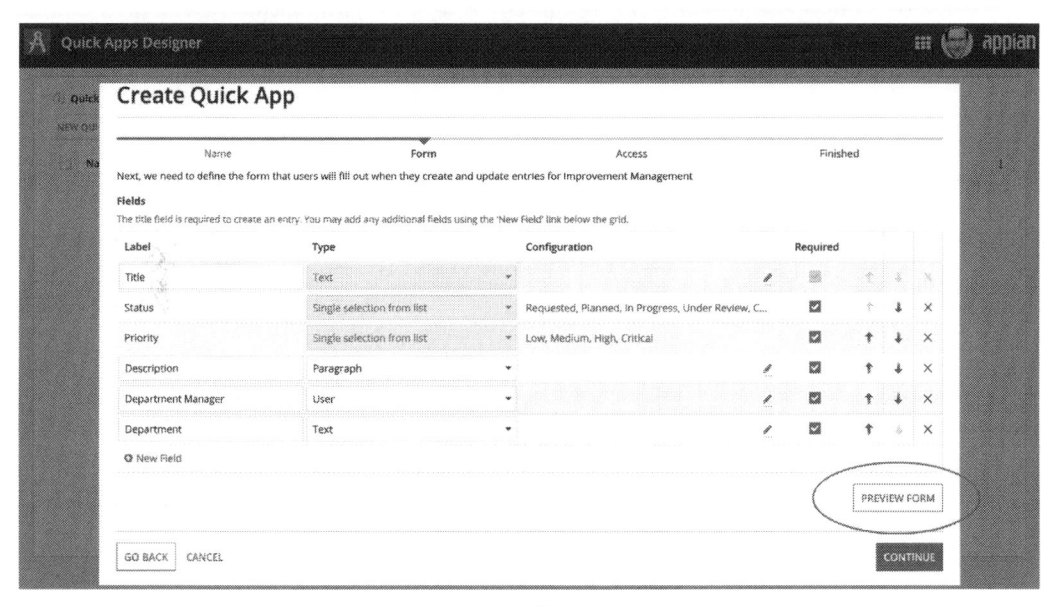

Figure 1.17 – All fields added

Appian will display a preview of the form, and you can already enter data to see whether it fits your requirements, as indicated in the following screenshot:

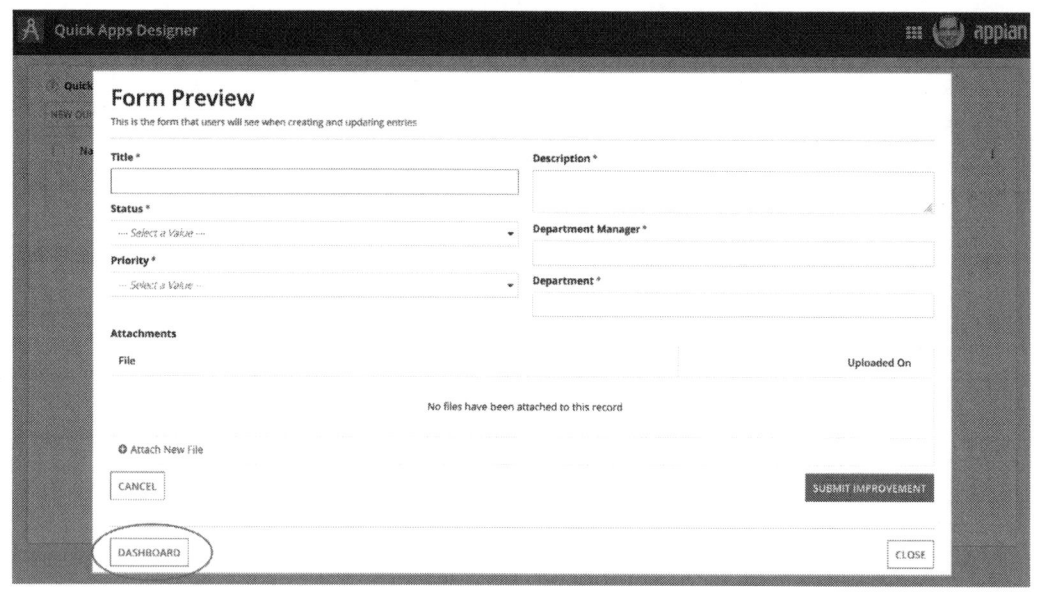

Figure 1.18 – Form preview

6. Click the **DASHBOARD** button highlighted in *Figure 1.17* to switch to a preview of how the screen for each improvement will look. This is the result:

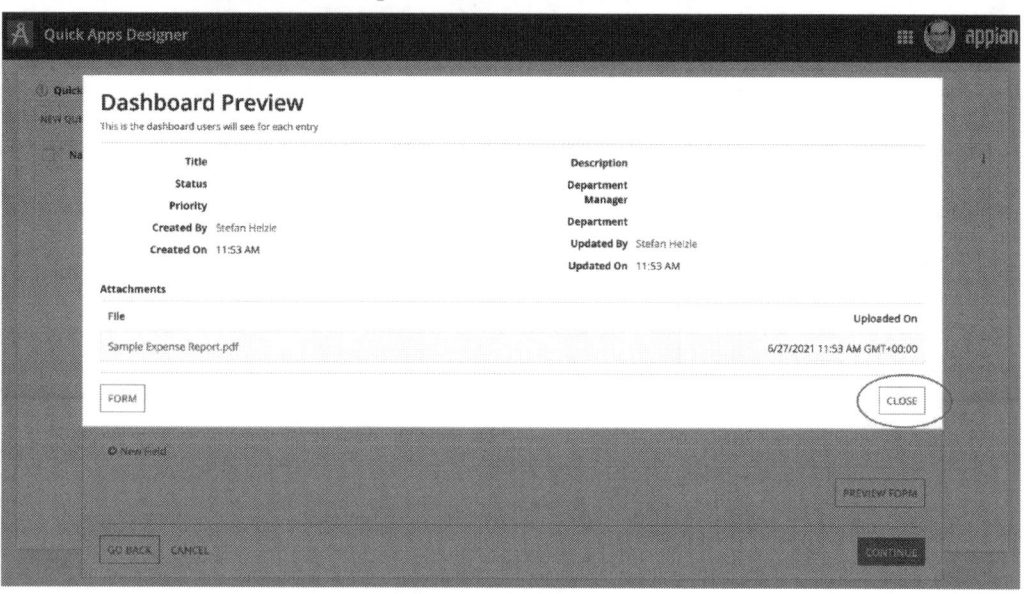

Figure 1.19 – The dashboard preview

7. Click the **CLOSE** button to close the review screen, followed by **CONTINUE** to get
    to the next step.

Setting permissions and generating an app

In the **Access** step, add users to the **Owners** field to define who is allowed to *modify* the
app—for example, to add another field. By adding users to the **Collaborators** field, you
enable them to participate in using the app.

Select an icon you'd like to represent the app's use case, as highlighted in the following
screenshot:

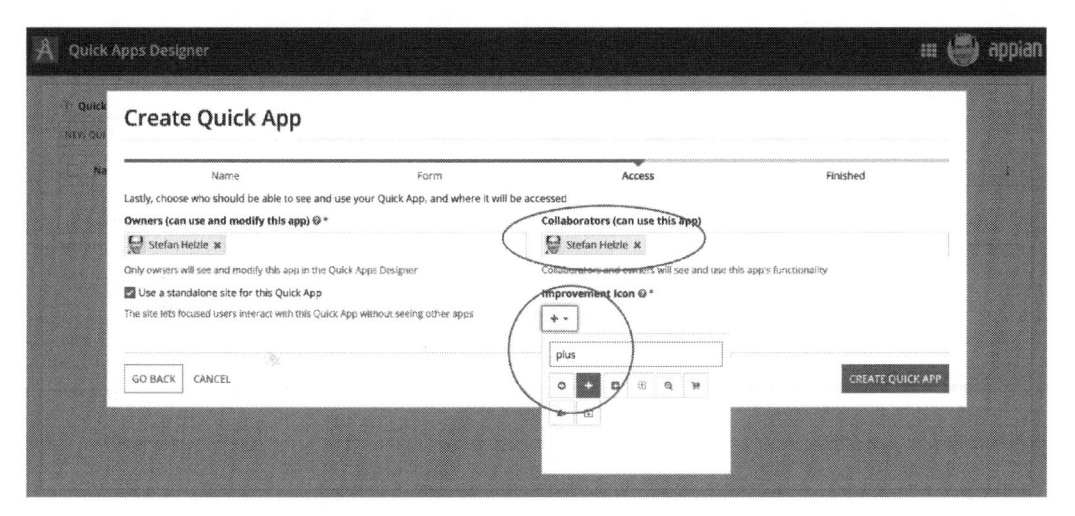

Figure 1.20 – Defining permissions and icon

Click the **CREATE QUICK APP** button to make Appian generate the final app. This takes
a bit of time, so let's use that to recap what you did to create a **Quick App**, as follows:

1. Define an app and record name.

2. Define a name and type for the record's fields.

3. Define who can work with the app and who can modify it later on.

4. Wait a bit…

5. Click the following link to open the Quick App:

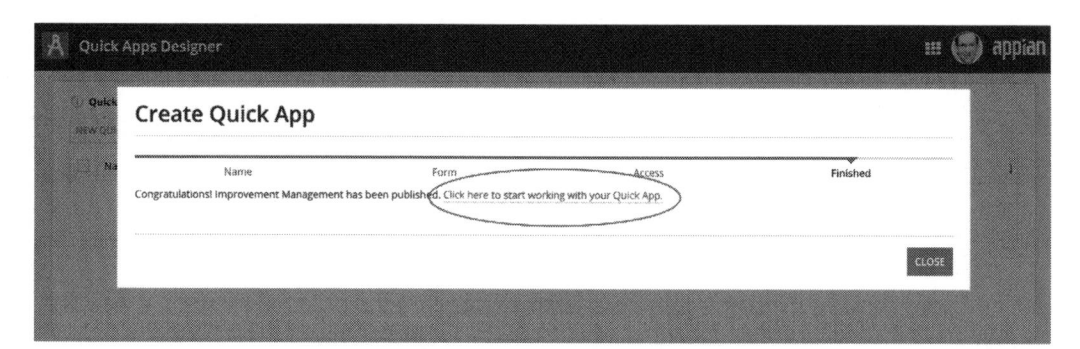

Figure 1.21 – Quick App is created

The generated **Quick App** contains the following three tabs:

- **IMPROVEMENTS**
- **TRENDS**
- **MY TASKS**

Check all the tabs. Since you have not entered any data yet, there is not much to see, as the following screenshot shows:

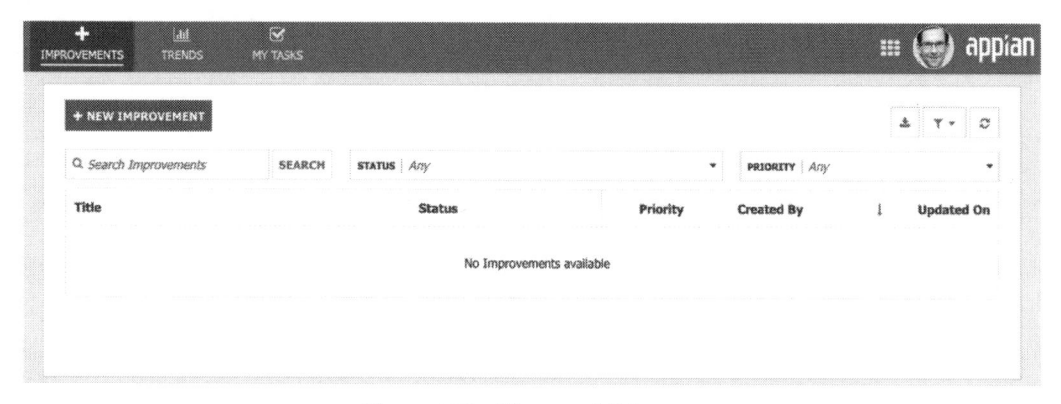

Figure 1.22 – The record list screen

Testing your app

Testing is an important step in any software development, even in low-code with Appian and in a no-code approach when creating a **Quick App**. Later in this book, we will have a closer look at how testing and QA in Appian works. For now, let's create some new improvements to make sure the app works as designed. Proceed as follows:

1. Click the + **NEW IMPROVEMENT** button, as illustrated in the following screenshot:

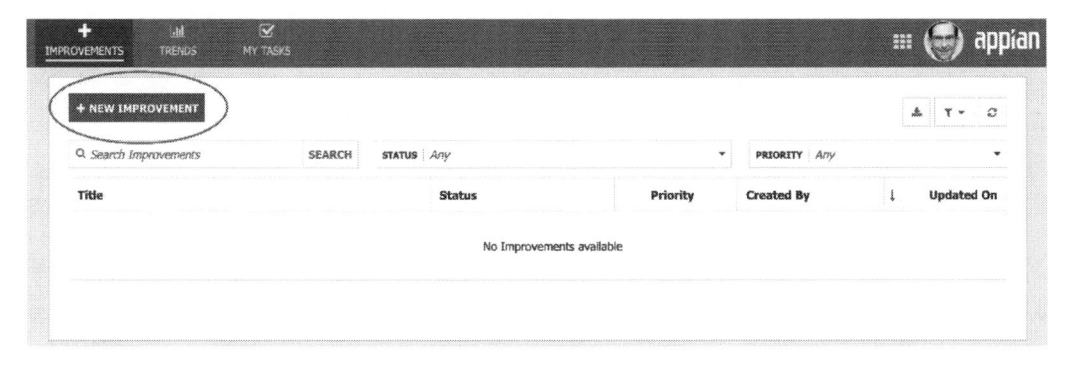

Figure 1.23 – Empty list, ready for adding items

2. You now see a screen to add a new improvement. This screen looks very similar to the one you saw just minutes ago in the preview function of the **Quick Apps Designer**, as we can see here:

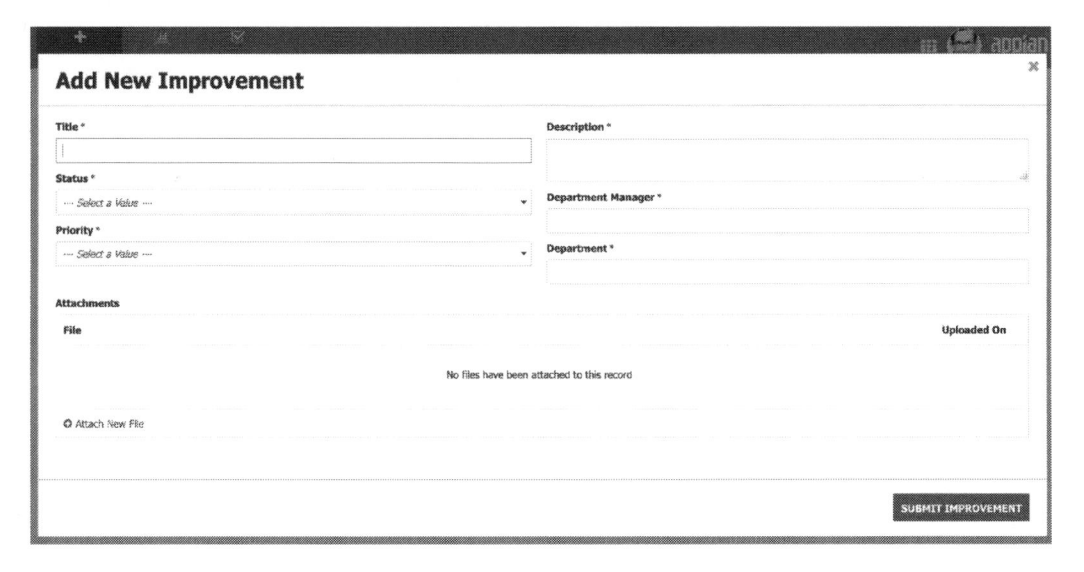

Figure 1.24 – Add New Improvement screen

3. Enter some data to create a new improvement record item. An example of what to add is provided in the following screenshot:

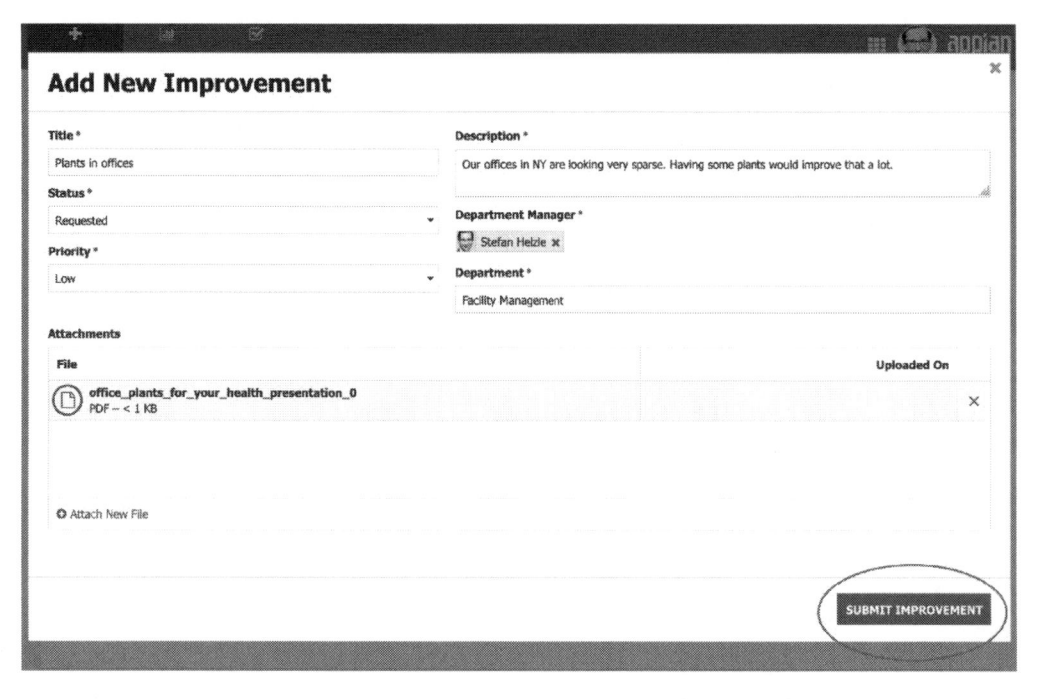

Figure 1.25 – New improvement with some data entered

4. After clicking the **SUBMIT IMPROVEMENT** button, you should see a list showing your just created item, as depicted in the following screenshot:

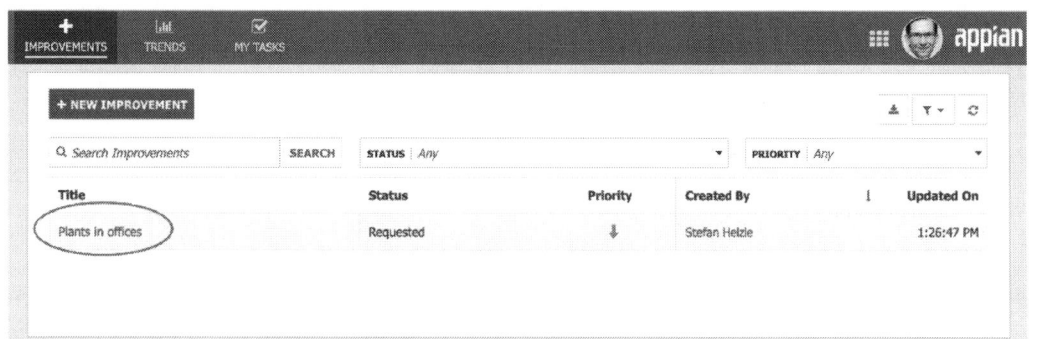

Figure 1.26 – The record list showing one item

5. Click the new item to open it. You will see the data you entered a moment ago in the format as defined in the **Quick Apps Designer**, as illustrated in the following screenshot:

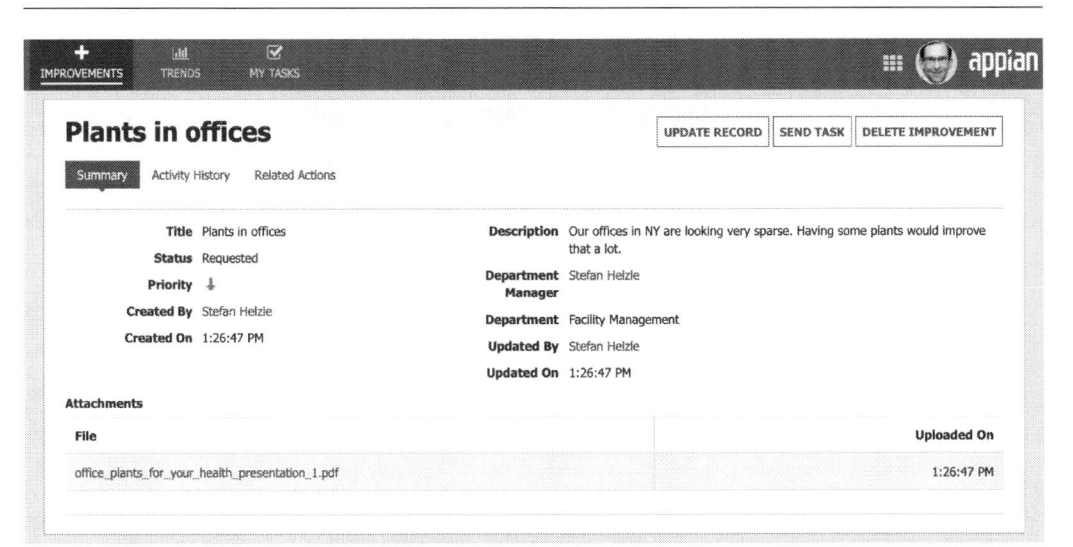

Figure 1.27 – The improvement record dashboard

This app is instantly available on your mobile device. Download the Appian app from your mobile app store, start it and follow these *four simple steps*:

1. Set up a new account.

2. Add a new account.

3. Enter the server name of your Appian environment.

4. Enter your credentials.

The preceding steps are illustrated in the following screenshot:

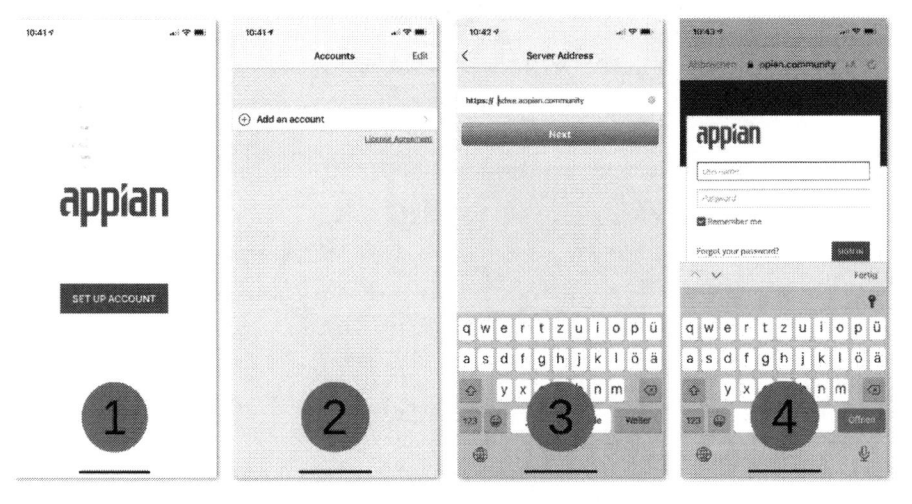

Figure 1.28 – Account setup steps

Voilà—your first mobile app! Take a look:

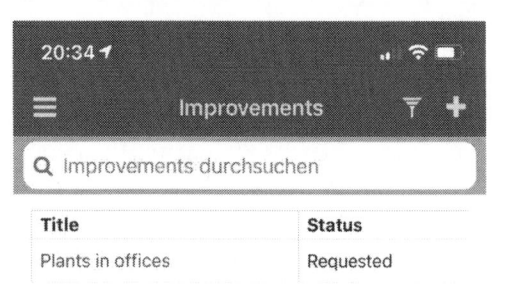

Figure 1.29 – List of improvements on mobile

Tap that list item to open the improvement. The following information is shown in the next figure:

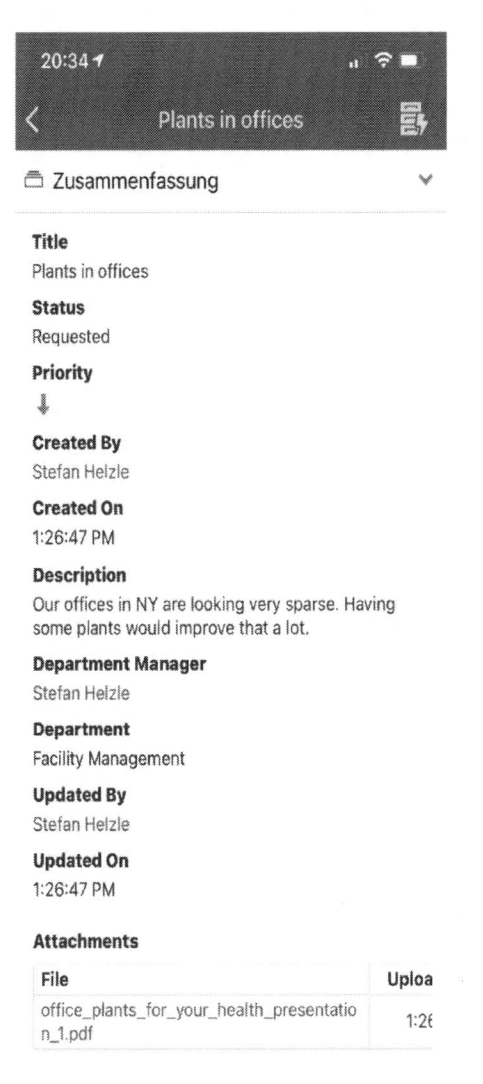

Figure 1.30 – Improvement dashboard on mobile

Hence, with this we are done with testing our very first application.

Summary

There you go—congratulations! This is your first app in Appian: your personal *Hello World*. You learned how to open the **Quick Apps Designer**, assign a name, define the data and collaborators, and finally have Appian generate a **Quick App**. Play with your new app and collaborate with the colleagues you added. If you find out that there is a field missing, go back to the **Quick Apps Designer** and add it. And by adding more users as collaborators, you have your whole team on board in no time.

This is just the first chapter in this book, and there is so much more to discover in Appian. In the next chapter, you will learn more about how to get the most out of your new **Quick App**.

Further reading

Here are some further sources of information for you to take a look at:

- `https://docs.appian.com/suite/help/latest/Getting_Started_with_Quick_Apps.html`
- `https://docs.appian.com/suite/help/latest/Quick_Apps_Designer.html`

2
Features and Limitations of Appian Quick Apps

The new **Quick App** has a fair number of built-in functionalities that you already know about. From managing record items to tasks and document upload, to reporting, Quick Apps are small and simple applications that can be an enormous aid in daily work. But they have their limitations. You will now learn what a Quick App can do.

There are also a few tweaks to improve functionality and increase the scope of viable use cases, which we will learn about in this chapter.

We'll be covering the following topics in this chapter:

- Managing record items in Quick Apps
- Managing tasks in Quick Apps
- Managing documents in Quick Apps
- Reporting in Quick Apps
- Modifying a Quick App

Managing record items in Quick Apps

Create, read, update, and delete are the basic methods of managing record items in a Quick App. Each record represents an improvement that you can look up. When you start working on an improvement, you set the status to **In Progress** by clicking the **UPDATE RECORD** button. After selecting the new status, make sure to click the **Update this Improvement** button to save your changes.

Let's go! Proceed as follows:

1. Click the **UPDATE RECORD** button to modify the selected item, as illustrated in the following screenshot:

Figure 2.1 – Record item summary and UPDATE RECORD button

2. Select the **In Progress** value as the new status and click the **UPDATE IMPROVEMENT** button to save your changes, as illustrated in the following screenshot:

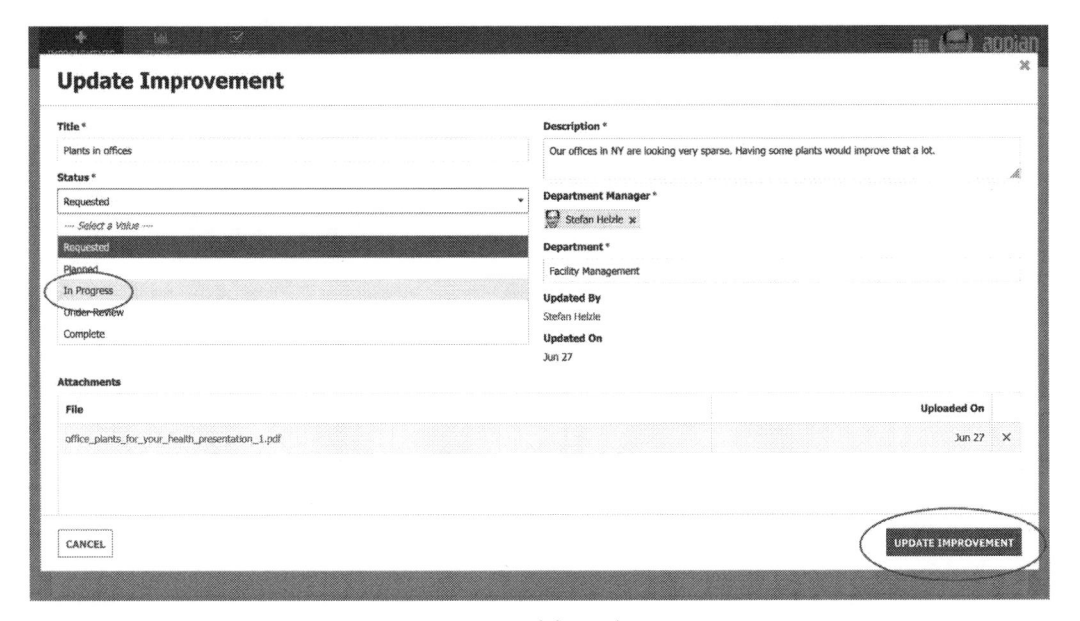

Figure 2.2 – Modifying the status

3. After your team has implemented that improvement, set the status to **Complete** to indicate the successful implementation.

But there's more! The **Priority** field can be used to aid in planning resources for future improvement activities, and the **Department** field helps to distribute your resources evenly to everybody.

When checking the **History** tab, you will see that the Quick App tracks all changes made to the record, including details such as who did the modification, when, and which fields have changed. This is a massive benefit compared to the Excel tables you might be used to.

A downside is that all users who have access to the application can create new items and update existing ones. There is no way to restrict access to individual items.

Managing tasks in Quick Apps

Collaborating with colleagues often means delegating a specific task. Task management is part of each **Quick App**.

Let's give it a try, as follows:

1. Click the **SEND TASK** button, as highlighted in the following screenshot:

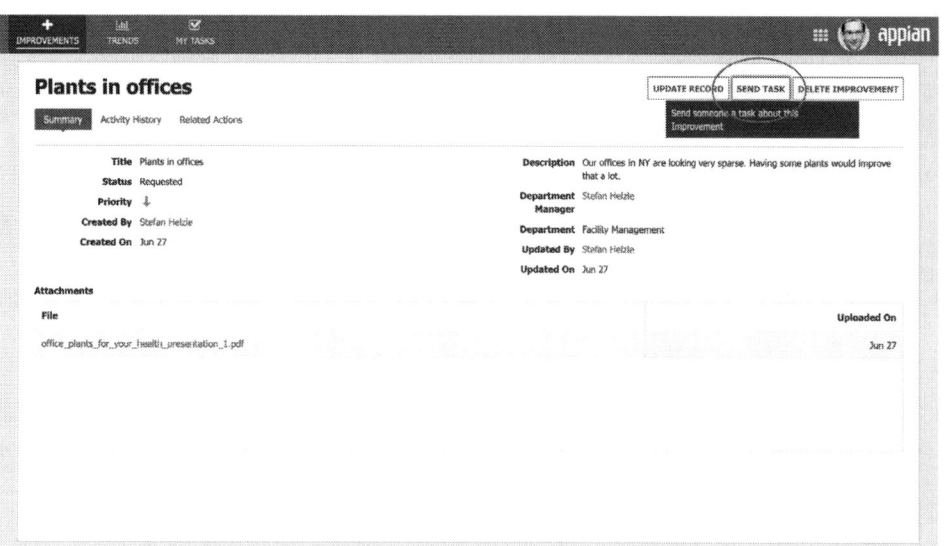

Figure 2.3 – Record item summary and SEND TASK button

2. Fill out the form and click **SEND TASK**. Enter a deadline to indicate when you expect the task to be completed, as illustrated in the following screenshot:

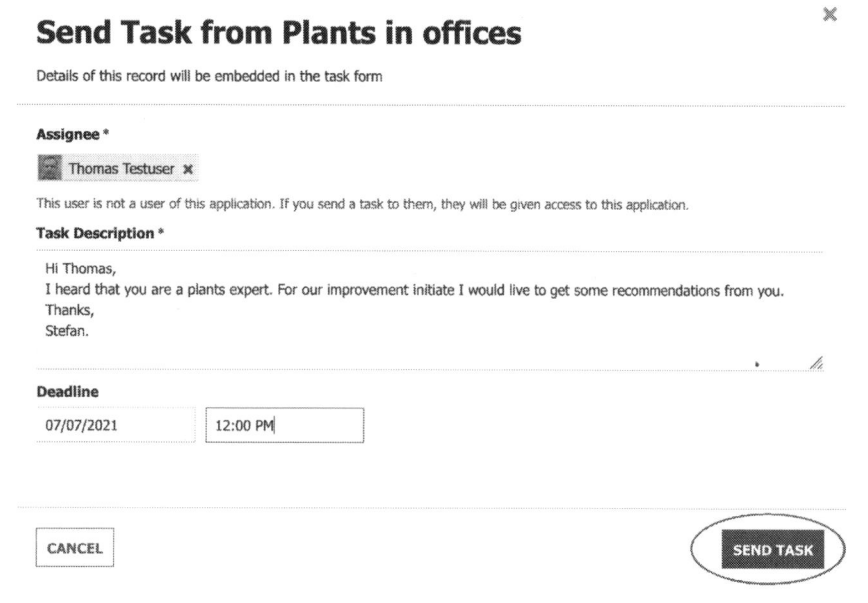

Figure 2.4 – The Send Task screen

3. This step only applies if you selected a user you did not add to the collaborators group before. The selected user is not a member of the Quick Apps collaborators group and does not have access to the application. A warning message makes you aware of what it means to add that user to the application. Click **YES** to add that user to the application, as illustrated in the following screenshot:

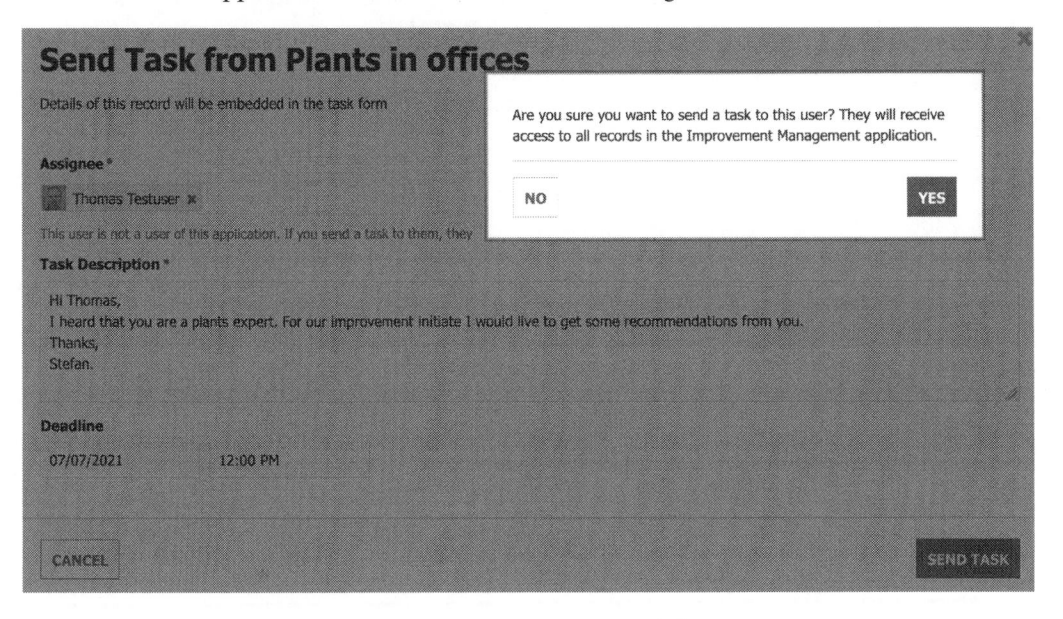

Figure 2.5 – New user warning dialog

4. Done. The task is assigned, as indicated in the following screenshot:

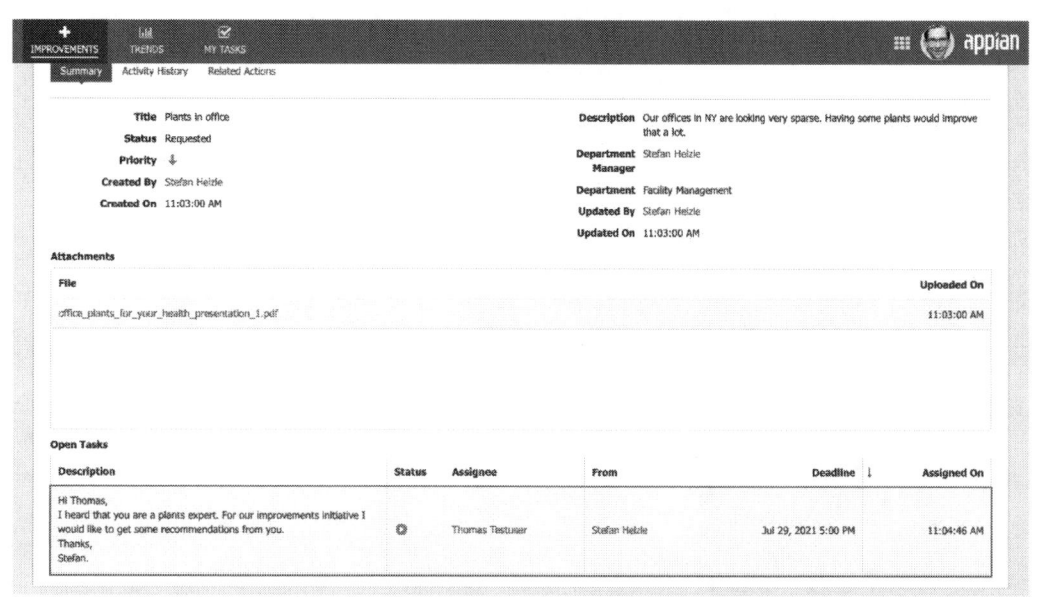

Figure 2.6 – List of tasks on the item summary

The user now gets an email notification including a link to the task, as illustrated in the following screenshot:

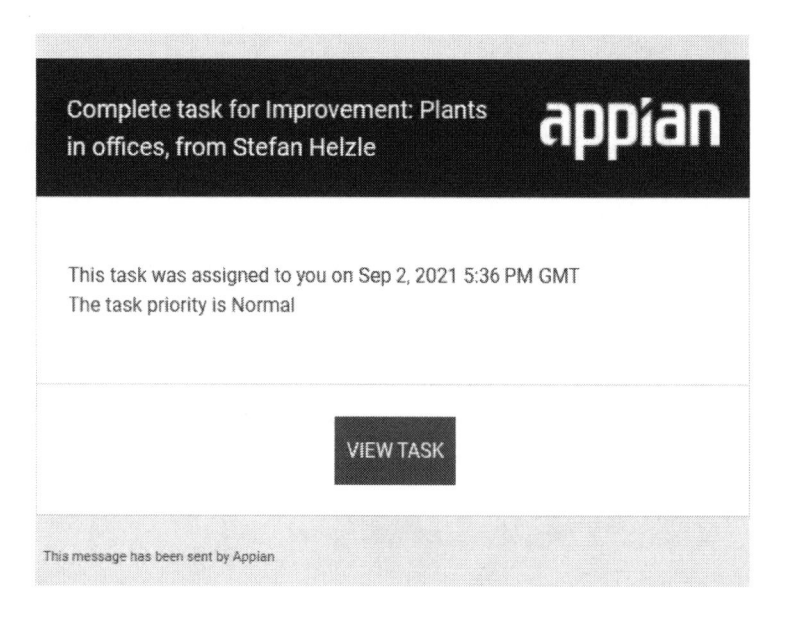

Figure 2.7 – Task assignment email notification

They can also log in to Appian, open the improvement management application in the waffle menu and find their task in the **MY TASKS** tab. Besides managing your tasks, you can also send new tasks.

Let's see how this works, as follows:

1. On the **MY TASKS** tab, click the task description to open it, as highlighted in the following screenshot:

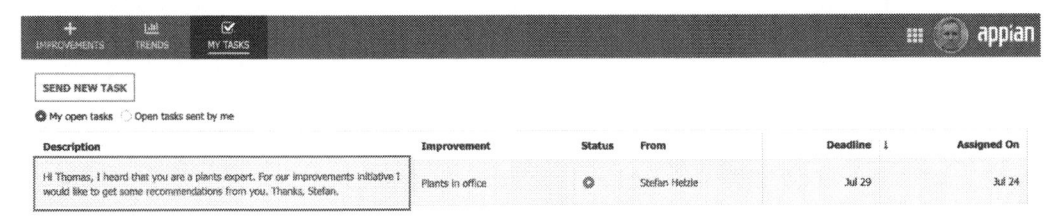

Figure 2.8 – The MY TASKS tab

2. Enter some text in the **Comments** field and click **TASK COMPLETED** to complete the task, as illustrated in the following screenshot:

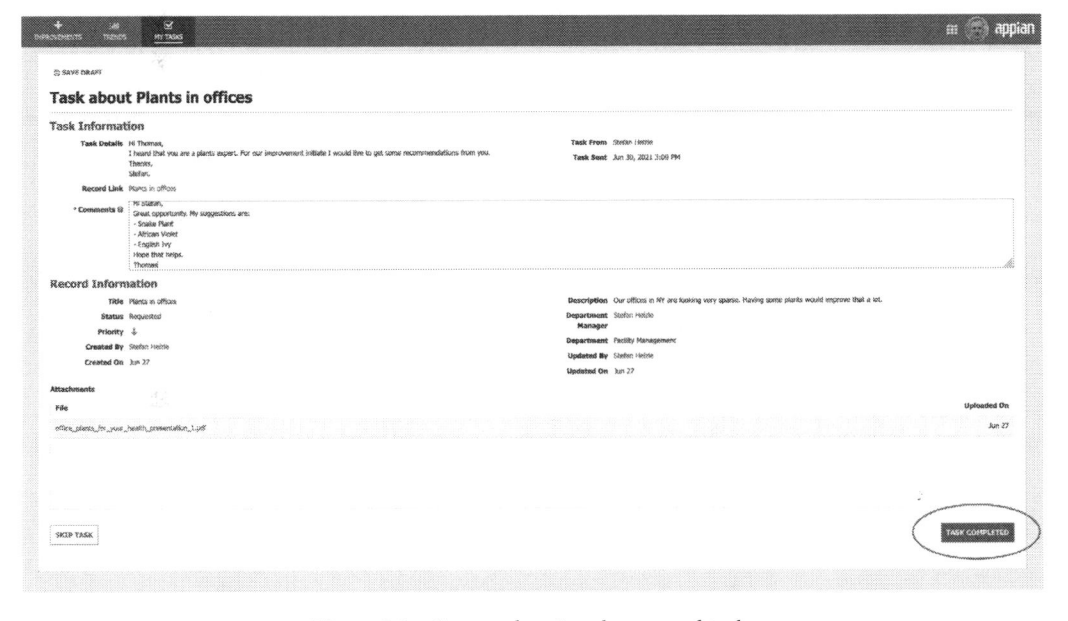

Figure 2.9 – Screen showing the opened task

When completing the task, the person who assigned the task will get a notification. There is no need to email or call others to find out whether they completed a task or not, and entered data is written to the activity history, as illustrated in the following screenshot:

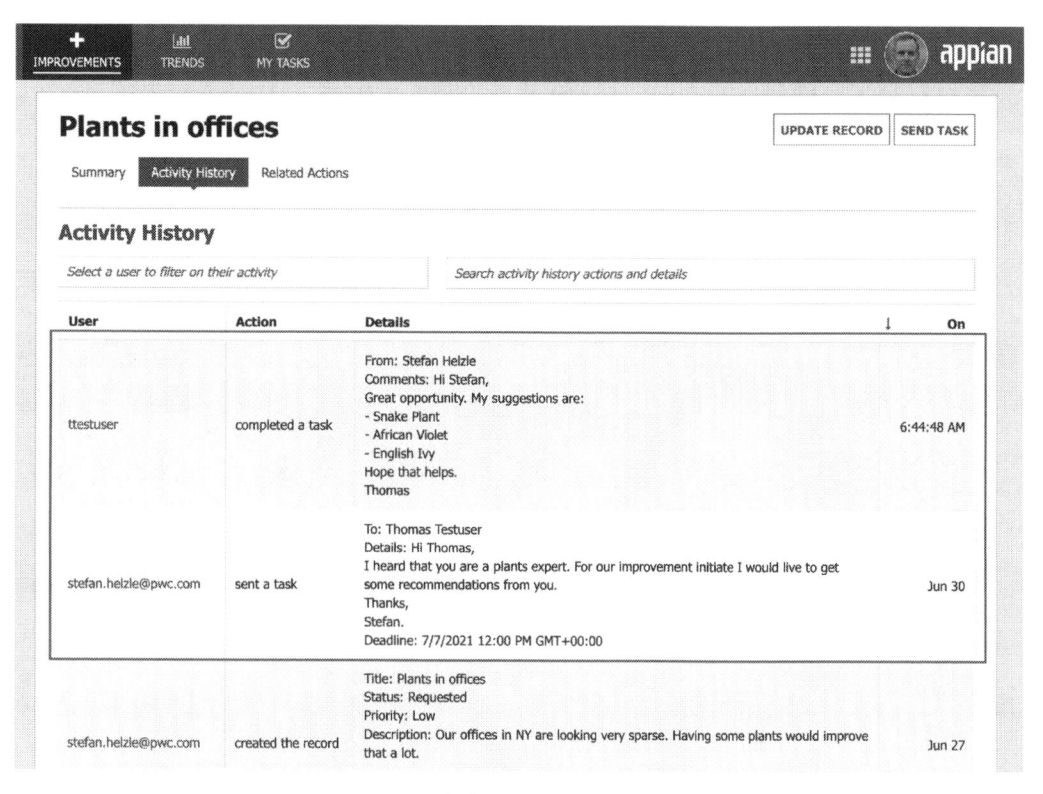

Figure 2.10 – Task details in Activity History view

> **Note**
>
> Remember that a user who gets assigned to a task is then a full member of the application's user group and is permitted to create or update any record. Keep that in mind when managing sensitive data.

Another drawback is that there is *no task escalation configured*. If the assigned colleague does not complete the task in time, no notifications will be sent. You need to check the list of open tasks on the item summary to see the status.

Managing documents in Quick Apps

While working on our improvement example, **Plants in offices**, you might get some brochures or offers from suppliers. Add them to the record, and you never need to search for documents anymore. That also includes colleagues who take over while you are on sick leave.

Click **UPDATE RECORD**, then click **Attach New File** to upload another document, as highlighted in the following screenshot:

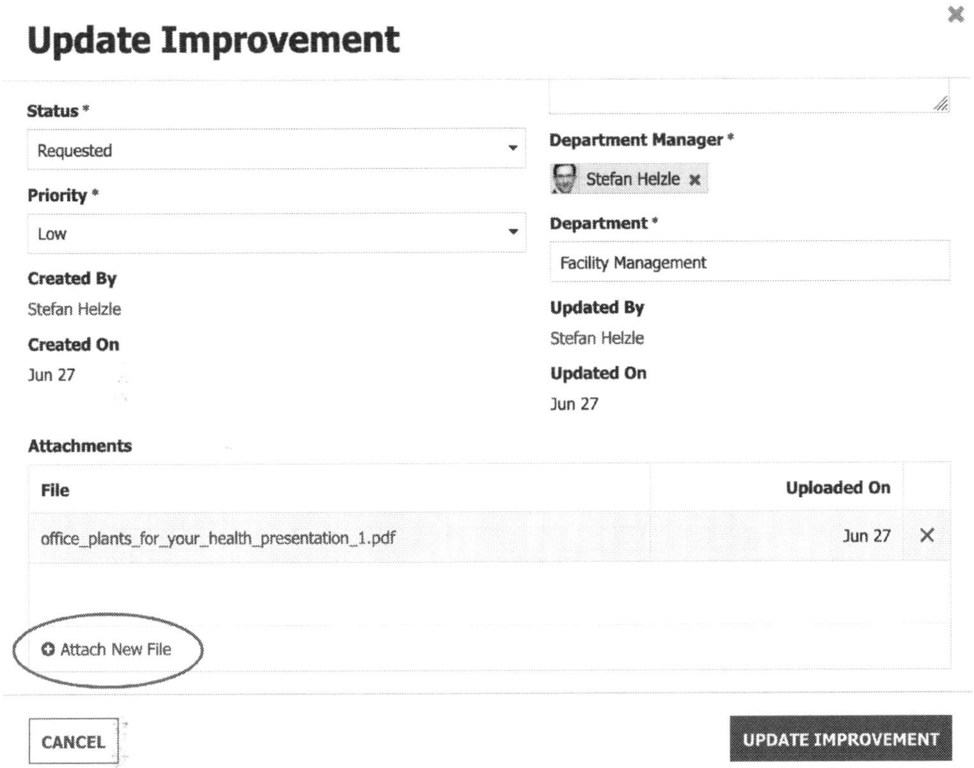

Update Improvement

Status *		**Department Manager** *
Requested		Stefan Helzle **x**
Priority *		**Department** *
Low		Facility Management
Created By		**Updated By**
Stefan Helzle		Stefan Helzle
Created On		**Updated On**
Jun 27		Jun 27

Attachments

File	Uploaded On	
office_plants_for_your_health_presentation_1.pdf	Jun 27	X

⊕ Attach New File

CANCEL   UPDATE IMPROVEMENT

Figure 2.11 – Update Improvement screen when adding a document

A small downside is that you cannot modify documents directly and there are no document versions, so you need to download each file you want to modify and open it in the appropriate application. Before uploading it back to Appian, you might want to change the name to reflect the new version.

Reporting in Quick Apps

Each **Quick App** includes a basic reporting dashboard to support important decision-making, called **TRENDS**. It provides basic indications on team performance, demand estimation, and planning. You can see an overview of the **TRENDS** dashboard here:

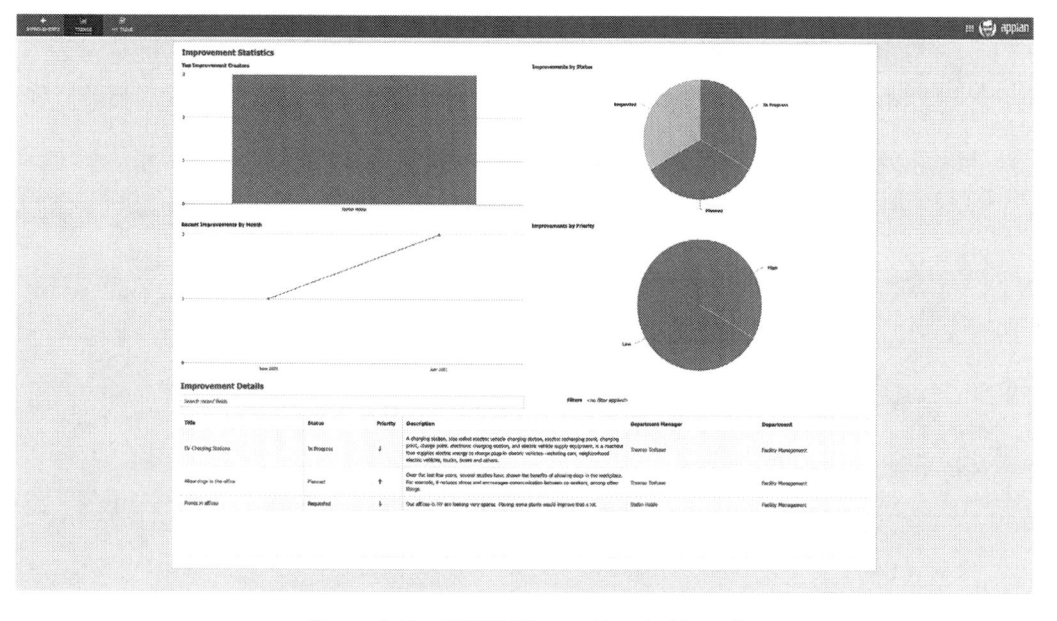

Figure 2.12 – TRENDS reporting dashboard

The two pie charts—**Improvements by Status** and **Improvements by Priority**—as well as the **Top Improvement Creators** chart are interactive. Click them to apply filters to the data displayed in the grid below. A combination of **High** priority and **Requested** status gives you a good overview of which improvement to start next.

The **Recent Improvements By Month** line chart shows an overview of what has been going on recently and helps to plan the team size for the expected upcoming workload.

Do you want to reward colleagues by pointing out improvements? The **Top Improvement Creators** chart should help you to do this.

When searching for a specific record, **TRENDS** can be a better option than the records list in the **IMPROVEMENTS** tab as it shows all fields you added. Combine searching and filtering to get a better overview.

That's pretty much what you can do with **TRENDS**. It is not highly sophisticated but gives some neat details and is a real benefit in your daily work.

Modifying a Quick App

An important feature of a **Quick App** is that you can modify it at any time. You may rename the application, add or remove team members, and even modify the fields captured for each record. To achieve this, proceed as follows:

1. Navigate to the **Quick Apps Designer** and open your application by clicking its name, as illustrated in the following screenshot:

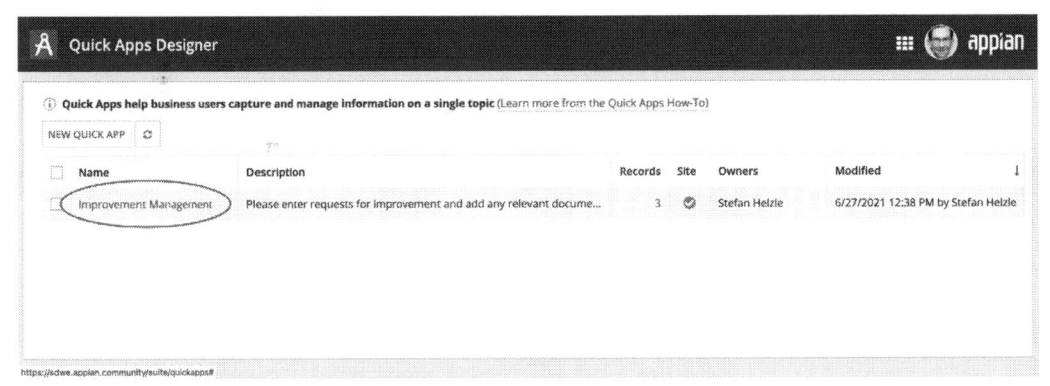

Figure 2.13 – Quick Apps Designer

2. For now, please leave the name as it is and proceed to the **Form** step. You already know how to add fields, but I want you to focus on the details you can configure for each field. Click the pencil icon for the **Title** item, as highlighted in the following screenshot:

Update Quick App

Name	Form	Access	Finished

Changes here will be reflected immediately on all existing entries in your Quick App. Deleting a field does not delete its data, but that field will no longer be visible to any user.

Fields

The title field is required to create an entry. You may add any additional fields using the 'New Field' link below the grid.

Label	Type	Configuration		Required			
Title	Text		✎	☑	↑	↓	✕
Status	Single selection from list	Requested, Planned, In Progress, Under Review, Co...		☑	↑	↓	✕
Priority	Single selection from list	Low, Medium, High, Critical		☑	↑	↓	✕
Description	Paragraph		✎	☑	↑	↓	✕
Department Manager	User		✎	☑	↑	↓	✕
Department	Text		✎	☑	↑	↓	✕

⊕ New Field

PREVIEW FORM

GO BACK   CANCEL   CONTINUE

Figure 2.14 – Form step with pencil icon and list selections

3. Add one or more of these configurations to support your users in entering the right values, as illustrated in the following screenshot:

Configuration for Title

Instructions Text ⊚

Placeholder Text ⊚

Help Tooltip Text ⊚

CANCEL   UPDATE FIELD

Figure 2.15 – Input field options

4. Let's see what these configuration texts are about, as follows:

    I.   **Instructions Text**: This is displayed below the input field and used when that text is so important that it needs to be displayed all the time.

    II. **Placeholder Text**: This is shown inside the field as long as the user did not enter any value. Use for hints in formatting—for example, phone number.

    III. **Help Tooltip Text**: This adds a question mark icon to the field name. The user can click that icon to see the text. Used to explain details or give examples.

5. Click **UPDATE FIELD** to close that dialog.

6. Now, click the list of selections for the **Status** field. With this field, the user selects one or more items from a list and has the option to modify selectable values, as illustrated in the following screenshot:

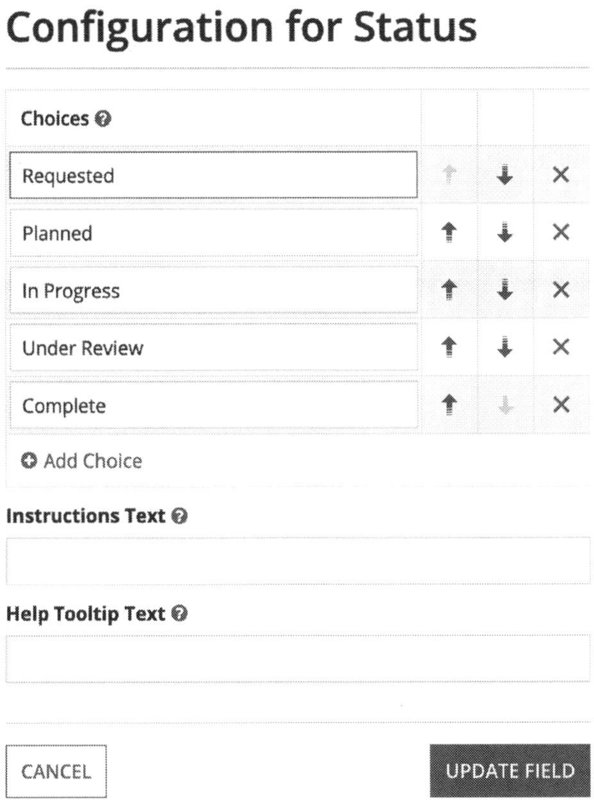

Configuration for Status

Choices ❷

Requested		⬆	⬇	✕
Planned		⬆	⬇	✕
In Progress		⬆	⬇	✕
Under Review		⬆	⬇	✕
Complete		⬆	⬇	✕

➕ Add Choice

Instructions Text ❷

Help Tooltip Text ❷

CANCEL   UPDATE FIELD

Figure 2.16 – Selecting field options

7. Click **Continue**, then **Update Quick App** to store the modifications.

Please don't hesitate to modify these values at any time. The **Instructions Text** and **Help Tooltip Text** fields have the same behavior as previously described.

> **Note**
>
> There is one thing I must point out. If you delete a field in the **Form** field and regenerate the **Quick App**, the data already entered is lost. Later, adding a field of the same name will not bring it back.

Summary

In a few minutes and some clicks, you created a small application providing real business value. This is what Appian thinks about it.

Quick Apps are best suited for ad hoc business processes without rigid workflows. A marketing collateral application is a great example, and business users in Marketing can create it themselves in less than an hour, replete with records, actions, review tasks, and a report.

You now understood the basic features of Quick Apps in Appian. You managed records, assigned a status, and prioritized to enable planning. Not only that, but you also uploaded related documents and assigned tasks. You used the **TRENDS** dashboard in your weekly planning meetings.

That's it for this chapter. In the next chapter, you will learn how a Quick App works under the hood.

3
Building Blocks of Appian Quick Apps

Now we have a good understanding of what a **Quick App** can do, we will look under the hood to see how it works. This chapter will introduce the individual objects in **Appian** and explore how they interact.

In this chapter, you will use the **Appian Designer** environment. This is the place where we can develop any Appian application. To understand how a Quick App works, I will give you a brief introduction. In *Chapter 3, Building Blocks of Appian Quick Apps*, we will go into more detail on objects and how they are created.

We'll be covering the following topics in this chapter:

- The basics of the Appian Designer environment
- An introduction to Appian Records
- Checking the Appian process models
- Learning about Appian interfaces
- Understanding Appian expressions rules

> **Note**
>
> As you open objects in their respective designers, please do not modify them. The Quick Apps feature in Appian is designed to allow quick and easy modifications only from the Quick Apps Designer. If you change an object manually, the Appian platform will recognize it, convert your Quick App into a normal Appian application, and remove it from the Quick Apps Designer.

The basic workings of the Appian Designer environment

The Appian Designer is the development environment in the Appian platform. We will now show you how to open it and explore the basic principles of how it works:

1. Click the waffle icon to open the menu and click the **Appian Designer** option.

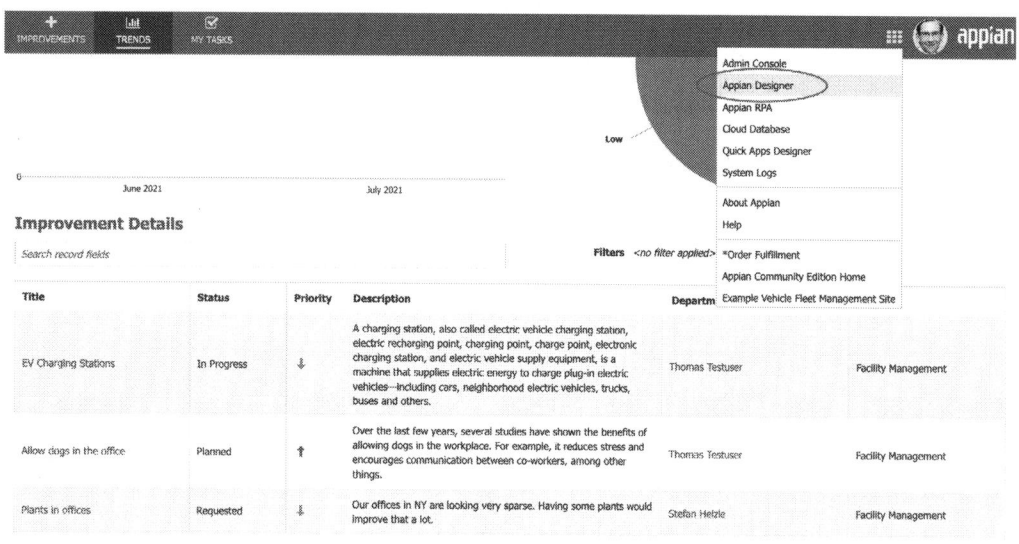

Figure 3.1 – The Appian Designer option in the Appian waffle icon menu

2. Now, you will see the **APPLICATIONS** view listing all of the applications you have permission to view or modify. On the top-left side of the screen, you will see a search field. This can be used if you cannot find the Quick App in the **Name** column. Click the application name to open it.

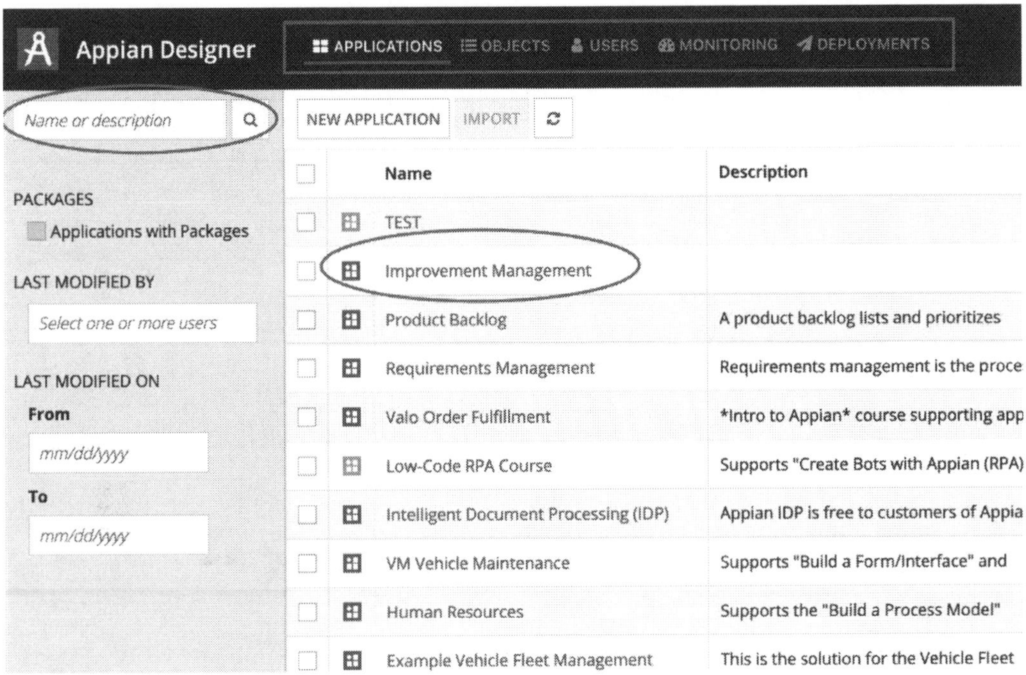

Figure 3.2 – Appian Designer showing all of the applications

The main screen of the Appian Designer is divided into three parts:

- On *top*, there is a menu bar with some tabs and buttons.
- The search and filter pane to the *left* makes finding application objects a breeze.
- The objects list to the *right* takes up the most space, showing the name, description, and modification date of each application.

For now, please stay on the **Objects** tab – you will get to know the other areas later on.

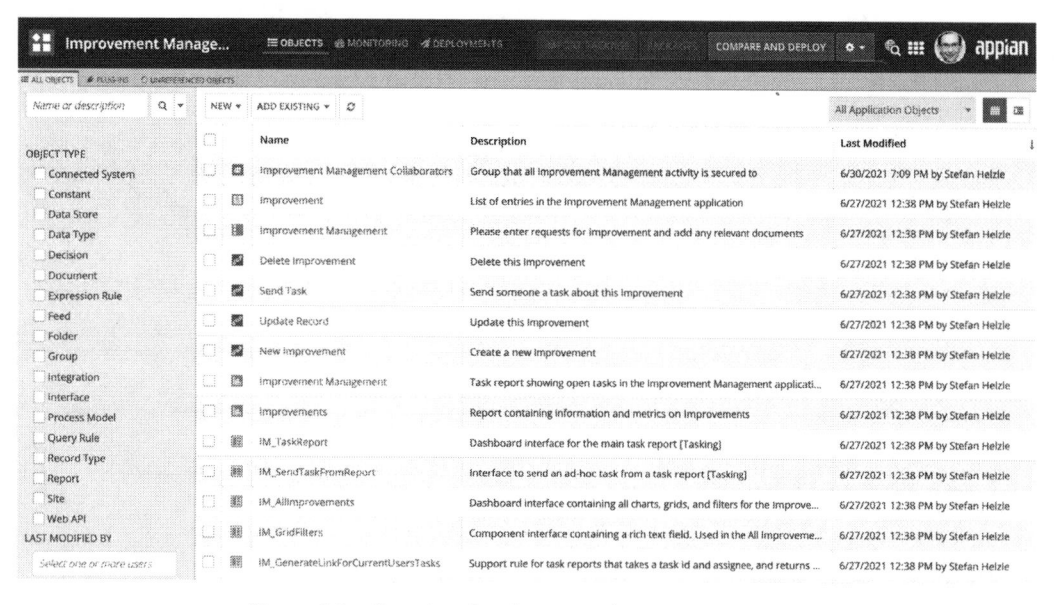

Figure 3.3 – Opening Quick apps in the Appian Designer

To make the Quick App work, Appian generated a set of 77 objects of various kinds. We will now have a look at the four central object types of each Appian application. These are **records**, **processes**, **interfaces**, and **expression rules**. Together, they make up 39 of the 77 objects.

When clicking objects, Appian either opens a pop-up window or a new tab in your browser. This depends on the object's complexity and the number of configuration options. Over time, you may have many open tabs, so keeping your browser tabs organized will stop you getting lost.

Introduction to Appian Records

As you created your Quick App, you defined the data structure as the core. Each improvement is stored as a single record item. An Appian record brings together data, interfaces (for display), and process models (for taking action). Search for the Improvement record type, and then click its name to open it in the **Record Designer**, as shown here:

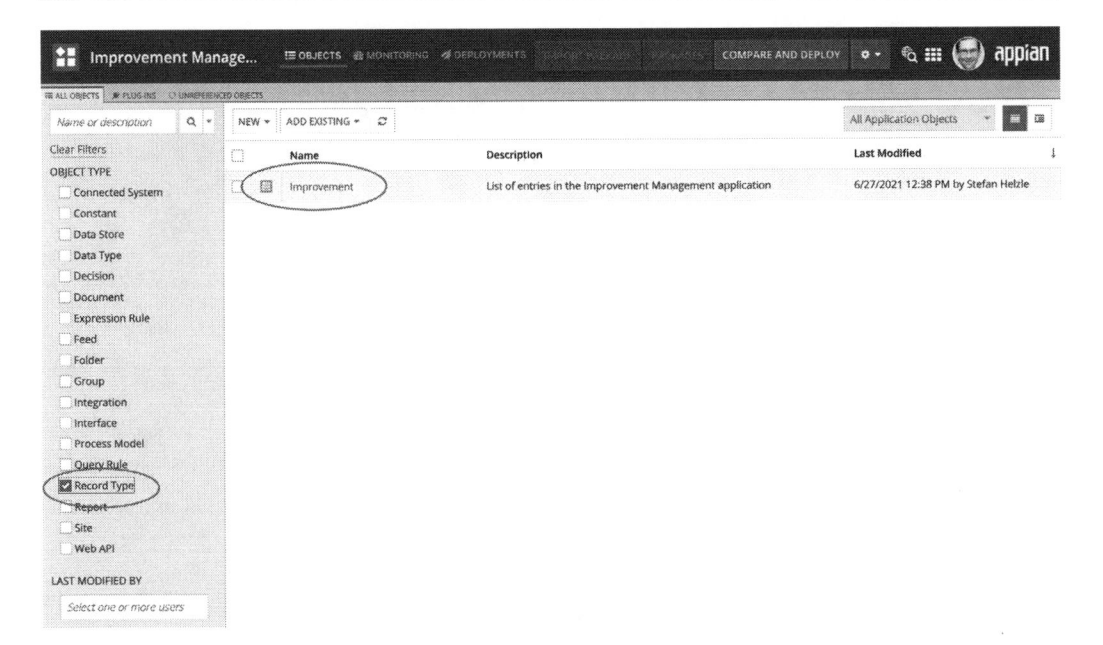

Figure 3.4 – Objects filtered by Record Type

Once you click on **Improvement**, you will see the following screen:

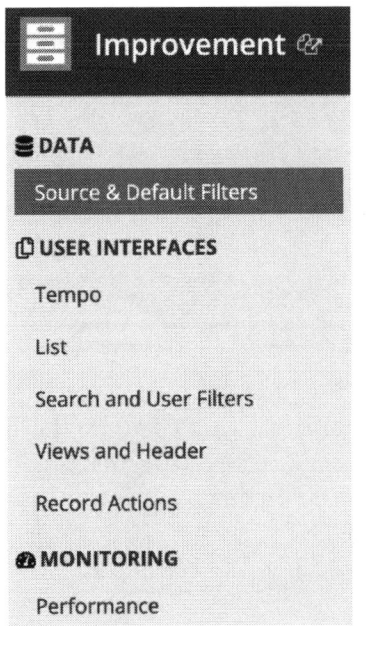

Figure 3.5 – The Improvement dashboard

This menu has the following sections:

- **DATA**: This tells Appian where to fetch the data for this record.
- **USER INTERFACES**: This configures the visual representations of the data.
- **MONITORING**: This analyzes performance to avoid slow user interfaces.

Let's take a look at a few of the fields in this menu in the next subsections.

Source & Default Filters

The **Source & Default Filters** tab is the first menu item. In the context of an Appian record, the *source* means where the data managed through that record is coming from. In our case, the source type shows **Data Store Entity**, which is the Appian term for a relational database. Don't worry, you will not write any SQL statements in this book.

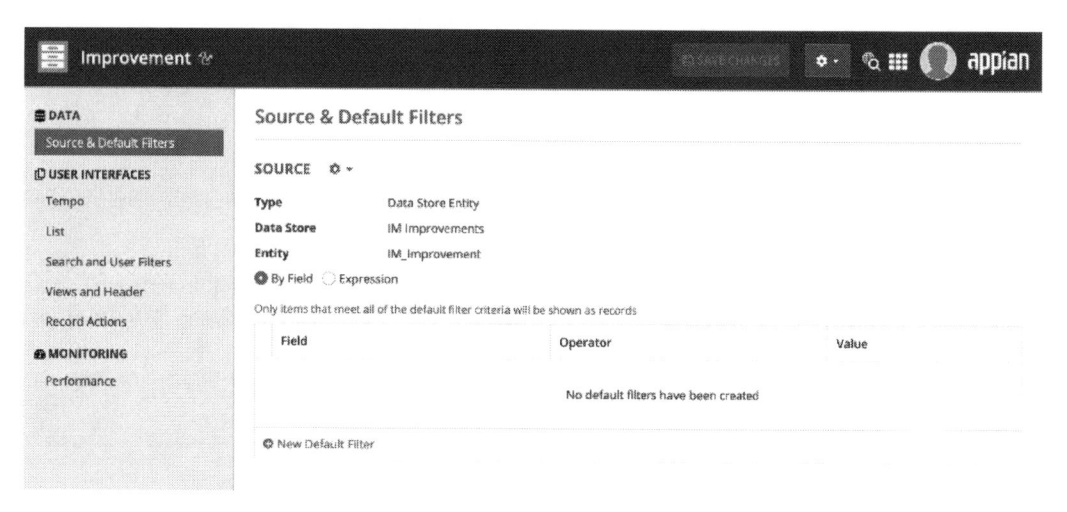

Figure 3.6 – The Record Designer

Tempo

The Appian **Tempo** user interface is a legacy feature and will not be covered in this book. Appian supports legacy features for a long time to allow us to upgrade to the latest versions without breaking our applications.

List

In the **List** tab, you can configure how Appian will display the list of records. In your Quick App, this is the first tab called **IMPROVEMENTS**.

In the **Action** section, you see that the **New Improvement** action relates to the process model, **New Improvement**. We will have a look at process models later. Click the **EDIT LIST** button to open the list editor.

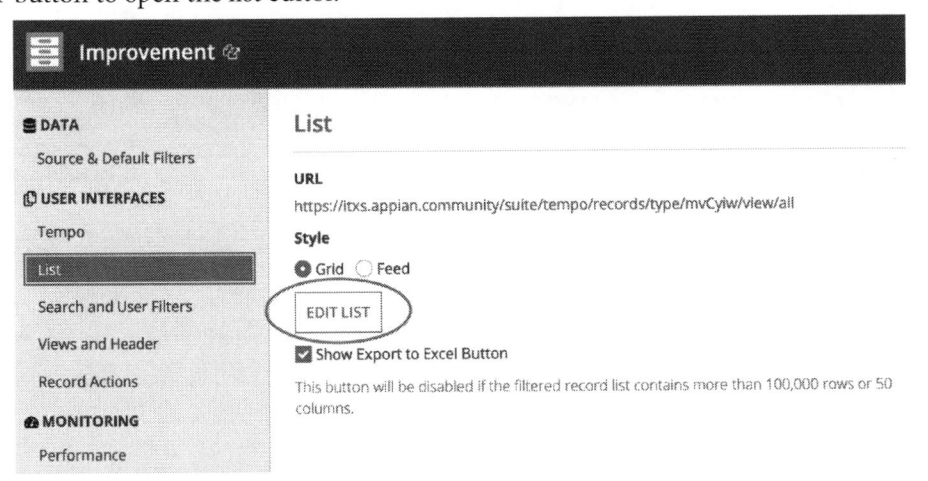

Figure 3.7 – The Record list configuration options

In the list editor, you can configure which columns to show and how they are displayed. Compare this to the list of improvements in the Quick App. Text of various formats, icons, images, and buttons are typically used here. Close the list editor.

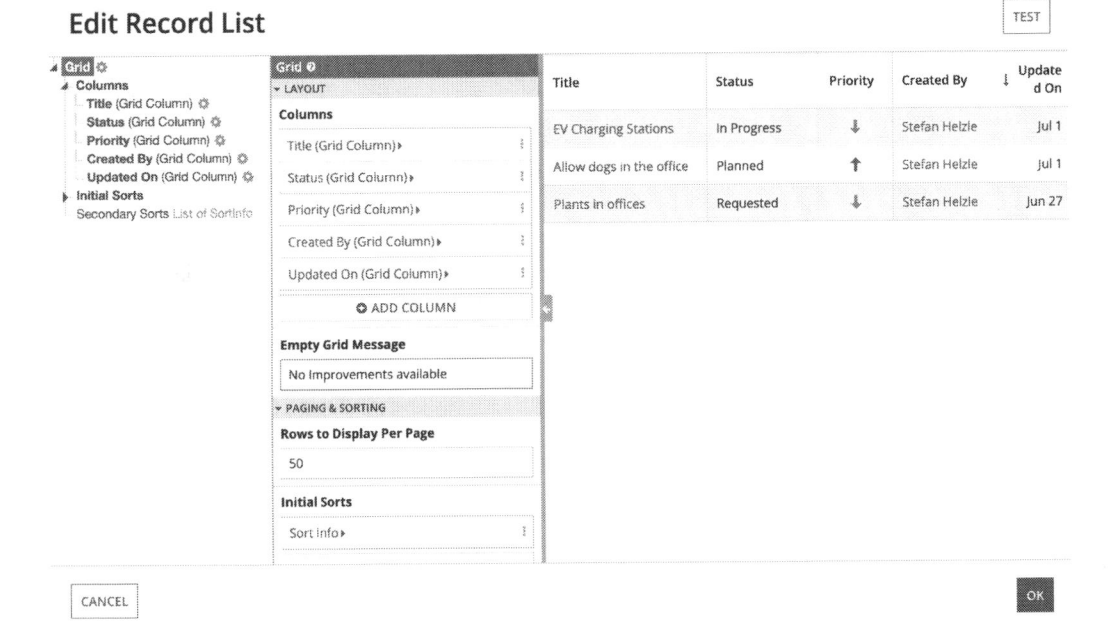

Figure 3.8 – Record list details

User filters

Above the records list in the Quick App, you have some filter options that can be set in the **STATUS**, **PRIORITY**, and **CREATED BY** fields.

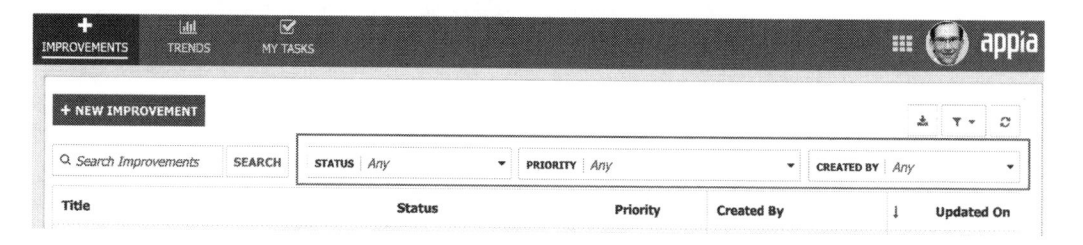

Figure 3.9 – User filters in the Quick App

These filters are configured in the **User Filters** tab. You will recognize some sort of programming code in the **Definition** column. This code dynamically creates the items in the filter dropdown, and it also calculates the item count to each. Static filters can be easily configured without a single line of code.

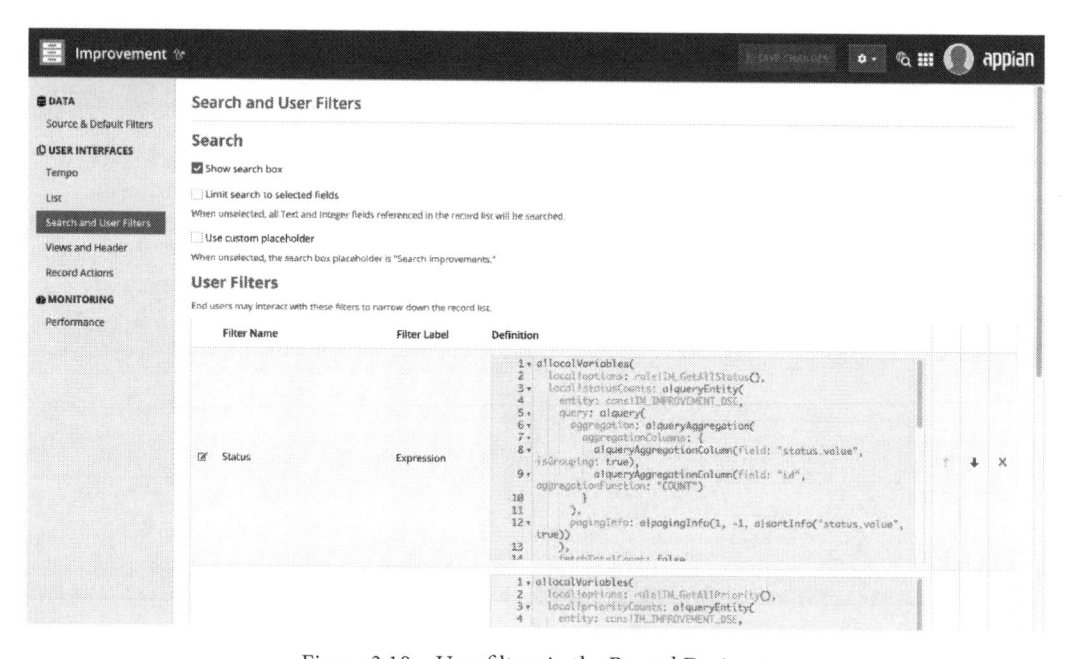

Figure 3.10 – User filters in the Record Designer

Views

Next, we will have a look at the **Views** tab. This is the term for the tabs on the screen that show the details for a single record item.

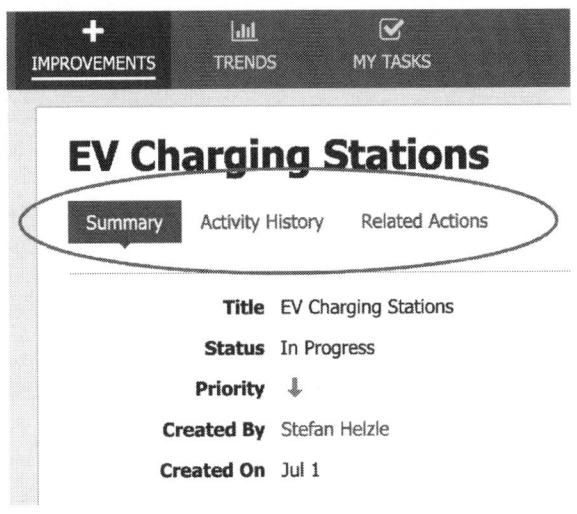

Figure 3.11 – Record views in the Quick App

Each record view is defined by a name and a corresponding user interface object.

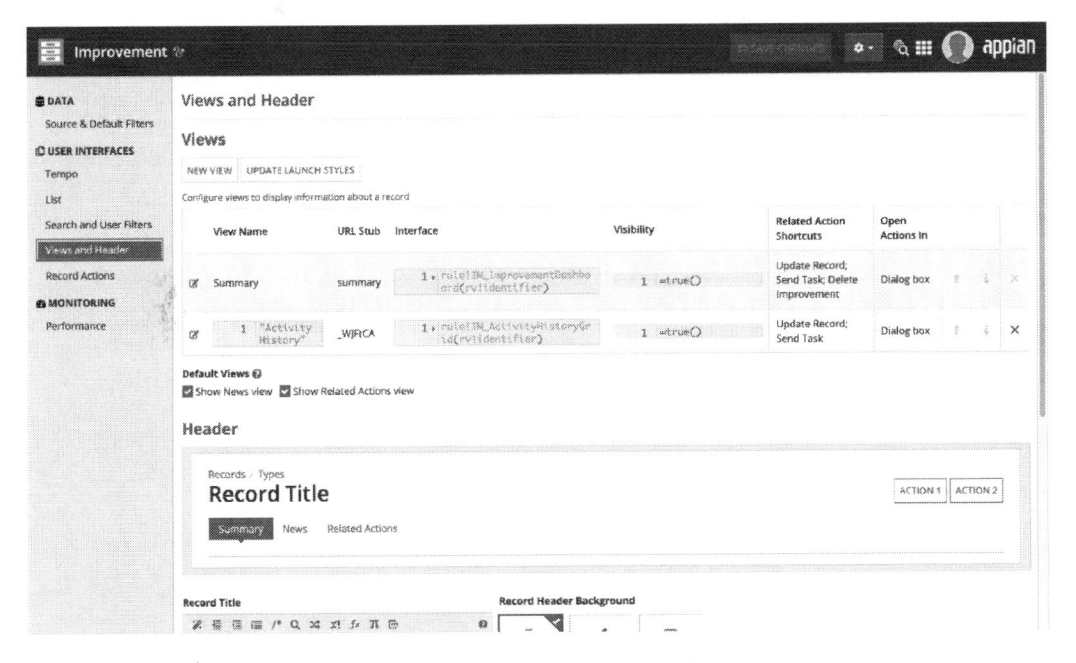

Figure 3.12 – The Views tab in the Record Designer

The selected record can display any related actions in the **Related Actions** section, or show them as buttons on the top right of the screen.

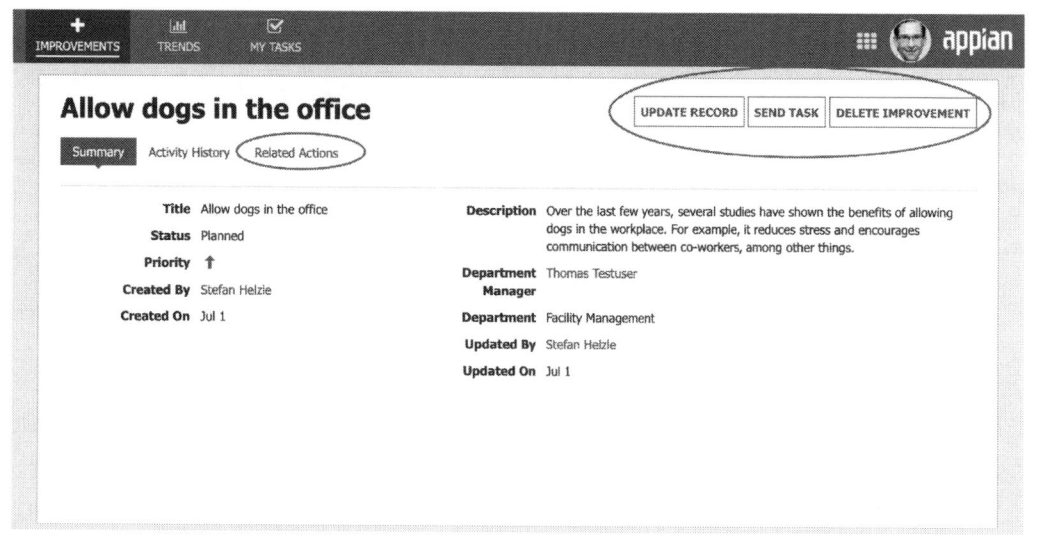

Figure 3.13 – Views and related actions in the Quick App

Now, let us look at the related actions.

Related Actions

In the **Related Actions** tab, you can define which process models are available to the user to interact with the record. In the **Context** column, you will see some code. This code is used to pass data to the process when it is started so that it knows which record item to work with. We will dive into the details of this later in this chapter.

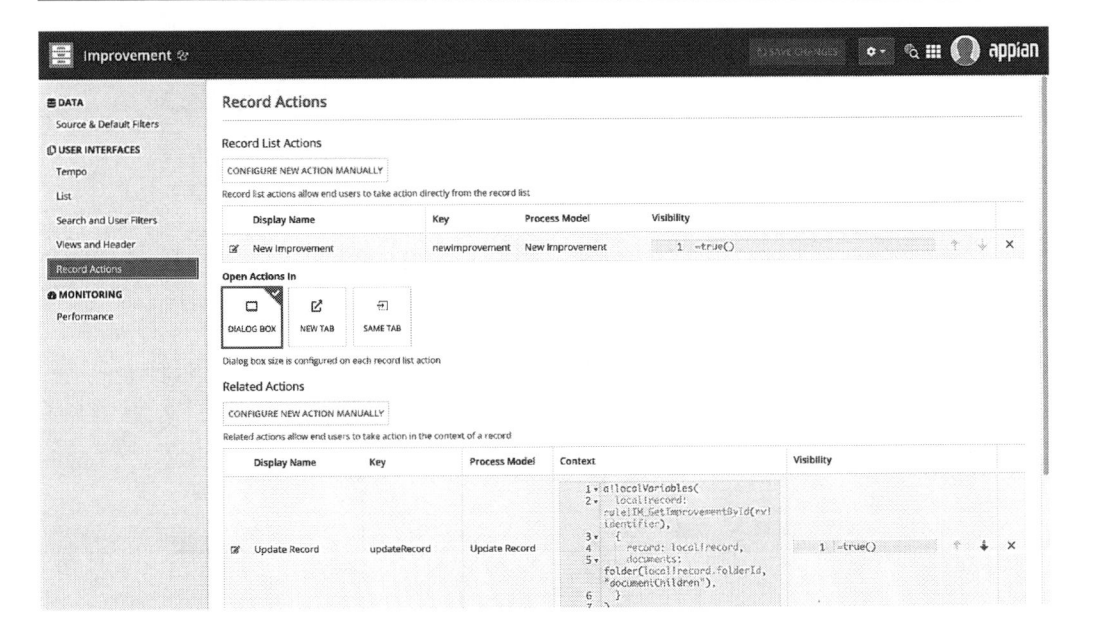

Figure 3.14 – The Related Actions tab in the Record Designer

By default, a record has a view showing all of its related actions. In addition, each record view can show selected related actions, as shown in the top-right buttons.

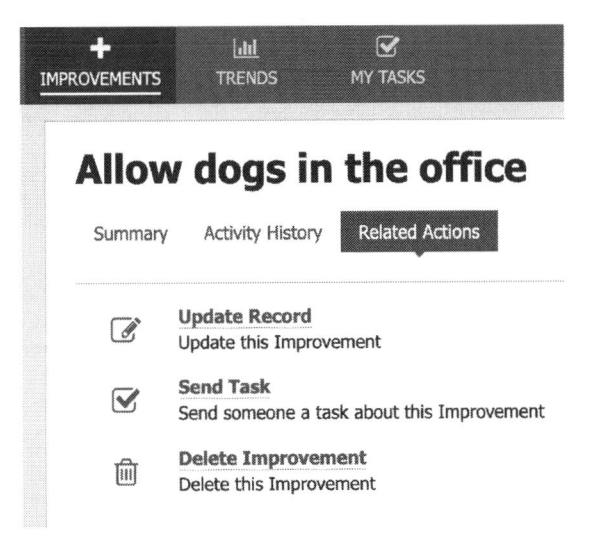

Figure 3.15 – Related actions in the Quick App

Performance

I will guide you through the process of performance analysis in detail in *Chapter 3, Building Blocks of Appian Quick Apps.*

For now, close the **Record Designer** browser tab and navigate back to the Appian Designer main screen.

Checking the Appian process models

When introducing Appian records in the previous section, I mentioned that you can attach process models as related actions. Now, let's have a closer look at the process model object type. In the Appian Designer **OBJECTS** tab, make sure that only the **Process Model** filter checkbox is checked. Appian will now display objects of that type:

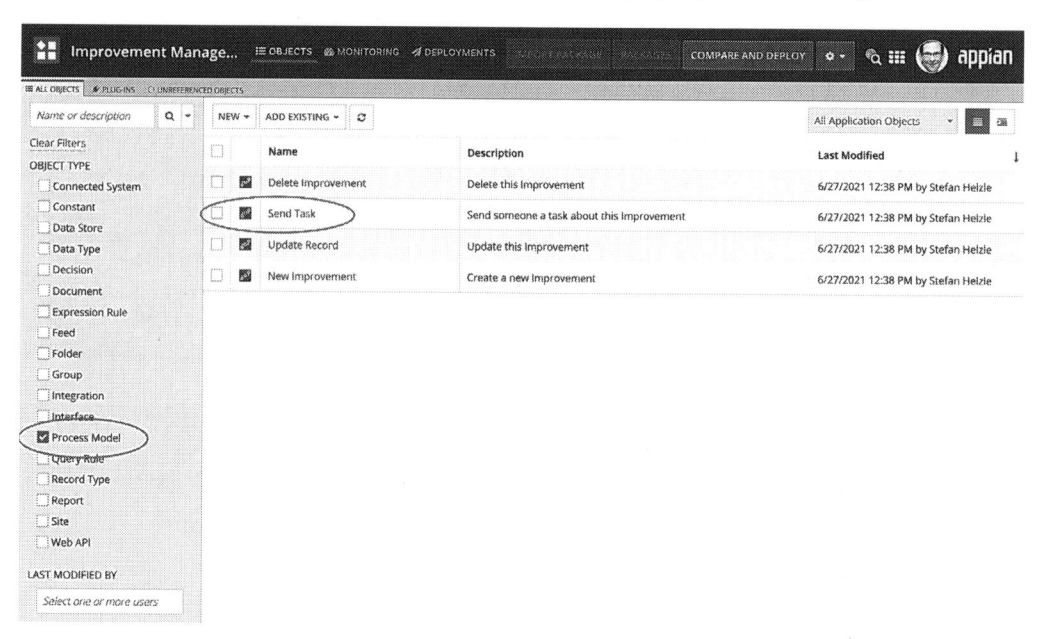

Figure 3.16 – Appian Designer showing process models

We will now have a closer look at the **Send Task** process model. Click its name to open it in the **Appian Process Modeler** window.

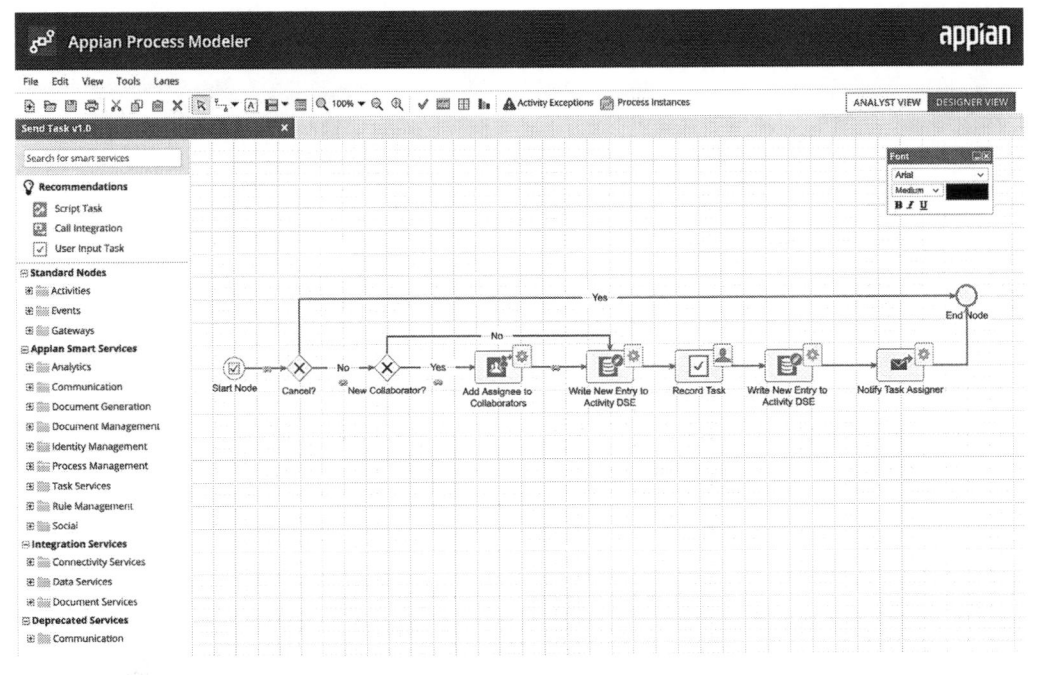

Figure 3.17 – The Appian Process Modeler interface

The model in the preceding figure is using a subset of visuals defined in the official standard for business process modeling, **BPMN (Business Process Modeling Notation)**. This standard is based on the use of boxes and arrows. Each box or process node has a specific purpose, and the arrows or connectors indicate the process flow. Think about how you would draw a business process on a whiteboard to discuss it with your colleagues. It would probably look pretty similar.

When checking the library of available process nodes to the left, you will see that Appian distinguishes between certain types. You will learn how to use them later in this book.

Now, let's have a look at each node:

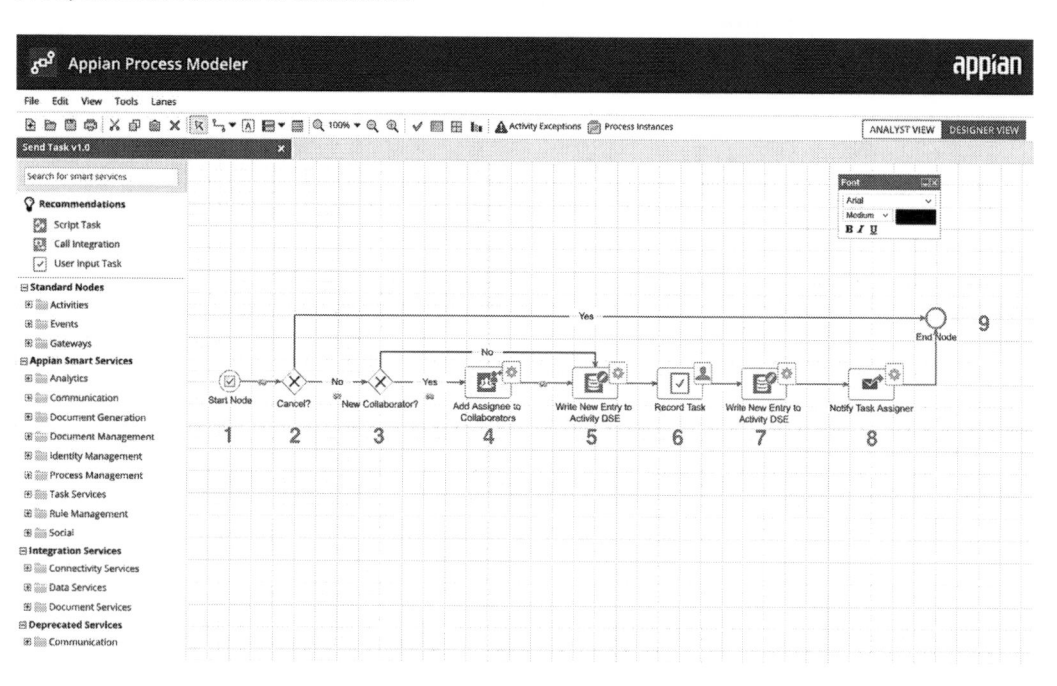

Figure 3.18 – Nodes in Appian Process Modeler

1. **Start Node**: This node contains the interface display when you click the related action, **Send Task**. When the user submits the form, the process is initiated.

2. **Cancel**: If you click the **CANCEL** button, the process flows directly to **End Node**.

3. **New Collaborator**: The process checks whether the assigned user is already allowed to use the application. We discussed this feature already in *Chapter 2*, *Features and Limitations of Appian Quick Apps*.

4. **Add Assignee to Collaborators**: If the user needs to be added to the application, this node will do it.

5. **Write New Entry to Activity DSE**: Again, this is a special type of node. This time, it writes a new item to the improvement record's history in the Appian database.

6. **Record Task**: In Appian, this is called a User Input Task. Nodes of this type have an interface attached. As the process flow activates this node, the assignee gets an email notification and can open the task from their email or tasks list.

7. **Write New Entry to Activity DSE**: As the user completes the task, another history item is saved to the database.

8. **Notify Task Assigner**: This node sends an email to the sender of the task to notify them of the task completion.

9. **End Node**: This is the end. Task completed. Process done.

You now have a basic understanding of what a process model looks like in Appian and have seen an overview of how a process drawn on a whiteboard might be transferred into Appian. Feel free to open the other process models to compare them to the behavior of their respective Quick Apps. Close the **Appian Process Modeler** tab before you continue.

Learning about Appian interfaces

When introducing Appian records and process models, I mentioned *interfaces* a few times already. Let's get into this now. An **interface** is the type of object an application user sees and interacts with. In the record, the *list* itself is configured in the Record Designer, but the *views* are created by assigning an *interface* to it.

In the Appian Designer, filter for interfaces only. You now should see 18 items on the list. Look up the **IM_SendTask** interface and click its name to open it in the **Interface Designer** window:

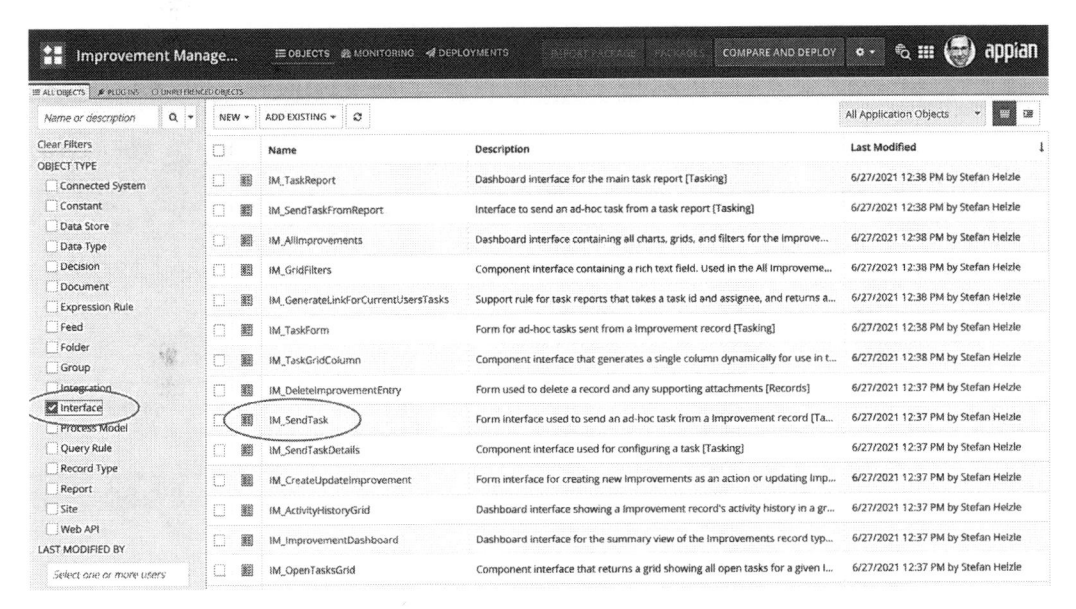

Figure 3.19 – Filtering by interface

The introduction video you will see is worth watching once, but the checkbox below allows you to prevent it from showing up every time. Click **CLOSE** to leave that dialog:

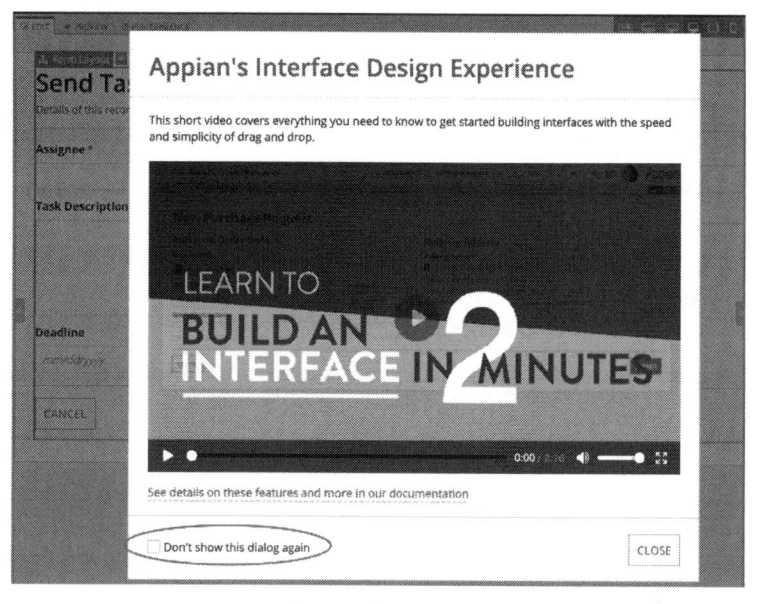

Figure 3.20 – The Interface Designer intro video

The Appian Interface Designer window shows the **Send Task** user interface with the **Edit** tab selected.

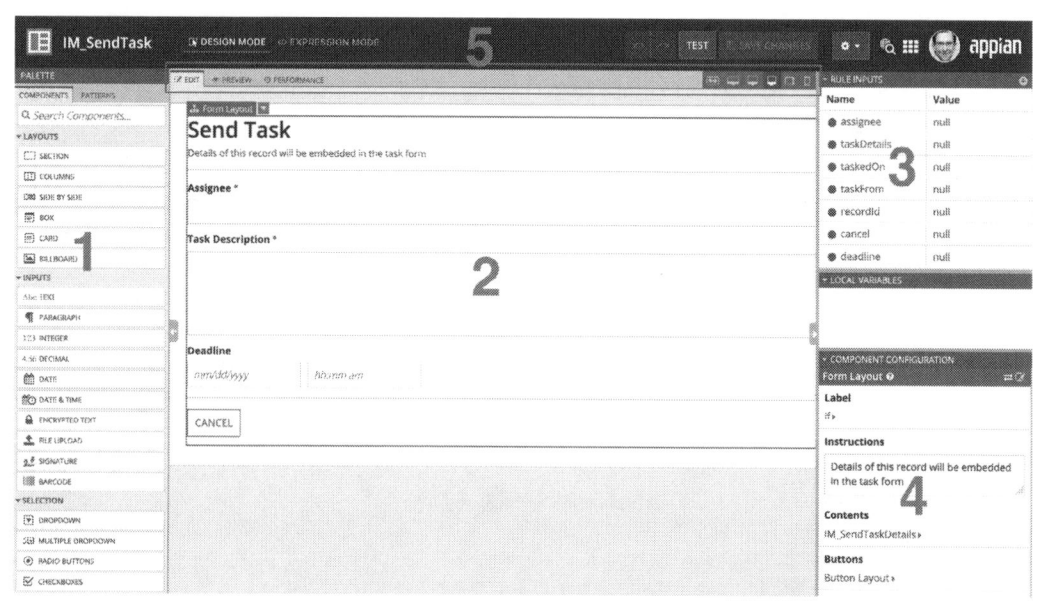

Figure 3.21 – The Appian Interface Designer window with its five areas highlighted

Let's have a look at the highlighted fields in the previous figure:

1. The palette **COMPONENTS** menu shows all of the available user interface components we can use in Appian.

2. In the main area, we add components to create the actual user interface.

3. In the **RULE INPUTS** panel, you can define the data going in and out of the interface when you assign it as a view in a record or a User Input Task in a process model.

4. The **COMPONENT CONFIGURATION** panel allows you to modify all the attributes a component has.

In the top bar, you can switch between the **EDIT** and **PREVIEW** tabs. In the preview mode, the interface behaves exactly as your users would see it, and you can already do some testing. To the right, you choose the kind of device on which to preview or edit the interface.

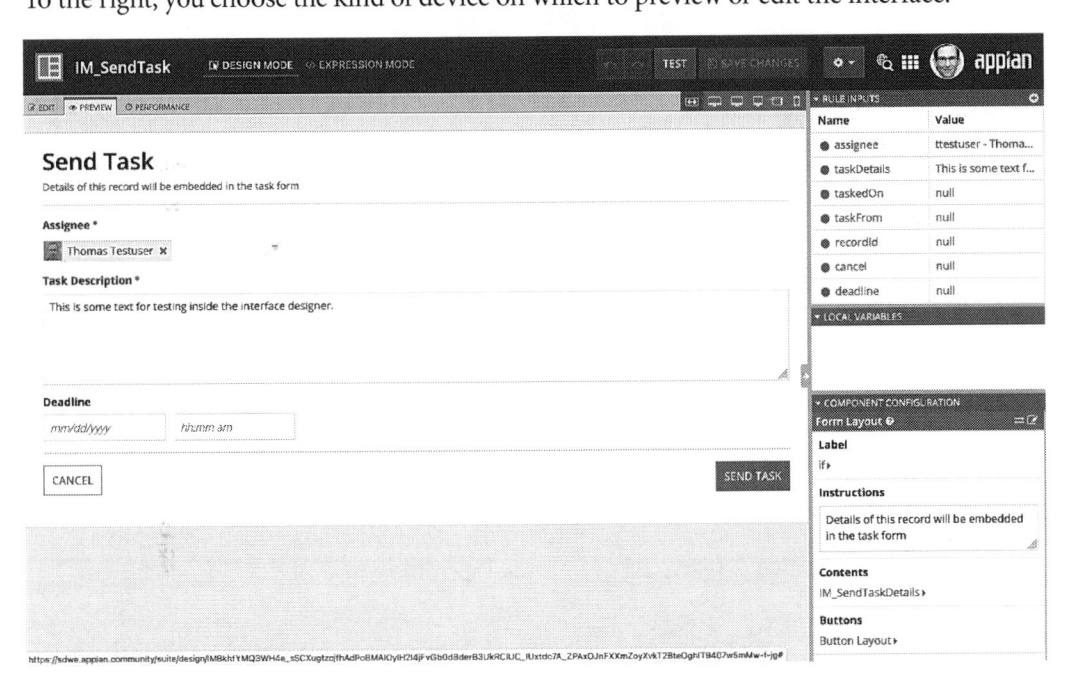

Figure 3.22 – An interface preview in Fit mode

Appian will automatically adapt the interface to the screen size of each device.

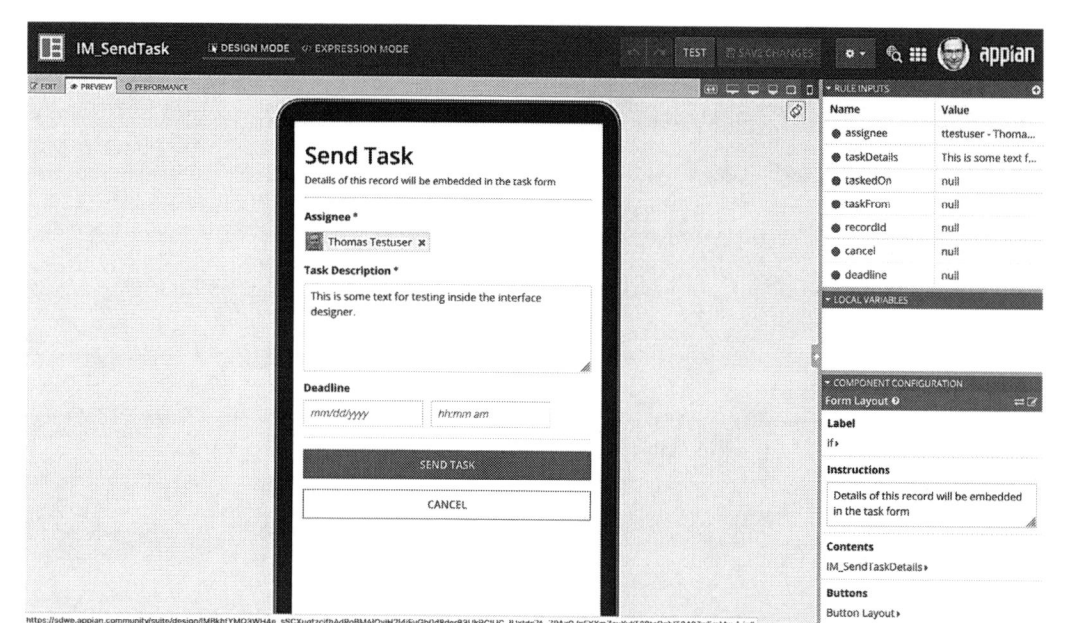

Figure 3.23 – An interface preview in phone mode

The Appian Interface Designer window is the part of Appian in which you will spend the most time. Designing great user interfaces takes some experience. Typically, we revise user interfaces several times until we achieve a good result. Later in this book, I will give you some guidelines to follow to make that an efficient process.

You are welcome to open other interfaces as well. Check the **Views** tab in the Record Designer (*Figure 3.11*) to see which interfaces are used and then look them up. You will then see how the record passes data to the interface. If you see a red error message when opening an interface (for example, **IM_ImprovementDashboard**), this is because the interface expects a value to be passed to the rule input **id**:

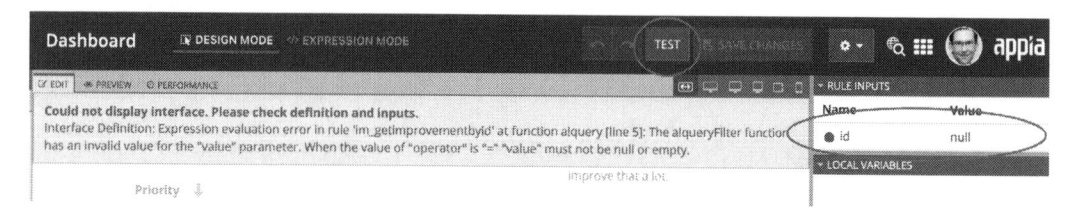

Figure 3.24 – An error message detailing missing input data

Click the **TEST** button, enter `1` in the **Value** field, and then click **TEST INTERFACE**.

Test Inputs

Enter initial input values to test interface

Rule Input Name	Expression	Value
id (Number (Integer))	1	1

Set as default test values

CANCEL   TEST INTERFACE

Figure 3.25 – Testing the interface

Now, the interface knows which data to display, and it looks like this:

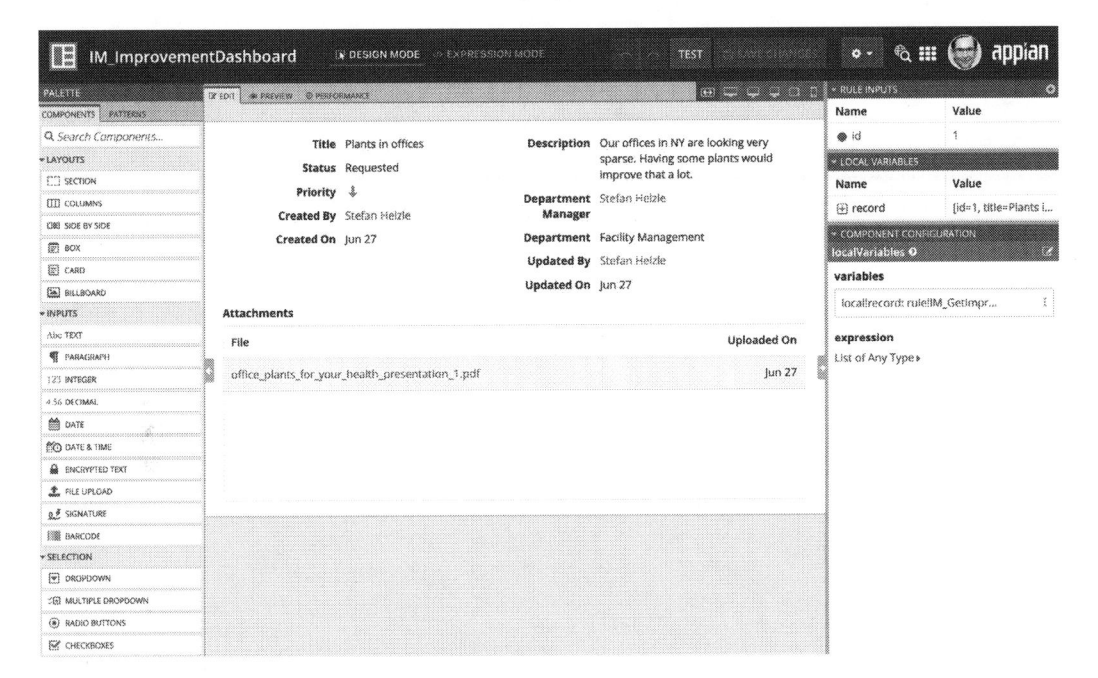

Figure 3.26 – IM_ImprovementDashboard displaying interface data

This was an introduction to Appian interfaces. There will be more details on interfaces, including how to create new ones, later in this book.

Understanding Appian expression rules

In Appian, **expression rule** objects are more code-oriented than any other object type. An important difference to normal software development is that, in Appian, we only use code to add the flexibility we need for building great business applications, instead of developing everything from scratch.

Let's have a look at expression rules. Go to the Appian Designer browser tab and check the **Expression Rule** filter checkbox.

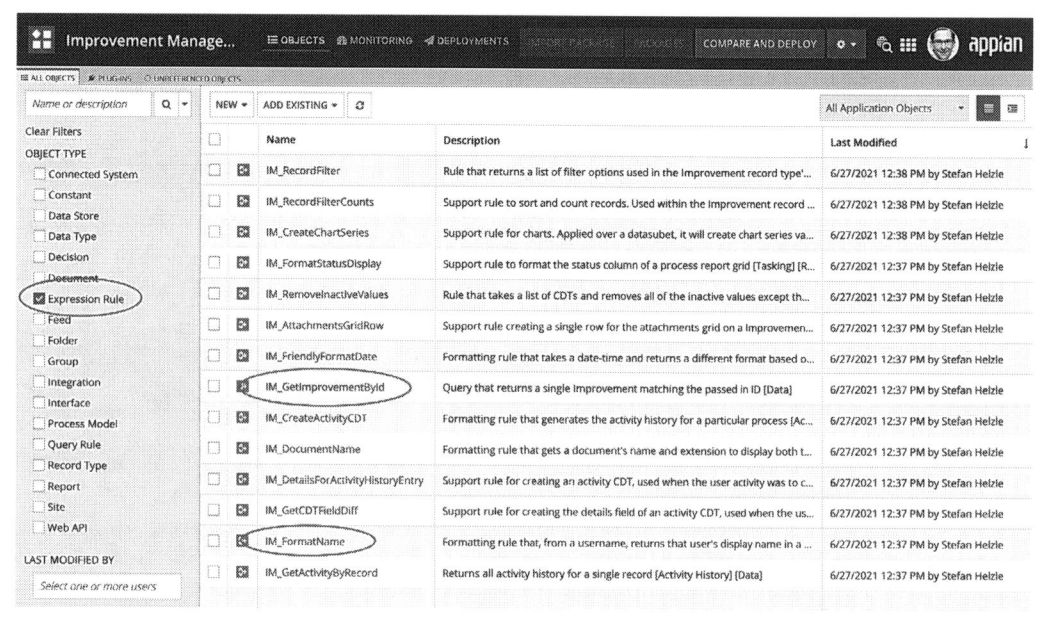

Figure 3.27 – Expression rules in Appian Designer

We are now going to open two expression rules. The first one is IM_FormatName. Its purpose is to take the internal name of a user (the name that you used to log in to Appian) and translate it into a human-readable string. This expression rule is used nine times in the Quick App. You already know one of these: the record list of your improvement record.

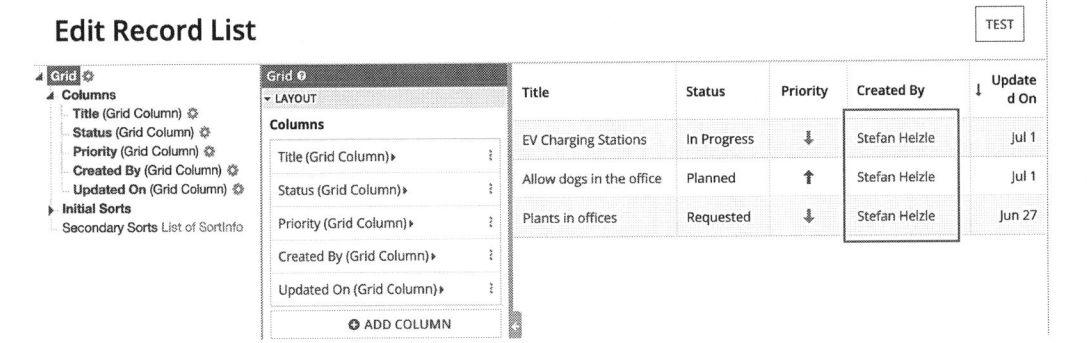

Figure 3.28 – The improvement record list using the IM_FormatName expression rule

Click the name of the expression rule to open it.

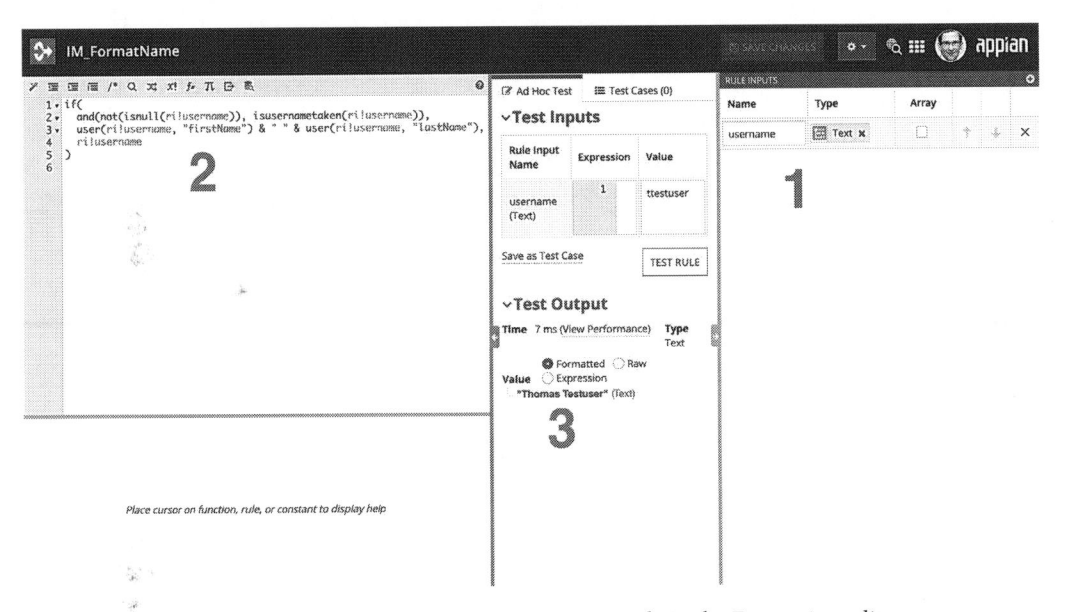

Figure 3.29 – The IM_FormatName expression rule in the Expression editor

In the **Expression Rule Designer** window, you again see three main areas:

1. **RULE INPUTS** is similar to what we saw in **Interface Designer**. This manages the data that can be passed into the expression rule.

2. This is the editor for the expression language code itself.

3. This section has the test input at the top and the evaluated output at the bottom.

Now, try to enter your login name and click the **TEST RULE** button. You will see that the output is a concatenation of your first name, a space, and your last name. This is what the code in line three looks like:

```
user(ri!username, "firstName") & " " & user(ri!username,
"lastName")
```

In Appian, the ampersand (&) character concatenates strings. The Appian built-in function, user(user, attribute), takes the name of the user and the name of the to-be-returned attribute as inputs and returns the requested value.

Close the **Expression Rule Designer** window and look up the second expression rule named IM_GetImprovementById. The purpose of this expression is to fetch the data for a single improvement record item from the database. The item itself is identified by its ID, passed into the expression rule via the rule input **id**. Test this by entering 1 in the **Value** field and clicking the **Test** button. In the **Test Output** section, you will now see the data of the first improvement you created.

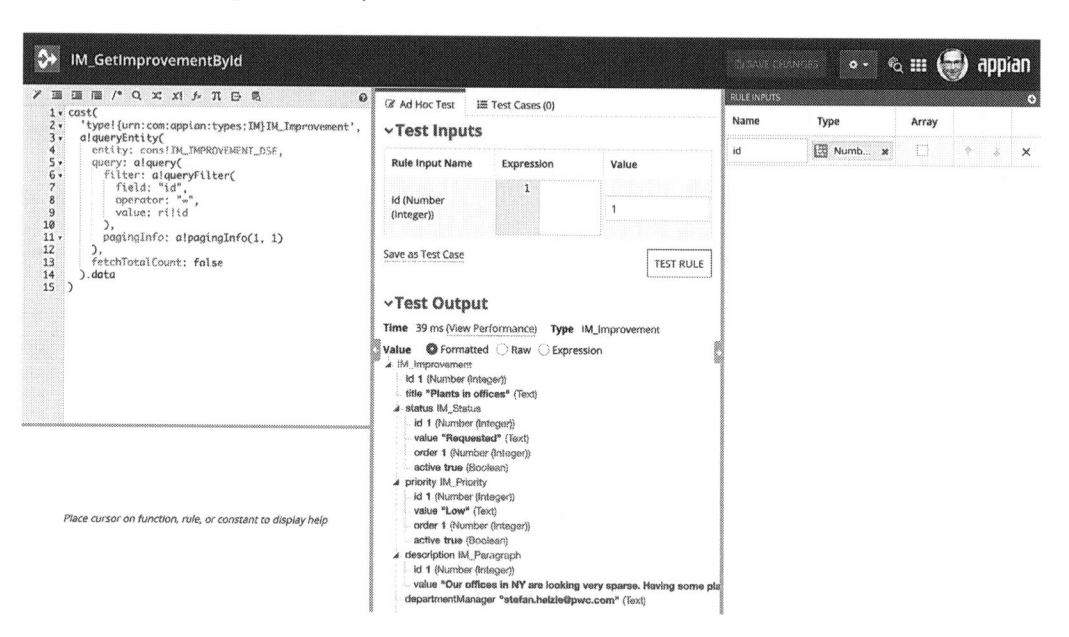

Figure 3.30 – IM_GetImprovementById in the Expression Rule Designer window

The IM_GetImprovementById expression rule is also used several times in the Quick App. Again, one place where it is used is your improvement record, but this time it is used in the related actions.

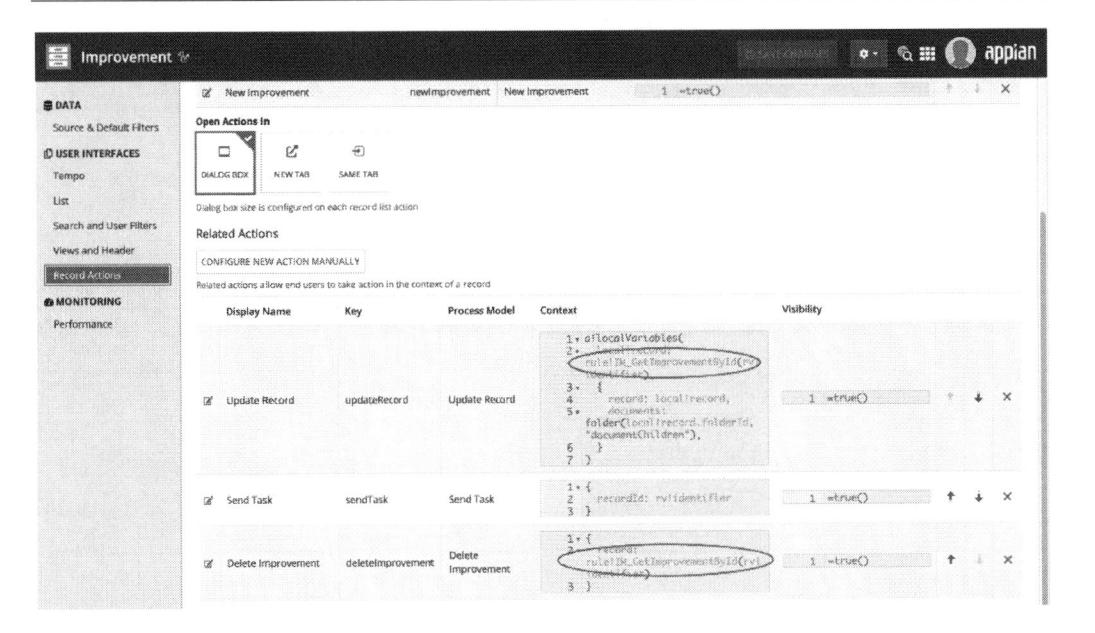

Figure 3.31 – The use of the IM_GetImprovementById expression rule in the related actions

When you click the button or link of the related action, this expression rule is executed to fetch the data for that improvement from the database. This data is then passed into the process as defined for that related action:

```
cast(
   'type!{urn:com:appian:types:IM}IM_Improvement',
   a!queryEntity(
      entity: cons!IM_IMPROVEMENT_DSE, /* Data Store Entity */
      query: a!query(
         filter: a!queryFilter( /* Filter for given id */
            field: "id",
            operator: "=",
            value: ri!id
         ),
         pagingInfo: a!pagingInfo(1, 1) /* Fetch only one item */
      ),
      fetchTotalCount: false
   ).data
)
```

We will go into much more detail about this later in this book. And no, you will not need to constantly write this much code. Remember this; expression rules are about adding flexibility, not about building everything from scratch. And to make this kind of expression rule even easier to create, there is a graphical user interface available. It is called the **Query Editor**, and it pops up when you position the cursor inside the `queryEntity()` function and click the **Query Editor** icon above the code.

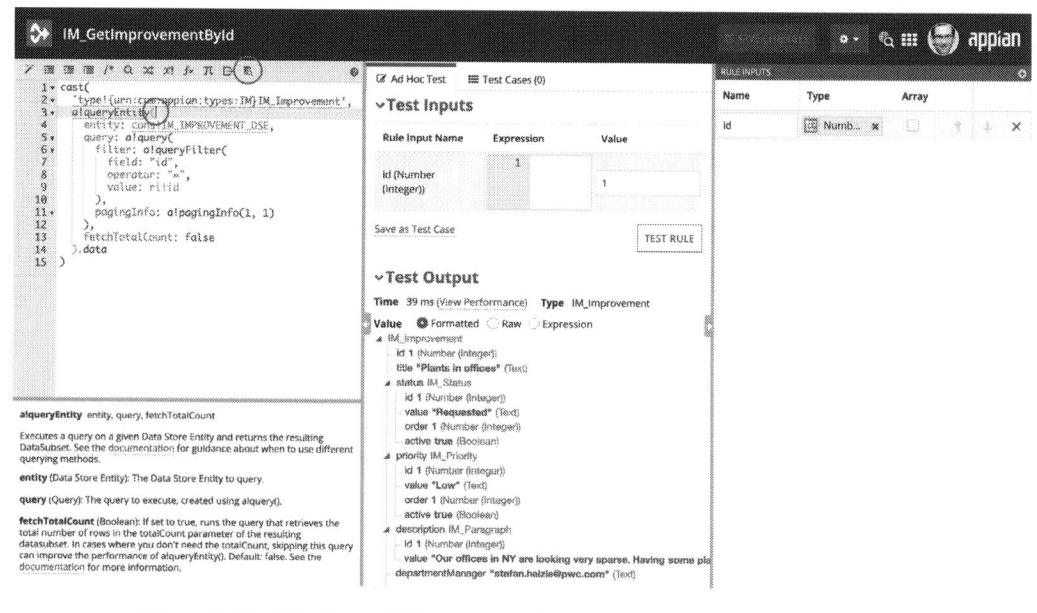

Figure 3.32 – The Query Editor icon in the Expression Rule Designer window

When we click the icon, we get the next screen:

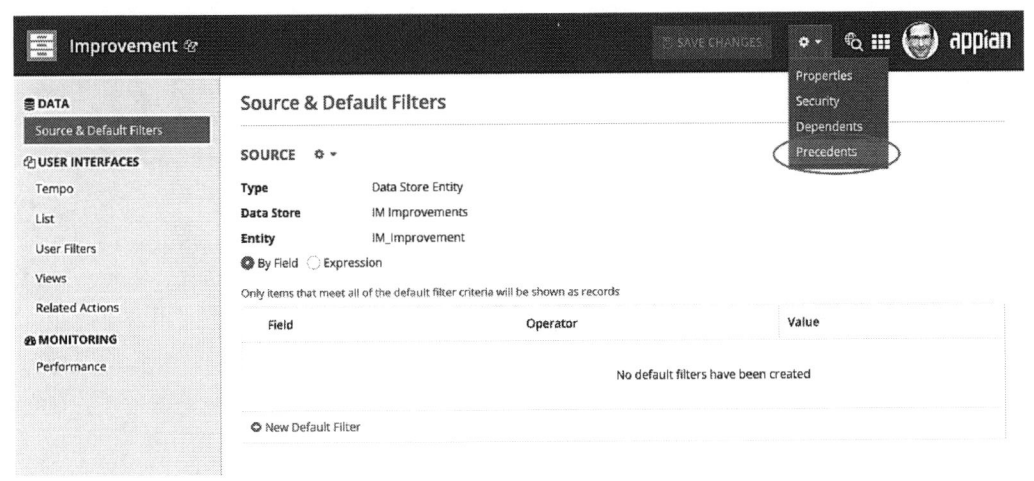

Figure 3.33 – Query Editor

This editor makes modifying expression rules and fetching data from the database straightforward.

Object dependencies in Appian

Appian keeps track of the dependencies of all objects. Open the **Improvements Record** tab in **Record Designer** and open the **Precedents** screen from the gear-icon menu to see all the objects used by the record.

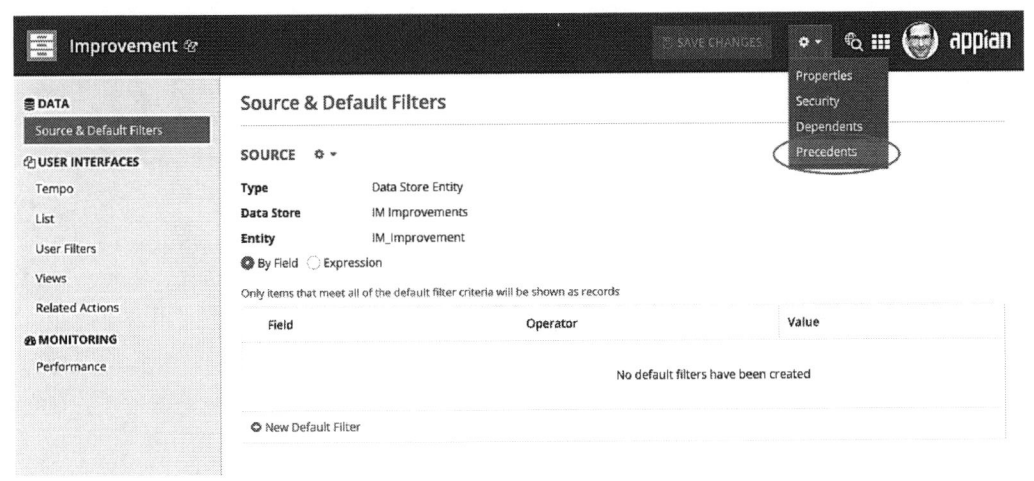

Figure 3.34 – Opening the Precedents screen from Record Designer

Once we click that, we get the following screen:

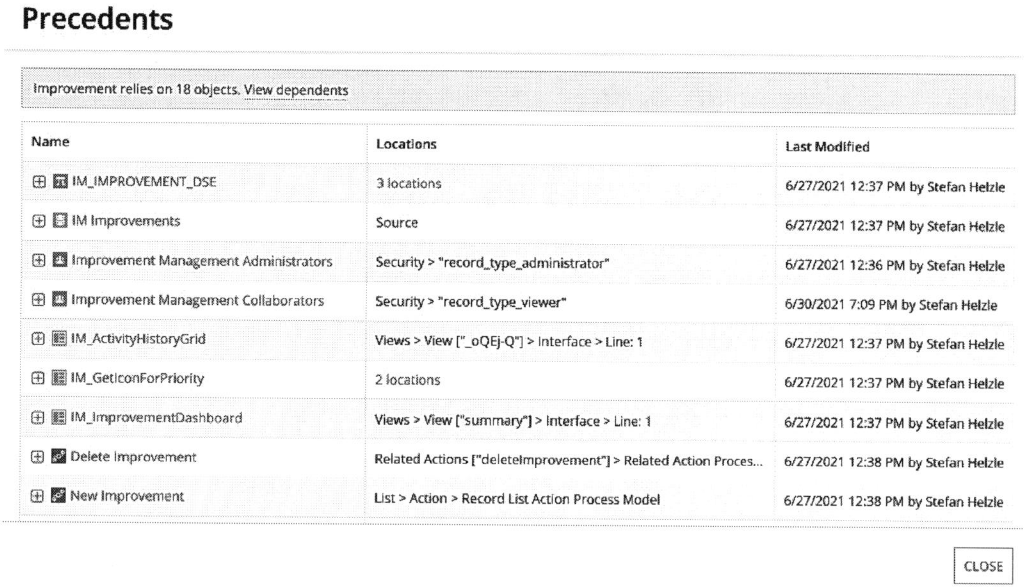

Precedents

Name	Locations	Last Modified
⊞ 🔢 IM_IMPROVEMENT_DSE	3 locations	6/27/2021 12:37 PM by Stefan Helzle
⊞ 📋 IM Improvements	Source	6/27/2021 12:37 PM by Stefan Helzle
⊞ 👥 Improvement Management Administrators	Security > "record_type_administrator"	6/27/2021 12:36 PM by Stefan Helzle
⊞ 👥 Improvement Management Collaborators	Security > "record_type_viewer"	6/30/2021 7:09 PM by Stefan Helzle
⊞ 🖼 IM_ActivityHistoryGrid	Views > View ["_oQEj-Q"] > Interface > Line: 1	6/27/2021 12:37 PM by Stefan Helzle
⊞ 🖼 IM_GetIconForPriority	2 locations	6/27/2021 12:37 PM by Stefan Helzle
⊞ 🖼 IM_ImprovementDashboard	Views > View ["summary"] > Interface > Line: 1	6/27/2021 12:37 PM by Stefan Helzle
⊞ 🖼 Delete Improvement	Related Actions ["deleteImprovement"] > Related Action Proces...	6/27/2021 12:38 PM by Stefan Helzle
⊞ 🖼 New Improvement	List > Action > Record List Action Process Model	6/27/2021 12:38 PM by Stefan Helzle

Improvement relies on 18 objects. View dependents

CLOSE

Figure 3.35 – The Precedents screen

In the gear-icon menu, there is also an option to see all the dependents. This will bring up a similar list of objects referencing this record.

Open a few of them to see what they are and what they do. Make sure not to modify them. Appian would recognize any modifications and disable the option to modify that application from the Quick Apps Designer window.

Summary

This was an interesting trip into your Quick App. It was created with just a few clicks, but it is still powerful. More importantly, it is made of the same building blocks as any other Appian application.

You now have a first impression of what the four main Quick App object types are, what they do, and how they are created, as well as how they interact and how they can be reused.

We learned that Appian records represent the data in an application. Attached as Related Actions, we have process models, which enable the user to interact with records. Using interfaces, we define the Quick App user interfaces and attach them to records and process models. Finally, we can add a bit of program code in expression rules to gain flexibility.

In the next chapter, we are going to have a look at a few use cases suited to Quick Apps.

4
The Use Cases for Appian Quick Apps

Simple apps for simple problems – this is what **Quick Apps** are made for. In this chapter, we are going to explore the use cases that are a good fit and examine how Quick Apps can give power to people.

The most important aspect of Quick Apps is that everything happens directly in the production **Appian environment**. There is no complicated deployment process or waiting for the IT department. Do you have any specific requirements? No worries! You can create a Quick App yourself and instantly manage your team and your data.

In this chapter, we will discuss the following Quick Apps use cases:

- Managing conference attendees
- Advanced task management
- The simple software development process

As we discuss these three use cases in more detail, try to create them directly in Appian.

Managing conference attendees

Let's consider the following scenario: a marketing department has been given the task to organize a small conference. Managing attendees is a big part of it and it involves a lot of manual work. With a Quick App, you will not be able to reduce the amount of manual work, but you can make management a lot easier and add transparency to that process.

The steps in that process for each attendee are as follows:

1. Invite each attendee by email.
2. Request payment details.
3. Check for a received payment.
4. Send out brochures to each attendee.
5. Book a hotel room for the attendee.
6. Check in the attendee at the conference.
7. Hand out promotional gifts only once.
8. After the conference, send out a link to the presentations and recordings.
9. Send a survey by email.

This requires quite a lot of fields in which to store all the data. Some basic fields include the following:

- **Name** (renamed from the **Title** field, as this allows you to search for the name in the records list)
- **Address**
- **Email**
- **Company**
- **Phone**
- **Credit card**
- **Requires a hotel room**
- **Survey results**

> Tip
> You can add as many fields as you think you might need.

Let's think about how to manage the process itself. For instance, you could use a *Status* field for that purpose. Modify the selected status values accordingly.

You should, at the very least, be able to view which attendee was *invited*, *accepted*, and *showed up*. An even more important aspect is to keep track of what each attendee needs and what has been done already. Add two fields of **Multiple selection from list** type:

- The first one can be called **Requirements**.
- The second one is a list of **To-Dos**.

The following is an example of the conference management configuration for this use case:

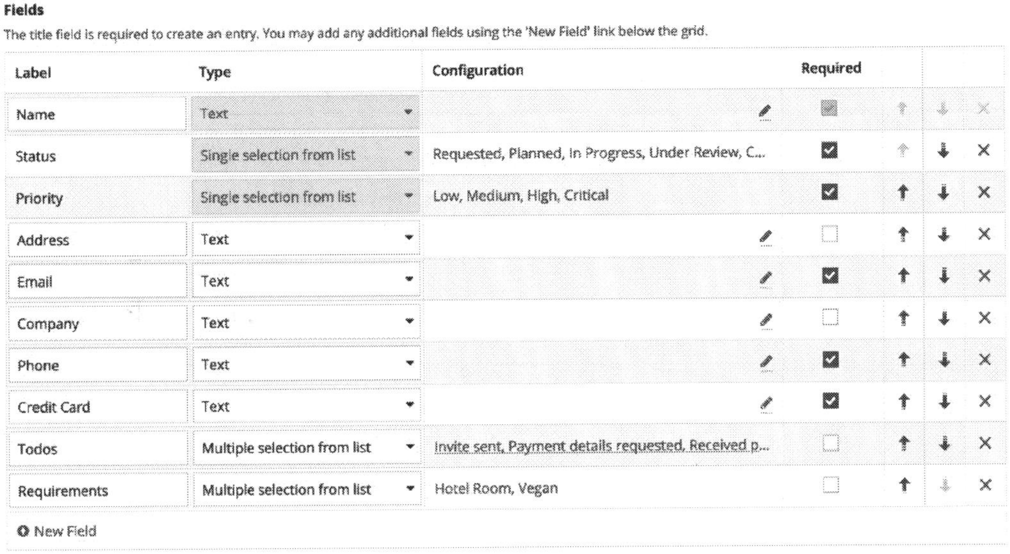

Fields

The title field is required to create an entry. You may add any additional fields using the 'New Field' link below the grid.

Label	Type	Configuration	Required			
Name	Text ▼	✎	☑	⬆	⬇	✕
Status	Single selection from list ▼	Requested, Planned, In Progress, Under Review, C...	☑	⬆	⬇	✕
Priority	Single selection from list ▼	Low, Medium, High, Critical	☑	⬆	⬇	✕
Address	Text ▼	✎	☐	⬆	⬇	✕
Email	Text ▼	✎	☑	⬆	⬇	✕
Company	Text ▼	✎	☐	⬆	⬇	✕
Phone	Text ▼	✎	☑	⬆	⬇	✕
Credit Card	Text ▼	✎	☑	⬆	⬇	✕
Todos	Multiple selection from list ▼	Invite sent, Payment details requested, Received p...	☐	⬆	⬇	✕
Requirements	Multiple selection from list ▼	Hotel Room, Vegan	☐	⬆	⬇	✕

⊕ New Field

Figure 4.1 – An example of the conference management configuration

Now, let's view an example of the configuration preview:

Form Preview

This is the form that users will see when creating and updating entries

Name *

Company

Status *

--- Select a Value --- ▼

Phone *

Priority *

--- Select a Value --- ▼

Credit Card *

Address

Todos

☐ Invite sent

☐ Payment details requested

☐ Received payment checked

☐ Brochures sent

☐ Hotel room booked

☐ Checked in

☐ Promotional gifts handed out

☐ Link to presentations and recordings sent

☐ Survey sent

Email *

Requirements

☐ Hotel Room

☐ Vegan

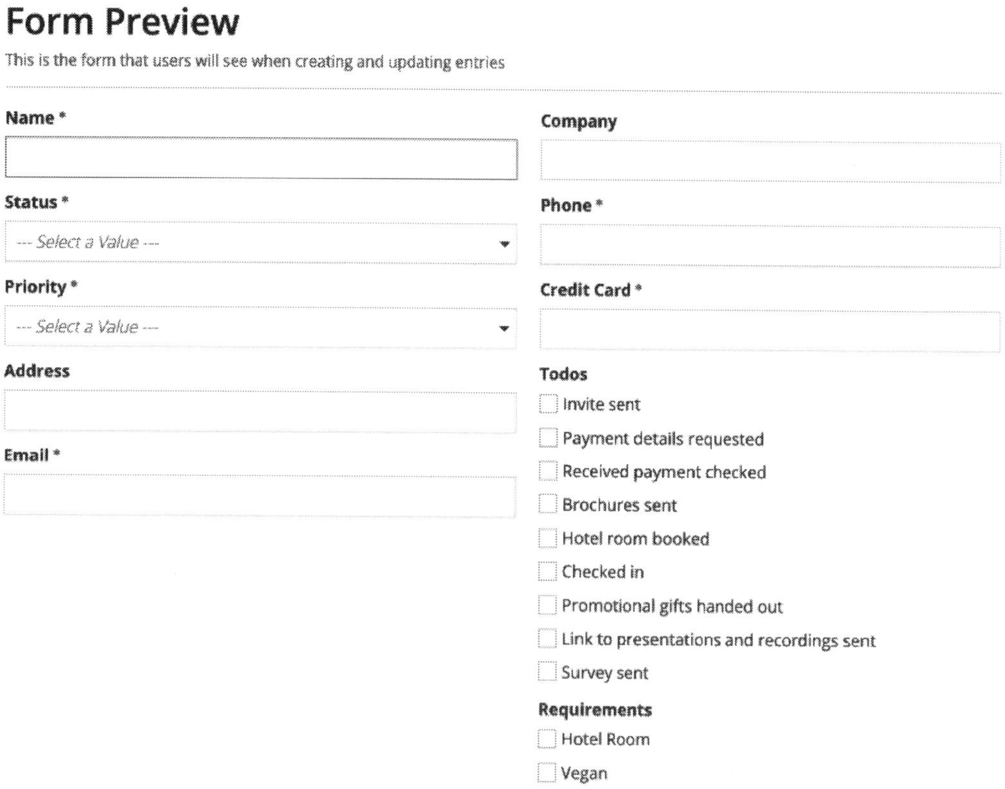

Figure 4.2 – An example of the configuration preview

Now when your team is busy checking in attendees, they can search for that person because the former **Title** field, now renamed to **Name**, is shown in the record list. Following this, modify the record and check the **To-Do** boxes: **Checked in** and **Promotional gifts handed out**.

If you need to perform additional tasks, such as an automated sending of email invitations, integration to your **Salesforce** system to fetch attendee data, or managing the final survey using SurveyMonkey, then you will need to invest a bit more. This can easily be implemented with Appian but is not possible with a Quick App.

So, you just learned how to manage and track the progress of a lengthy and highly manual process using a Quick App. And it makes collaboration a lot easier.

Let's use another great feature of Quick Apps for our next use case.

Advanced task management

We are now talking about a more generic use case with a twist, which is **task management** within a team. You are probably used to managing tasks using email and phone calls. This generally happens without asking, and you never know the status of a task that you assigned to your colleague. Hence, there is *zero transparency*.

It would be a massive benefit for your team if you used a Quick App for this. This is because all information is in one place, including any documents created along the way.

The basic fields in a **Quick App** record are as follows:

- **Title**
- **Status**
- **Priority**

Now, let's add some more fields, such as the following:

- **Description (Paragraph)**
- **Due Date (Date)**

To make task management a bit more professional, let's add a **simple RACI-Matrix**. Here, **RACI** stands for **Responsible, Accountable, Consulted**, and **Informed**. It is used in business analysis to define the roles of stakeholders for a specific task. For each of the keywords, you add a field of the user type. Now everybody will know who the stakeholders are and what their role is:

- Responsible (User)
- Accountable (User)
- Consulted (User)
- Informed (User)

Think about which of the fields are mandatory and which are optional.

Fields of the **Multiple selection from list** type allow you to define certain attributes. In a highly regulated environment, you might need to store the outcome of some tasks in a document management system.

Additionally, there might be certain important steps that you want to track. Create two fields of the **Multiple selection from list** type with the same list of values: one to define the required steps and the other one to track completion. Remember, the Quick App tracks all changes in the history so any unintentional changes in the wrong list do not go unnoticed.

The following is an example configuration for this use case:

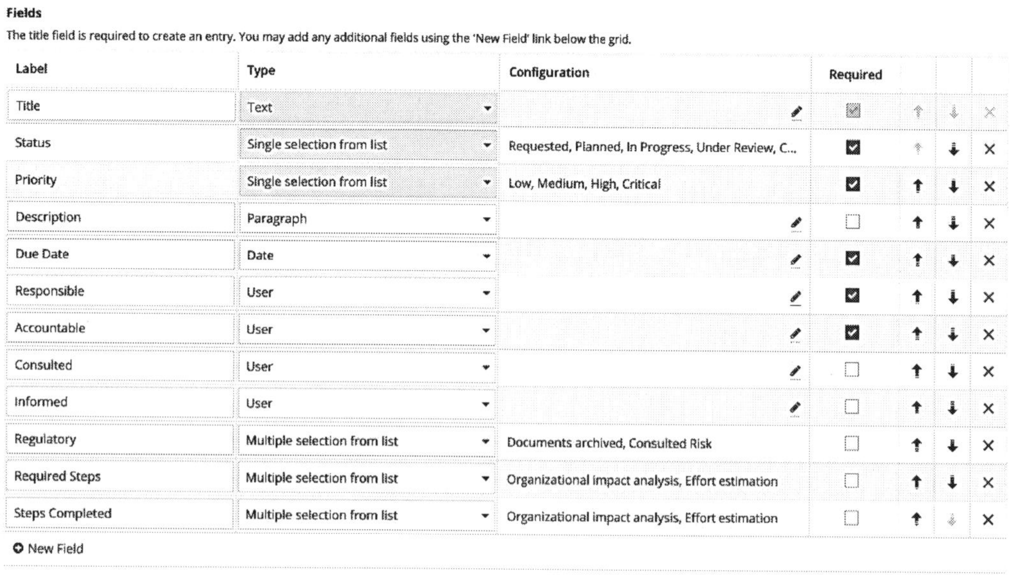

Fields

The title field is required to create an entry. You may add any additional fields using the 'New Field' link below the grid.

Label	Type	Configuration	Required			
Title	Text	✎	☑	↑	↓	✕
Status	Single selection from list	Requested, Planned, In Progress, Under Review, C...	☑	↑	↓	✕
Priority	Single selection from list	Low, Medium, High, Critical	☑	↑	↓	✕
Description	Paragraph	✎	☐	↑	↓	✕
Due Date	Date	✎	☑	↑	↓	✕
Responsible	User	✎	☑	↑	↓	✕
Accountable	User	✎	☑	↑	↓	✕
Consulted	User	✎	☐	↑	↓	✕
Informed	User	✎	☐	↑	↓	✕
Regulatory	Multiple selection from list	Documents archived, Consulted Risk	☐	↑	↓	✕
Required Steps	Multiple selection from list	Organizational impact analysis, Effort estimation	☐	↑	↓	✕
Steps Completed	Multiple selection from list	Organizational impact analysis, Effort estimation	☐	↑	↓	✕

⊕ New Field

Figure 4.3 – An example of an advanced task management configuration

Now, let's view an example of the configuration preview:

Form Preview

This is the form that users will see when creating and updating entries

Title *	Accountable *

Status *	Consulted
--- Select a Value --- ▼	

Priority *	Informed
--- Select a Value --- ▼	

Description

Regulatory
- ☐ Documents archived
- ☐ Consulted Risk

Required Steps

Due Date *

mm/dd/yyyy

- ☐ Organizational impact analysis
- ☐ Effort estimation

Responsible *

Steps Completed
- ☐ Organizational impact analysis
- ☐ Effort estimation

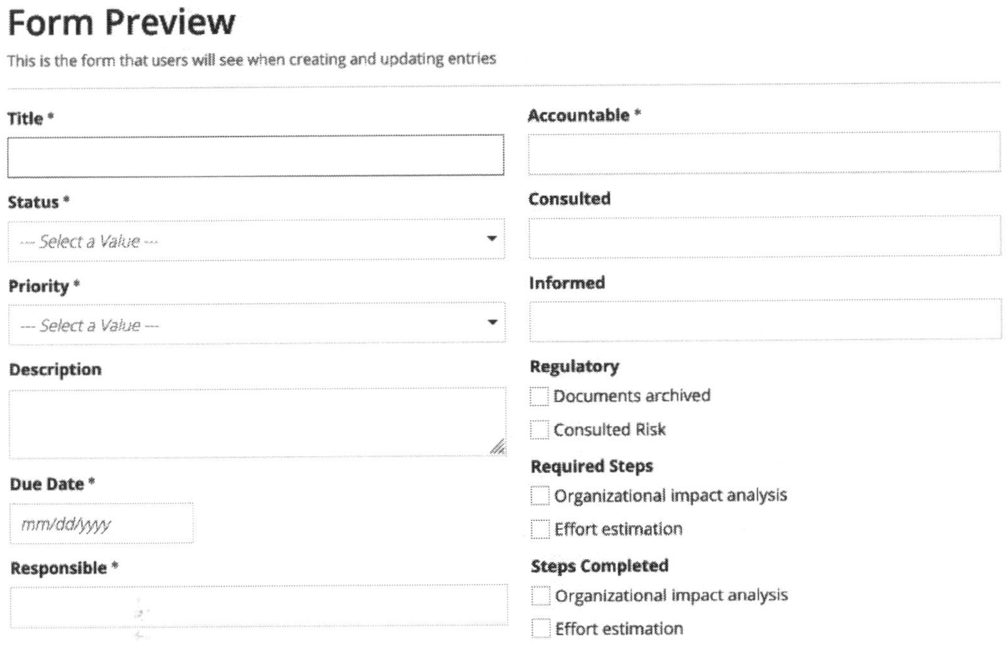

Figure 4.4 – An example of the configuration preview

Now you have added another useful feature to your app. Create a task management item and make sure that you also take advantage of the other built-in features such as tasks and reporting. The related **Send Task** action can be used to split up a larger task into smaller and more manageable steps.

This way, planning and assigning work in teams or even larger departments becomes straightforward. A user can split up larger tasks into smaller ones and track their completion.

This was a nice use case for **Quick Apps**. Do you want even more? Let's examine what we can do with the last use case.

The simple software development process

This book is about software development. The basic idea of software development is to perform a proper analysis of what is required and turn that into software. With Appian and the low-code approach, the actual development is easy. However, the method of turning visions, wishes, and ideas into **Appian Records**, **Process Models**, and **Interfaces** requires well-structured methodologies. These are called **Requirements Management** and **Agile Development**. For additional details, please refer to the following articles:

- `https://www.pmi.org/learning/library/requirements-management-planning-for-success-9669`

- `https://www.agilealliance.org/agile101/`

Now we are going to create a Quick App that implements these methodologies. Note that it needs a bit more than just a plain Quick App like the first two use cases. A great feature of Quick Apps is that you can relate an item in one app to another item in another app. This is what the field of the record type is made for.

To simplify this a bit, we can join requirements management and agile development and draw a process diagram similar to the following:

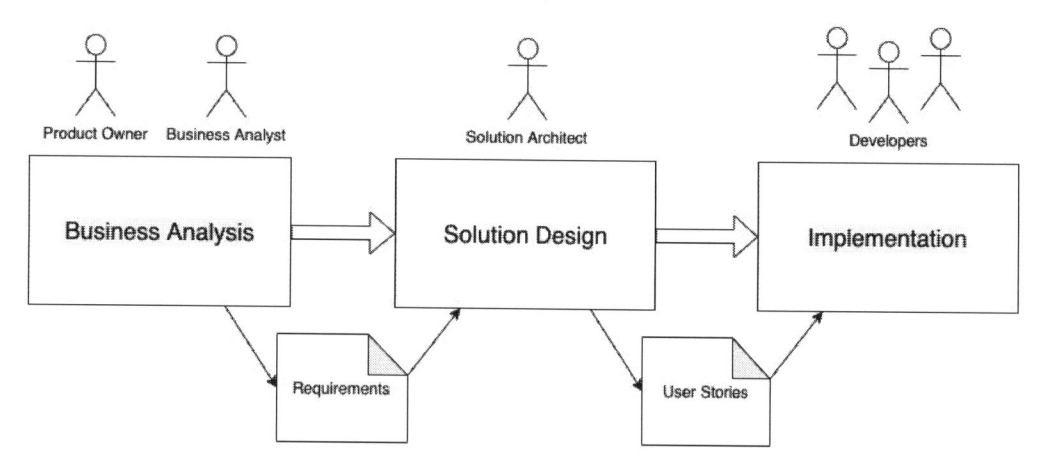

Figure 4.5 – A simplified development process

We will discuss the purpose of this process in *Chapter 5, Understanding the Business Context*, in more detail. You can observe that we have four roles, three major activities, and two deliverables. For our requirements management Quick App, we will focus on the two **Requirements** and **User Stories** deliverables.

A larger application is made of hundreds or even thousands of requirements and user stories. This makes them perfect candidates for Quick Apps, as we need to manage them individually. Additionally, as each user story does exist to implement a requirement, we need to relate them to each other.

Requirements management

First, create the **Requirements Management** Quick App. Add one additional **Description** paragraph field and change the values of the **Status** field to the following:

- **New**
- **Approved**
- **Rejected**
- **Implemented**

Click on the **Continue** button to enable Appian to generate the Quick App. Create a few example requirements in the app. You'll need them later.

Product backlog

Now, create the second Quick App, and name it **Product Backlog**. This is a term used in Agile software development. The items are called **User Story**. I will explain some of these details in *Chapter 5*, *Understanding the Business Context*. For now, perform the following steps:

1. Change the values of the **Status** fields to the following:

    - **New**: Just created and needs refinement.
    - **Ready for Development**: Approved and estimated by the development team.
    - **Developing**: Development team is working on it.
    - **Development Done**: Development team completed implementation and testing.
    - **Accepted**: Accepted by the business.
    - **Rejected**: Rejected by the business.

2. We also need to add some fields here:

- **Description (Paragraph)**: Add the `As a [ROLE], I want [WHAT] so that [BENEFIT]` text as a placeholder and help tooltip. This is a template for a properly formulated user story.

- **Acceptance Criteria (Paragraph)**: Add the text of an instruction that says *Acceptance Criteria describes a set of predefined requirements that developers must meet to finish working on a user story.*

- **Requirement (Record)**: Select **Requirement** as the **Record Type** setting:

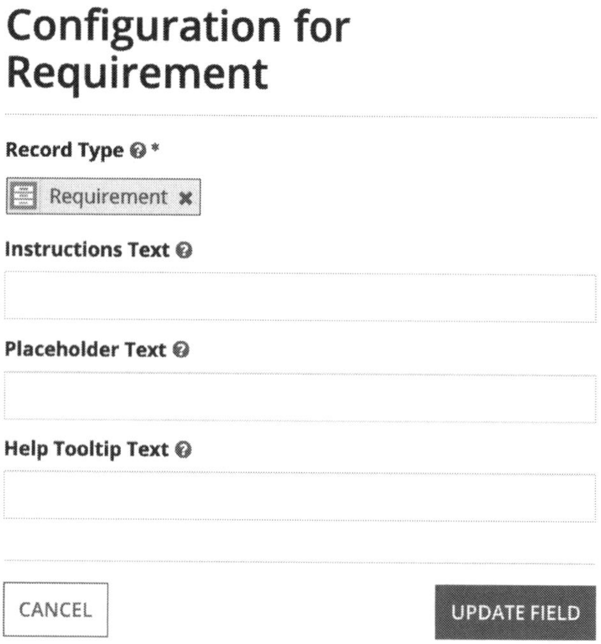

Configuration for Requirement

Record Type ❷ *

> 📇 Requirement ✖

Instructions Text ❷

Placeholder Text ❷

Help Tooltip Text ❷

CANCEL   UPDATE FIELD

Figure 4.6 – The configuration of the requirement field

3.   After adding the fields, the configuration should look like this:

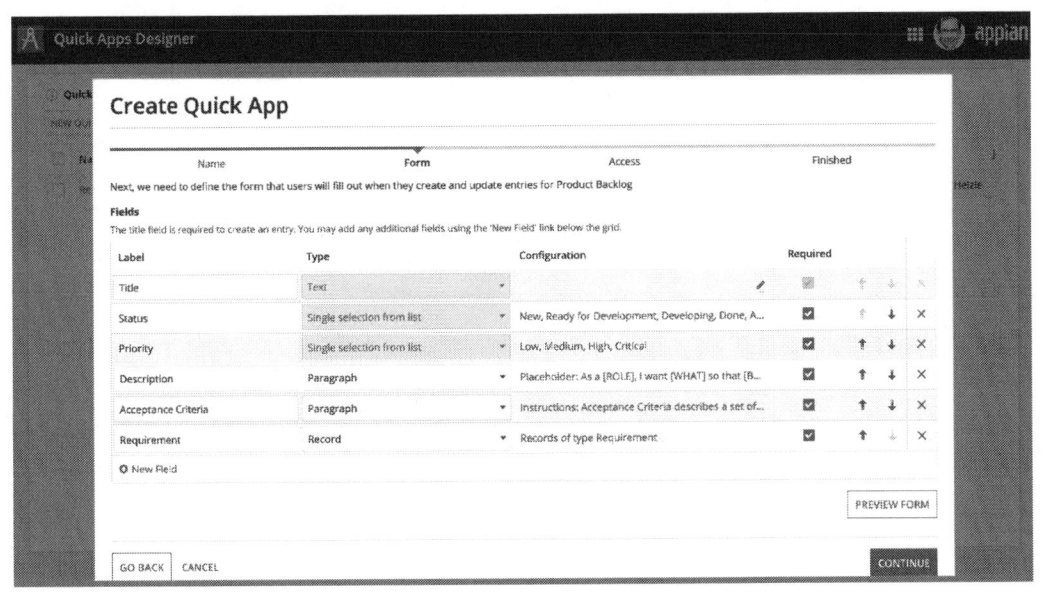

Figure 4.7 – The product backlog configuration

4.   In the form preview, you can observe what the configured fields will look like:

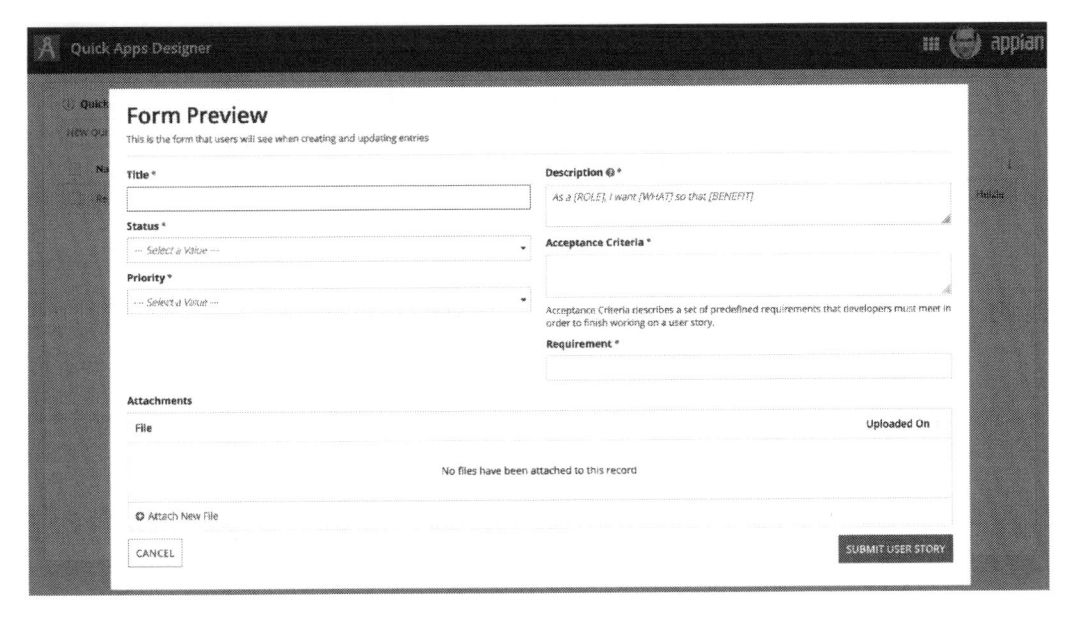

Figure 4.8 – The product backlog preview

5. Again, have Appian generate the Quick App. As you create a few example user stories, you will see that you can relate them to the requirements of the other Quick App:

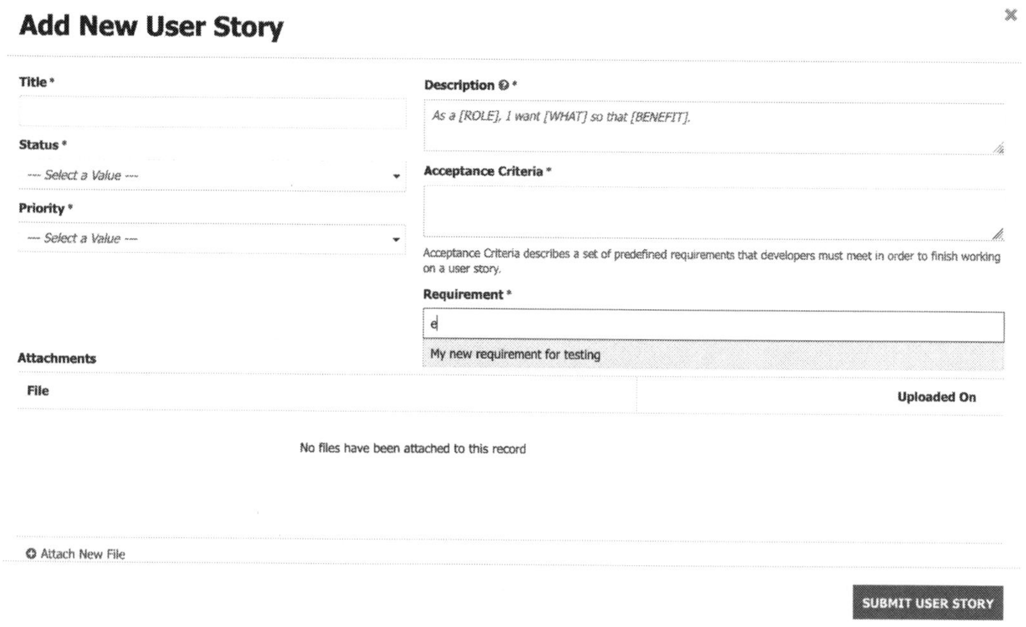

Add New User Story   ✕

Title *	Description @ *
	As a [ROLE], I want [WHAT] so that [BENEFIT].
Status *	Acceptance Criteria *
--- Select a Value --- ▾	
Priority *	Acceptance Criteria describes a set of predefined requirements that developers must meet in order to finish working on a user story.
--- Select a Value --- ▾	Requirement *
	e|
Attachments	My new requirement for testing

File	Uploaded On

No files have been attached to this record

⊕ Attach New File

SUBMIT USER STORY

Figure 4.9 – A new user story

Use the built-in tasks feature (as discussed in *Chapter 2, Features and Limitations of Appian Quick Apps*) to split up user stories into smaller chunks and assign them to your development team. This is probably no competition to tools such as Jira, but it can be sufficient for smaller projects.

So, you just learned how to combine multiple Quick Apps to implement even more challenging use cases. If you wish to read more about this topic, please refer to `https://docs.appian.com/suite/help/latest/Getting_Started_with_Quick_Apps.html`.

Summary

In this chapter, you learned about a few interesting use cases. Each of them uses Quick Apps differently. You now understand how to define a process for items in an app and how to keep track of the completion of individual steps. Managing stakeholders using a RACI matrix is also straightforward. Additionally, you created two interdependent Quick Apps that support the software development process, which we will discuss in the next chapters.

And you have done all of this without writing a single line of code. Awesome! But you should now also recognize that both Quick Apps and a no-code approach have their limitations. The use cases described, including the tricks, are as far as you can probably go.

In the next chapter, you will learn how to create a powerful business application leveraging the process automation capabilities of Appian.

Section 2: A Software Project with Appian

Quick Apps can be a huge benefit for your business but is just a tiny part of what the Appian platform has to offer. Appian enables you to develop full-scale, secure, and mobile-enabled, enterprise-ready business applications with low-code in just a few weeks. In this part of the book, you will learn how to prepare for such a project at our fictional company Tarence Limited.

The meaning of software development

As with all kinds of development or engineering, software development is not child's play. We want software that does the following:

- Fulfills all our requirements
- Is a joy to use and looks great
- Is easy to maintain and enhance

Using low-code and Appian makes implementing software itself less complicated by some orders of magnitude. But the overall process is still the same. We need to understand what to implement in detail. This is the most important part of any software project. This is no new insight by any means and this book is about Appian and not about how to do software development.

Software development using Appian

Why still spend four chapters on software development? The reason is that the way software is developed using Appian is different. And this has a huge impact on a lot of aspects of that process.

In my experience, the most important difference is that we implement the process itself and not a tool to merely optimize some steps in that process. The idea of intelligent business process automation is to make the software run the process and have it reach out to humans only when needed.

This is a significant change in how to look at business software. Up to now, most business applications have just displayed data, allowing the user to modify some fields and write it back to the database.

Now we need to think differently. Let me give you some examples.

Business user: "I need a dashboard showing graphical reports that I can check in the morning to find out what to do."

Why not have the system assign concrete tasks to people? You have your sorted tasks list. Click the first item to get started.

Business user: "I need a screen showing the tasks assigned to colleagues so I can ask them what the status is."

Let's add a due date to tasks and configure escalations to have tasks manage themselves. Why not reassign a task to a manager before it's too late?

Business user: "I need to see all the data of a case on one screen. If the case has the status 'Review,' I want to be able to modify the 'Review Comment' field."

Seems like we have a process that includes a review step. What data will be reviewed? We add a task to the process that shows exactly that data to the user and allows them to enter a review comment.

Starting a software project using Appian

You will now learn what is important in a software development project with low-code using Appian and what is different from what you may be used to. Keep in mind: it's all about the process!

This section contains the following chapters:

- *Chapter 5, Understanding the Business Context*
- *Chapter 6, Understanding Business Data in Appian Projects*
- *Chapter 7, Understanding Business Processes in Appian Projects*
- *Chapter 8, Understanding UX Discovery and UI in Appian Projects*

5
Understanding the Business Context

In this chapter, you will be introduced to the fictional company of **Tarence Limited**. It is a well-established firm, selling a wide variety of products to customers all over the world. Tarence Limited will be our background scenario for creating a feature-complete Appian application.

In this chapter, we will cover the following topics:

- The people at Tarence Limited

- Discovering the IT landscape

- Motivation for the project

- Why use a low-code approach?

The business challenge that our fictional company wants to solve is the high-process costs for the validation of incoming supplier invoices. There is already a system in place that automates the simple steps of matching bank transfers to invoices. This works well, but if the matching fails, the process ends up with a lot of manual work, such as email, Excel, and phone calls. The estimated effort for each manually processed bank transfer is about 15 minutes. Outliers with a processing duration of several days happen frequently as there is no standard procedure for communicating with suppliers.

Tarence Limited is a new Appian client and has grand expectations regarding the speed of its development. Let's discover the motivations and drivers for starting a low-code project using Appian.

Further, you will learn how to create personas and fictional characters based on common characteristics. This approach is designed to help you better understand the user's needs, behaviors, experiences, and goals.

Additionally, we will discuss how to find out what the real drivers are for starting this particular project. We already know about the high-process cost, but most of the time, there is more going on behind the scenes. At the end of this chapter, you will find more information about the mentioned methodologies.

The people at Tarence Limited

The board of management at Tarence Limited has decided to use Appian for all future process automation projects. This is a strategic decision.

However, the people are what powers a company. For a successful Appian project, we need to understand their needs and motivations. Let us now describe the key stakeholders in our project. With this at hand, we can later design the application to perfectly fit their real needs.

Christine – Business Owner

Figure 5.1 – Business owner Christine

The company has grown like crazy in the recent years. However, some processes, conducted by an ever-increasing workforce of clerks, have shown increasing signs of bad efficiency and a lack of transparency. The board of management commissioned *Christine*, the COO of Tarence Limited, to start a business process automation initiative. As a dedicated supporter of processes and KPI-based management, she decided to go with Appian.

Paul – Product Owner

Figure 5.2 – Product owner Paul

As *Paul*, the manager of the accounting department, decided to start an improvement project to increase the efficiency of invoice validation. He was not happy as he heard that Appian was the tool of choice. *Paul* is an analytics person. He likes to use Excel to drill down into data to find out what is going on. He was hoping to make the upgrade to big data and business intelligence. Making decisions on these insights gives him the feeling of doing the right thing. For him, invoice validation is a matter of going through lists of invoices and bank transactions and finding the right match.

Melanie – Key Stakeholder

Figure 5.3 – Key stakeholder Melanie

Melanie is the manager of the team taking care of all the manual invoice validations. She spends a lot of time training new hires, as the level of fluctuation is higher than in other departments. *Melanie* is a people person. She is concerned about the current way in which the assignment and tracking of validation cases works. Her goal is to reduce process costs and increase transparency. To improve employee satisfaction, she wants better software support, leading to reduced training efforts and longer-enduring employments.

Igor – IT Architect

Figure 5.4 – IT architect Igor

Igor has been with the company for many years and has a profound knowledge of most parts of the enterprise IT landscape. He has a background in computer science and used to work as a system administrator. Data flows between systems and the required transformations are what he cares most about. As part of recent system consolidation initiatives, he was responsible for the design of the company's operational data and services integration layer. While being skeptical about the promises of business process automation, he hopes to be able to better support the business departments in the future.

Beth – Key User

Figure 5.5 – Key user Beth

In the two years since *Beth* joined the invoice validation team, she has become a real expert in the subject and is one of the most experienced associates. She has tried to improve the process of operations and efficiency using tools such as Excel. In training conducted by *Melanie*, she supports the knowledge transfer of the trickier details. She is eagerly awaiting to start the project and hopes for a substantial leap forward. She will be in a multiplier role in the project, helping to onboard and train the team.

You

Figure 5.6 – You

You will need to cover all the other roles in this project. The most relevant roles are as follows:

- **Business analyst**: Conduct workshops with the team and turn insights into concrete requirements.

- **Solution designer**: Create an application design that meets all functional and non-functional requirements.

- **Appian designer**: Implement the application according to the design and requirements.

Your main concern is to make the project an enormous success.

Discovering the IT landscape

Any new software at a company will become part of the existing IT landscape. To understand how the individual components work together, we need to understand the structure. In general, this structure is called **enterprise architecture**.

The enterprise architecture itself is split up into three parts:

- **Business architecture**: This is the business structure from an organizational and operational perspective.

- **Information architecture**: This is the structure of enterprise data, including how to find and understand it.

- **Technology architecture**: This is the structure of supporting systems and operational aspects.

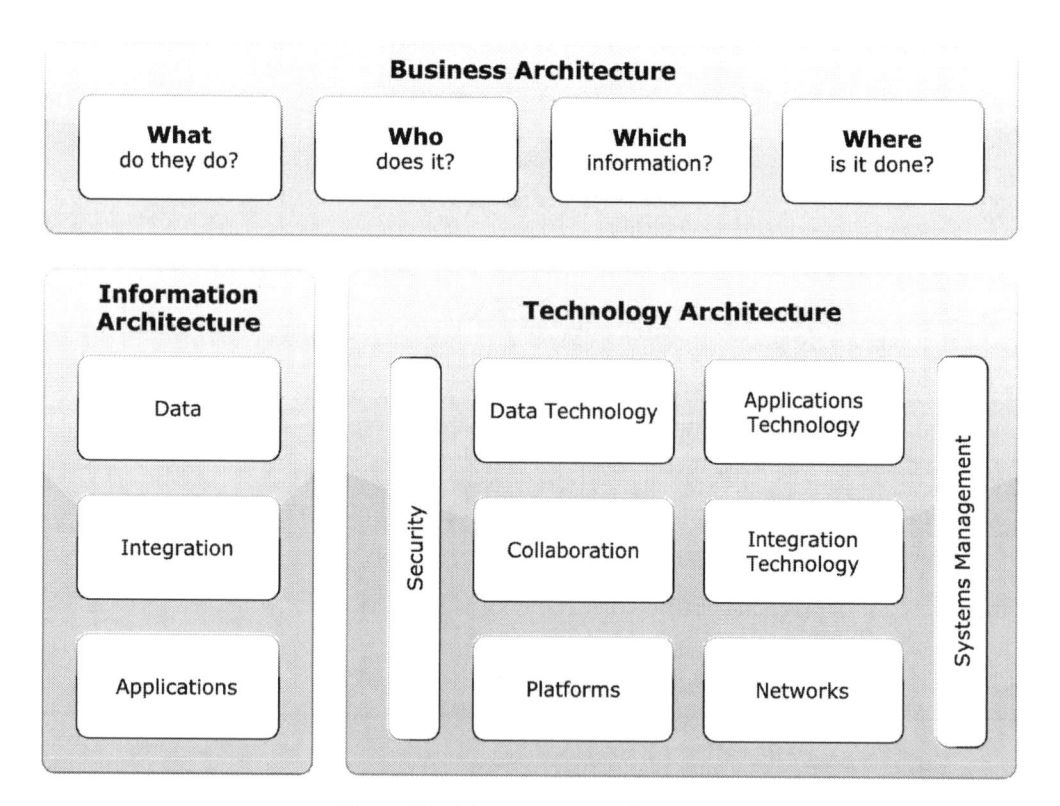

Figure 5.7 – The enterprise architecture

Now we will examine how this works at the level of sophistication required for this book. You can read more about **enterprise architecture** by following the references at the end of this chapter.

Business architecture

At the core of business architecture is the business strategy. It defines what the actual business goals are and where the company wants to go in the future.

Business processes are developed in such a way that the created outputs optimally support that strategy. This is the level you are most interested in, as you are going to implement an application that executes such a process.

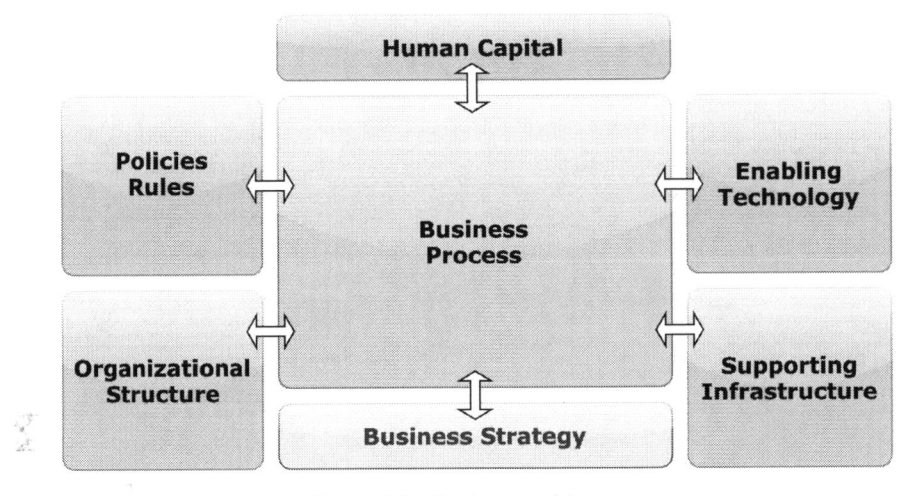

Figure 5.8 – Business architecture

For a successful project, you also need to understand the surrounding context. To get started, we will look at the lean management methodology of Six Sigma. There is an interesting tool called **SIPOC**, which stands for the following:

- **Supplier**: This is the provider of the input. It can also include the trigger that starts the process.

- **Input**: This is the material or data the process is working with.

- **Process**: This includes the activities required to create the necessary output.

- **Output**: This is the material or data the process creates.

- **Customer**: This is the receiver of the output.

Using this simple methodology, you will gain a better understanding of which parts of the business architecture are relevant for your project. Additionally, you will learn, on a business level, what you need for your application to work and whom to talk to.

Information architecture

Information architecture is the structuring of data relevant to the company's business and their interrelations, along with rules and guidelines for their creation and usage.

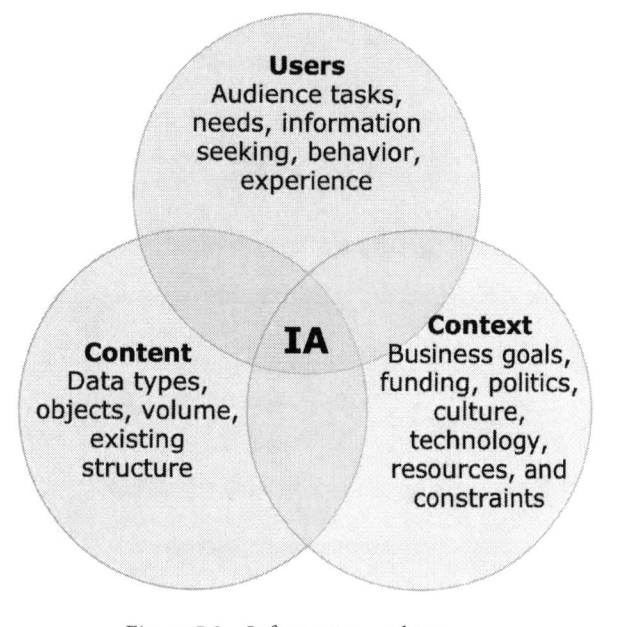

Figure 5.9 – Information architecture

Content

In the context of implementing an application with Appian, let's focus on the **content** part. You will need to understand the individual data entities in detail. Additionally, you need to find out what data you need for your application, what is available, and where to get it. Make sure that you get the following:

- **Structure**: Are there any field names? Is the data flat or nested? Are there singular items or lists?

- **Data types**: Fields can be text, numbers, or dates.

- **Constraints**: Restrictions in length or valid values.

Additionally, bear in mind that you should check for regulations such as data security, data protection, deletion deadlines, and retention periods. Most likely, other departments are also interested in the data your application will need and create.

All the data entities will have a data owner that is responsible for structure, usage, and evolution over time. Additionally, the owner designates a system of records as the sole source of truth.

Context

Context incorporates business goals and provides resources such as technology and funding.

Users

Users are the target audience. They get tasks assigned to them and have specific requirements for information.

So, now that we have understood the basic gist of information architecture, we can move on to technology architecture.

Technology architecture

After talking about processes and data in the last two sub-sections, we will now take a look at the technical infrastructure needed to run all this. The technology architecture structures the following technical components:

- **Hardware**: Servers, storage, and locations
- **Software**: Databases, applications servers, and cloud components
- **Connections**: Network, integrations, and protocols

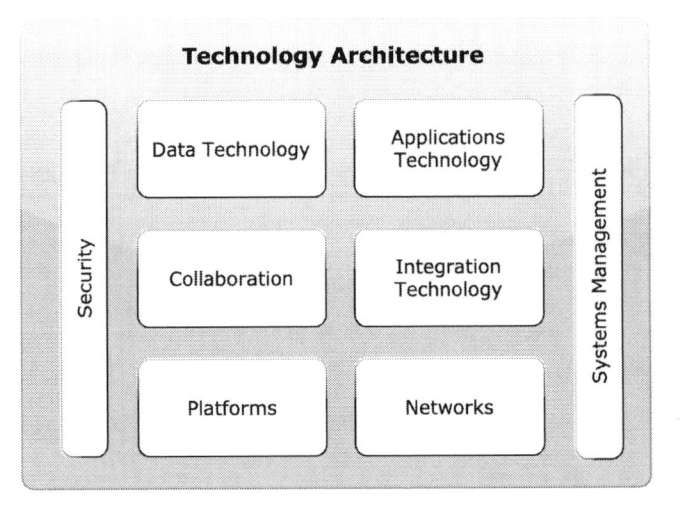

Figure 5.10 – Technical architecture

As all these components need to be operated safely and securely, **Technology architecture** covers the required organizational aspects and procedures.

You will need to identify the technical components and connections necessary for your application. For each connection, you need to cover the protocol, data format, and authentication.

Motivation for the project

Tarence Limited wants to achieve several goals with its project. It is important to understand these goals and use them as guidance when making any design decisions. As goals might be conflicting in certain situations, a clear order of priority helps.

Cost reduction

Reduce the average 15-minute handling time down to less than 5 minutes for 90% of all manual validations.

Scaling up

Manage invoice validations for an expected year-by-year growth of 25% without increasing the workforce. This means that the effort required must be reduced by 25% every year.

Team upskill

Reduce and simplify manual steps to decrease fluctuation. This frees up time to responsibly manage more complex cases. Upskilling turns the team from a participant into the owner of the process.

Implementing low-code Business Process Management (BPM)

In the last section of our chapter, we need to discuss the potential versus the expectations of low-code software development in general and Appian in particular. Ignoring this leads to an increased risk of overlooking important aspects of a project or the whole program.

Appian has the power to initiate a disruptive transformation in the way a company operates, thinks, and makes decisions. It has a profound impact on the technology used, but far greater are the potential changes at the human and cultural levels.

The potential of Appian

Appian has the potential to be a *transformative force*. In the non-manufacturing parts of a company, people drive the actual process, supported by systems for individual steps. For example, high-volume data processing is typically automated, but this is mostly only a single step in an overarching business process.

The reason for this is that in the predigital age, information was created, stored, and transferred on paper in files. Storing information meant having a clever numbering system to be able to find a specific record in a paper archive with levels, rooms, racks, and boxes.

Figure 5.11 – The National Archive

Before, working with information meant having to look up a file, open it as a whole, and search for the right information within it. Following this, you had to add or modify some data following the steps you learned in training or from written documentation. In the end, you closed the file and placed it back into the archive.

Let's fast-forward a few centuries.

Working with information means looking up files, PDFs, emails, and reports in an ERP system, and searching for the right information. Then, you add or modify some of the data following the steps you learned in training or from written documentation. In the end, you save the files.

Sounds familiar, right? It is you who needs to understand and execute all steps in the process.

This is what **BPM, process automation,** and **low code** are about to change. With tools as flexible as **Appian**, we can finally transfer the process itself into a system. The software understands, based on simple business rules or sophisticated machine learning algorithms, what the next task is. If this task cannot be completed by a system, it is assigned to a human, along with all the necessary information required to complete it. To ensure timely completion, tasks are managed by due dates, reminders, and escalations.

Appian orchestrates resources in a process; silicon-based and carbon-based ones.

This is the potential. Next, let's take a look at the business expectations.

The expectations of companies

A company or department starts with Appian to solve a specific problem. Typically, the goal is to introduce or replace a tool. Such a tool is meant to support a step or multiple steps in a process with the idea of increased speed and reduced cost. Other goals can be improved transparency or adherence to upcoming regulations.

A typical Appian project is considered to focus on technical transition.

Most companies expect to achieve these goals without changing their way of working. Doing that would require an organizational and cultural transformation way beyond the scope of a departmental project. Typically, companies are very hesitant to make major organizational changes.

So what happens when expectations meet potential in a project?

Goals versus potential versus change

As you might have guessed, there is a conflict. Introducing a new tool, without changing the way of working, will sacrifice most of the potential that the company expects to make use of.

This conflict must be considered as a potential risk for an Appian project. Making the step too small might give the users the feeling that nothing has changed with the new application. Additionally, you risk losing the users when the leap is too large.

A well-defined process landscape is a good indicator of an organization's willingness to change. To find out where the company stands right now, conduct a process maturity assessment at the beginning of a project. Adjust your level of pushing toward a process organization accordingly.

Changing an organization is a complex endeavor, and it is probably not your responsibility. It still helps to have a basic understanding of change management and to know some of the related methodologies.

Summary

You now understand why Tarence Limited has started its project, the goals it wants to achieve, the people involved and their motivations, the potential for conflicts, and what architecture means on an enterprise level. A process maturity assessment and basic change management know-how can help you to navigate around potential risks and make the project a success.

Bearing this in mind, in *Chapter 6, Understanding Business Data in Appian Projects*, we will begin designing an application in Appian. The first step is to analyze the required data and define a data model.

6
Understanding Business Data in Appian Projects

Tarence Limited needs to manage a massive pile of data to be able to serve its customers. You need to develop a good understanding of what that data is in detail and how to model it. You already know about enterprise architecture and information architecture. We will now create a real-world data model for our application, following well-known methodologies and Appian best practices.

In this chapter, we will cover the following topics:

- **Main business data entities**: These represent our most important business objects.
- **Adding relations**: Define how our business objects relate to each other.
- **Adding details**: Define data fields that make our objects.
- **Adding application data**: Have a place for processes to persist data.
- **Finding the right level**: Find the right level between too simple and too complex.

Learning objectives

In this chapter, you will conduct your very first workshop with the team to get an initial idea of the business data. We will then go through an iterative process to create a data model ready to be used for implementation.

The main methodology used is an **entity-relationship model** (**ERM**). In a typical Appian project, there is no need to have extensive knowledge of it, hence I will discuss it only to the required level of detail.

An ERM consists of data objects, entities, and their relations. For each entity, the model also contains all the fields and their data types.

I will guide you on how to use all of this while creating a concrete model. You can see an example of an ERM here:

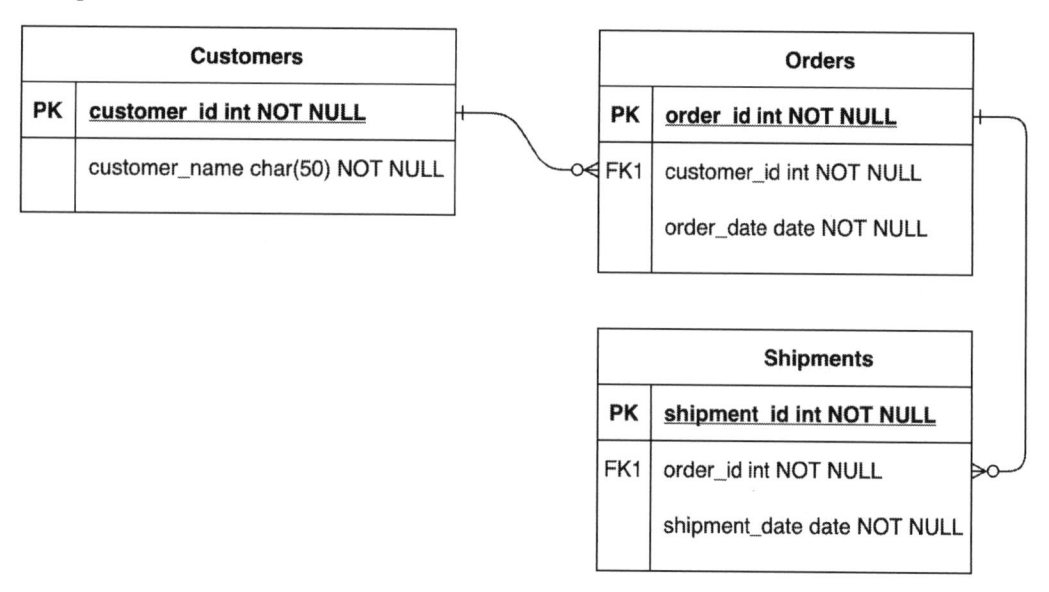

Figure 6.1 – Example ERM

Primary Key and Foreign Key

In a technical data model, we need a **unique identifier** (**UID**) for each entity. This is called the **primary key** (**PK**). In the implementation, we will use this to load specific items from the Appian database.

When creating relations in our model, each entity needs to store the PK of the other entity it relates to. To distinguish it from the entity's own PL, it is called the **foreign key** (**FK**).

In the next section, we will determine which main business data entities are required.

Main business data entities

To find out what the main business entities are, prepare and conduct a workshop with **Igor**, the **information technology (IT) architect**, and **Melanie**, the **subject-matter expert (SME)**. They will probably have different perspectives on the data, and you will need to moderate accordingly to achieve the set goals.

Melanie knows all the **user interfaces (UIs)** in detail and can tell stories about the weird data her team sometimes needs to cope with. In her day-to-day business, she manages the validation process with suppliers and knows exactly what to do. She will need some support from you to get structure into the data she uses.

Igor knows all the involved database tables by heart. That structure seems to be way more complicated than you would expect from Melanie's description. To develop a simplified data model, Igor will need some help.

> **Note**
>
> It is your job to help them both to take a step toward each other and develop an understanding of each other's perspectives. Remember to get started with the high-level business objects. We will add the details later.

In the workshop, we use a whiteboard for collaboration. After an initial discussion about the business data entities at their highest level, the whiteboard looks like this:

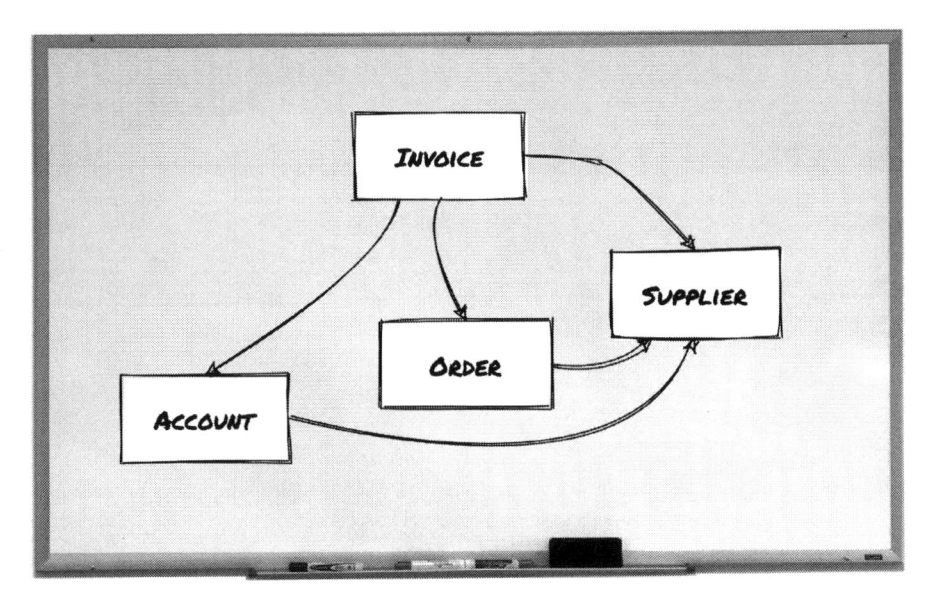

Figure 6.2 – Draft ERM

You really need to drill down into each aspect. Remember—this exercise is about creating a data model you will need to build an application on. All the data entities needed for invoice validation must become a part of the model! Better to be on the safe side and ask questions like this:

- Do you pay invoices before or after delivery and incoming inspections?

- Does an invoice sometimes cover more than a single delivery?

- Is the delivery itself important in the process?

The output of our initial workshop is shown in the following draft diagram:

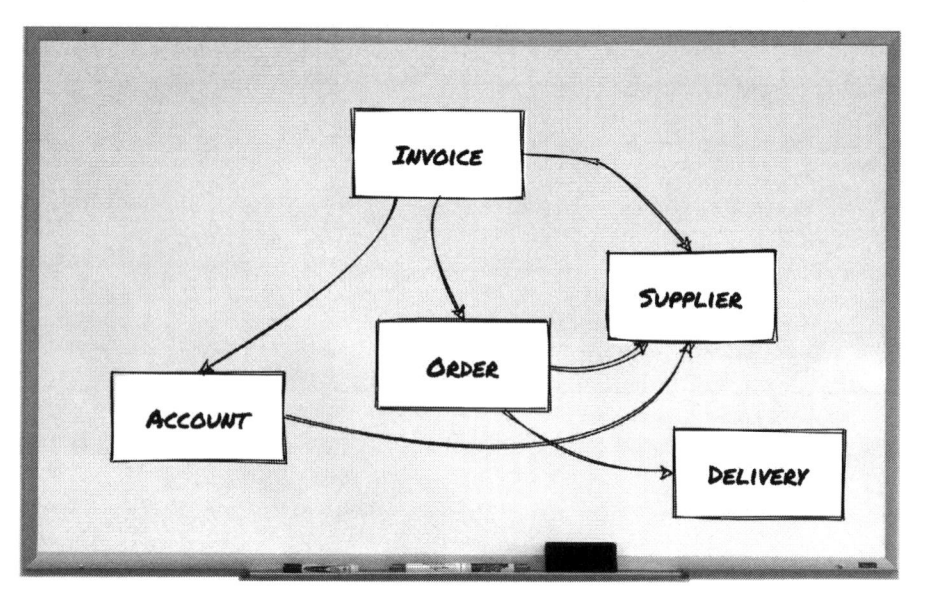

Figure 6.3 – Diagram showing the added delivery entity

Now, you need to take the whiteboard diagram and turn it into a real ERM. Make sure to keep the same entity names as you will use this diagram throughout the project in stakeholder discussions.

> **Software Tools**
>
> In this book, I am using the free software *diagrams.net* (`https://www.diagrams.net`). You are welcome to use any other modeling software, such as **Microsoft Visio** or **Sparx Systems Enterprise Architect**.

You can see the first iteration of the ERM here:

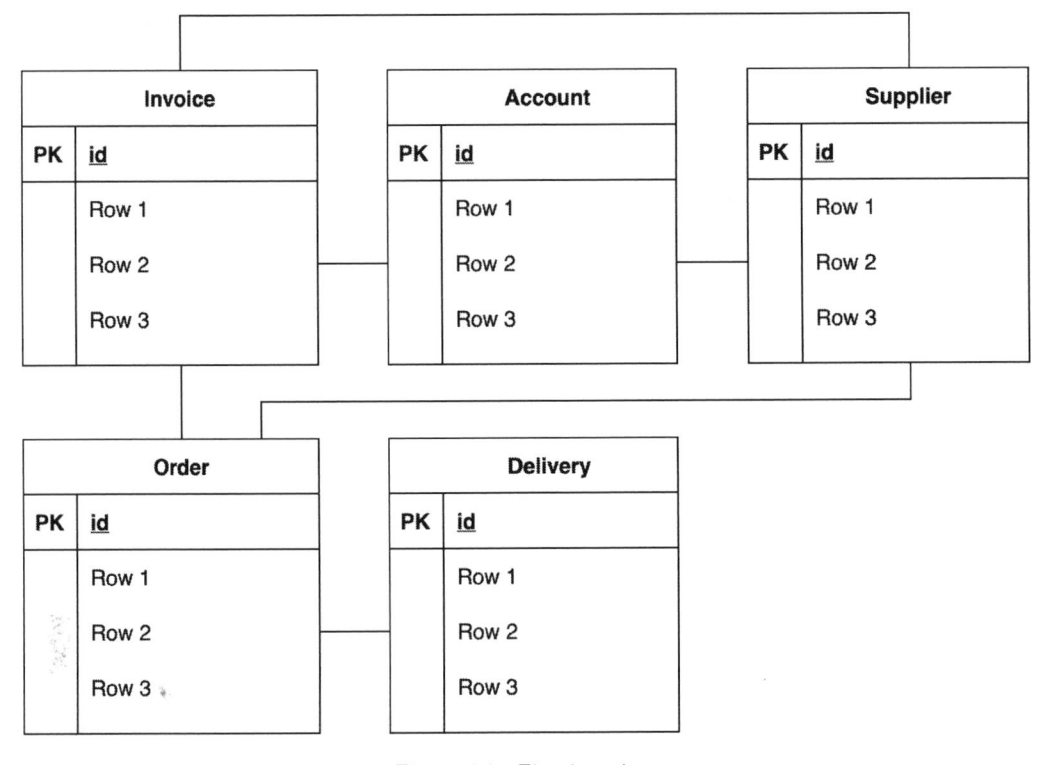

Figure 6.4 – First iteration

In this first step, all the entities are basic placeholders. We will add the individual fields after we have spent time on the relations. Make sure to add an id field to each entity. We will use this unique value as a PK to identify items of the same entity type.

In this section, you identified all the relevant entities. Now, we need to specify the relations.

Adding relations

Your first draft model already shows that some entities have relations to some others. Now, we specify these relations in more detail to get an even better understanding of our business data model.

We will use the following simplified visual representation, ignoring that some relations can be mandatory or optional:

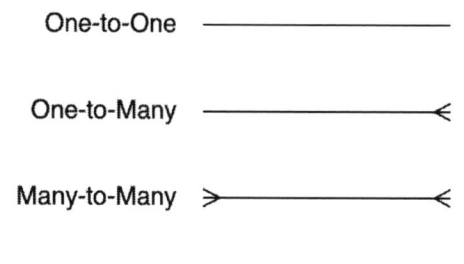

Figure 6.5 – Types of relations

One-to-one

One "A" entity relates to exactly one "B" entity.

The relation between **Supplier** and **Account** is a good example of this kind of relation. Each supplier has only one account, and each account belongs to only one supplier.

One-to-many

One "A" entity relates to one or more "B" entities.

Our model contains more than one one-to-many relation. They are **Supplier-Invoice**, **Account-Invoice**, and **Supplier-Order**. So, one supplier can submit many invoices and we can order many different products from a single supplier.

Many-to-many

One or more "A" entities relate to one or more "B" entities.

In our ERM, the **Order-Invoice** and **Order-Delivery** relations are of the many-to-many type. This means that each order belongs to one or more invoices, and each invoice belongs to one or more orders. This also means that each order belongs to one or more deliveries, and each delivery belongs to one or more orders.

Most of the time, we have simple one-to-one relations here. These cases can be automatically checked. An automated check fails if items on orders, deliveries, and invoices are mixed. This makes invoice validation a complicated matter and is what our application tries to make easier.

You can see a diagram of the ERM model and the relations within it here:

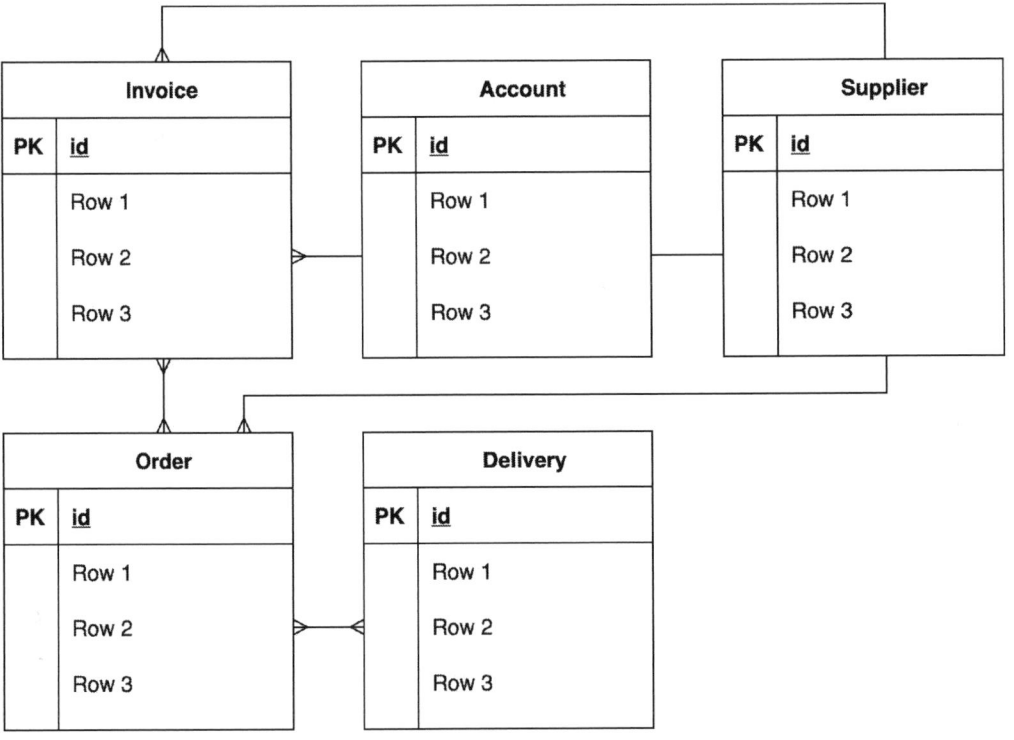

Figure 6.6 – Model showing relation details

Upon completing relations, you added an important aspect to the model. Now, let's define the details for each entity.

Adding details

In this section, you will add data fields to all entities. From the initial workshop, you might have already got some ideas. If this is not the case, conduct another one to share the state of the ERM and discuss the fields for each entity relevant to the process.

> **Tip**
> Existing data structures in an IT enterprise are large and complex. Make sure to not just copy the ERM, but strip it down to fit the purpose of our process application.

We will ignore field-level data types for now, as these are technical implementation details and not relevant for the current project phase.

In addition to the required fields, you will typically want to add other fields to all entities in your model. Some are optional, so read the description to decide which of them you need.

> **Tip**
> Our data model needs to reflect all required data, and we are free in how we design it. In a real project, most of the data would be sourced from other systems, and we have to accept it as-is. Make sure to understand the purpose and meaning of each field.

UID

I already told you to add an `id` field to each entity. This is our own numeric UID or PK. Whenever you want to refer to a specific item, use this number.

External IDs

As we are dealing with data coming from other systems, we will also have to store IDs that the external system is using. Good examples of external IDs are provided here:

- Invoice number
- Account number
- Supplier number

Keep these external IDs separate from the internal UID. Systems do not always guarantee the uniqueness of these values, and duplicates will become a problem if our application relies on them.

Name

Add this field in case you want to give items a name that helps users to identify them. This field will be maintained by users and there might be duplicates. This means it cannot be used as a technical UID.

Add that field at least to the **Supplier** entity.

Description

Users may want to add descriptive text to some of the entities—for example, to the **Supplier**, **Order**, and **Invoice** entities.

Created

Add two fields to each entity to store who created an item and when.

Modified

Add two fields to each entity to store who modified an item and when.

Status

Most entities have a status—for example, an invoice might have an **Open** or **Paid** status. Add that status field to all entities.

Our ERM now looks like this:

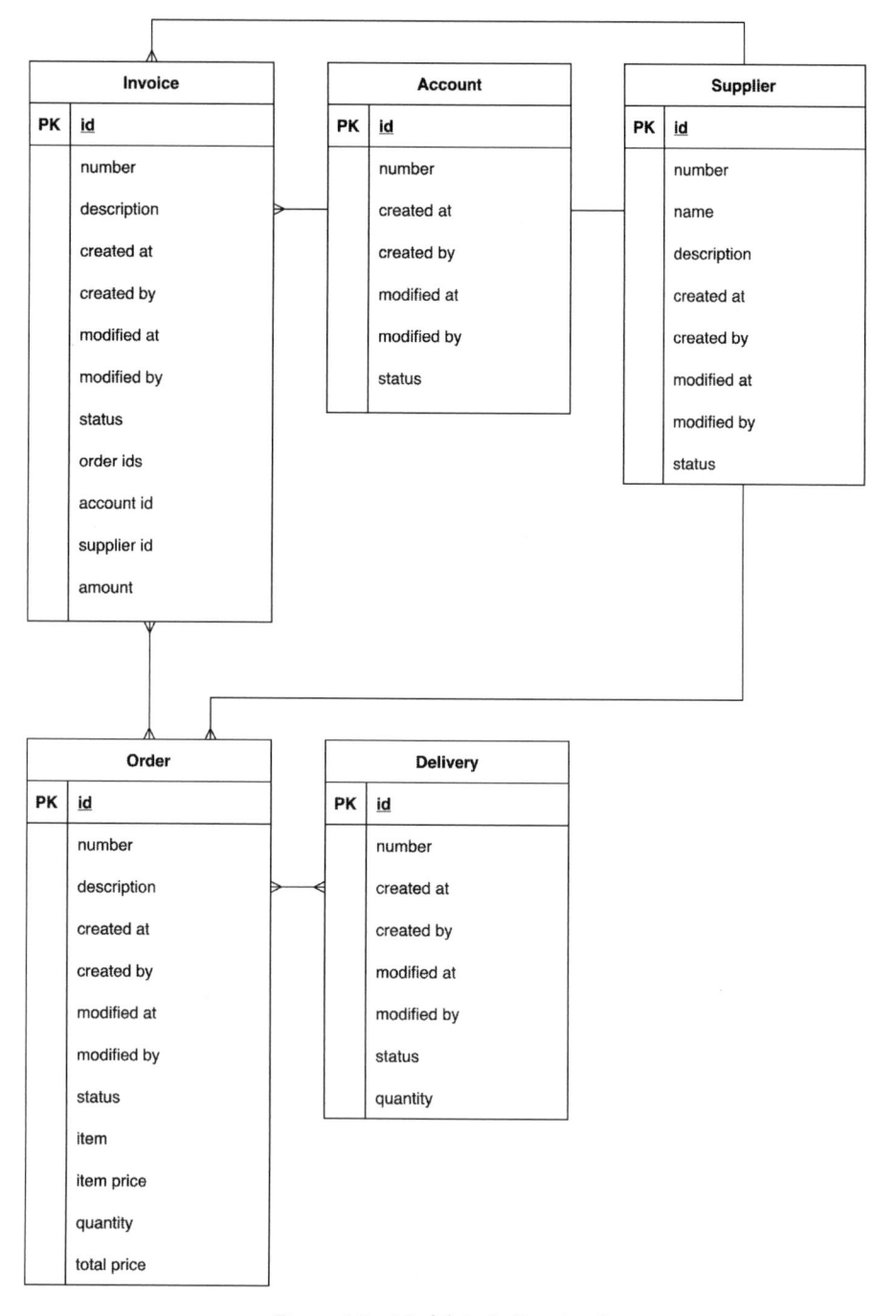

Figure 6.7 – Model, including details

> **Note**
> This is a simplified data model to develop an application within the scope of this book. A real data model would be much more complex. For example, a purchase order would consist of several items.

Adding application data

Your application, or, to be more specific, the implemented processes, also need a place to persist data. In contrast to the functional data already in the data model, we are now talking about operational data. We also need to think about specific requirements regarding process persistence, auditing, monitoring, and reporting.

Let's have a look at the important aspects of application data in the data model.

Process data

Each instance of the invoice validation process needs to store some data. I added the **Case** entity as a good baseline to the model shown in *Figure 6.8*.

Audit trail

The **Activity** entity is used to store information about who performed any case-related activities. The application will display the top time-consuming activities by analyzing the `duration` field.

Monitoring

Making management aware of the current performance of active process instances is called **monitoring**. To identify any additional required fields, let's discuss which **key performance indicators** (**KPIs**) make sense.

Current open cases

No additional fields are required—just count the items where the **is completed** field equals `false`.

Cases at risk

A **case at risk** is an open case for which the due date is near or in the past. We will use the `is completed` field in combination with the `due at` field.

Case ownership

Management wants to know the distribution of open cases to people. For this indicator, we will use the `is completed` and `owner` fields. In the application, we will implement a recommendation for ownership based on this distribution.

Reporting

With reporting, we want to support management in longer-term planning and optimization. This typically requires displaying the variation of certain performance indicators over time to see the impact of changes in the organization or process.

Assuming that the application's process will have several steps or phases reflected in the status field, it would be great to know the duration of each step or phase. To persist that data, I added a **Status Transition** entity to the model. The **Activity** entity is not sufficient, as there can be more than a single activity during a status.

Here, you can see the final ERM for your application:

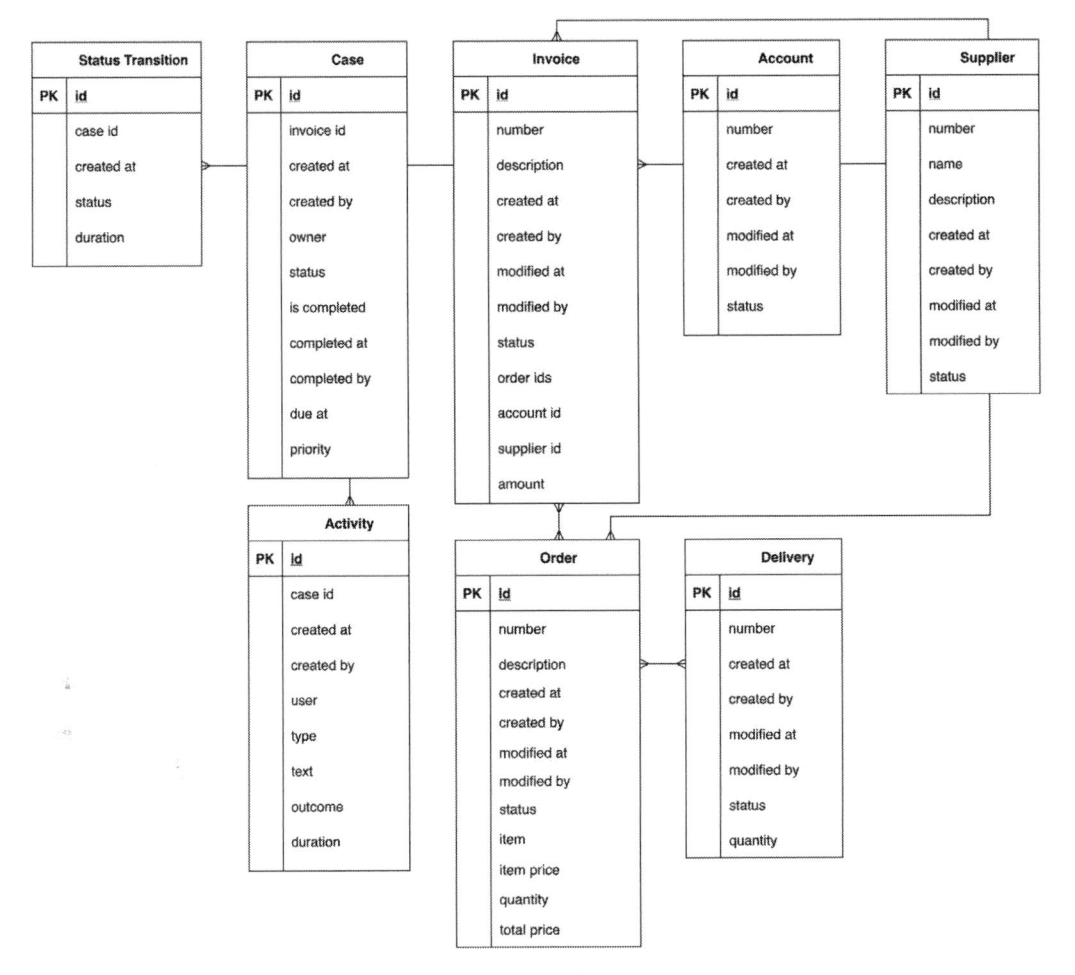

Figure 6.8 – Final data model

It is not necessary to know 100% of the fields at this stage. Add only the ones you already know you will need. The requirements for the details of the data model usually change prior to the completion of a project.

I have tried my best to guide you through the creation of that data model. In the following section, I will give you some guidelines for your ventures.

Finding the right level

In general, try to adhere to the **Pareto** principle: make sure to get the entities right, and then try to get 80% of the fields in 20% of the time. Remember—this book is about low code using Appian. Things can easily be changed once created. Just make sure not to start before reaching 80% of confidence so as not to miss an important aspect.

> **Pareto Principle**
>
> This is also known as the 80/20 rule. In projects, it is often used to describe the invested effort versus the completion of work. Typically, 20% of the effort is spent on the first 80% of the work. For the remaining 20% of the work, you need 80% of the effort.

Start with the basic functional data the business process needs. This data is probably already available from other systems. Talk to an IT architect to understand the data structures and determine which parts you need. In case your process needs data from multiple systems, make sure to identify common IDs needed to relate the data throughout the process.

Next, add the parts required by the application itself. Start with a container for actual process activity. Typically, this is called a case. In the UI, you can use a different one that is more familiar to the users. Many companies already have defined their own wording. If that wording is good, accepted, and consistent, feel free to go with that. If the existing wording is confusing, take the opportunity to introduce a new application and try to define a new naming scheme.

For monitoring and reporting, it is important to keep this separate. You may prefer not to create a generic data layer or Excel export and then force your users to find out how to aggregate data on their own. Challenge your stakeholders and try to develop a purposeful monitoring and reporting approach that effectively supports management.

A final word—if you are not sure that you need it, skip it. In case you find out later that you do need it, you can easily add it.

Summary

In this chapter, you learned how to approach the design of an ERM. You now know the different parts of that model, their purpose, and why they are important. It is the foundation of your low-code application in Appian. You will need this model from now on throughout the development of your application. You can keep it updated and pull it out of your pocket during discussions with stakeholders.

In the next chapter, you will go to the next step and design some business process models.

7
Understanding Business Processes in Appian Projects

With a solid data model, you will now learn how to discover and analyze the business processes in **Tarence Limited**. Processes are the second building block in your application's foundation. Asking the right questions while following some well-known methodologies is the key to success.

The importance of thinking in processes, as part of a digital transformation initiative, is crucial. With Appian, you deal with a business process management platform. You will want the software to conduct the process with the help of humans, which is generally the opposite of humans who conduct the process with the help of some software tools. In this chapter, we will cover the following topics:

- Useful methodologies: Simplifying a challenging process
- As-is process: Capturing the process as currently conducted
- Software-driven processes: Automating your processes

- Task-driven processes: Making peoples' strengths part of the process

- Case management: Coping with non-linear processes

- To-be process: Designing the future process

Learning objectives

In this chapter, you will conduct another series of workshops with your team. This time, we will discuss the current flow of activities required to validate an invoice. Then we will convert it into a proper business process that focuses on automation and implementation in Appian. We will use commonly known methodologies as well as Appian-tailored best practices to make this a success.

Useful methodologies

Before we analyze the current business process situation, I would like to introduce you to four helpful methodologies:

- Business-Process-Modeling-Notation

- Five-Whys method

- Ishikawa diagram

- SIPOC

Business-Process-Modeling-Notation

Business-Process-Modeling-Notation (BPMN) is a way to create formal process models, just like the entity-relationship model for data models.

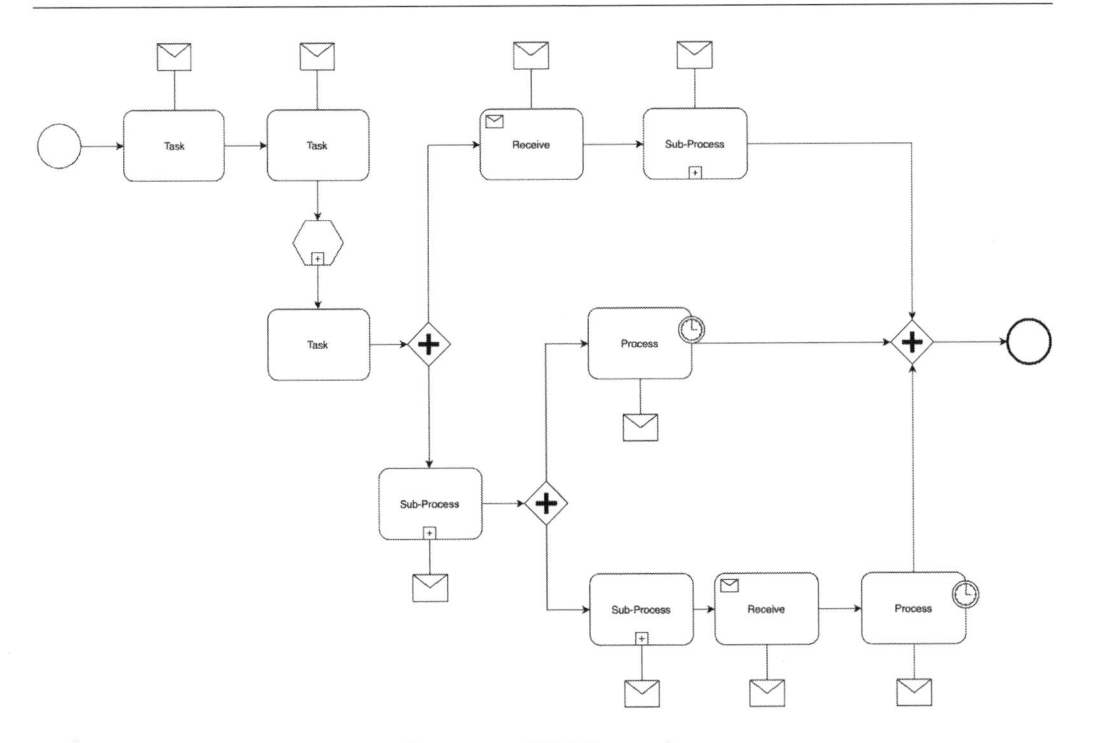

Figure 7.1 – BPMN example

These models look like the way a process is modeled in Appian.

I have had huge success using simplified BPMN models when conducting workshops with business stakeholders. In the latter half of my project, I will show the Appian process models and everyone will be able to successfully recognize the important parts. This makes the software development process a lot more transparent to my business users.

Five-Whys

When we try to analyze a human-driven workflow or process, it is necessary to understand the root causes for all activities and decisions. The Five-Whys method assists in identifying the underlying causes and contributing factors.

The method is as simple as this. Keep asking:

- Why do you do this?

- Why does this happen?

- Why is this necessary?

- Why is it taking time?
- Why is this done this way?

You will typically need five iterations to get to the root cause. I also use this method to challenge the way of how stakeholders think about the business process and their way of working.

Ishikawa diagram

When you discuss a more complex situation with your stakeholders, the Five-Whys method might not be sufficient. Going with an Ishikawa diagram gives you a more visual tool that allows you to analyze a situation where multiple causes are leading to the problem. You can use the Five-Whys method to analyze each cause.

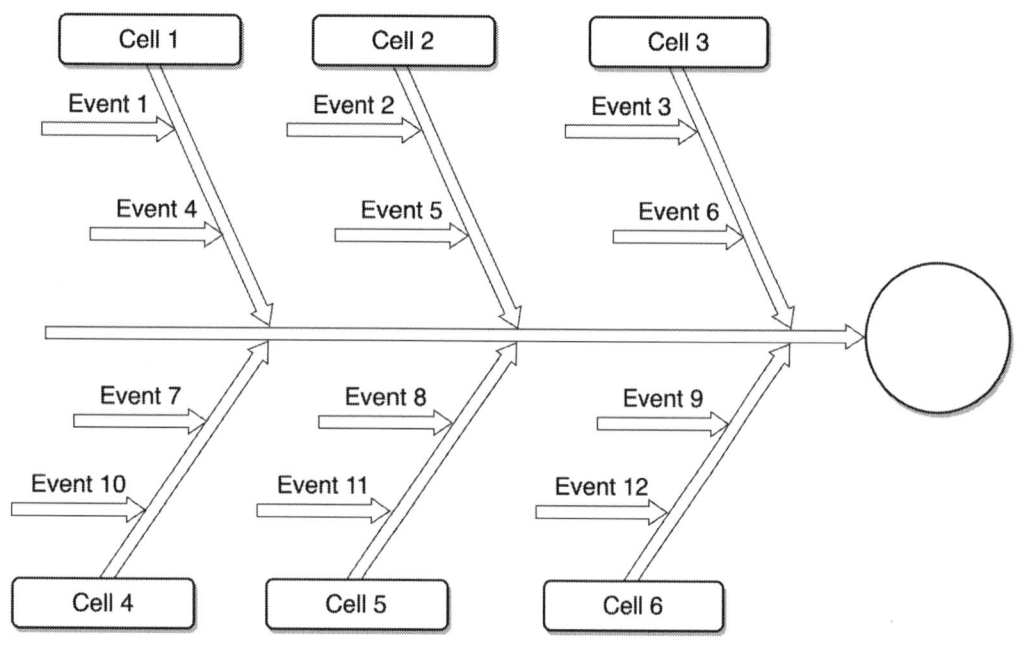

Figure 7.2 – Ishikawa diagram example

SIPOC

SIPOC is a well-known tool used to define a business process from beginning to end and stands for:

- **Supplier**: Can be internal or external
- **Input**: Materials, services, or data

- **Process**: High-level steps only
- **Output**: Materials, services, or data
- **Customer**: Can be internal or external

Create the SIPOC table in the following order:

1. **Process**:

   Write a few steps to outline the process. The focus, however, is on the inputs and outputs.

2. **Output**:

   Recall the data model you created and note down the actual outputs of your process.

3. **Customer**:

   List other processes or departments that need the outputs for further processing.

4. **Input**:

   Check the data model again and identify the entities your process requires.

5. **Supplier**:

   Identify the processes or departments supplying the required inputs.

Supplier	Input	Process	Output	Customer

Figure 7.3 – SIPOC table template

These methodologies will assist you in challenging situations in workshops with business stakeholders. I have given you a quick introduction, but do not hesitate to spend some time learning more about them. You might need them when analyzing the *as-is process* in the next section.

As-is process

In this series of workshops, you will need to discover how invoices are validated currently. We are going to invite Paul, Melanie, and Beth, introduced in *Chapter 5, Understanding the Business Context*.

- **Paul**, the department manager, in his role as product owner, needs to fully understand the current process. He is responsible for the project's vision and overall goals. He might have to make tough decisions when we design the to-be process later.

- **Melanie**, the team manager, represents the operations management perspective. She knows the overall process, as well as connections to other systems and departments, and is responsible for process performance and transaction costs.

- And you need **Beth**, as the expert in the actual invoice validation process. She knows all the nitty-gritty details. Later, she will tell her colleagues about the new process, application, and the huge improvements for everybody.

The main goal of the as-is process analysis is to get everybody at the same level of understanding of how the current process works. Do not leave any questions open, especially in difficult cases where your stakeholders disagree or are even surprised by the actual way of working.

> **Tip**
> Note down any misunderstanding, conflict, or disagreement and make them a topic when designing the to-be process.

Depending on the level of disagreement, you might want to initiate risk management activities. The earlier you start to manage project risks, the better.

The output of the initial workshop is the following whiteboard draft:

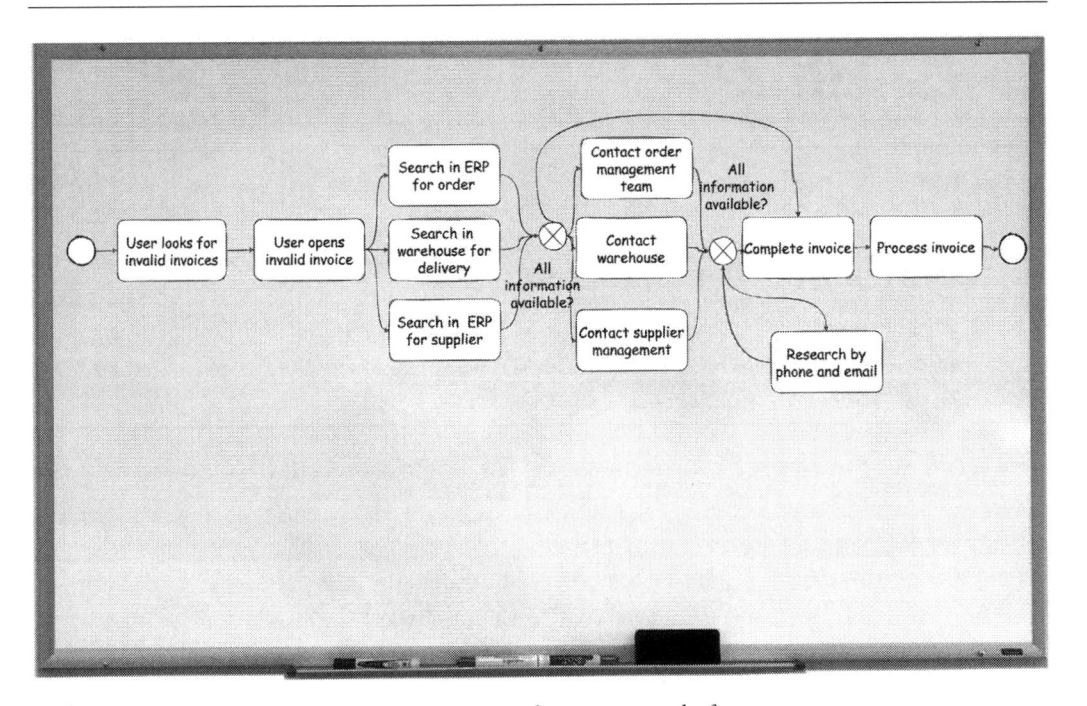

Figure 7.4 – Initial as-is process draft

In addition to the whiteboard, you also took some notes:

- Users spend a lot of time chasing responses from other departments.

- Users seem to cherry-pick the easier invoices.

- The invoice is a PDF, plus the data is already extracted and structured. About 30% of the data is incorrect.

- Users track the status of invoices in a shared Excel sheet. Users must check whether the invoice they want to select is already being processed.

> **Tip**
>
> It is not necessary to copy that draft into a modeling tool. Take a photo and make that part of the project documentation, together with the notes and any other output created.

This seems to be a highly manual, people-driven, and transparent process, a perfect candidate for a redesign and implementation in low code with Appian.

Before jumping into the design of the new process, let me give you a few more thoughts along the way.

Software-driven processes

We try to digitalize a process. This is more than going from paper to PDFs. Currently, most applications are tools to support a human who is executing the process. We want to implement an application that executes the process itself and reaches out to humans for support if needed.

"Appian orchestrates resources, silicon-based and carbon-based ones."

Silicon-based resources are any kind of simple business logic, such as AI and machine learning algorithms trying to understand the situation and make decisions. In case that does not work out, their duty is to prepare the data in a way that the carbon-based, or human, resource can focus on what they do best, which is being creative, understanding complex situations, and making decisions.

> **Tip**
> Try to automate as much as possible, then prepare the data and hand it over to a human.

Task-driven processes

But what does it mean for the way we work in the future, with Appian driving the process and assigning tasks to people to get input? In short, it means: *"No task, no work!"* This is a bold statement and probably only valid for a typical business process automation use case. But this is a huge change in how an organization or department perceives itself.

Also, this does not make any person redundant but relieves them from boring manual work and allows concentration to be focused on more complex tasks and decisions.

This organizational change must be discussed with all business stakeholders! It is part of your project by nature, whether you like it or not. Ignoring it is a threat to your project's success.

Case management

In recent years, some colleagues and I have developed a set of theses that we use to direct attention to certain aspects of typical process improvement scenarios. These theses are formulated aggressively to challenge the existing ways of thinking about business processes, process automation, and implementation in Appian.

The theses are not laws, but guidelines. You can use them to initiate discussions and adapt them carefully to your actual requirements. All the theses give tips for business analysis. Some also provide concrete hints for the implementation in Appian.

> **Tip**
> These theses are meant to make people reconsider their own points of view. Do your own thinking before using them in a workshop. You must be able to explain the thesis and answer any questions that arise.

Basic principles

Let's understand the basic principles for case management:

- A *business process* is a *concrete description* of the *transformation* of an *input* to an *output*.

- There is business data and a separate, related case, that contains the process information. Within the scope of the case, activities act on that business data.

There is a path of critical steps driving the process and optional supporting steps. Each critical step must be executable, have a defined purpose, a concrete description, and can be completed within a short period.

Theses

1. **A business process begins at the client and ends at the client**:

    I.   Think big!

    II.   Who is the client?

    III. Why does the process even exist?

    IV.   What is the purpose?

    V.   Narrow down the focus and scope later.

2. **Work is dictated by process tasks**:

   I.   A task is executable.

   II.   A task has a concrete description.

   III. A task can be completed within a short period, typically, a single session on the computer.

   IV.   Assign a task if the process requires the help of a user.

   V.   What do I do if there is no task assigned to me?

   VI.   Users do not need to monitor the application to find work.

   VII. No task → get some coffee.

   VIII. A notification is not a task.

3. **Only critical activities drive the business process**:

   I.   A critical activity is a logical part of a process.

   II.   Can contain one or more actual tasks.

   III. Stores its results in a separate data structure.

4. **Only one critical activity can exist at a given time**:

   I.   In the scope of a critical activity, parallel process flows can exist.

5. **A critical activity is followed by another critical activity**:

   I.   These activities drive the process.

6. **A critical activity that cannot be completed now will be assigned again in a follow-up**:

   I.   Waiting for an external event is no activity.

   II.   A follow-up is set up to keep track.

   III. The user may start the task via a related action in case they can complete the task before the follow-up.

7. **Avoid modifying business data in critical activities**:

     I.   Critical activities have a result that is stored separately.

     II.   Results can "overlay" business data.

     III. Results can be jointly displayed with business data.

     IV.   If you need to modify business data, take care of conflicting modifications, and restrict support activities.

8. **The process is based on clearly defined business objects**:

     I.   Store business data separate from case data and activity data.

9. **Business data and process data are clearly separate entities**:

     I.   Business data does not reflect process status.

10. **Monitoring and reporting are separate things**:

     I.   Monitoring is about actual operational performance.

     II.   Reporting is about supporting strategic decision making and analytics by aggregating data.

11. **A completed case stays completed**:

     I.   Resuming an activity is a new case and a different process.

To-be process

Finally, armed with all these insights, let's design the new process. Typically, this phase is the most challenging. Therefore, I put all the methodologies, guidelines, and philosophical discussions ahead of this section.

For the scope of this book, we assume that Terence Limited and the people in our project are willing to make a bold step forward and overcome their old way of working. Organizational change management is in progress and they can't wait to get to know the new process:

1. You will want to set up another series of workshops with Paul, Melanie, and Beth.

2. Start with a high-level SIPOC diagram:

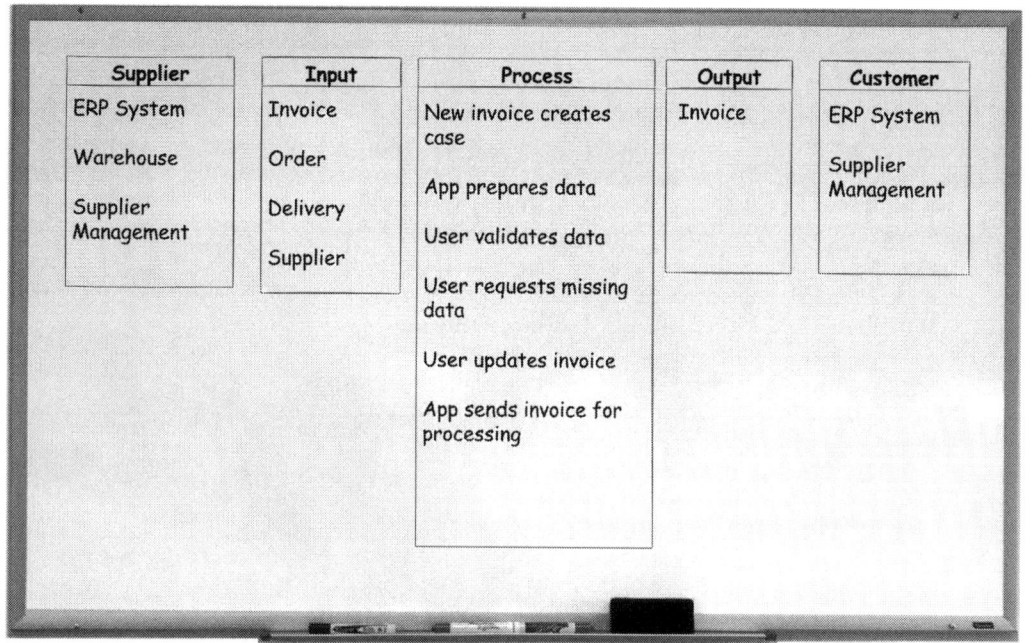

Figure 7.5 – SIPOC for a new process

This result is not a surprise, but it gives more structure to your discussions. Many people are not trained to think in highly abstract models. SIPOC helps you to guide them up and down the different levels of abstraction.

3. Next, you will guide your team in developing the concrete business process model. Keep in mind that each stakeholder has their own requirements and views on how to improve the process.

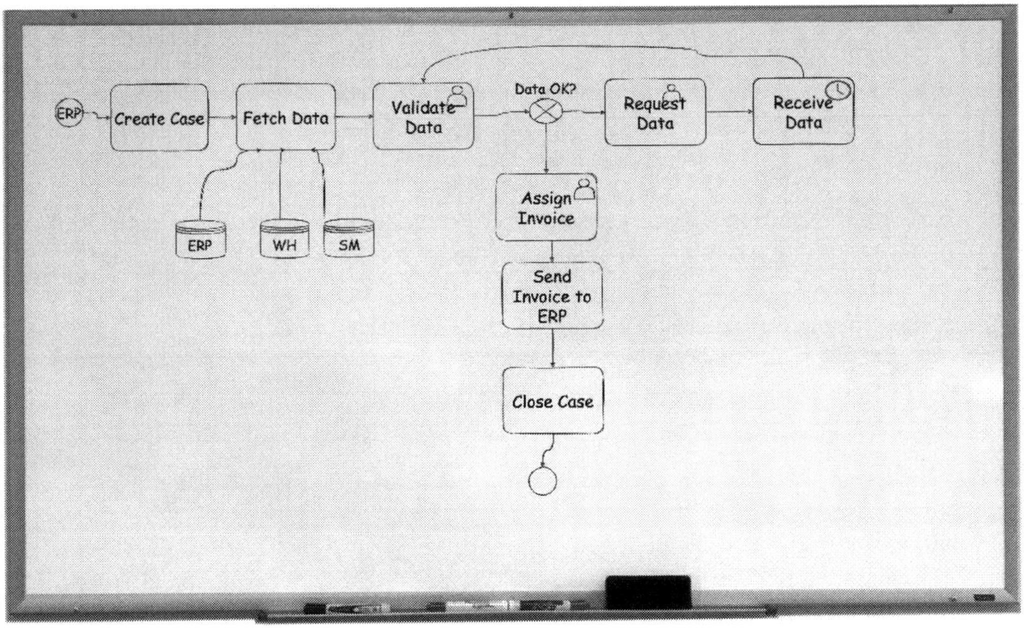

Figure 7.6 – To-be process draft

Basically, this is not much different from the as-is process. However, one important improvement is the fact that the user does not need to dive into other systems to get data about the invoice, while the need to track requests to other departments becomes obsolete.

Some additional notes are the following:

- The application will assign a priority to each created case. For now, this will be based on the invoice amount. Above 100,000, the priority is high.

- The application will assign tasks to the team based on current workload. The member with the least number of assigned tasks will get the new task assigned.

- The reaction time is set to 4 business hours. The task will be reassigned to the team manager for manual assignment after 4 business hours. For high-priority cases, this is only 2 business hours.

- The expected response time for external information requests is 8 business hours. After 8 business hours, a reminder is to be sent and the priority of the task is increased. For high-priority cases, this is only 4 business hours.

In the workshops, it was decided to start with a minimum viable product approach. Then, each quarter, a new iteration will be released. This way, the team gains experience of the new way of working and the application. This iterative approach is a great way to refine new applications. Low code with Appian makes it easy to change applications with a high frequency.

Together with the data model, the process model is the foundation for your application. Create a proper process model in your tool of choice. Whenever you discuss process behavior with stakeholders, pull out that model as a reference. Please do not hesitate to add details you might discover later while implementing the application.

Summary

In this chapter, you created the process model, the second part of the application's foundation. You learned about the BPMN, Five-Whys, Ishikawa, and SIPOC methodologies. And you learned how to approach a software-driven and task-driven process implementation project. The case management theses are excellent guidance for discussions with stakeholders and certain aspects of the implementation.

In the next chapter, we will discuss what makes great user interfaces, the third and last building block in your application's foundation.

8
Understanding UX Discovery and the UI in Appian Projects

Records and processes need a **User Interface** (**UI**), which is the third and last part of your application's foundation. In the olden days, we had paper forms; in the 21st century, we have screens on computers and mobile devices. Designing UIs requires a profound understanding of what will drive and motivate people at Tarence Limited.

In this chapter, we will cover the following topics:

- Understanding UX discovery – the user experience determining the user interface
- Supporting people doing their tasks – creating efficient UIs
- Understanding management needs – creating monitoring and reporting dashboards
- A wireframing introduction and tools – when and how to create UI mock-up
- Designing screens in an Appian context – screen design for business process automation

Throughout this chapter, you will learn how to conduct **User Experience** (**UX**) discovery with a focus on business process automation. Then, we will turn these insights into user interface mock-up. These mock-up, in combination with business process models, are perfect to discuss and refine the to-be-implemented application with your business stakeholders.

With this chapter, you will be able to complete the application's foundation, and we will finally start the actual application design in Appian.

Understanding UX discovery

The biggest challenge in designing UIs for an application is to make the right choices. These choices can be about screen layout, the display of data, color, icons, or font. The questions you ask yourself will be based on what selection you want to make.

When you talk to your business stakeholders, they will say things such as the following:

- "I need an overview of all the items."

- "Can we have more icons?"

- "In Excel, we had all fields on one screen and could zoom in and out!"

This will not help you to make selections by any means. This is where UX discovery kicks in. But first, let's have a look at the difference between UX and UI.

User experience

In short, UX is about understanding what a user is doing, why they do it, how they do it, and what their requirements are to perform any action. This also means that UX is not about how things look. It is about how the user is interacting with the application to achieve a specific goal. Once you understand the UX requirements, you have a rock-solid basis to make the right decisions when designing user interfaces.

> **Important Note**
>
> The *Appian UX Design Guide* is a great resource for diving deeper into the details of UX and UI. It is specifically tailored to the Appian platform and filled with guides, best practices, examples, and tips. You can find it here: `https://docs.appian.com/suite/help/latest/ux_getting_started.html`.

User interface

Derived from UX, UI design tries to create a visual user interface that enables the user to perform their tasks in an efficient and effective way. Here, we are talking about the relevancy and importance of data, layout, user focus, style, color, buttons, and icons.

Although UX and UI are in no way specific to Appian, you need to learn both to be successful as an Appian designer. In my experience, people like to talk about what things should look like but not about what their actual goals are or the underlying problem to be solved. As I need to understand why they need to do certain tasks, I use the **five whys method**, introduced in *Chapter 7, Understanding Business Processes in Appian Projects*, to learn about their way of working.

Let me tell you a short real-life story to explain the relation between UX and UI:

> *An investment company needed an application to manage investment guidelines because of compliance regulations. In the past, this was done with shared Excel spreadsheets. In a demo session, users requested an overview of a selection of guidelines to be able to compare them. They had that in Excel and wanted that function also in the new application. We created a small mock-up in Appian using a grid to show what that could look like.*
>
> *In the demo the other day, they said that it was not acceptable to have to scroll the columns and the column headers must be fixed, and they wanted to be able to zoom in and out.*
>
> *I then inquired, "Why?" a few times to get the team to think about the purpose instead of the looks. We then tried to formulate this in a short sentence.*
>
> *"As a user, we want to be able to quickly determine the differences between multiple guidelines to select the appropriate one."*
>
> *This sentence is fundamentally different from "I want an overview like I had in Excel!" Once I understood the requirement of the actual user interaction, I was able to implement a user interface that directly supported the user in achieving their goal. I switched from a grid-style UI to a list UI, showing the common values on top and then just the differences for each guideline below. The user could also select certain attributes they were interested in and display only those.*

*This UI was then an "interactive-guidelines-differences-analyzer" and
supported the user toward achieving their goal in a better way than the old
Excel overview.*

Keeping this story in mind, we will now discuss how to translate a user's wish to
a purpose-based requirement.

Supporting people doing their tasks

When you implement business process automation applications in Appian, you need to
know the purpose of the user's interactions with the system. Typically, users will only
tell you what they want in terms of a solution to a given problem. This is because they
have already faced the problem in the past and found a solution using the tools they are
familiar with.

> Tip
> Figure out the actual underlying need and the purpose it serves.

The tricky thing about process automation is that your application will be developed
for specific needs and not be a generic tool that users can use, in any way they want, to
conduct the process they have in mind (Excel or Outlook).

> Tip
> Identify each task in the process and figure out how to best support the user.

For each of these tasks, you must define the inputs, the action, and the outputs. This is
similar to human tasks and system tasks. To support a human in conducting a task, they
need a visual UI, while a system expects you to communicate with its technical interface.

Think about how that matches my story about investment guidelines from the last section.

A UI needs the following items to enable a user to complete a task in a responsible,
efficient, and effective way.

Scope

A user must know what kind of task it is and to which process it belongs. Tell the user
what they are expected to do and why. If the process has multiple roles, it can help to tell
the user within which role they are expected to act.

Information

Try to provide the user with all the information they need to complete their task. Forcing the user to look up data in another system reduces the efficiency of the process. Make sure to prepare the data in a way that is easy for the user to understand. Use layout, style, and color to highlight the most important data.

For example, you want the user to decide about a leasing request. The requester must be older than 18. Do you display the date of birth, the age, or an icon indicating that the requester is old enough?

Input

A task always requires the user to enter or interact with data. This part of the UI must be structured, simple, logical, and unambiguous. Separate large interfaces into multiple sections or create a wizard-style interface for more complex or multistep data acquisition needs.

Orientation

Tell the user about the next steps in the process. This prevents the user from perceiving the application as a black box. For example, if the next step is a review of the data entered, tell the user that they will be notified if they need to rework.

With this guide at hand, you should be able to design UIs that fit the purpose and are easy to use. Now, let's have a look at the management side.

Understanding management needs

First, let's talk a bit about what management is about. It's about using management tools and making decisions about how to use them. To make these decisions, you need the appropriate facts.

You need to understand these facts and their purpose and design the application to deliver them.

In many organizations, people deliver these facts in a handcrafted Excel document to their boss once a month. We want to transform this, using the reporting and visualization capabilities of Appian. Design one or more dashboards that give each interested manager the facts they need for making their decisions.

There are typically two different types of management that need answers to two simple questions:

- Is that process good?

- Does that process run?

The question is about the definition of the process itself, the quality of the output, the costs, and the performance. Typically, a dashboard shows overall performance, the change in process volume over time, and values that allow conclusions to be drawn about the quality of the output delivered. Facts and figures should lend themselves to supporting improvements in the next iteration of the process and application.

Does that process run? This question cares about organizing daily business. This includes workforce management, assignment, availability, and training. A dashboard might display individual workload, current adherence to performance requirements, and the number of process escalations. Also think about situations where a user has been assigned a task and suddenly becomes unavailable. This might require some abandoned task management features.

Let's now transform the insights from the last three sections into something more tangible using wireframes.

A wireframing introduction and tools

Let's address the elephant in the room. Why would you want to create wireframes for UIs when creating the final UI in Appian is so quick and easy? It doesn't really need to be done; however, let's talk about what wireframes are and their pros and cons.

There are many specialized wireframing tools on the market. Most of them are made for more demanding tasks such as websites or magazines. We will focus on creating business applications using low-code in Appian. This limits the possibilities for visual design. Therefore, we can also use a simpler tool for wireframing. I use the already-introduced free software *diagrams.net* (`https://diagrams.net`).

Wireframes are also a great tool for sketching UIs collaboratively on a whiteboard or paper. You can also prepare them using software and get them printed out in a large format. In the workshop, you can then use Post-its and markers for refinement.

Understanding wireframes

Have a look at this simple web page example:

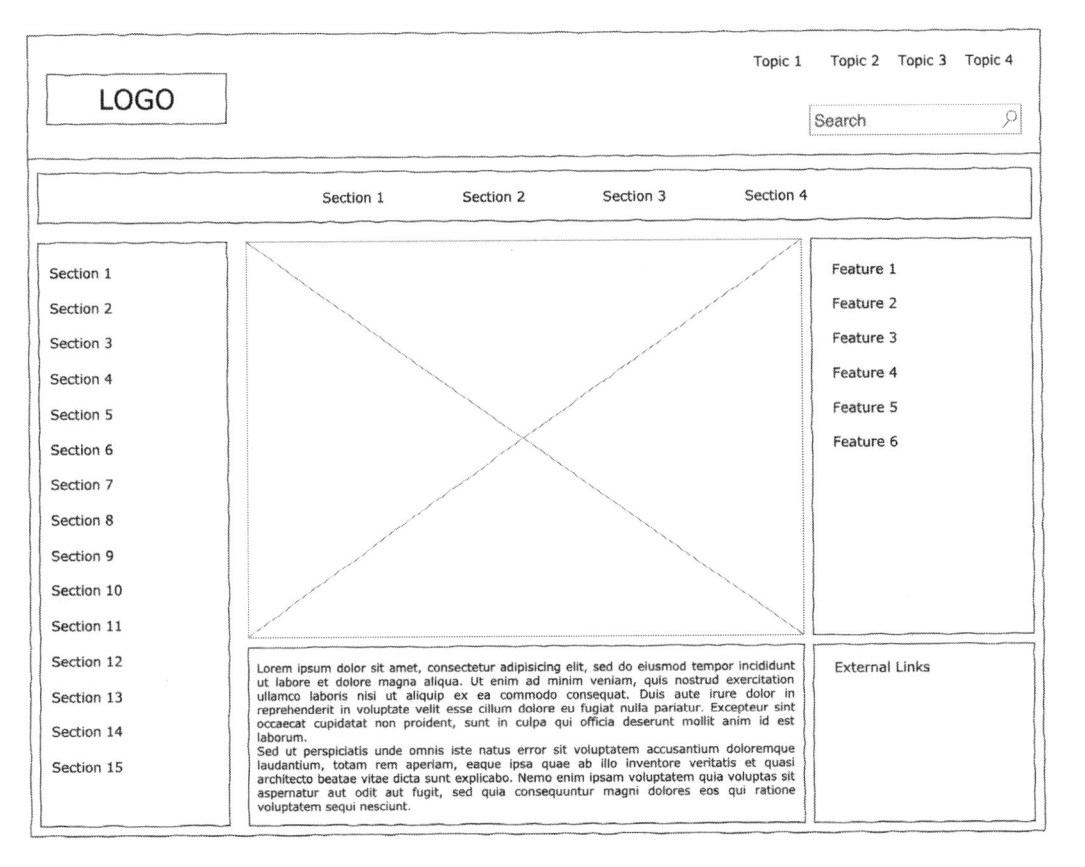

Figure 8.1 – A wireframe example

The idea of a wireframe is to turn the purpose of a specific UI into an arrangement of visual elements. The sketchy style, and the lack of color and detail, allows you to concentrate on how the individual elements work together instead of the look. This is an important benefit, as your business stakeholders prefer to talk about button colors rather than the actual purpose of certain screen elements.

When creating a wireframe, we focus on the following:

- The available functions
- The structure and priority of data and functions
- The conditions for showing or hiding certain sections

A more concrete example is shown in the following figure:

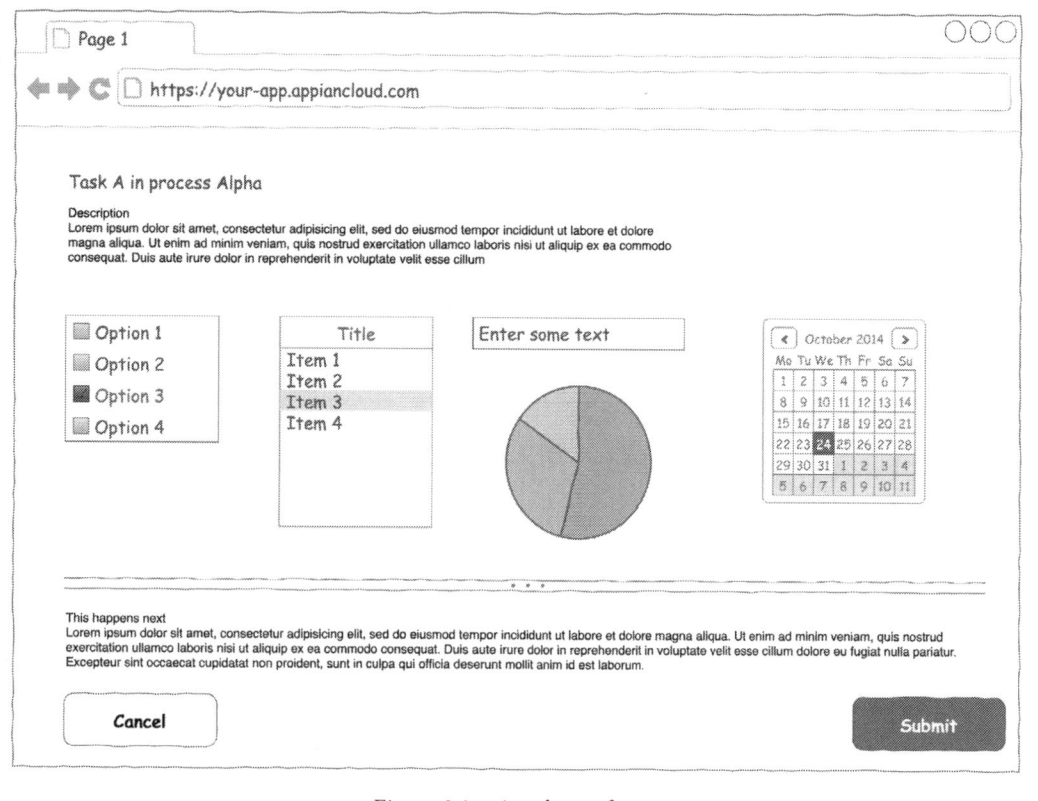

Figure 8.2 – A task wireframe

This example loosely mimics a typical Appian task. It contains the four important sections – scope, information, input, and orientation – introduced in this chapter in the *Supporting people doing their tasks* section.

The benefits of wireframes

The main benefits of wireframes are simplicity, collaboration, speed, and the focus on function over form. Use wireframes to show your UI ideas to your business stakeholders. This way, they can join your creative path and imagine how it would affect their daily work. Creating a UI directly in Appian might be a tempting idea, but it is easy to get sidetracked by the form. If your business stakeholders see a UI that already looks like the real application, they tend to stop thinking about the purpose. But that's exactly why we do UX discovery in the first place.

With the power of wireframes in your hands, let's talk about the specific needs of Appian screen design.

Designing screens in an Appian context

In Appian, we differentiate three basic types of UIs:

- A **record**: Shows the details about a specific business object item

- A **task**: The UI for a human task in a process

- A **report**: Displays aggregated data for reporting purposes

The following screenshots are taken from the **order fulfilment** demo application that is part of Appian Community Edition:

Record

In Appian, a **record** represents the details of a specific business object item.

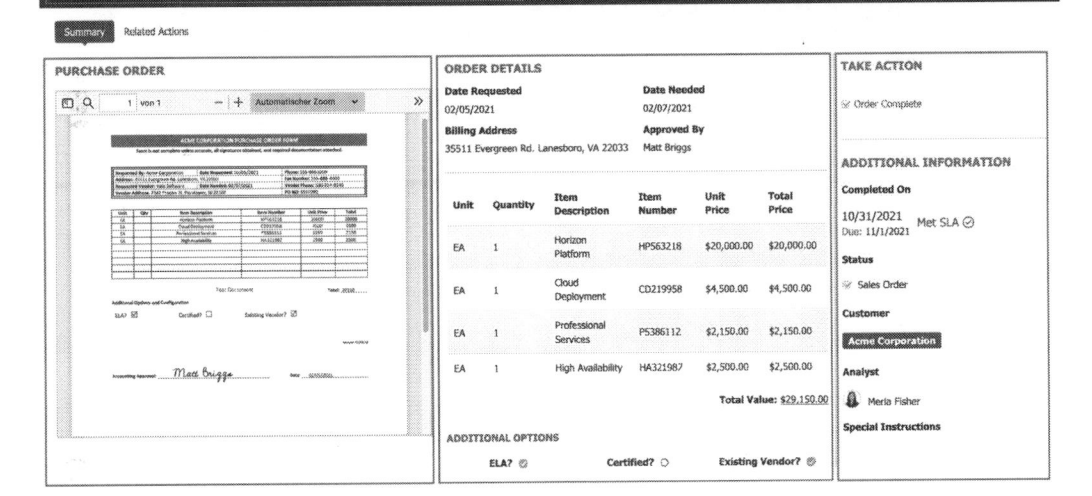

Figure 8.3 – An order record view example

You define the top-left title and the overall content below. The title defines the scope, telling the user which item they are looking at currently.

This example splits the content into three columns, as follows:

- The order document on the left

- The extracted order details in the middle column

- The additional details on the right

Let's check a second example:

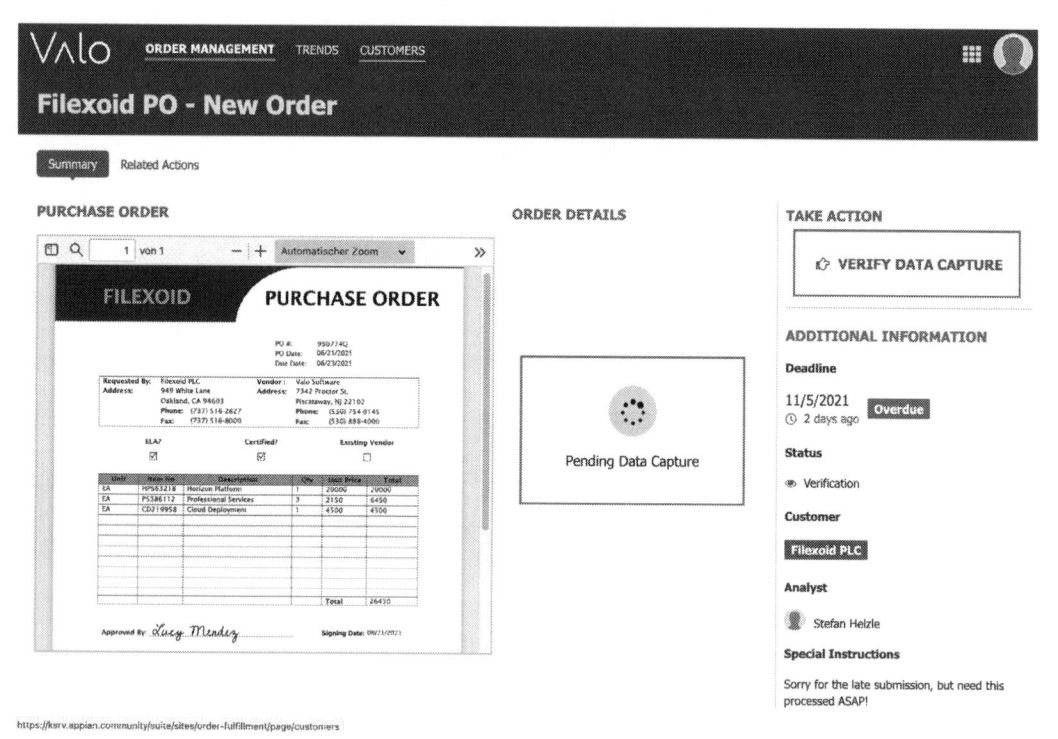

Figure 8.4 – An incomplete order record view

This example makes it clear that the order has not been processed completely by showing an icon in the middle column. In the right column, in the **TAKE ACTION** section, you can see a clearly visible link to complete the data capturing process.

To sum it up, this record has a clear scope, the displayed data is easy to understand, and the required action is highlighted.

Task

We already discussed the high-level sections of a typical Appian task interface – scope, information, input, and orientation:

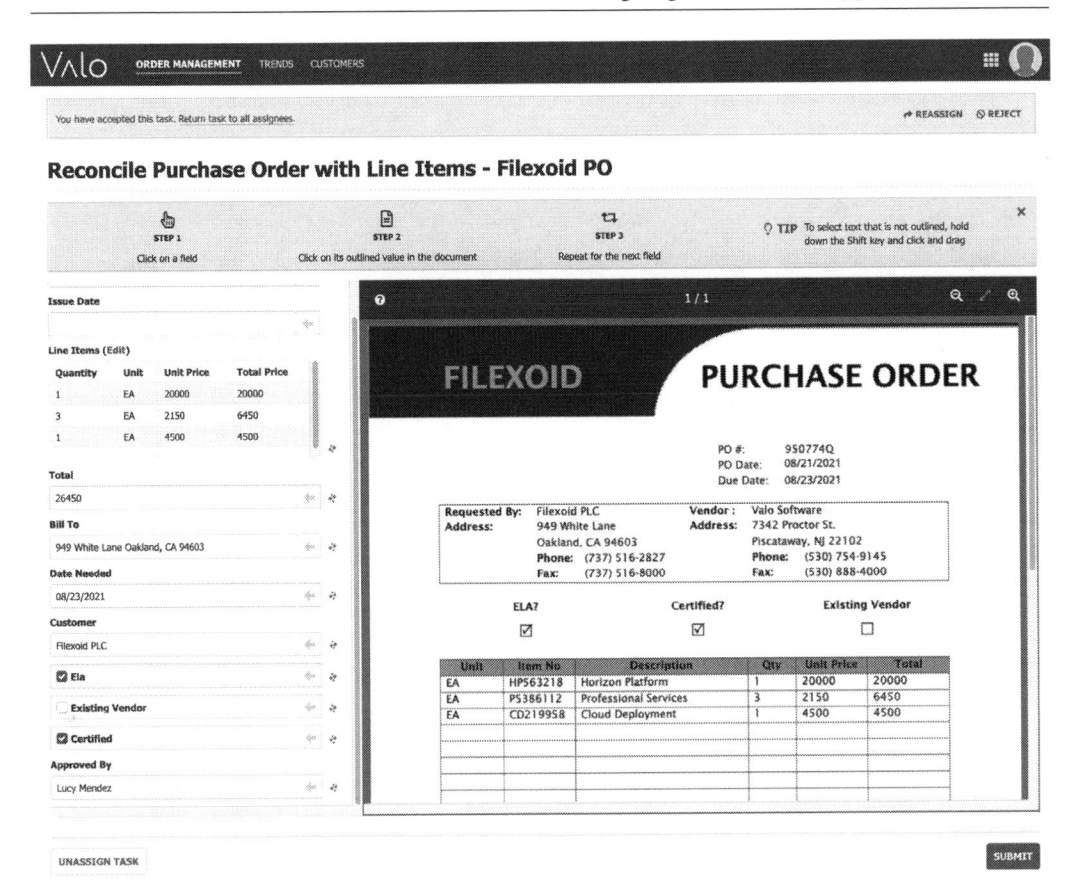

Figure 8.5 – A task example

Try to identify these sections in the previous example. They are pretty easy to see and understand, with the orientation section obviously missing.

The orientation section is most important for a user who does not do the same tasks every day. A daily user might read that information a few times but will ignore it after a while. So, you might want to discuss the usage frequency of individual tasks with your business stakeholders and tailor the UI accordingly.

The gray section at the top of the screen shows a small **x** button at the top right. This allows me to close this instruction as soon as I know what to do. A similar pattern can also be used for the orientation section:

Report

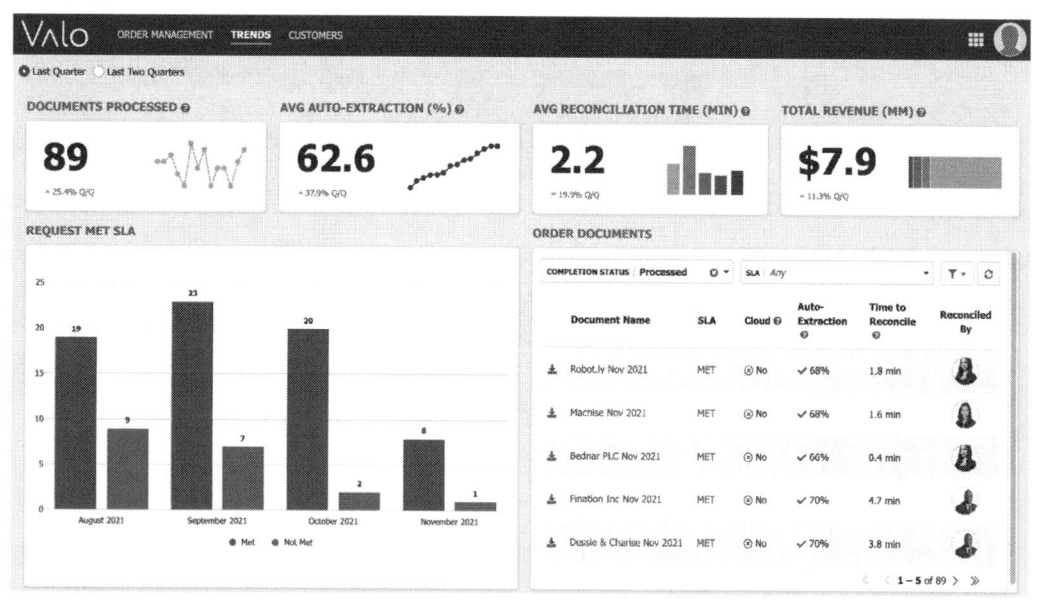

Figure 8.6 – A reporting dashboard example

This is an excellent example of a combined report. It covers both strategic and operational reporting, and I can act if required.

The **DOCUMENTS PROCESSED, AVG AUTO-EXTRACTION, AVG RECONCILIATION TIME,** and **ORDER DOCUMENTS** sections cover the operational reporting. The other sections, **REQUEST MET SLA** and **TOTAL REVENUE,** target the strategic reporting demands.

The **ORDER DOCUMENTS** list allows me to filter for status and SLA, and I can drill down to a certain order if I want to see the details.

Summary

In this chapter, you learned about the difference between UI design and UX discovery, and why it is important to do UX first and UI second. We discussed how to best support a user in completing their tasks, the specific needs of management, and how to wireframe to screens in Appian.

This chapter concludes the preparation phase. You learned many methodologies, conducted workshops with the business stakeholders, and created a data model, process models, and wireframes.

The next part of this book, starting with *Chapter 9, Modeling Business Data with Appian Records*, is all about working with Appian to create an application for our invoice validation process.

Section 3: Implementing Software

With all the preparation in the last four chapters completed, it is time to implement your application using Appian. This part of the book heavily relies on the outcomes of *Section 2*. Make sure you have your data model, business processes, and wireframes to hand.

Did you try to challenge the way you think about what that application in Appian can do for you and your organization?

You learned the important object types in *Chapter 3, Building Blocks of Appian Quick Apps*, in which we analyzed the objects Appian creates for a Quick App. I'm now going to walk you through creating an application with all the required objects from scratch.

You'll learn how to create Appian Records from your business data model, turn your business process models into executable technical processes, and turn your wireframes into real working user interfaces. The application object you will create first is the container for all subsequent objects.

This section contains the following chapters:

- *Chapter 9, Modeling Business Data with Appian Records*
- *Chapter 10, Modeling Business Processes in Appian*
- *Chapter 11, Creating User Interfaces in Appian*
- *Chapter 12, Task Management with Appian*
- *Chapter 13, Reporting and Monitoring with Appian*

9
Modeling Business Data with Appian Records

You are going to create custom data types in Appian to implement the prepared Entity-Relationship model. Appian Records are a powerful way to integrate data from a variety of sources, such as databases, processes, and integrated web services.

The records created will then be the central elements to which we add user interfaces to display the data for a given record. We also add processes as related actions to allow the user to take action.

In this chapter, we will cover the following topics:

- **Creating the application object**: The container for all objects that make up your application.

- **Custom data types**: Define the concrete data structures, as in your Entity-Relationship model.

- **Data stores**: The technical connection to the Appian database.

- **Records**: The central place for users interacting with data.

- **Relationships**: Defining relationships of Appian Records, as in your Entity-Relationship model.

- **Best practices**: Guidelines for efficient data design in Appian.

All the examples and screenshots in this and the following chapter are created on *Appian version 21.4*. If you use a different version, check the release notes and try to identify what has changed.

Creating the application object

The application is the container for the objects you create and the topmost structural element in Appian. Let's see the steps to create an application object:

1. Navigate to Appian Designer and click the **NEW APPLICATION** button.

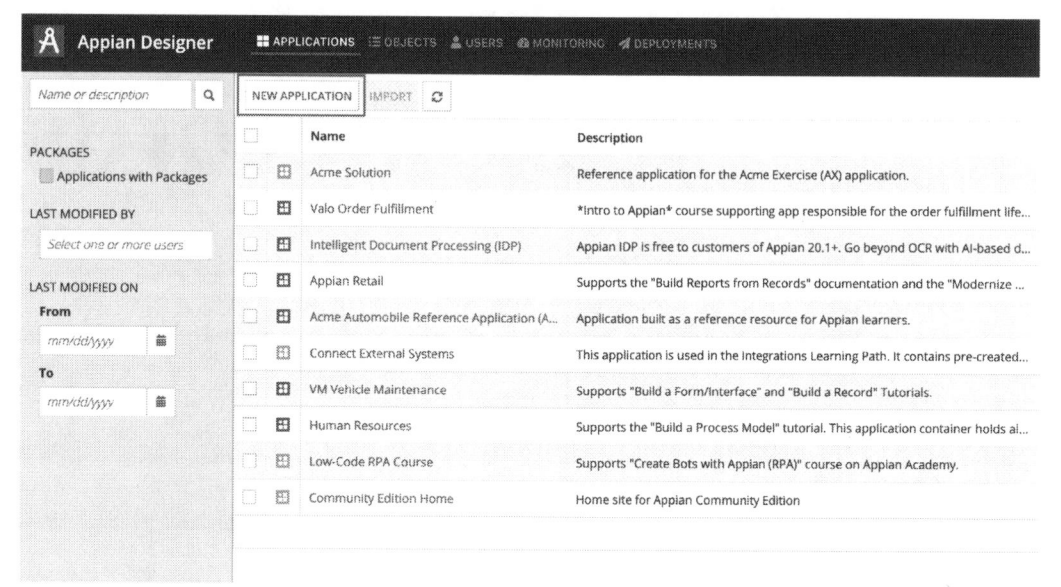

Figure 9.1 – New application in Appian Designer

2. For the dialog that has now opened, please observe the following screenshot, where you can freely select the entries for the **Name**, **Prefix**, and **Description** fields.

> **Prefix**
>
> The **Prefix** is part of the naming convention in Appian, used to show that an object belongs to a certain application. Typically, this uses three uppercase letters. Follow this to avoid object naming confusion, as there is no package structure concept in Appian.

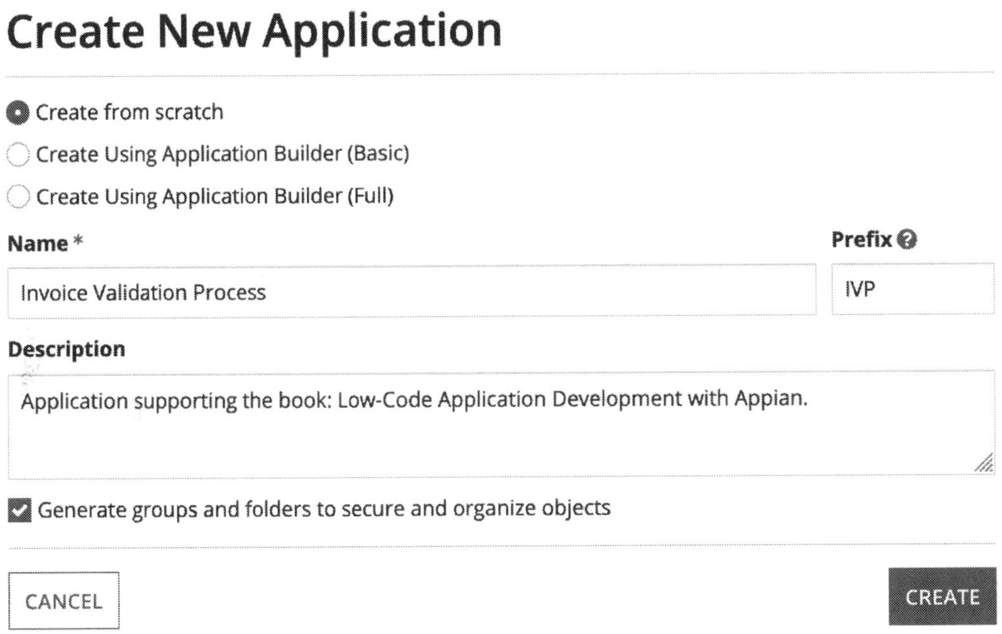

Create New Application

◉ Create from scratch

◯ Create Using Application Builder (Basic)

◯ Create Using Application Builder (Full)

Name *   **Prefix** ❷

| Invoice Validation Process | IVP |

Description

Application supporting the book: Low-Code Application Development with Appian.

☑ Generate groups and folders to secure and organize objects

CANCEL   CREATE

Figure 9.2 – Create New Application

We select the creation process **Create from scratch** as it only creates the basic application objects. The other two options, **Create Using Application Builder**, will create more objects, like the **QuickApps** approach we discussed in *Chapter 1, Create an Appian Quick App*. While this may help in certain situations, my experience is that I always end up having to heavily modify most created objects. And this takes longer than creating them myself. However, your mileage may vary, so do not hesitate to try this yourself.

3. Clicking **CREATE** will show the next dialog, in which you can review the security settings for the new application object:

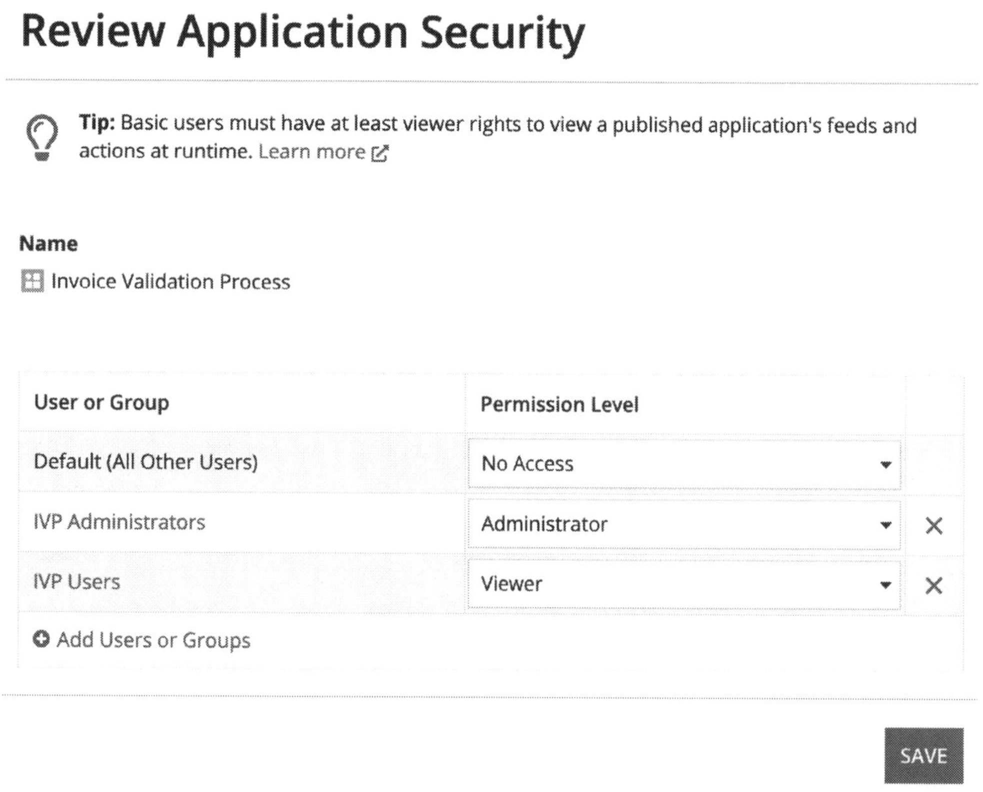

Review Application Security

> **Tip:** Basic users must have at least viewer rights to view a published application's feeds and actions at runtime. Learn more ☑

Name

 Invoice Validation Process

User or Group	Permission Level	
Default (All Other Users)	No Access ▾	
IVP Administrators	Administrator ▾	✕
IVP Users	Viewer ▾	✕
⊕ Add Users or Groups		

SAVE

Figure 9.3 – Review Application Security

4. You can leave the settings as they are and click **SAVE** to close the dialog. In Appian Designer, you will now see the basic objects every application needs.

> **Tip**
>
> **Objects** in Appian exist outside any application in a global context, and applications are containers that retain object references. This means that two objects cannot have the same name. Objects can be referenced by zero or more applications, and deleting an object also deletes it from other applications having a reference to it.

In Appian, all objects exist in a flat hierarchy. The object's security settings define what individual users can do with them. Applications are containers that reference objects. Make sure not to reference any objects created in other applications as long as they are not explicitly created as global reusable objects.

		Name	Description
		IVP Administrators	Group that all Invoice Validation Process activity is secured to
		IVP Users	Group that all Invoice Validation Process activity is secured to
		IVP Models	Process models folder for the Invoice Validation Process application
		IVP Rules & Constants	Rules and constants folder for the Invoice Validation Process application
		IVP Artifacts	Artifacts folder for the Invoice Validation Process application
		IVP Application Documentation	Application Documentation folder for the Invoice Validation Process application
		IVP Knowledge Center	Knowledge Center for documents in the Invoice Validation Process application

Figure 9.4 – Initial list of objects

> **Application Security**
>
> Application security assigns object permission roles to Appian groups and defines what designers can do with the application. The **Application** object has the security roles **Administrator**, **Editor**, **Viewer**, and **Deny**. Both **Administrator** and **Editor** can change the application, but only the administrator can change the security settings. **Viewers** can just see it, and users in **Deny** will not get any access. For more details, check the Appian documentation: `https://docs.appian.com/suite/help/21.4/applications-view.html#application-security`.

> **Folder Security**
>
> Folder security assigns object permission roles to Appian groups. A folder has the roles **Administrator**, **Editor**, **Viewer**, and **Deny**. Folders inherit security from their parent folder by default, but this can be overwritten. Folder security defines users' access to contained documents and folders. A user in the **Viewer** role has read-only access to folder content. An **Editor** may store and overwrite documents. The **Administrator** role allows security settings to be modified. For more details, check the Appian documentation: `https://docs.appian.com/suite/help/21.4/object-security.html`.

Hence, you have created the application and know about basic security settings. Now, you can create the *custom data types* based on your Entity-Relationship model.

Custom data types

A **custom data type** (**CDT**) in Appian defines a data structure made up of fields with a data type. The data type can be simple, such as `Text` or `Date`. A field can also use another CDT as a type, which creates a nested data structure. A field can be rendered as an array, which allows you to store a list of values in a single field.

While we will use CDTs to persist data to the database, the CDT **does not** do that on its own. It is just a data structure we use to define the types of objects and variables in the following places:

- Variables in process models
- Variables and rule inputs in expressions and interfaces
- Entities in data stores
- Exchanging data in integrations and Web APIs

> **Tip**
>
> There is no behind-the-scenes magic in Appian. If you want something to happen, you need to configure, model, or code it. All this is easy to do, but still needs to be done.

Creating the CDT

Follow these steps to create a new CDT:

1. To create a new object in Appian, click the **NEW** button.

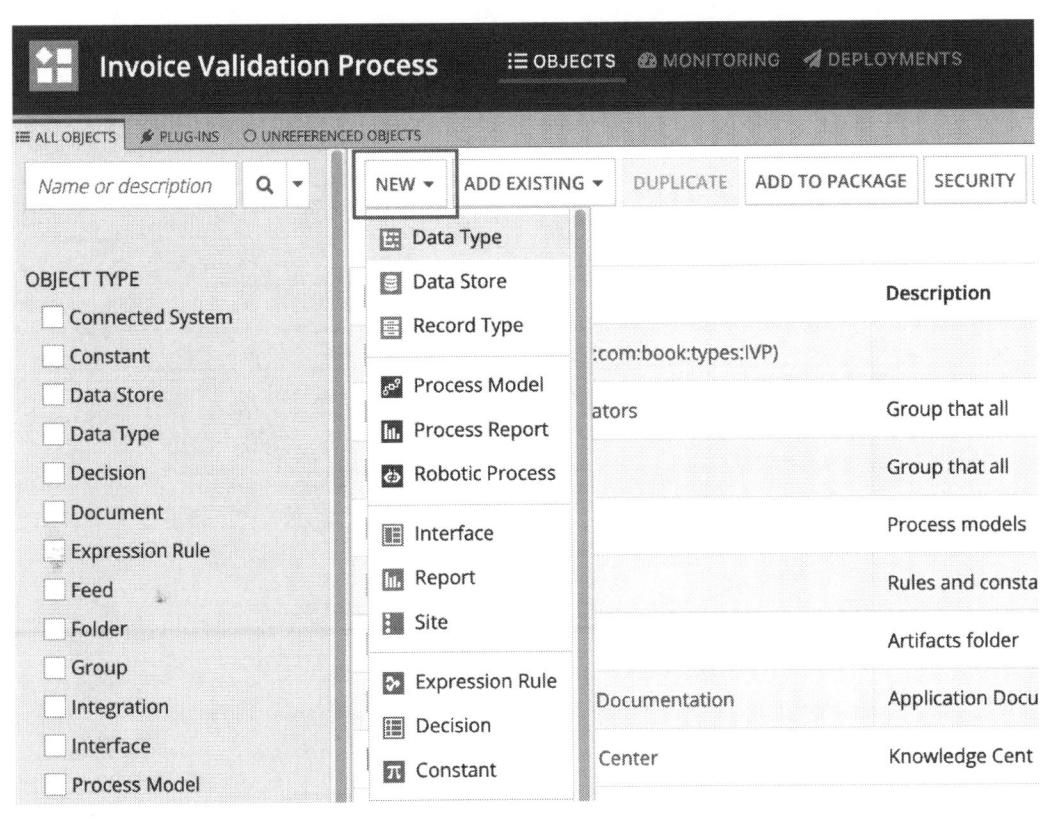

Figure 9.5 – The NEW button

2. In the menu, select the **Data Type** item to start creating the CDT for the entity case.

Tip

Whenever you want to create a new object, click the **NEW** button.

In the dialog that opens, you can also create a copy of an existing object for some object types. Alternatively, select one of the existing objects and press the **DUPLICATE** button.

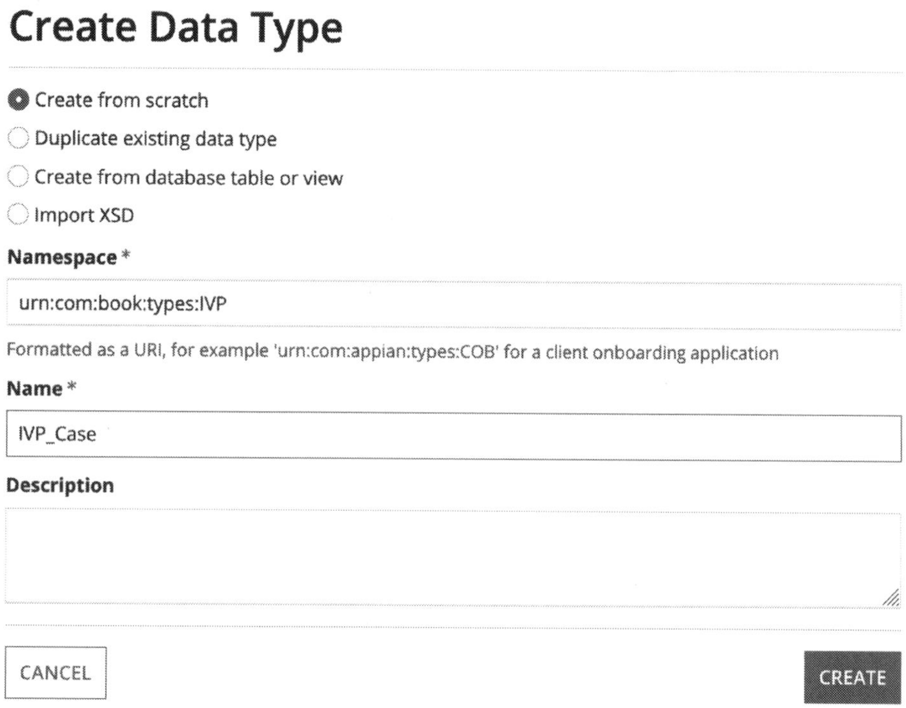

Create Data Type

◉ Create from scratch

○ Duplicate existing data type

○ Create from database table or view

○ Import XSD

Namespace *

    urn:com:book:types:IVP

Formatted as a URI, for example 'urn:com:appian:types:COB' for a client onboarding application

Name *

    IVP_Case

Description

    CANCEL   CREATE

Figure 9.6 – Creating the data type case

3. In the **Create Data Type** dialog, select the **Create from scratch** option and enter values for **Namespace** and **Name**. Follow these patterns to achieve uniform object naming:

    ▪ For **Namespace**: `urn:com:<your_company>:types:<APP_PREFIX>`

    ▪ For **Name**: `<APP_PREFIX>_NameOfDataType`

4. The pattern after the prefix is called **Pascal casing**. Each word starts with an uppercase letter, and there are no spaces between words. Use this naming convention for all objects you create in Appian.

5. Click **CREATE** to get to **Data Type Designer**.

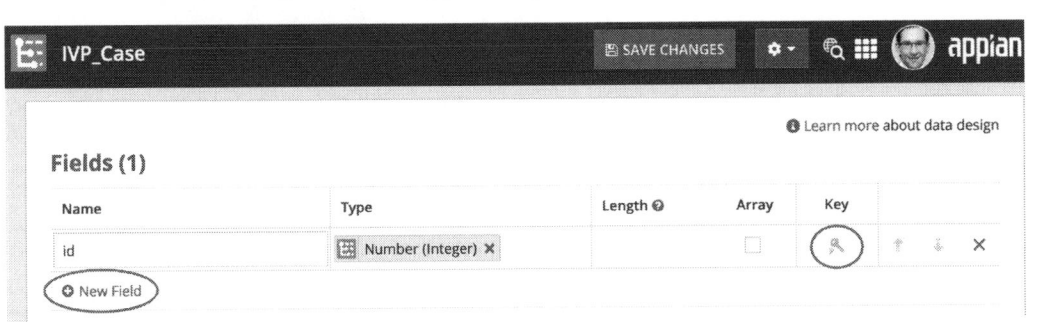

Figure 9.7 – Data Type Designer

6. Click **New Field**, enter id for **Name** and Number (Integer) for **Type**. Click the **Key** icon to configure the **Primary Key** field.

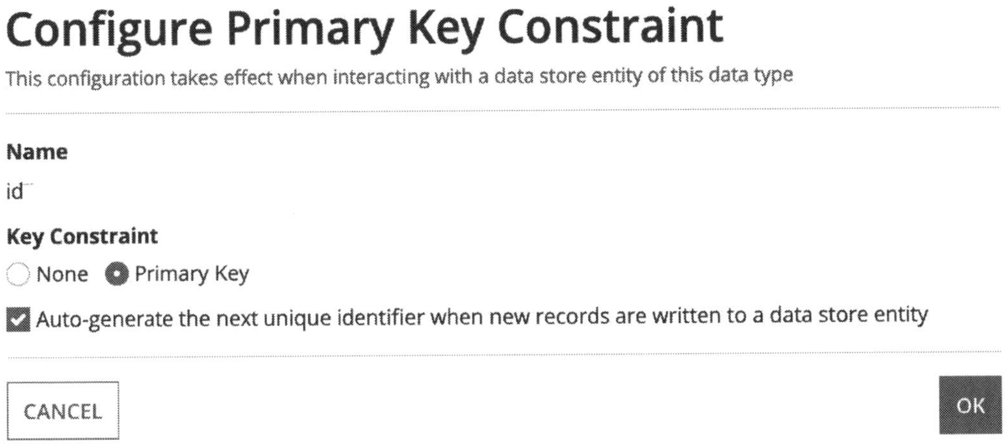

Configure Primary Key Constraint

This configuration takes effect when interacting with a data store entity of this data type

Name

id

Key Constraint

◯ None ⬤ Primary Key

☑ Auto-generate the next unique identifier when new records are written to a data store entity

CANCEL   OK

Figure 9.8 – Configuring the primary key

7. In the dialog, select **Primary Key** for **Key Constraint** and check the **Auto-generate** checkbox. Click **OK** to close that dialog. As the name **Primary Key** implies, you can only configure a single field as the primary key for a CDT.

You might ask, *why is it important to configure a primary key if I just define a data structure?* In the next section of this chapter, we will use this CDT to make Appian automatically manage the tables in the database. Appian will then use the field configuration in the CDT to set up the tables and fields in the database. In the event that you do not use the CDT in an Appian data store, you can ignore the primary key configuration.

Creating more fields

Now, let's create all the fields defined for that entity.

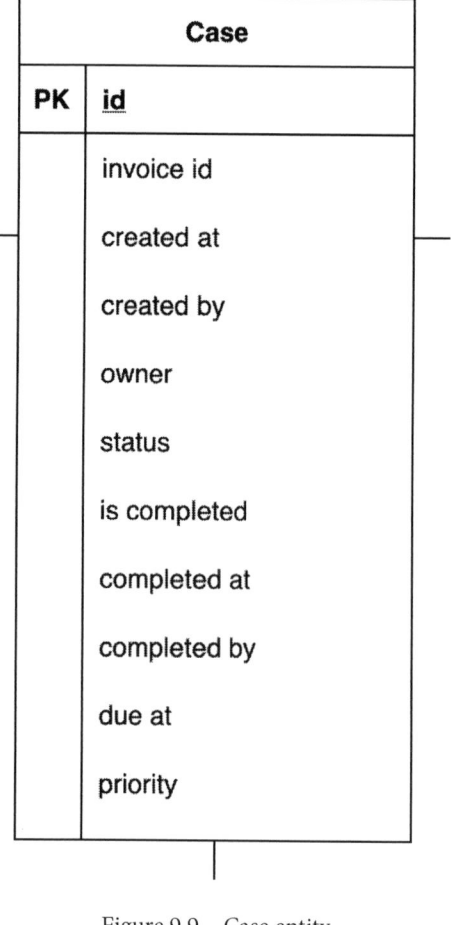

Figure 9.9 – Case entity

> **Tip**
>
> The naming pattern to use is called **Camel casing**. It starts with a lowercase letter. Each subsequent word starts with an uppercase letter, with no spaces in-between. Use this naming convention for CDT fields, variables, and parameter names.

For the fields in the entity, use the data types as follows:

- **Text**: createdBy, owner, status, completedBy
- **Number (Integer)**: invoiceId, priority
- **Date Time**: createdAt, completedAt, dueAt
- **Boolean**: isCompleted

You should end up with a screen like this:

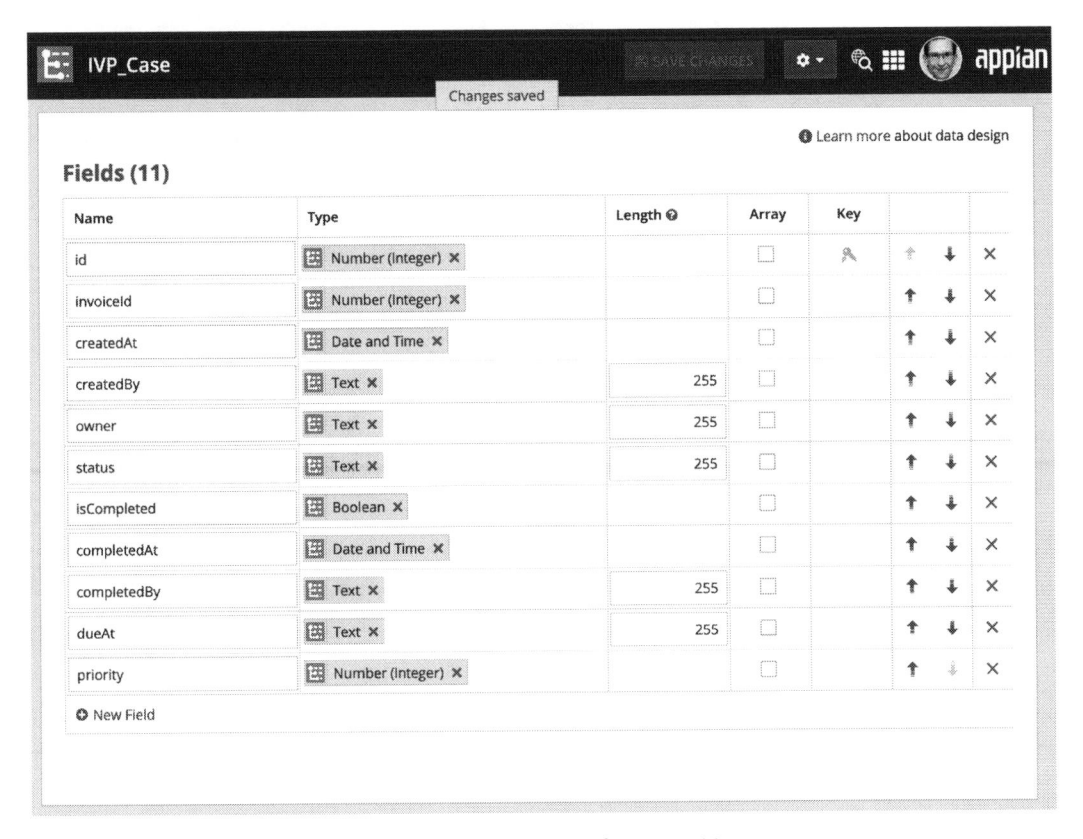

Figure 9.10 – Completed Case CDT

Creating more CDTs

Now, create CDTs for each entity in your Entity-Relationship model. I added the data types for each field in the model.

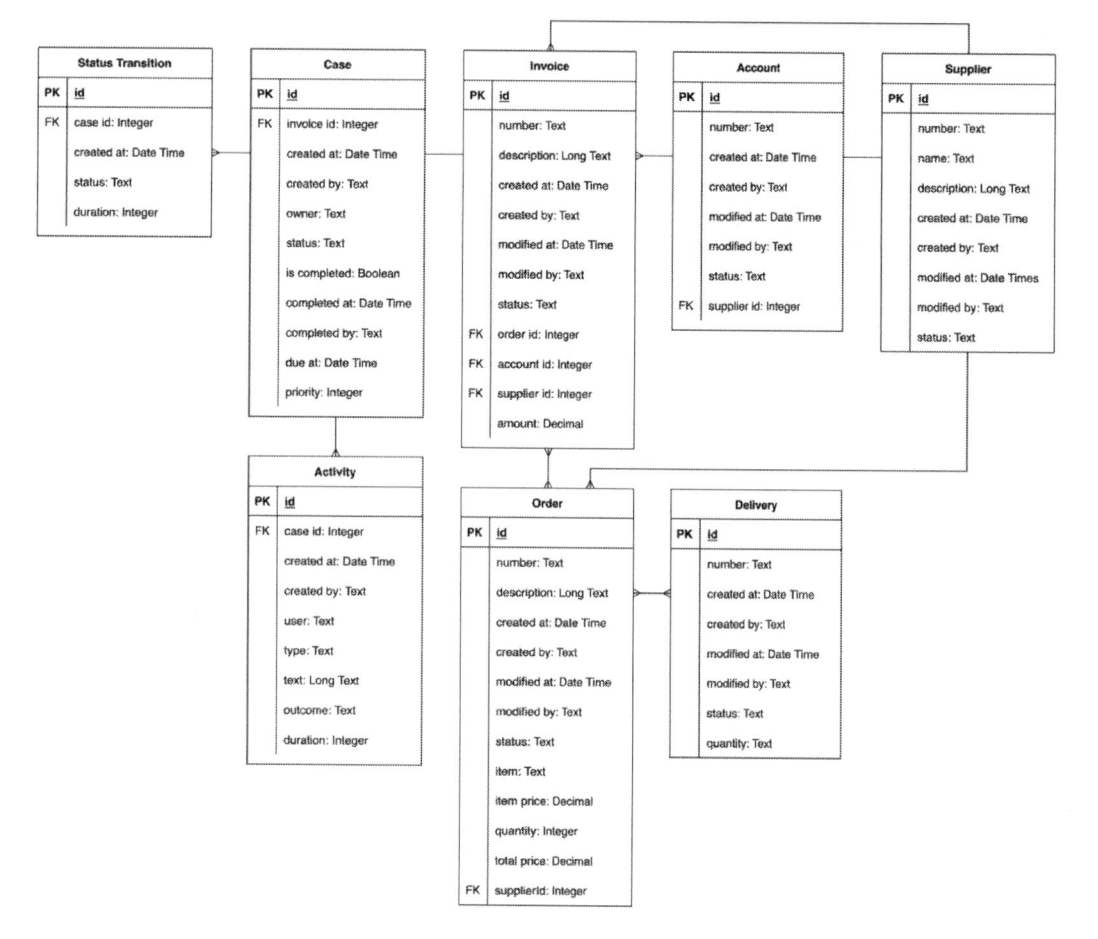

Figure 9.11 – Entity-Relationship model with data types

Create the ID fields, as in the Case CDT, and remember to configure it as the primary key and enable **Auto-generate**. Create the other fields using the following Appian data types:

- **Integer**: Number (Integer)
- **Date Time**: Date Time
- **Text**: Text (255)

- **Long Text**: Text (4000)

- **Boolean**: Boolean

- **Decimal**: Number (Decimal)

For some of the fields, such as the description in the **Invoice** field, or text in the **Activity** field, you might want to make the text field a bit larger. Enter 4000 for **Length**.

With all **custom data types** created, you will now create a data store to be able to persist data to the database later.

Data stores

A **data store** in Appian is used to define a connection to a database and the CDTs to store. You will learn later how to store and query data to and from the database using that data store.

An important feature of a data store is that it allows Appian to automatically manage tables and fields in the database. This feature must be enabled in the Appian Administration Console.

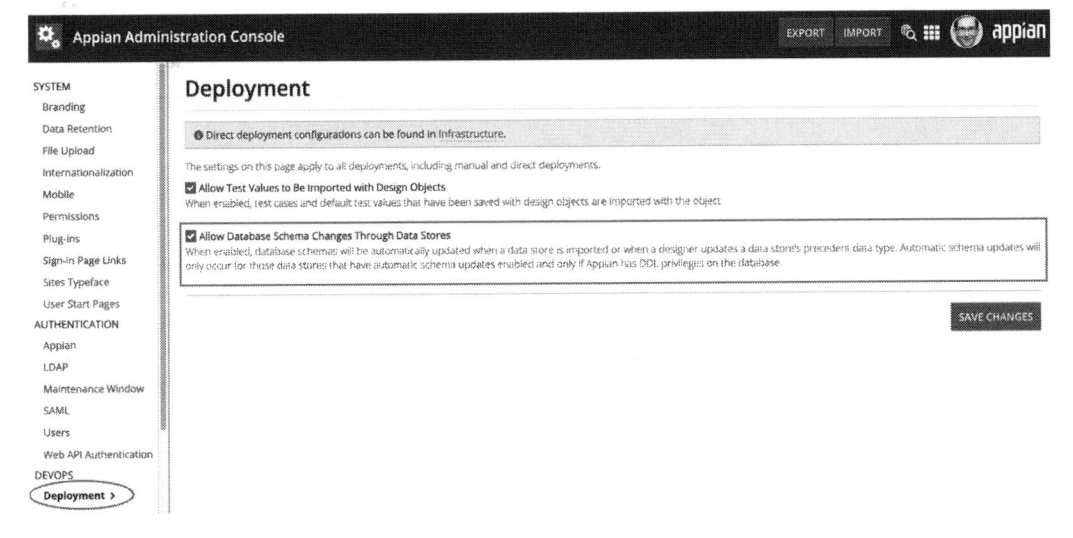

Figure 9.12 – Enabling schema management in the Administration Console

When this is enabled, Appian will perform non-destructive changes automatically. Appian will never delete any tables or fields, leading to the loss of data. It will also never modify the *type* of an existing field, as this also might lead to data loss.

I highly recommend this way of managing the database, as it makes overall development in Appian a lot easier. There are other opinions on this approach. A database admin might want to enforce certain naming conventions for database objects. Some developers may try to put a lot of logic and validation into the database. In my experience, this makes application development with Appian more complicated without any tangible benefits. From an Appian perspective, the database is mostly simple storage for data, structured in CDTs.

Creating the data store

For now, in the following steps, we will create a data store using the **NEW** button in Appian Designer:

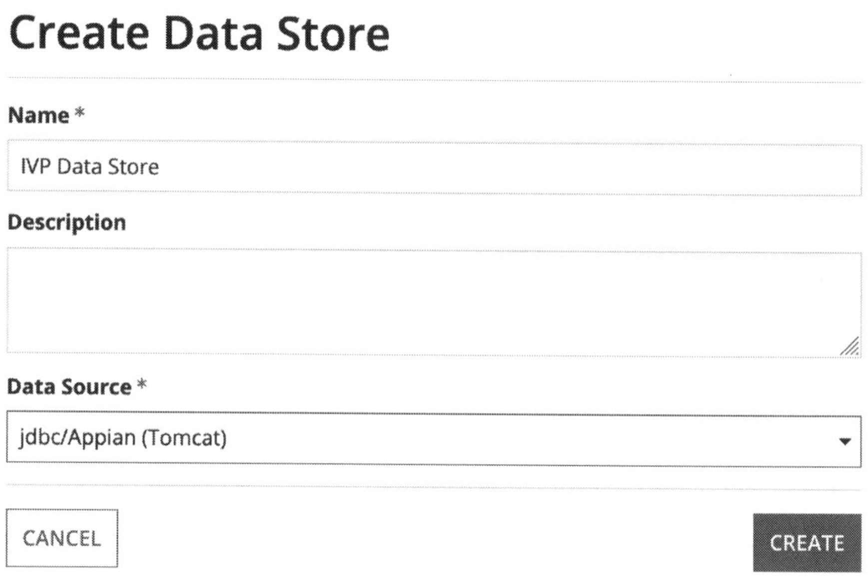

Figure 9.13 – Create Data Store

In a typical Appian application, there is only a single data store, so a generic name fits the purpose. If there are multiple database systems connected to Appian, select yours in the **Data Source** dropdown:

1. Click **CREATE** and then **SAVE** in the **Review Data Store Security** dialog.

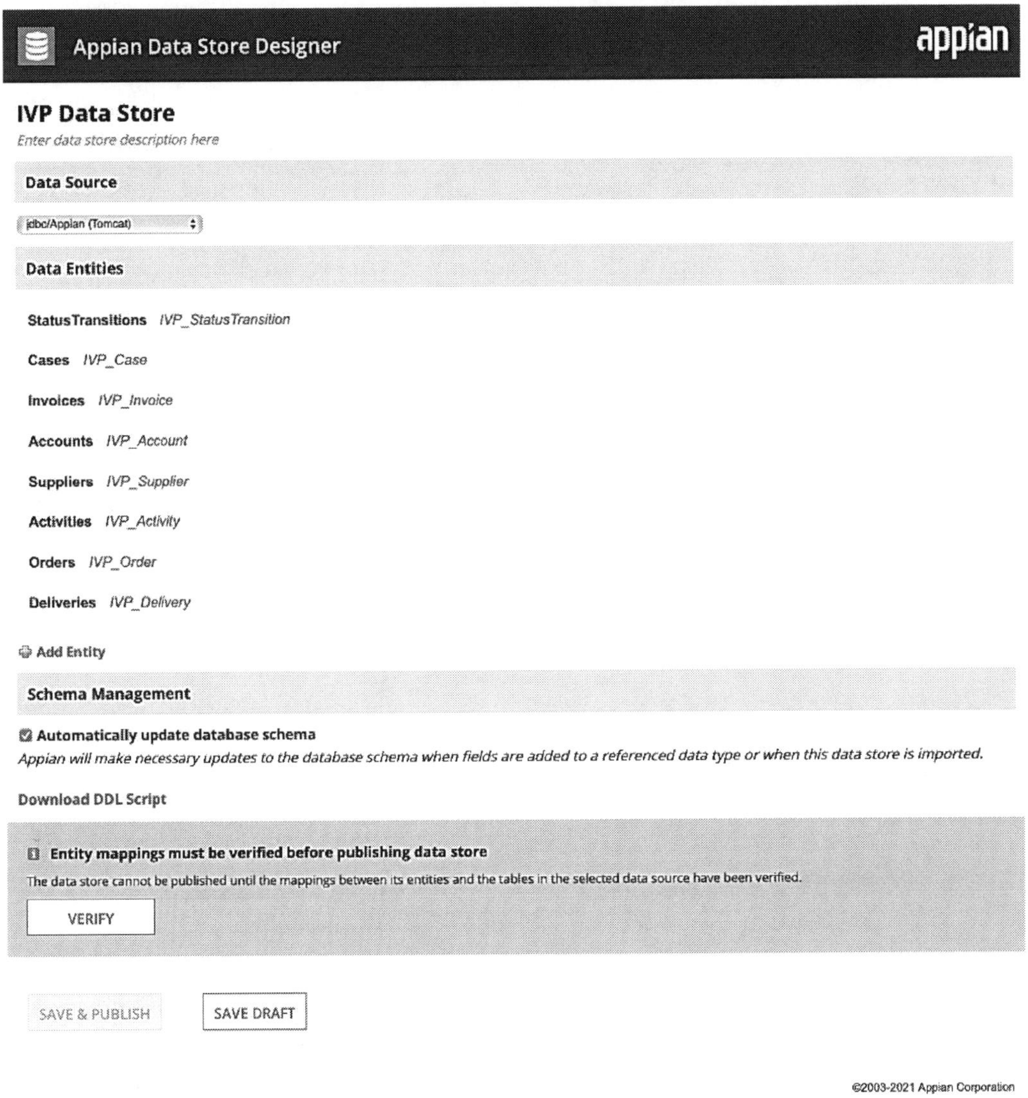

Figure 9.14 – Data store and entities

Now, create entities for each CDT. The naming convention here is to use the plural form of the CDT name without the prefix and Pascal casing once again, with all words starting with an uppercase letter and no spaces.

2. Make sure to enable the **Automatically update database schema** checkbox.

3. As discussed, this enables Appian to manage tables and fields for you. If you add a field in a CDT, Appian will then add the field in the database automatically.

4. After clicking **VERIFY**, Appian will show the following warning:

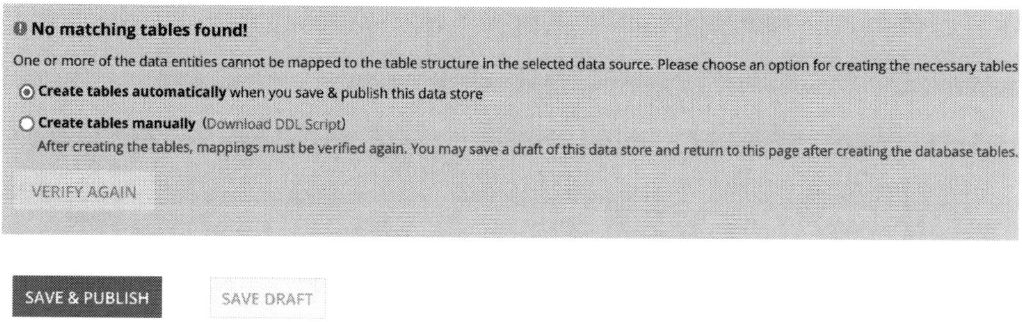

Figure 9.15 – Data store validation warning

5. Appian checks the database for already existing tables and fields and does not find any. As you want Appian to do the hard work, select the **Create tables automatically** option. Then, click **SAVE & PUBLISH**.

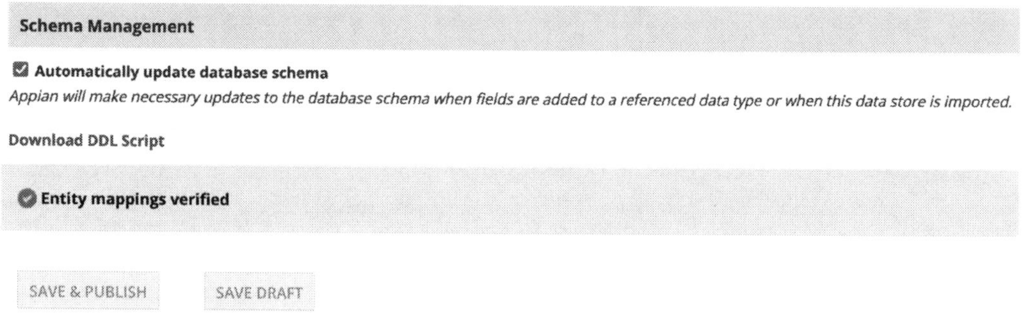

Figure 9.16 – The data store is created

Managing the database

The data store is created, and Appian manages the database for you. Let's have a look. Close the **Data Store Designer** tab, navigate to **Appian Designer**, and, in the top-right waffle menu, click **Cloud Database**.

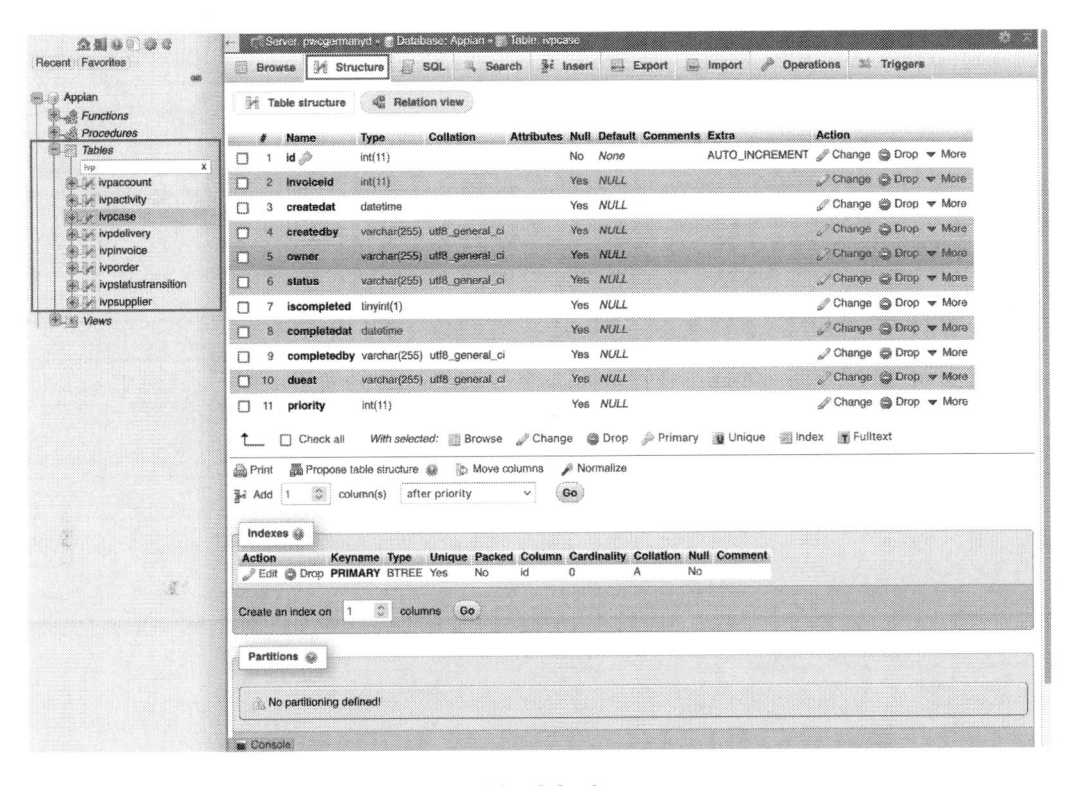

Figure 9.17 – Cloud database manager

In the left panel, open the **Tables** item and search for ivp and hit *Enter*. All your tables should show up. Click a table, followed by **Structure**, to display all the fields and their data types. The cloud database manager allows you to do more advanced database operations. In this book, I will cover just the basics.

An important activity is the deletion of fields and tables. If you modify the types of existing fields, primary key settings, or CDTs in Appian, you need to delete tables or fields manually. In database terminology, deleting something is called **Drop**.

In the table structure view, use the **Drop** icon on each field to delete that field. To delete, or drop, a table, go to the **Operations** tab, scroll down, and click the **Delete the table (DROP)**. After doing this, open the **Data Store** tab in Appian and click the **VERIFY** button, followed by **SAVE & PUBLISH** to make Appian recreate the deleted fields or tables.

In a situation where the data store cannot be published, delete the recently modified tables and then try to publish it again.

Tip

The default database in Appian Cloud is `MariaDB`, which can be managed using the Appian Cloud Database tool. Appian directly supports the integration of the following database management systems:

Amazon Aurora

IBM DB2

MariaDB

Microsoft SQL Server

MySQL

Oracle

PostgreSQL

To manage these databases, use the tools of the respective vendor.

Now, as you have the data storage in place, it is time to map that into Appian.

Records

Appian Records are the most important object type in Appian and integrate data, the UI, and processes. In our invoice validation application, the central record is called **Case**. It represents a single instance of the validation process, displays the relevant data, and allows a user to act.

Appian has the feature of synchronizing record data into an internal data store that is highly optimized for complex queries, aggregation, and analytics. This allows easier and more flexible application design. I will bring it to your attention when we use a functionality based on synchronized records.

Creating records

I will now walk you through creating one record. Once done, please create records for all entities in the same way. You will then have generated the following list of objects:

- IVP case
- IVP order
- IVP supplier
- IVP account
- IVP invoice
- IVP delivery
- IVP status transition
- IVP activity

In Appian Designer, click the **NEW** button, followed by **Record Type**.

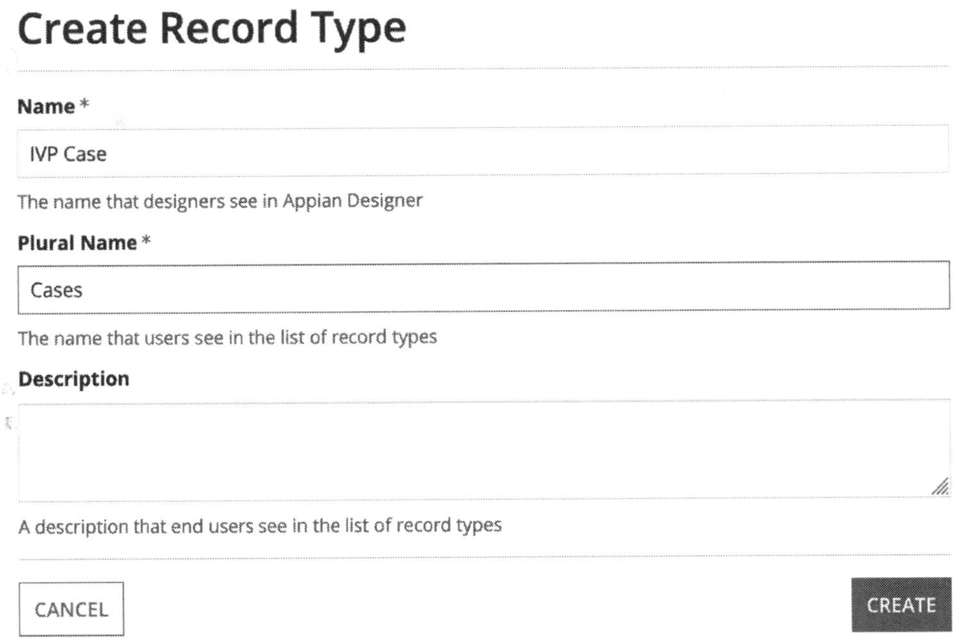

Create Record Type

Name *

> IVP Case

The name that designers see in Appian Designer

Plural Name *

> Cases

The name that users see in the list of record types

Description

>

A description that end users see in the list of record types

CANCEL   CREATE

Figure 9.18 – Creating a new record type

1. Enter the name using the following pattern:

    ```
    <PREFIX> Record Name
    ```

2.   In the **Plural Name** field, enter the name in plural form without the prefix. Click the **CREATE** button, and then **SAVE** in the next dialog, to go to Appian Records Designer.

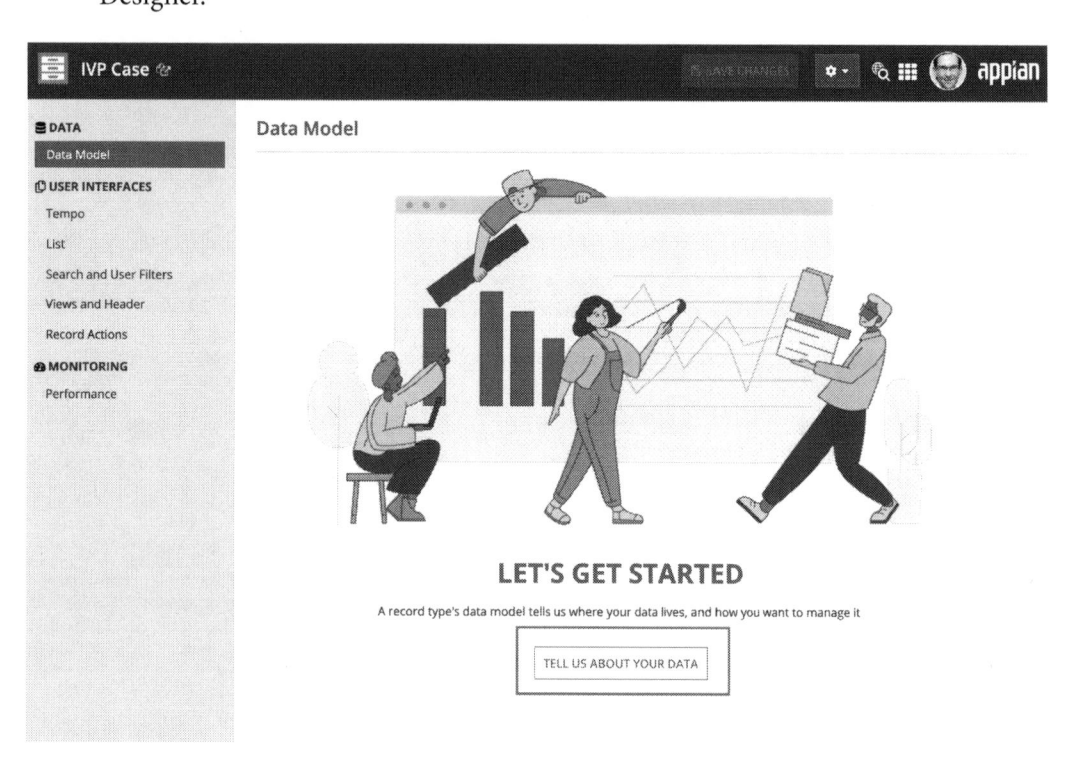

Figure 9.19 – New record in Records Designer

3.   Click **TELL US ABOUT YOUR DATA** to start the initial wizard and select **Database** as the source type. Then, click **NEXT**:

Configure Data Source

Data Sync

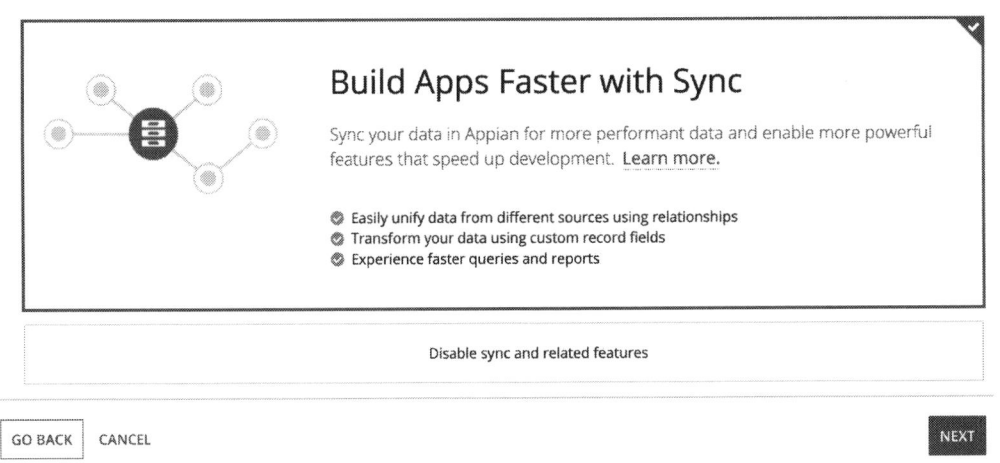

Figure 9.20 – Configuring record data sync

4. As already explained, this is about the data synchronization feature. As we want to use that, just click **NEXT**:

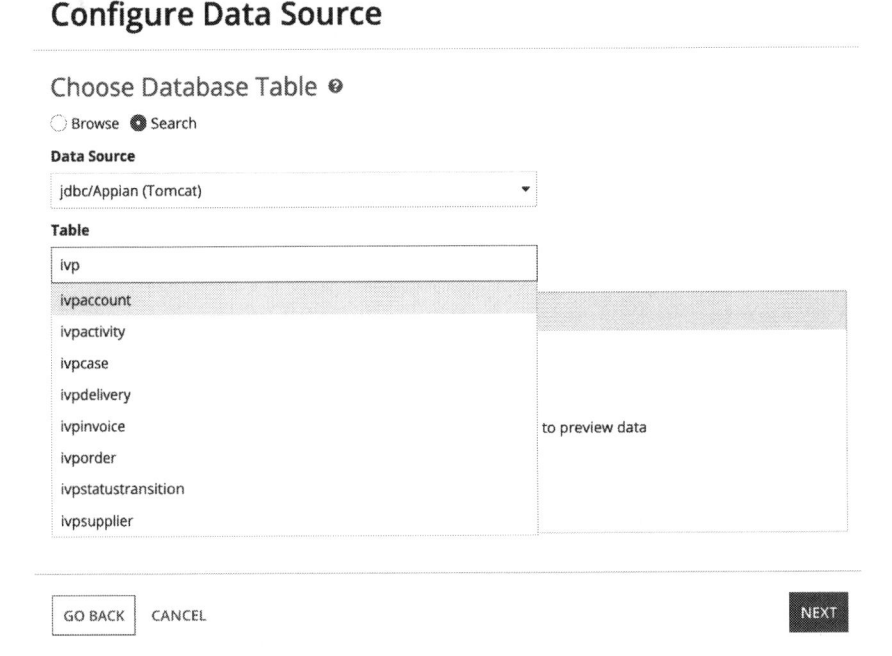

Figure 9.21 – Lookup table for a new record

5. In this step of the wizard, you will select the database table the record will work with. Switch from **Browse** to **Search** and type `ivp` in the **Table** field to search for the tables you just created as you published the data store. Select the `ivpcase` table and then click **NEXT**.

6. In the *Configure Source Filters* step, you can define a filter to only synchronize a subset of the data into Appian. As we want all data, just click **NEXT**:

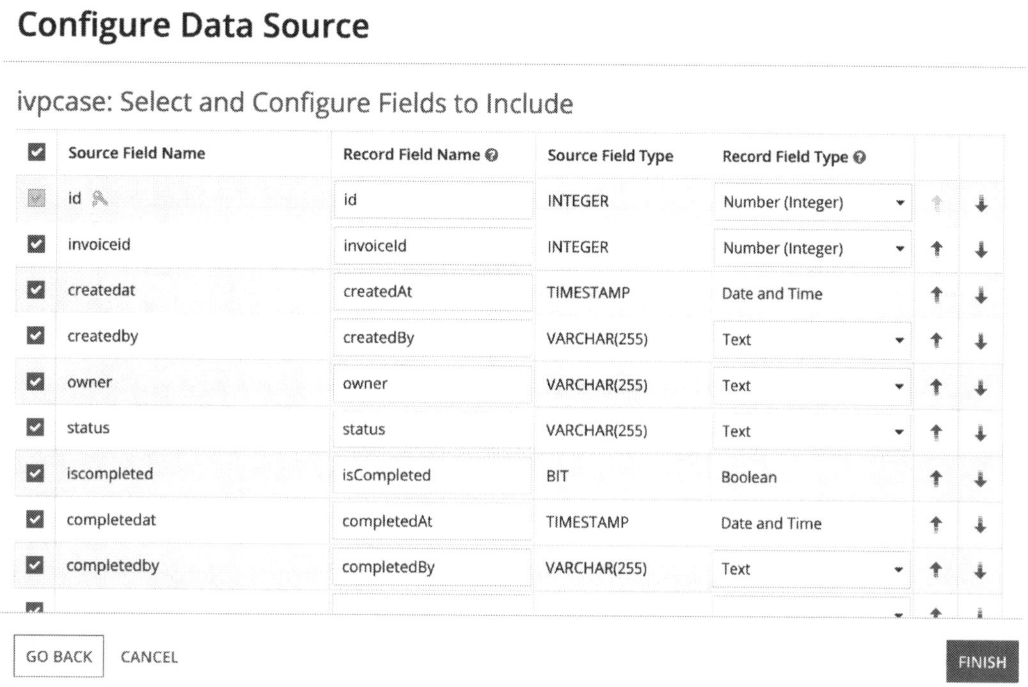

Configure Data Source

ivpcase: Select and Configure Fields to Include

☑	Source Field Name	Record Field Name ❷	Source Field Type	Record Field Type ❷		
☑	id 🔍	id	INTEGER	Number (Integer) ▼	↑	↓
☑	invoiceid	invoiceId	INTEGER	Number (Integer) ▼	↑	↓
☑	createdat	createdAt	TIMESTAMP	Date and Time	↑	↓
☑	createdby	createdBy	VARCHAR(255)	Text ▼	↑	↓
☑	owner	owner	VARCHAR(255)	Text ▼	↑	↓
☑	status	status	VARCHAR(255)	Text ▼	↑	↓
☑	iscompleted	isCompleted	BIT	Boolean	↑	↓
☑	completedat	completedAt	TIMESTAMP	Date and Time	↑	↓
☑	completedby	completedBy	VARCHAR(255)	Text ▼	↑	↓
☑				▼	↑	↓

GO BACK   CANCEL   FINISH

Figure 9.22 – Defining the fields to synchronize

7. In the last step of the wizard, you can select the field to be synchronized into Appian and have the option to map the data type to a different one. In our case, we want all fields and hence, will not change the data types. However, make sure to change the field names to the same camel casing pattern as used in the CDT. Click **FINISH** to complete the wizard.

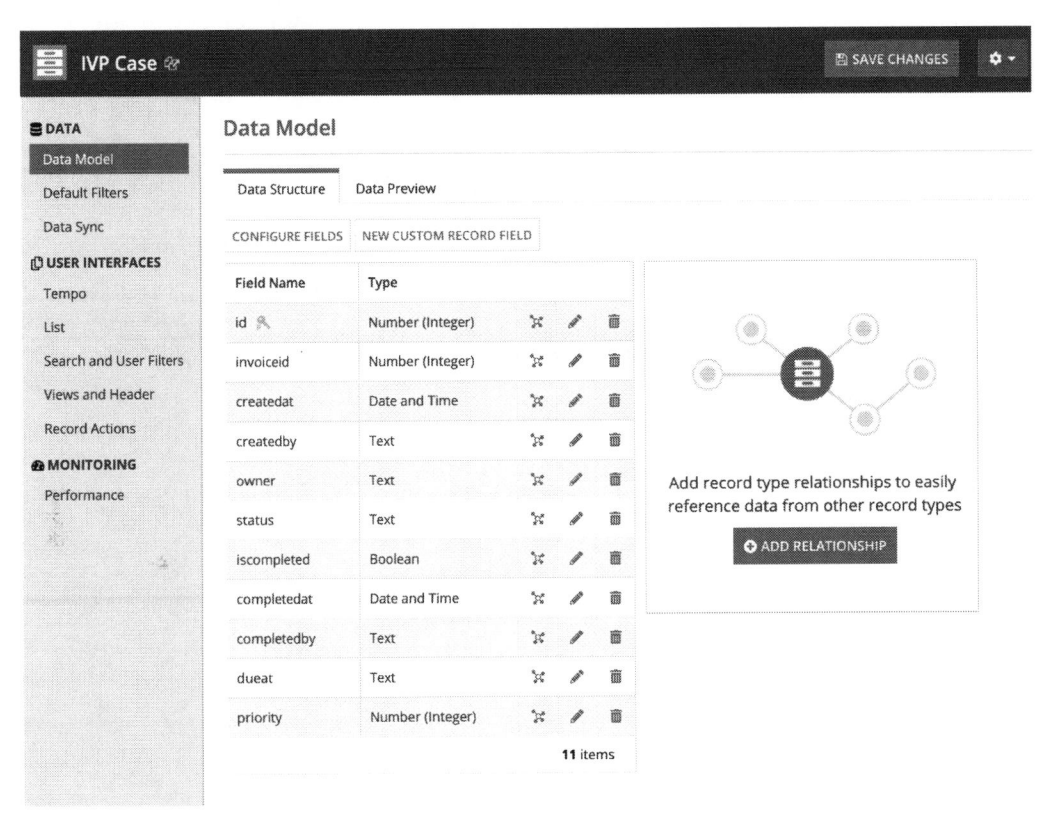

Figure 9.23 – The new record type

8. Click the **SAVE CHANGES** button in the top-right corner and then repeat these steps for all entities in the Entity-Relationship model.

Once done, I will show you how to translate the relations from that model into Appian Records.

Relationships

From a development perspective, records are the way to express relations between individual record types. You have already defined these relations in the Entity-Relationship model. From the perspective of a database developer, you would want to model these relations inside the database using foreign-key constraints. Then you would create views to join and aggregate multiple tables to make that data accessible to the user.

With Appian synchronized records, we define these relationships within Appian, which makes working with a data model with complex relationships much easier.

We start with the **Case** record, and add three relations to **Status Transition**, **Invoice**, and **Activity**:

1. Open **Case Record** in Appian Records Designer.

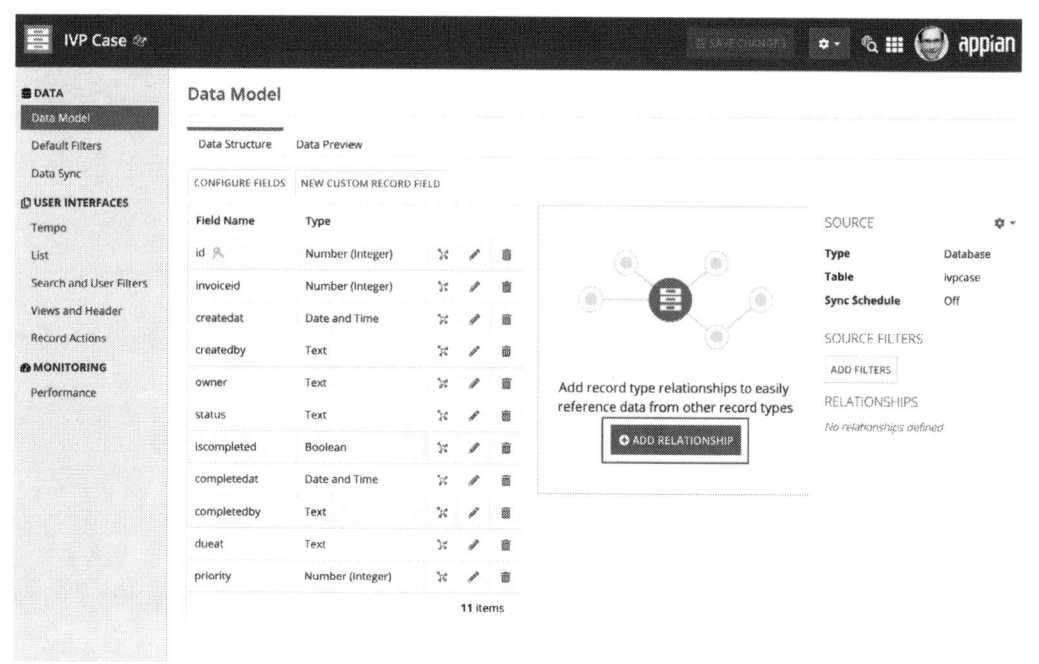

Figure 9.24 – Case Record in the Designer

2. Click **ADD RELATIONSHIP** and type ivp in the dialog that opens.

Add Relationship to IVP Case

Figure 9.25 – Selecting the related record

3. Select **IVP Status Transition**, which can be seen at the bottom of *Figure 9.26*, and then click **NEXT**.

Add Relationship to IVP Case

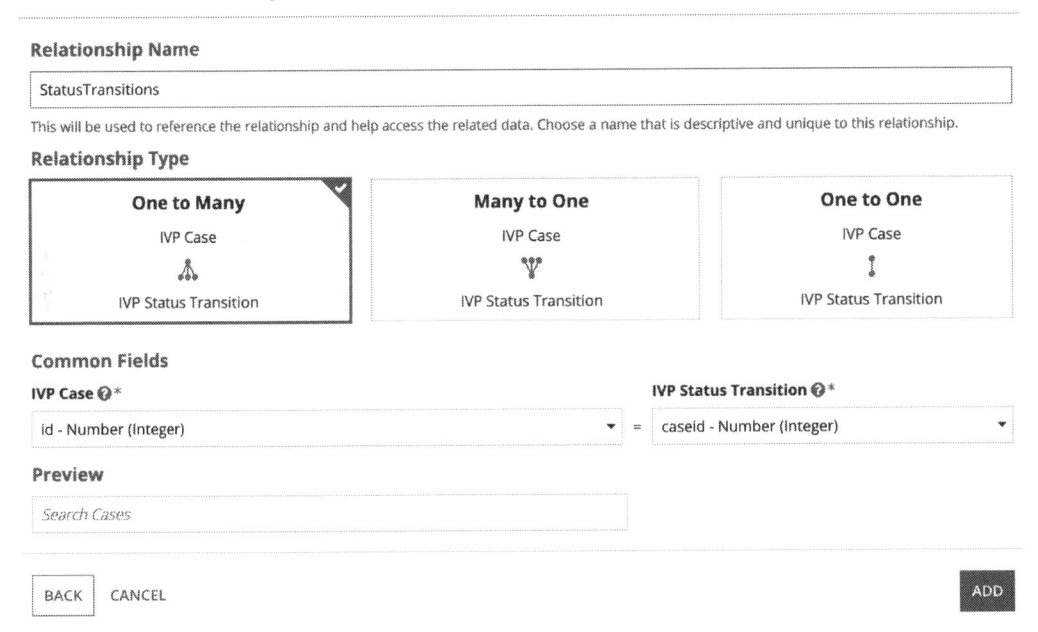

Figure 9.26 – Relationship configuration

4. Enter a descriptive name. From the perspective of the **Case** record, the relation will point to all status transitions belonging to a given case. So, it makes sense to use the name `StatusTransitions`.

    - The relationship type is one-to-many, as defined in the Entity-Relationship model.
    - The two fields that define how these two records belong to each other are `id` for **Case** and `caseId` for **Status Transition**. Then, click **ADD** to complete the wizard.

5. Create the relation to **Invoice** as follows:

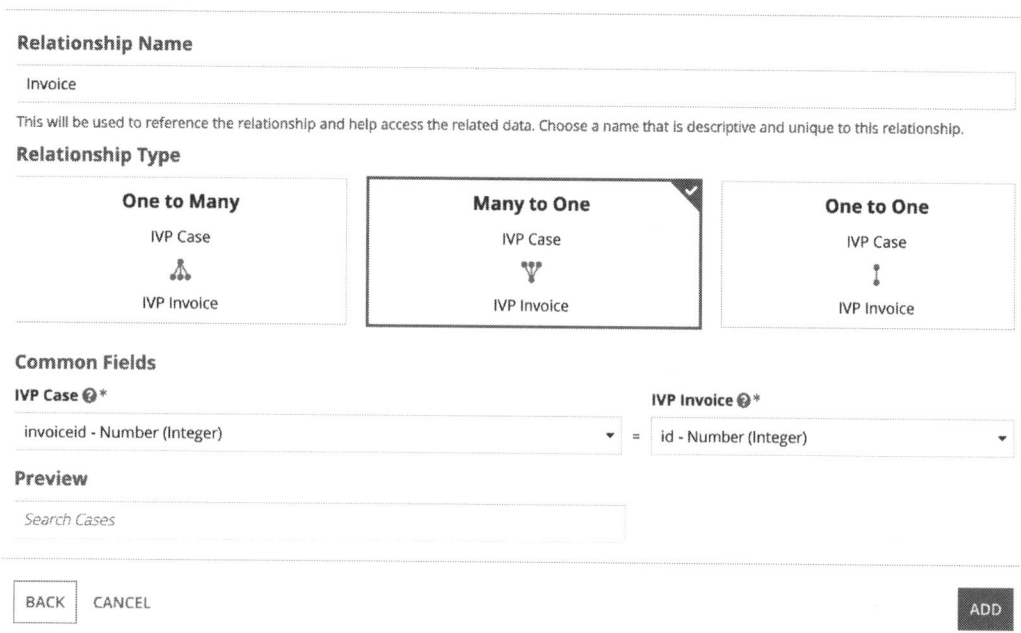

Figure 9.27 – Case to Invoice relationship

6.   Then, create the relation to **Activity**.

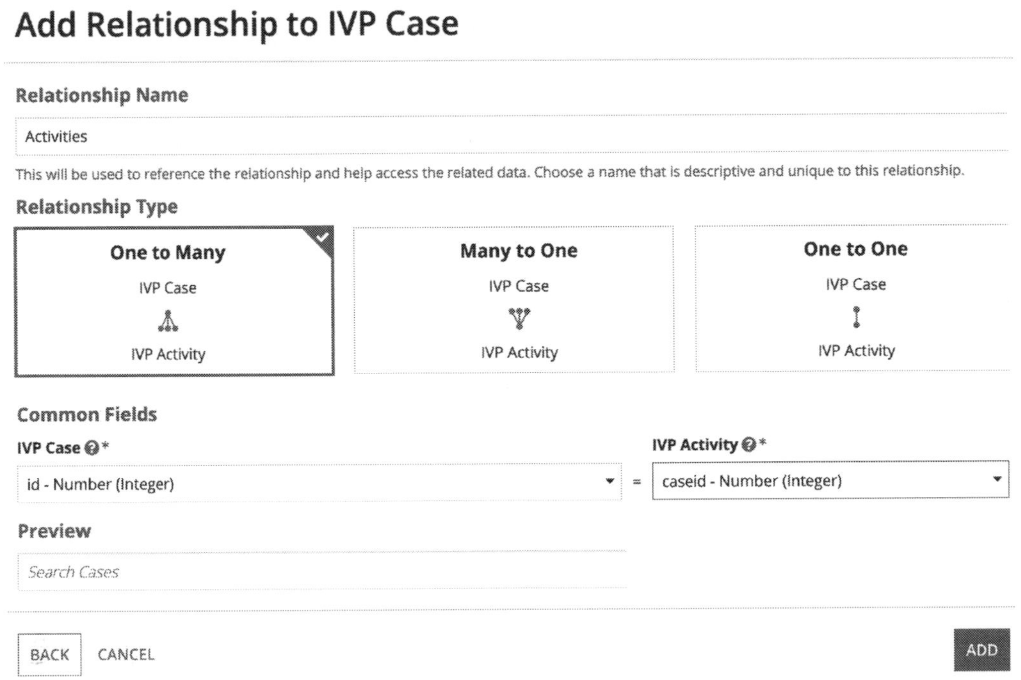

Add Relationship to IVP Case

Relationship Name

Activities

This will be used to reference the relationship and help access the related data. Choose a name that is descriptive and unique to this relationship.

Relationship Type

One to Many	Many to One	One to One
IVP Case	IVP Case	IVP Case
⚠	⚠	⚠
IVP Activity	IVP Activity	IVP Activity

Common Fields

IVP Case ❓*

| id - Number (Integer) ▾ |

=

IVP Activity ❓*

| caseid - Number (Integer) ▾ |

Preview

Search Cases

BACK   CANCEL   ADD

Figure 9.28 – Case to Activity relationship

7. The **Case** record in Records Designer is shown as follows:

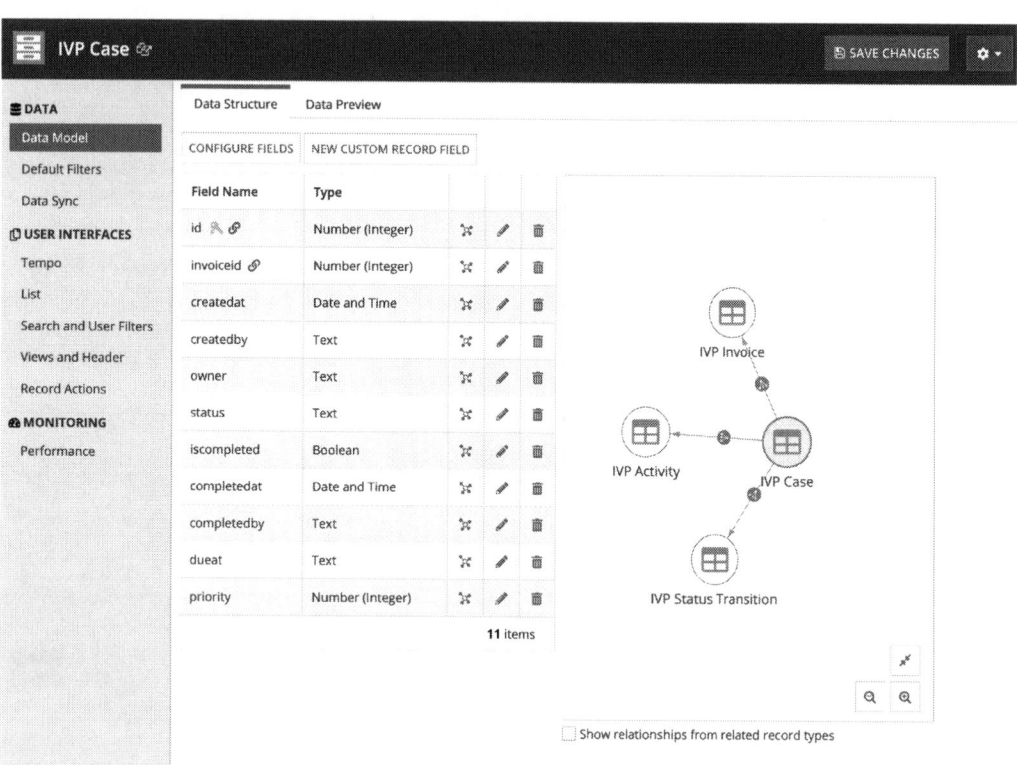

Figure 9.29 – The Case record and its relations

8. Click **SAVE CHANGES** to save the modifications you just made.

9. You will then create more relationships. Appian will suggest creating reverse relationships.

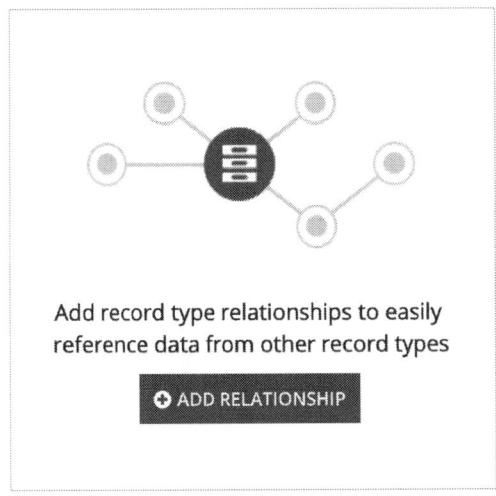

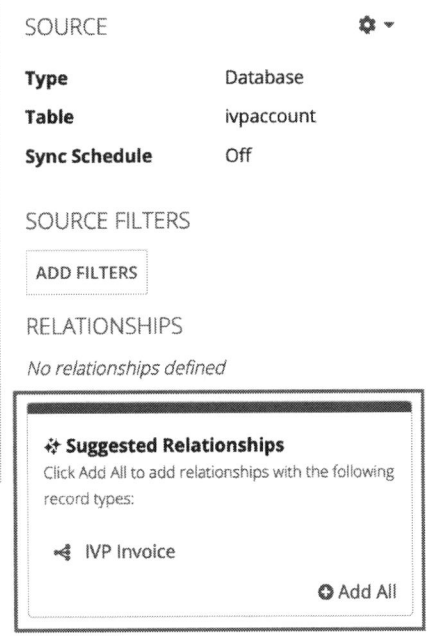

Figure 9.30 – Suggested reverse relationships

10. Add these, clicking the **Add All** link. Then, change the names to more descriptive ones.

11. Once you are done with the above process, you can now create the following list of relationships:

- **Invoice to Account**:

    - Name: `Account`
    - Type: many-to-one
    - Fields: `accountId` and `id`

- **Invoice to Supplier**:

    - Name: `Supplier`
    - Type: many-to-one
    - Fields: `supplierId` and `id`

- **Supplier to Order**:

    - Name: `Orders`

    - Type: one-to-many

    - Fields: `id` and `supplierId`

- **Account to Supplier**:

    - Name: `Supplier`

    - Type: many-to-one

    - Fields: `supplierId` and `id`

- **Supplier to Order**:

    - Name: `Orders`

    - Type: one-to-many

    - Fields: `id` and `supplierId`

Adding many-to-many relations

For the two many-to-many relationships between **Invoice** and **Order**, and **Order** and **Delivery**, we need to add two more entities. The reason is that a relational database, such as our MariaDB, cannot store multiple values in a single field. But this is what we need to express, that a single invoice can belong to multiple orders, and that a single order can belong to multiple invoices.

We solve that problem by creating two more CDTs by doing nothing more than connecting **Orders** to **Invoices** and **Orders** to **Deliveries**:

1. The first CDT is called `IVP_InvoicesToOrders`:

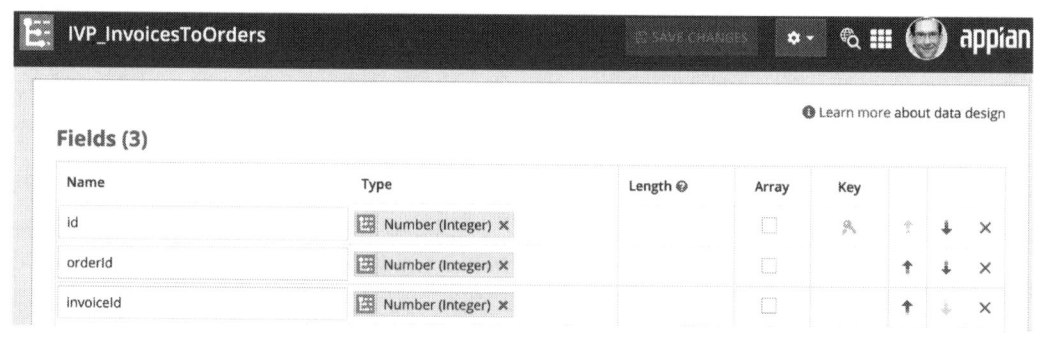

Figure 9.31 – InvoicesToOrders CDT

2. The second CDT is called `IVP_OrdersToDeliveries`:

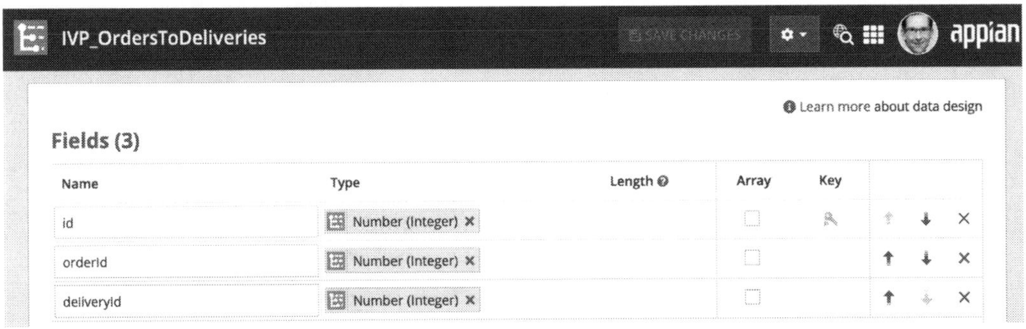

Figure 9.32 – OrdersToDeliveries CDT

3. Add both the already existing data store, and then **Verify** and **Save** & **Publish** it.

4. Now, create two new record types named **IVP Invoices To Orders** and **IVP Orders To Deliveries** based on the respective tables. Both will have many-to-one relationships.

Now, create four new relationships:

- **Invoice** to **Invoices to Orders**

    - Name: `OrderIds`
    - Type: one-to-many
    - Fields: `id` and `invoiceId`

- **Invoices to Orders** to **Invoices**

    - Name: `Order`
    - Type: many-to-one
    - Fields: `orderId` and `id`

- **Order** to **Orders to Deliveries**

    - Name: `DeliveryIds`
    - Type: one-to-many
    - Fields: `id` and `orderId`

- **Orders to Deliveries** to **Deliveries**

  - Name: `Delivery`

  - Type: many-to-one

  - Fields: `deliveryId` and `id`

When you enable the option to also show relationships from related record types in Appian Records Designer, it should show a Record relationship diagram like this:

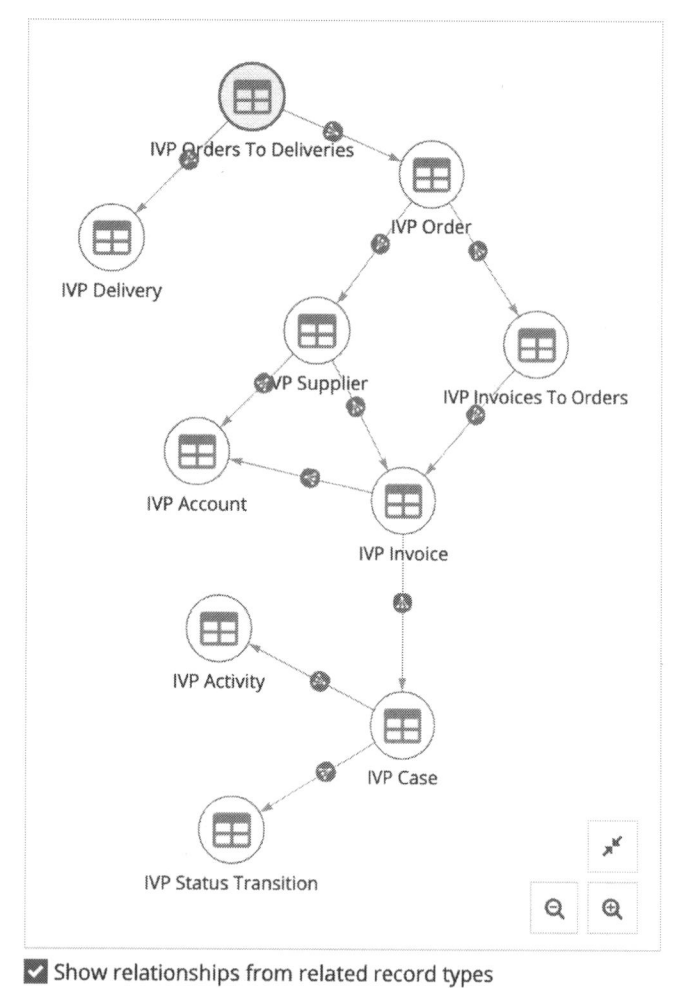

Figure 9.33 – Final Record relationship diagram

In *Chapter 6, Understanding Business Data in Appian Projects*, in the *Adding relations* section, we discussed the fact that suppliers sometimes split one purchase order into multiple deliveries or deliver multiple purchase orders in a single delivery, which complicates matters. A similar problem exists with the relationship between invoices and purchase orders. Both are many-to-many relationships and make the process, as well as our data model, more complex.

Adding such relationship tables is standard for all cases in which many-to-many relationships must be modeled in a relational database such as our MariaDB database.

Let's now discuss some best practices for modeling business data in Appian.

Best practices

The most important best practice is to create an entity relationship model before you start in Appian. It is not a problem to make minor changes, as you have seen, but without good preparation, you may have to recreate large parts of your CDTs and records.

The second best practice is the **naming convention**. In Appian, each field has a defined type. This type is visible in all places. Do not add the data type itself into the field name. Then, give the primary key field the same name in all CDTs. I use id for that. A field, referring to the primary key of another CDT, gets the name by following this pattern:

```
<nameOfOtherCdt>Id
```

Finally, keep the logic out of the database. From a pure Appian perspective, the database is just another integration, much like an integration with a SalesForce system or SAP. Try to implement most logic in Appian to reduce the complexity of your overall development.

Summary

In this chapter, you learned how to turn an Entity-Relationship model into tangible CDTs and records in Appian. You now know that a CDT itself cannot store data but, used in a data store, it defines the structure of a database table. On top of these tables, you created records, which synchronize the data into a high-performance data layer that you then use to model complex record relationships.

This is the required foundation for the next chapter, where you will learn how to create executable process models in Appian.

10
Modeling Business Processes in Appian

Process models are the way to implement resource orchestration in Appian. This orchestration typically includes the following:

- Carbon-based systems (humans) by assigning a task.
- Silicon-based systems where a computer performs a task, such as data persistence, **Artificial Intelligence (AI)**, **Robotic Process Automation (RPA)**, or **Optical Character Recognition (OCR)**.

We'll model these processes using a subset of the **Business Process Modeling Notation (BPMN)**, which will look like the business processes you already know. While the models might look similar, the big difference is that the models in Appian are directly executable, like a computer program. You will even be able to monitor a process during execution. To make this work, you will add different types of nodes and configure logic, user interfaces, and data flows.

As our processes will interact with people, we will need to create **User Interfaces (UI)**. For this chapter, we will focus on the process modeling and keep it simple. In *Chapter 11, Creating User Interfaces in Appian*, we will have a closer look at designing UIs.

In this chapter, we will cover the following topics:

- **A first simple process**: Creating an invoice and starting a validation process
- **Persisting data**: Writing data to a database
- **Adding the process to the record**: Attaching a validation process to a case record
- **Adding related actions and record actions**: Adding data management processes to an application
- **Completing the process**: Completing s validation process
- **Best practices**: When, why, and how to use a process

A first simple process

As our application is about a fictional process in a fictional company, you will need to model a small process that creates an invoice we can then use in an invoice validation process.

Creating the model

Just like any other object in Appian, you create a new process model with the **NEW** button in Appian Designer:

1. You will need to enter a name (following the naming convention) for process models:

   ```
   <PREFIX> This Is My Process Model Name
   ```

2. A good name would be IVP Create New Invoice.
3. Click the **CREATE** button and accept the default values in the security settings. Then, **Appian Process Modeler** will open.

We already had a look at the Process Modeler in *Chapter 3*, *Building Blocks of Appian Quick Apps*, but this time, we will take a closer look:

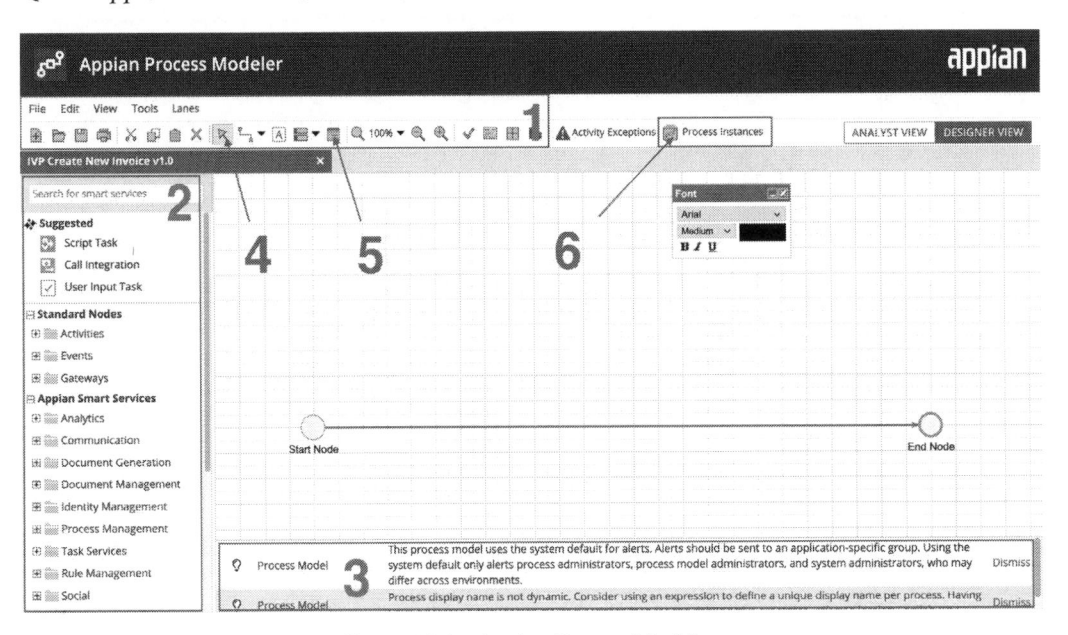

Figure 10.1 – Appian Process Modeler

1. **Menu bar**: The most relevant activities are in the icon in the menu bar. It is a good idea to explore the individual menus and menu items. Increase your efficiency by remembering the keyboard shortcuts that are given with some menu items.

2. **Smart services palette**: This consists of the available node types you can add to your process model. Since most of them implement complex behavior, Appian calls them Smart Services.

3. **Validations and suggestions**: The Process Modeler will constantly check your model for any issues and adherence to general best practices.

4. **Select tool**: The mouse cursor can have two modes of operation – **Select** or **Connect**. With **Select**, you move or configure nodes. **Connect** allows you to connect individual nodes. Keep the **Select** tool activated and switch between **Select** and **Connect** by holding the *Shift* key.

5. **Process model properties**: Click the icon to open a dialog that allows you to configure the process model.

6. **Process Instances**: This icon will open a dialog showing all active process instances of your model. Click individual instances to load them into the modeler for monitoring and debugging.

There are three additional steps to go through before adding the first node to the model:

1. **Data management**: In Appian, data management for process models defines the behavior of a system after a process is completed. To keep memory consumption low, you want the completed process to be deleted as soon as possible. For debugging purposes, I recommend setting the deletion period to **1 day**. Do not use the archive, as this fills up disk space and is typically not needed:

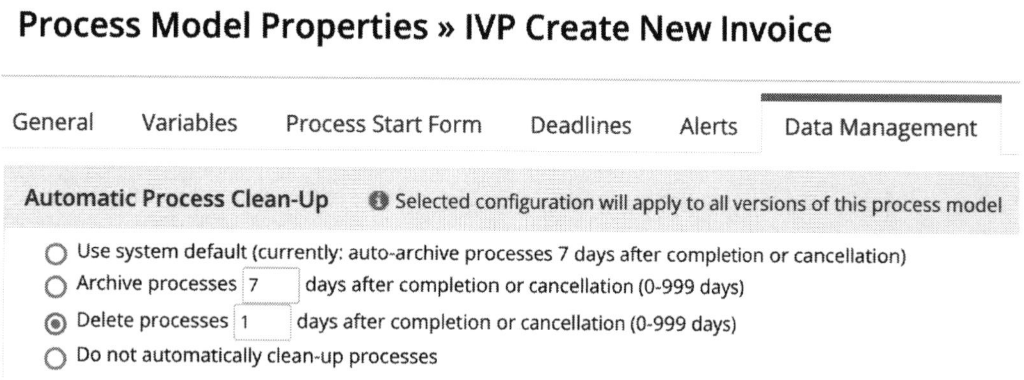

Process Model Properties » IVP Create New Invoice

General	Variables	Process Start Form	Deadlines	Alerts	**Data Management**

Automatic Process Clean-Up   ⓘ Selected configuration will apply to all versions of this process model

○ Use system default (currently: auto-archive processes 7 days after completion or cancellation)
○ Archive processes [7] days after completion or cancellation (0-999 days)
◉ Delete processes [1] days after completion or cancellation (0-999 days)
○ Do not automatically clean-up processes

Figure 10.2 – Process model data management

Click the **Process Model Properties** icon, go to the **Data Management** tab, and set it to delete the process after 1 day.

> **Tip**
> You will persist any relevant data to a database before completing the process. Keeping completed processes in memory is not considered best practice, as it can affect system stability.

2. **Process alerts**: If there is an error in process execution, the process will halt and send a notification:

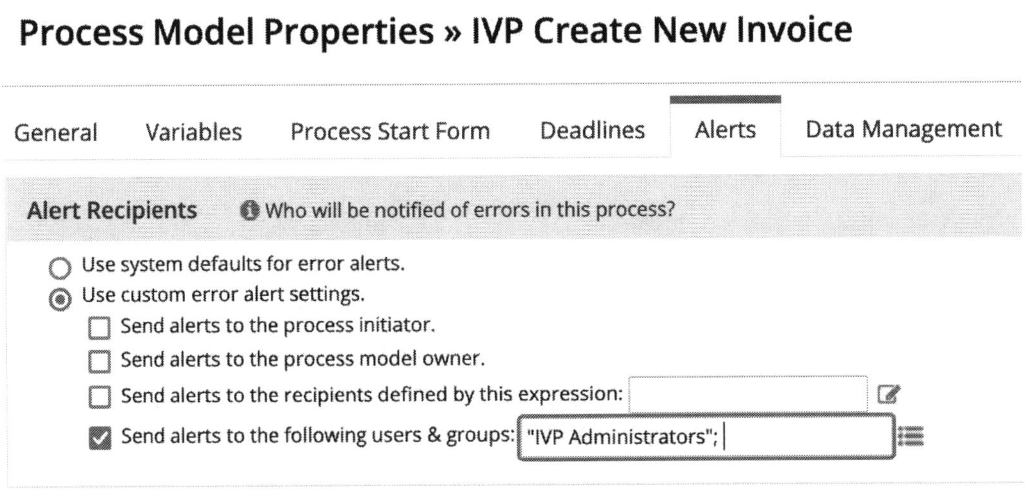

Process Model Properties » IVP Create New Invoice

General   Variables   Process Start Form   Deadlines   **Alerts**   Data Management

Alert Recipients   ⓘ Who will be notified of errors in this process?

○ Use system defaults for error alerts.
◉ Use custom error alert settings.
   ☐ Send alerts to the process initiator.
   ☐ Send alerts to the process model owner.
   ☐ Send alerts to the recipients defined by this expression: [   ] ☑
   ☑ Send alerts to the following users & groups: ["IVP Administrators"; |] ☰

Figure 10.3 – Process model alert settings

Make sure to send these notifications only to users in your administrator group.

3. **Straight (Direct) versus angle connectors**: Make sure to use angle connectors as a default. This makes a larger process model more comprehensible. Toggle between the modes using the icon in the menu bar:

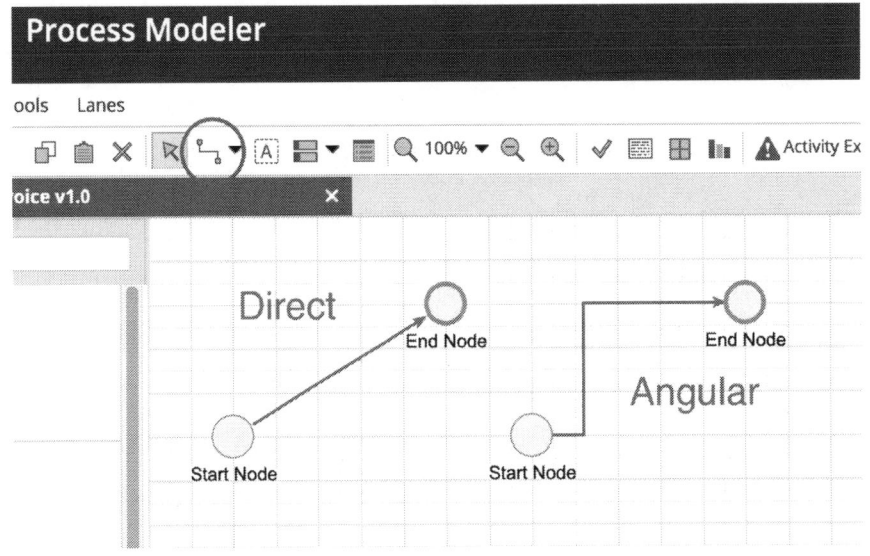

Figure 10.4 – Direct versus Angular connectors

In rare cases where a node has many connectors, it can help to use some straight connectors to avoid overlapping. The connector in the just-created process model is a straight one. You might want to replace it with an angle one. Click the connector, then click the *Delete* icon in the menu bar or hit the *Delete* key, and connect the two nodes again.

Next, you will learn how to add variables to the process model.

Adding a process variable

The process model needs a place to store data while the flow goes from one node to the next. In Appian, we use process variables with a defined type to do that:

1. Set up these variables in the **Process Model Properties** dialog on the **Variables** tab:

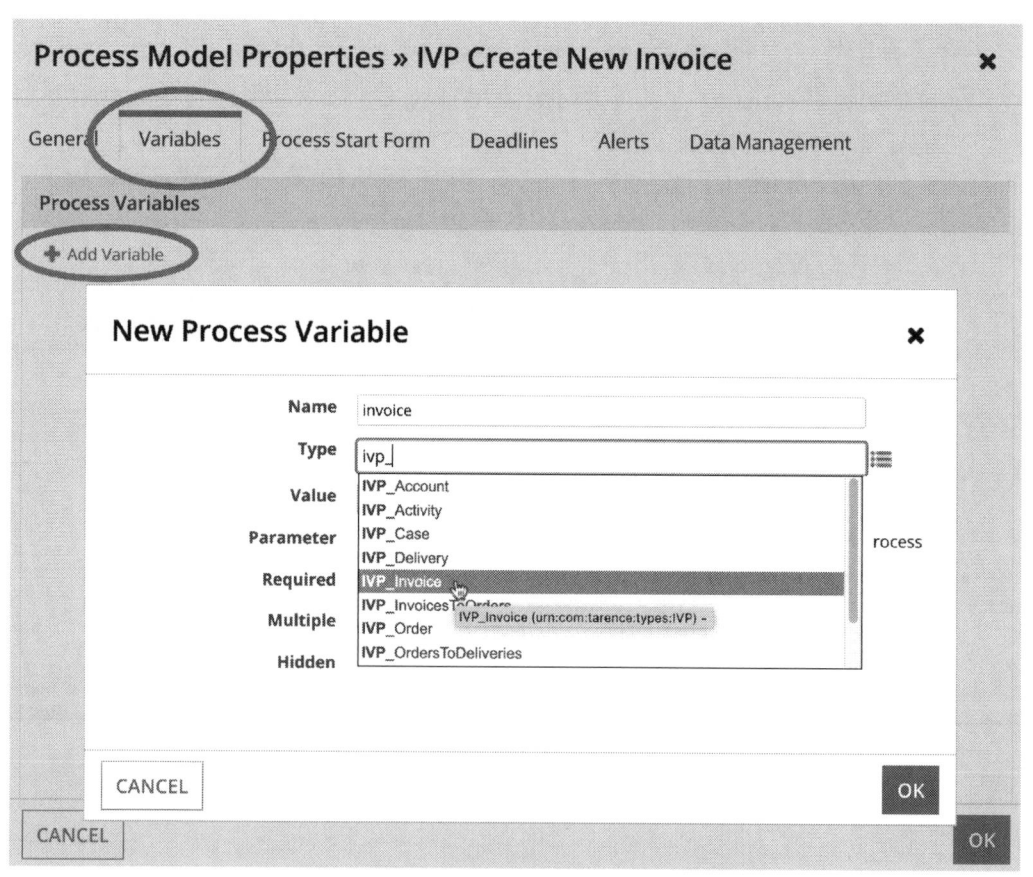

Figure 10.5 – Adding a process variable

2. Click **Add Variable** and type a descriptive name in camel casing. There is no added value in adding the application prefix or the type to the name. In the **Type** field, you can start typing, and Appian will show up matching CDTs. Select the **IVP_ Invoice** type.

Make sure to check the **Parameter** checkbox. This allows you to pass data into the process as it is started. When you do not see the data being passed to the process variables as expected, the reason might be that you forgot to define the process variable as a parameter.

Adding a process start form to the model enables the user to capture data when initiating the process.

Adding the start form

Now, create the first UI and add it to the process to allow the user to capture the invoice data.

Follow these steps in the **Process Model Properties** dialog on the **Process Start Form** tab:

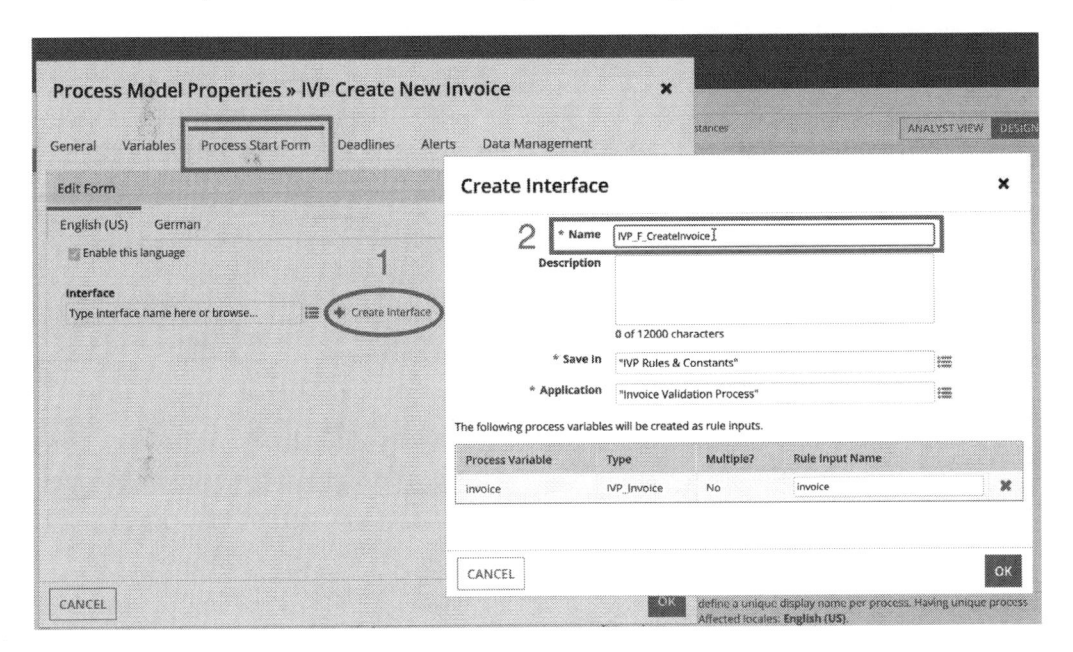

Figure 10.6 – Create a process start form

3. Click **Create Interface**.

4. Enter a name following the following pattern, where **F** indicates that this is a special type of interface.

    Check the *Best practices* section in this chapter for the full list of interface types:

    ```
    <PREFIX>_F_<MyNewInterface>
    ```

5. Click **OK** to create the interface. Appian will now show the **Edit Interface** button.

Click it to open the new interface in the Appian Interface Designer. Then, follow these steps to create a basic interface to capture the invoice data:

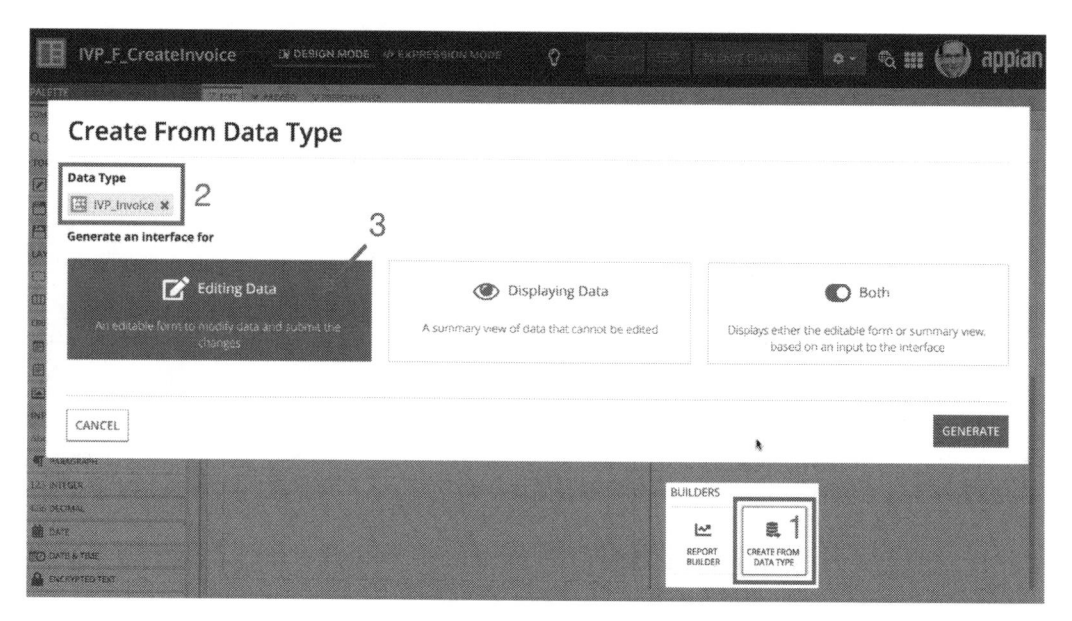

Figure 10.7 – Create a basic interface from the CDT

6. In the right panel, scroll all the way down and click **CREATE FROM DATA TYPE** to open a new dialog.

7. Click in the **Data Type** field and start typing IVP to look up your **IVP_Invoice** CDT.

8. Select the **Editing Data** option and click **Generate**. We will later create a separate interface for display purposes:

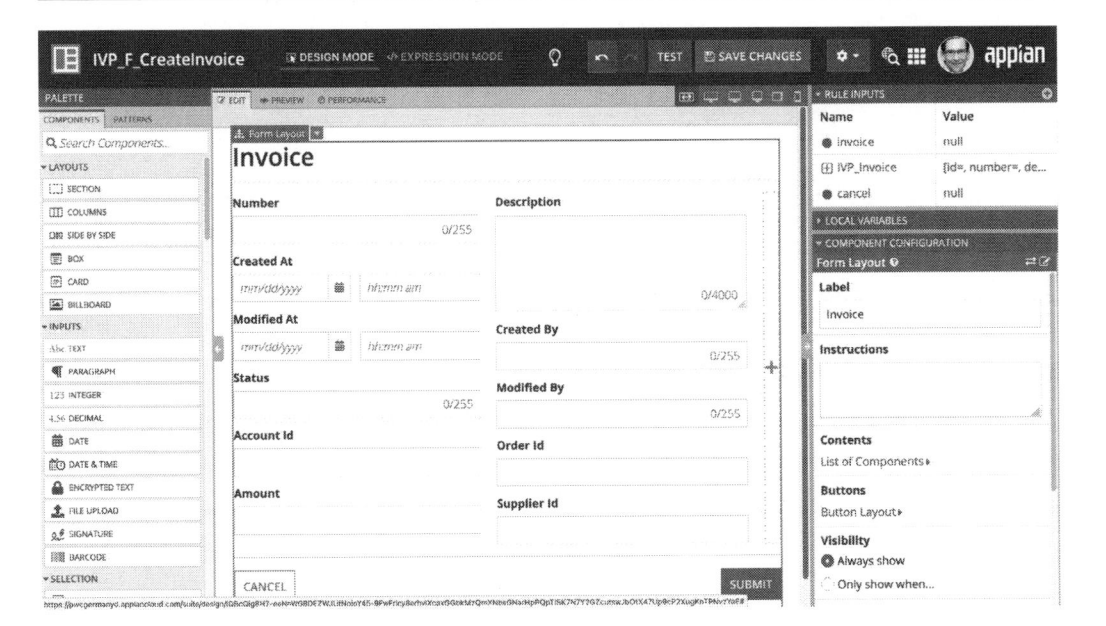

Figure 10.8 – A basic interface for the IVP_Invoice CDT

As Appian generated the interface automatically, it does not know about our specific requirements. This results in one unnecessary rule input and a rule input with an unsightly name. You will now modify these rule inputs:

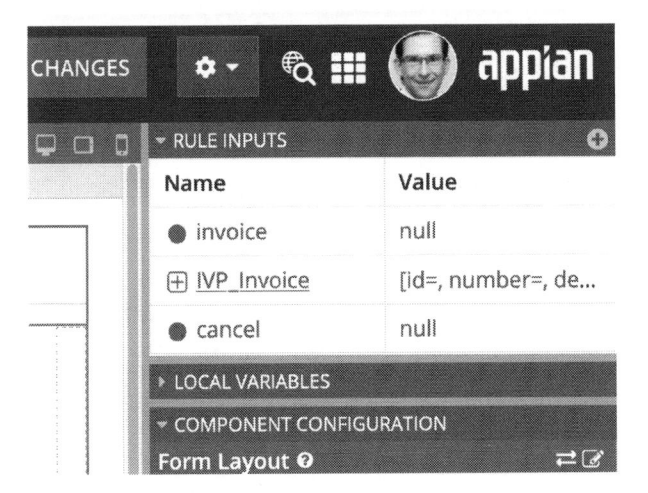

Figure 10.9 - Modify the rule inputs

9. In the **RULE INPUTS** panel, click the **invoice** rule input and then delete it.

10. Click the **IVP_Invoice** rule input and rename it `invoice`.

11. Click **SAVE CHANGES** to complete your modifications.

12. Navigate back to the process model and click **Refresh**:

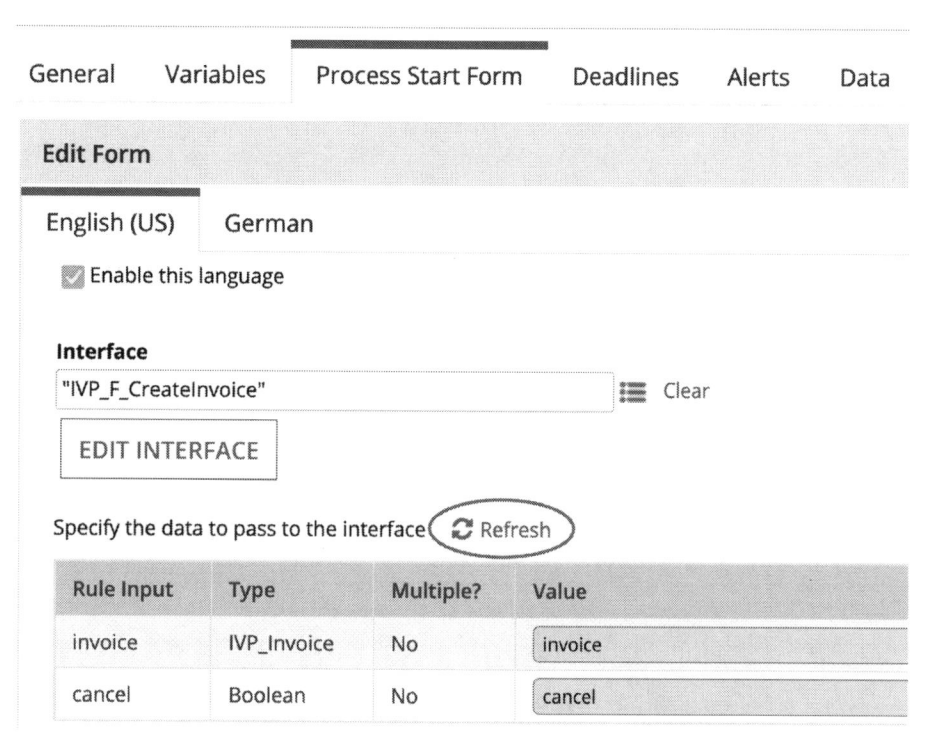

Process Model Properties » IVP Create New Invoice

| General | Variables | Process Start Form | Deadlines | Alerts | Data |

Edit Form

| English (US) | German |

☑ Enable this language

Interface

"IVP_F_CreateInvoice"   ☰ Clear

EDIT INTERFACE

Specify the data to pass to the interface ⟳ Refresh

Rule Input	Type	Multiple?	Value
invoice	IVP_Invoice	No	invoice
cancel	Boolean	No	cancel

Figure 10.10 – Refresh after interface modification

13. Appian will now check the rule inputs in your interface against the process variables. If the interface has a new rule input, Appian will ask you whether you want to have them automatically mapped to process variables. Click **YES** to accept.

14. Close the **Process Model Properties** dialog by clicking **OK**.

15. Open the **File** menu and click **Save & Publish** to store your modifications as a new version of the model.

Next, we will test the new process model for the first time.

Testing the model

I design all my process models in small increments to minimize the risk of errors. To verify that my changes meet my expectations, I test each increment. Adopt this habit, and don't build complex process models all at once without testing in between.

Let me introduce you to process model testing and monitoring. Open the **File** menu and click **Start Process for Debugging**. Appian will display the interface you configured as the process start form. Enter some data and click **SUBMIT**:

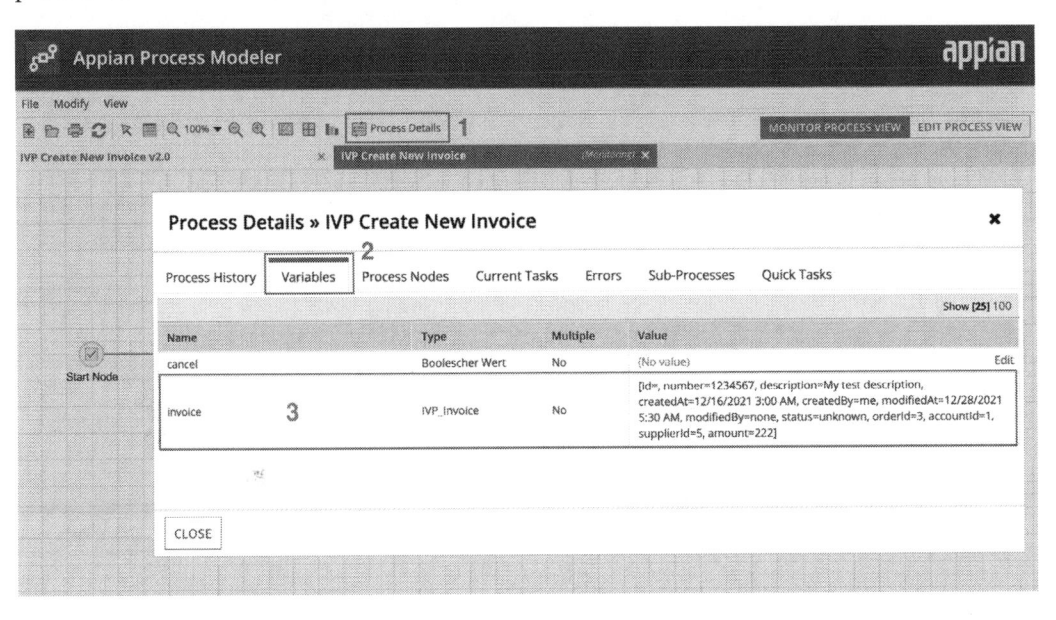

Figure 10.11 – The active process and Process Details

1. Open the **Process Details** dialog.

2. Navigate to the **Variables** tab.

3. Validate the process variables and their values.

This is the way to test and debug a process model in Appian. In the **Process History** tab, you will see all actions that happened during process execution and which process variables have been modified:

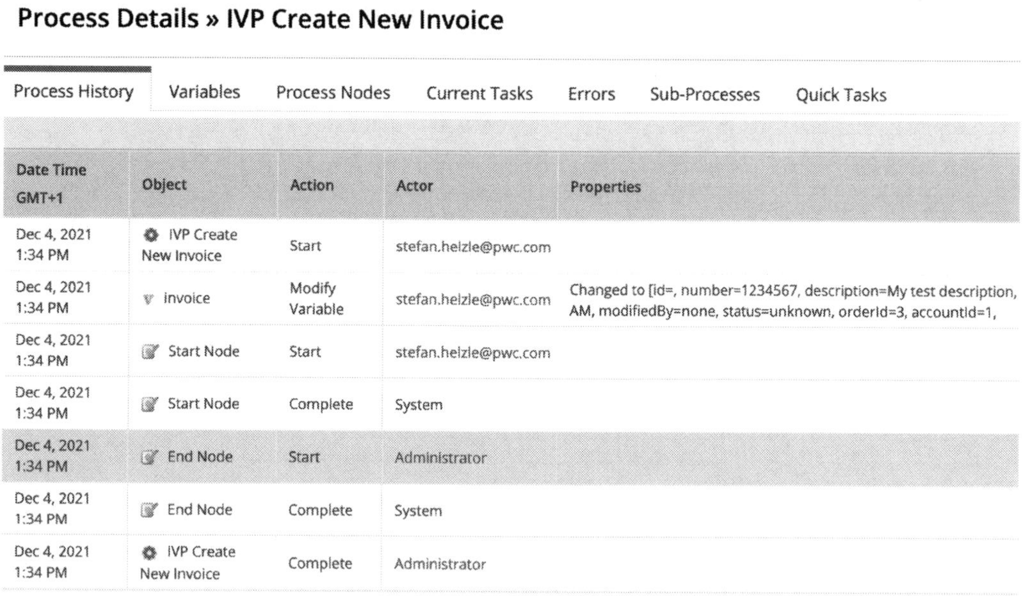

Process Details » IVP Create New Invoice

Process History	Variables	Process Nodes	Current Tasks	Errors	Sub-Processes	Quick Tasks

Date Time GMT+1	Object	Action	Actor	Properties
Dec 4, 2021 1:34 PM	⚙ IVP Create New Invoice	Start	stefan.helzle@pwc.com	
Dec 4, 2021 1:34 PM	ⅴ invoice	Modify Variable	stefan.helzle@pwc.com	Changed to [id=, number=1234567, description=My test description, AM, modifiedBy=none, status=unknown, orderId=3, accountId=1,
Dec 4, 2021 1:34 PM	📝 Start Node	Start	stefan.helzle@pwc.com	
Dec 4, 2021 1:34 PM	📝 Start Node	Complete	System	
Dec 4, 2021 1:34 PM	📝 End Node	Start	Administrator	
Dec 4, 2021 1:34 PM	📝 End Node	Complete	System	
Dec 4, 2021 1:34 PM	⚙ IVP Create New Invoice	Complete	Administrator	

Figure 10.12 – Process History in Process Details

You now have a process you can start, and you can see the captured data. In *Chapter 11, Creating User Interfaces in Appian*, I will show you how to enhance a very basic process start form. Now, let's see how to persist the captured data to a database.

Persisting data

The captured data is already stored in a process variable. Our goal is to write the data to a database and then make it visible in the **Invoices** record. Let me walk you through how to do this:

1. Open the **IVP Create New Invoice** process model in the modeler:

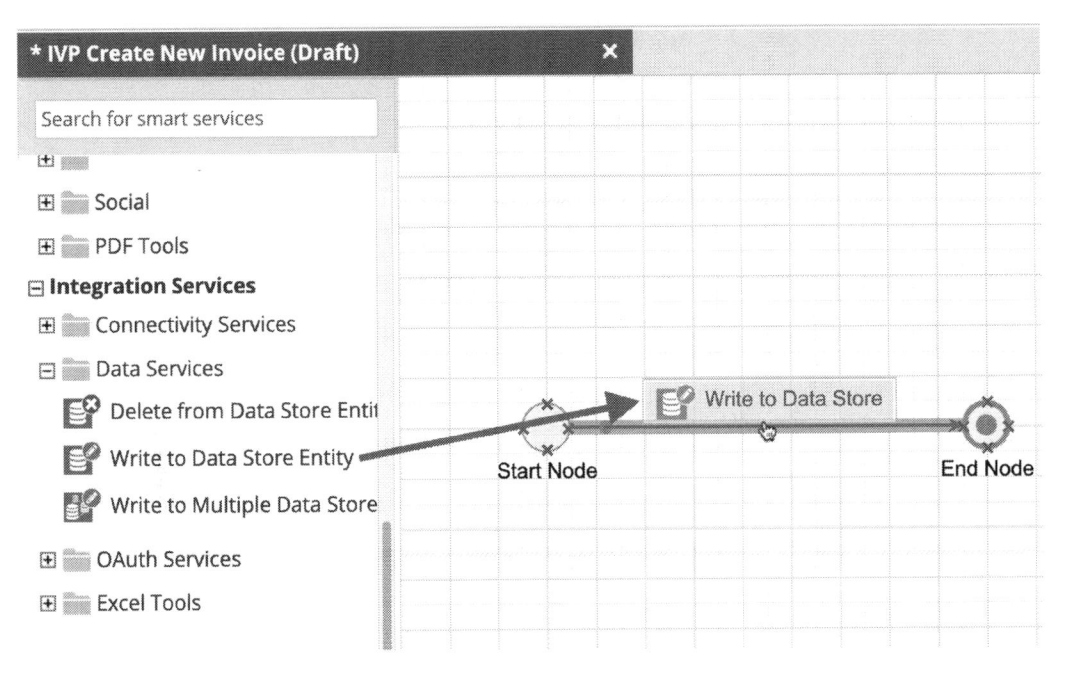

Figure 10.13 – Adding a Write to Data Store Entity node

2. From the Smart Services palette, navigate to the **Data Services** subsection in the **Integration Services** section, and drag and drop a **Write to Data Store Entity** node on top of the connector.

3. To validate that the node is connected, look for the small arrow on the left side of the node.

> **Tip**
>
> When adding a node, make sure that the connector is highlighted in blue before you release it. If you drop the node slightly off, it will look like it is connected, but it is not:

Start Node   Write to Data Store Entity   End Node

Figure 10.14 – Check the connection on the new node

> **Tip**
>
> You cannot move a node from one connection to another. Appian will not release the old connection, and you might end up with a loop. Disconnect a node before you move it to another place.

You now configure the node to define where to store the data and what data to use. Double-click the node to open the properties dialog. Go to the **Data** tab, then the **Inputs** tab, and follow these steps:

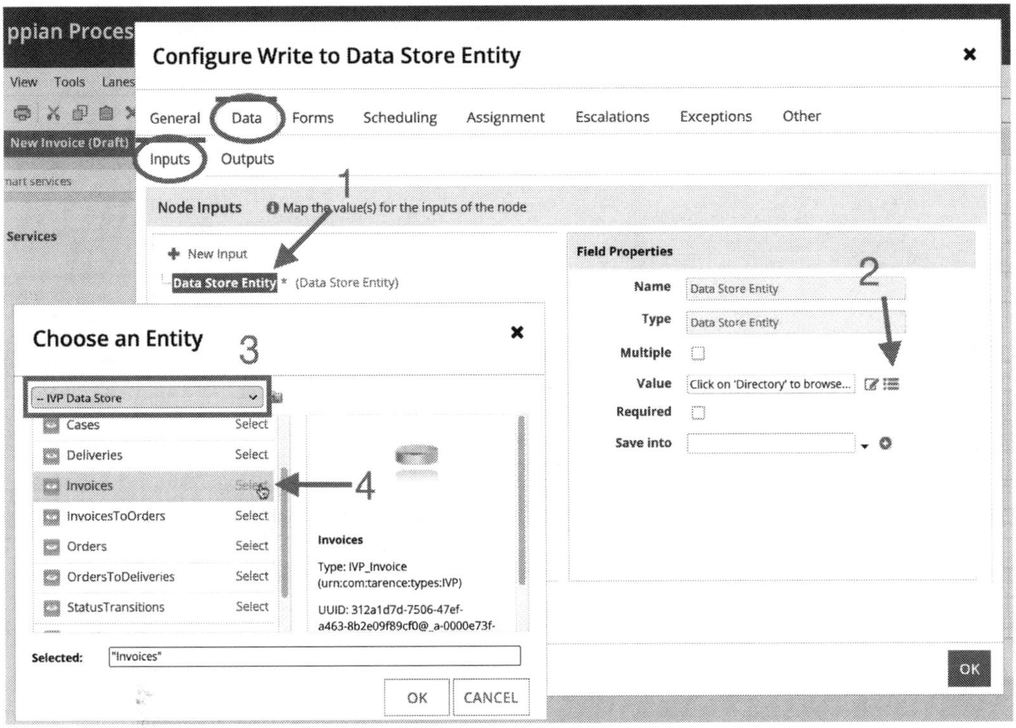

Figure 10.15 – Configure Data Store Entity

1. Click **Data Store Entity**.

2. Click the **Directory** icon.

3. Navigate to your **IVP Data Store** data store.

4. Look up **Invoices** and click the **Select** link:

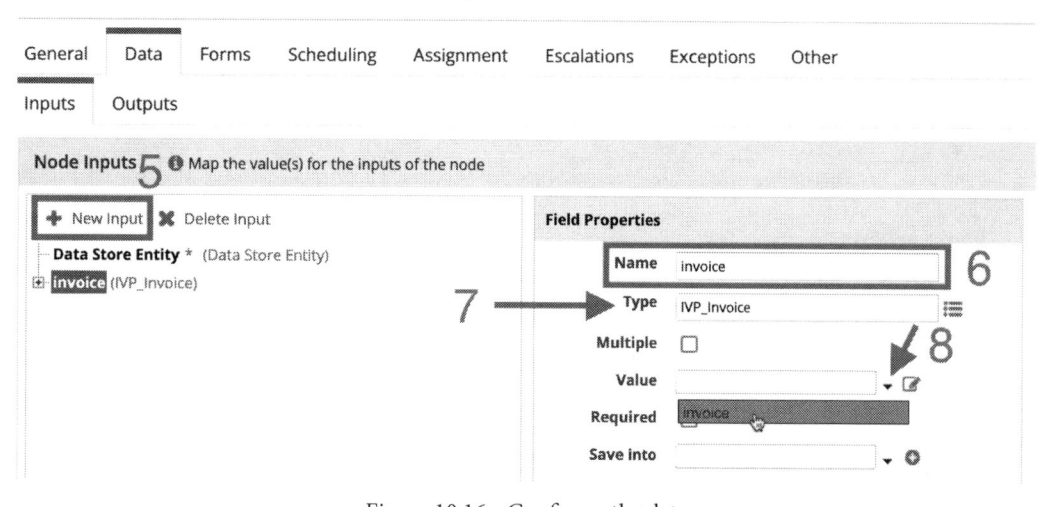

Figure 10.16 - Configure the data

5. Click **New Input**.

6. Type `invoice` in the **Name** field.

7. Type `IVP` to look up your CDTs and select **IVP_Invoice**.

8. Click the small arrow icon to select the process variable as input:

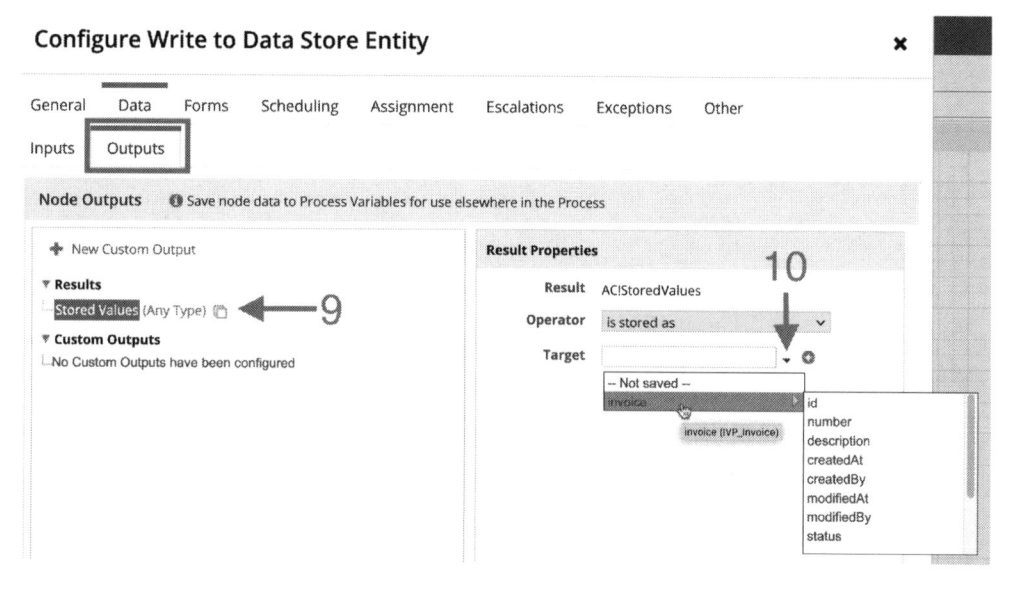

Figure 10.17 – Configure the node output

9. On the **Outputs** tab, click **Stored Values**.

10. Click the small arrow and select the **invoice** process variable as the target.

Click **OK** to complete the configuration. Then, click **Start Process for Debugging** in the **File** menu to test the process once more:

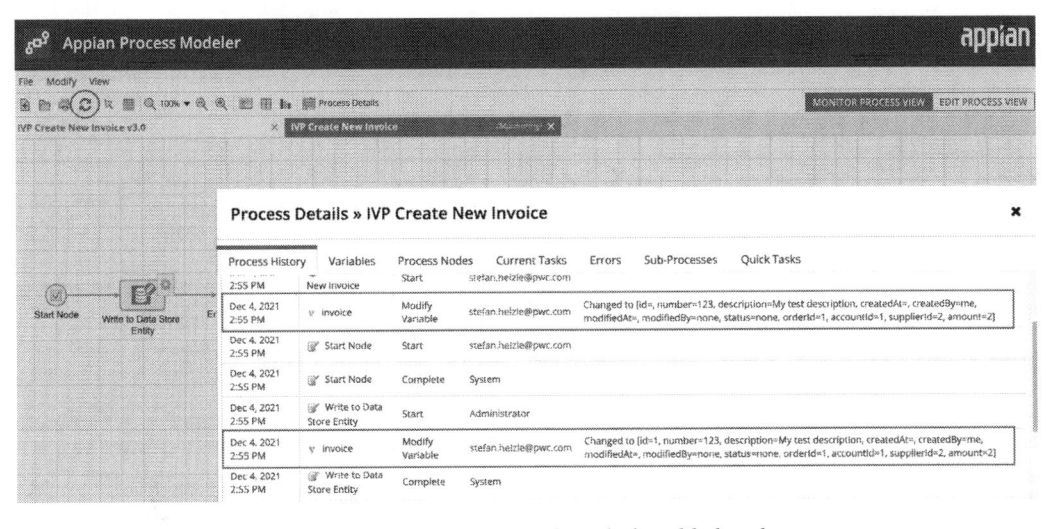

Figure 10.18 – Process Details with the added node

In the process monitoring, make sure that the **Write to Data Store Entity** node is completed. Click the **Refresh** icon in the menu bar in case the node is not highlighted in blue. In **Process Details**, you see how the process flow got the data from the start form, and the **invoice** variable is modified a second time by the **Write to Data Store Entity** node.

Let's now check whether Appian wrote any data to a database. Open the Cloud database from the *waffle* menu in Appian Designer:

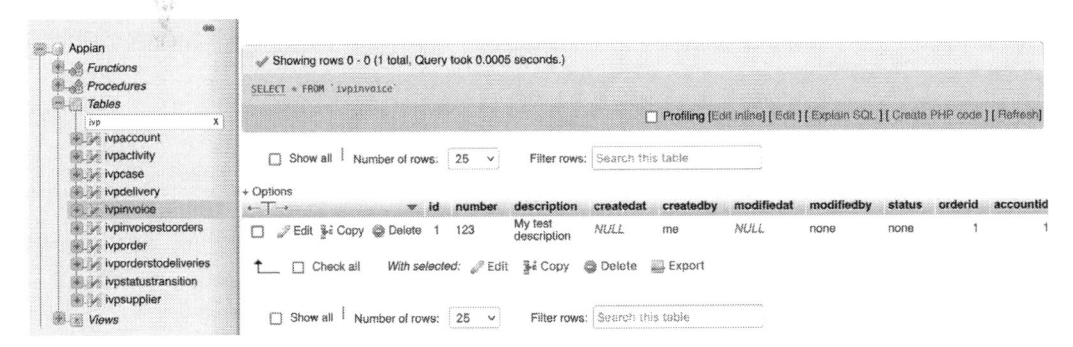

Figure 10.19 – Persisted data in a database

You should see the data as entered in the interface. In *Chapter 9*, *Modeling Business Data with Appian Records*, you created an Appian record on top of this database table. Check that you see the data there as well.

Open the **IVP Invoice** record in Appian Designer:

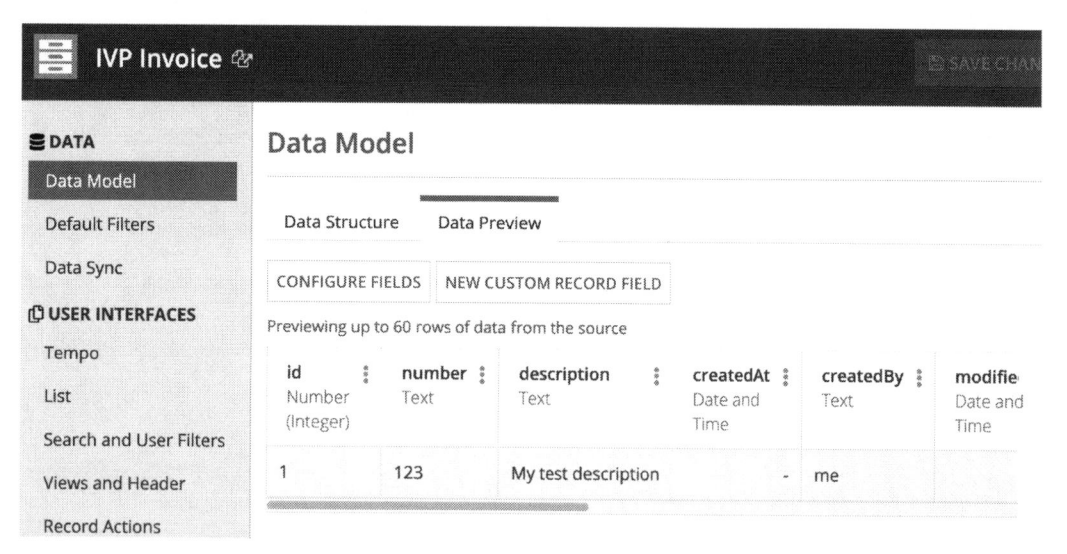

Figure 10.20 – Persisted data in the record

In the **Data Preview** tab, you should see the same data.

You now have two related objects – the **IVP Invoice** record from the last chapter, and the process model that creates new record items. It's time to put these pieces together.

Adding the process to the record

An Appian record as the center of Appian applications makes data accessible to the user but also allows interaction. I will show you how to add the just-created process model to the record.

Assigning the process

1. Start by opening the **IVP Invoice** record from Appian Designer:

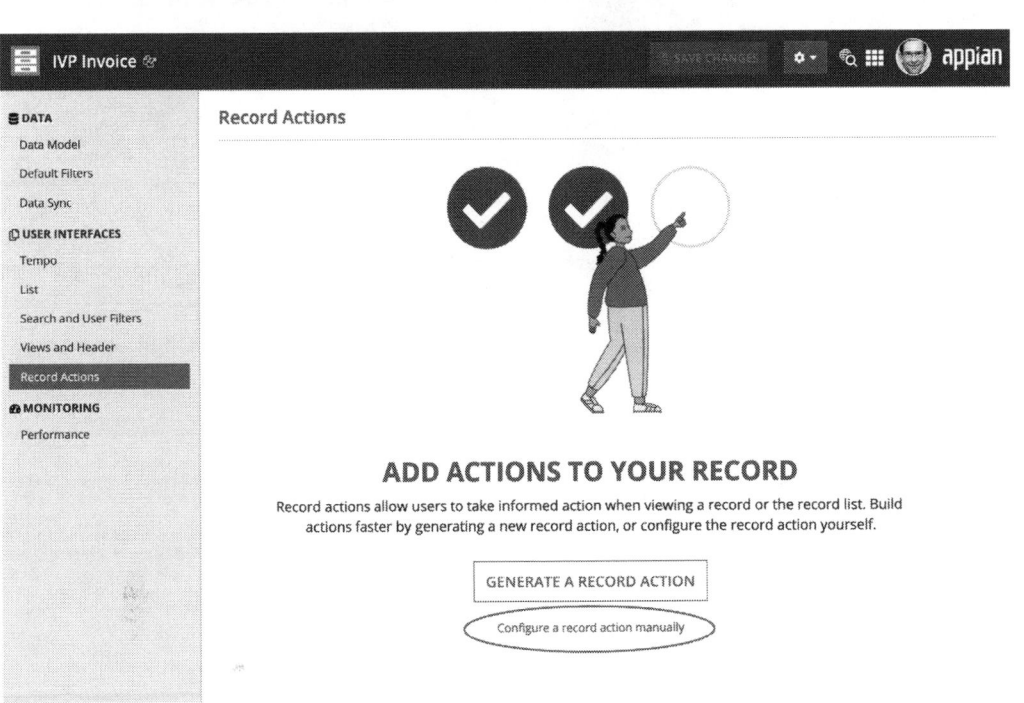

Figure 10.21 – The Record Actions tab in the Invoice record

2.   Click **Configure a record action manually** to switch to manual mode:

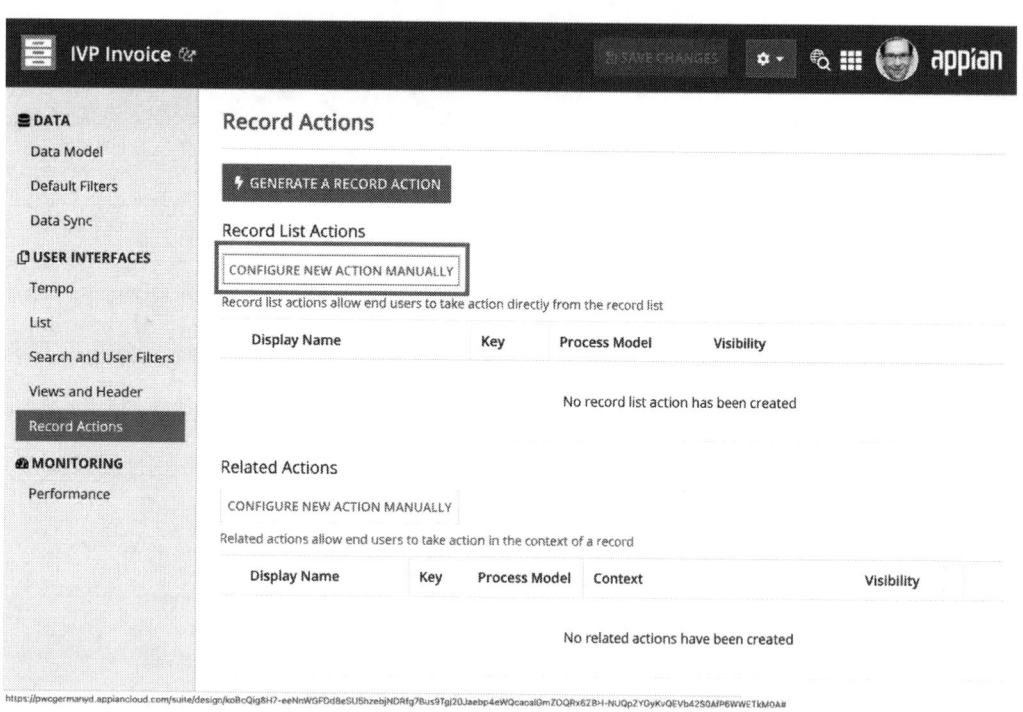

Figure 10.22 – Record Actions in manual mode

3. Now, click **CONFIGURE NEW ACTION MANUALLY** to get started:

Create New Action

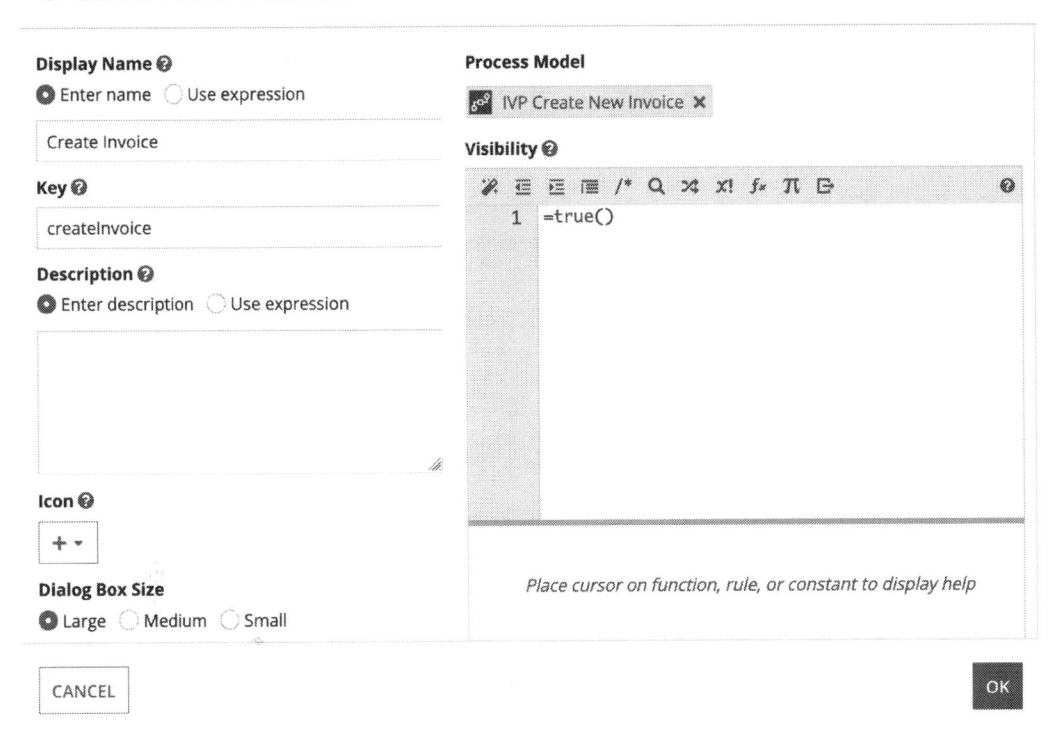

Figure 10.23 – The Create New Action dialog

4. Enter a name for the new action and select the **IVP Create New Invoice** process model. Click **OK** to complete the configuration. Then, click **SAVE CHANGES**. To check how that looks for the end user, navigate to the **List** tab:

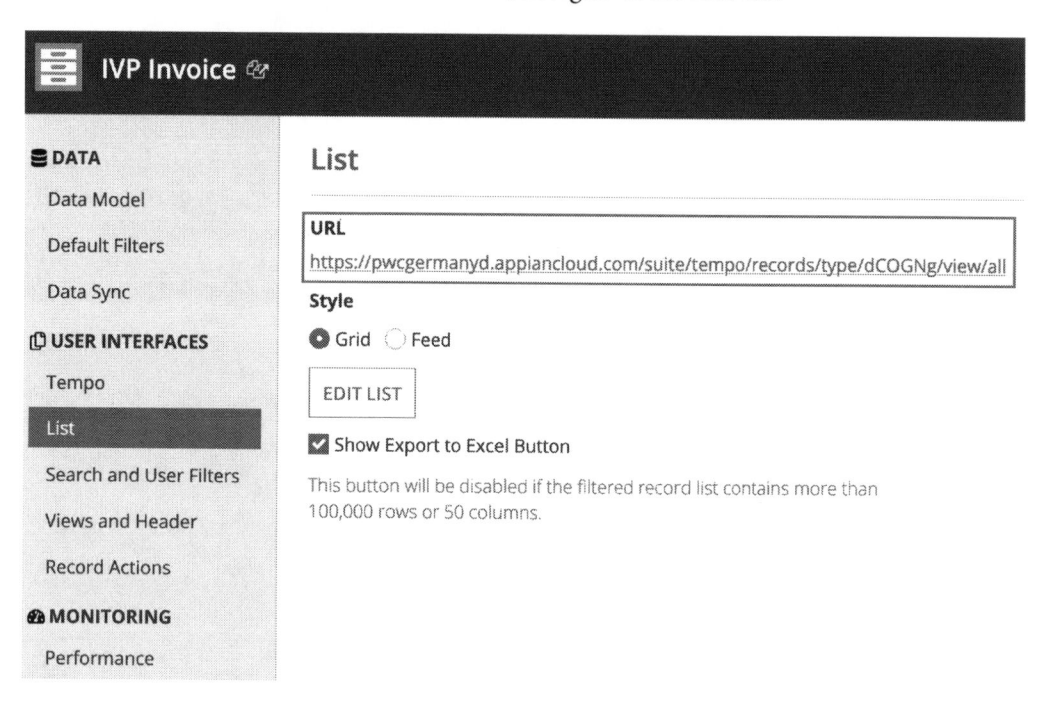

Figure 10.24 – The invoice record List tab showing the record URL

5. Click the highlighted link. Appian will open a new tab and load the record list:

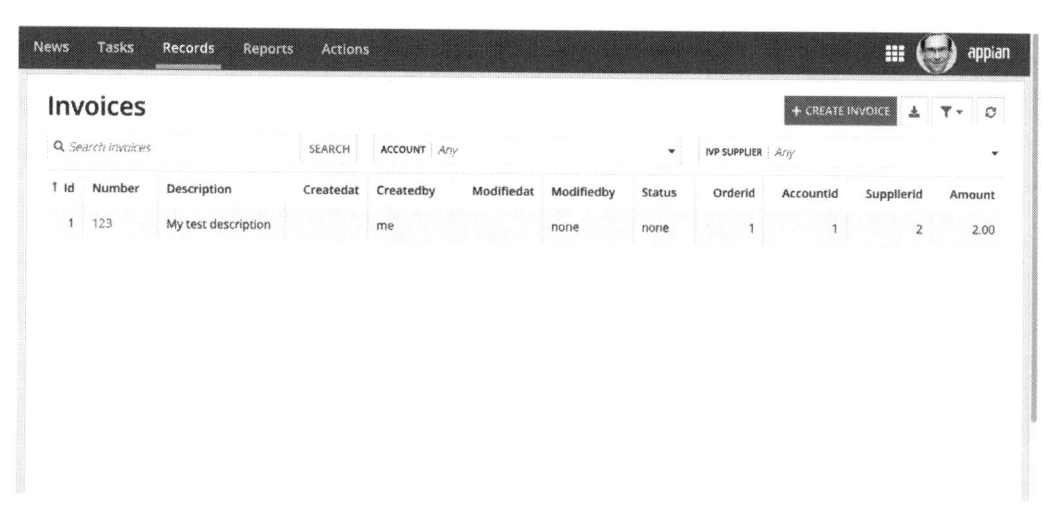

Figure 10.25 - The Invoices record List

6. Click the **CREATE INVOICE** record action button at the top right of the screen. This shows the interface you created in a dialog window:

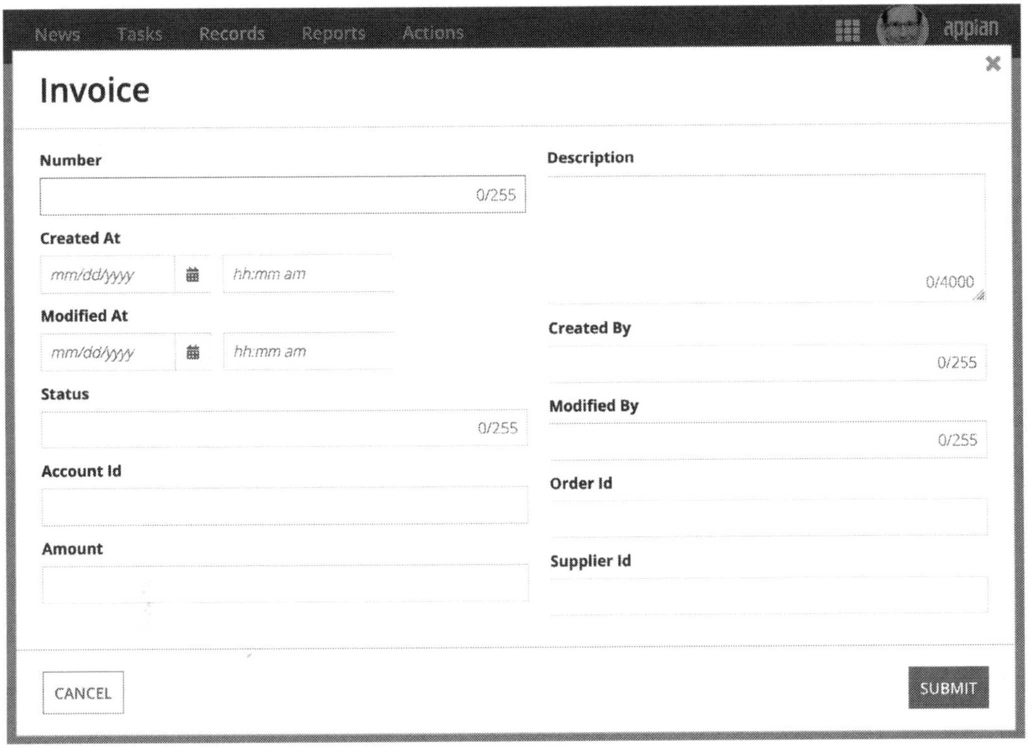

Figure 10.26 – The end user creates a new invoice

Enter some data, and you will see that the list displays the new item after you submit it. Did you also try to click the **CANCEL** button? Before you continue reading, give it a try and find out what happens and why.

Cancel behavior

A **CANCEL** button on Appian interfaces is just a button with no hard-wired behavior. When you just click the **CANCEL** button without entering any data, your process should look like this:

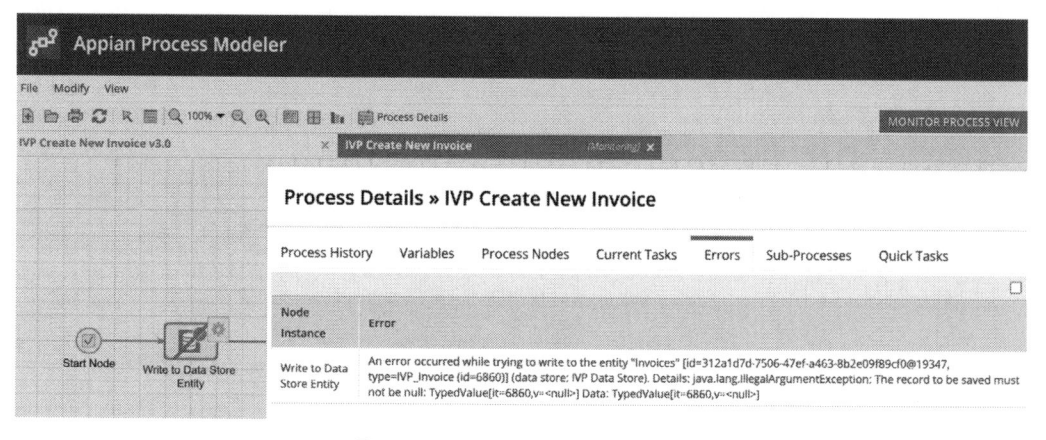

Figure 10.27 – An error in Process

This error message means that Appian cannot write an empty CDT to the database. To prevent that, we can use the **CANCEL** button to add some logic to our process model to interpret the intention of the user. Let's have a look at the details of the **CANCEL** button first:

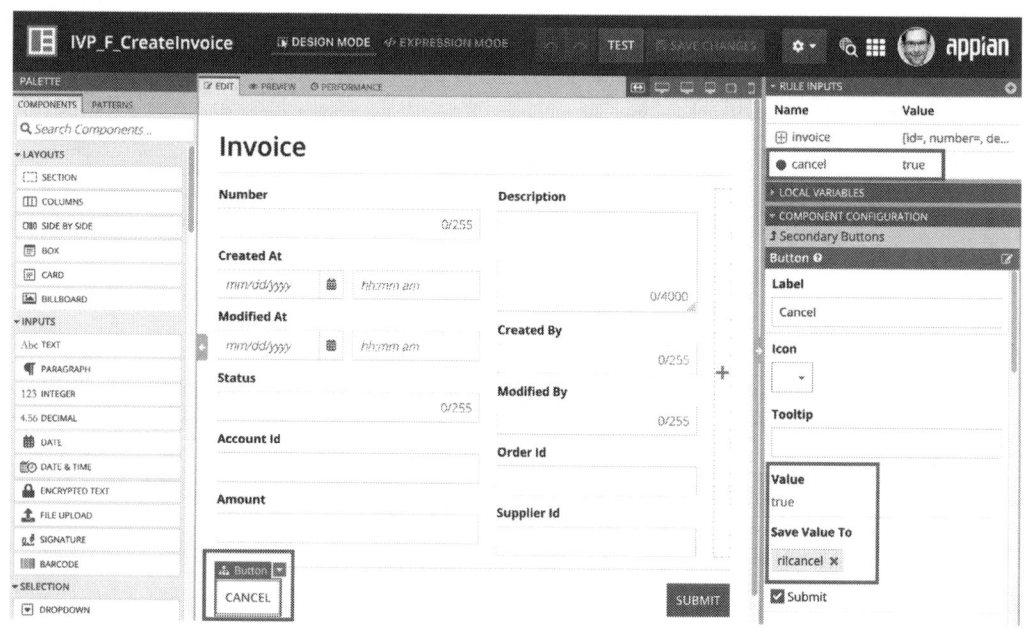

Figure 10.28 – CANCEL button logic

The button has the `true` Boolean value, which it writes to the **cancel** rule input when clicked. This means that your process model already *knows* whether the user clicked the **CANCEL** button. Let's add a bit of logic to make the model react properly.

Open the process model and add an **XOR** node between **Start Node** and the **Write to Data Store Entity** node. Then, rename it `Cancel?` by clicking the node name:

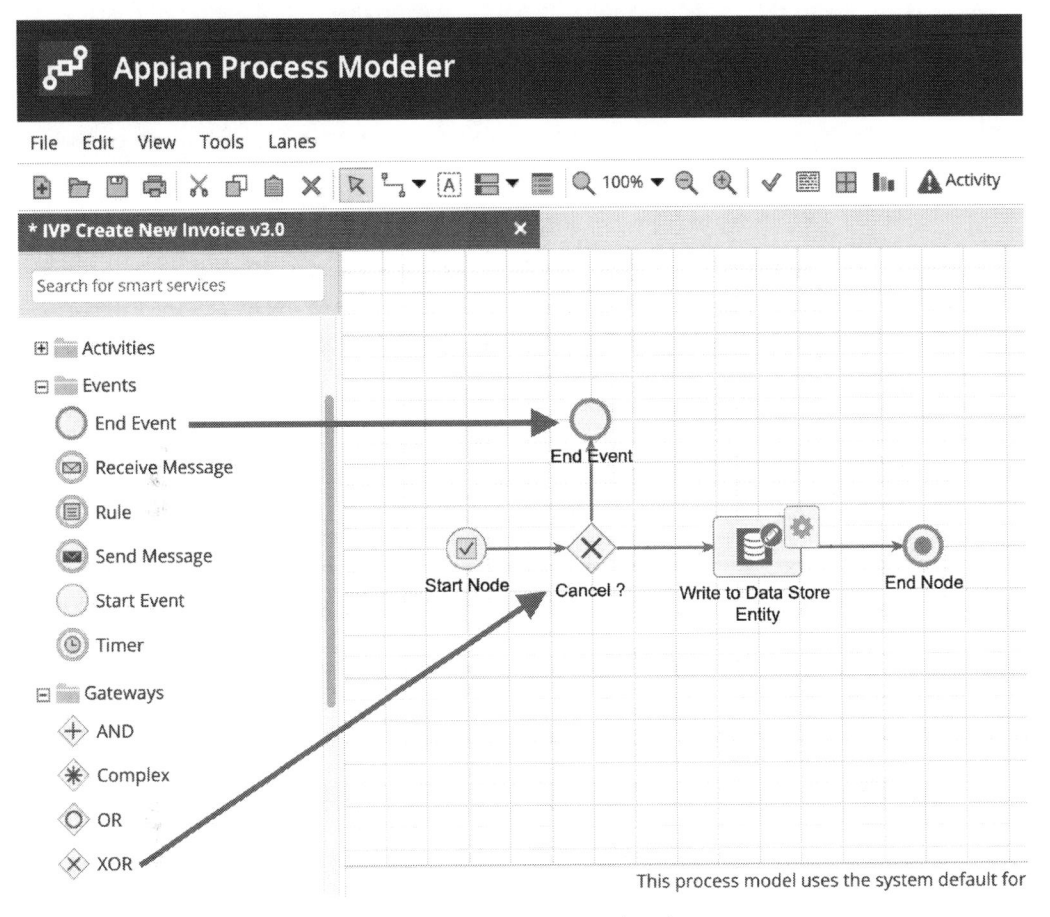

Figure 10.29 – Adding XOR and End Event

Then, add a second **End Event** node above the **XOR** node and add a connector from the **XOR** node to the **End Event** node. Next, double-click the **XOR** node. In the configuration dialog, navigate to the **Decision** tab and click **NEW CONDITION**:

Conditions				
Condition		**Result**	**Path Label**	**Order**
✖ If `=pv!cancel` 📝 is True		go to [End Event ⌄]	[　　　]	
Else if no rules are TRUE		go to [Write to Data Store Entit... ⌄]		
[NEW CONDITION]				

Figure 10.30 – Configure a condition in the XOR node

Enter `=pv!cancel` as the condition. If the condition evaluates to **True**, the process flow will go to the **End Event** node; otherwise, it will go to the **Write to Data Store Entity** node. Click **OK**, and then save and publish the model. Go to the **Invoices** record, click **CREATE INVOICE**, and then **CANCEL**. Back in the process modeler, click **Process Instances** and load the latest instance:

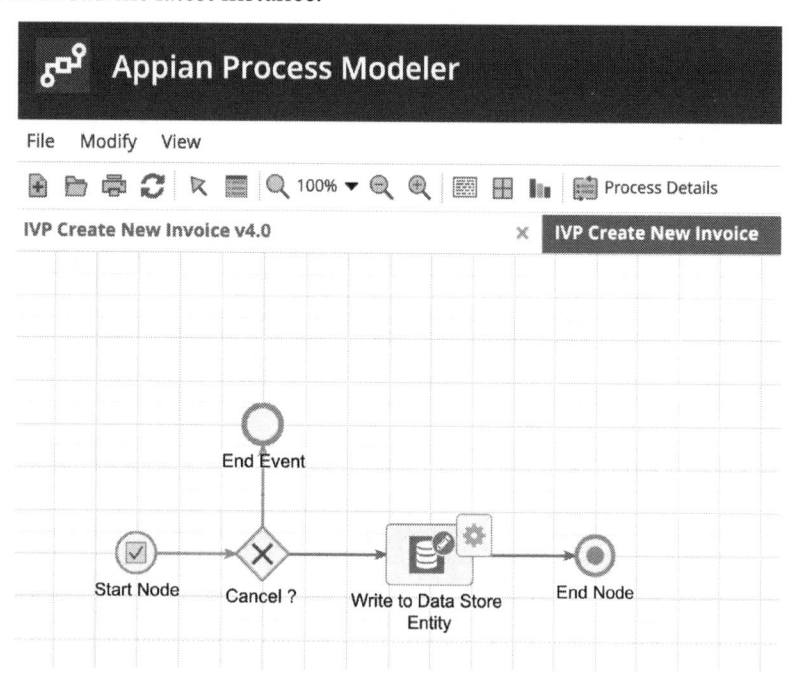

Figure 10.31 – The Cancel flow in the process model

You added logic to the process, which allows the user to control the flow. This works for simple cancel logic and in the same way for any other user-initiated logic.

> **Tip**
>
> When you add any kind of cancel logic to your process, keep in mind that Appian is about business processes. Implementing cancel logic like the preceding in a business process would just stop the technical process, but what about the functional process? From a business perspective, any process must have a specific outcome and cannot be just canceled. Remember the **SIPOC** table – if your specific business process can be canceled at certain steps, add a proper cleanup flow.

When you click a record item, you will see an error message because you did not assign a UI. Create a very basic record view interface by clicking **GENERATE INTERFACE** in the **Views and Header** tab of the records designer:

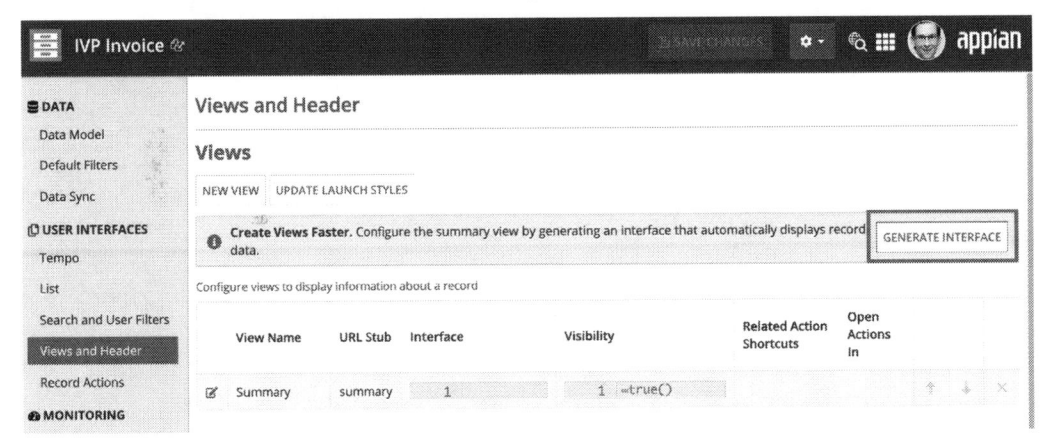

Figure 10.32 – Creating the summary view

Name the new interface IVP_D_InvoiceSummary. Leave that interface as it is for now. The error message should be gone, and you should see the data of the invoice when clicking an item in the records list.

For some of the other records, you will create more of these small data management process models in the next section.

Adding related actions and record actions

Our application requires some master data such as `supplier` and `account`, but also some transactional data such as `order` and `delivery`. In a real IT infrastructure, this data would be managed by other systems and Appian would integrate them. Since these other systems are missing in our case, we have to manage this data ourselves.

This kind of data management requires separate operations to create, read, update, and delete data. In Appian, this translates to a record to make the data accessible and three record actions to create, update, and delete it.

> **Tip**
> The focus of Appian is the implementation of business processes. As a result of this design decision, there is no strong support for data locking mechanisms to prevent users from overwriting data by starting related actions in parallel. My opinion on this is that strict data locking should not be an important design goal for Appian applications. In a process design that is oriented towards a business process, there are usually no situations in which the same records are manipulated in parallel.

You already know how to build a process to create a new record item. I will now show you how to create the two models to update and delete records.

Updating a record

To update an existing record, we need a process model that accepts the data, shows a UI, and writes the data back to the database on submission. This is similar to the process model that creates a new record item. But most of the time, you might want to use a different UI for modifying the data – for example, you want to prevent the user from modifying the **supplier number**. Simple requirements can be implemented by some logic in a single interface. In my experience, it is better to maintain two interfaces in the long run.

Most object types in Appian have an option to duplicate an existing one in the **NEW** dialog. Use that to duplicate the **IVP Create Invoice** process model and the **IVPFCreateInvoice** interface. Use the word `Update` instead of `Create` in the names. Then, modify the process model to use the new interface as a process start form. Open the **Invoice** record in the Records designer and navigate to the **Record Actions** tab:

IVP Invoice
DATA
Data Model
Default Filters
Data Sync
USER INTERFACES
Tempo
List
Search and User Filters
Views and Header
Record Actions
MONITORING
Performance
Record Actions
GENERATE A RECORD ACTION
Record List Actions
CONFIGURE NEW ACTION MANUALLY
Record list actions allow end users to take action directly from the record list
Display Name
Key
Process Model
Visibility
Create Invoice
createInvoice
IVP Create New Invoice
1 =true()
Open Actions In
DIALOG BOX
NEW TAB
SAME TAB
Dialog box size is configured on each record list action
Related Actions
CONFIGURE NEW ACTION MANUALLY
Related actions allow end users to take action in the context of a record
Display Name
Key
Process Model
Context
No related actions have been created

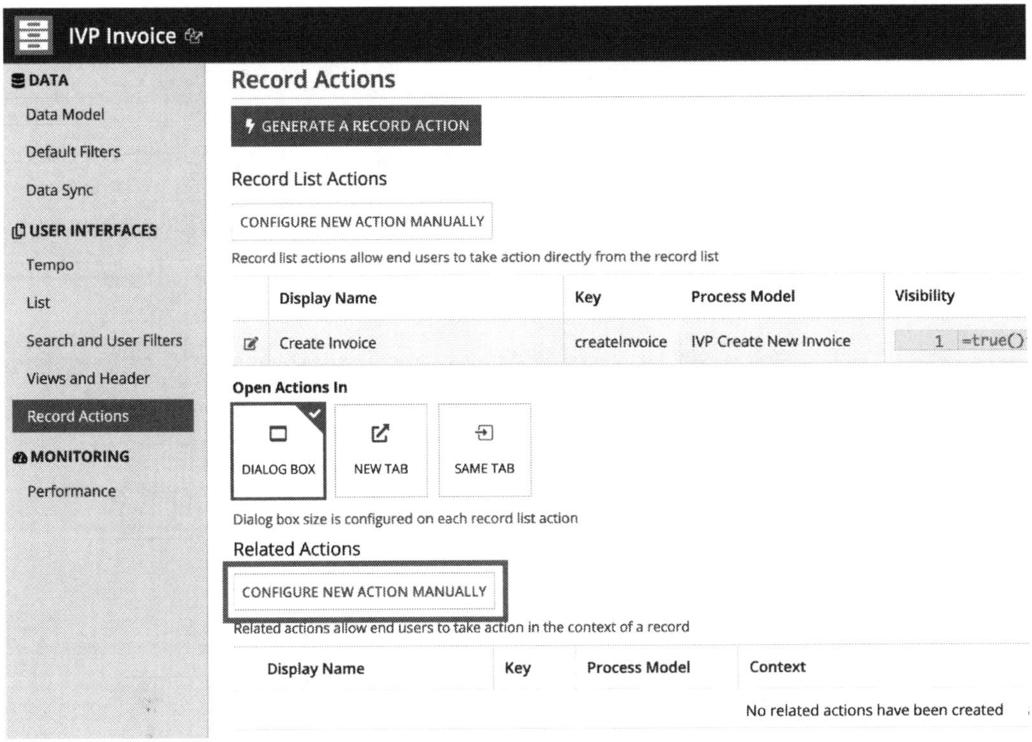

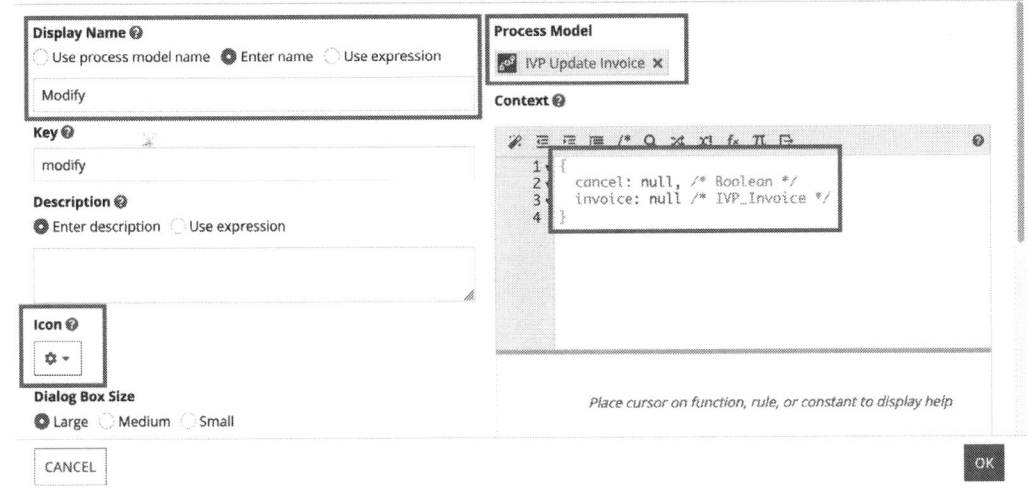

Figure 10.33 – Adding a related action

1. Click **CONFIGURE NEW ACTION MANUALLY** to get started:

Create New Related Action
Display Name
Use process model name
Enter name
Use expression
Modify
Key
modify
Description
Enter description
Use expression
Icon
Dialog Box Size
Large
Medium
Small
CANCEL
Process Model
IVP Update Invoice
Context
1 {
2 cancel: null, /* Boolean */
3 invoice: null /* IVP_Invoice */
4 }
Place cursor on function, rule, or constant to display help
OK

Figure 10.34 – The Create New Related Action dialog

2. Enter a name and choose an icon, and then select the new **IVP Update Invoice** process model.

   The **Context** field is specific to related actions and does not exist for record actions, as these are meant to create new data. Related actions are meant to work with existing data, which we need to pass to the process using the **Context** field. The context is a simple data structure that you use to assign values to process variables. In our case, we have **cancel** and **invoice**.

3. Keep the `null` value for **cancel**, as we leave it up to the user whether they cancel or not. The value assigned to **invoice** has to be the current value from the database.

Follow these three steps to create an **expression rule** to query the data for a specific invoice from the database:

1. Create a constant named **IVP_ENTITY_INVOICES** of the **Data Store Entity** type, pointing to **IVP Data Store** and the **Invoices** entity:

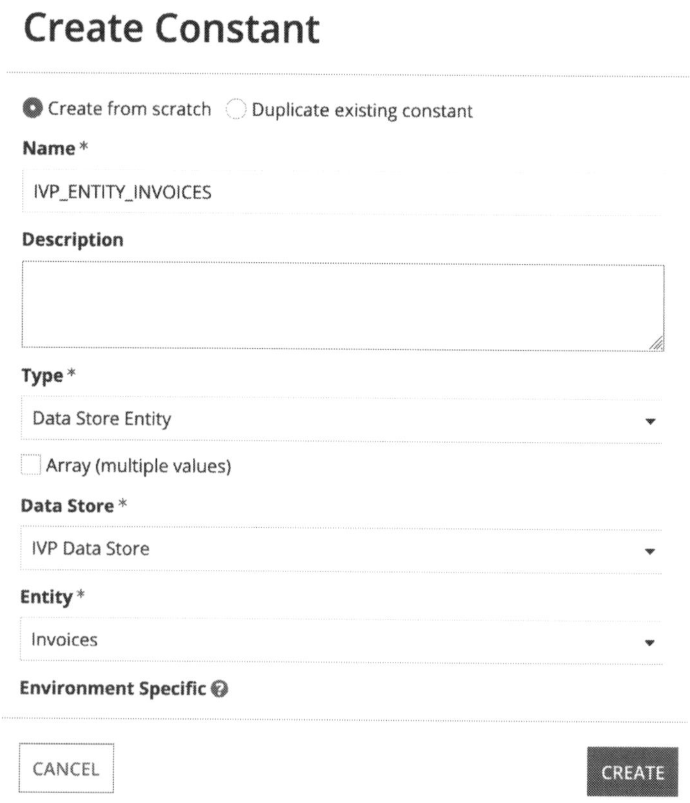

Create Constant

◉ Create from scratch   ○ Duplicate existing constant

Name *

IVP_ENTITY_INVOICES

Description

Type *

Data Store Entity ▼

☐ Array (multiple values)

Data Store *

IVP Data Store ▼

Entity *

Invoices ▼

Environment Specific ❓

CANCEL   CREATE

Figure 10.35 – Create the IVP_ENTITY_INVOICES constant

2. Create a new **Expression Rule** object in Appian Designer and name it `IVPQGetInvoiceById`. Add a rule input of the `Integer` type named `id` and enter the following code:

```
cast(
  'type!{urn:com:tarence:types:IVP}IVP_Invoice',
  if(
    isnull(ri!id),
    null,
    index(
      a!queryEntity(
        entity: cons!IVP_ENTITY_INVOICES,
        query: a!query(
          filter: a!queryFilter(
            field: "id",
            operator: "=",
            value: ri!id
          ),
          pagingInfo: a!pagingInfo(1, 1),
        )
      ).data,
      1,
      null
    )
  )
)
```

3. Type 1 as a test value and click **TEST RULE** to execute the code. You should see the data for the first invoice:

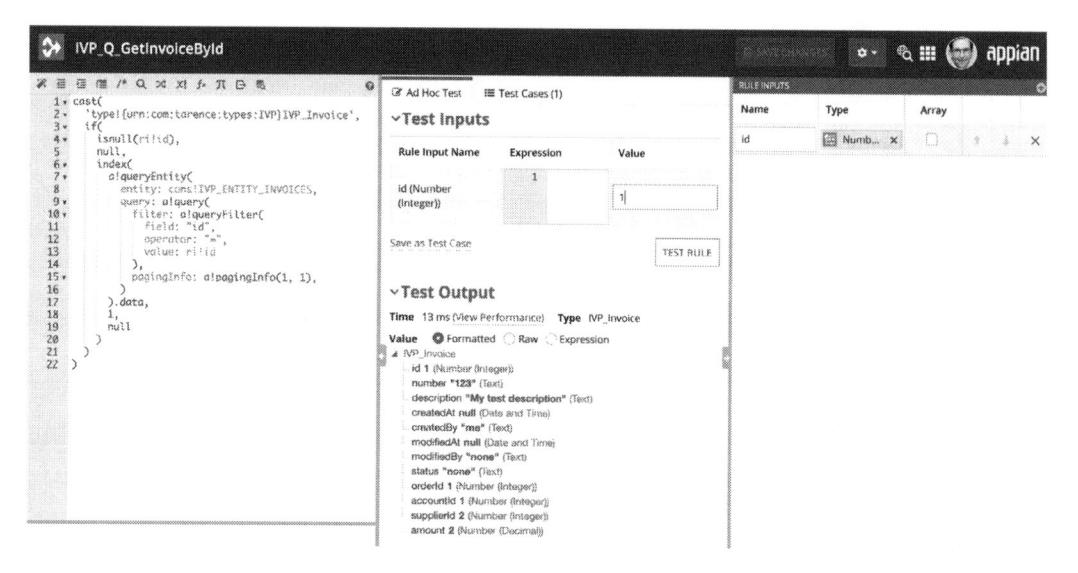

Figure 10.36 – The new expression rule showing the test values

Now, modify the context in the Records Designer to call the new expression rule, and for the **id** rule input, pass the identifier of the invoice that the user clicked on:

```
{
    cancel: null, /* Boolean */
    invoice: rule!IVP_Q_GetInvoiceById(
        id: rv!identifier
    )
}
```

Save your modifications in the record, then select an invoice from the records list, navigate to the **Related Actions** tab, and click **Modify** to edit the invoice. Clicking **SUBMIT** should save your modifications.

Let's now have a look at how to delete data from a database.

Deleting a record

Deleting data is always a difficult topic. In a typical application, data relates to each other. Deleting an item would break this relationship. And from an auditor's perspective, you would never delete any data. But let's look at how to delete data from a database anyway:

1. Create a new process model and modify the alert **Settings and data management**, as before.

2. Add a single process variable of the **Integer** type, give it the name `invoiceId`, and make it a parameter.

3. Add a **Delete from Data Store Entities** node:

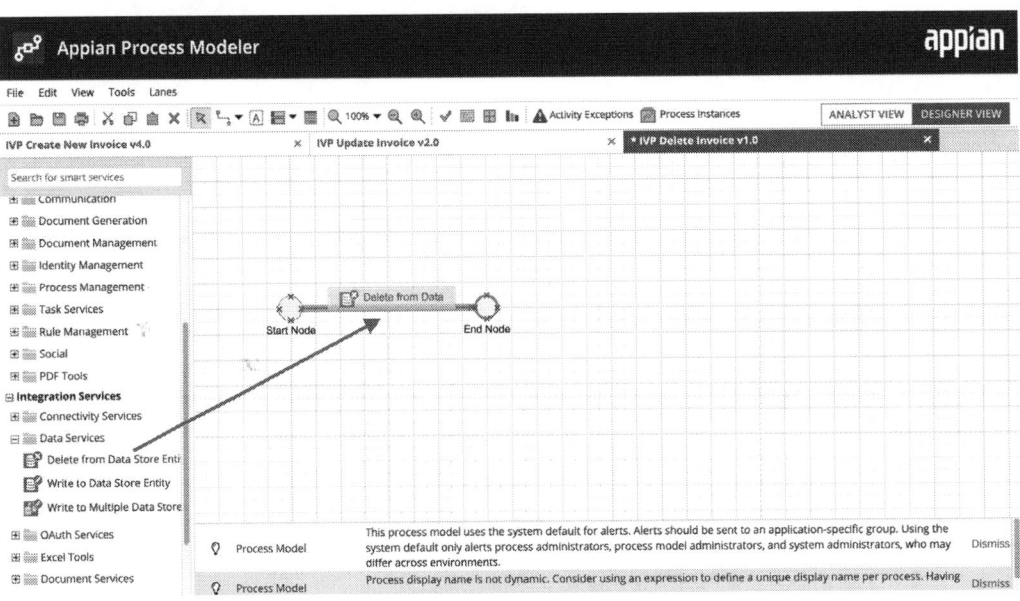

Figure 10.37 – Add the Delete from Data Store Entities node

4. Double-click the node, navigate to the **Data** tab, and open the editor for the **Data to Delete** input:

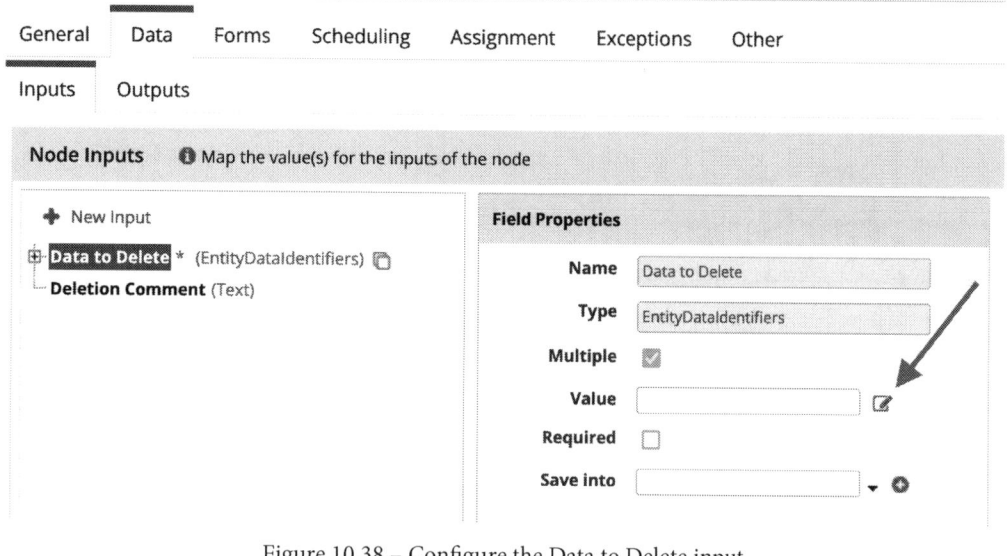

Figure 10.38 – Configure the Data to Delete input

5. Enter the following code:

```
a!entityDataIdentifiers(
    entity: cons!IVP_ENTITY_INVOICES,
    identifiers: pv!invoiceId
)
```

This creates the data structure holding the required configuration for the node.

6. When assigning the process model to the **Invoices** record, use the following code as context to pass the ID of the selected record item to the process:

```
{
    invoiceId: rv!identifier /* Number (Integer) */
}
```

Save all your changes in the process model and the record and test it. The record might now display an error message because Appian still tries to display the now-deleted invoice.

You now have the tools to add the missing data management actions to the following records:

*   Supplier
*   Account
*   Order
*   Delivery

The application now has all the required data management capabilities, so we will continue with the actual business process.

Completing the process

The **IVP Create New Invoice** process can't really do much so far. One reason is that the invoice has relationships to a supplier, an account, a case, and orders. Plus, we had no data management capabilities.

This situation has improved, so let's add more data to the invoice.

Modifying the Create Invoice interface

I will walk you through replacing the simple **Integer** fields that refer to another data entity with **RECORD PICKER** fields, which allow the user to search and select existing records of a specific type:

1. Open the **IVP_F_CreateInvoice** interface:

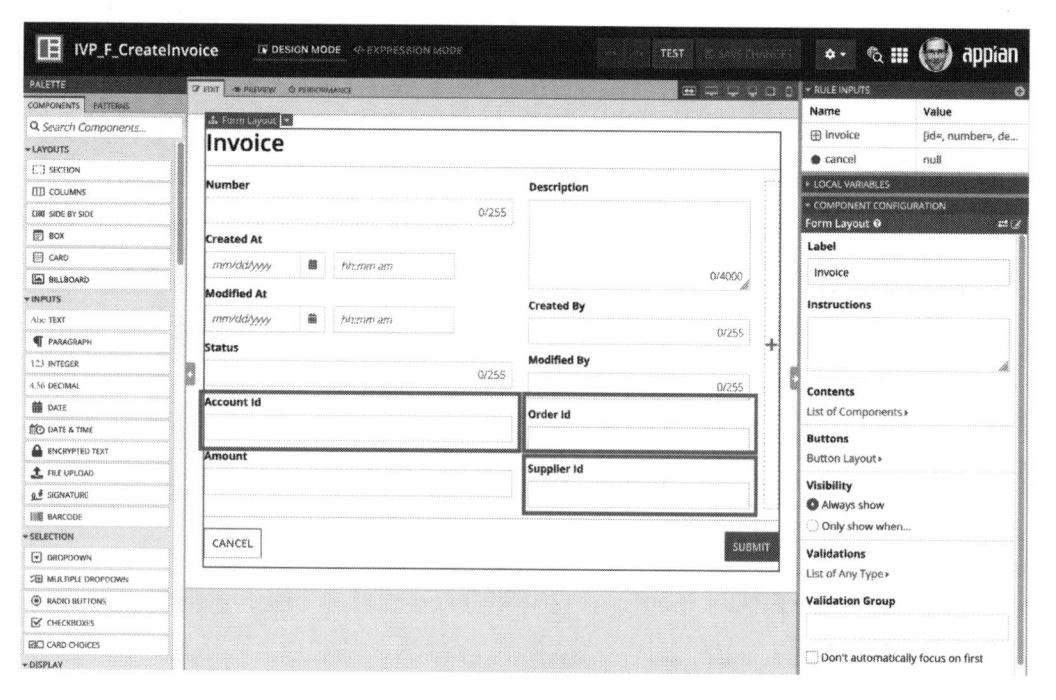

Figure 10.39 – The simple number fields to replace

2. Search in the **COMPONENTS** palette and add a **RECORD PICKER** field just below the **Account Id** field:

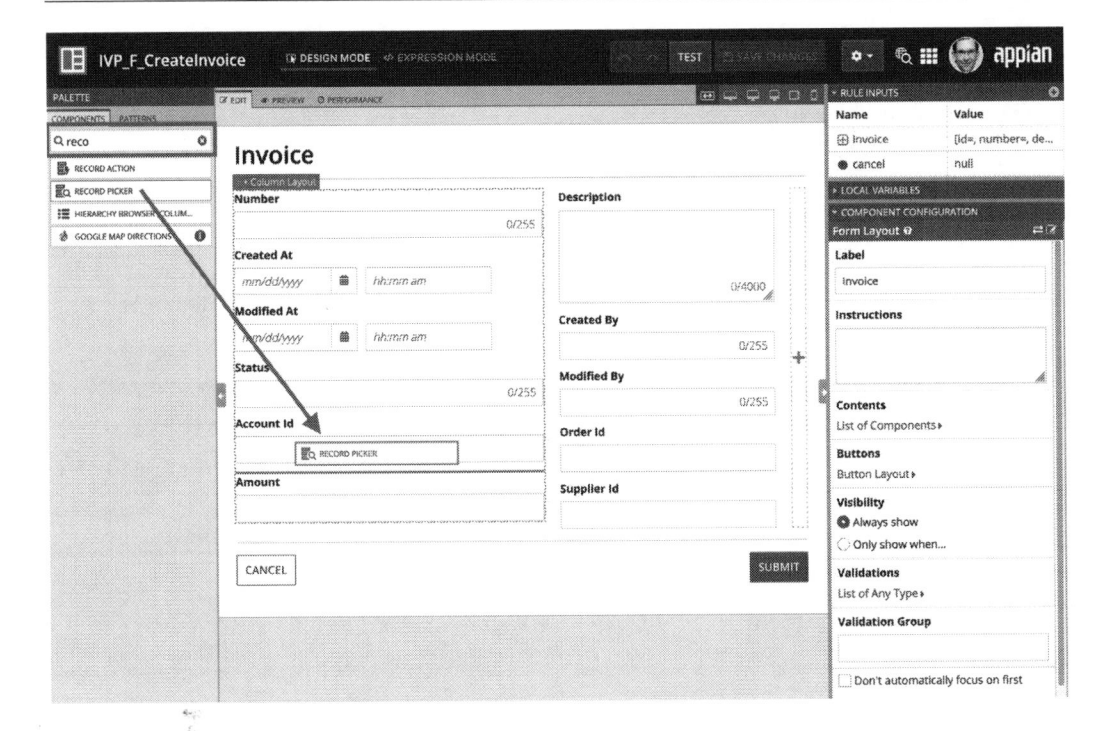

Figure 10.40 – Adding a RECORD PICKER field

3. Name the field `Account` and complete the configuration as follows:

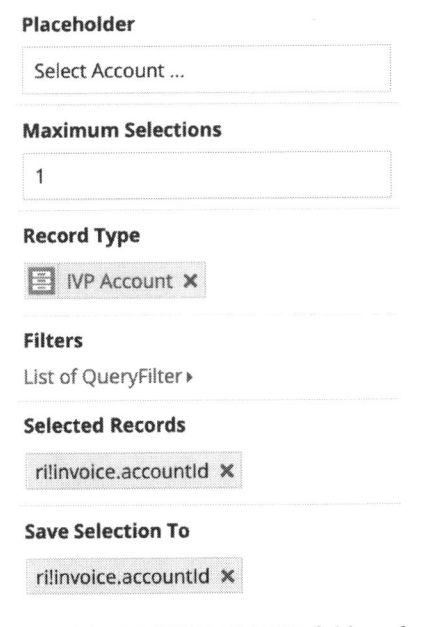

Placeholder

Select Account ...

Maximum Selections

1

Record Type

IVP Account ✕

Filters

List of QueryFilter ▸

Selected Records

ri!invoice.accountId ✕

Save Selection To

ri!invoice.accountId ✕

Figure 10.41 – The RECORD PICKER field configuration

4. Delete the **Account Id** field:

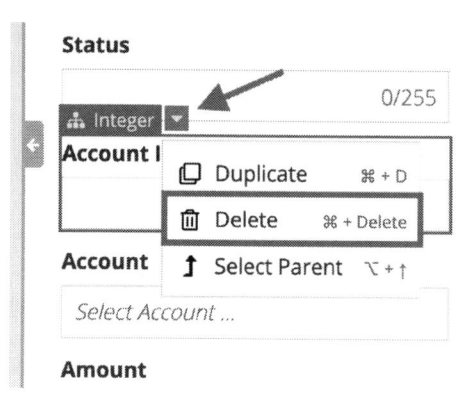

Figure 10.42 – Delete the Account Id field

Repeat these steps for the **Order Id** and **Supplier Id** fields. Make sure that they refer to their specific record type and fields.

Create some **Account Record** items, **Order Record** items, and **Supplier Record** items, and check that you can select them from the new fields. This completes the data required to start our actual business process.

Setting up the case

As already discussed, the case is your container for keeping track of any business activity. This means that as you create a new invoice for validation, you need to create a new case. Let's see how to do that.

Create a new process model named IVP Create Case. Make sure to check the alert settings and data management. Then, add three **Write to Data Store Entity** nodes and name them:

- [Case]
- [Activity]
- [StatusTransition]

Figure 10.43 – Adding three Write to Data Store Entity nodes

Create these constants in Appian Designer:

- `IVP_CASE_STATUS_INITIATED` (text) = INITIATED
- `IVP_CASE_PRIORITY_LOW` (integer) = 1
- `IVP_CASE_PRIORITY_MEDIUM` (integer) = 2
- `IVP_CASE_PRIORITY_HIGH` (integer) = 3
- `IVP_ACTIVITY_TYPE_USER` (text) = USER
- `IVP_ACTIVITY_TYPE_SYSTEM` (text) = SYSTEM

Configure the nodes as follows:

The case node

Here I have shown how to configure the case node with a small snippet of code:

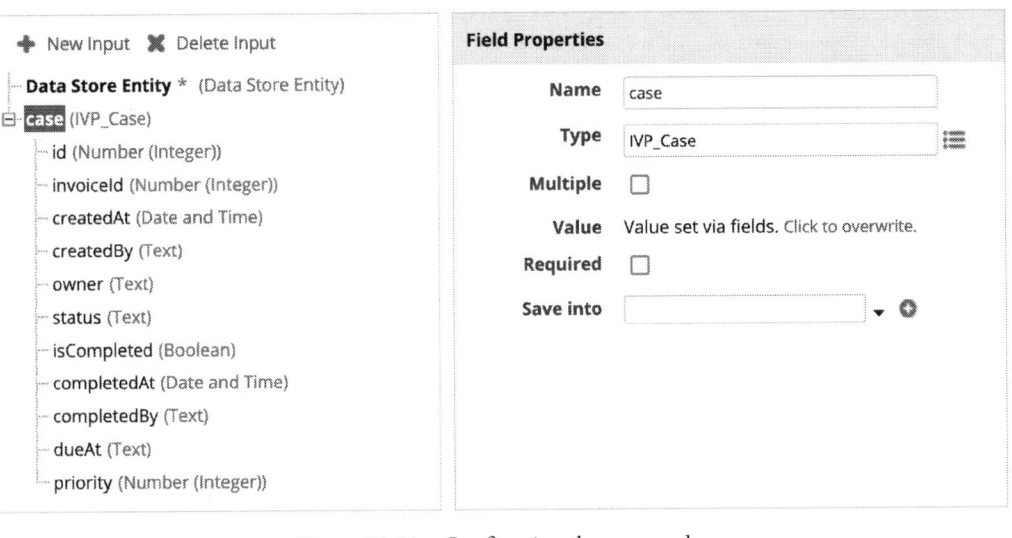

Figure 10.44 – Configuring the case node

The code to configure the **Case** node is as follows, which is quite self - explanatory:

```
id =
invoiceId = pv!invoice.id
createdAt = now()
createdBy = pp!initiator
owner = pp!initiator
status = cons!IVP_CASE_STATUS_INITIATED
```

```
isCompleted = false
completedAt =
completedBy =
dueAt = caladddays(today(), 3)
priority = cons!IVP_CASE_PRIORITY_LOW
```

Now, let's understand the **activity** node.

The activity node

Here I have shown how to configure the **Activity** node with a small snippet of code:

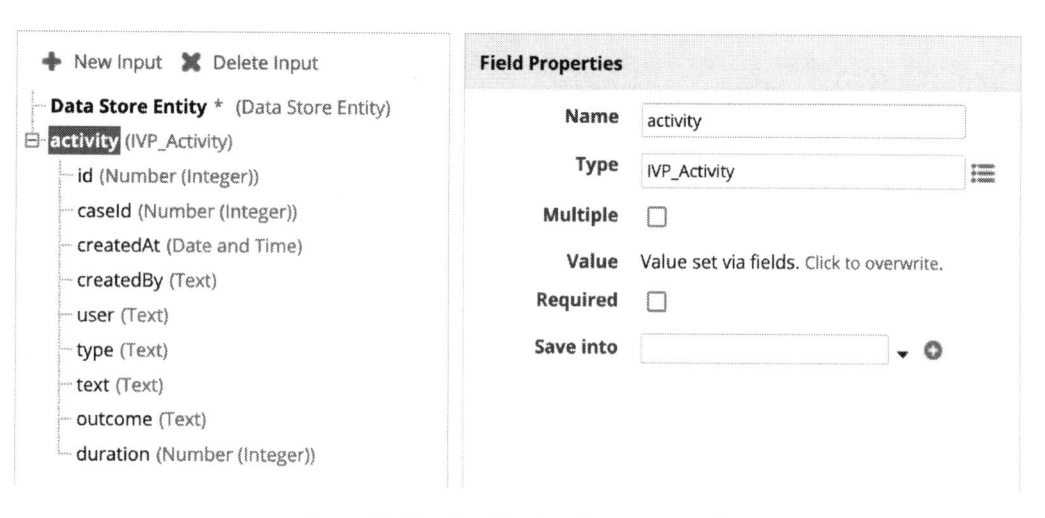

Figure 10.45 – Configuring the activity node

The code to configure the **Activity** node is as follows, which is quite self - explanatory:

```
id =
caseId = pv!case.id
createdAt = now()
createdBy = pp!initiator
user = pp!initiator
type = cons!IVP_ACTIVITY_TYPE_SYSTEM
text = "Created"
outcome =
duration = 0
```

Now, let's understand the **statusTransition** node.

The statusTransition node

Here I have shown how to configure the **statusTransition** node with a small snippet of code:

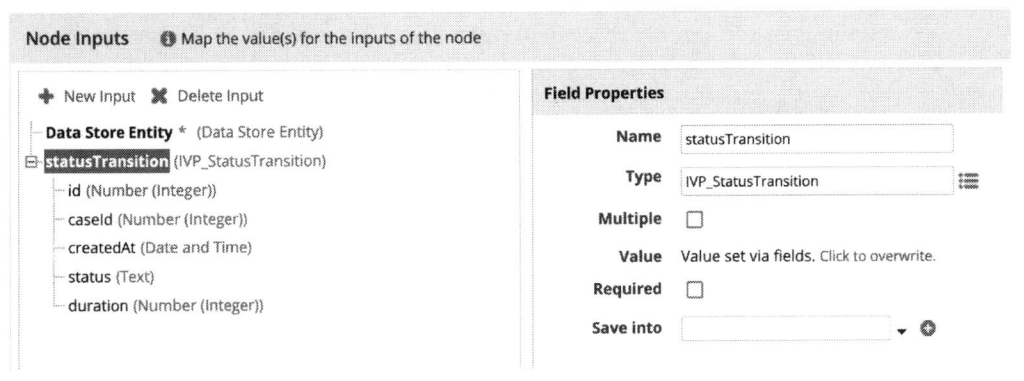

Figure 10.46 – Configuring the statusTransition node

The code to configure the **satusTransition** node is as follows, which is quite self -explanatory:

```
id =
caseId = pv!case.id
createdAt = now()
status =
duration = 0
```

After this we will configure the output to assign **Stored Values** to their respective process variable:

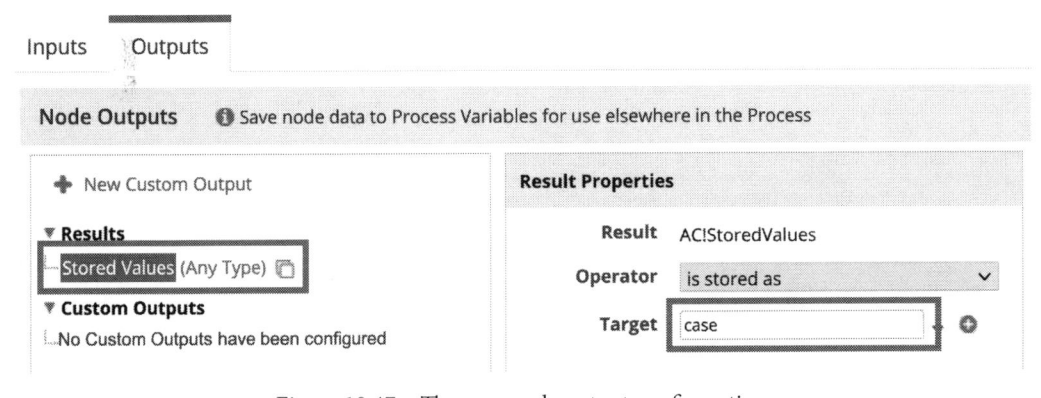

Figure 10.47 – The case node output configuration

Okay, that was quite a piece of work. Now, we must change perspective for a moment. The business process is about the validation of invoices, and the case is our logic container for it. So, we must make sure that for each new invoice, the application creates a new case. Let's see how to do that.

1. Save and publish the model, and then open the **IVP Create New Invoice** model:

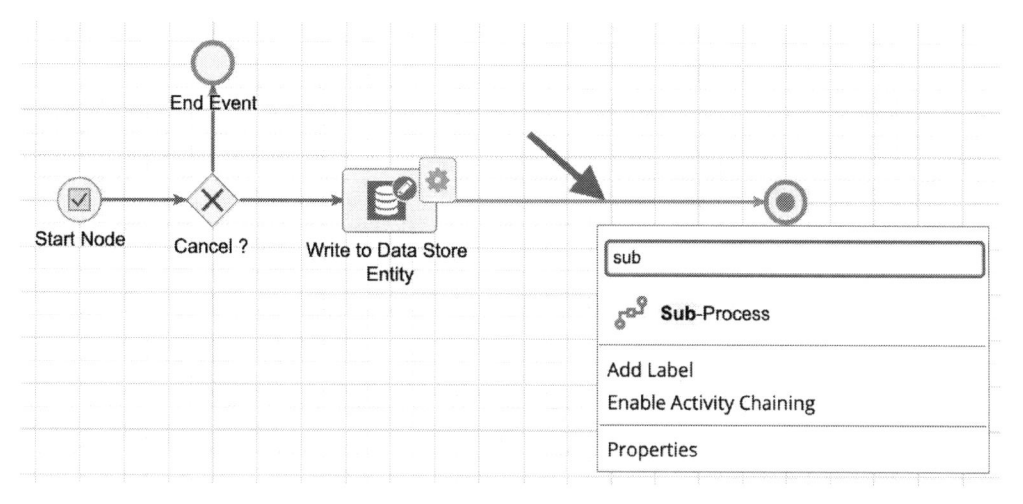

Figure 10.48 – Adding a Sub-Process node

2. Right clicking a connector and searching for a specific node is a quick way to add new nodes to a process model.

3. Add a **Sub-Process** node after the **Write to Data Store Entity** node and name it `Initiate Case`.

4. Double-click it to open the properties dialog:

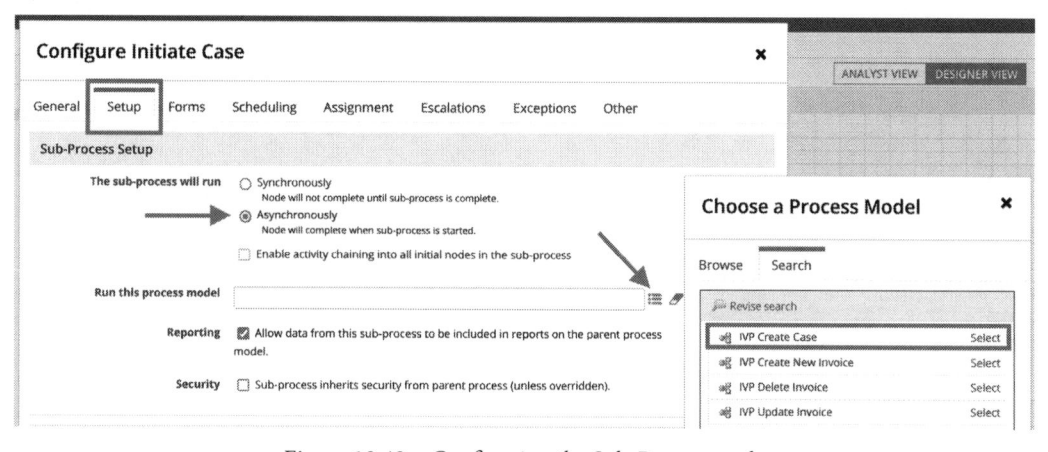

Figure 10.49 – Configuring the Sub-Process node

5. Make it run **Asynchronously** and search and select your **IVP Create Case** process model.

In the **Input Variables** dialog section, Appian shows all process variables configured as parameters. Assign the local **invoice** process variable to the **invoice** input variable to pass the invoice data.

Save and publish the process model and create a new invoice to test the modifications. In Appian Designer, switch to the **MONITORING** tab and then to the **PROCESS ACTIVITY** sub-tab. You will see all the recently started process instances.

6. Click **Process Name** to open it for monitoring:

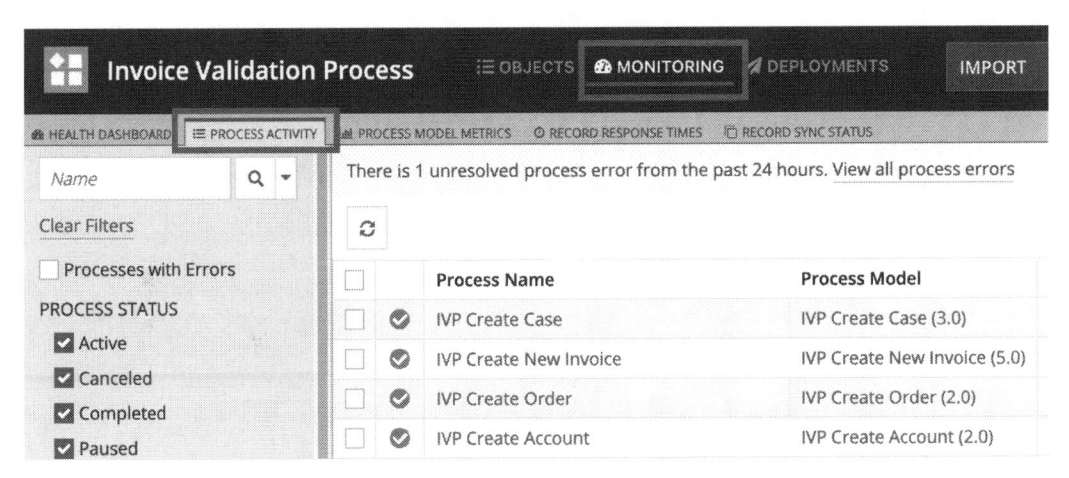

Figure 10.50 – Process monitoring

7. In the monitoring view, click the tiny + icon in the **Sub-Process** Node:

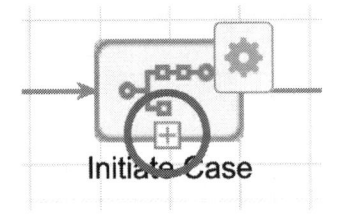

Figure 10.51 – Open the Sub-Process

8.   This will open the **Sub-Process** for monitoring:

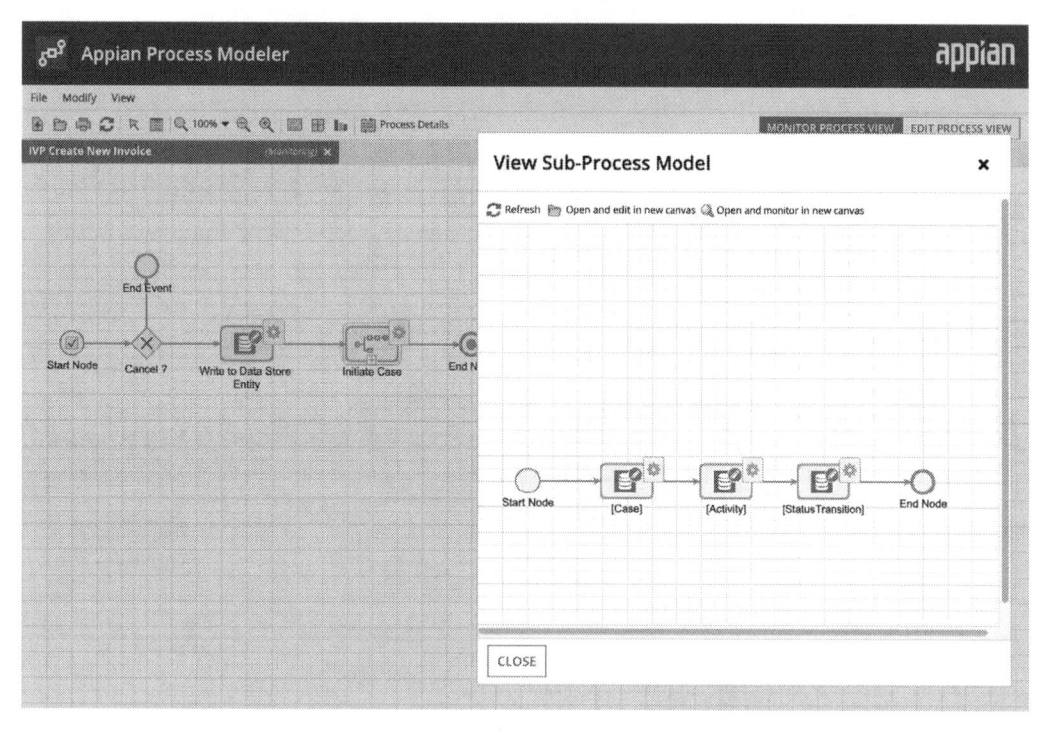

Figure 10.52 – IVP Create New Invoice and IVP Create Case completed

This looks promising. All nodes have been completed successfully. Do not hesitate to also check the Cloud database.

Now we have written data to a database captured from a few simple interfaces. Appian is about business processes and assigning tasks to people, so let's do that now.

Assigning the first task

As a case is created, we want to assign a task to a human to have an initial look. In the following chapters, you will add more processes and interfaces to the application, but let's start with the first one:

1.   Add a user input task to the **IVP Create Case** process model right after the last **Write to Data Store Entity** node.

2.   Assign the task to the **IVP Users** group on the **Assignment** tab:

3. Create a new interface from the **Forms** tab and name it IVP_F_
   InitialVerification.

4. Use the **CREATE FROM DATA TYPE** wizard, select the **IVP Case** data type, and
   generate the interface for editing purposes.

5. Rename the rule input case.

6. Delete the **CANCEL** button from the interface.

7. Delete the **cancel** rule input.

8. Rename the form Initial Verification.

9. Rename the **SUBMIT** button COMPLETE VERIFICATION.

The interface should look like this:

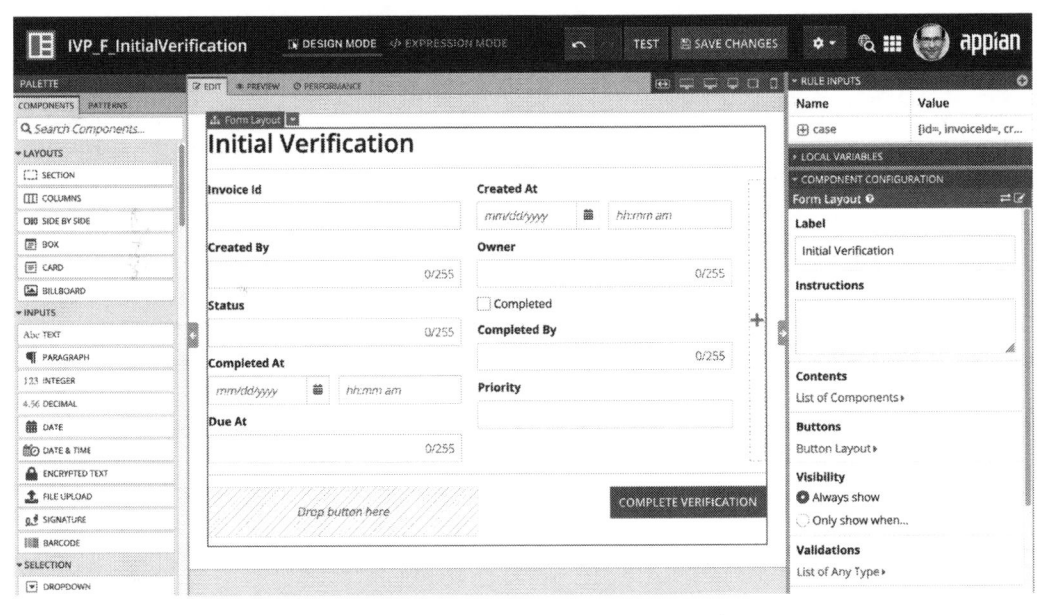

Figure 10.53 – The Initial Verification interface

It's still basic, but in *Chapter 11*, you will learn how to create more attractive UIs. Back in the process modeler, click **Refresh** to update the rule inputs. Then, click the small + icon to create a new node input and configure it as shown in the following screenshot:

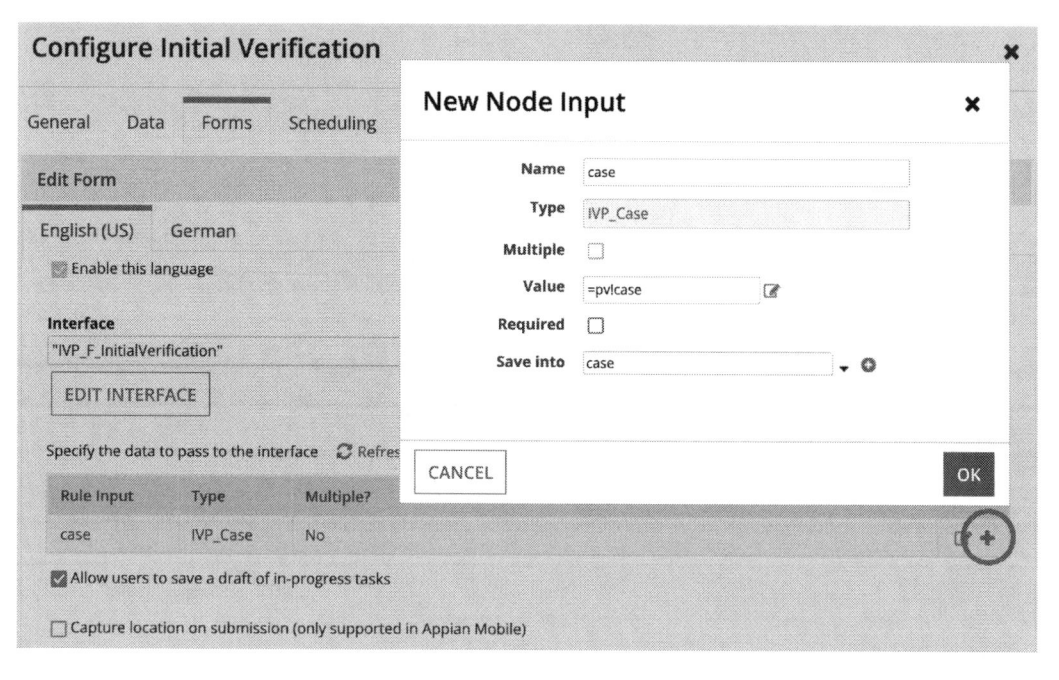

Figure 10.54 – Configure the new node input

This is required, as the interface is backed by a variable in the user input task to which you pass the case data from the process variable. The assignment in the **Save into** field passes the data back to the process variable as the user submits the interface.

Save all the changes in the interface and the process model. Before testing, add yourself to the **IVP Users** group so that the user input task in the process will be assigned to you. Then, create another invoice to test the added task:

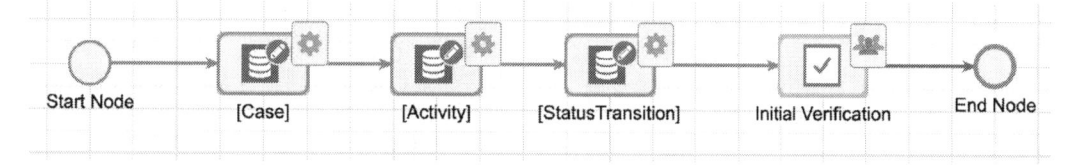

Figure 10.55 – Initial Verification in the process monitoring

In monitoring, the **Initial Verification** task is highlighted in green. Right-click it and select **View Form** to see the interface.

But that's still not the whole process. Your application needs a nice UI first. And as you have probably already noticed, without UIs, we don't get anywhere with the processes either.

Best practices

Although best practices always depend on personal habits, situations, and experiences, I've tried to compile a list that has stood the test of time and many teams and projects.

Process modeling habits

- Right after you have created the model, configure data management and alert settings.

- Use angle connectors instead of straight connectors.

- Give nodes descriptive names. Use a question for decision nodes. Use [EntityName] for Write to Data Store Entity nodes.

- Name connectors if it helps to understand the flow.

- Skip the swim lanes unless you actually use them for assigning tasks.

- Try to keep process models less than 25 nodes in size.

Process data flow

In a process model, you deal with three kinds of data. Have a look at *Figure 10.54*. The red warning symbols indicate variable assignments that you need to configure:

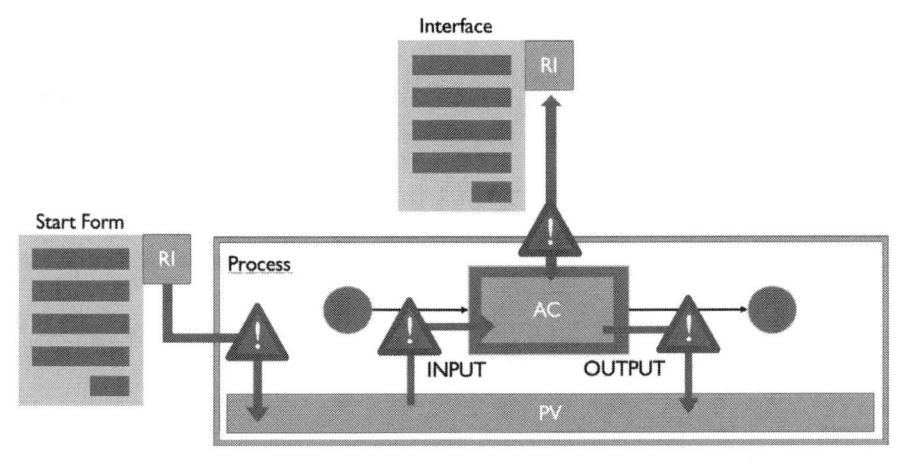

Figure 10.56 – Data flow in a process

These are **Process Variables** (**PVs**), which can store data in the process. Data can be passed into the process when it is started and modified using process nodes.

Process nodes can have their own set of internal variables called **Activity Class** (**AC**) variables. You can pass data from the process into ACs and also from ACs back into the process. The assignments on the **Inputs** tab are evaluated as the node is started, while the assignments on the **Outputs** tab are evaluated as the node completes. You can execute logic in **Inputs** and **Outputs** to manipulate data.

> **Tip**
>
> Assignments on the **Inputs** and **Outputs** tabs are evaluated in parallel. This means you cannot use the output of the first assignment as the input of the next one.
>
> When you assign an interface to a user input task, you need to create AC variables for each rule input in the interface. It will then use them to store data entered by the user.

Summary

In this chapter, you learned how to model, test, and debug process models in Appian. You use them for data management as well as to implement the functional business process. You now understand how the data flow in processes works, how to pass data into processes, and how process data flows in and out of process nodes.

Furthermore, you realized that processes strongly interact with UIs. In the next chapter, you will learn how to transform a plain and simple UI into an experience your users will embrace. Also, lest we forget, we're going to add a few more steps to what is so far just a tiny business process.

11
Creating User Interfaces in Appian

As of now, our records are pretty boring, and the processes have only the most basic user interfaces. You will now learn how to create great-looking user interfaces for records and process models. Starting with a simple interface, you will add dynamic behavior and custom validation rules. All of this will be based on what you learned about UX, UI, and wireframing in *Chapter 8, Understanding UX Discovery and UI in Appian Projects*.

In this chapter, we will cover the following topics:

- **Creating interfaces from scratch**: Designing for specific use cases
- **Adding validation logic**: Simple and complex validations for fields and sections
- **Creating dynamic interfaces**: Dynamic display of components and wizards
- **Creating reusable interface components**: When and how to reuse components
- **Assigning interfaces to records and processes**: Ways of using interfaces
- **Best practices**: The dos and don'ts of Appian interface design

In conversations about user interfaces, your business users like to talk about what certain aspects of the interface should look like, and document that as requirements. You will need to guide your project team to understand that business requirements are functional, may include visual suggestions, but are not binding design-wise.

With low-code in Appian, we use out-of-the-box visual design capabilities to realize these functional requirements: fast, agile, and with an extremely low error rate. Let's see what that means in practice.

Technical requirements

You will find the code mentioned in this chapter placed here:

```
https://github.com/PacktPublishing/Low-Code-Application-
Development-with-Appian.
```

Creating interfaces from scratch

Up to now, you have used the **Appian interface designer** only to automatically generate very basic interfaces. There is a lot more to discover. You can use templates, ready-made patterns, and specific layout, display, or input components. You can modify your interface in the drag and drop design mode for easy layout and add dynamic behavior in the code-oriented **expression mode**. You can test the whole interface while working on it, then analyze the performance to make sure to meet the performance requirements.

We will now discuss the various kinds of **interfaces**, and how to build them tailored to their specific requirements.

Record views

In the context of a **record**, we use interfaces to display the data of an individual record item selected by the user. By default, a record has three views:

- **Summary**: This view is meant to display the most important data, immediately relevant for a user, at first glance. It cannot be removed or renamed.

- **News**: Appian has strong messaging and collaboration features built in. The **News** view displays messages related to that record item. Most companies already have their means of messaging. This view can be disabled.

- **Related Actions**: A fundamental concept of records is the related action, and you already used it to implement data management. The **Related Actions** view shows all related actions currently available to the user. This view can be disabled.

Basic record configuration

Let's have a brief look at the **Views and Header** tab in **Records Designer**. Open the **IVP Case** record.

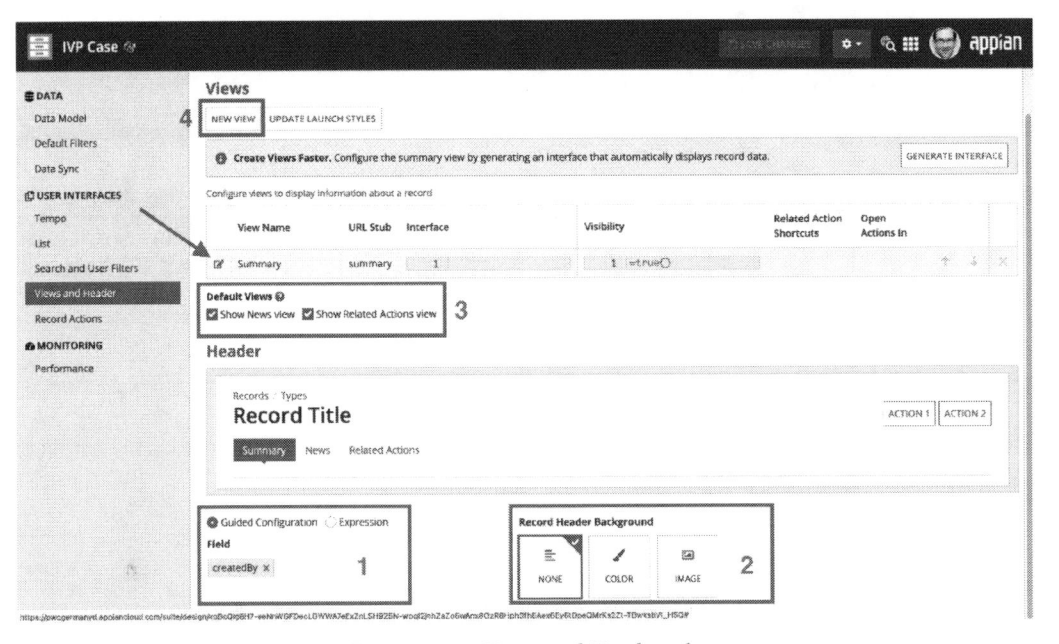

Figure 11.1 – Views and Header tab

1. Configure which fields of the record data you want to use as the **Record Title**.

> **Tip**
> The record title is also used in the **Record Picker** field components. Make sure to define descriptive values for this field, so users can identify the record they want to select.

2. We can use no background, a color, or an image as the background for the record header. Use an image in cases of a record that has images for each individual item, but be aware that an image also adds visual clutter and can be distracting. A color can help to align the record views with corporate style guides.

3. We can control the visibility of the default views with the **Show News view** and **Show Related Actions view** checkboxes.

4. Click the **NEW VIEW** button to create a new view or click the small *Editor* icon to modify an existing one.

Start with some basic configuration.

5. In **Record Title**, switch from **Guided Configuration** to **Expression**, and type the following:

```
"#" &
rv!record[recordType!IVP Case.fields.id] &
"-" &
rv!record[recordType!IVP Case.relationships.Invoice.
fields.number]
```

This results in a record title such as #53-76492, and allows the user to identify the case by the case number as well as the invoice number.

6. Disable the default **News** views.

Creating a new view

Now, create a new interface in Appian Designer, name it IVP_D_CaseSummary, and add the rule input case of type Record Type IVP Case.

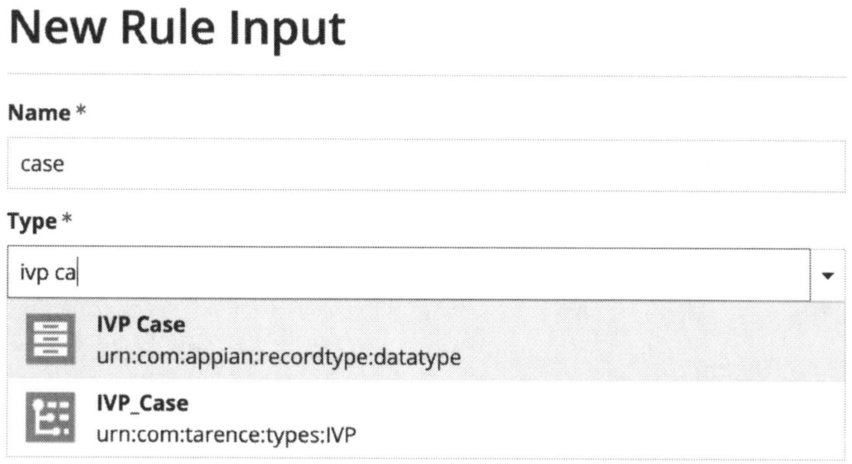

New Rule Input

Name *

case

Type *

ivp ca

IVP Case
urn:com:appian:recordtype:datatype

IVP_Case
urn:com:tarence:types:IVP

Figure 11.2 – CDT Type versus Record Type

Be careful to select the **Record Type** data type but not **CDT Type**. Save the changes and return to **Records Designer** to assign the newly created interface to **Case Record Summary View**. Click the **Editor** icon, and type the following:

```
rule!IVP_D_CaseSummary(
  case: rv!record
)
```

In Appian, interfaces are like an **expression rule**. This code snippet is evaluated when the user navigates to the summary view to render the screen. The interface has a Rule Input that accepts the data of the record the user has selected from the **Record List.**

You now have an interface assigned to the record and can pass the data. From the UX and wireframing exercises, you should have a good idea of how the interface should look. While we take a look at my wireframe, I'll briefly explain my thought process on this:

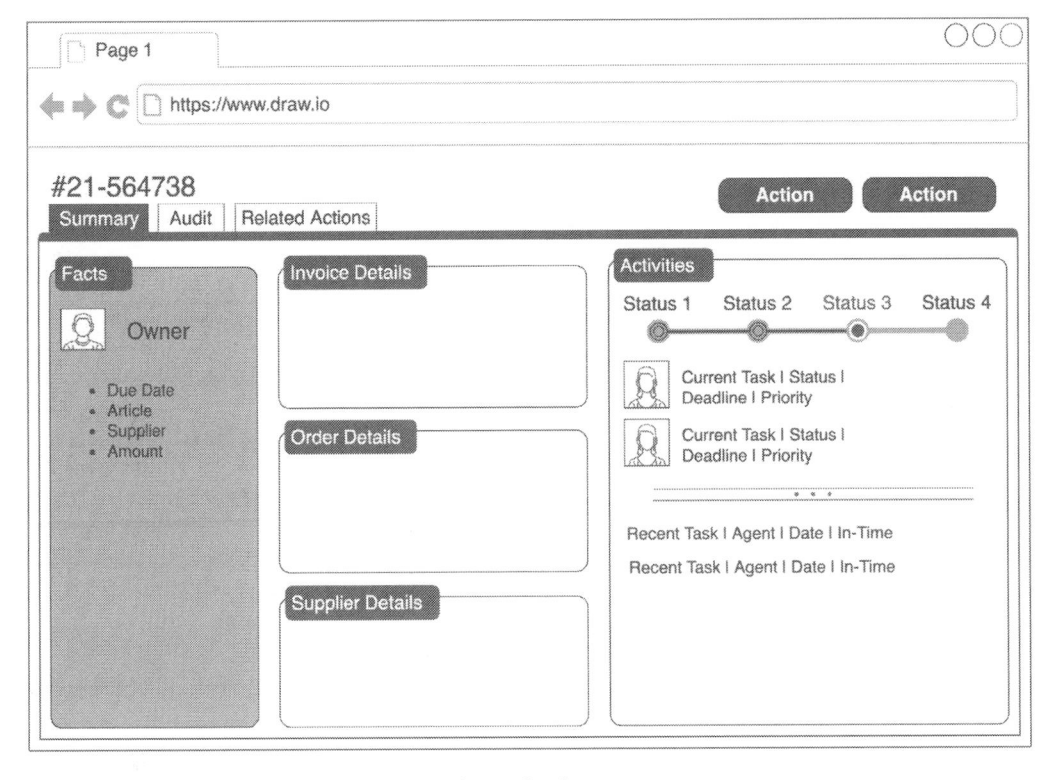

Figure 11.3 – Wireframe for the case summary view

The first and most important aspect is that this is a process-driven application. This means that users do not open the application to find something to do. If there is a task, it will be assigned. The impact is that our user primarily uses this dashboard to get information, but not to interact with the process. We can consider it to be the last stage in a drill-down report.

Since it is the record summary, we need to make sure that only information is displayed that is so critical that *every* user must *always* see it at a glance. Any other information can be placed on additional views or made visible by some form of interaction.

The hierarchy of importance of information is as follows:

1. **Identification**: Use the record title to identify a record item.

2. **Performance**: The owner (accountable person), deadline, and priority. This becomes the left column. As visual reception goes from dark to light, I gave it a gray background.

3. **Status**: Process status, assigned tasks, and recent activities. I placed that into the right column.

4. **Further information**: Any other information a user needs goes into the middle column.

Basic layout

Let's understand the basic layout with a few steps.

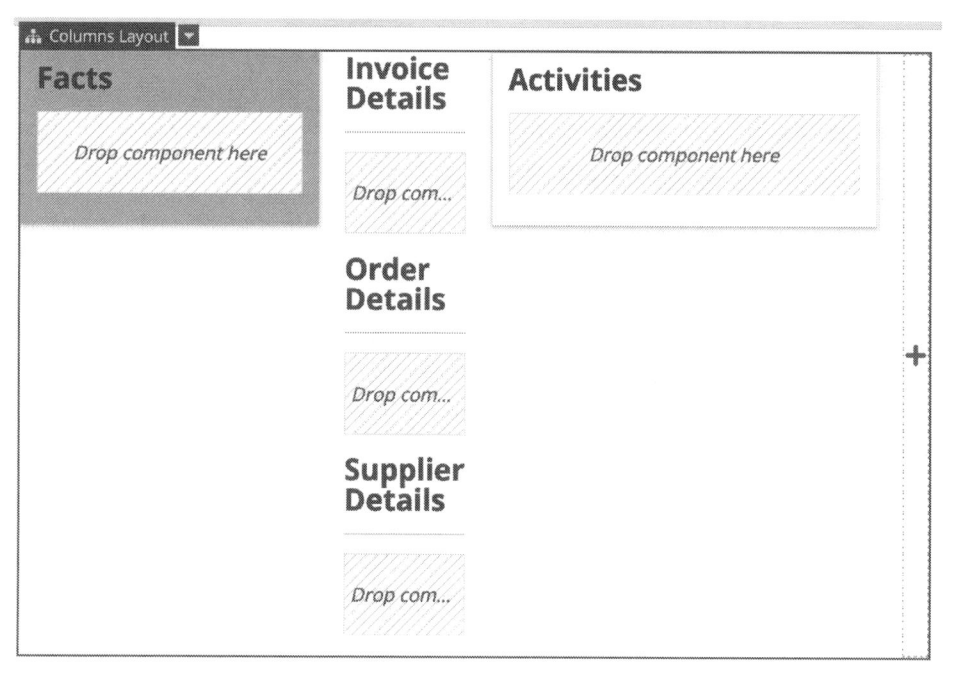

Figure 11.4 – Basic layout

Let's now start with adding layout and components in the design mode:

1. Add **Columns Layout**. It already has three columns that we require. Configure the widths of the columns, from left to right, to `Narrow Plus`, `Automatically Distribute`, and `Medium`.

2. Add a card layout to the left column, disable the border, enable the shadow, and give it a light gray background color. Add a section layout inside the card and name it `Facts`.

3. Add three section layouts to the middle column. Select the **Secondary** pre-defined color, set **Divider Lines** to **Above Content**, and name them `Invoice Details`, `Order Details`, and `Supplier Details`.

4. Add another card layout to the right column, disable the border, and enable the shadow. Add a section layout inside and give it the name `Activities`.

> **Tip**
> Use columns layouts to implement the rough layout first, then add **Side By Side** layouts within columns to arrange individual components in rows.

With this layout, we achieve a clear hierarchy in the importance of information, as well as an unobtrusive structure.

Before adding more components to display data, we use the Appian testing capabilities to load some data into the interface designer. Click the **Test** button at the top of the screen. Then, enter the following code snippet into the expression field:

```
a!queryRecordType(
    recordType: recordType!IVP Case,
    pagingInfo: a!pagingInfo(1,1)
).data
```

> **Tip**
> To reference a record type in code, just start typing the name of the record and Appian will auto complete it.

As shown in *Figure 11.5*, click the **Set as default test values** link, then click **TEST INTERFACE** to evaluate the code:

Test Inputs

Enter initial input values to test interface

Rule Input Name	Expression	Value
| case (IVP Case) | ```
1 ▾ a!queryRecordType(
2     recordType: ▦ recordType!IVP Case ,
3 ▾   pagingInfo: a!pagingInfo(1,1)
4 ).data
``` | IVP Case<br>id: 1<br>invoiceId: 3<br>createdAt: 12/5/2021 5:55 PM GMT+01:00<br>createdBy: "stefan.helzle@pwc.com"<br>**...More** |

Set as default test values

CANCEL   TEST INTERFACE

Figure 11.5 – Loading record data in the test dialog

In the **RULE INPUTS** panel, you will now see the data of the first record:

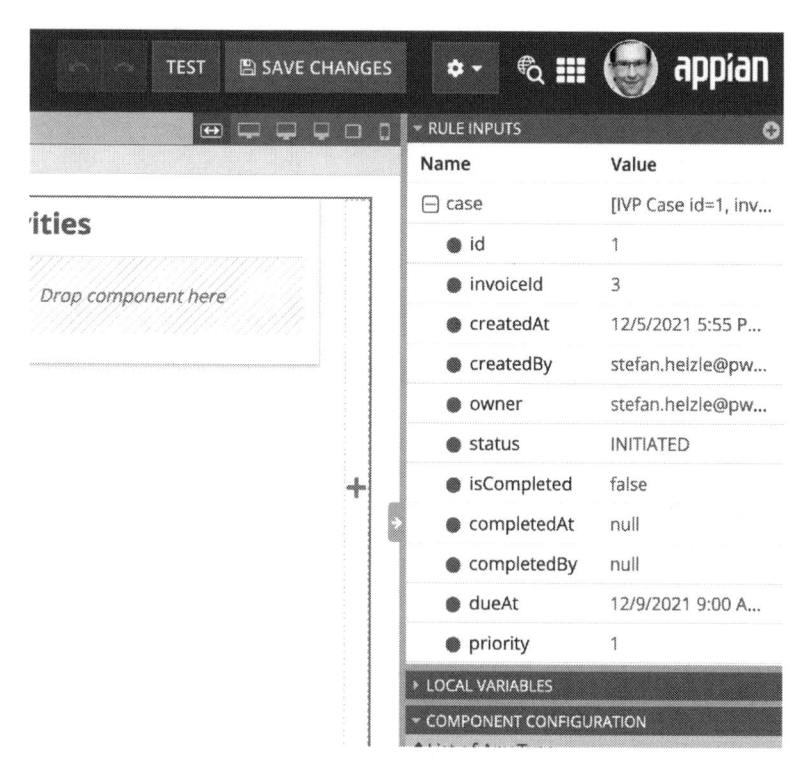

Figure 11.6 – Record data in the RULE INPUTS panel
```

Now, let's look at how to add details.

Adding details to the Facts column

Now that we have some real data available, let's populate the **Facts** card:

1. Add a **Side By Side** layout, make sure you configure the vertical alignment to **Middle**, then add **Image** and **Rich Text** to that layout.

2. Switch to **EXPRESSION MODE** and change the `imageField` component as follows:

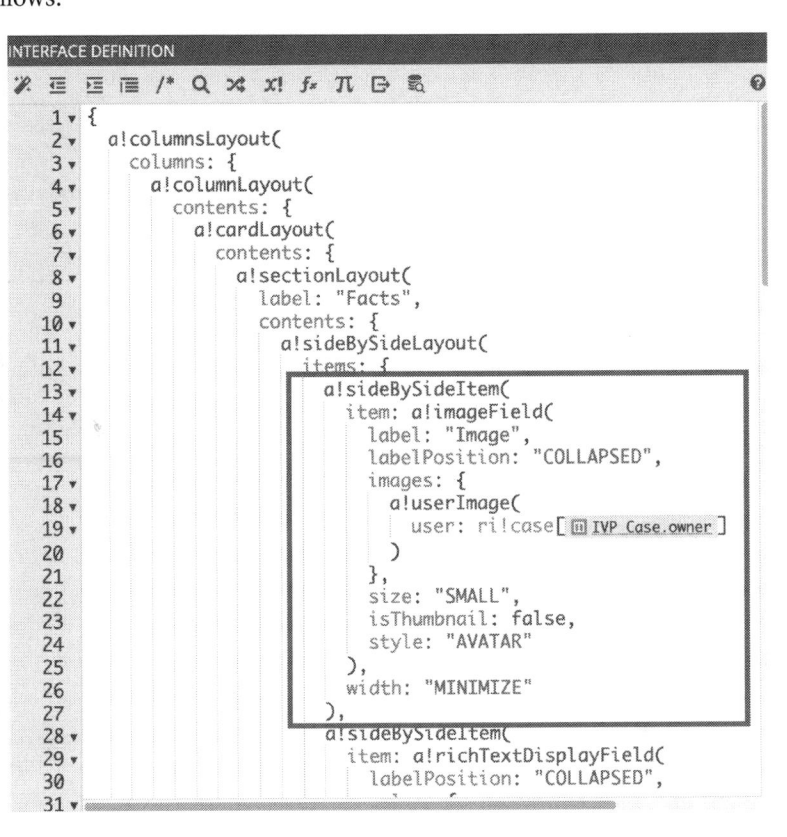

Figure 11.7 – Modifying the imageField code

In this code snippet, you see how to display the user's profile image.

3. Change the `richTextDisplayField` component as follows:

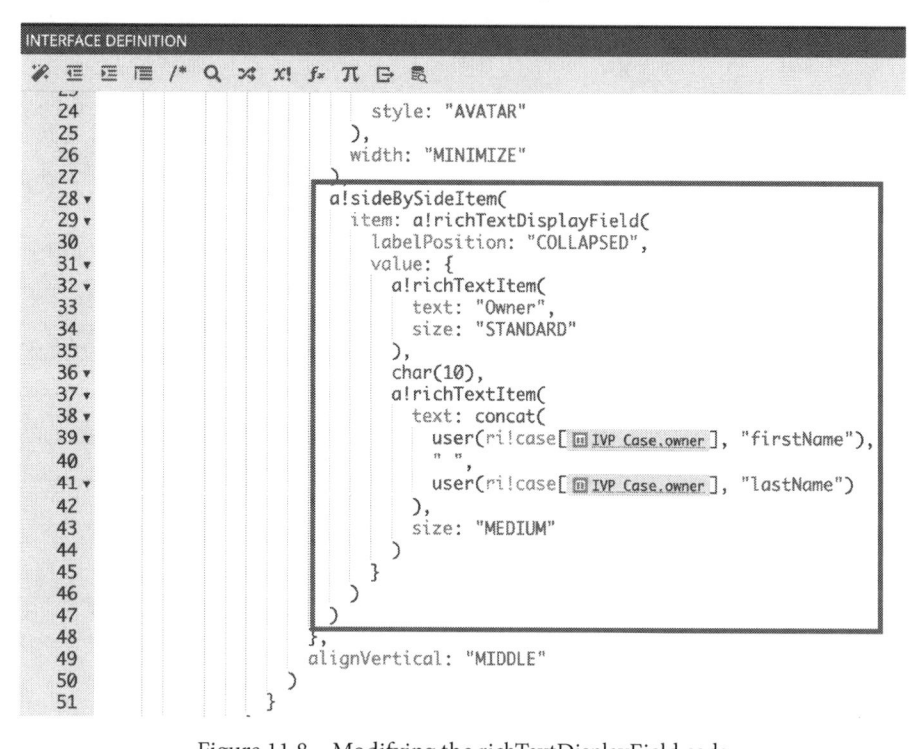

Figure 11.8 – Modifying the richTextDisplayField code

Here, we use the `user()` function to access attributes of an Appian user account.

Expression Mode Help

Navigate the cursor on any function to display detailed information in the help panel below. This includes all parameters, their data types, default values, valid values, and which functions to use to create specific input values.

Your interface should now look like this:

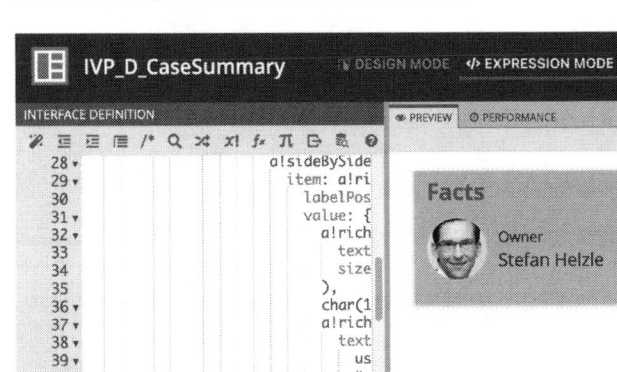

Figure 11.9 – Facts showing case owner information

Back in **DESIGN MODE**, add two date fields to display the case creation and due dates. Configure the label positions to **Justified** and enable **Read-only**. Using normal input fields in read-only is the easiest way to display values. To define the displayed values, click the small **editor** icon that pops up when the mouse cursor hovers over a field.

Label Positions

You typically use only three of the four label positions. Following the Appian UX Design Guide (https://docs.appian.com/suite/help/ latest/ux_getting_started.html), I recommend using Above for editable fields, and Justified for read-only fields. Use Hidden, or COLLAPSED, which is the expression mode value, whenever you want to hide the field label. Leaving it empty, without hiding it, will still use up some space and result in excessive white space between components.

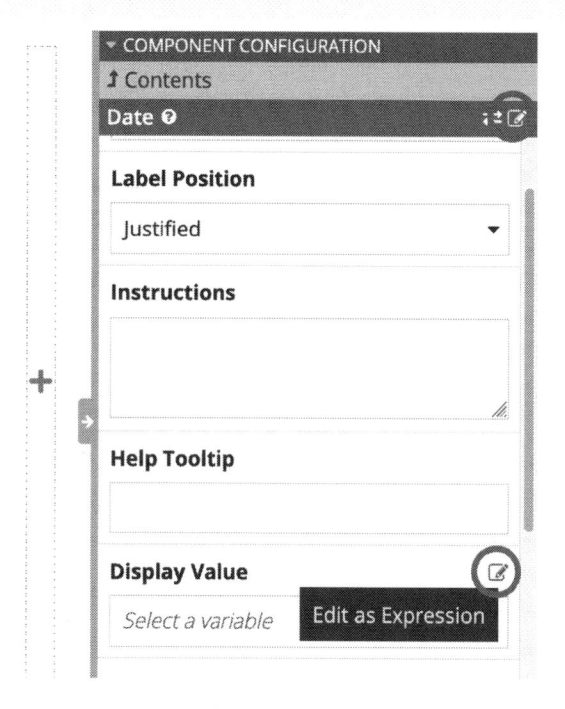

Figure 11.10 – Editor icons in the design mode

Enter the values:

```
ri!case[recordType!IVP Case.fields.createdAt]
```

and

```
ri!case[recordType!IVP Case.fields.dueAt]
```

The editor on each field allows you to modify the passed value just for that field. There is another editor icon at the component level that you can use to modify the whole component as an expression without switching to **EXPRESSION MODE**.

> **Tip**
> Beyond a very basic interface, and with raising complexity, it becomes more and more necessary to switch between **DESIGN MODE** and **EXPRESSION MODE**. Both modes have their benefits and with more experience, you will find your personal way in interface design.

Adding details to the middle column

In the middle column, we want to display related data from the invoice, order, and supplier. Because we added all these relations to the records, we can easily query related data and display the values of fields using the dot-notation and the relationships attribute.

Switch to **EXPRESSION MODE** and wrap your existing code in the following snippet:

```
a!localVariables(
  local!relatedData: a!queryRecordType(
    recordType: recordType!IVP Case,
    pagingInfo: a!pagingInfo(1,100),
    filters: a!queryFilter(
      field: recordType!IVP Case.fields.id,
      operator: "=",
      value: ri!case[recordType!IVP Case.fields.id]
    ),
    fields: {
      recordType!IVP Case.relationships.Invoice,
      recordType!IVP Case.relationships.Invoice.relationships.
        OrderIds.relationships.Order,
      recordType!IVP Case.relationships.Invoice.relationships.
        Supplier,
      recordType!IVP Case.relationships.Activities,
    },
relatedRecordData: {
    a!relatedRecordData(
      relationship: recordType!IVP Case.relationships.
      Activities,
      sort: {
        a!sortInfo(
          field: recordType!IVP Activity.fields.createdAt,
```

```
            ascending: false
        )
    },
        limit: 1
    )
  },
) .data,
<EXISTING CODE>
)
```

> **Tip**
>
> Sections in the Appian code can be collapsed to gain a better overview of the structure. Click the small arrow to the right of the line numbers to collapse or expand a section of code.

This will create a local variable holding the values of the case, including a nested structure of related data as defined in the `queryRecordType` field parameter. In the `relatedRecordData` parameter, we define the sort order of the activities to show the latest on top:

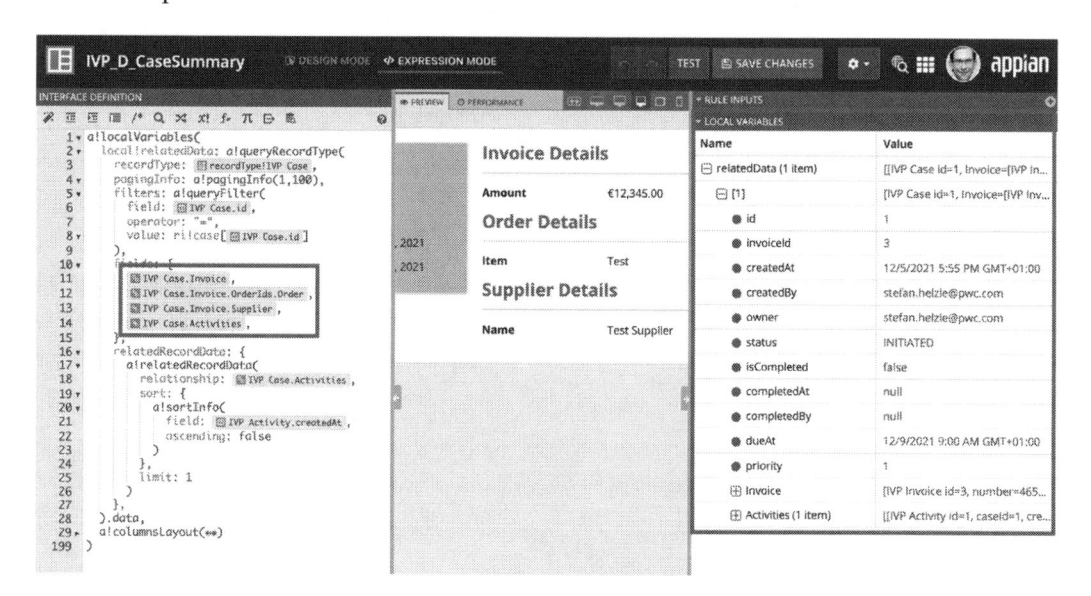

Figure 11.11 – Related data in a local variable

Back in **DESIGN MODE**, add a read-only text field to the **Invoice Details** section, name it
Amount, and select the correct label position. Edit the value parameter as expression
and enter the following code:

```
if(
    isnull(local!relatedData[recordType!IVP Case.relationships.
       Invoice.fields.amount]),
    "--",
    euro(local!relatedData[recordType!IVP Case.relationships.
       Invoice.fields.amount])
)
```

This formats the decimal value properly and adds €-character. The euro() function
does not handle Null values. You need to check for Null values and display a default
value.

There is also a dollar() and yen() function available. If you want a more custom
format, use the text() function, which accepts a formatting string as in this example:

```
text(local!relatedData[recordType!IVP Case.relationships.
   Invoice.fields.amount], "€ ###,###,###.00")
```

Creating the list of actions

In the card layout that we added to the right, we want to display a list of all the activities
incurred during the process. In Appian, you can easily create dynamic user interfaces. The
method I will show you now uses the forEach function to create a UI component for
each activity. Also, have a look at how I use the text function to format the timestamp of
the createdAt field:

```
a!forEach(
   items: a!flatten(local!relatedData[recordType!IVP Case.
      relationships.Activities]),
   expression: a!richTextDisplayField(
      label: text(
         fv!item[recordType!IVP Activity.fields.createdAt],
         "mm/dd/yyyy hh:mm"
      ),
      value: concat(
         fv!item[recordType!IVP Activity.fields.type],
```

```
          "  |  ",
        fv!item[recordType!IVP Activity.fields.user],
          "  |  ",
        fv!item[recordType!IVP Activity.fields.text],
      )
    )
  )
```

Add the prceeding snippet inside the curly braces of the `contents` parameter of the **Activities** section layout.

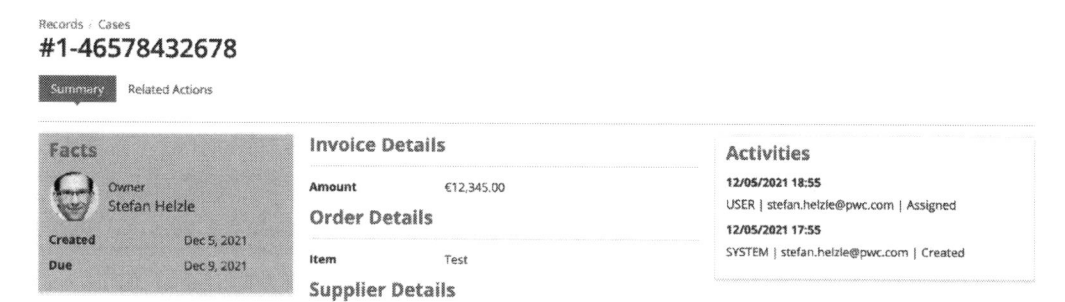

Figure 11.12 – Final record view

This is a very simple interface. I want to encourage you to add more information yourself. Maybe a status? Put yourself in the role of a user and think about what concrete information they need to do their job. But remember that we are implementing a process and the actual work is done in individual tasks and not by the user searching for a case, looking at this interface, and then having to decide for themselves what to do next.

In my daily work, I frequently come back to certain interfaces to check whether they still meet my ever-growing understanding of the matter. When I add another field to a record, I also need to check whether I have to include that field on the **Record Summary** view.

Process start forms

In *Chapter 10, Modeling Business Processes in Appian*, in the first section, *A first simple process*, we already created a **Process Start Form** named `IVP_F_CreateInvoice`. As the name implies, the purpose of that form is to capture the data required to initiate the process. The process itself is started when the user clicks the **submit** button in the interface.

In *Chapter 10, Modeling Business Processes in Appian*, in the first section, *Simple Process*, we also made Appian create the interface automatically. It works but doesn't look good. Let's start with a clean table. Open the interface, switch to **EXPRESSION MODE**, delete all existing code, then go back to **DESIGN MODE**.

Let's have a quick look at an example, and then I will explain the implementation details:

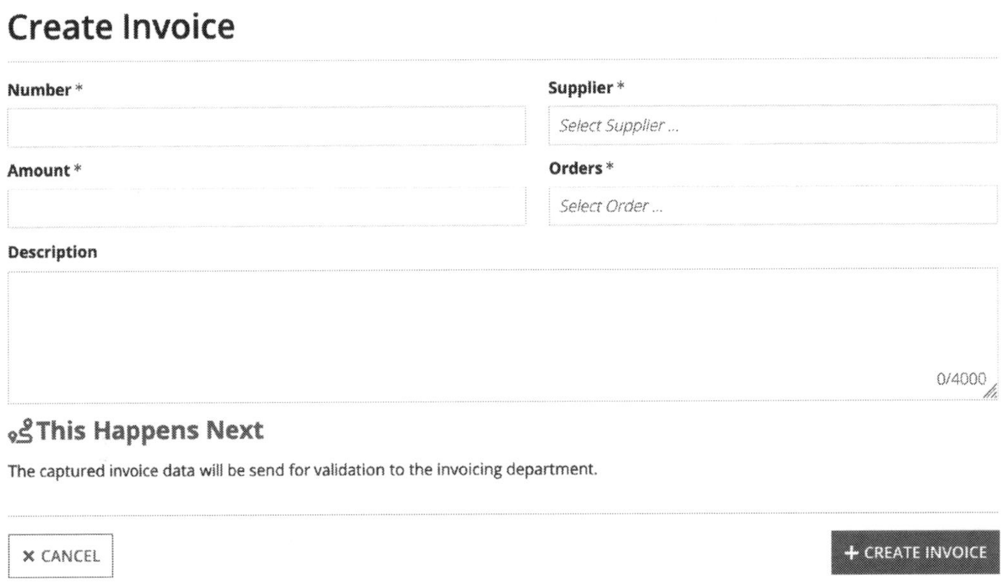

Create Invoice

Number *

Supplier *

Select Supplier ...

Amount *

Orders *

Select Order ...

Description

0/4000

⚙ This Happens Next

The captured invoice data will be send for validation to the invoicing department.

✕ CANCEL

+ CREATE INVOICE

Figure 11.13 – Example interface

In *Chapter 8, Understanding UX Discovery and UI in Appian Projects,* we discussed the basic requirements for an interface. They are as follows:

- Scope
- Information
- Input
- Orientation

Out of these four, we need to cover **input** and **orientation**. As the user will trigger the **Start Form** because they want to capture the data for a new invoice and start the process, we do not need **scope** and **information**:

1. Click the **Two Column Form** template from the right-hand **Forms** template to get started.

2. Modify the basic layout to consist of a two-column layout on top, followed by a section layout. Add the components for the **Number, Amount, Description**, and **Supplier** fields.

3. Configure the **Display Value** and **Save Input To** properties to their respective fields in the **invoice** rule input. Set **Maximum Selections** for the **Supplier** record picker to 1. The icon for the lower section is called **route** and the component used is **Rich Text**.

   The picker field for **Orders** requires a bit more attention. In our data model, the invoice has a many-to-many relationship to **Orders** as suppliers might want to combine multiple orders in a single invoice.

4. Add an **Order** record picker and leave **Maximum Selections** empty to allow the user to select multiple orders. Then, create a new `orderIds` rule input of the `Integer` type, make it an array, and use it for the picker field. You can now select multiple orders and should see the rule input display the IDs.

5. You will later need to update the `IVP Create New Invoice` process to accept the new rule input from the start form and to persist that many-to-many relationship from **Invoice to Orders** to the database.

6. The last detail of this interface is that we need to assign a few technical values not directly entered by the user. These are `createdAt`, `createdBy`, and `status`. These fields are controlled by our application.

7. Modify the **+ Create Invoice** button and add the **saveInto** parameter as in the following snippet:

```
a!buttonWidget(
  label: "Create Invoice",
  icon: "plus",
  submit: true,
  style: "PRIMARY",
  saveInto: {
    a!save(
      target: ri!invoice.createdAt,
```

```
        value: now()
    ),
    a!save(
        target: ri!invoice.createdBy,
        value: loggedInUser()
    ),
    a!save(
        target: ri!invoice.status,
        value: cons!IVP_CASE_STATUS_INITIATED
    ),
    }
)
```

This stores the current timestamp, the username of the submitting user, and the value of the status constant to the respective fields in the invoice rule input.

> **Tip**
>
> There are multiple ways to set the initial values of a data structure. The other commonly used way is to add a script task to the process, which sets these values. I prefer to do that in the interface because I need to check only one spot in case something is wrong with the data passed into the process.

Now, complete the interface and test it. The following are some basic technical tests that you should do before leaving any interface:

- Did you use the components matching the field type?

- Is entered data stored in the correct fields?

- Is the correct required parameter set up for all fields?

Open the **IVP Create New Invoice** process model, go to **Process Model Properties**, and navigate to the **Process Start Form** tab. The added rule input will show up with no value assigned.

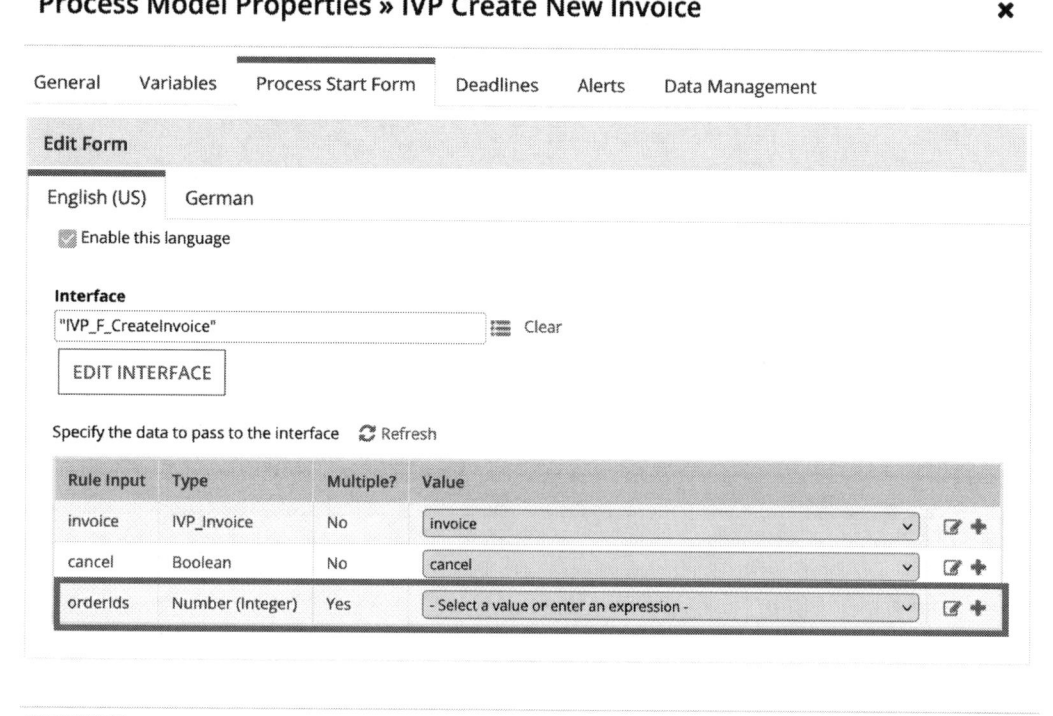

Figure 11.14 – Updated Process Start Form

Click the + icon to create a new process variable of the Integer (Multiple) type. **Save** and **Publish** the model, then start it for debugging. Enter some data and make sure to select at least two orders. Then, submit the form and check the variables in **Process Details**. You should see multiple values in the **orderIds** process variable.

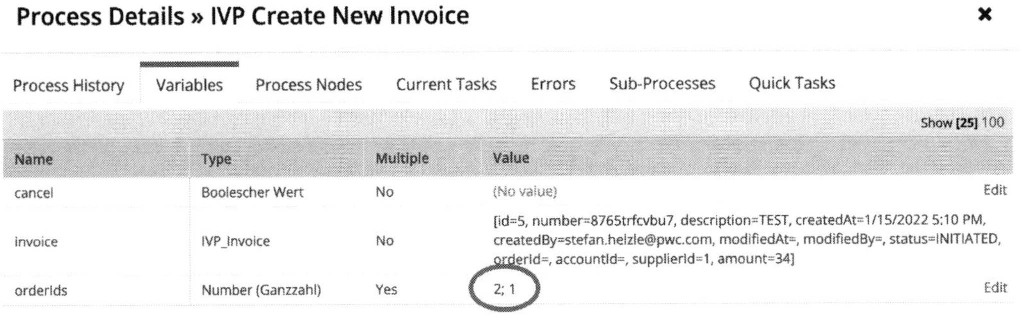

Process Details » IVP Create New Invoice   ✖

Process History	Variables	Process Nodes	Current Tasks	Errors	Sub-Processes	Quick Tasks

Show **[25]** 100

Name	Type	Multiple	Value	
cancel	Boolescher Wert	No	(No value)	Edit
invoice	IVP_Invoice	No	[id=5, number=8765trfcvbu7, description=TEST, createdAt=1/15/2022 5:10 PM, createdBy=stefan.helzle@pwc.com, modifiedAt=, modifiedBy=, status=INITIATED, orderId=, accountId=, supplierId=1, amount=34]	
orderIds	Number (Ganzzahl)	Yes	2; 1	Edit

Figure 11.15 – Process variable storing multiple values

If this doesn't work, check for the following:

- Is the **orderIds** process variable of type Integer (Multiple)?
- In the interface, is the rule input **orderIds** of type Integer (Multiple)?
- Does the picker field save the value into the **orderIds** rule input?

Next, add a new **Write to Data Store Entity** (**WDSE**) smart service to the model between the existing WDSE and the sub-process node. Rename it to [OrderIds]. Configure the data inputs of the node to the following:

```
Data Store Entity = IVP Datastore
```

Add a new invoicesToOrders input of the IVP_InvoicesToOrders type and make it a multiple. Click the small + at the input and configure the fields as follows:

```
orderId = pv!orderIds
invoiceId = repeat(count(pv!orderIds), pv!invoice.id)
```

This will store multiple IVP_InvoicesToOrders records in the database, one for each combination of orderId and invoiceId. Appian detects that the target data structure is a multiple and will map the data accordingly. As invoiceId is always the same, we need to make sure to repeat that ID as many times as there are items in orderIds.

Debug the model again, check the process variables, and also check that all values have been stored in the database.

You now know how to design a process start form and how to set initial values. Let's take a look at interfaces used during process execution.

User Input Task

A User Input Task in a process model has four basic requirements as discussed in *Chapter 8*. These are as follows:

- Scope
- Information
- Input
- Orientation

Let's see what we can do for the `IVP_F_InitialVerification` interface, which has also been automatically created.

Our process is the exception to an otherwise completely automatic process. This means that we have to deal with all sorts of mismatching of orders and invoices. Think about how you could analyze the data and give clear indications of errors.

> **Hint**
>
> A small example I had to deal with in a project was when a user had to check that the applicant for a loan was older than 18. What would you display on the interface?
>
> -The age in years?
>
> -An icon indicating whether the applicant is older than 18?
>
> -The date of birth?

I created an example that includes the following checks:

- The sum of totals of all orders must be equal to the amount of the invoice.
- The suppliers of the orders must be the same as on the invoice.

I present the results of these checks prominently to the user:

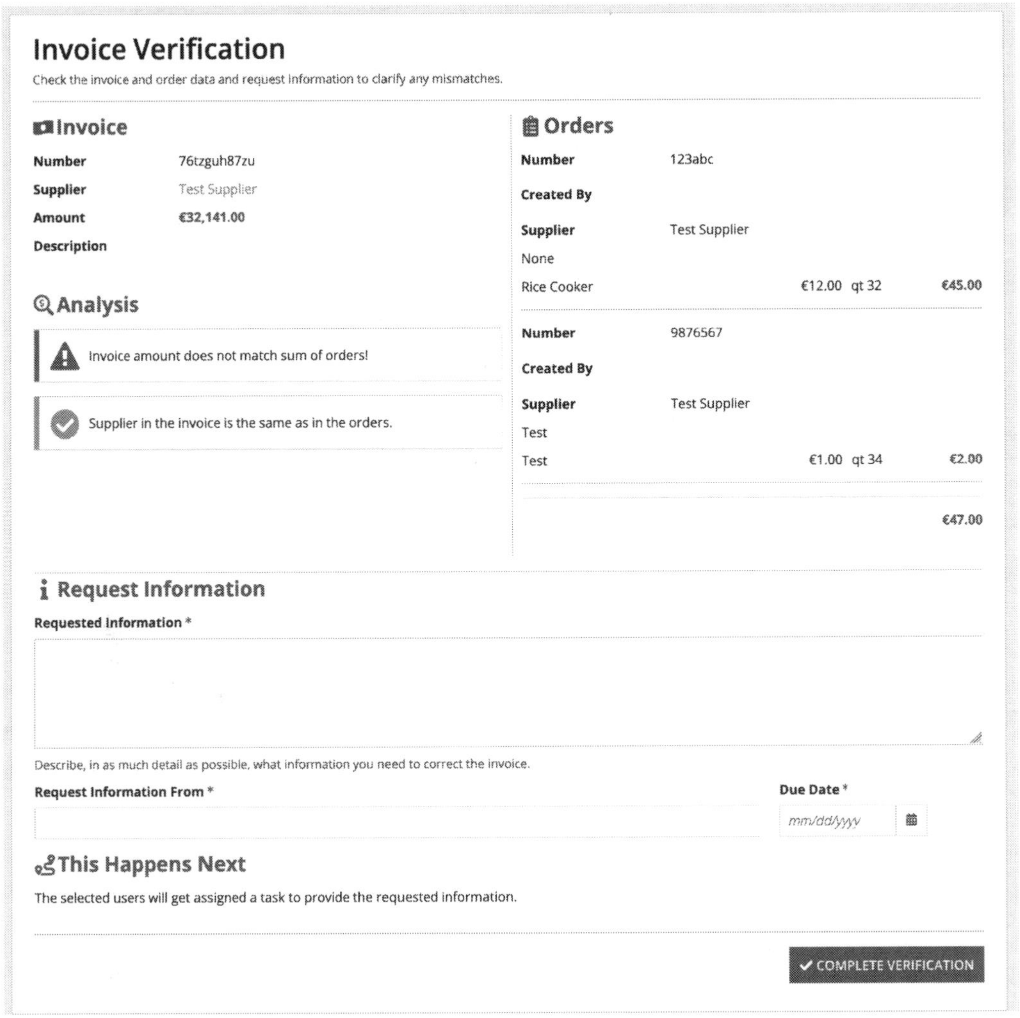

Invoice Verification

Check the invoice and order data and request information to clarify any mismatches.

📷 Invoice

Number	76tzguh87zu
Supplier	Test Supplier
Amount	€32,141.00
Description	

🔍 Analysis

⚠ Invoice amount does not match sum of orders!

✅ Supplier in the invoice is the same as in the orders.

📋 Orders

Number	123abc
Created By	
Supplier	Test Supplier
None	
Rice Cooker	€12.00 qt 32 €45.00

Number	9876567
Created By	
Supplier	Test Supplier
Test	
Test	€1.00 qt 34 €2.00

€47.00

ℹ Request Information

Requested Information *

Describe, in as much detail as possible, what information you need to correct the invoice.

Request Information From *

Due Date *

mm/dd/yyyy 📅

🔗 This Happens Next

The selected users will get assigned a task to provide the requested information.

✔ COMPLETE VERIFICATION

Figure 11.16 – Example verification interface showing errors

Depending on the checks, I show or hide various components:

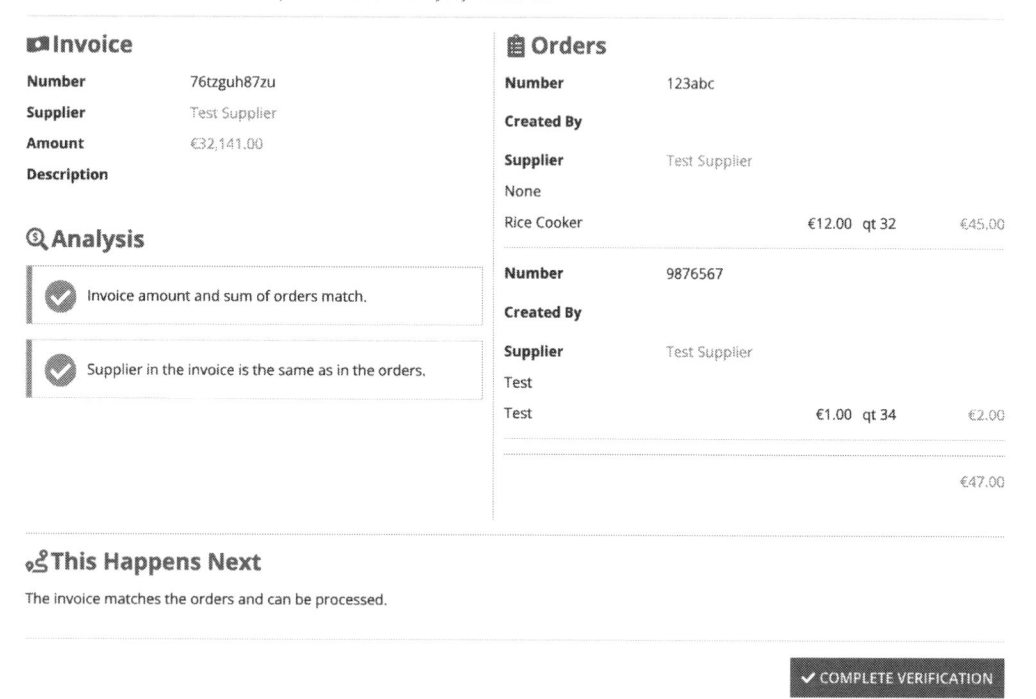

Figure 11.17 – Example verification interface showing success

Try to design that interface yourself. I will now discuss some remarkable implementation details. You will find the whole code on GitHub following this link: `https://github.com/PacktPublishing/Low-Code-Application-Development-with-Appian`.

Loading related data

To have all the data at hand, you will need to add more fields to a `!queryRecordType`:

```
local!relatedData: a!queryRecordType(
    recordType: recordType!IVP Invoice,
    pagingInfo: a!pagingInfo(1,100),
    filters: a!queryFilter(
        field: recordType!IVP Invoice.fields.id,
        operator: "=",
```

```
        value: ri!case.invoiceId
    ),
fields: {
    recordType!IVP Invoice.relationships.OrderIds.
      relationships.Order,
    recordType!IVP Invoice.relationships.OrderIds.
      relationships.Order.relationships.Supplier,
    recordType!IVP Invoice.relationships.Supplier,
    recordType!IVP Invoice.relationships.Account,
    recordType!IVP Invoice.relationships.Supplier,
    }
  ).data,
```

Storing validation results

Create two more local variables to hold the results of the validations. You will need them multiple times, and this way you have to write the logic only once:

```
local!invoiceAmountEqualsSumOfOrders:
 local!relatedData[recordType!IVP Invoice.fields.amount]
= sum(a!flatten(local!relatedData[recordType!IVP Invoice.
relationships.OrderIds.relationships.Order.fields.
totalPrice])),
```

This takes `totalPrice` of all orders and feeds it into the `sum()` function. The result is then compared to the amount of the invoice:

```
local!suppliersMatch: count(
  union(
    local!relatedData['recordType!IVP Invoice.fields.
      supplierId'],
    tointeger(local!relatedData['recordType!IVP Invoice.
    relationships.OrderIds.relationships.Order.fields.
      supplierId'])
  )
) = 1
```

This uses another nice trick. We want to know whether the supplier of the invoice is the same as for all orders. The `union()` function helps us in a way that takes two lists and returns the unique values. Feeding that into the `count` function gives us the number of unique suppliers. If the suppliers are the same, this number is 1, otherwise, it is 2 or higher.

> **Tip**
>
> Make it a habit to frequently visit the list of Appian functions following this link: `https://docs.appian.com/suite/help/latest/Appian_Functions.html`. Learn the functions by heart and do your own research and development using them to become an efficient Appian designer.

Conditional color and style

Use an `if` statement to give individual parameters different values, depending on simple checks or more complex logic:

```
a!richTextItem(
    text: euro(local!relatedData[recordType!IVP Invoice.fields.
        amount]),
    color: if(
        local!relatedData[recordType!IVP Invoice.fields.
        amount] = sum(a!flatten(local!relatedData[recordType!IVP
        Invoice.relationships.OrderIds.relationships.Order.fields.
        totalPrice])),
        "POSITIVE",
        "NEGATIVE"
    ),
    style: if(
        local!relatedData[recordType!IVP Invoice.fields.
        amount] = sum(a!flatten(local!relatedData[recordType!IVP
        Invoice.relationships.OrderIds.relationships.Order.fields.
        totalPrice])),
        "PLAIN",
        "STRONG"
    )
)
```

Showing and hiding components

Use the showWhen parameter to show or hide individual components, depending on logic:

```
a!sectionLayout(
  label: "Request Information",
  labelIcon: "info",
  showWhen: or(
    not(local!invoiceAmountEqualsSumOfOrders),
    not(local!suppliersMatch)
  ),
  contents: {
    ....
```

> **Tip**
>
> When you use showWhen to hide components, these are not just hidden from the user but do not exist in the interface the user is looking at. This is important regarding data security, as a malicious user would try to get access to the HTML content loaded into the browser. As a result, a user has no chance to get access to any information in a hidden component.

As of now, the **IVP Create Case** process model, which uses this interface, does not know about the added rule inputs. We will return to this model and add the required logic in the next chapter when completing the overall process.

Sites

You have now learned about most types of interfaces in Appian, but we are missing an essential piece. Our users still have no place to find their records, tasks, and reports. In Appian, you create a **Site** object for this purpose.

A site is composed of up to five pages, and each page can be configured to take a **Record**, a **Process**, a **Report**, or an **Interface** as content.

1. Create a new site object, name it IVP Invoice Validation Process, and accept the security defaults.

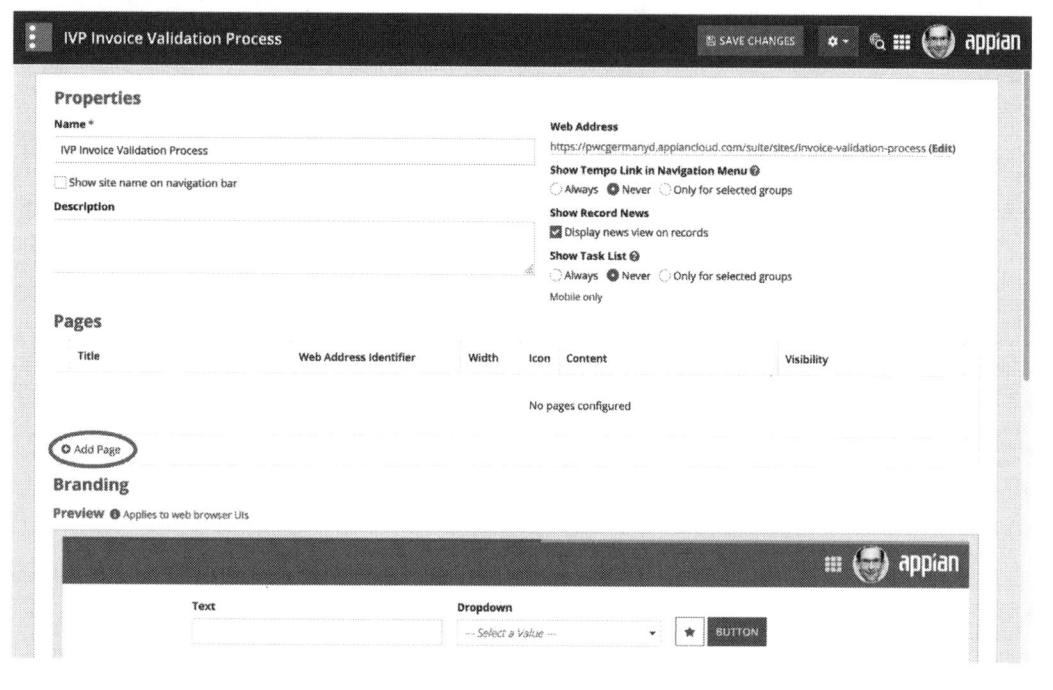

Figure 11.18 – Site editor

2. Click the **Add Page** link to add a new page, then configure the new page as follows:

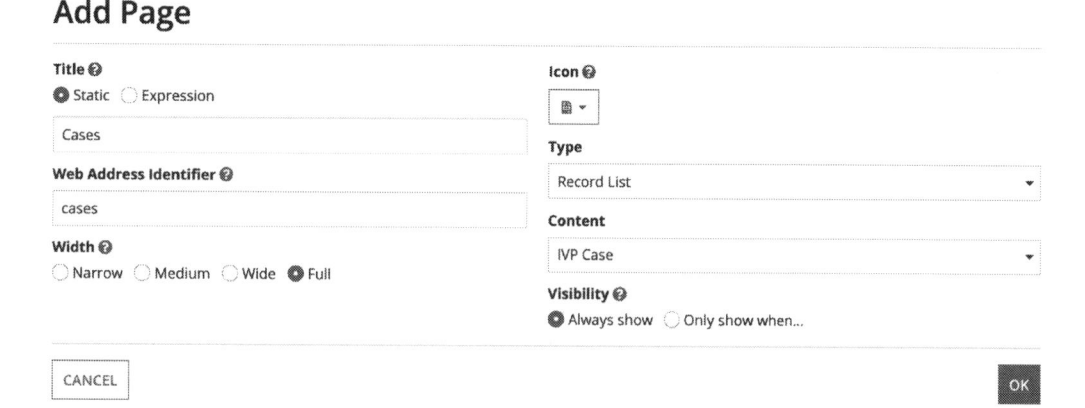

Figure 11.19 – Configuring the new page

The name of the icon is `file-invoice`, but do not hesitate to select any icon you like. Click **OK** to close the dialog, then click **SAVE CHANGES**. To open the site in a new browser tab, click the **Web Address** link at the top right of the screen. The new site is also accessible from the waffle menu at the top right of the screen.

A user can now bookmark the site URL in the browser or open the application site using the waffle menu.

So much for now about building whole interfaces. We will now have a look at some specific topics, starting with field-level validations.

Adding validation logic

Data validation in interfaces is important and can go way beyond making a field mandatory. I will show you how to implement the following validations:

- A selected date must be in the future.

- An entered number must be in a specific range.

An important aspect is that Appian only executes validations if the field has any value. So, you cannot implement a validation that checks for an empty field. Set the `required` parameter to `true` to do that. Validations can then check any entered values. Make the `required` parameter `false` to create an optional field that can still have validations.

While I use a simple literal in the examples, it is a good idea to store values such as thresholds or range definitions in constants. This way these values can be reused and use the **Update Constant** smart service in a process model to let a user modify values stored in constants.

Date validation

Use a simple `if()` statement to check whether the entered value is later than today:

```
a!dateField(
  label: "Due Date",
  value: ri!dueAt,
  saveInto: ri!dueAt,
  required: true,
  validations: if(
    ri!dueAt > today(),
    null,
```

```
        "The due date must be in the future."
    )
)
```

The preceding code will display the following **Due Date** field in an interface:

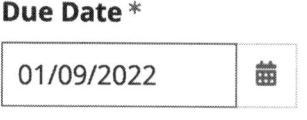

Figure 11.20 – Date field with validation

Range check

Implementing a range check is just as easy as the date validation. Add another condition and combine them with a logical AND.

```
a!integerField(
  label: "Quantity",
  value: ri!quantity,
  saveInto: ri!quantity,
  required: true,
  validations: if(
    and(
      ri!quantity > 0,
      ri!quantity <= 100
    ),
    null,
    "The quantity must be between 1 and 100."
  )
)
```

That code will display a field taking integer values:

Quantity *

    123

The quantity must be between 1 and 100.

Figure 11.21 – Integer field with range check

If you decided to store the lower and upper boundary as constants, the code would be like this:

```
a!integerField(
  label: "Quantity",
  value: ri!quantity,
  saveInto: ri!quantity,
  required: true,
  validations: if(
    and(
      ri!quantity > cons!IVP_QUANTITY_MIN,
      ri!quantity <= cons!IVP_QUANTITY_MAX
    ),
    null,
    concat(
      "The quantity must be between ",
      cons!IVP_QUANTITY_MIN,
      " and ",
      cons!IVP_QUANTITY_MAX
      "."
    )
  )
)
```

In general, you can use any kind of logic in validation. This includes expressions, decision tables, and integrations. Yes, you can do a call to an external web service to validate a value!

Let's now have a look at how to create dynamic interfaces.

Creating dynamic interfaces

You already know about the showWhen parameter and how to assign different values to parameters depending on logic, and you implemented a dynamic list of components to display multiple orders using forEach.

The important part of creating dynamic interfaces is that you need a way to store the state. State means one or more local variables you use to control which parts of the interface to show. To understand how that works, we will dissect one of the interface patterns provided by Appian:

1. Create a new interface, just for this investigation, and name it `IVP_F_Test`. You can delete this interface at the end of our small workshop. Switch to the **PATTERNS** palette and add the **TABS** pattern to the empty interface:

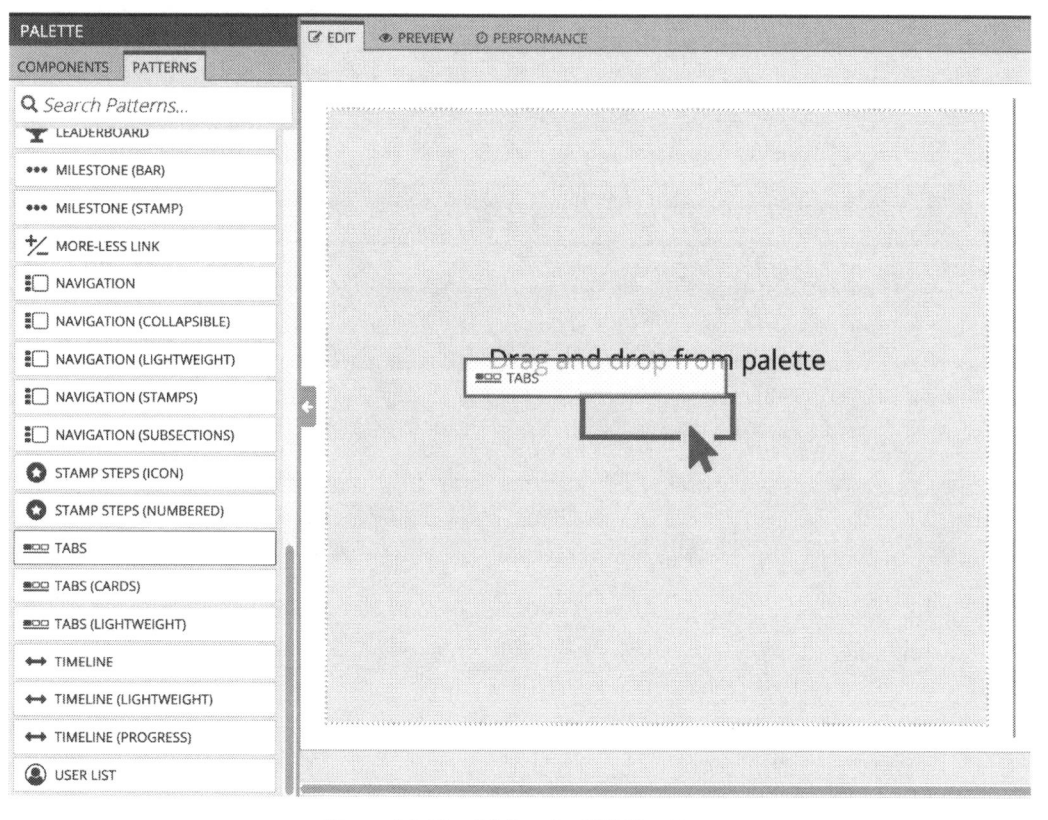

Figure 11.22 – Adding the TABS pattern

2. Then, switch to **EXPRESSION MODE**. The first few lines define a local variable and `buttonArrayLayout` containing a list of buttons:

```
{
  a!localVariables(
    local!selectedTab: 1,
    {
      a!buttonArrayLayout(
```

```
buttons: {
    a!buttonWidget(
        label: "Summary",
        saveInto: if(
            local!selectedTab = 1,
            {},
            a!save(local!selectedTab, 1)
        ),
        size: "SMALL",
        width: "MINIMIZE",
        style: if(local!selectedTab = 1, "PRIMARY", "LINK")
    ),
    ....
```

3. The visual style of the buttons depends on the value of the local variable. Each button stores a number in the local variable to indicate which one is the selected one. This means that the `selectedTab` local variable stores the state of the interface.

4. A few lines later, you will find the following snippet:

```
....
choose(
  local!selectedTab,
  {
    a!richTextDisplayField(
      labelPosition: "COLLAPSED",
      value: {a!richTextItem(text: "The contents of the first
        tab would go here", style: "EMPHASIS")},
      align: "CENTER"
    )
  },
  ....
```

This is the code that uses the state to determine which part of the interface to display.

The `choose()` function takes a number and a list of expressions, and it will only evaluate the expression at the index of the number. The expressions can be simple rich text fields, as in the example. My recommendation is to create a separate interface component for each tab to reduce the complexity of the main interface.

Talking about the main interface, assuming that the main interface has a rule input of a CDT type, and you want to enter individual fields on the tabs, just pass the rule input from the main interface to the sub-interfaces using the same data type. Then, add the fields in the usual way.

You have learned that managing state is the key to dynamic interfaces and that you can pass data from the main interface to a sub-interface.

Next, we will have a look at how to create interface components.

Creating reusable interface components

In Appian, an interface is basically like any other expression, with the added benefit of the design mode in the interface designer. This also means that you can create your own reusable interfaces tailored to a specific need. Let's have a look at the interfaces we built and try to identify candidates for building an interface component.

This happens next

Create a new interface with the name `IVP_C_ThisHappensNext`. The letter *C* indicates that the purpose of this interface is for it to be used as a component inside other larger interfaces.

Add a rule input named `text` of the `text` type. Enter the following code snippet:

```
a!sectionLayout(
  label: "This Happens Next",
  labelIcon: "route",
  contents: {
    a!richTextDisplayField(
      labelPosition: "COLLAPSED",
      value: ri!text
    )
  }
)
```

From now on, use this component in interfaces instead of recreating it over and over again. Try to rework the `IVP_F_InitialVerification` and `IVP_F_CreateInvoice` interfaces.

Formatted amount field

Let's now create a field in which the user can enter an amount and get it formatted nicely. Create an interface named `IVP_C_AmountField` and add the following rule inputs:

- `label` of the `Text` type
- `value` of the `Decimal` type
- `saveInto` of the `Save multiple` type
- `required` of the `Boolean` type

The code looks pretty simple:

```
a!textField(
  label: ri!label,
  align: "RIGHT",
  value: if(isnull(ri!value), null, dollar(ri!value)),
  saveInto: a!save(
    target: ri!saveInto,
    value: todecimal(save!value)
  ),
  required: ri!required
)
```

The trick here is that the value passed in is a decimal, which is turned into a string using the `dollar()` function. As the user modifies the value, which may include that dollar character, the `todecimal()` function parses the entered value back into a decimal.

As this component does not make any assumption of where the value is stored, it can be used in place of a decimal field like this. Let's see what that looks like in `IVP_F_CreateInvoice`. The old code is shown here:

```
a!floatingPointField(
  label: "Amount",
  labelPosition: "ABOVE",
  value: ri!invoice.amount,
  saveInto: ri!invoice.amount,
  required: true
)
```

The new code is shown here:

```
rule!IVP_C_AmountField(
  label: "Amount",
  value: ri!invoice.amount,
  saveInto: ri!invoice.amount,
  required: true
)
```

The interface now displays this.

Figure 11.23 – Amount component

An important aspect of creating reusable components is to make them behave as similarly to the standard components as possible. For `AmountField`, this means to create all the rule inputs a normal `floatingPointField` has. Map these inputs to their respective parameters of `textField`. Take the `required` parameter as an example. This makes it a real drop-in replacement.

Try to start with simple reusable components. Then, with more experience and a more in-depth understanding of the Appian expression language, you will be able to implement more complex components.

In the last section, I want to share some best practices with you.

Best practices

Over the years, I've found that I spend most of my development time on refining interfaces. I would like to give you some tips to keep this time under control.

User experience

Make sure you perform at least basic UX discovery procedures before you start implementing interfaces in Appian. Investing time in UX will save you twice as much implementation time later because stakeholders will build a better understanding of each user interaction, its feasibility, and benefits earlier.

Expression mode versus design mode

Start in the design mode and draft your rough layout using column layouts:

1. Place structural elements, such as section and card layouts, to structure information. Then, add the required fields and configure them.

2. To add local variables, query data, and add logic, switch to the expression mode.

3. Use the design mode if you need to rearrange larger parts of your interface.

This is done faster in the design mode than in the expression mode.

Performance view

As soon as your interface becomes larger and you query data, keep an eye on the performance view.

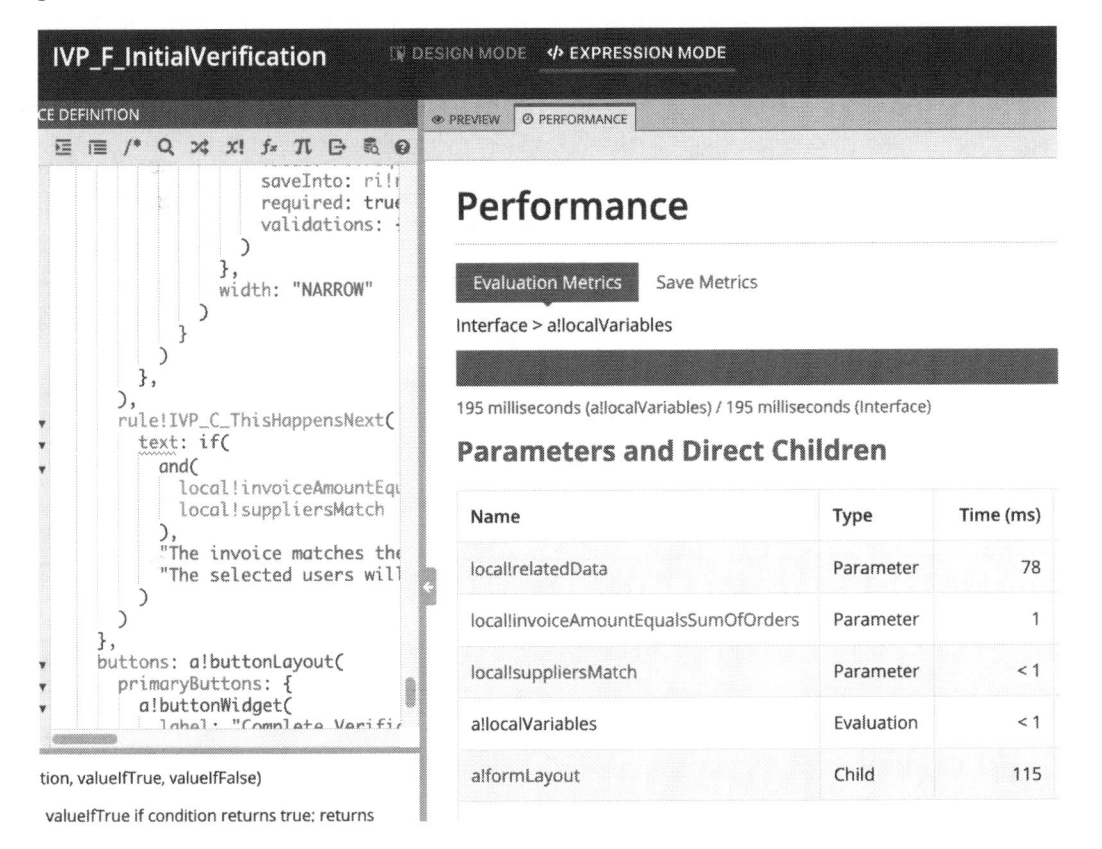

Figure 11.24 – Performance view showing evaluation time

Try to keep your interfaces below 500 milliseconds.

Variable flow

When composing an interface out of multiple reusable components, try to query and manage necessary data in the main interface and pass it to the sub-interfaces.

Every so often, this does not work, for example, when the component uses a **Record** grid. Then, make sure to not query the same data multiple times. If this is also not possible, you might have to redesign some components or create a new one specifically tailored to that use case.

Local variables

Use local variables only for state management and to query additional data. Any data entered by the user is stored in rule inputs.

Rule inputs

Use rule inputs to store data entered by the user. Store the interface state in local variables. There is one exception. By default, a user can save the draft of an interface and come back later to complete it. If you want to save the state of the interface for the user, then you need to do that in rule inputs. Any local variable will lose its value when the user navigates away.

Reusable components

Try to use the standard Appian components as much as possible. Adapt your way of designing an interface to how these components work.

Do not try to design a component for reusability in the first place. This leads you to make assumptions about how this component will be used. The risk of being wrong is extremely high, especially when just starting with Appian and regardless of your experience with other software development environments.

Debugging

While building the interface, keep testing it. Enter data into each field and check the values in the rule inputs. If you have local variables, keep an eye on their values as well.

Occasionally, you might want to implement some logic or calculations in the interface, or you might need to drill down into a nested structure. It can become a challenge to find the right place. To make that easier, add a paragraph field to the interface and define its value like this:

```
a!paragraphField(
  value: tostring(
    count(
      union(
        local!relatedData[recordType!IVP Invoice.fields.
          supplierId],
        tointeger(local!relatedData[recordType!IVP Invoice.
          relationships.OrderIds.relationships.Order.fields
          .supplierId])
      )
    ) = 1
  )
)
```

You might remember this logic from the `IVP_F_ InitialVerification` interface. Use this method to understand what the data looks like, see the results of functions, and iterate towards a working solution.

Summary

In this chapter, you learned how to build and test interfaces in Appian. You learned how to manage data in rule inputs and local variables, analyze their performance, and debug them. You created dynamic interfaces showing lists of items and understand how to show or hide components based on conditions.

Not only that, but you also know how to create your own reusable interface components and why this is sometimes a bad idea.

In the next chapter, we will discuss how to assign and manage tasks in Appian, and we will complete our invoice validation process.

12
Task Management with Appian

We use Appian to bring business process management to a file. Looking at your application, you will immediately see that the Appian process models represent the business process. But what about the management?

You will now learn how to assign tasks to groups and individuals, and how to use Appian to automate the management of your business process using escalations and exceptions.

In this chapter, we will cover the following topics:

- **Assigning tasks**: Defining the pool of users that should complete a task
- **Dynamic task assignment**: Assigning tasks based on business logic
- **Escalations and exceptions**: Managing tasks and business exceptions
- **Process reports**: Querying real-time process and task data
- **Completing the process**: Adding the final task to the invoice validation process
- **Best practices**: Considerations on task assignment

Technical requirements

- You will find the code mentioned in this chapter here: `https://github.com/PacktPublishing/Low-Code-Application-Development-with-Appian`.

Assigning tasks

In *Chapter 7, Understanding Business Processes in Appian Projects* in the *Task-driven processes* section, I claimed, *"No task, no work!"*

This means that we have to assign concrete tasks to people so that they have something to do. But this does not mean reducing people to brainless robots. In the end, the intellectual challenge lies more in completing a specific task than in knowing what to do next.

Let's have a look at the details of how task assignment in Appian works.

In the **IVP Create New Invoice** process model, you already added the **Initial Verification** User Input Task activity and assigned it to the **IVP Users** group:

1. Open the properties dialog of that node in the model:

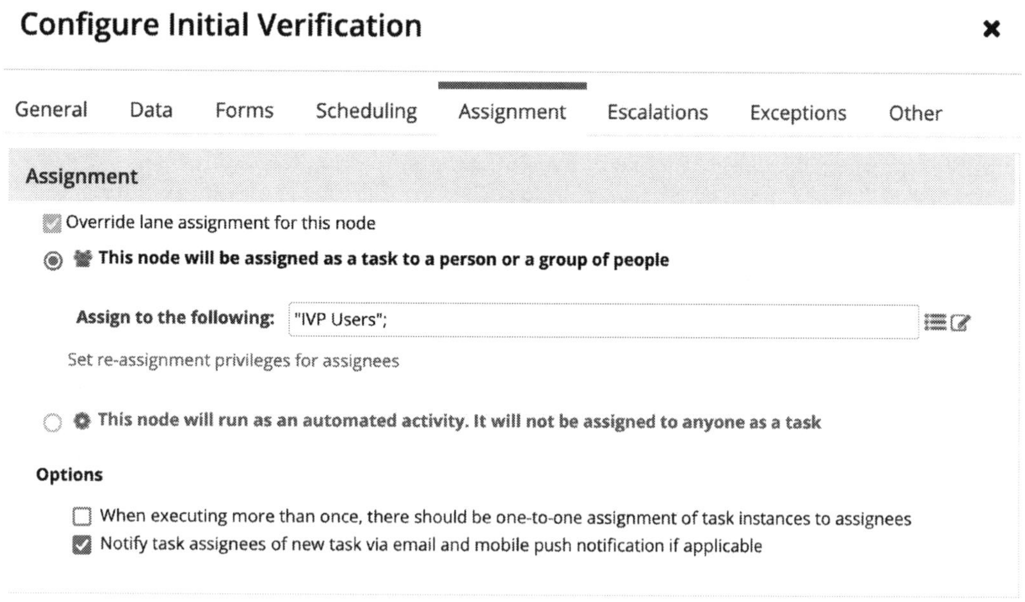

Configure Initial Verification   ✖

General   Data   Forms   Scheduling   **Assignment**   Escalations   Exceptions   Other

Assignment

☑ Override lane assignment for this node
◉ 👥 **This node will be assigned as a task to a person or a group of people**

      Assign to the following: "IVP Users";   ☰ ✎

     Set re-assignment privileges for assignees

○ ⚙ **This node will run as an automated activity. It will not be assigned to anyone as a task**

Options

    ☐ When executing more than once, there should be one-to-one assignment of task instances to assignees
    ☑ Notify task assignees of new task via email and mobile push notification if applicable

Figure 12.1 – The assignment of the Initial Verification task

The configured behavior allows any member of the **IVP Users** group to accept and then complete the task. By accepting a task, the user takes over responsibility for the outcome of that specific task. Typically, this user will then complete the task. If the user accepted a task mistakenly, they can then return the task to the original assignees.

2. Next, let us have a look at this simple task status diagram as explained previously:

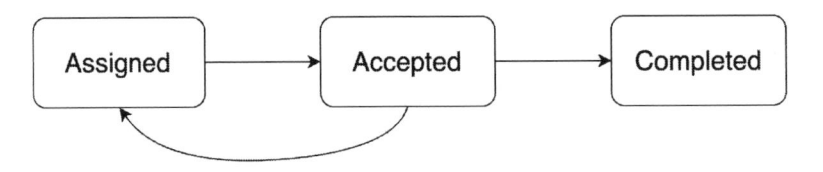

Figure 12.2 – The task status diagram

But that's not the end of it. Appian adds more interesting features to the topic of task assignment.

Reassignment behavior

After you have accepted a task, you can reject or reassign it.

Rejecting a task means that you have actively chosen not to do it. You are then removed from the list of assignees and any other assignee can accept the task.

If you think that someone else was a better fit for a given task, you can reassign an accepted task to other users. Then, the users or groups you selected define the new pool of assignees.

> **Important Note**
> A task describes a concrete activity. If a user is unable to complete this task due to incorrect or missing information, reassigning this task to another user will usually not solve the problem. Help the user by implementing an alternative flow that allows them to request support. Assign a task to users who can give that support, and then return to the first user to enable them to complete the original task.

Re-assignment privileges

Open **Re-assignment privileges** to control which functionality is available to each group of assignees:

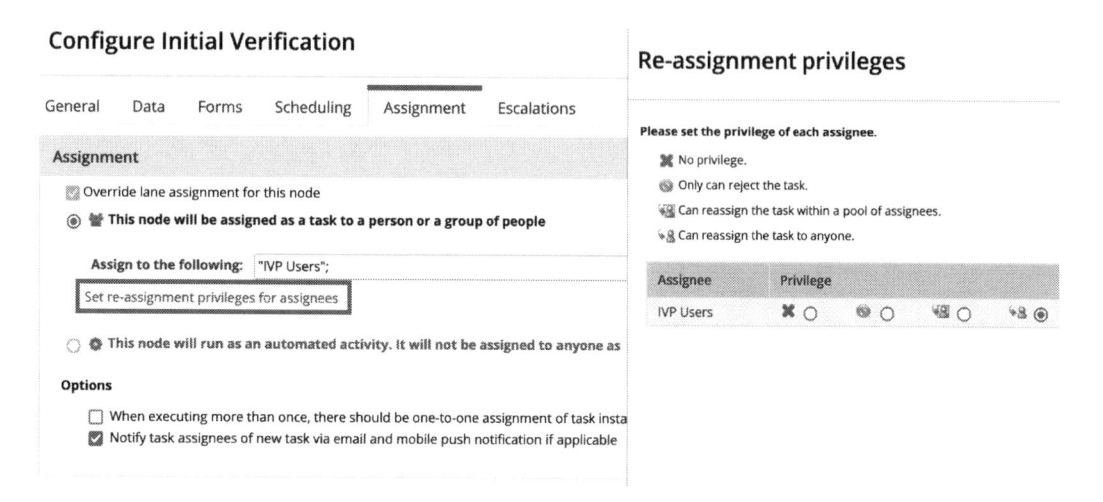

Figure 12.3 – Re-assignment privileges

- **No privilege**: Once a user had accepted a task, they must complete it.

- **Only can reject the task**: This can be used to allow a user to communicate that they are the wrong person for this specific task.

- **Can reassign the task within a pool of assignees**: A user trying to reassign a task is restricted to the users and groups currently in the pool of assignees.

- **Can reassign the task to anyone**: A user may reassign a task to any Appian user. It is possible to restrict visibility between users so that *any user* actually means instead *visible users*. I do not cover user-to-user visibility in this book.

Process model security and reassignment

The previously described behavior can be overruled by the configuration of the process model security roles. In the Process Modeler, open the **Security** dialog from the **File** menu:

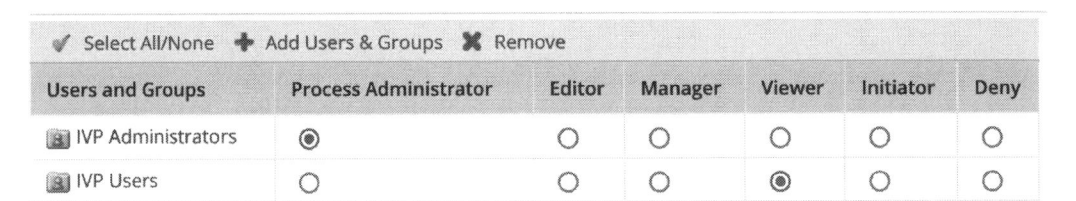

Process Model Security for: IVP Create Case ✖

Users and Groups	Process Administrator	Editor	Manager	Viewer	Initiator	Deny
IVP Administrators	◉	○	○	○	○	○
IVP Users	○	○	○	◉	○	○

Figure 12.4 – Process model security

- When we talk about reassignment, the difference between the **Viewer** role and the **Manager** role is especially important for us.

- A user in the **Viewer** role can only reassign tasks assigned to them. Use **Re-assignment privileges** to restrict permissions.

- A user in the **Manager** role may reassign any task in that process, ignoring **Re-assignment privileges**. Use this role to allow a team or department manager to manage task assignments.

> **Appian Documentation**
>
> You can find more details in the Appian documentation: `https://docs.appian.com/suite/help/latest/process-model-object.html#process-model-security`.

That's all the secrets of task assignment. Now, let's see how to make that more dynamic.

Dynamic task assignment

When closely looking at the **Assign to the following** field in the node properties dialog, you will see that you can define the field value using expressions by clicking the small editor icon:

☑ Override lane assignment for this node

◉ 👥 **This node will be assigned as a task to a person or a group of people**

Assign to the following: "IVP Users";

Set re-assignment privileges for assignees

Figure 12.5 – The assignment field and expressions

> **Attention**
>
> Any value or expression you enter in the editor will always be appended to the list of existing values in that field. This can be confusing and lead to unexpected behavior. Clear the field before opening the editor and make sure that the content of the field matches your expectations.

We will now discuss two examples and then use one of them to extend our invoice validation process.

Assigning tasks using process variables

Appian identifies a user by its login name and a group by its numeric ID. You already do that in the **owner** field in the IVP Case CDT. To store a group, you would use a field of the `integer` type.

To assign a task to the owner of a case, you enter the following code in the expression editor of the **Assign to the following** field:

```
touser(pv!case.owner)
```

The `touser()` function converts the text stored in the owner field into a value of type user. If you want to assign a group, stored as an integer in a CDT, use the `togroup()` function. And there is even a special data type in Appian that can store a user, or a group called `people`. Use the `topeople()` function to convert the user's login name or a group's ID. All these types can be made multiple according to the conversion functions handle lists.

As constants can also store references to groups, you can combine them to create a list of the following:

- A group constant
- A user stored in a CDT
- The person who started the process:

```
topeople(
  {
    cons!XYZ_GROUP_USERS,
    pv!cdtData.user,
    pp!initiator
  }
)
```

Data from the `Process Variables (PV)` and `Process Properties (PP)` domains are only available inside a process model. Using `pp!`, you have access to properties such as the process initiator or the process start time.

Please visit the Appian documentation for more details about domains:

- `https://docs.appian.com/suite/help/21.4/domain_prefixes.html`

- `https://docs.appian.com/suite/help/21.4/Process_and_Report_Data.html`

Since this is still not very dynamic, I will now show you how to add business logic for more flexibility.

Assigning tasks using decision tables

A decision table is a simple way to express low-to-medium complexity business logic. In our example, we want to assign a task to two different groups, depending on the amount of the invoice.

Follow these steps:

1. Create the **IVP Validators Low** group, setting the group type to **Custom**, visibility to **Public**, and privacy to **Low**.

2. Create the **IVP Validators High** group, setting the group type to **Custom**, visibility to **Public**, and privacy to **Low**.

3. Add both new groups as members to the **IVP Users** group.

4. Create the **IVP_DetermineAssigneeForInitialValidation** decision:

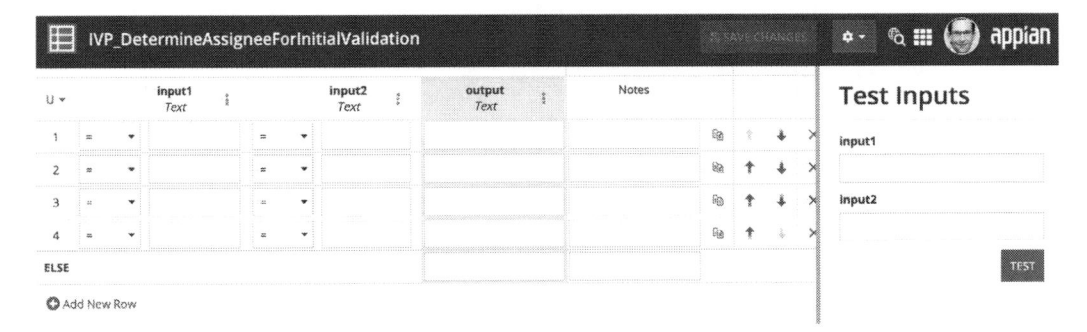

Figure 12.6 – The initial view of the decision

5. Modify **output** by clicking the three-dots menu in the column. Rename it `assignee` and change the type to a single group.

6. Delete **input2**.

7. Rename **input1** `amount` and change the type to decimal.

8. Configure the first two rows to look like this:

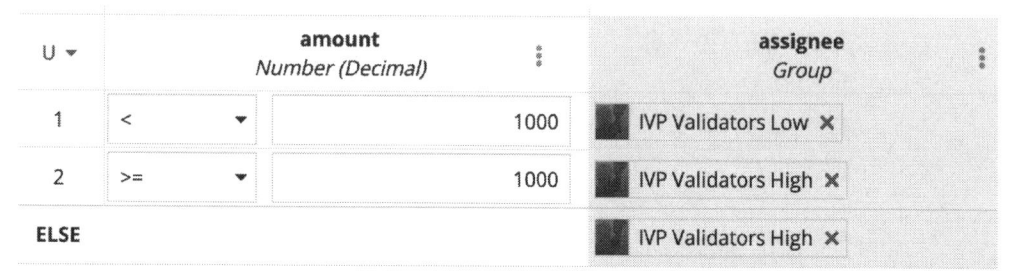

Figure 12.7 – Configure the first two rows

9. Enter some values below and above **1000** in the **Test Inputs** panel to validate the logic.

10. Save your changes.

With the decision created, go back to the Process Modeler and open the node properties of the user input task. Then, navigate to the **Assignment** tab, clear the **Assign to the following** field and, enter the following code in the assignment field expression editor:

```
rule!IVP_DetermineAssigneeForInitialValidation(
   amount: pv!invoice.amount
)
```

Then, save and publish the modified model.

Now, you will want to test this modification. The way we've done it so far is getting a little elaborate. To make it easier, we will add a record action to the IVP Case record. Then, we can easily start it from our Appian site. This is just a few simple steps away:

1. Open the IVP Case record, navigate to **Record Actions**, and click **Configure a record action manually**:

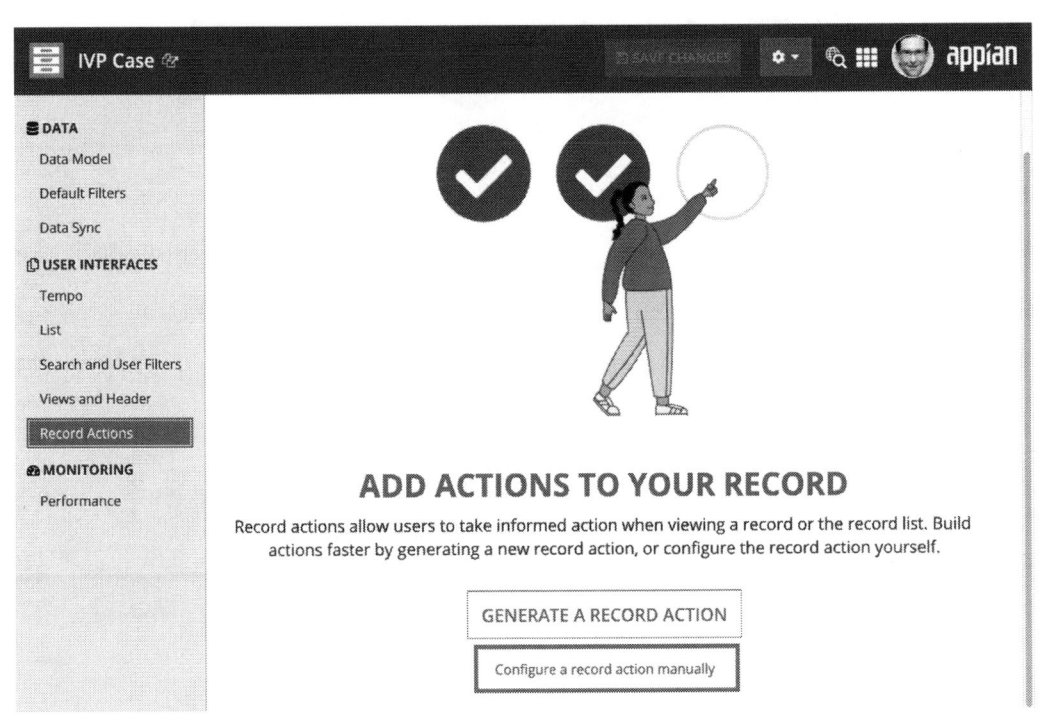

Figure 12.8 – Manual record action configuration

2. Under **Record List Actions** at the top of the screen, click the **CONFIGURE NEW ACTION MANUALLY** button.

3. Configure the action as shown in the following screenshot. It is important to select the **IVP Create New Invoice** process model, as this is the one that eventually creates a new case:

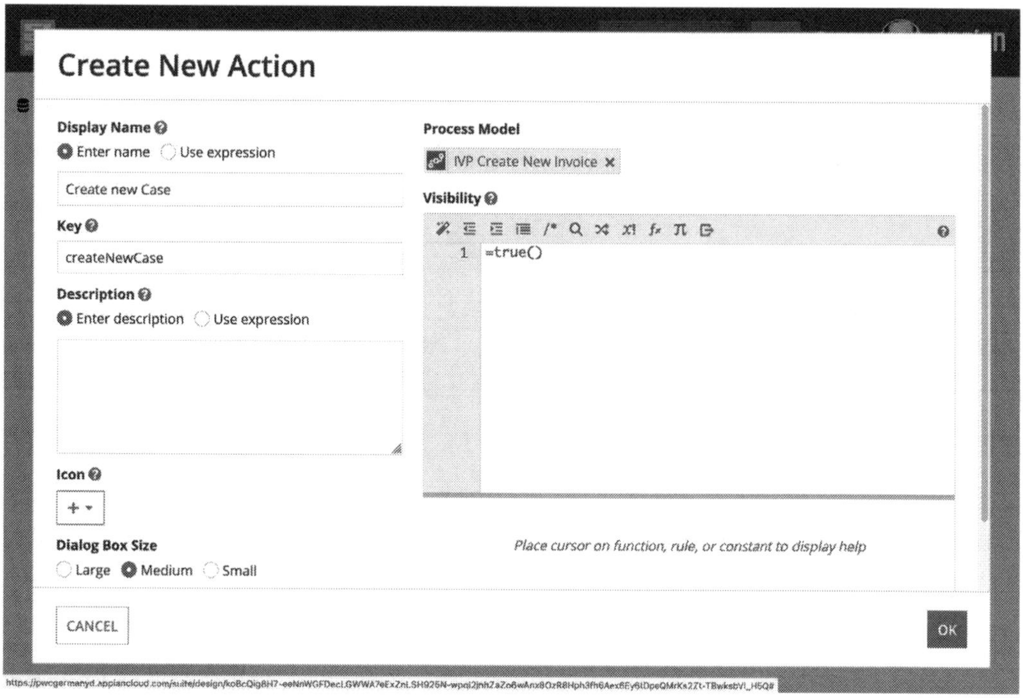

Figure 12.9 – Configure a new action

4. Click **OK** and then **SAVE CHANGES**.

Now, open the site from the waffle menu and initiate a few new processes with values above and below the threshold. To see what is going on, go to process monitoring and open an active instance. In the **Current Tasks** tab in **Process Details**, you will see the variations in the assignment:

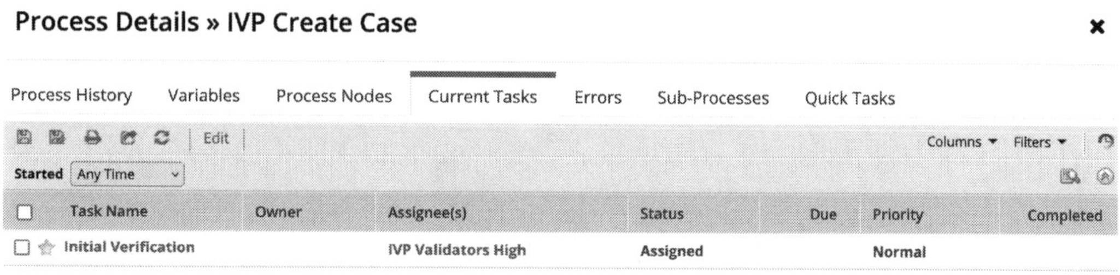

Figure 12.10 – The current task's in-process monitoring

Let's wrap this up. When assigning a task, you need to provide one or more users or groups, and it does not matter how you create that list. Some examples of what I have seen are as follows:

- A web service call to the HR system to get the supervisor.

- Dynamic assignment to teams based on the current workload.

- For multi-stage approval, create an initial list of assignees, and then remove the approver from that list for the next stage. This way, an individual cannot approve all stages.

When you assign a task, you should have an idea of when it should be completed and what to do if this is compromised. Let's dive into that in the next section.

Escalations and exceptions

Let's quickly revisit our business process diagram:

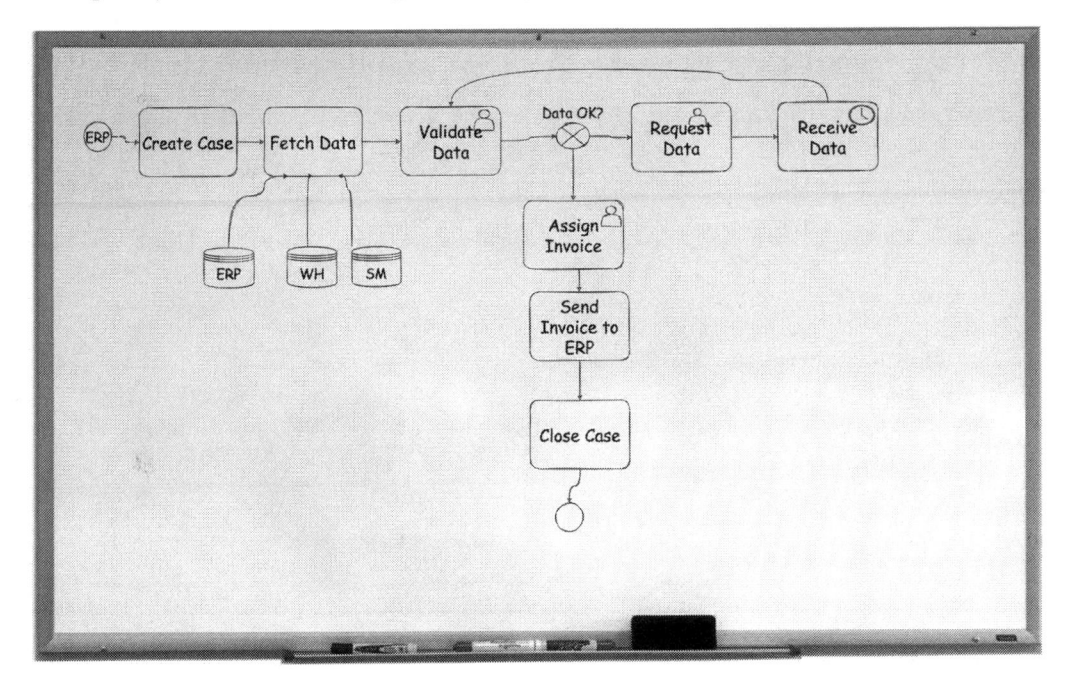

Figure 12.11 – The invoice validation process diagram

The last task interface you created is **IVP_F_InitialVerification**. You added a date picker field to allow the user to define a due date for the next task in the process. Let's complete that task and create the next one, **Receive Data**, which already has a clock symbol next to it, indicating that it should have a due date:

1. Open the **IVP Create Case** process model and open the properties dialog of the **Initial Verification** task. In the **General** tab, change the value for **Task Display Name** to the following:

```
"Verify Invoice #" & pv!invoice.number
```

This allows your users to identify a specific task by the invoice number. We will use that in the next section when discussing task reports.

2. Then, go to the **Forms** tab, which looks like this:

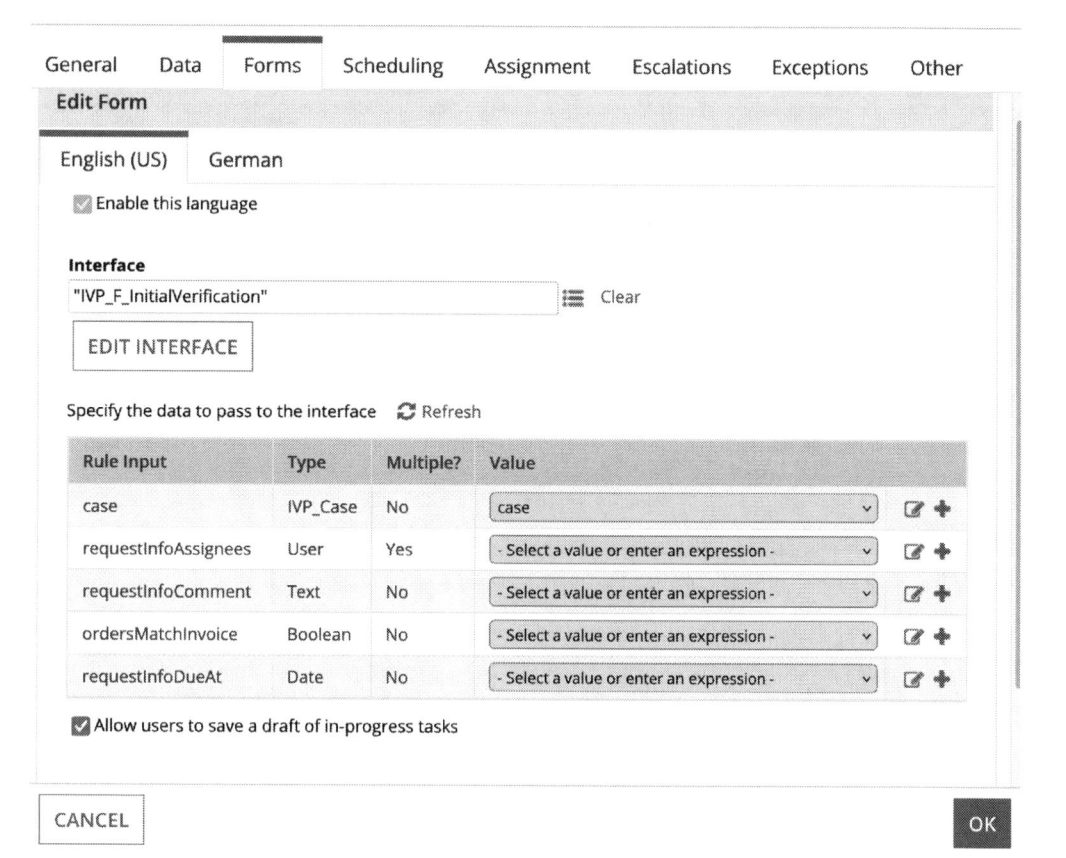

Figure 12.12 – Completing the initial verification form

3. Create a new process variable for each of the four interface rule inputs that are missing a value.

Let's now understand the steps to create missing process variables:

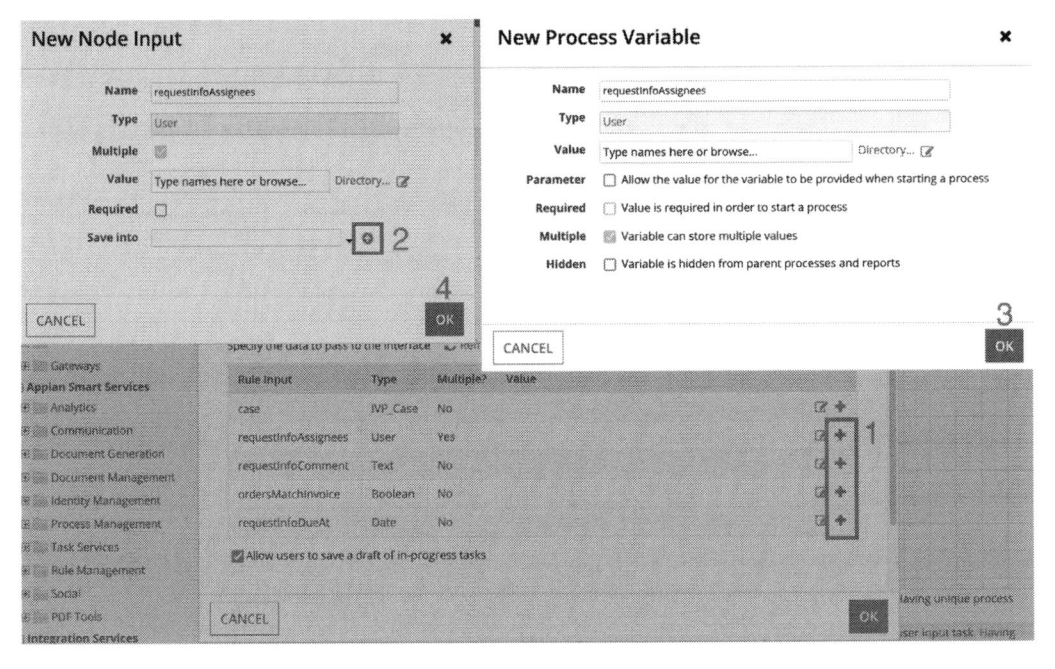

Figure 12.13 – Create missing process variables

4. Click the small + symbol at the end of the row to create a node variable. Appian suggests that the name and type should match the rule input.

5. Click + in the next dialog to create the process variable with a matching name and type.

6. Click **OK**.

7. Click **OK**.

This configuration defines that once the user has clicked the **submit** button in the interface, the values flow from the rule inputs to the node variables, and then to the process variables.

Now, we can use these variables to pass values entered by the user to the next User Input Task. Follow these steps:

1. Add an **XOR** gateway and another User Input Task to the model. Copy the node layout and connections from the screenshot:

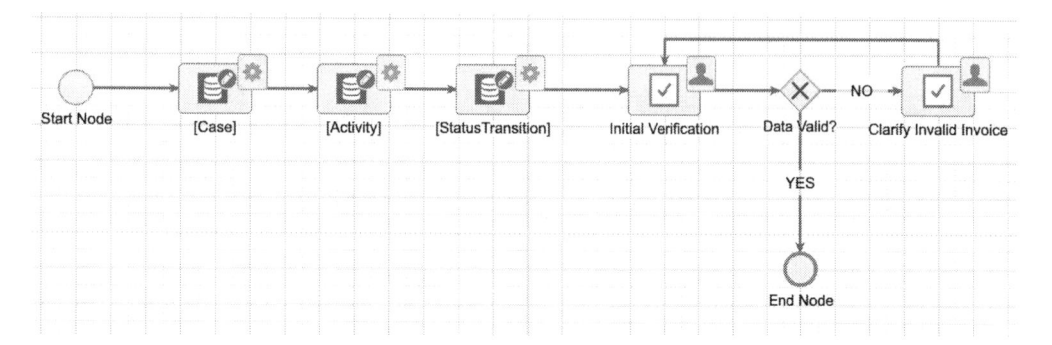

Figure 12.14 – The updated process model

2. Add a condition to the **XOR** gateway and configure the results as shown in the screenshot:

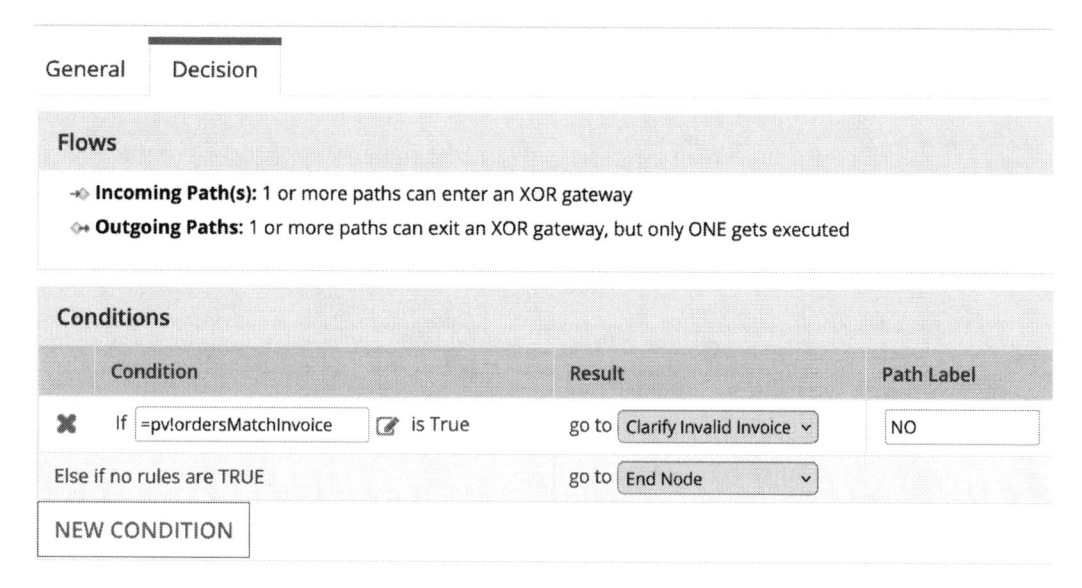

Figure 12.15 – The data valid condition

3. Change the **Task Display Name** of the User Input Task to the following:

```
="Clarify Invalid Invoice #" & pv!invoice.number
```

4. Change the assignment of the User Input Task to the following:

```
=pv!requestInfoAssignees
```

That's it. Depending on the validation logic in the verification task, the process flow goes to the **Clarify Invalid Invoice** task or **End Node**.

Escalations

But we are talking about escalations in this section, so let's add one. We already have the **requestInfoDueAt** process variable storing the due date. We can do that in two steps. First, define the due date, which in Appian is called the deadline, like this:

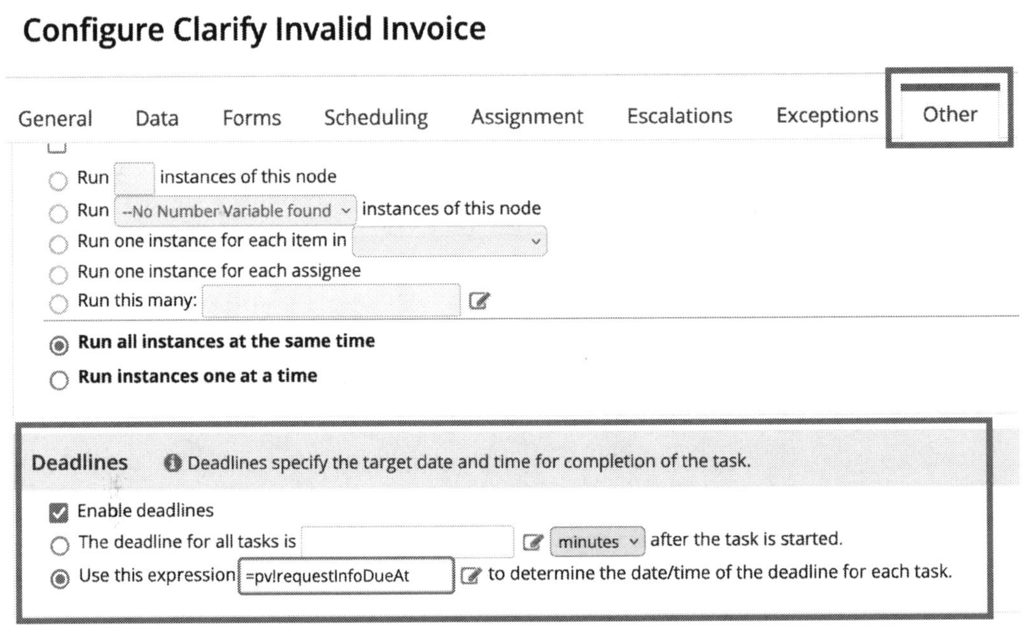

Configure Clarify Invalid Invoice

General	Data	Forms	Scheduling	Assignment	Escalations	Exceptions	Other

○ Run ___ instances of this node

○ Run --No Number Variable found ∨ instances of this node

○ Run one instance for each item in ___ ∨

○ Run one instance for each assignee

○ Run this many: ___ ☑

◉ **Run all instances at the same time**

○ **Run instances one at a time**

Deadlines   ❶ Deadlines specify the target date and time for completion of the task.

☑ Enable deadlines

○ The deadline for all tasks is ___ ☑ minutes ∨ after the task is started.

◉ Use this expression =pv!requestInfoDueAt ☑ to determine the date/time of the deadline for each task.

Figure 12.16 – Configure the task deadline

Next, on the **Escalations** tab, configure a new escalation:

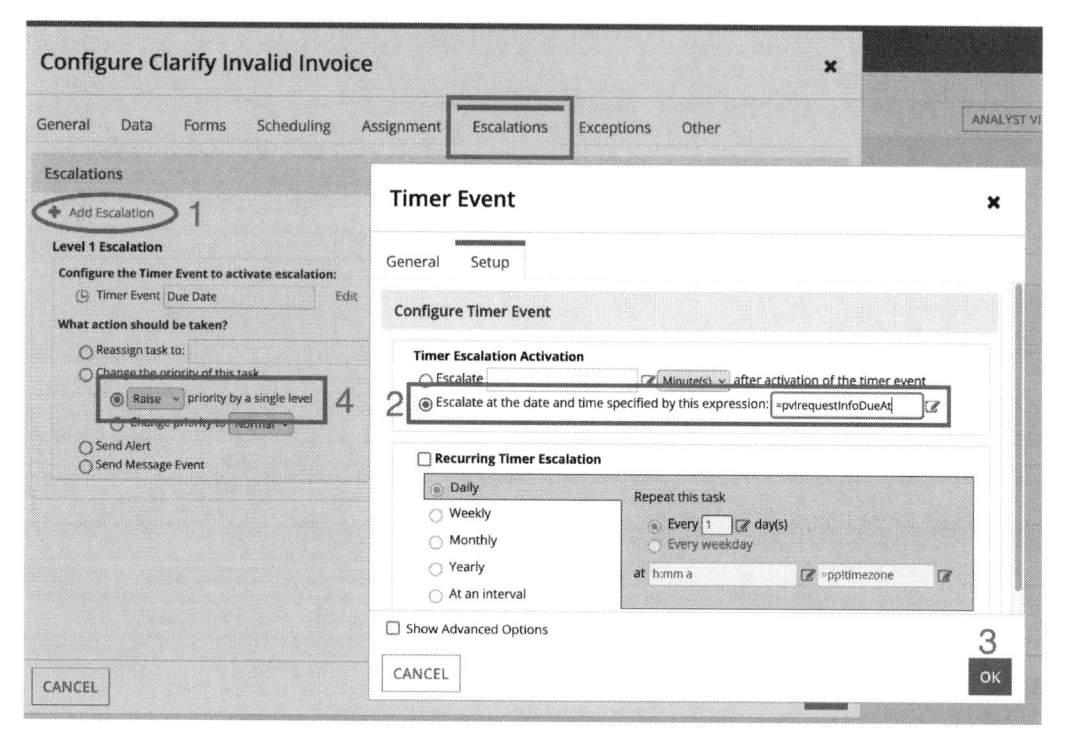

Figure 12.17 – Configure new escalation

1. Click **Add Escalation**.
2. Use the **requestInfoDueAt** process variable as **Timer Escalation Activation**.
3. Click **OK**.
4. Select **Raise priority by a single level** for **What action should be taken?**.

This escalation will increase the priority, but we also want to send a notification to the assigned users to make them aware that this task is waiting to be completed. Add a second escalation, with the same timer configuration as the first one:

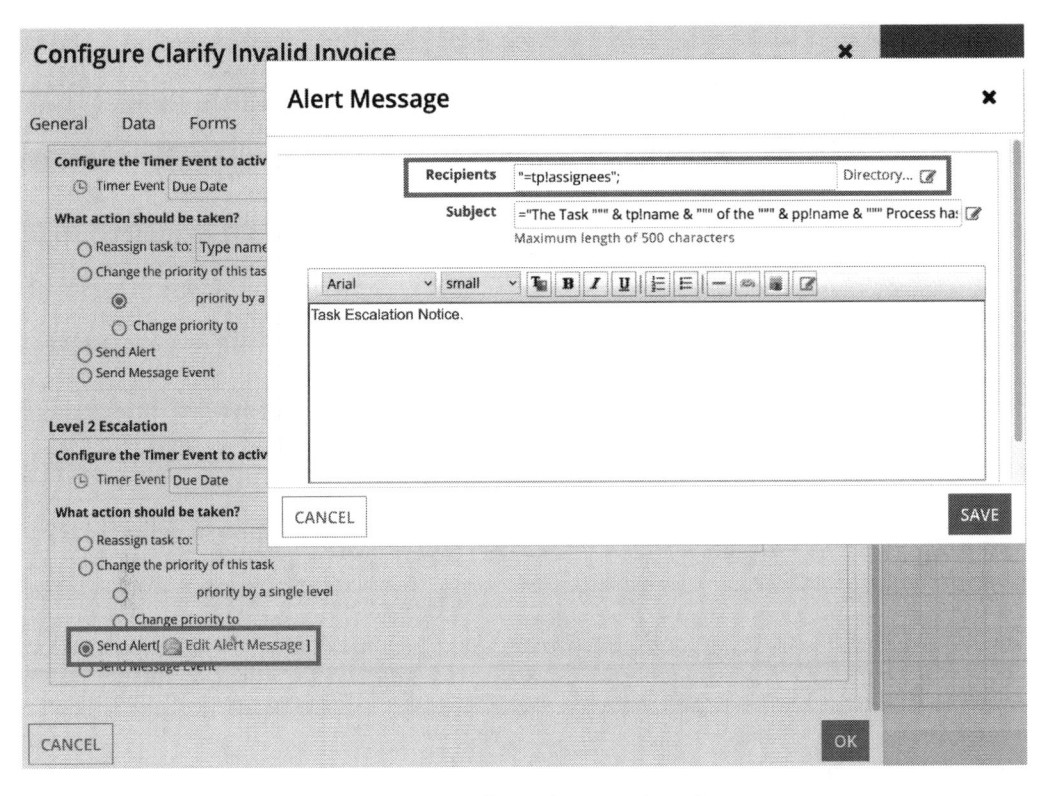

Figure 12.18 – Configure the second escalation

Then, configure **Send Alert** instead of configuring **Change Priority**, as shown in the screenshot.

This is a basic configuration that you should do for most user input tasks.

You can implement interesting things using escalations – for example, you want to prevent users from accepting tasks but then not completing them. Configure an escalation with a recurring timer set to 1 hour. Make sure to set the initial timer to the same interval. The recurring timer will only start after the initial one:

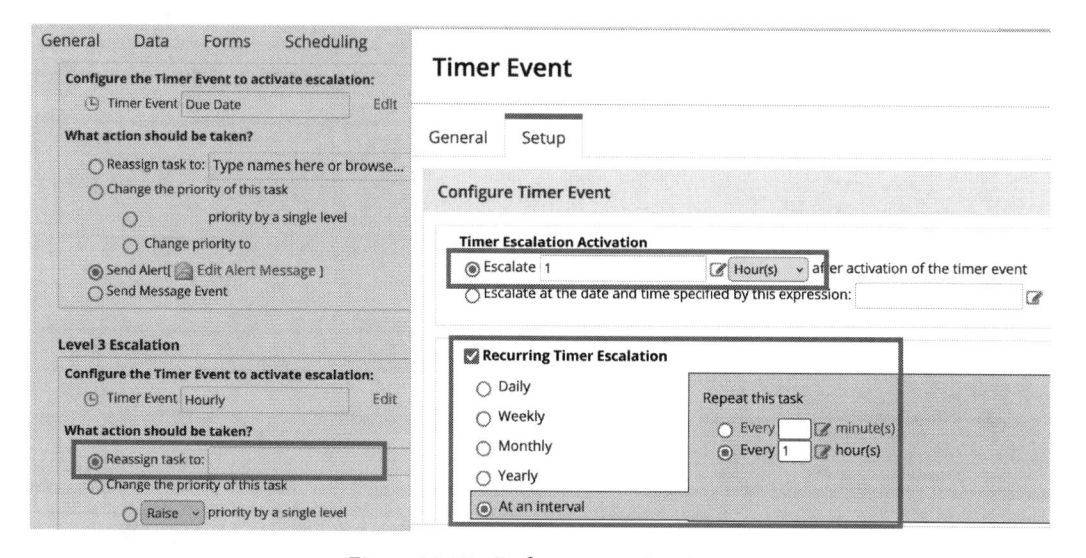

Figure 12.19 – Define a recurring timer

Now, the task will be reassigned to the initial pool of assignees every hour, and no user can pile up tasks.

Exceptions

The noun **exception** has a different meaning in Appian than you might be used to. In commonly used programming, an exception indicates a technical error condition. In Appian, an exception does not handle any technical hiccups but is instead used to define an alternative process flow as an exception to the default flow.

To give you a better understanding of what this means, let me give you an example.

Imagine a process where the demands for completing a task are very high. What do you do when a task takes longer? One way to handle this might be to send the waiting customer an email apologizing and saying that it's taking a little longer than promised. Then, you assign a task to a supervisor to manage this escalation. This task allows them to complete the task with more authority:

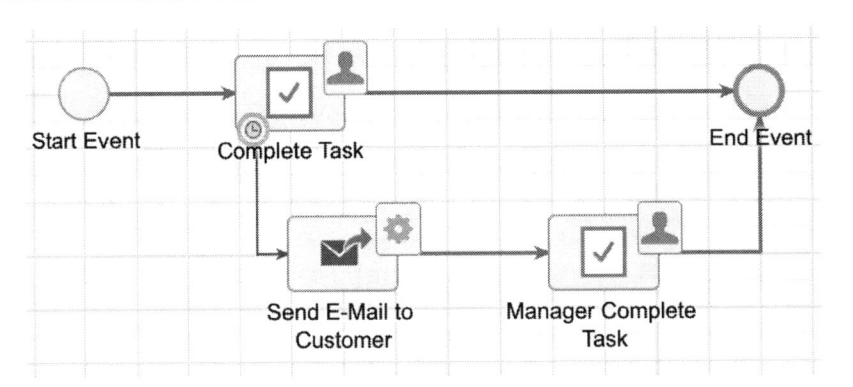

Figure 12.20 – An example exception flow

> **Technical Exceptions**
>
> When a technical exception occurs in an Appian process, the process is stopped and the users defined in the alert settings receive an email notification. They investigate and resolve the underlying problem and restart the failed node. This is the default behavior of Appian and is good enough for almost all situations – at least as far as the scope of this book is concerned.

Escalations and exceptions sare a great way to automate the management of a process. The idea is to free people from having to look for work in a system. With smart process design in Appian, our application can automatically bring people in when needed. Appian comes with everything needed to do this – even when things go wrong.

The application is capable of assigning work to people and sending notifications. Now, we will take a look at how to make that list of tasks tangible.

Process reports

In Appian, processes are running inside an in-memory high-performance transaction management system. Metadata of running processes and tasks is made available by the **Process Analytics** component in real time. Think of it as a database that you can use to query data about processes and tasks.

I will now show you how to create a process report that shows the tasks assigned to a user. Then, we will create an interface to make this data visible.

Creating a process report

Appian includes a selection of ready-made process report templates. Never change these templates, but create a copy. Then, modify this copy to fit your requirements.

To get started, use the **Tasks for User** template to create the new **IVP Tasks for User** process report. Store the new report in the IVP Artifacts folder:

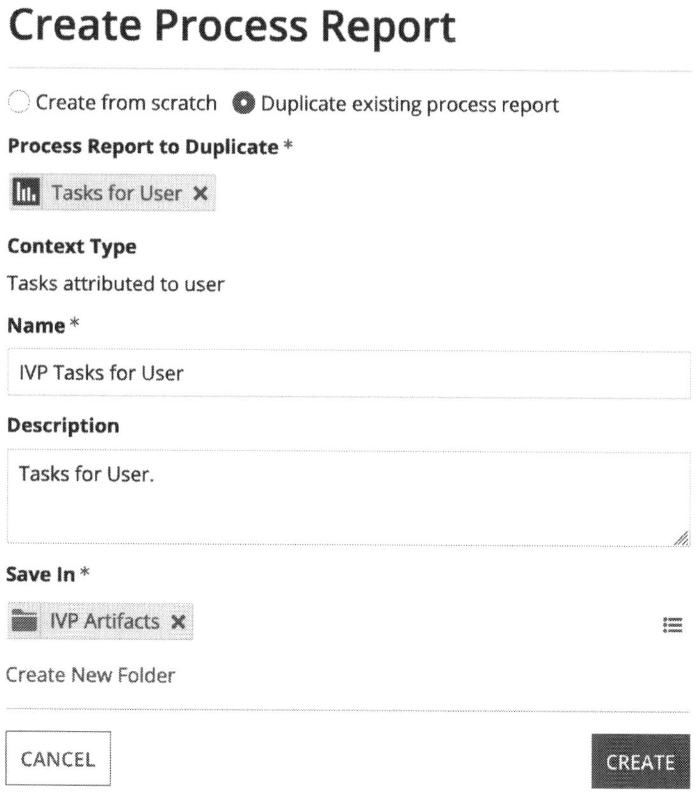

Create Process Report

○ Create from scratch   ● Duplicate existing process report

Process Report to Duplicate *

▮ Tasks for User ✕

Context Type

Tasks attributed to user

Name *

> IVP Tasks for User

Description

> Tasks for User.

Save In *

📁 IVP Artifacts ✕   ☰

Create New Folder

CANCEL   CREATE

Figure 12.21 – Create a process report

Appian will not directly open the **Process Report Designer**, so click the name to open it. You will now see the report, showing some tasks. In case you do not see any tasks, make sure to start a few **Invoice Validation** processes.

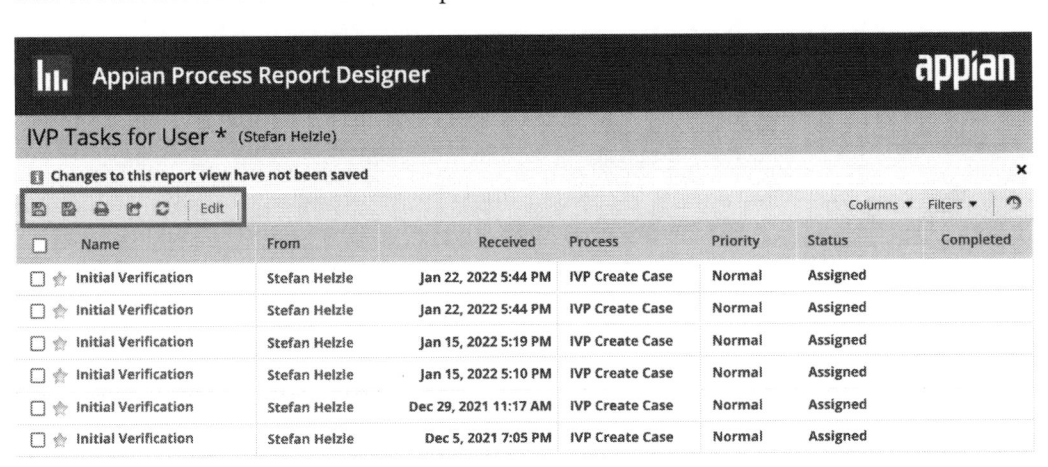

Figure 12.22 – The process report showing tasks

While most data is already there, the due date is missing. Add it by following these steps:

1. Click **Edit** in the highlighted menu bar.

2. On the **Filters** tab, click **Active** in **Default Filters**. We are only interested in tasks that still need to be done.

3. On the **Data** tab, click **+ New Data**, and type `Due Date` for the name and `=tp!deadline` for the definition:

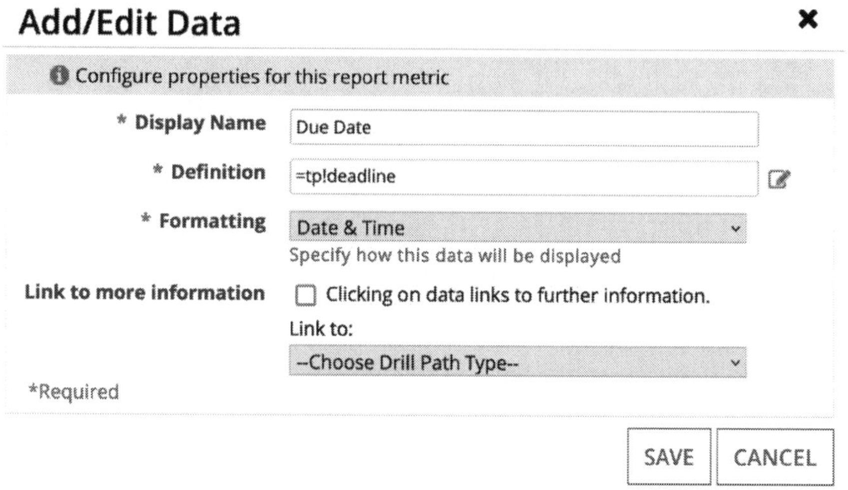

Add/Edit Data   ✖

ⓘ Configure properties for this report metric

* **Display Name**	Due Date
* **Definition**	=tp!deadline ▣
* **Formatting**	Date & Time ⌄
	Specify how this data will be displayed
Link to more information	☐ Clicking on data links to further information.
	Link to:
	--Choose Drill Path Type-- ⌄

*Required

SAVE   CANCEL

Figure 12.23 – Adding the Due Date column

4. Click the left-most floppy disk icon to save your changes.

We are only scratching the surface here. In the next chapter, I will show you how to do real-time visual reporting using **process reports**.

In the next section, we will make the report visible to our users.

Display a process report

I will now walk you through adding a grid component to a new interface and configuring it to show the new process report:

1. Create a new **IVP_REPORT_TASKS_FOR_USER** constant of the **Document** type pointing to the **IVP Tasks for User** document.

2. Create the new **IVPDTasksForUser** interface.

3. Add a **READ-ONLY GRID** component to the canvas:

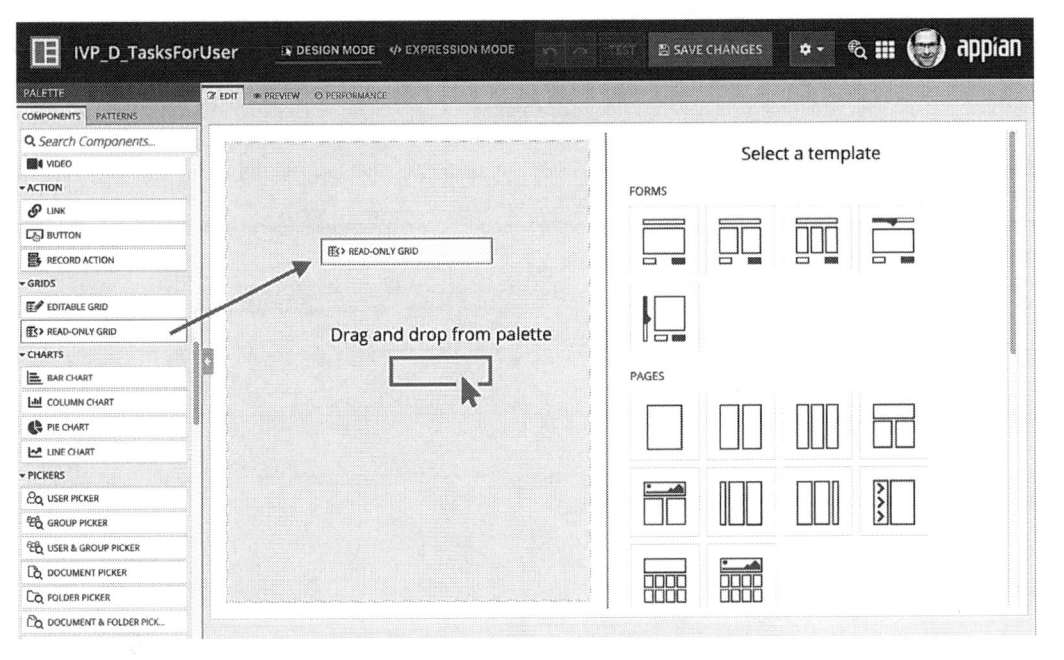

Figure 12.24 – Adding a read-only grid

4. In the right-hand **COMPONENT CONFIGURATION** panel, click **EXPRESSION** and **Edit**.

5. Enter the following code snippet:

```
a!queryProcessAnalytics(
  report: cons!IVP_REPORT_TASKS_FOR_USER,
  query: a!query(
    paginginfo: fv!pagingInfo
  )
)
```

6.   The grid will now show a list of tasks similar to this screenshot:

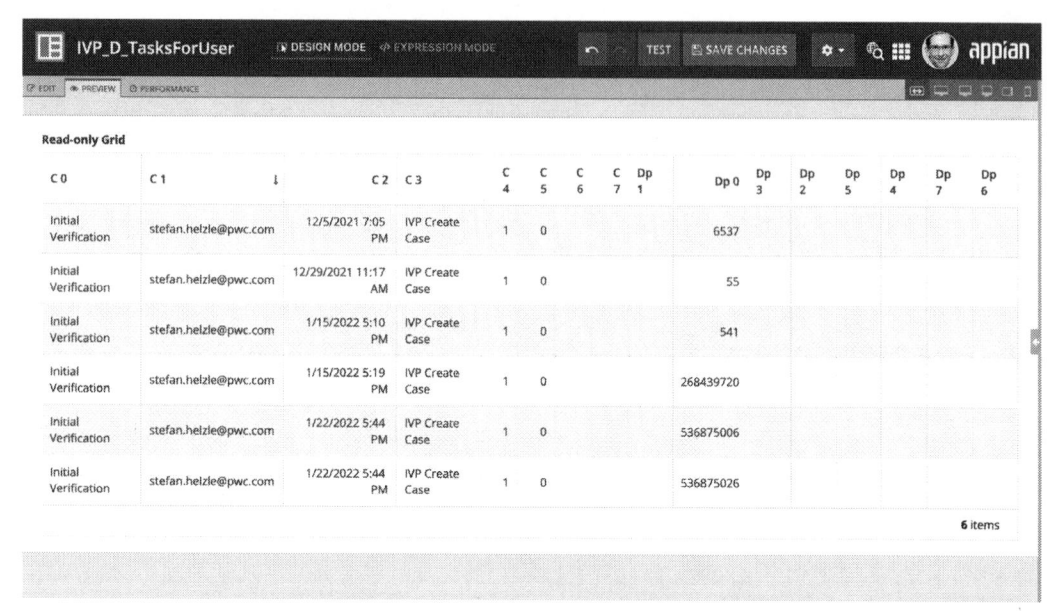

Figure 12.25 – The grid showing tasks

7.   Click the **X** icon in the hovering menu to remove all the columns starting with **Dp**, as well as the **C6** column:

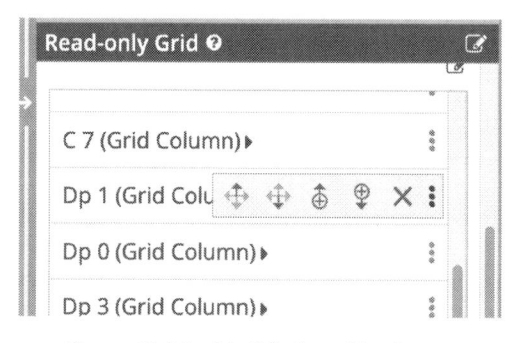

Figure 12.26 – Modify the grid columns

8.   Click the editor icon on each of the columns and change the names according to the names in the process report:

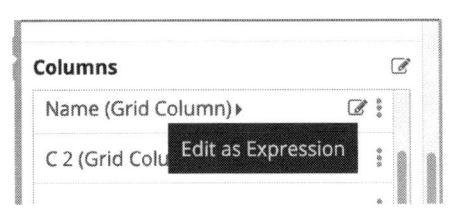

Figure 12.27 – Modify a column

9. The first column should be a link to the task. To make this work, change the column like this:

```
a!gridColumn(
  label: "Name",
  sortField: "c0",
  value: a!richTextDisplayField(
    value: a!richTextItem(
      text: fv!row.c0,
      link: a!processTaskLink(
        task: fv!row.dp0
      )
    )
  )
),
```

10. Change the label position to Hidden.

To make this task list visible to the user, add it as a new page to the existing site:

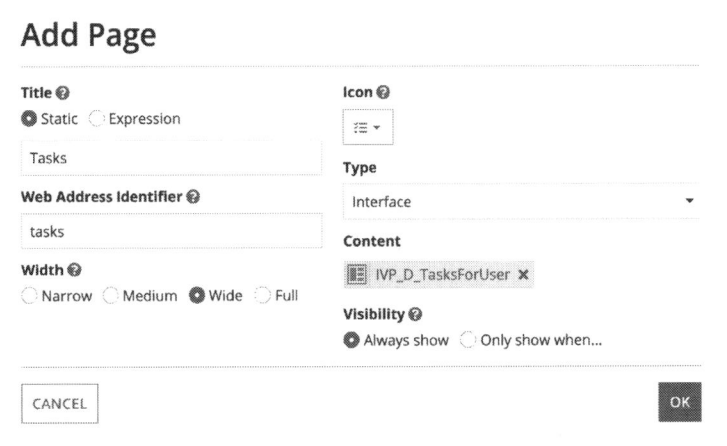

Figure 12.28 – Adding the task list to the site

The user interface for your application users should now look like this:

Name	From	↓ Received	Process
Initial Verification	stefan.helzle@pwc.com	1/22/2022 5:44 PM	IVP Create Case
Initial Verification	stefan.helzle@pwc.com	1/22/2022 5:44 PM	IVP Create Case
Initial Verification	stefan.helzle@pwc.com	1/15/2022 5:19 PM	IVP Create Case
Initial Verification	stefan.helzle@pwc.com	1/15/2022 5:10 PM	IVP Create Case
Initial Verification	stefan.helzle@pwc.com	12/29/2021 11:17 AM	IVP Create Case
Initial Verification	stefan.helzle@pwc.com	12/5/2021 7:05 PM	IVP Create Case

Figure 12.29 – The site with the new TASKS tab

Clicking the name of a task will directly open the task form. With the user interface taking shape, it's now time to complete our invoice validation process.

Completing the process

At this point in the book, you have all the necessary basics to complete a business process. You know about records, processes, interfaces, and the other small pieces to turn that into an application. Let's now identify and create the missing parts.

Currently, your Appian process model should look like this:

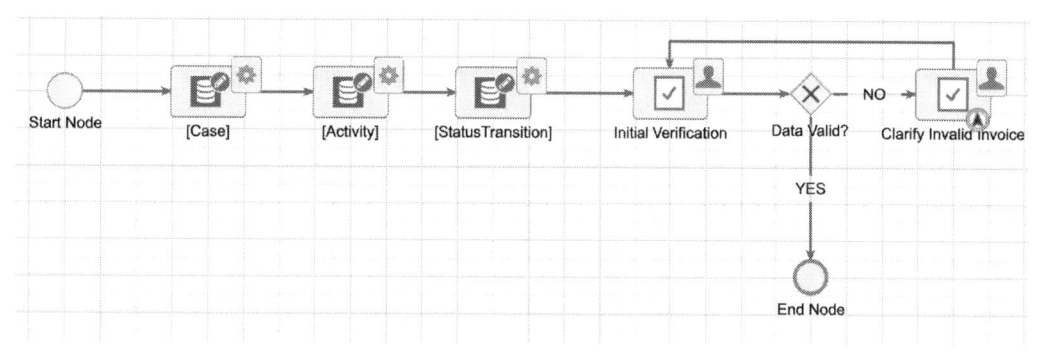

Figure 12.30 – The Appian process model

Your business process model should look like this:

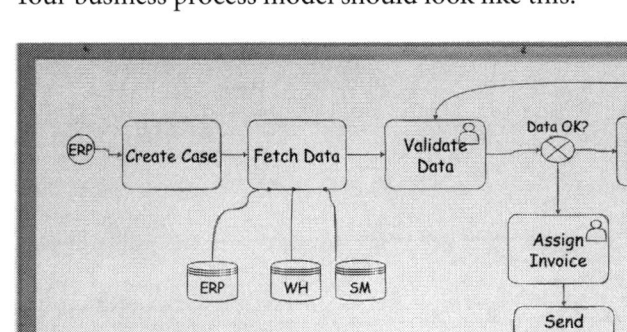

Figure 12.31 – The invoice validation process diagram

The missing parts are as follows:

- An interface for **Clarify Invalid Invoice**
- Modification of the **Initial Verification**
- A task and interface for **Assign Invoice**
- Logic to finalize the invoice and the case

Let's understand each in detail.

An interface for Clarify Invalid Invoice

Let's think briefly about the tools that we need to provide to a user to resolve the discrepancy between the orders and the invoice. We will focus on two options.

The first option allows the user to simply accept the deviation of the amount. Such a deviation may occur in the case of a discount granted by the supplier.

The second option allows the user to adjust the amount of the invoice to the sum of orders.

This is probably a gross oversimplification of the real complexity, but it helps us not to go beyond the scope of this book. After working through the last chapter, you should know enough about Appian to modify this basic application and add more complex behavior yourself.

I will walk you through these steps:

1. Create a new interface, duplicating the existing **IVP_F_InitialVerification** interface.

2. Modify the rule inputs to the following: **case**: IVP_Case **requestInfoReply**: Text **requestInfoComment**: Text **resolution**: Text

3. Modify the label and instructions so that they are similar to this screenshot:

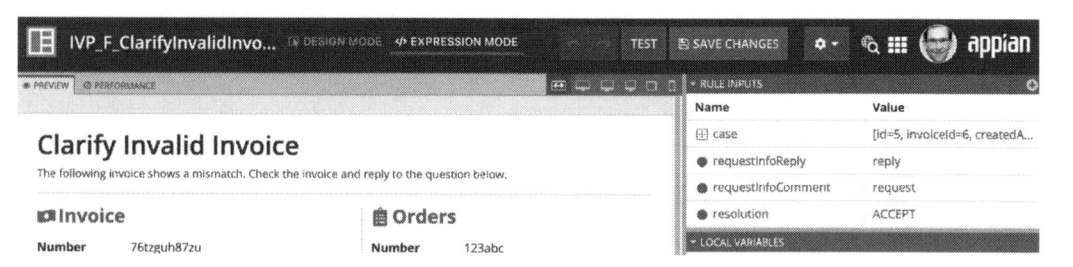

Figure 12.32 – The new interface – the upper part

4. Remove the user picker and the **Date** field from the lower part.

5. Make the existing **Paragraph** field read-only and add another **Paragraph** field assigned to the requestInfoReply rule input.

6. Create two text type constants:

   • IVP_RESOLUTION_ACCEPT with the ACCEPT value

   • IVP_RESOLUTION_ADJUST with the ADJUST value

7. Add a radio button and change the expression to this:

```
a!radioButtonField(
    label: "Resolution",
    choiceLabels: {"Accept deviation", "Adjust invoice
        to sum of orders"},
    choiceValues: {cons!IVP_RESOLUTION_ACCEPT,
        cons!IVP_RESOLUTION_ADJUST},
```

```
value: ri!resolution,
saveInto: ri!resolution,
required: true,
choiceStyle: "CARDS"
)
```

8. Remove the value and the `saveInto` parameter from the **submit** button.

9. Remove the `showWhen` parameter from the **Request Information** section.

10. Design the interface like this:

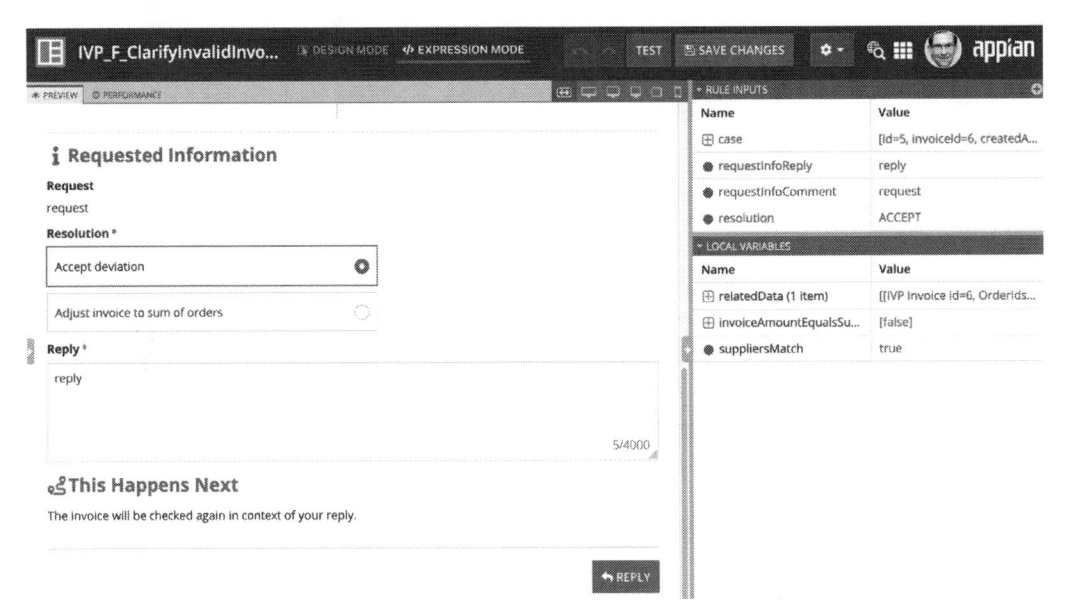

Figure 12.33 – The new interface – the lower part

11. In the process model, assign the new interface to the **Clarify Invalid Invoice** node. Let Appian create all the added rule inputs as node inputs:

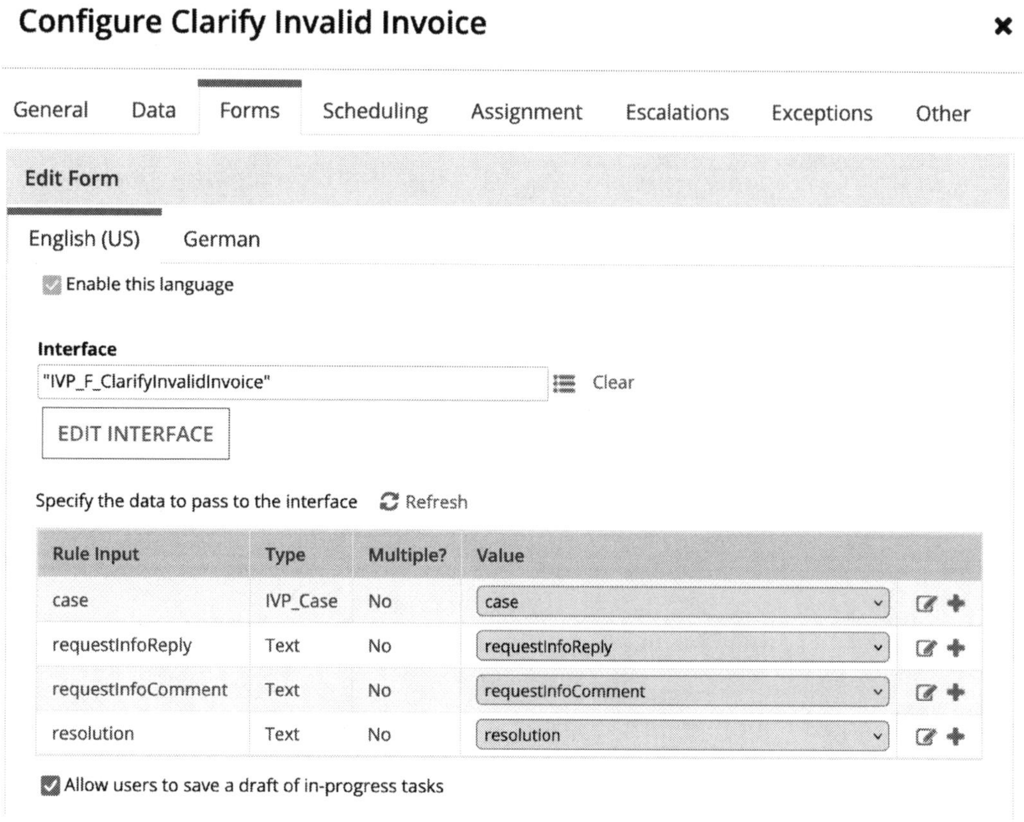

Configure Clarify Invalid Invoice   ✖

| General | Data | Forms | Scheduling | Assignment | Escalations | Exceptions | Other |

Edit Form

English (US)   German

☑ Enable this language

Interface

"IVP_F_ClarifyInvalidInvoice"   ☰   Clear

[EDIT INTERFACE]

Specify the data to pass to the interface   ↻ Refresh

Rule Input	Type	Multiple?	Value
case	IVP_Case	No	case ∨
requestInfoReply	Text	No	requestInfoReply ∨
requestInfoComment	Text	No	requestInfoComment ∨
resolution	Text	No	resolution ∨

☑ Allow users to save a draft of in-progress tasks

Figure 12.34 – The new interface and rule inputs

12. Configure the node inputs to the following while creating new process variables as required:

- **case**: In the **Value** field, type `pv!case`, and in the **Save into** field, type `pv!case`.

- **requestInfoReply**: In the **Save into** field, type `pv!requestInfoReply`.

- **requestInfoComment**: In the **Value** field, type `pv!requestInfoComment`.

- **resolution**: In the **Save into** field, type `pv! resolution`.

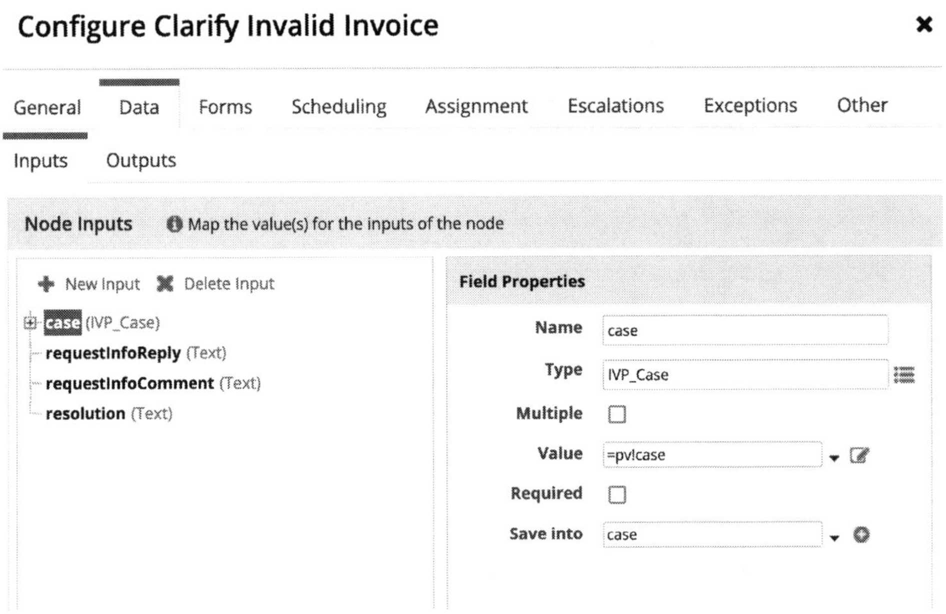

Configure Clarify Invalid Invoice   ✖

General   **Data**   Forms   Scheduling   Assignment   Escalations   Exceptions   Other

Inputs   Outputs

Node Inputs   ❶ Map the value(s) for the inputs of the node

➕ New Input   ✖ Delete Input

⊞ **case** (IVP_Case)
  requestInfoReply (Text)
  requestInfoComment (Text)
  resolution (Text)

Field Properties

Name	case
Type	IVP_Case
Multiple	☐
Value	=pv!case
Required	☐
Save into	case

Figure 12.35 – The Clarify Invalid Invoice input configuration

Again, perform some tests and check whether the interface works as expected.

Modify initial verification

You now have a loop in this process. In the **Clarify** task, the user enters some data that then flows back to the **Verify** task. However, the interface for this task cannot yet process this information. This requires a few modifications of the IVP_F_ InitialVerification interface, as explained in the following steps:

1. Add the **resolution** and **requestInfoReply** rule inputs of the text type.

2. The following code snippet defines a new section. Add it above the **Request Information** section. This section will only show up if there is a value in the **resolution** rule input. I am displaying the resolution using just the word. If you want to display it more nicely, do not hesitate to add a decision table to turn the constant values into a descriptive sentence:

```
a!sectionLayout(
   label: "Resolution",
   labelIcon: "check",
   showWhen: not(a!isNullOrEmpty(value: ri!resolution
     )),
```

```
    contents: {
      a!textField(
        label: "Resolution",
        labelPosition: "JUSTIFIED",
        value: proper(ri!resolution),
        readOnly: true
      ),
      a!paragraphField(
        label: "Comment",
        labelPosition: "COLLAPSED",
        value: ri!requestInfoReply,
        readOnly: true
      )
    }
  ),
```

3. Add another code snippet below the existing button widget. The visibility of that new button also depends on the **resolution** rule input:

```
a!buttonWidget(
  label: "Resolve Mismatch",
  icon: "check",
  submit: true,
  style: "PRIMARY",
  validate: false,
  value: true,
  saveInto: ri!ordersMatchInvoice,
  showWhen: not(a!isNullOrEmpty(value: ri!resolution
    )),
),
```

4. Modify the following parameters of the existing **Request Information** button:

```
icon: "info",
saveInto: {
  ri!ordersMatchInvoice,
  a!save(
    target: {ri!resolution, ri!requestInfoReply},
```

```
        value: null
      )
    },
    style: if(
      a!isNullOrEmpty(value: ri!resolution),
      "PRIMARY",
      "SECONDARY"
    )
```

This allows the user to accept the suggested resolution or request further information from someone else. Once accepted, we keep the proposed resolution and add some logic to implement it.

To accomplish this, we need to load the invoice data and the orders. Then, we need to modify the invoice amount to the calculated sum of the orders. I will now show you an easy way to do that:

1. Create the new `IVP_AdjustInvoiceAmountToSumOfOrders` expression and add an `invoiceId` rule input of the `integer` type.

2. Enter the following code:

```
a!localVariables(
  local!invoice: index(
    a!queryRecordType(
      recordType: 'recordType!IVP Invoice',
      pagingInfo: a!pagingInfo(1,1),
      filters: a!queryFilter(
        field: 'recordType!IVP Invoice.fields.id',
        operator: "=",
        value: ri!invoiceId
      ),
      fields: {
        'recordType!IVP Invoice.relationships.OrderIds
          .relationships.Order',
      }
    ).data,
    1,
    null
  ),
```

```
    local!invoice
)
```

3. Test by using an existing invoice ID. You will see that this shows the invoice and its related orders. `a!queryRecordType()` returns a data structure that holds a list of items in the `data` field. I use the `index()` function to pick the first item from this list:

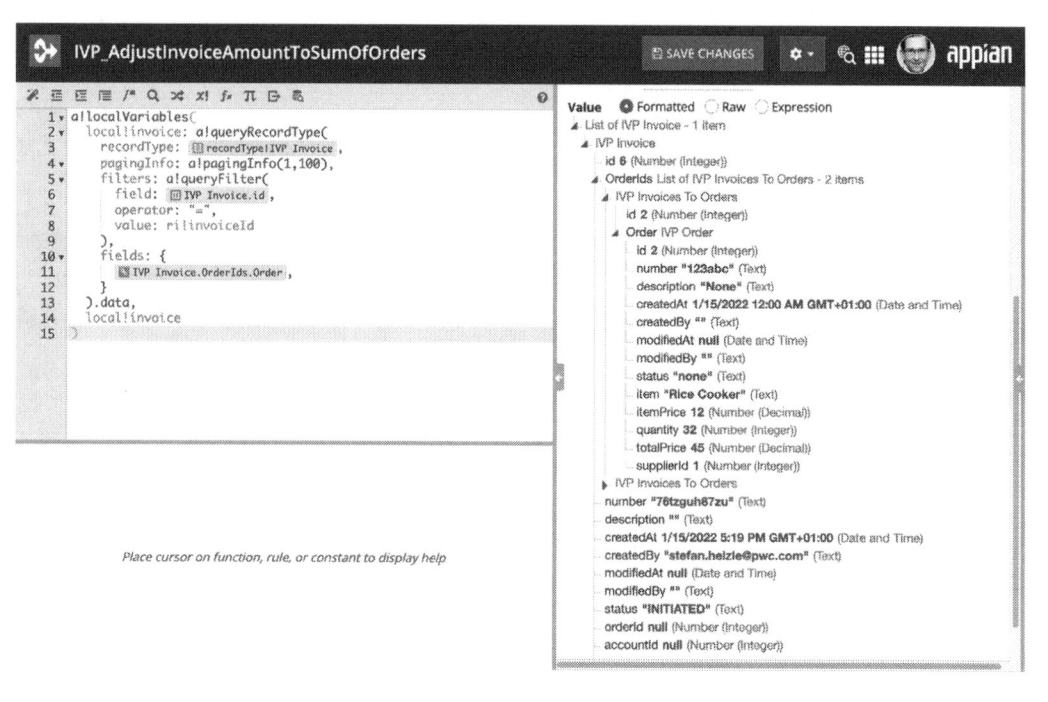

Figure 12.36 - Loading invoice and order data

4. Then, replace the second last line with the following snippet. Read it, starting at the innermost statement. It takes all `totalPrices` values of the orders, adds them up, updates the `amount` field of the invoice, and turns the result into the CDT `IVP_Invoice` data type:

```
cast(
    'type!{urn:com:tarence:types:IVP}IVP_Invoice',
    a!update(
        data: local!invoice,
        index: {'recordType!IVP Invoice.fields.amount'},
        value: {
```

```
sum(a!flatten(local!invoice['recordType!IVP
    Invoice.relationships.OrderIds.relationships
        .Order.fields.totalPrice'])),
    }
 )
)
```

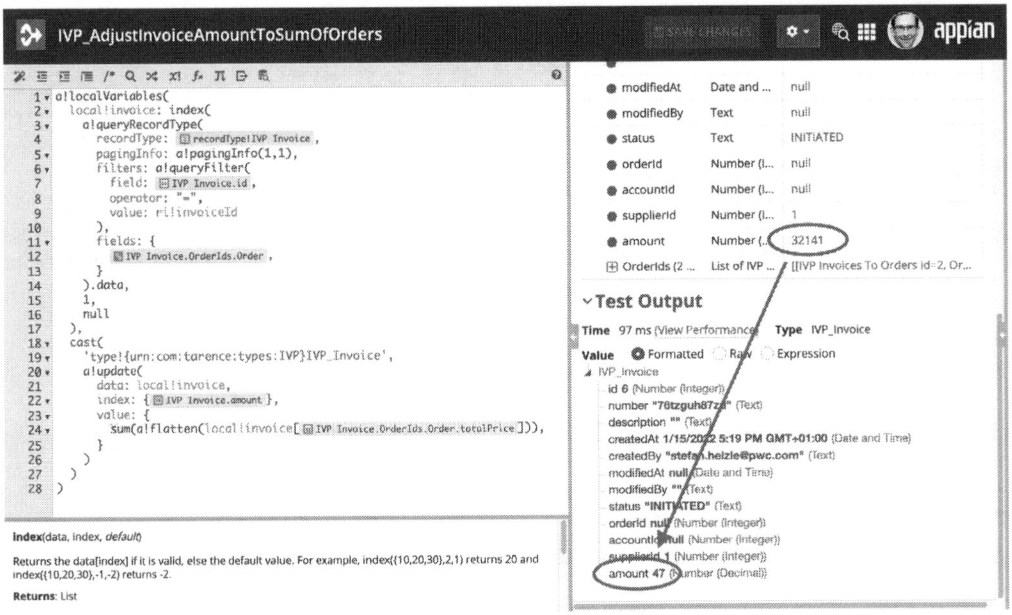

Figure 12.37 – The final expression, showing the updated invoice amount

5.   Modify the process model like this:

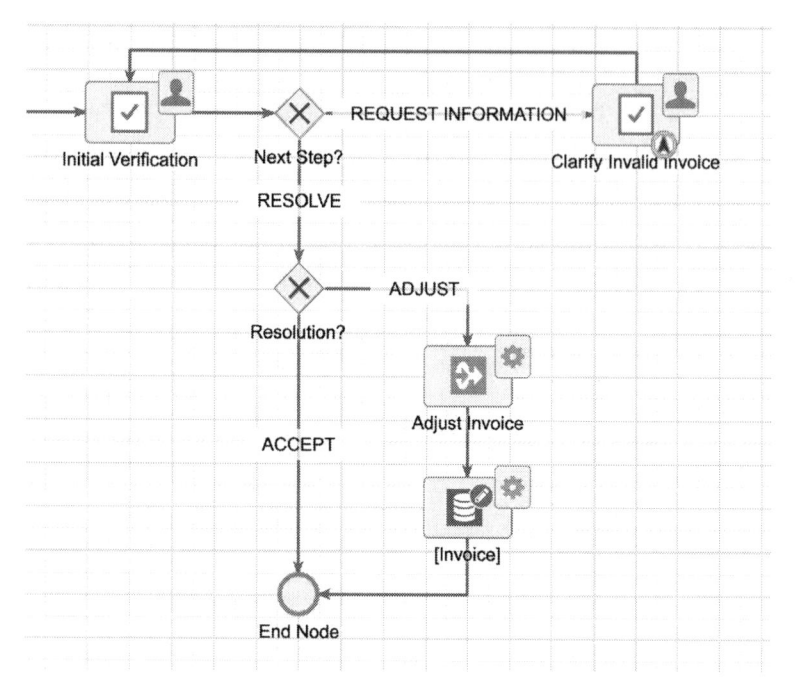

Figure 12.38 – The updated process model

6.   Define the conditions in the **Resolution** XOR node:

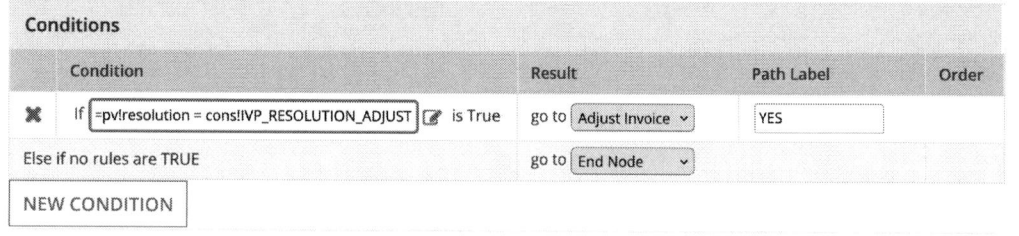

Figure 12.39 – The XOR conditions

7. In the **Adjust Invoice** script task, use the **IVP_ AdjustInvoiceAmountToSumOfOrders** expression in an output to update the invoice stored in the process variable with the modified invoice returned by the expression:

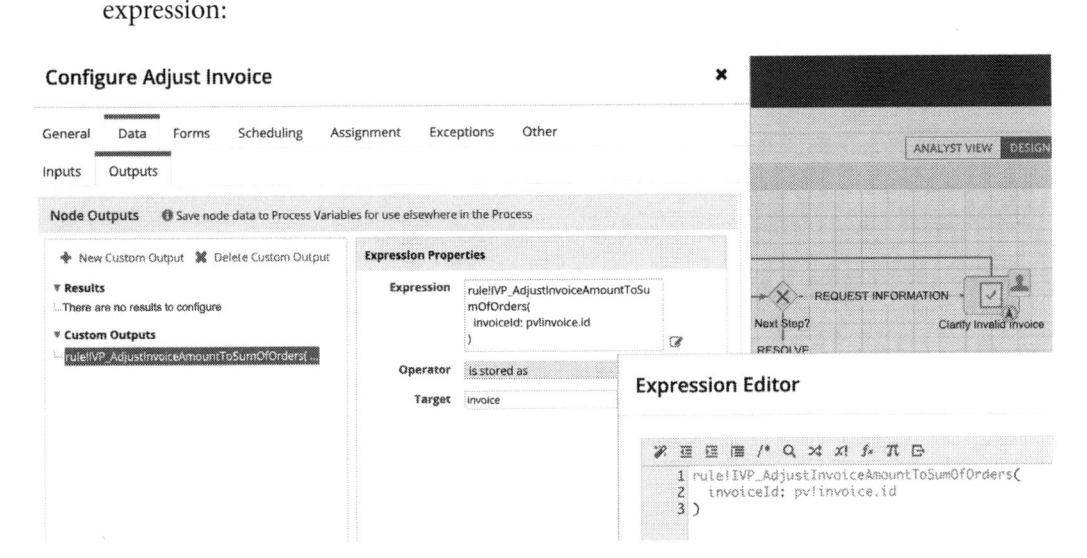

Figure 12.40 – The script task output definition

8. Configure the WTDSE to store the modified invoice in the same way as the other similar nodes in this process model.

The task and interface for Assign Invoice

In this step of the process, we would like to post the invoice in our ERP system. This can be a manual step assigned to a human, or an automated step performed by a function in the ERP system itself. Since we prefer not to bother humans with repetitive manual work, we will call a web service in this step. In *Chapter 15, Using Web Services with Appian Integrations*, we will return to this step, and I'll show you exactly how to implement it.

For now, let's close up our business process and our case.

Logic to finalize the invoice and the case

To complete the process and the case, you need to set a few values in the case process variable and store it in the database. Modify the process model to look like this:

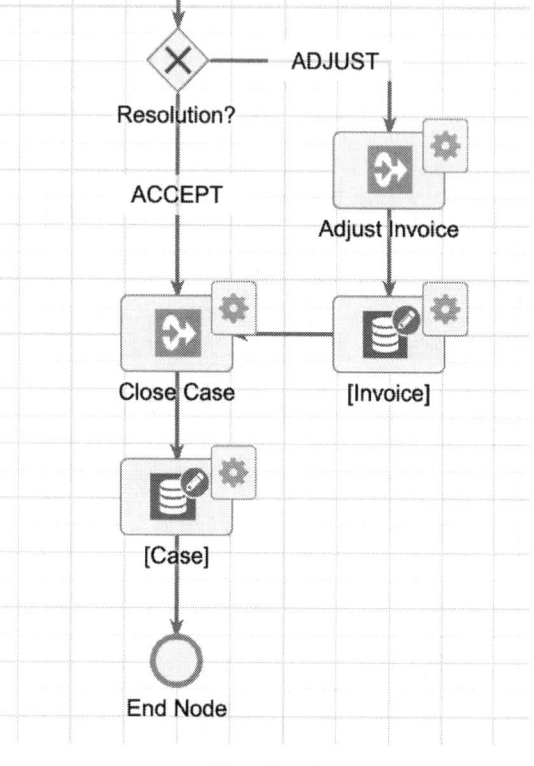

Figure 12.41 – Add nodes, finalizing the case

Before configuring the script task, create a new constant named IVP_CASE_STATUS_ COMPLETED of the text type with the COMPLETED value. In the **Initial Verification** User Input Task, add a new output that stores the **tp!owner** value to the new **taskOwner** process variable:

Inputs
Outputs
Node Outputs
Save node data to Process Variables for use elsewhere in the Process
New Custom Output
Delete Custom Output
Results
There are no results to configure
Custom Outputs
tp!owner
Expression Properties
Expression
tp!owner
Operator
is stored as
Target
taskOwner

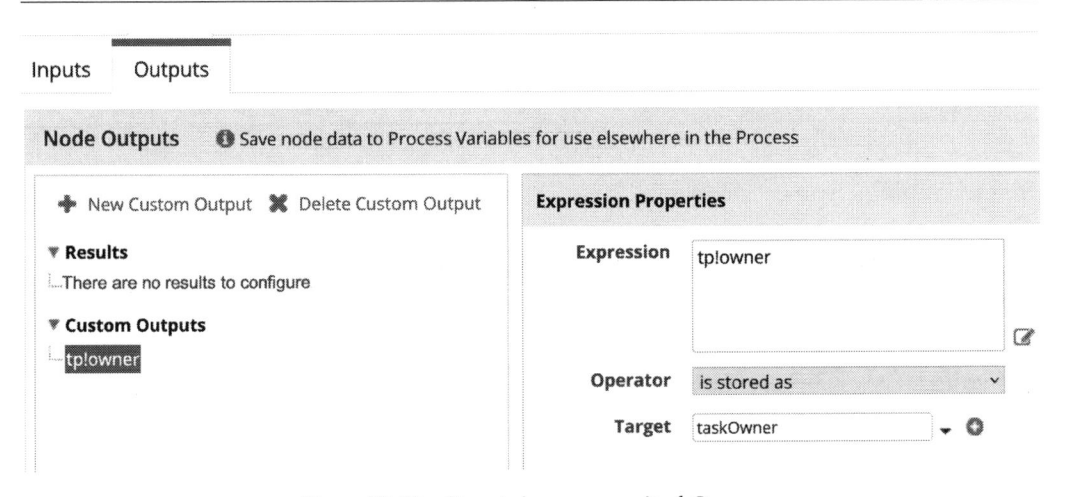

Figure 12.42 – Store tp!owner as pv!taskOwner

This will store the user, completing the task of the process variable. We will need that in a second to store that value in the case.

Then, configure the script task to assign the following values:

- **cons!IVP_CASE_STATUS_COMPLETED**: `pv!case.status`
- **true**: `pv!case.isCompleted`
- **now()**: `pv!case.completedAt`
- **pv!taskOwner**: `pv!case.completedBy`:

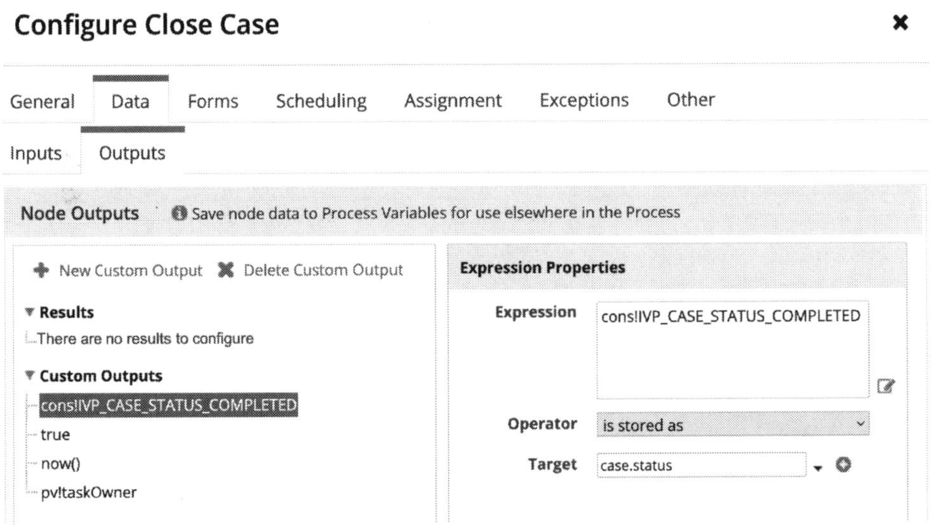

Configure Close Case
General
Data
Forms
Scheduling
Assignment
Exceptions
Other
Inputs
Outputs
Node Outputs
Save node data to Process Variables for use elsewhere in the Process
New Custom Output
Delete Custom Output
Results
There are no results to configure
Custom Outputs
cons!IVP_CASE_STATUS_COMPLETED
true
now()
pv!taskOwner
Expression Properties
Expression
cons!IVP_CASE_STATUS_COMPLETED
Operator
is stored as
Target
case.status

Figure 12.43 – Configuring the closed task

Configure the WTDSE node as usual.

This completes our business process and closes the case. Test your implementation thoroughly. We will enhance and modify it in the following chapters.

Best practices

We discussed many aspects of assigning tasks in Appian in detail. I would like to recap the most important ones.

Using groups

When talking about task assignments in Appian, the most essential best practice is to use groups whenever possible. When you need to split up groups to reflect certain organizational structures, just do that.

Let's discuss an example in more detail. We want to assign tasks based on specific skills to maximize efficiency. First, create groups for each skill and add people based on their individual skills. Then, create groups for each task and add the skill groups that best match the specific requirements.

The assignment of people to skill groups as well as the assignment of skill groups to tasks can be made available to managers, allowing them a maximum of flexibility.

Task due date

Next, each task has a due date! Why would you assign a task if you aren't concerned about when it is completed? Add escalations to make people aware of the urgency of the task. Send alerts and use task priority.

Task exceptions

Important tasks need an exception flow that allows a manager to act if a due date is at risk. Talk to stakeholders about what they typically do when tasks are left undone for too long. Turn this into a small escalation process. This adds automation to process management on top of process automation.

Summary

With this chapter, you have completed the first iteration of your invoice validation business process in Appian! And you've learned a lot about assigning tasks, using groups and users, and even dynamic assignment based on business logic.

You are now familiar with variables in the process, tasks, and interfaces, and how data flows in an Appian process model. You can also load data from the database, modify it, and save it back.

In the following chapters, we will enhance this process together, adding better status tracking, activity logging, and so on. Specifically, in the next chapter, we will take care of the topics of monitoring and reporting.

13
Reporting and Monitoring with Appian

With Appian, we try to implement the process itself in software. But this is only half the story. We also need to consider process management in our application. After all, there's a reason it's called **business process management**.

Management is about making decisions. You will learn how to enable managers to make these decisions using reports that give insight into process performance and display **Key Performance Indicators (KPIs)**. Interactive and actionable reports enable managers on an operative or strategic level to improve Tarence Limited's process performance.

In this chapter, we will cover the following topics:

- **Data sources and preparation**: Designing data for reporting requirements
- **Aggregating data**: Preparing data in the database and query-time aggregation
- **Visualizing data**: Turning raw data into appealing visual representations
- **Adding interaction**: Using interactive charts to filter and drill down data
- **Best practices**: Basic principles and some tricks

Data sources and preparation

In the process of designing data for reporting, it is important to first think about what specific questions you wish to answer. You must conduct a workshop with management stakeholders to get started. Try to get an understanding of the following key topics.

Monitoring process activity

Monitoring is mostly about the current state of process operations and the organization of day-to-day work. Usually, the management is interested in the following:

- How many active processes do we have?
- What is the compliance to deadlines and **Service Level Agreements (SLAs)**?
- What is the workload of the teams?

Management uses these questions to identify any need for changing process operations, staffing, or the organization of the teams.

In Appian, we use a process analytics engine and the database to query real-time data for visualization.

Reporting

Stakeholders for reporting are usually higher up in the management hierarchy and, therefore, have completely unique issues. Some of the questions raised can be the following:

- How does the number of processes change over time?
- How does the number of complaints and service level violations change over time?
- How do process cost and team efficiency change over time?

These performance indicators help management understand the impact of changes in the environment and identify the need for action.

In Appian, we do not have direct support for analyzing historical data – for example, to get the number of active processes from last Thursday, we would need to measure this data point daily and store it in the database.

Periodic data measurement

Create a new process model called `IVP Measure Reporting Data`. As usual, adjust the data management and alert settings. Then, follow these steps:

1. Double-click the start node to open the configuration dialog.

2. Navigate to the **Triggers** tab:

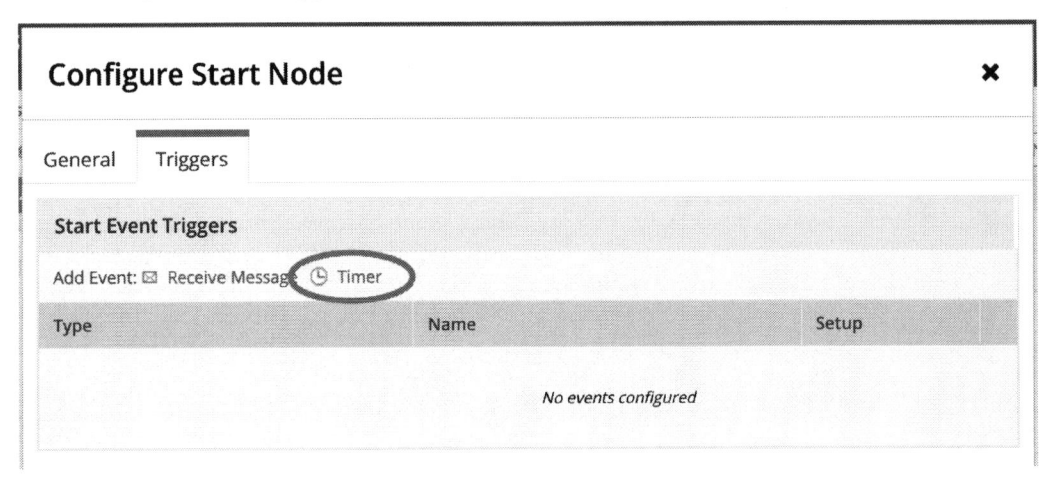

Figure 13.1 – The triggers in the start node

3. Click **Timer** to add a new timer and name it `Daily`.

4. Click **Configure** and then navigate to the **Setup** tab:

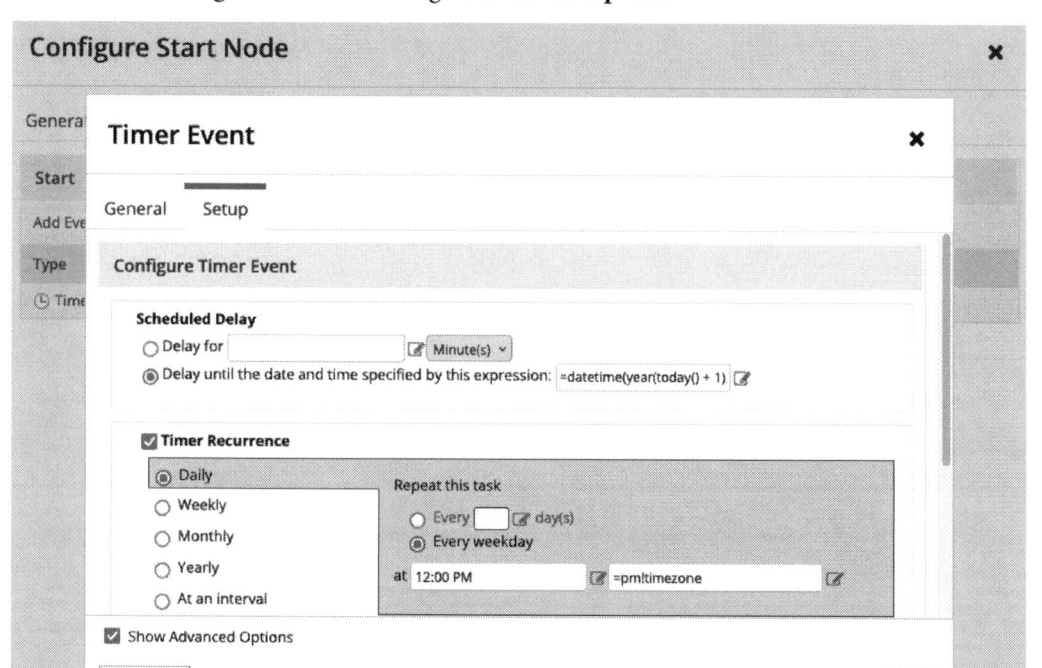

Figure 13.2 – Setting up a timer event

5. Set the scheduled delay to the following:

```
=datetime(year(today() + 1), month(today() + 1),
    day(today() + 1), 12)
```

6. This way, the process is started the first time on the day after deployment, and duplicate rows in the database are avoided.

7. Activate the timer recurrence and set it to 12:00 AM every weekday.

In the next sections, I will walk you through adding the necessary features.

Storing measurements

Create a new `IVP_DailyReportingData` data type to store the measured data. Add the following fields:

-   **id**: `integer`, primary key, and auto-increment
-   **date**: `date`

- **numCreated**: `integer`
- **numActive**: `integer`
- **numCompleted**: `integer`

Then, add the new data type to the exiting data store and create a new record, using that new database table as the source.

Preparing the case record

As of now, the Case CDT has two fields to store the creation and completion timestamps as date and time. To filter valid records for our daily measurements, we need these values as dates only. Add two custom **Record** fields to make this easier by following these steps:

1. In **Case Record**, click **NEW CUSTOM RECORD FIELD**.
2. Select **Extract Partial Dates** and click **NEXT**.
3. Select **createdAt** as the field and **Date** for **Unit of Time**, and click **NEXT**:

Create Custom Record Field

Select a Template	Configure Values	Set Name and Type

CONFIGURE VALUES

☐ EXTRACT PARTIAL DATES

Field ❷	Unit of Time
createdAt ✕	Date ▼

TEST

◉ View Record Data ◯ Enter Test Values   [TEST]

id Number (Integer)	createdAt Date and Time	▦ Custom Record Field Date
1	12/5/2021 5:55 PM GMT+01:00	12/5/2021
2	12/5/2021 7:05 PM GMT+01:00	12/5/2021
3	12/29/2021 11:17 AM GMT+01:00	12/29/2021
4	1/15/2022 5:10 PM GMT+01:00	1/15/2022
5	1/15/2022 5:19 PM GMT+01:00	1/15/2022
6	1/22/2022 5:44 PM GMT+01:00	1/22/2022

Figure 13.3 – Creating a custom record field

4. Accept the values for **Name** and **Type** and click **CREATE**.
5. Repeat these steps for the **completedAt** field.

Measuring data

Let us understand how to measure data in this section:

1. To measure the data, create a new `IVP_MeasureReportingData` expression and enter the following code snippet:

```
a!localVariables(
  local!numCreated: 0,
  local!numActive: 0,
  local!numCompleted: 0,
  'type!{urn:com:tarence:types:IVP}
    IVP_DailyReportingData'(
    date: today(),
    numCreated: local!numCreated,
    numActive: local!numActive,
    numCompleted: local!numCompleted
  )
)
```

   This creates a data structure of the `IVP_DailyReportingData` type with all fields set to zero. Now, replace the declarations of the local variables in lines 2, 3, and 4 with the following code snippets.

2. The following code queries cases from the IVP Case record, which has been created today. To minimize data transfer, it queries only a single case and only the `id` field. But it fetches the total count of matching cases, which is the number we are interested in:

```
local!numCreated: a!queryRecordType(
  recordType: 'recordType!IVP Case',
  filters: a!queryFilter(
    field: 'recordType!IVP Case.fields.createdAtDate',
    operator: "=",
    value: today()
  ),
  pagingInfo: a!pagingInfo(1,1),
  fields: 'recordType!IVP Case.fields.id',
```

```
    fetchTotalCount: true
).totalCount,
```

3. The next snippet fetches the total count of all uncompleted cases:

```
local!numActive: a!queryRecordType(
  recordType: 'recordType!IVP Case',
  filters: a!queryFilter(
    field: 'recordType!IVP Case.fields.isCompleted',
    operator: "=",
    value: false
  ),
  pagingInfo: a!pagingInfo(1,1),
  fields: 'recordType!IVP Case.fields.id',
  fetchTotalCount: true
).totalCount,
```

4. The last snippet fetches the number of cases that have been completed today:

```
local!numCompleted: a!queryRecordType(
  recordType: 'recordType!IVP Case',
  filters: a!queryFilter(
    field: 'recordType!IVP Case.fields.completed
      AtDate',
    operator: "=",
    value: today()
  ),
  pagingInfo: a!pagingInfo(1,1),
  fields: 'recordType!IVP Case.fields.id',
  fetchTotalCount: true
).totalCount,
```

5.   When testing, you should see output similar to this:

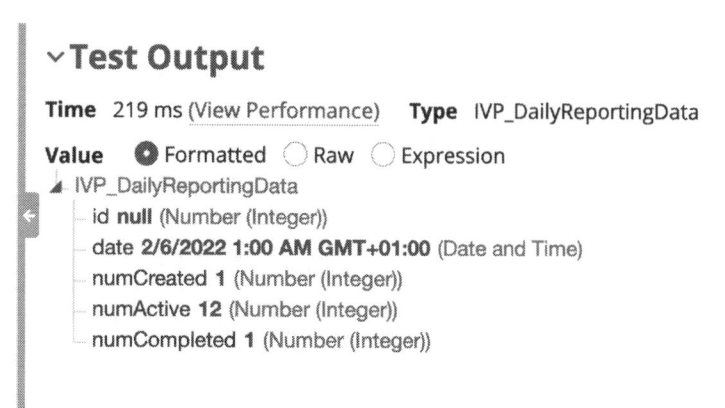

Figure 13.4 – Reporting the data test output

Now that you are measuring the data, we add the expression to the process to run it every day.

Completing the measuring process model

Complete the process by following these steps:

1.   Add the **reportingData** process variable to the model:

Process Model Properties » IVP Measure Reporting Data   ✕

| General | Variables | Process Start Form | Deadlines | Alerts | Data Management |

Process Variables

✚ Add Variable

Name	Type	Value	Parameter?	Required?	Multiple?	Hidden?	
reportingData	IVP_DailyReportingData	(No Value)	No	N/A	No	No	✕

Figure 13.5 – Adding the reportingData process variable

2. Add a script task and a WTDSE node to the model, and change the names according to the following screenshot:

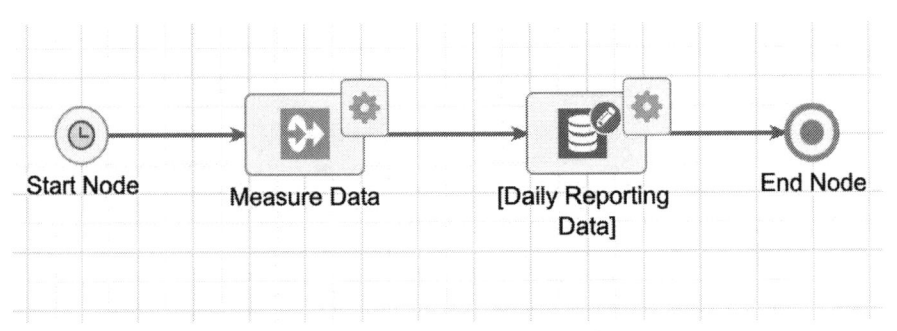

Figure 13.6 – The added nodes in the model

3. Configure the **Measure Data** node:

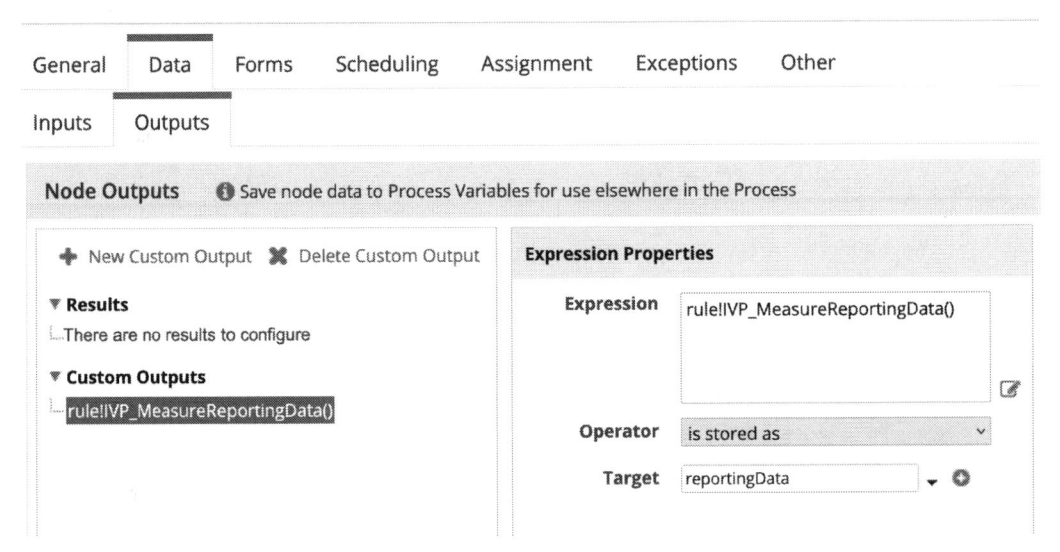

Figure 13.7 – Configure the script task

4.   Configure the **Daily Reporting Data** node:

Configure [Daily Reporting Data]   ✖

General	Data	Forms	Scheduling	Assignment	Escalations	Exceptions	Other

Inputs	Outputs

Node Inputs   ❶ Map the value(s) for the inputs of the node

➕ New Input   ✖ Delete Input

Data Store Entity * (Data Store Entity)
➕ **reportingData** (IVP_DailyReportingData)

Field Properties

Name	reportingData
Type	IVP_DailyReportingData ☰
Multiple	☐
Value	=pv!reportingData ▾ ☑
Required	☐
Save into	▾ ➕

Figure 13.8 – Configure the Daily Reporting Data node

Let's have a quick recap of what this process is doing. It will run every weekday at 12 AM and call the expression that performs the measurement. This measurement is stored in a process variable and is picked up by the next node, which writes it to the database:

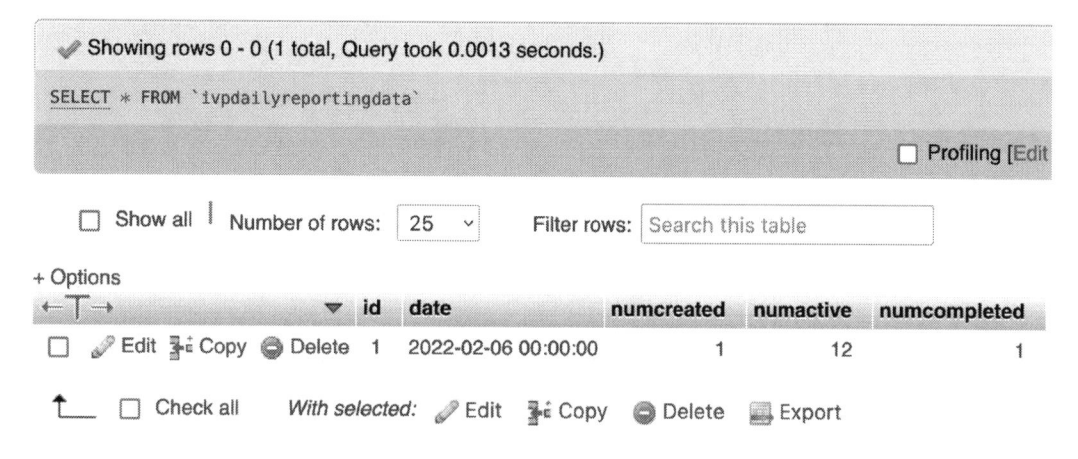

Figure 13.9 – The measurements in the database table

That was all we had to do to save daily measurement values into the database. In the next section, I will give you an introduction to data aggregation using Appian records.

Aggregating data

We will now create some expressions to aggregate and prepare data for visualization.

Cases over time

The `IVP_Q_ReportingCasesOverTime` expression is a simple one, as it fetches our daily reporting data and sorts it by date:

```
a!queryRecordType(
  recordType: 'recordType!IVP Daily Reporting Data',
  pagingInfo: a!pagingInfo(
    startIndex: 1,
    batchSize: 1000,
    sort: a!sortInfo(
      field: 'recordType!IVP Daily Reporting Data.fields
        .date',
      ascending: true
    )
  )
)
```

Current case status

In the `IVP_Q_ReportingCurrentCaseStatus` expression, we need to exclude all completed cases and group by the status and count the ID:

```
a!queryRecordType(
  recordType: 'recordType!IVP Case',
  filters: a!queryFilter(
    field: 'recordType!IVP Case.fields.isCompleted',
    operator: "=",
    value: false
  ),
  fields: a!aggregationFields(
    groupings: a!grouping(field: 'recordType!IVP
```

```
        Case.fields.status', alias: "status"),
     measures: a!measure(field: 'recordType!IVP Case.fields
       .status', function: "COUNT", alias: "count")
  ),
  pagingInfo: a!pagingInfo(1, 1000)
)
```

When you execute this expression, you will notice that all cases are in the INITIATED status. This is because we did not modify the case status in our process flow.

1. Let's add that now.

> **Iterative Design in Appian**
>
> It is perfectly normal to refine existing objects in Appian. Start doing this as soon as you think your solution approach is good enough. As you gain experience, your personal level of "good enough" will change as you become better at assessing the impact of certain design decisions.
>
> Just make sure to keep any dependencies in mind. And when testing your modifications, look left and right to make sure you did not break existing functionality.

2. Modify the process model like this:

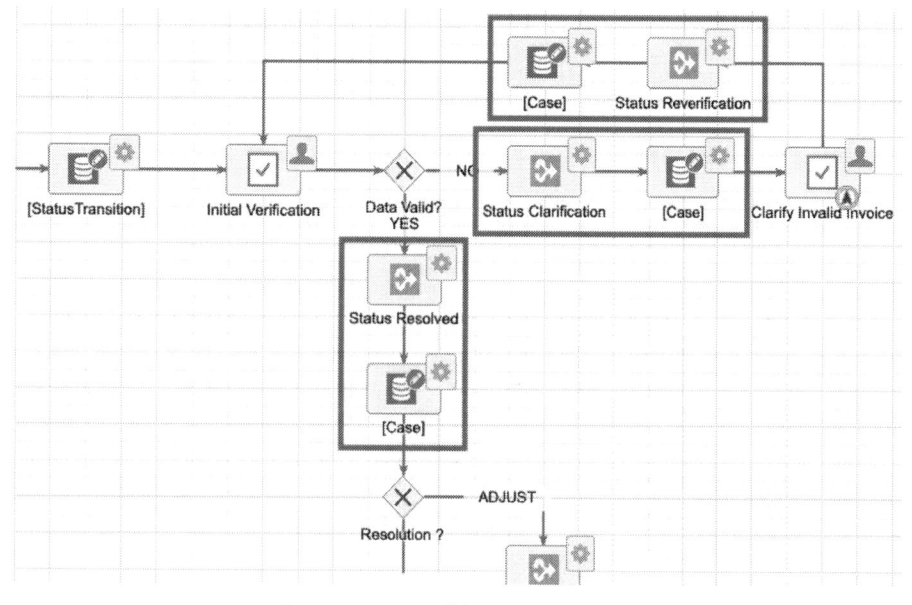

Figure 13.10 – Adding status updates

3. Create the new constants:

    - `IVP_CASE_STATUS_RESOLVED`

    - `IVP_CASE_STATUS_CLARIFICATION`

    - `IVP_CASE_STATUS_REVERIFICATION`

4. Assign these constants to the **status** field of the case in the respective script tasks. Do this in the same way as in the **Close Case** script task. The WTDSE nodes just store `pv!case` to the **Cases** data store entity.

5. Run a few new processes to see how the status values change over time. Your reporting expression should now create an output similar to this:

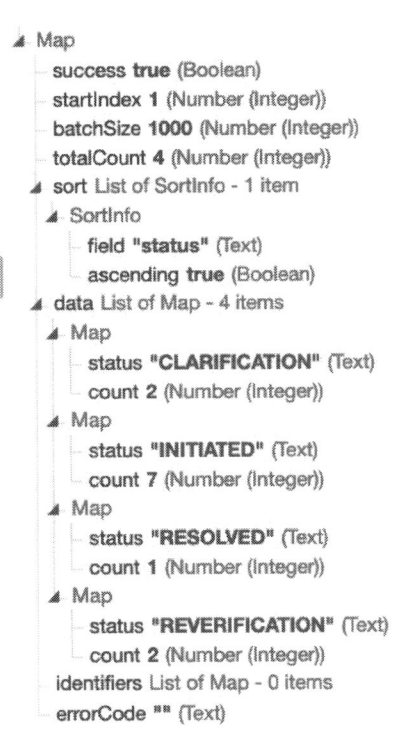

Figure 13.11 – The status aggregation output

In the next section, I will show you how to turn that raw data into a visual report.

Visualizing data

A visual report should be more than just a white canvas with some numbers on it. In Appian Designer, create a new `IVP_D_Reporting` interface. Then, add a card header and replace the card layout with a billboard layout to give the screen a nice-looking header. Replace the billboard background with an image of your choice. To do so, create a new document in Appian designer, select your image, and create a constant pointing to that image. Then, change the **Background Media** attribute to this:

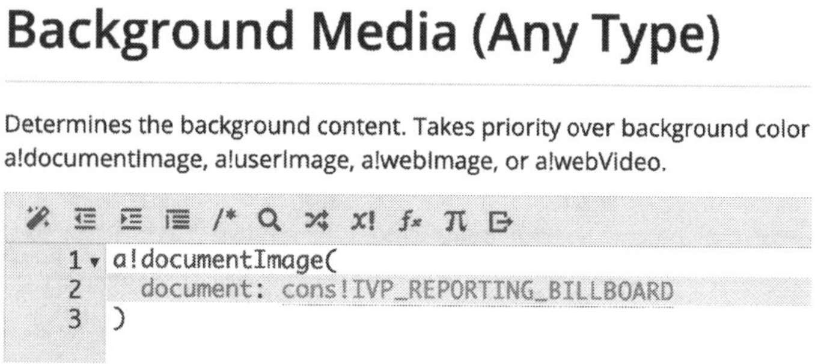

Background Media (Any Type)

Determines the background content. Takes priority over background color a!documentImage, a!userImage, a!webImage, or a!webVideo.

```
1 ▾ a!documentImage(
2       document: cons!IVP_REPORTING_BILLBOARD
3   )
```

Figure 13.12 – Modifying the billboard background

In **Expression Mode**, your code should look like this:

```
a!headerContentLayout(
  header: {
    {
      a!billboardLayout(
        backgroundMedia: a!documentImage(
          document: cons!IVP_REPORTING_BILLBOARD
        ),
        backgroundColor: "#f0f0f0",
        overlay: a!barOverlay(
          contents: {}
        )
      )
    }
  },
  contents: {}
)
```

Save your changes, and then add this interface as a new page to the existing **IVP Invoice Validation Process** site:

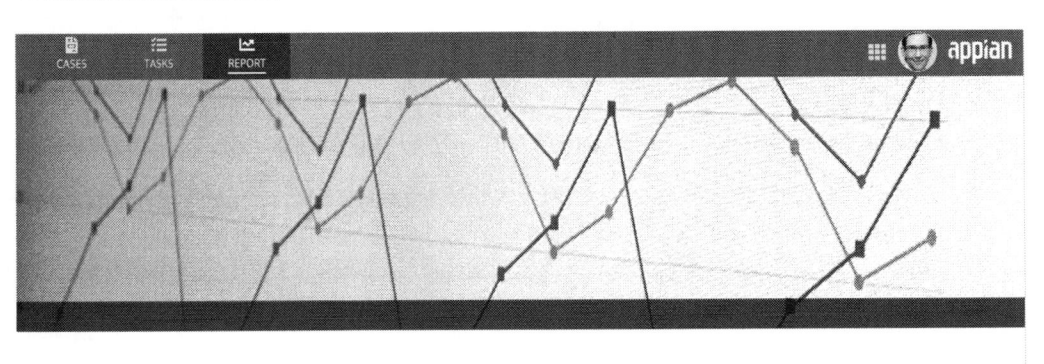

Figure 13.13 – The draft report added to the site

Now, I will walk you through adding content to this interface.

Status over timeline chart

As we did with the query expressions, we will also put each chart into a separate interface component. Create the `IVP_C_ReportingStatusOverTime` interface and enter the following code snippet:

```
a!localVariables(
  local!data: rule!IVP_Q_ReportingCasesOverTime().data,
  a!lineChartField(
    label: "Status over Time",
    categories: local!data['recordType!IVP Daily Reporting
      Data.fields.date'],
    series: {
      a!chartSeries(
        label: "Started",
        data: local!data['recordType!IVP Daily Reporting
```

```
            Data.fields.}numCreated']
        ),
        a!chartSeries(
            label: "Active",
            data: local!data['recordType!IVP Daily Reporting
                Data.fields.numActive']
        ),
        a!chartSeries(
            label: "Completed",
            data: local!data['recordType!IVP Daily Reporting
                Data.fields.numCompleted']
        ),
        }
    )
)
```

This stores the output of our query expression in a local variable. Then, it creates a line chart field, defining the measurement dates as categories and the three measurements as chart series. It will then look like this:

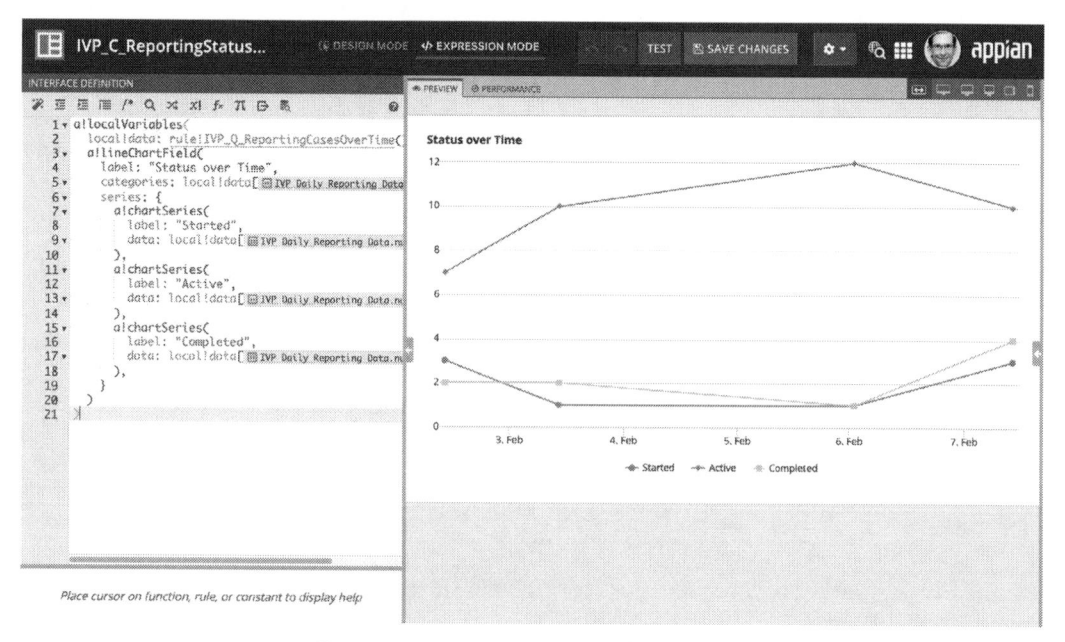

Figure 13.14 – Case activity in the line chart

Appian has some built-in functionality for line charts. You can toggle series by clicking the name in the legend, and you can zoom into the chart, which is handy when the data volume becomes larger. Just select a range using the mouse:

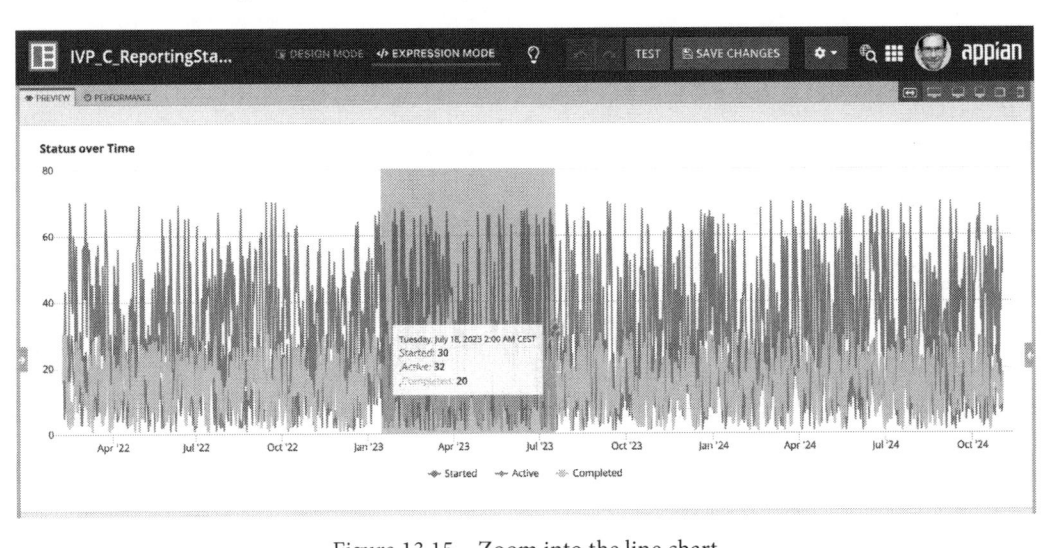

Figure 13.15 – Zoom into the line chart

Appian will now display the zoomed-in range and a button to reset the zoom level:

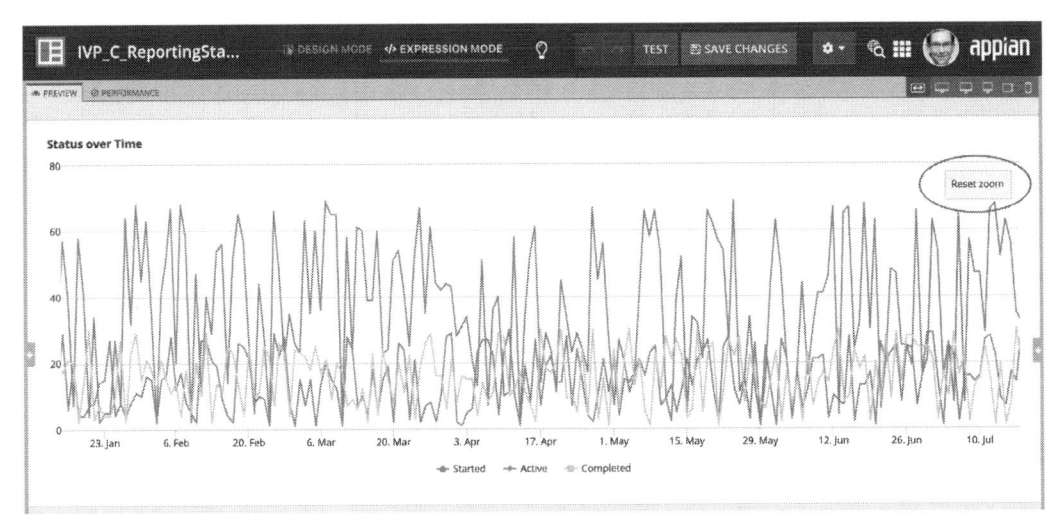

Figure 13.16 – Zoomed in

To add the chart to the report, modify the `contents` parameter of the report interface like this:

```
contents: {
    rule!IVP_C_ReportingStatusOverTime()
}
```

Case status donut chart

The simplest way to create a donut chart, showing the current case statuses, is to use the built-in aggregation capabilities:

1. Create a new `IVP_C_ReportingCurrentCaseStatuses` interface, add a pie chart, and configure it like this:

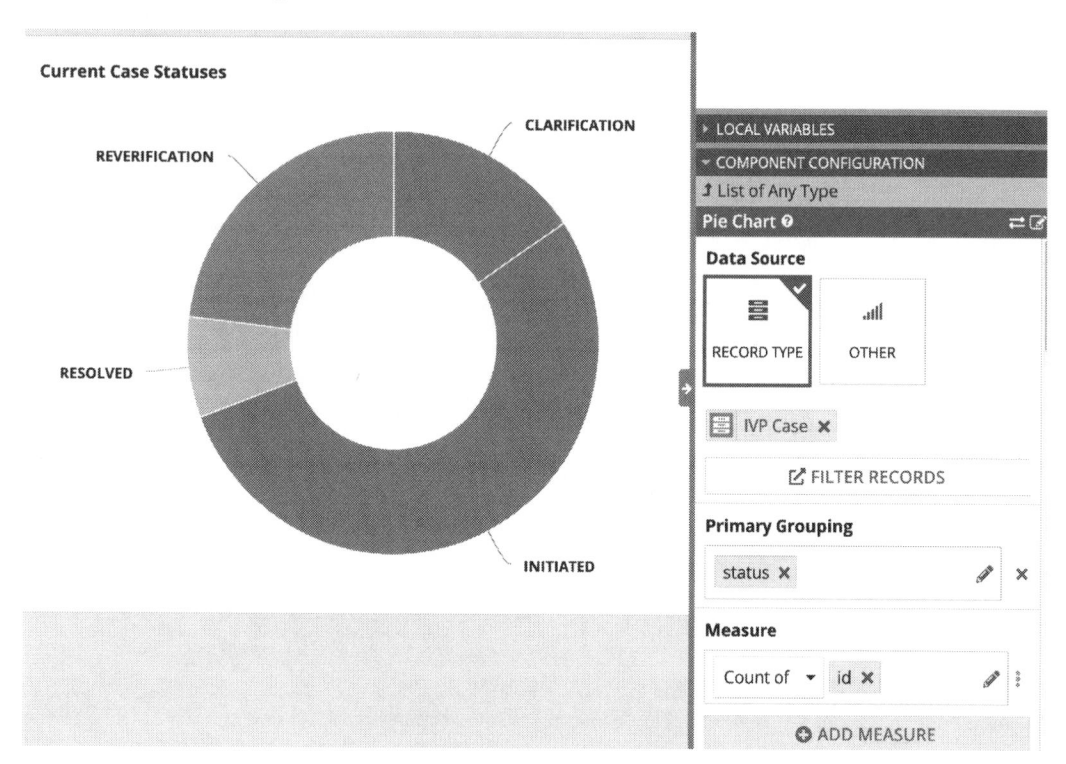

Figure 13.17 – A pie chart aggregating data

2. Now, go back to the main **IVP_D_Reporting** reporting interface and add a columns layout to place the line chart to the left and the donut chart to the right. Split the space to about **3:1**.

3. Change the height of the billboard layout to **Short** to give the charts a bit more space. Try the different color schemes and choose the one that fits best:

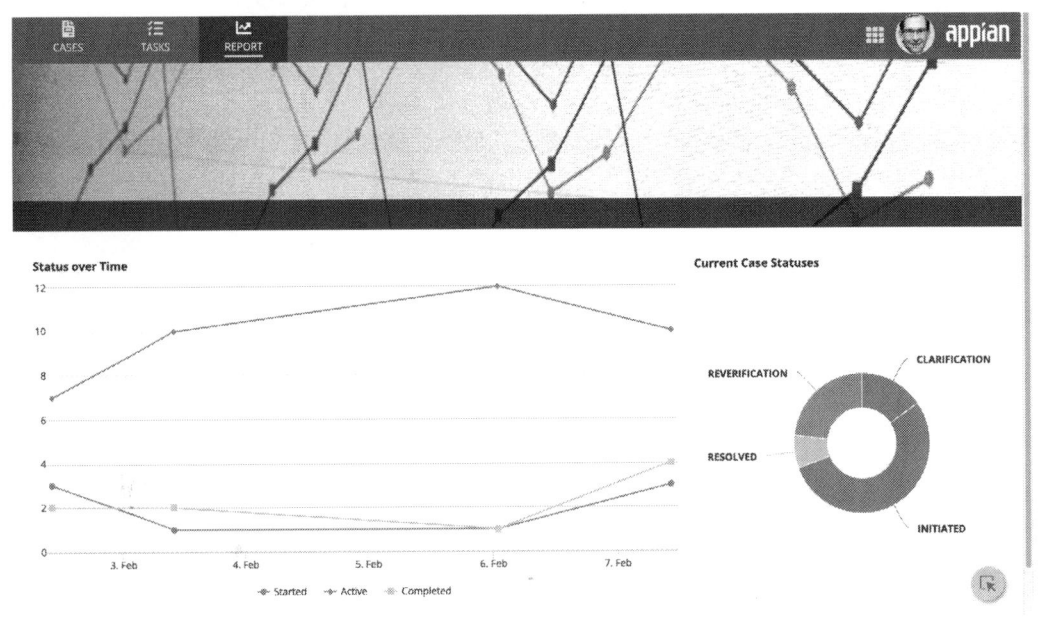

Figure 13.18 – The report showing the added donut chart

In case you are wondering why we created a query expression to aggregate the data for the donut chart, we will change this diagram later, and then we will need this expression.

But for now, I will show you how to add a case grid to the report.

Case grid

Let us add a case grid to the report:

1. Create a new `IVP_C_ReportingCaseGrid` interface, add a **Read-Only Grid** component, and then select the **IVP Case** record as the data source. In the background, Appian copies the configuration from the record list, and the base grid is ready:

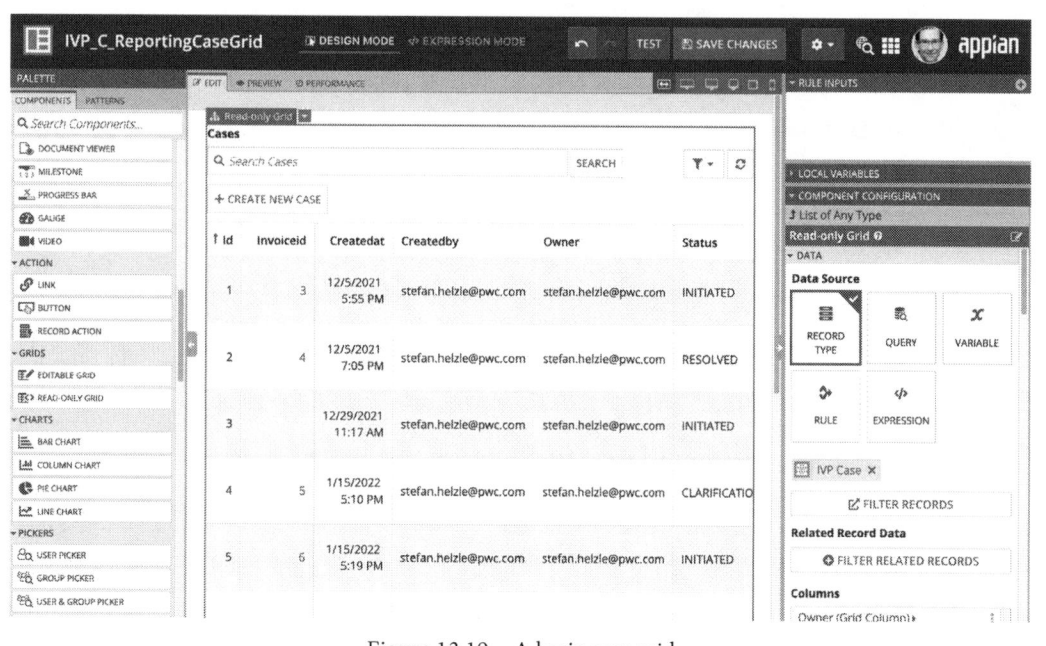

Figure 13.19 – A basic case grid

2. Remove some columns, but keep at least the following:

   - ID
   - Created At
   - Owner
   - Status
   - Due At
   - Priority

3. Now, change the status column to display the status properly:

```
a!gridColumn(
  label: "Status",
  sortField: 'recordType!IVP Case.fields.status',
  value: proper(fv!row['recordType!IVP Case.fields
    .status'])
)
```

4. Add this new component to the reporting interface below the column's layout.

We can now move to the next section and understand Billboard cards.

Billboard cards

The last visualizations we add are some cards in the billboard overlay showing the KPIs. We will display the following numbers:

- The number of cases per year to date
- The median of case duration
- Compliance with the due date

This time, we will create interface components for each card, which also include the query logic. Then, we will combine them in a column's layout. All three components consist of a side-by-side layout inside a card layout:

Figure 13.20 – The KPI card layout

Use four side-by-side items, setting the width of the middle ones to **MINIMIZE**. This way, they align to the center. Leave the outer ones empty and add a **Rich Text** component to the inner. Add a large, styled icon to the left one, and text to the right. Make the text center-aligned.

1. Now, for any concrete implementation, create the first `IVP_C_ReportingKpiCasesYearToDate` component and modify the code to include the record query:

```
a!localVariables(
  local!kpi: a!queryRecordType(
    recordType: 'recordType!IVP Case',
    fetchTotalCount: true,
    pagingInfo: a!pagingInfo(1,1),
    filters: a!queryFilter(
      field: 'recordType!IVP Case.fields.createdAt',
      operator: "between",
      value: {
        datetime(year(today()), 1, 1, 0, 0, 0),
        datetime(year(today()) + 1, 1, 1, 0, 0, 0)
      }
    ),
    fields: 'recordType!IVP Case.fields.id'
  ).totalCount,
  a!cardLayout(
    contents: {
```

2. Then, change the value of the rich text to the following:

```
value: {
  a!richTextItem(
    text: local!kpi,
    size: "LARGE"
  ),
  char(10),
  a!richTextItem(
    text: year(today()),
    color: "SECONDARY"
```

```
        )
    },
```

The second component, `IVP_C_ReportingKpiMedianCaseDuration`, needs another quick visit to the case record. We will add a custom field to calculate the number of business hours between the start date and the end date of the case.

3. Create a new custom record field and select **Write Your Own Expression** as the type. Then, configure it like this:

Edit Custom Record Field

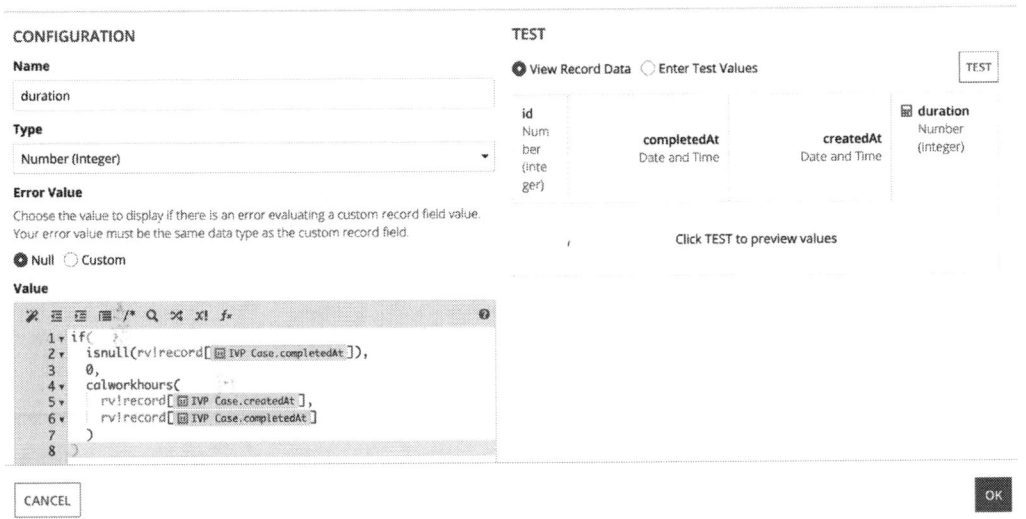

Figure 13.21 – The duration record field

4. This time, the code to calculate the `kpi` value is as follows:

```
local!kpi: median(
  index(
    a!queryRecordType(
      recordType: 'recordType!IVP Case',
      fetchTotalCount: false,
      pagingInfo: a!pagingInfo(1,5000),
      filters: {
        a!queryFilter(
          field: 'recordType!IVP Case.fields
            .createdAt',
          operator: "between",
          value: {
            datetime(year(today()), 1, 1, 0, 0, 0),
            datetime(year(today()) + 1, 1, 1, 0, 0, 0)
          }
        ),
        a!queryFilter(
          field: 'recordType!IVP Case.fields
            .isCompleted',
          operator: "=",
          value: true
        ),
      },
      fields: 'recordType!IVP Case.fields.duration'
    ).data,
    'recordType!IVP Case.fields.duration',
    0
  )
),
```

I queried the duration of completed cases created this year. Then, I used the `index()` function to get the list of durations and fed that into the `median()` function:

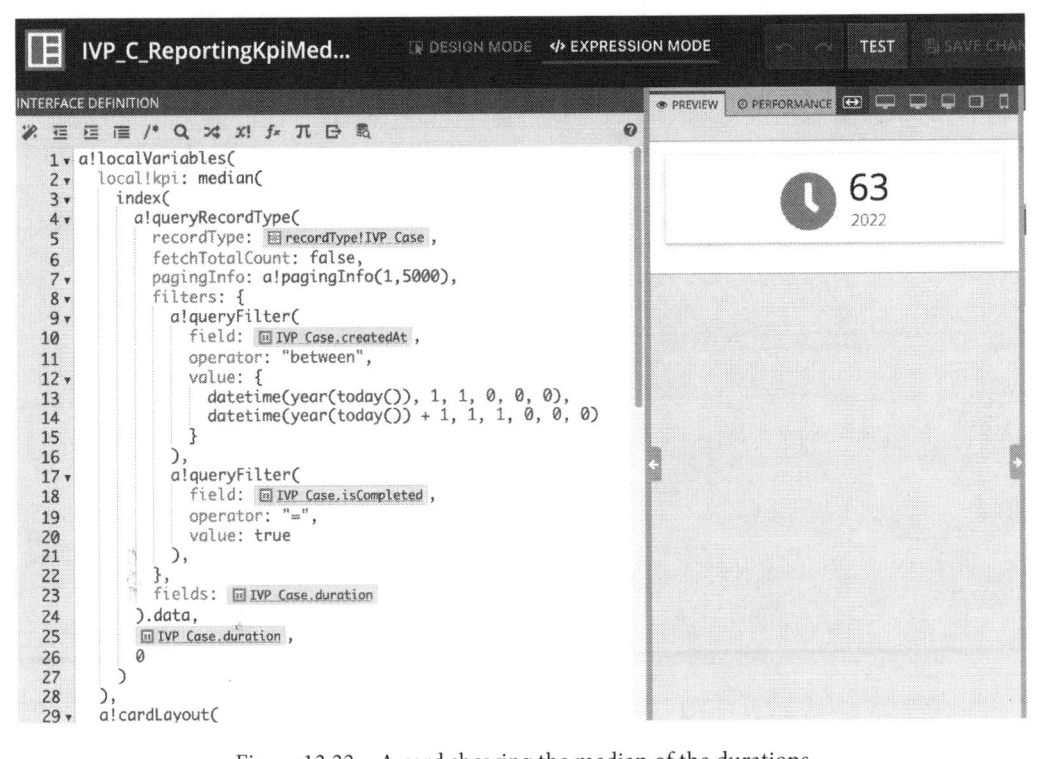

Figure 13.22 – A card showing the median of the durations

I also selected a different icon and color. For the last card, we need to identify cases with the end date before or after the due date. This calls for another custom record field. Then, we can use that for aggregation.

5. Create a new custom record field of **Groups Based on a Date Difference** type and configure it like this:

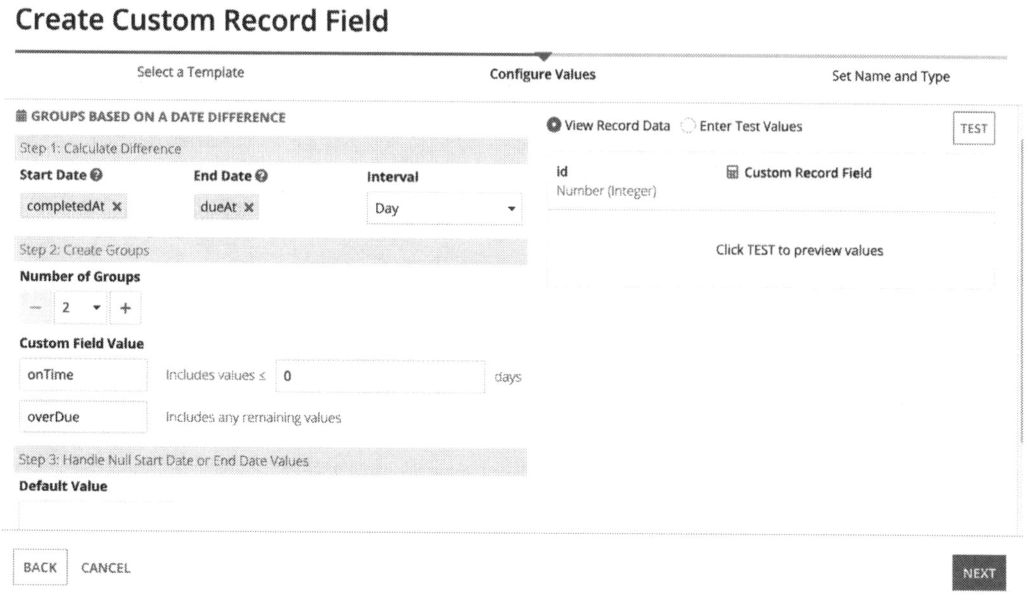

Create Custom Record Field

Figure 13.23 – The slaCompliance custom record field

6. Give it the name `slaCompliance`.

7. Create the last card component, `IVP_C_ReportingSlaCompliance`, following the same pattern as the last two. The query part is now as follows:

```
local!kpi: a!queryRecordType(
  recordType: 'recordType!IVP Case',
  fetchTotalCount: false,
  pagingInfo: a!pagingInfo(1,10),
  filters: {
    a!queryFilter(
      field: 'recordType!IVP Case.fields.createdAt',
      operator: "between",
      value: {
        datetime(year(today()), 1, 1, 0, 0, 0),
        datetime(year(today()) + 1, 1, 1, 0, 0, 0)
      }
    ),
```

```
    a!queryFilter(
      field: 'recordType!IVP Case.fields.isCompleted',
      operator: "=",
      value: true
    ),
  },
  fields: a!aggregationFields(
    groupings: a!grouping(
      field: 'recordType!IVP Case.fields
        .slaCompliance',
      alias: "slaCompliance"
    ),
    measures: a!measure(
      field: 'recordType!IVP Case.fields.id',
      function: "COUNT",
      alias: "count"
    )
  )
).data,
```

Again, I query completed cases created this year, and then grouped them by the custom **slaCompliance** field and counted the IDs.

To display the data, I used the `displayvalue()` function:

```
item: a!richTextDisplayField(
  labelPosition: "COLLAPSED",
  value: {
    a!richTextItem(
      text: displayvalue(
        "onTime",
        index(local!kpi, "slaCompliance", null),
        index(local!kpi, "count", 0),
        0
      ),
      size: "LARGE",
      color: "POSITIVE",
    ),
    a!richTextItem(
      text: " / ",
      size: "LARGE"
    ),
    a!richTextItem(
      text: displayvalue(
        "overDue",
        index(local!kpi, "slaCompliance", 0),
        index(local!kpi, "count", 0),
        0
      ),
      size: "LARGE",
      color: "NEGATIVE",
    ),
```

LOCAL VARIABLES	
Name	Value
⊟ kpi (2 items)	[[slaCompliance:onTime,count:1]; [slaC.
⊟ [1]	[slaCompliance:onTime,count:1]
● slaCompliance	onTime
● count	1
⊟ [2]	[slaCompliance:overDue,count:1]
● slaCompliance	overDue
● count	1

Figure 13.24 – Displaying values

This takes a value and two lists. Then, it looks up the index of the value in the first list and returns the value from the second list at that index. You can combine the `lookup()` and `index()` functions to get the same result, but I always try to use a function with functionality that is closest to what I am looking for.

8. That was the last card. Add it to the column's layout in the overlay of the billboard layout. Your report should now look like this:

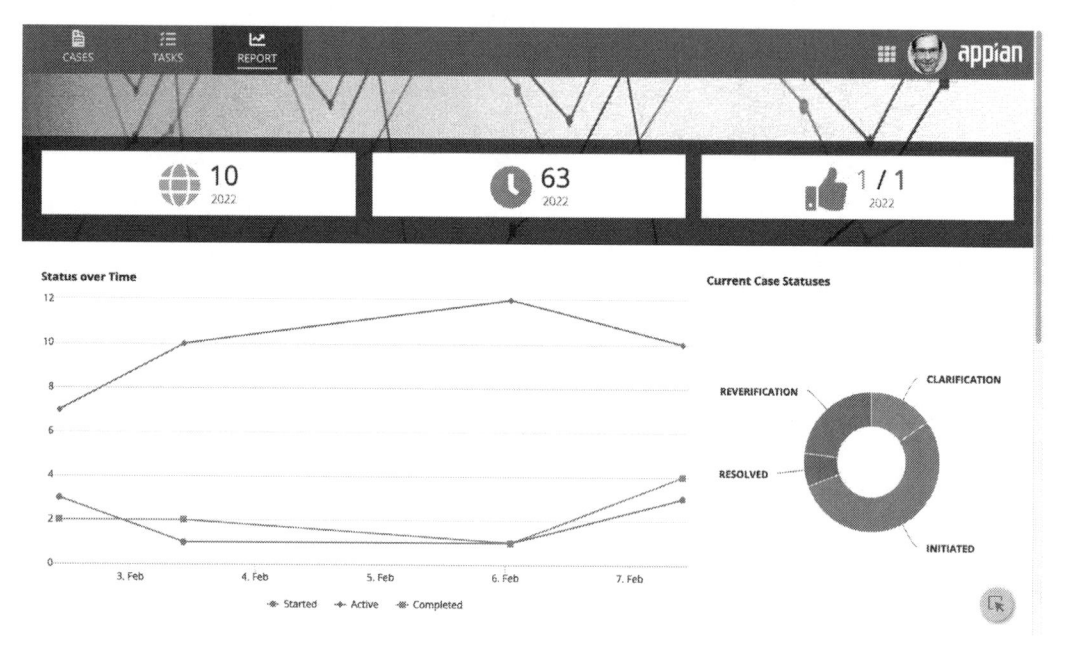

Figure 13.25 – The completed report

Do not hesitate to add your own visualizations, which you just learned how to do. In the next section, I will show you how to add an interaction to that dashboard.

Adding interaction

In this dashboard, we have two components that would be perfect for interacting. The donut shows the statuses and the grid below all the cases. Why not use the donut to filter the grid by the selected status?

To make this work, I first need to explain to you the simple principle of how nested components can interact:

A rule input or a local variable can be shared to one or more nested components!

Updates in one spot are immediately shared to any other places where that value is shared to.

To make use of this, follow these steps:

1. Create a new rule inputs named `selectedStatus` at the **IVP_C_ReportingCaseGrid** and **IVP_C_ReportingCurrentCaseStatuses** interfaces.

2. Add a local variable to the **IVP_D_Reporting** interface:

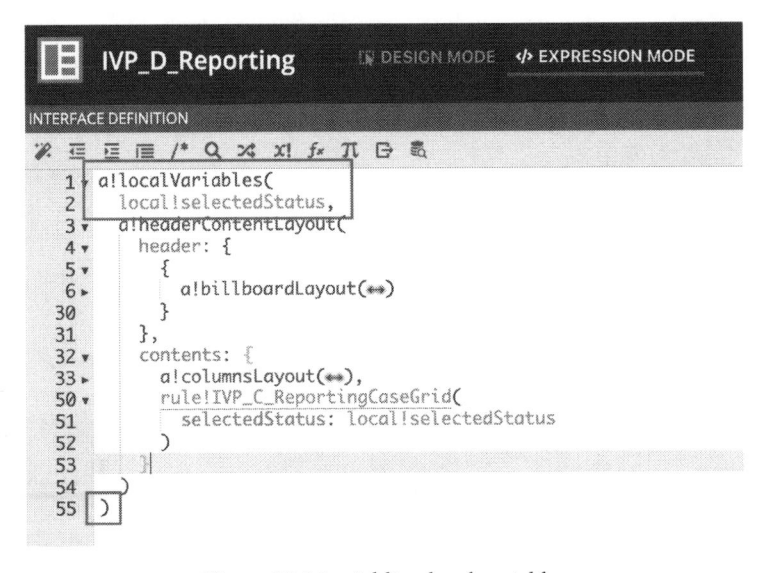

Figure 13.26 – Adding local variables

3. Pass the local variable to the donut chart and the case grid:

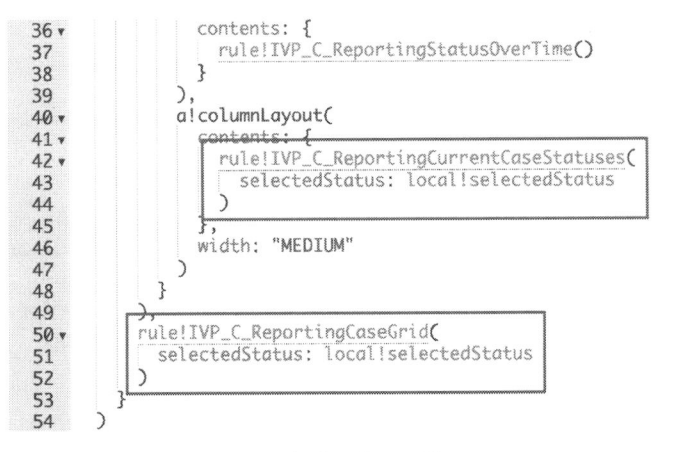

Figure 13.27 – Passing the local variable to components

4. Change the code in the case grid to be able to filter queried data using the status passed to the rule input:

Figure 13.28 – Add a filter to the case grid

5. Remove the parameters data and config from the donut chart:

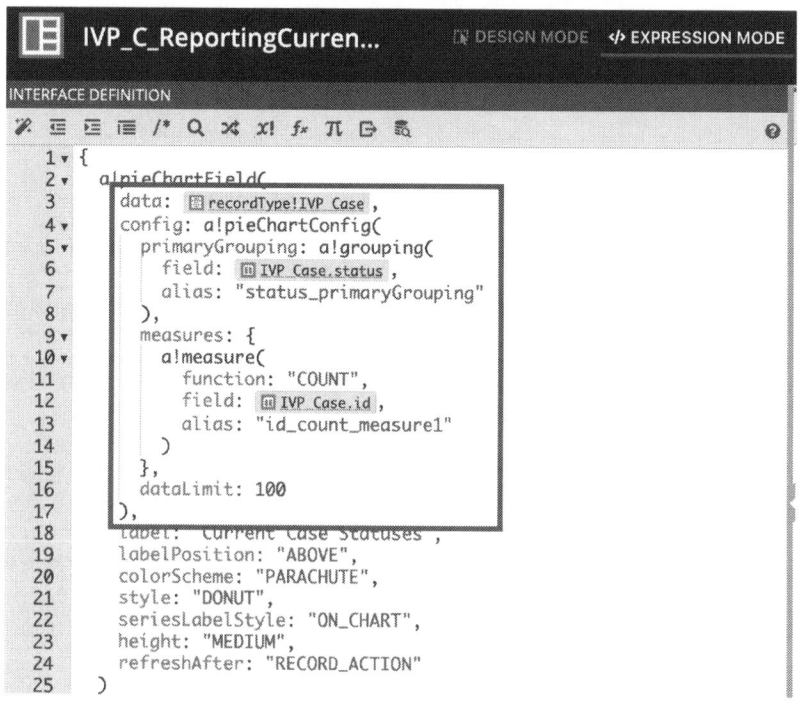

Figure 13.29 – Remove data and config

6. Add a local variable to the donut chart to store the data returned by our IVP_Q_ ReportingCurrentCaseStatus expression:

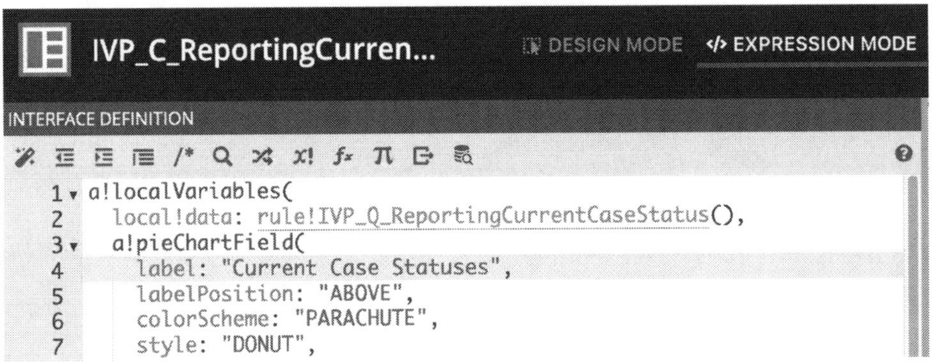

Figure 13.30 – Adding a local variable

7. Add the series parameter:

```
series: a!forEach(
  items: local!data.data,
  expression: a!chartSeries(
    label: proper(fv!item.status),
    data: fv!item.count,
    links: a!dynamicLink(
      value: if(
        ri!selectedStatus = fv!item.status,
        null,
        fv!item.status
      ),
      saveInto: ri!selectedStatus
    ),
    color: if(
      or(
        isnull(ri!selectedStatus),
        ri!selectedStatus = fv!item.status
      ),
      null,
      "#e0e0e0"
    )
```

```
    )
  )
```

This needs a bit of explanation. Our expression returns a list of data structures containing a status and a count stored in the local variable. Each `chartSeries` represents a section of the donut charts. We use the status as the label and the count as the value for `chartSeries`.

`dynamicLink` allows us to modify a variable when the user clicks that link. In our case, the chart sections are now clickable. Clicking a section will store the status of that section in the `selectedStatus` rule input.

To indicate the selected status, we make the color of the section depending on the selected value. If no status is selected or the selected status matches the status of a section, we do not assign a color. Appian will use a default color palette. If any other status is selected, we give the section a gray color:

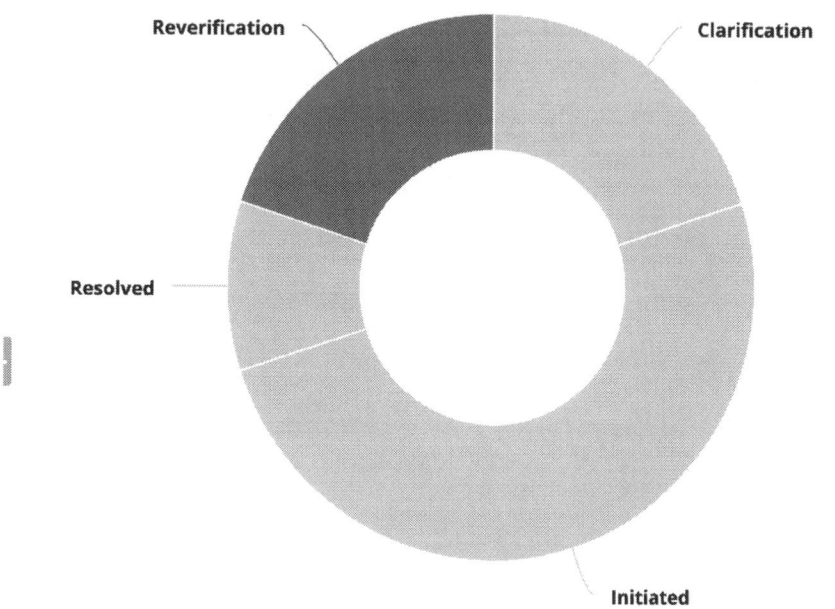

Figure 13.31 – A donut chart showing the selected statuses

The user can now click any section to select a status. Clicking a selected status will unselect it.

Now, by putting the pieces together, we can make our dashboard interactive:

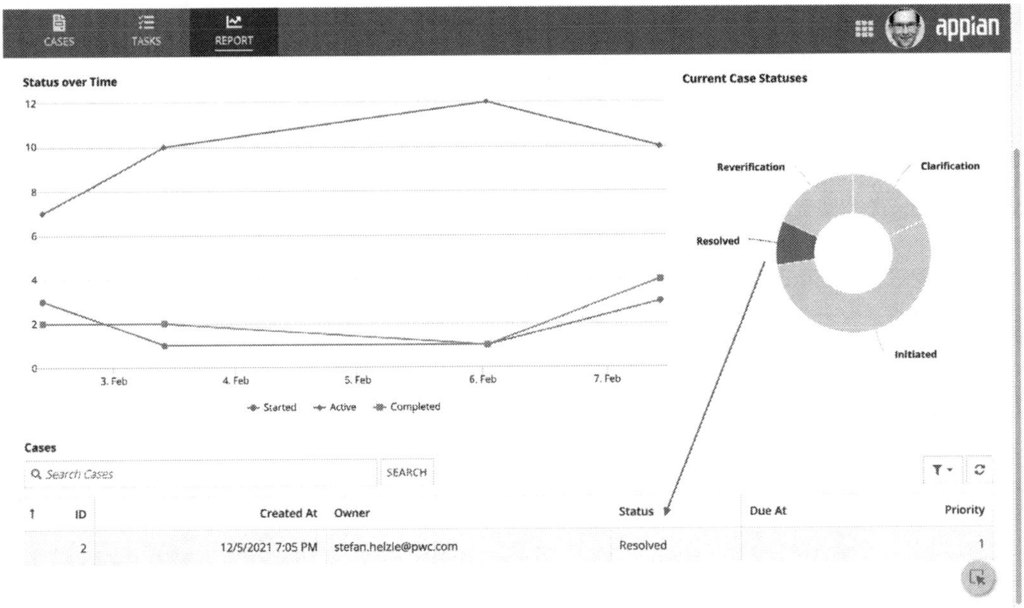

Figure 13.32 – Filter the grid by clicking the donut

Let's now recap reporting and monitoring in Appian and give you some best practices.

Best practices

The following are some best practices regarding stakeholder groups, historic reporting, report interaction, and report composition.

Stakeholder groups

Your target groups for the reports each have their own requirements. The executive board is more interested in the longer-term effects of implemented measures. For a department head, the impact of changes in an environment or process improvements is more important. The operational team leader wants to be able to control his employees based on the reports.

Develop a set of performance indicators for each group of stakeholders and design reports to meet the specific needs of the presentation format. After all, a board meeting is different from a daily team meeting.

Historic reports

Especially for reporting, which shows change over time, you will need to take periodic measurements and persist that data to the database. Sometimes, this is not that easy – for example, you may want to store how many cases have been in a certain status for each day. A simple periodic measurement can only count that number for a specific moment. When counting in the morning, you will not see the cases that enter that status in the afternoon. And what about a case that is in that status for only 15 minutes?

In my experience, the information value of a report that counts a single case in more than one category for a given period of time is rather questionable. Keep in mind that reporting is about identifying problems and the effects of measures taken. That is not an easy task! Take the reporting issue seriously.

Make reports interactive

An interactive reporting dashboard can be a considerable benefit. Zooming into a larger dataset in a line chart or clicking a chart to filter a grid is easily implemented. You can also allow the user to switch between a chart and a grid to display data. Use a local variable to know which part to display. Add conditions to the showWhen parameter of the respective components and links or buttons to switch the state of the local variable.

Again, while an interactive report can be an eye-catcher, everything you do should support a specific requirement and purpose.

Composing reports

Reporting dashboards are a mix of data queries and visualization. Try to create components that combine a query and the visualization for that specific dataset. In a case where you have two charts based on the same data, place both charts into the same component to avoid multiple queries of the same data.

Rule inputs and local variables can be shared to rule inputs of nested components, and updates to these variables can be used for interaction between components.

Summary

In this chapter, you got a good understanding of how to design a reporting dashboard, prepare and measure performance indicators, and visualize data for individual groups of stakeholders.

This chapter concludes the third part, *Implementing Software*, of this book. I want to encourage you to make use of all the things you learned and enhance the invoice validation application. There are quite a few loose ends for you to pick up – for example, there is the **IVP Activities** record, which can store a few more items, and that can become an audit trail of the case. Think about attaching a scan of the invoice to the case.

In the next part of this book, we will deal more intensively with the subject of coding, expressions, and logic in Appian. And in *Chapter 15, Using Web Services with Appian Integrations*, we will return to the application to add a web service integration to post the invoice.

Section 4: The Code in Appian Low-Code

In the last few chapters, you learned how to create a process-driven application using only very little code. That is the standard way of working with Appian. To be honest, that is the only way. In the Appian platform, the closest you can get to coding is in Expression Rules. Unlike other low-code platforms, Appian does not generate Java code in the background that is then deployed and executed. And there is also no in-between layer that executes any scripting language.

> **Appian Plugins**
>
> Appian is a Java Enterprise application and can be enhanced by plugins written in Java and UI components built in HTML and JavaScript. But I recommend going that way only if it is absolutely necessary and is a deal-breaker for your project. Custom plugins will increase the efforts for initial development, testing, and maintenance tremendously.

The reason for this is that Appian can change the way it interprets our configurations and expression rules at any time. This allows Appian to improve the internal architecture over time while keeping compatibility.

In this section of the book, I will show you how to work with Expression Rules in detail. Next, we will have a look at integrating web services and add one to your application. To conclude the book, I will share a set of useful implementation patterns with you.

This section contains the following chapters:

- *Chapter 14, Expressing Logic with Appian*
- *Chapter 15, Using Web Services with Appian Integrations*
- *Chapter 16, Useful Implementation Patterns in Appian*

14
Expressing Logic with Appian

You already wrote some code in Appian expression rules to query data from records. I showed you how to use a **Decision** to implement dynamic task assignments as well. Let's now dive a bit deeper and learn more about how to implement flexible business logic in Appian.

In this chapter, you will get a detailed understanding of the following Appian objects:

- Decisions—simple logic in a visual designer
- Constants—managing literals and application configuration
- Expressions—complex logic expressed in text
- Best practices

Decisions – simple logic in a visual designer

Let's have a brief look here at the decision you created for a dynamic assignment:

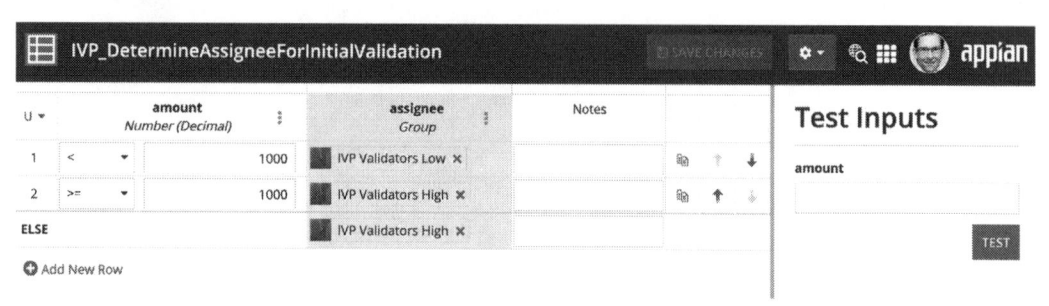

Figure 14.1 – Dynamic assignment decision

Here, we take the amount as input, and depending on a threshold we return one group or another. In general, a **Decision object** in Appian applies some logic to inputs and returns matching output. The limitation here is that we cannot define any dynamic runtime behavior such as data manipulation or database queries.

But we can configure a decision to do a bit more than just simple input-to-output mapping. Our options are presented here:

- **Hit Policy**: Define that only a unique single row can match the first or multiple rows (**Rule Order**)

- **Logical Operator**: Define in which way the input value should be compared

- **Multiple Inputs**: Create one or more inputs to implement multiple condition logic

- **Multiple Outputs**: Create one or more outputs to return groups of values

- **Rule Order**: Move rules up or down to define priority when using the **First Hit Policy**

See the **Hit Policy** options in the following screenshot:

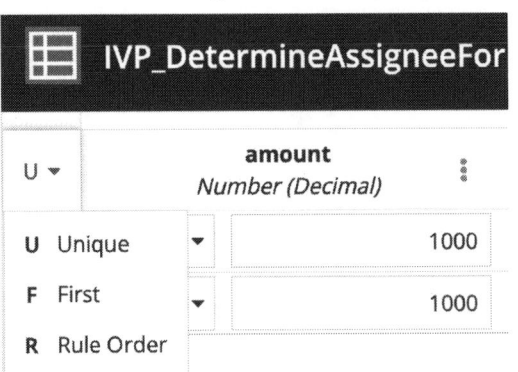

Figure 14.2 – Decision Hit Policy options

Select an **operator** from the dropdown, as seen in the following screenshot:

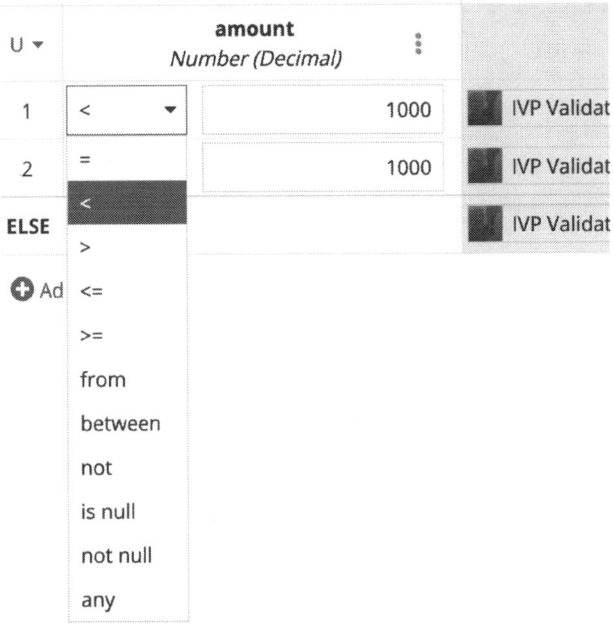

Figure 14.3 – Decision logic operators

The **Hit Policy** option defines the basic behavior of a decision and whether the output is a single item or a list. Then, use the operators according to the logic you have in mind.

Input configuration

When creating an input, you define a name and type. For `Integer` and `Text` types, you will see some additional options, as illustrated in the following screenshot:

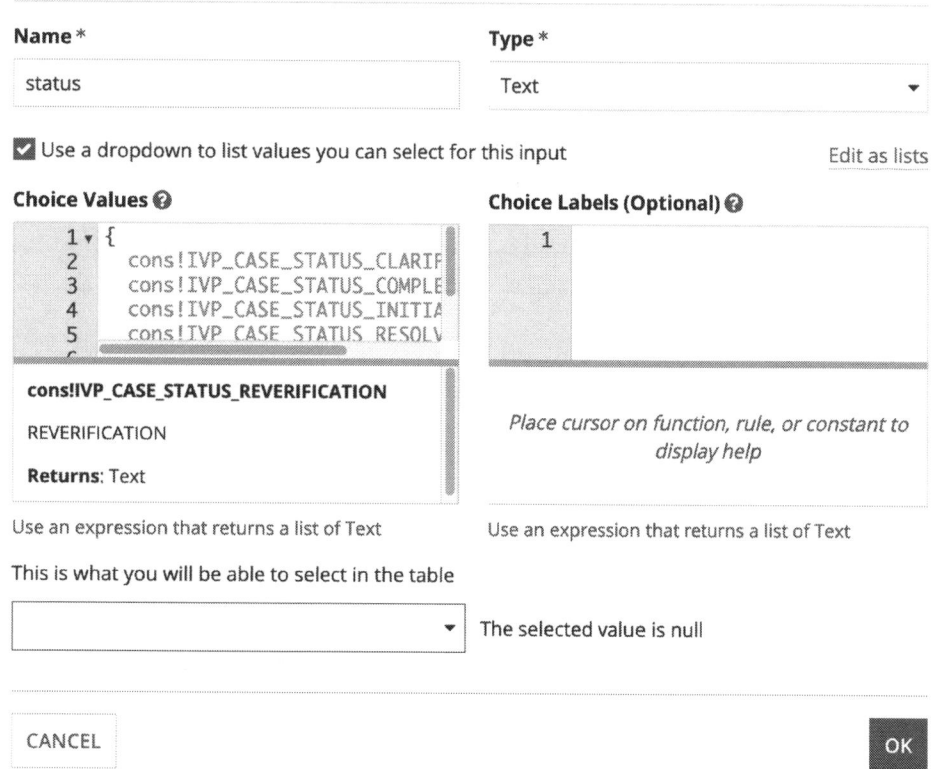

Figure 14.4 – Input configuration

Here, you can define a list of values used for comparison. This list can be entered directly, or as an expression that allows us to use constants.

For example, you want to display an icon on the case dashboard depending on the case status. Store the status values in constants. Use these constants in the decision when defining the input. Create an output of type `Text` and use the names of styled icons as values, as shown at this link: `https://docs.appian.com/suite/help/latest/ux_styled_icons.html`.

We can also use constants as user-managed values in **decisions**. The **Update Constant** smart service can update a constant from a **process model**. You will find it in the **Process Modeler** in **Appian Smart Services|Rule Management**.

Create a **user interface** (**UI**) for application configuration to allow the user to manage certain values stored in constants and add it as a start form to a process model. See *Chapter 10, Modeling Business Processes in Appian,* for how to do that. Then, use these constants in decisions. Make sure to restrict access to the process model to a select group.

> **Tip**
> When using the **Update Constant** smart service, make sure to define the assignment as **Run as whoever designed this process model**. This is always the account that deployed the application and is always a user of type **System Administrator**. This smart service, and a few more, requires elevated permissions. Find this information in the documentation of the respective smart service.

Output configuration

An output has a name, a specific type, and can be made into a list. Have a look at the following screenshot to view the configuration of an output:

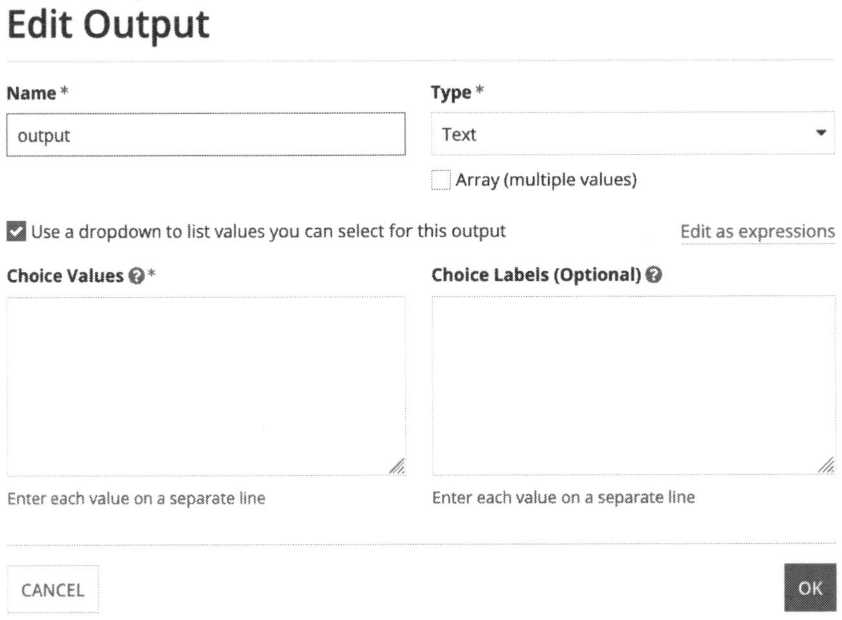

Edit Output

Name *	Type *
output	Text ▼
	☐ Array (multiple values)

☑ Use a dropdown to list values you can select for this output   Edit as expressions

Choice Values ❓ *	Choice Labels (Optional) ❓
Enter each value on a separate line	Enter each value on a separate line

CANCEL   OK

Figure 14.5 – Output configuration

You can also predefine a list of values to choose from when defining rules. Defining this as an expression allows user-managed values, as with inputs.

Similar to inputs, you can define multiple outputs. The decision will then return a data structure holding one field for each named output.

If you select the **Rule Order** hit policy and multiple rules match the input, the decision will return a list of outputs. This is just a list if you defined a single output and a list of data structures for multiple outputs, as illustrated in the following screenshot:

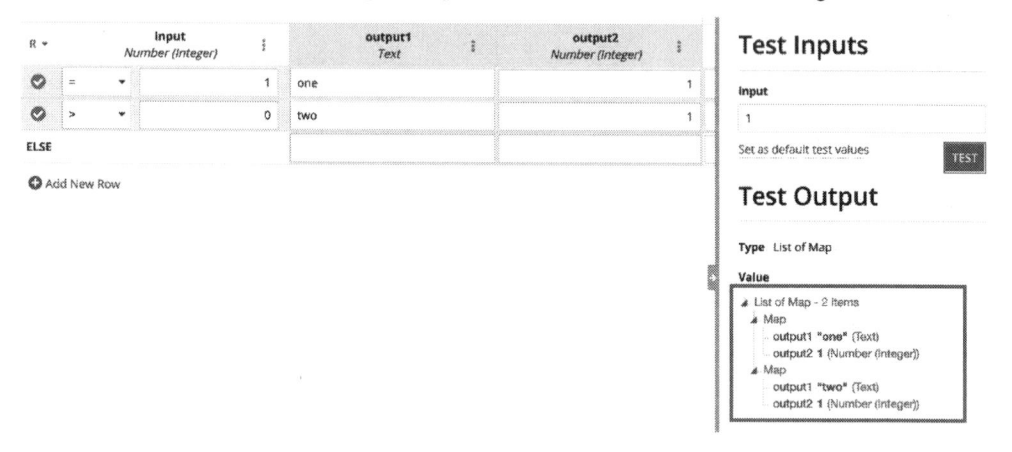

Figure 14.6 – List of data structures

Now, let's look at what the decision returns when we define an output as a list. Have a look at the following screenshot:

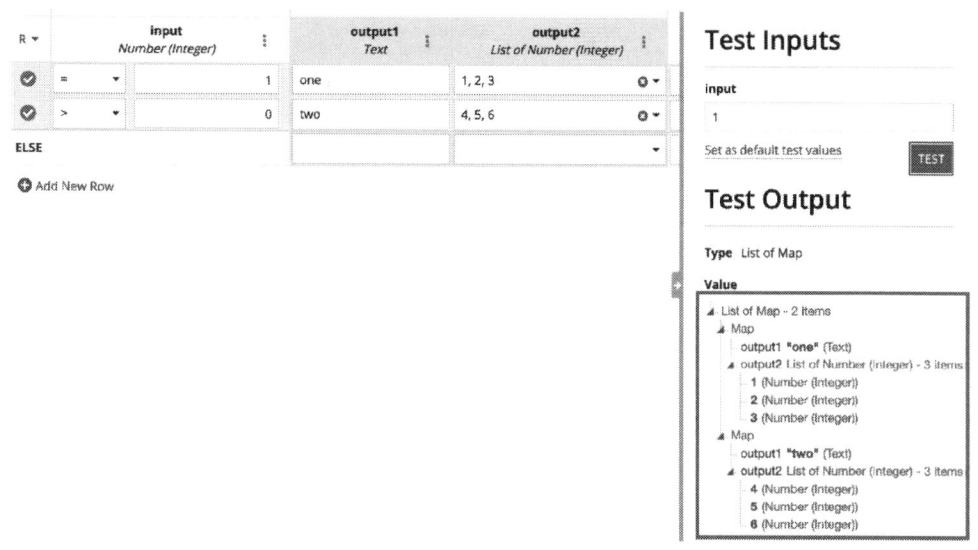

Figure 14.7 – List of data structures with a list-type output

As expected, this time, we get a list of data structures, with one field being a list.

Decisions summary

Decisions are a handy tool in Appian to express static business logic. Before writing a list of nested `if()` statements in an expression rule, check whether a decision could be the easier approach. Combine it with constants to make the behavior user-manageable.

While we're talking about constants, let's take a closer look at them now.

Constants – managing literals and application configuration

Constants are used in Appian to store specific typed values used in an application. Constants allow you to create a defined set of values for a given use case. Referencing a constant instead of typing the value repeatedly reduces the error rate and the effort required for debugging and maintenance.

When looking at your application, you will notice that you already created several constants. Most of them are of type `Text` and hold values used for status tracking and process control. In some of my projects, about a third of the several hundred application objects are constants. So, why so many, and what to use them for?

String literals

The biggest use case for constants is to store values for status tracking and decision-making in processes. Here, using a constant helps to assign the correct values, but also when displaying the status to the user; and in **decisions**, **expression rules**, and **queries**, you can reference these constants.

If you have a task in a process in which the user needs to make a decision, use constants to define possible outcomes. Then, in the process, use the same constants in an `XOR` gateway to control the process flow based on user selection.

I would like to give you a special tip regarding status values and constants. There are situations in which you need each value separate, but also situations in which you want all values as a list. In the past, I saw a single status constant, holding all the values as a list. Referencing a specific status was done like this:

```
cons!XYZ_CASE_STATUS[3]
```

Now, what happens when someone decides to change the order of the values in the constant?

The alternative solution I propose is this:

1. Create a constant for each status value

2. Create an expression rule that creates a list of all these status values

3. You can see an example of this in the following code snippet:

```
{
    cons!XYZ_CASE_STATUS_NEW,
    cons!XYZ_CASE_STATUS_WAITING,
    cons!XYZ_CASE_STATUS_COMPLETED,
}
```

Now, you have both requirements covered. Each value is separate, and when you need them all in a list, just call the expression. Make sure to update the expression if you add or remove any status value.

Groups

There are certain situations when you require a constant to reference a group. Most often, this is the case when you want to check if someone is a member of a certain group. Think of a UI in which you would like to show or hide certain content based on the role of the user. For a specific type of process report, you will also need a group constant when querying data using a!queryProcessAnalytics().

Data store entities

Constants referencing data store entities are used with functions that interact with a connected relational database, as listed here:

*   a!queryEntity(): Query data including filtering and aggregation from a connected relational database from any expression

*   a!writeToDataStoreEntity(): Insert or update data in a connected relational database from an interface or a web **application programming interface (API)**

*   a!deleteFromDataStoreEntities(): Delete data from a connected relational database from an interface or a web API

Documents

In the **Invoice Validation** application, we used a constant of type `Document` to reference the background image of the reporting dashboard. Whenever you want to add a custom icon, background, or illustration to your application, you upload an image and create a constant. Then, use this constant and the `a!documentImage()` function to turn the document into an image that can be displayed by an `imageField`, `richTextImage`, or `billboardLayout`.

Another common use case is **process reports**. These reports are stored as documents in the Appian document management system. To query data from a process report, we use the **Query Process Analytics in Process Models** smart service and the `a!queryProcessAnalytics()` function in expression rules and interfaces.

Process models

You use process model-type constants with the `a!queryProcessAnalytics()` function to define process models from which to retrieve data.

Constants summary

Although we usually create countless constants in applications, this is not a very extensive topic. Let's spend the rest of the chapter on the many possibilities of expressions.

Expressions – constant logic expressed in text

In Appian, you use low-code methods to design the largest parts of your applications. Although this is very powerful, there are situations where you need more flexibility, which only code can provide.

You can find all details about expressions on the following Appian documentation page:

`https://docs.appian.com/suite/help/latest/Expressions.html`

To be able to write expressions, you need to know the available functions. I highly recommend the following list of Appian functions: `https://docs.appian.com/suite/help/21.4/Appian_Functions.html`.

Programming paradigms

If you already have experience in other programming languages such as Java or C#, be aware that the Appian expression language is different—and by different, I mean not just the syntax; Appian expressions use an entirely different programming paradigm.

Java and C# are imperative languages in which you describe the individual steps of data transformation to solve a specific problem. This data transformation includes the mutation of any local data structure and internal or external storage or system.

The Appian expression language follows a functional paradigm. These functions, which we call expressions in Appian, are stateless and always return the same output for a given input. If your data does not meet your requirements, you pass it to another function or expression, but since variables in functional programming languages are immutable, this function does not change your original data. You get a new, transformed copy of the data as a return value.

In this book, I will cover functional programming in the scope of Appian only, and I will give you a few hints to adapt your existing way of problem-solving. To find out more about functional programming, find various books in the *Packt Publishing* library. I also recommend watching Russ Olsen talking about functional programming at the *GOTO* conference 2018 on YouTube: `https://www.youtube.com/watch?v=0if71HOyVjY`.

Let's have a brief look at a simple example. We have a list of numbers and want to multiply each number by a factor.

This is the code in Java:

```java
import java.util.Arrays;

public class Main {
    public static void main(String[] args) {
        System.out.println("Hello from Java!");
        int numbers[] = {2, 1, 7, 6, 4, 2, 9};
        System.out.println(Arrays.toString(numbers));
        multiplyArray(numbers, 3);
        System.out.println(Arrays.toString(numbers));
    }
    public static void multiplyArray(int array[], int factor) {
        for(int i = 0; i < array.length; i++) {
            array[i] = array[i] * factor;
        }
    }
}
```

The code in Appian is split into two parts.

- Here's the code for the main expression:

```
a!localVariables(
  local!numbers: {2, 1, 7, 6, 4, 2, 9},
  local!transformedNumbers: rule!helperExpression(
    numbers: local!numbers,
    factor: 3
  ),
  concat(
    local!numbers,
    char(10),
    local!transformedNumbers
  )
)
```

- And here's the code for the helper expression:

```
a!forEach(
  items: ri!numbers,
  expression: fv!item * ri!factor
)
```

Now, about the difference. In Java, the numbers variable is being modified in place, and the former state is lost. In Appian, the forEach() function creates a new, modified copy of the values and returns that. The numbers and transformedNumbers variables are completely separate, and numbers is unmodified.

To implement more complex behavior in Java, you write multiple lines of code, and each line modifies the data directly. In Appian, you just pass the output of one function to the next. Let's do a quick example, as follows:

```
text(
  date(
    year(today()),
    month(today()),
    ri!daysOfMonth
  ),
  "mmm ddd yyyy"
)
```

The idea is to turn the `daysOfMonth` rule input into a nicely formatted list of dates. The `date()` function detects that one parameter is a list and automatically creates a list with a dynamic day and the same month and year for all dates. Then, I pass this list of dates to the `text()` function, which applies the required format to all items in the list, as illustrated in the following screenshot:

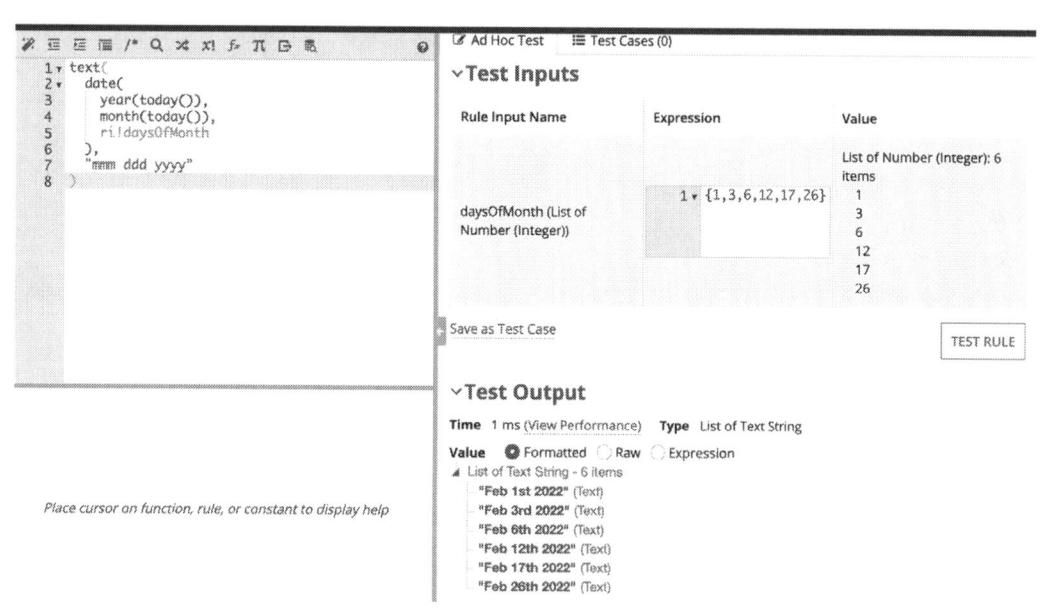

Figure 14.8 – Test and output in Appian

To transform data, just pass the output of one function to the next function by "wrapping" it. There is no need to do each step in a separate line by creating local variables for each, as in the following example:

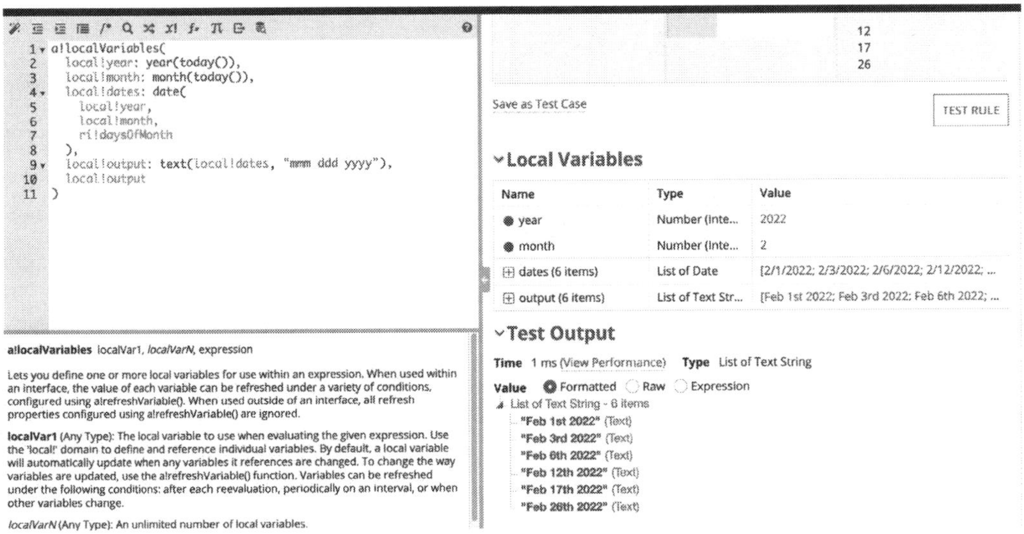

```
1 ▾ a!localVariables(
2      local!year: year(today()),
3      local!month: month(today()),
4 ▾    local!dates: date(
5          local!year,
6          local!month,
7          ri!daysOfMonth
8      ),
9 ▾    local!output: text(local!dates, "mmm ddd yyyy"),
10     local!output
11 )
```

                                                            12
                                                            17
                                                            26

Save as Test Case   TEST RULE

▾ Local Variables

Name	Type	Value
● year	Number (Inte...	2022
● month	Number (Inte...	2
⊞ dates (6 items)	List of Date	[2/1/2022; 2/3/2022; 2/6/2022; 2/12/2022; ...
⊞ output (6 items)	List of Text Str...	[Feb 1st 2022; Feb 3rd 2022; Feb 6th 2022; ...

▾ Test Output

Time 1 ms (View Performance)   **Type** List of Text String

Value ● Formatted ○ Raw ○ Expression
▴ List of Text String - 6 items
    "Feb 1st 2022" (Text)
    "Feb 3rd 2022" (Text)
    "Feb 6th 2022" (Text)
    "Feb 12th 2022" (Text)
    "Feb 17th 2022" (Text)
    "Feb 26th 2022" (Text)

a!localVariables localVar1, *localVarN*, expression

Lets you define one or more local variables for use within an expression. When used within an interface, the value of each variable can be refreshed under a variety of conditions, configured using a!refreshVariable(). When used outside of an interface, all refresh properties configured using a!refreshVariable() are ignored.

localVar1 (Any Type): The local variable to use when evaluating the given expression. Use the 'local!' domain to define and reference individual variables. By default, a local variable will automatically update when any variables it references are changed. To change the way variables are updated, use the a!refreshVariable() function. Variables can be refreshed under the following conditions: after each reevaluation, periodically on an interval, or when other variables change.

localVarN (Any Type): An unlimited number of local variables.

Figure 14.9 – Line-by-line transformation

While this technically works, it creates many unnecessary local variables and wastes memory, and it is just not the right way of writing expressions in Appian.

For more details on data in expressions, see the next section.

Inputs, locals, and outputs

Expressions in Appian have an optional input and a single function or operation that creates an output. When creating rule inputs, you define a data type to make it easier for developers to understand which values to pass in. Data queried from a database or web API can also act as a kind of input. A good example is IVP_MeasureReportingData.

In an expression, rule inputs define data available to your code. Use a!localVariables() to wrap your existing code to add local variables as the first parameters. The last parameter is your code, which now has access to any rule inputs plus local variables. Any functions or expressions used to declare local variables evaluate before your code does.

The output of an expression is defined by the function or operation. This might be confusing as most expressions consist of multiple lines of text, but this is just to make it more readable. Technically, this is a single function call wrapping another function call, and so on. Let's have a look at the following code, which you saw in *Figure 14.8*:

```
text(
  date(
    year(today()),
    month(today()),
    ri!daysOfMonth
  ),
  "mmm ddd yyyy"
)
```

The single function call is text(). The first parameter is created by the output of the date() function, which calls the year() and month() functions. The functions are called from outside in and their respective output is passed inside out. I will now add local variables to the game, as follows, then we will analyze the code again:

```
a!localVariables(
  local!today: today(),
  text(
    date(
      year(local!today),
      month(local!today),
      ri!daysOfMonth
    ),
    "mmm ddd yyyy"
  )
)
```

Now, the only function call is a!localVariables(), which first defines local!today. Then, it calls the text() function, followed by date(), year(), and month(), which use the local variable.

> **Tip**
>
> Create your expressions so that they produce the same type of output data in all circumstances. I have seen expressions returning three different types of output data. This leads to a fragile application and massively increased efforts for debugging. This is the reason for the typecast in `IVP_Q_GetInvoiceById`.

In the next section, we will have a closer look at data types.

Data types

Appian uses a mix of **static types** and **dynamic types**. Variables in processes have static types, which means that you need to define a type when creating a variable. Rule inputs in interfaces and expressions work in the same way. In contrast, local variables adopt the data type of the assigned data—in other words, they are dynamically typed.

When assigning values to a variable, Appian is extremely good at automatically doing the appropriate kind of conversion. For example, when you assign values such as `true`, `yes`, `y`, or `1` to a Boolean, the resulting value will be `true`.

On the other side, when comparing two values, the types must match; otherwise, Appian will display an error message complaining about a type mismatch, as illustrated here:

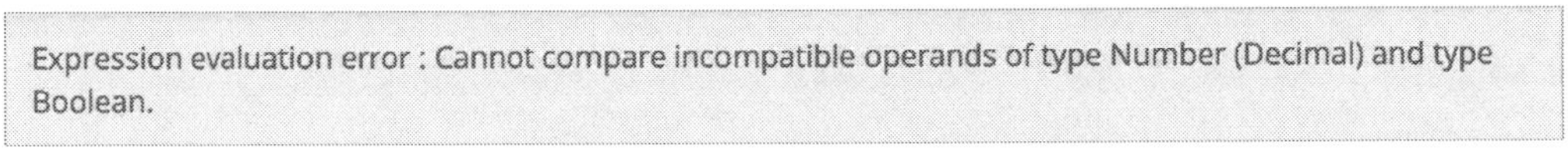

> Expression evaluation error : Cannot compare incompatible operands of type Number (Decimal) and type Boolean.

Figure 14.10 – Type mismatch error

To convert, or cast, a data type to another, Appian provides a list of functions such as `tostring()`, `toboolean()`, and `tointeger()`. Visit the following Appian documentation page for a comprehensive list of conversion functions: `https://docs.appian.com/suite/help/latest/Appian_Functions.html`.

> **Tip**
>
> Unlike some other functions in Appian, `tostring()` does not support lists. When you pass a list, the entire list is converted to a single string. Use the `touniformstring()` function to convert lists of data into lists of strings.

There is also a generic function to convert data to a specific type—the `cast()` function. It takes the data to be converted and a data type to which to convert, as illustrated in the following code snippet:

```
cast(
    'type!{http://www.appian.com/ae/types/2009}Text',
    123
)
```

This converts the number `123` into text. All data types in Appian can be referenced like this, and by adding the `?list` suffix to the type, as illustrated in the following code snippet, you can convert the whole list into another type:

```
cast(
    'type!{http://www.appian.com/ae/types/2009}Decimal?list',
    {"123", "7.1", "371", "61.34"}
)
```

The last stop on our journey through data types looks at the **custom data type (CDT)** types we created in our application. You already created a data structure from a type in the `IVP_MeasureReportingData` expression, as follows:

```
'type!{urn:com:tarence:types:IVP}IVP_DailyReportingData'(
    date: today(),
    numCreated: local!numCreated,
    numActive: local!numActive,
    numCompleted: local!numCompleted
)
```

And you can easily cast a data structure to that CDT type, like this:

```
cast(
    'type!{urn:com:tarence:types:IVP}IVP_DailyReportingData',
    {
        date: today(),
        numCreated: 0
    }
)
```

The data structure I define here is called a dictionary, which is a list of field names and their values. I intentionally skipped some fields, so in the created data structure, these will be empty. You can see the output in the following screenshot:

Value   ● Formatted   ○ Raw   ○ Expression

⌐ IVP_DailyReportingData

    id **null** (Number (Integer))

    date **2/10/2022 1:00 AM GMT+01:00** (Date and Time)

    numCreated **0** (Number (Integer))

    numActive **null** (Number (Integer))

    numCompleted **null** (Number (Integer))

Figure 14.11 – Typecast dictionary

You will use this technique, for example, when creating web APIs to allow external systems to send data to Appian. The incoming data must be converted into its internal data type for validation and further processing.

Now, we take a closer look at data structures.

Dictionaries and maps

In Appian, we have CDTs to define static and reusable data structures. Besides CDTs, we have two more ways to create ad hoc data structures.

With dictionaries, we can create a data structure whenever needed. Dictionaries are also used in other programming languages and work similarly. Create a dictionary using curly brackets, like this:

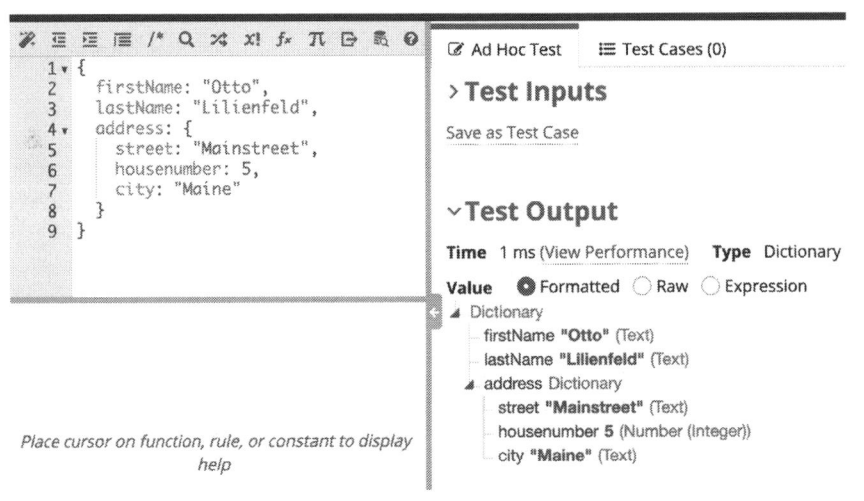

Figure 14.12 – Dictionary example

Consider dictionaries a legacy application. They have been replaced by maps recently.

Maps work very similarly to dictionaries, with one big difference: all fields have a defined data type and keep that type when extracting values from a structure.

First, let's have a look at a value extracted from a dictionary, as follows:

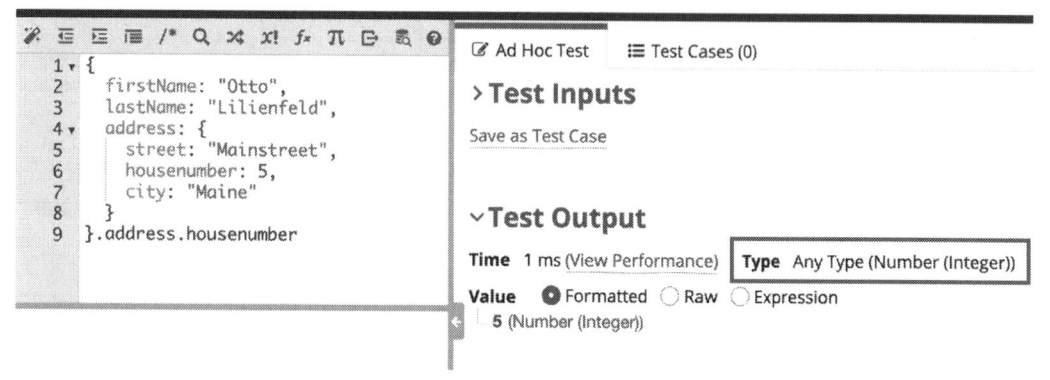

Figure 14.13 – Value extraction from a dictionary

Here's the same situation, but using a map:

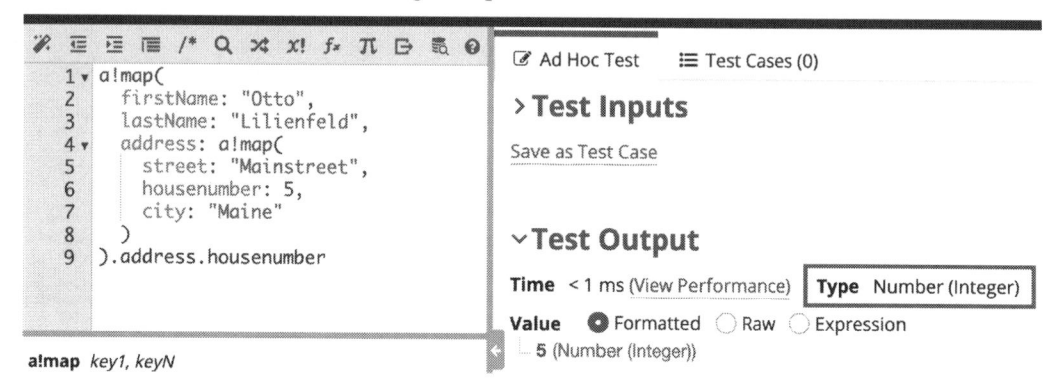

Figure 14.14 – Value extraction from a map

Although the difference does not seem to be large, there may be situations where the value no longer has an assignment type, and further processing fails.

Another important aspect of preferring maps to dictionaries is that maps are a supported data type for process variables, but dictionaries are not.

While you should know both ways of creating ad hoc data structures, the clear recommendation is to use maps.

In *Figure 14.14*, I used dot notation to define a path to drill down into the data structure of a specific field. Another option would be to use angular brackets, like so:

```
a!map(firstName: "otto")["firstname"]
```

This works well, as long as the fields exist. If any of the fields in the path do not exist, the expression just fails.

In Appian, we use the index() or property() function to access a certain field in a data structure or a specific item in a list in a safe way. To make this work, these functions allow us to define a default value in case the field or item does not exist. You can see the index() function in use in the following screenshot:

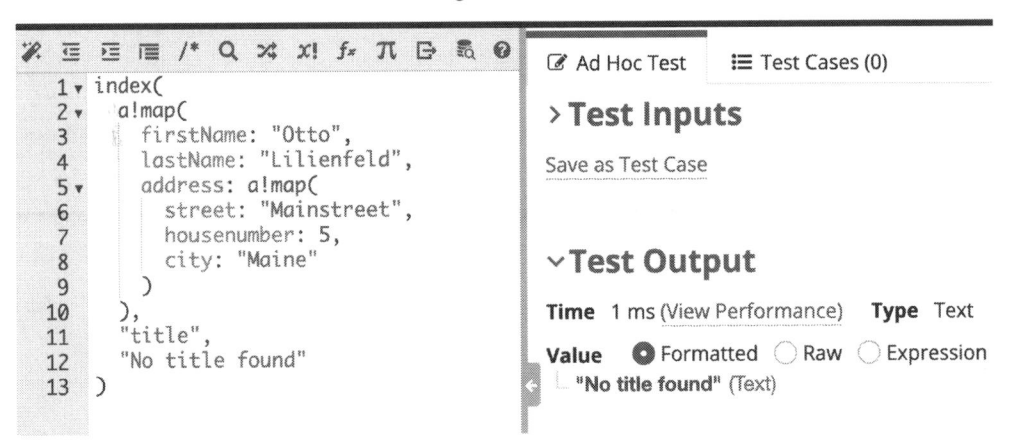

Figure 14.15 – Indexing into a data structure

The index() and property() functions can only drill down a single level. In *Chapter 16, Useful Implementation Patterns in Appian*, I will show you a more efficient way to drill into a deep data structure than to nest multiple index() or property() calls.

> **Tip**
>
> There is a major drawback when using index() or property() functions over dot notation or angular brackets. Both functions return a copy of the data, while dot notation and angular brackets return a reference to the data. When composing interfaces out of smaller components that implement editable fields, always pass partial data using dot notation or angular brackets. These reference parts of a local variable or rule input in which a field can store data. That does not work when passing the output of a function directly.

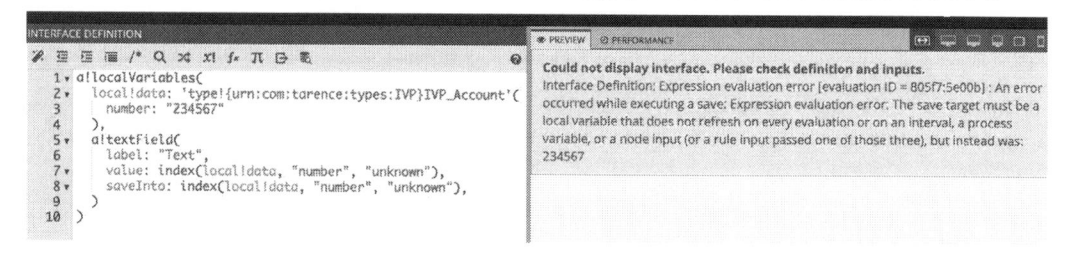

Figure 14.16 – Saving into index()

Since I mentioned lists, let's see how they work.

Working with lists

In our application, we already had some contact with lists. In Appian, a list is capable of containing any data type, and is created like this:

```
{1, 4, 6, 34}
```
```
{"John", "Jim", "Jack"}
```

This is a list of integers and a list of text. You can also create a heterogeneous list, like so:

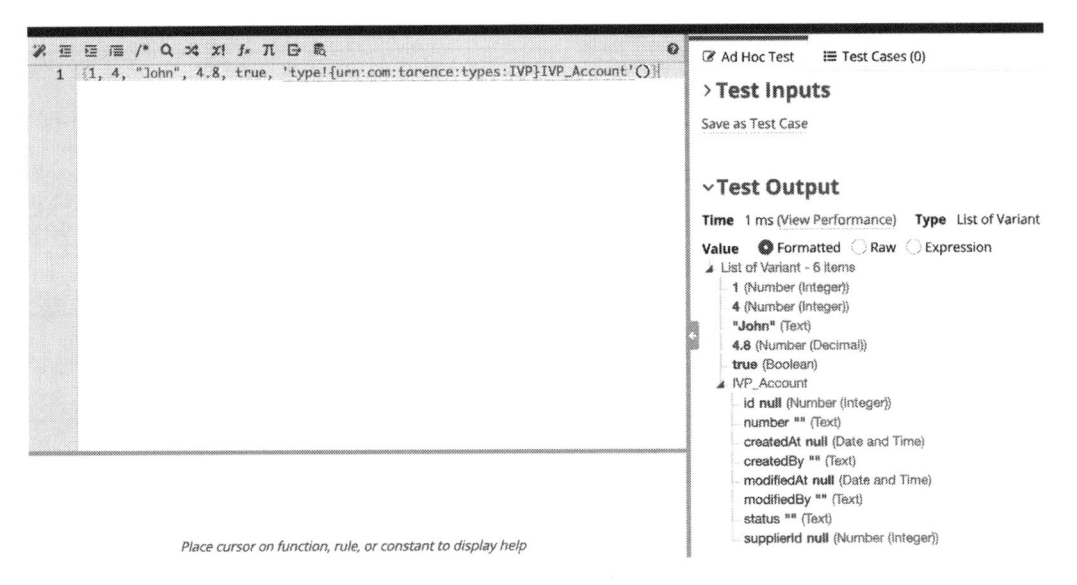

Figure 14.17 – Heterogeneous list

To access items in our flexible lists, we use angular brackets, `index()`, or `property()`. The limitations are the same as for data structures, with `index()` and `property()` returning a copy, and the angular brackets returning a reference that can be modified.

Now that you know how to create lists and access items, I want to explain how to implement typical use cases.

Iterating lists

Use `a!forEach()` to apply an expression to each item in a list. The output will have the exact same number of items as the input, as shown in the following screenshot. But before trying to solve any problem using `a!forEach()`, keep in mind that all operators and most functions in Appian can directly work with lists:

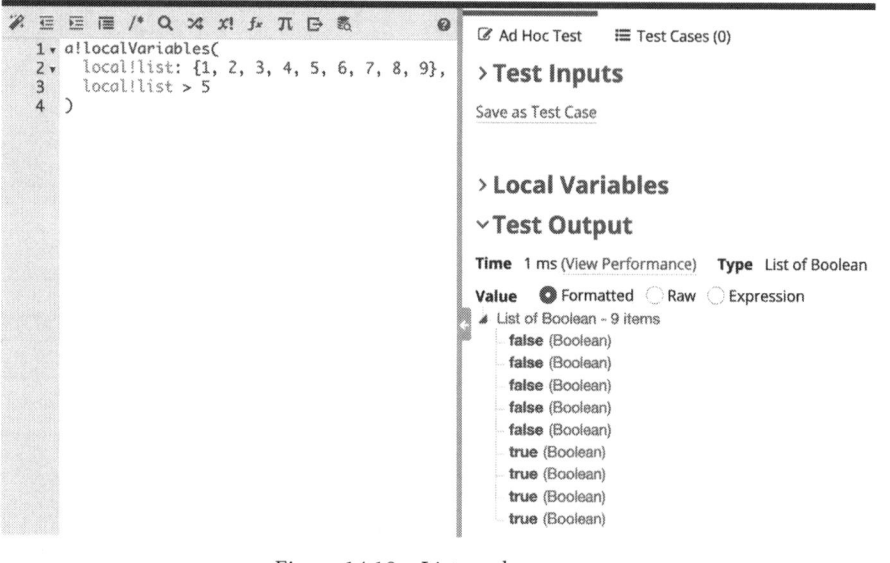

Figure 14.18 – Lists and operators

Here's a more meaningful example:

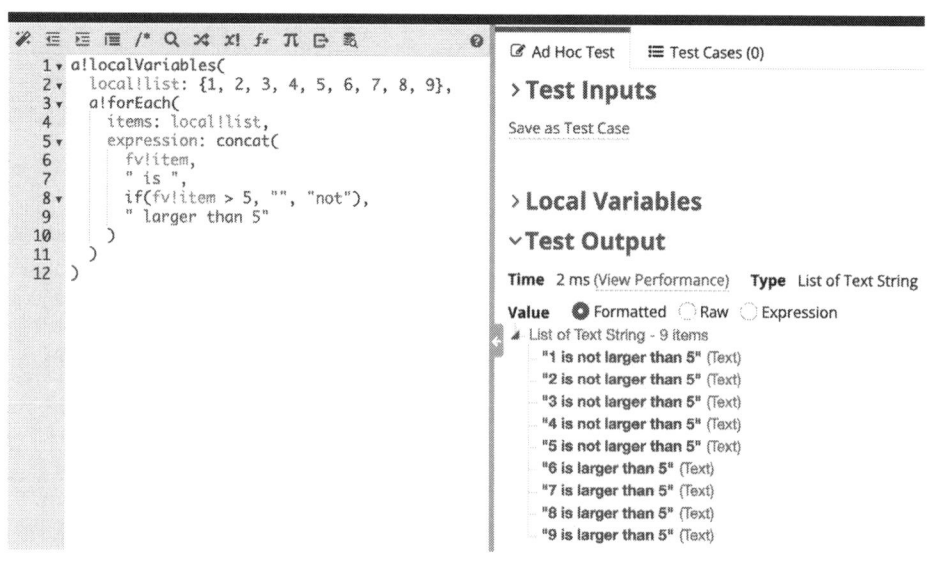

Figure 14.19 – Formatting text from a list

You can also generate a dynamic UI using a!forEach(), as we did in IVP_F_ InitialVerification to display a list of orders.

Now, because a!forEach produces exactly one element as output for each element of the input, a!forEach cannot be used to filter a list, as illustrated in the following screenshot:

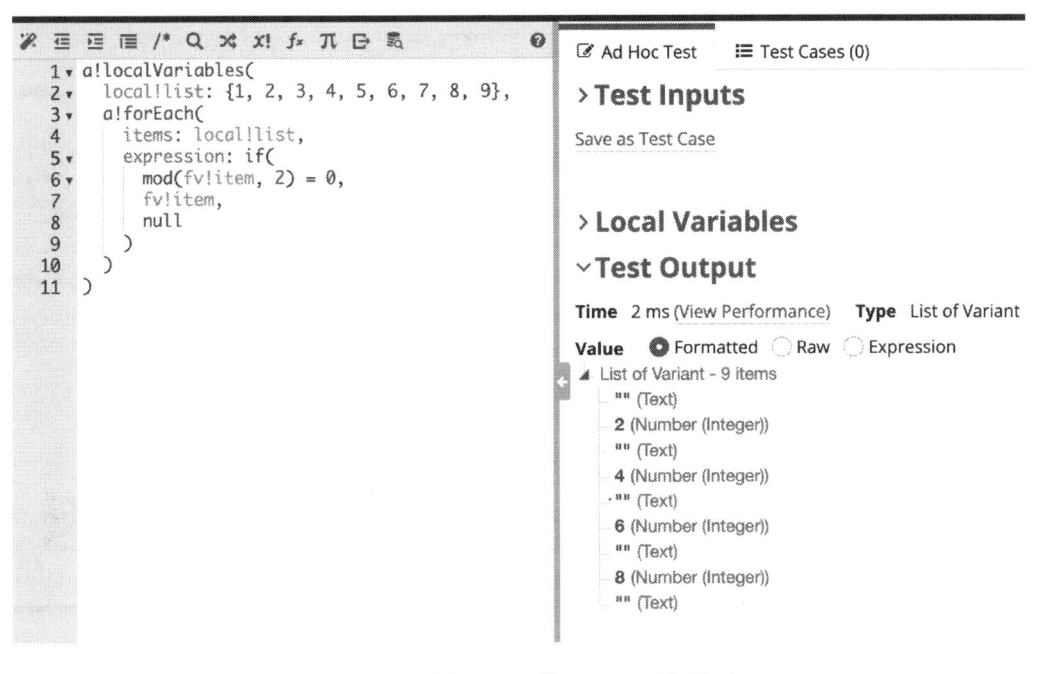

Figure 14.20 – Trying to filter using a!forEach

Tip

There is a lengthy discussion going on in the Appian community about whether to use a!forEach() for filtering or not. While I agree that it can be done, I don't think it's an elegant solution. My recommendation is to use the filter() function, as I describe later in this chapter.

There is one more thing to know about Appian and lists. Appian is pretty good at automatically merging lists of lists. Have a look at the following code snippet:

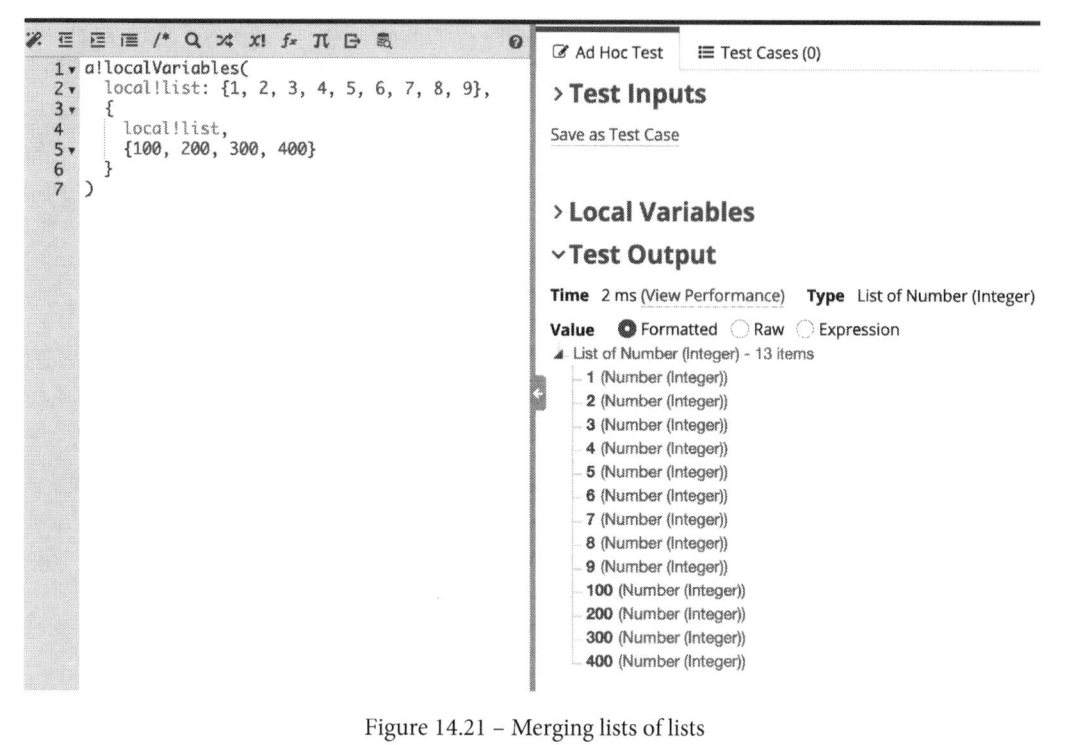

Figure 14.21 – Merging lists of lists

But this does not always work when using a!forEach(), as we can see here:

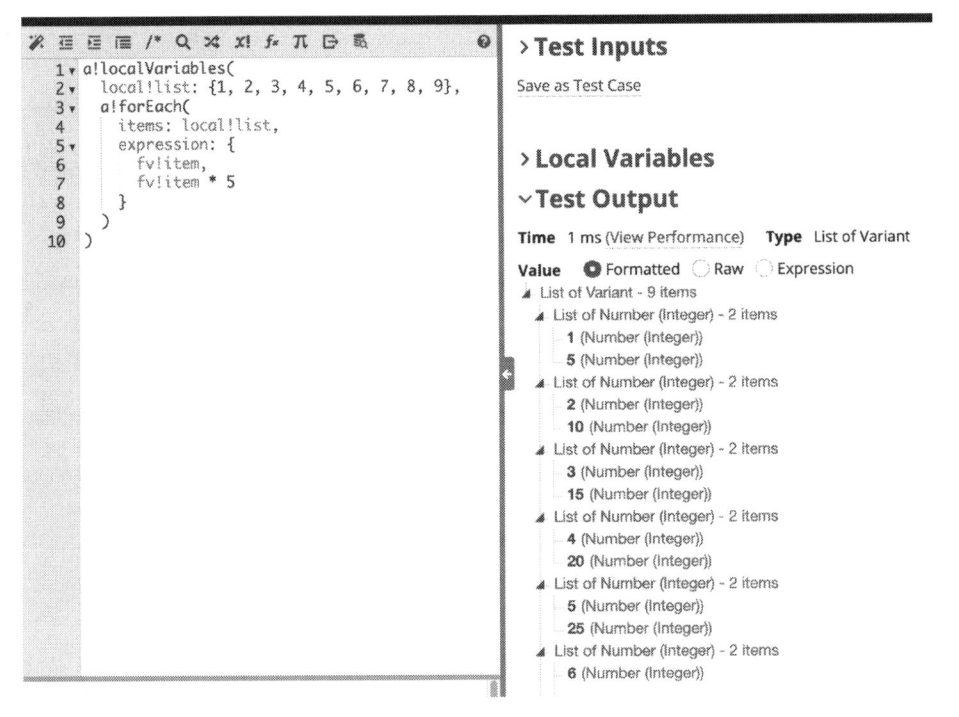

Figure 14.22 – a!forEach and lists of lists

If you get into such a situation, use the `a!flatten()` function to merge lists of lists into a single list, as illustrated in the following screenshot:

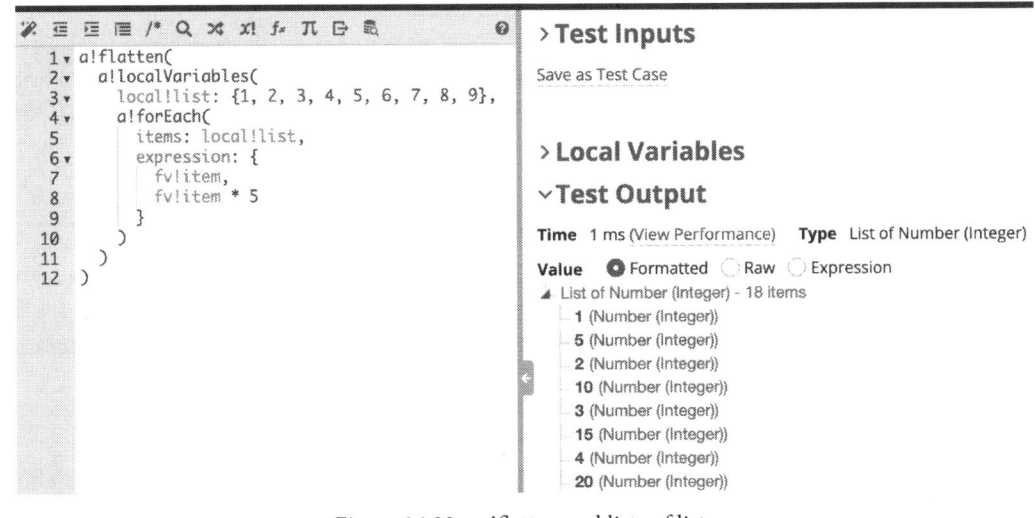

Figure 14.23 – a!flatten and lists of lists

That's enough about iterating lists. Let's now talk about how to filter lists.

Filtering lists

Appian provides some functions that are specifically designed for lists. They are called **looping functions**, and `a!forEach()` belongs to this category. The functions I want to explain now are `filter()` and `reject()`. As with any other looping function, they evaluate an expression—called a predicate—for each element in a list. These expressions must return a Boolean value, and depending on that, the element is either included in the returned list or not. You can see the `filter()` function in use in the following screenshot:

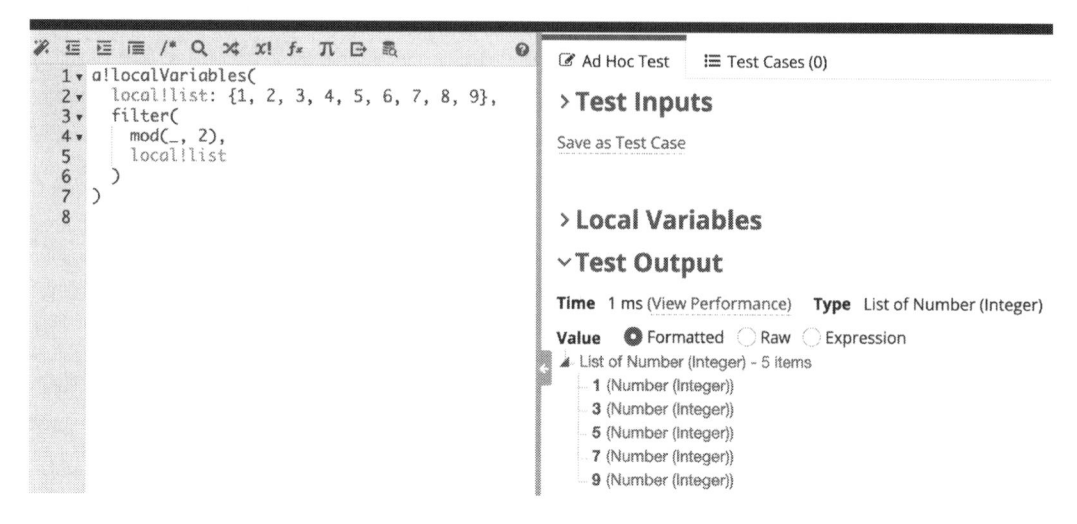

Figure 14.24 – Filtering using modulo

In this example, I use the `mod()` function, which returns 0 or 1, to get all uneven numbers from the list. Replace `filter()` with `reject()` to get all even numbers.

But what is this " _ " all about? This represents the item when calling the predicate expression for each list item.

As the predicate expression can be any function or expression, you can, of course, implement your own separate expression to implement more complex behavior.

Let's have a look at some of the siblings of `filter()` and `reject()`.

Evaluating lists

In some situations, you may need to check all items in a list for certain conditions. In Appian, you can use the following functions:

- `all()`: Returns `true` if all items match

- `any()`: Returns `true` if at least one item matches

- `none()`: Returns `true` if no item matches

The predicate expression works in the same way as the other looping functions, as illustrated in the following screenshot:

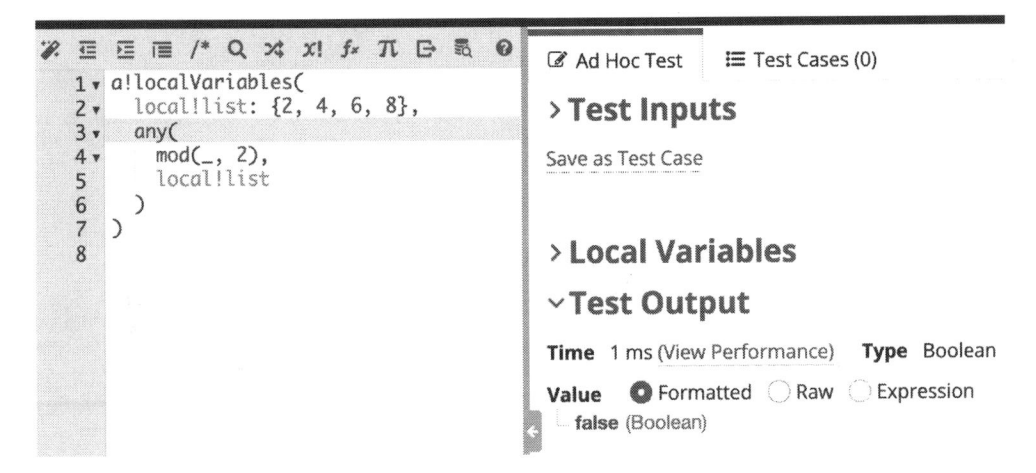

Figure 14.25 – Checking for uneven numbers

And now, at the very end, the most interesting looping function.

Reducing a list

The reduce() function is a simple one but can be used to implement some fascinating algorithms. Think of a block-based checksum algorithm such as the one the **International Bank Account Number** (**IBAN**) system uses. I will describe that in *Chapter 16, Useful Implementation Patterns in Appian*. Let's start with a simple example, as follows:

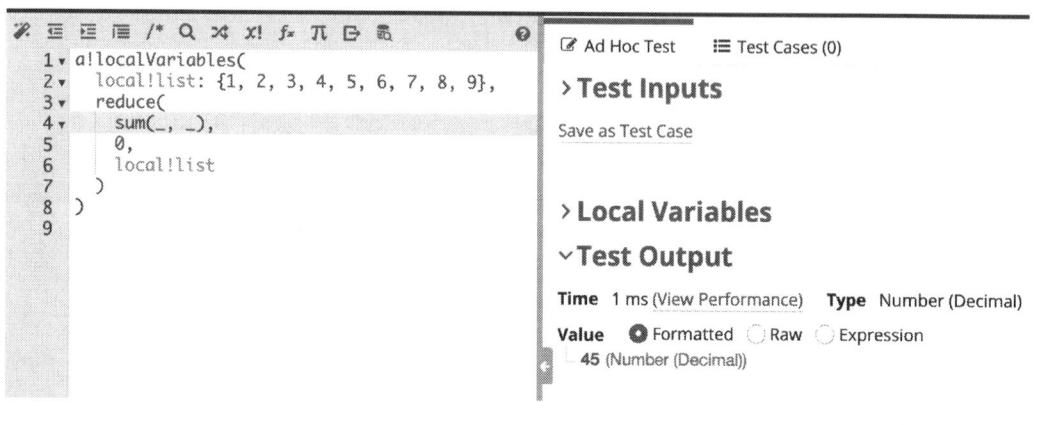

Figure 14.26 – Simple reduce() example

The reduce() function takes a predicate expression and a list, as with the other looping functions, but it also takes an initial value. It now passes two values to the predicate expression—first, the initial value; second, an item from the list. In the next iteration, the result of the first iteration becomes the new initial value.

In our example, the evaluated list looks like this:

```
( ( ( ( ( ( ( (0+1) + 2) + 3) + 4) + 5) + 6) + 7) + 8)
```

Let's add our own predicate expression to the game, as follows:

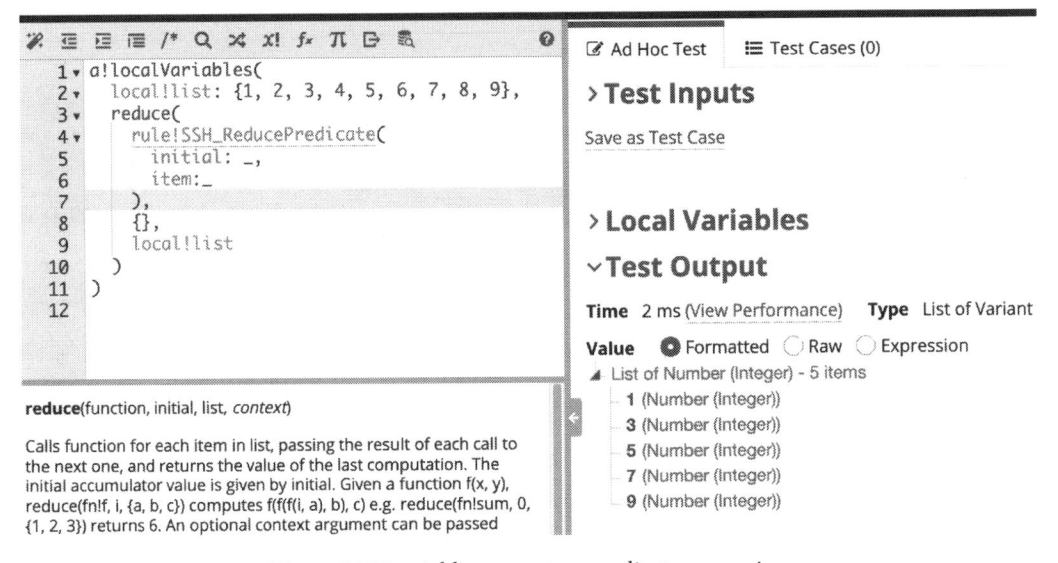

Figure 14.27 – Adding a custom predicate expression

The predicate expression looks like this:

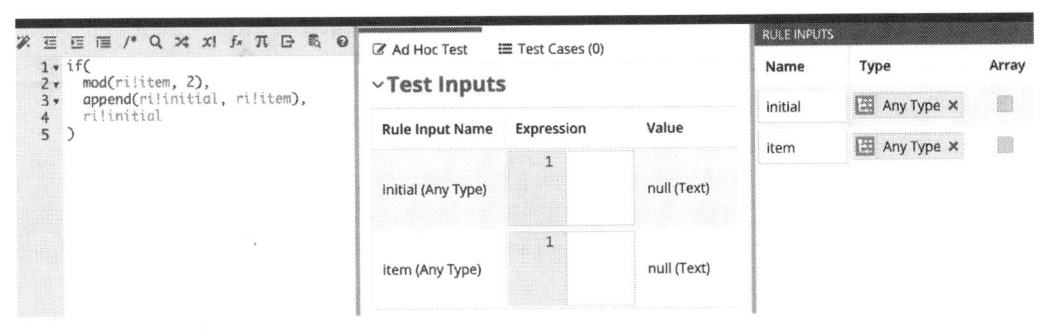

Figure 14.28 – Custom predicate expression

This expression checks whether the element is even. If it is, it returns the unchanged initial as output. Otherwise, the element is appended to the initial value as output. This way, the final list only contains uneven numbers.

OK—we have already done that in a simpler way. I know, but what if we make the initial a map? Let's make an expression that sorts random numbers into even and uneven numbers, as follows:

```
a!localVariables(
  local!list: ceiling(rand(12) * 100),
  reduce(
    rule!SSH_ReducePredicate(
      initial: _,
      item:_
    ),
    a!map(
      even: {},
      uneven: {}
    ),
    local!list
  )
)
```

The code in *line 2* creates 12 random numbers between 0 and 1. Then, it multiplies each item in the list by 100 and rounds them up to the nearest integer. Here's the code for the SSH_ReducePredicate expression:

```
if(
  mod(ri!item, 2),
  a!update(
    ri!initial,
    "uneven",
    append(ri!initial.uneven, ri!item)
  ),
  a!update(
    ri!initial,
    "even",
    append(ri!initial.even, ri!item)
  )
)
```

This snippet updates one of the two lists in the map passed as initial values. This way, we modify that map with each iteration.

But don't forget that this is not always the same map—`a!update` creates a new altered copy for the output, which becomes the input of the next iteration.

Best practices

I just want to give you some simple advice here. Try to understand how Appian expressions work and adapt your way of solving problems.

Oh, and before I forget, `a!forEach` is not the best solution for all kinds of difficulties you may encounter when working with lists. Use `filter` or one of the many functions that can handle lists, such as the `like()` function.

Summary

You just learned a lot about how to write expression rules in Appian. From simple decision tables to constants, to simple and more complex expressions, you can now add exciting new features to your applications.

Even with expression rules, low-code with Appian is still low-code. You will spend the most time building process models and refining interfaces. Expression rules give you just that level of flexibility you need to create a gorgeous application.

In the next chapter, we will learn how to integrate an external system using web services.

15
Using Web Services with Appian Integrations

The application you built needs to connect to some of the existing systems at our company, Tarence Ltd. You will learn the basics of how modern web services work and how to consume them in a low-code way using Appian.

To be more specific, I will walk you through calling a web service to initiate an invoice posting process. Since we do not have an existing ERP system to play with, we will implement that service ourselves in Appian.

In this chapter, we will talk about the following topics:

- **HTTPS, security, and JSON**: Basic communication and data transfer protocols
- **OpenAPI basics**: Defining the structure of a web API
- **Connected systems and integrations**: Utilizing web APIs
- **Using integrations**: Use cases for web APIs
- **Best practices**: Considerations when using and providing web APIs

Let's get started and dive into the shallows of encrypted communication between web services.

Technical requirements

You will find the code mentioned in this chapter here:

```
https://github.com/PacktPublishing/Low-Code-Application-
Development-with-Appian/tree/main/chapter%2015
```

HTTPS, authentication, and JSON

The way in which modern applications communicate is a vast and complex topic, but, in this book, I will ignore the first six of the seven layers of the **Open Systems Interconnection** (**OSI**) model and concentrate on the **Hypertext Transfer Protocol Secure** (**HTTPS**) as the protocol of choice. (For more information about the OSI model, go to `https://osi-model.com`).

In a real enterprise integration scenario, you will be supported by the IT department. They are responsible for all the firewalls, VPNs, proxy servers, DNS services, mail servers, and all the other parts that make up the enterprise IT landscape. They'll be able to help you with most challenges you encounter.

First, we need to discuss how two systems communicate using HTTPS.

HTTPS

HTTPS is one of the most used protocols in modern times to exchange structured information between two systems. To be more specific, with the *S* standing for *secure*, it means that all data is encrypted by one system and decrypted by the other system. This way, no other system in between can read the data.

The browser you use to work with Appian is using HTTPS to request a web page from the Appian server. Appian responds with data in the **Hypertext Markup Language** (**HTML**) format, which the browser can understand and display. Here, we are talking about a request-response pattern (the basic principle of HTTPS). The participants are the client, the system initiating the request, and the server returning the response.

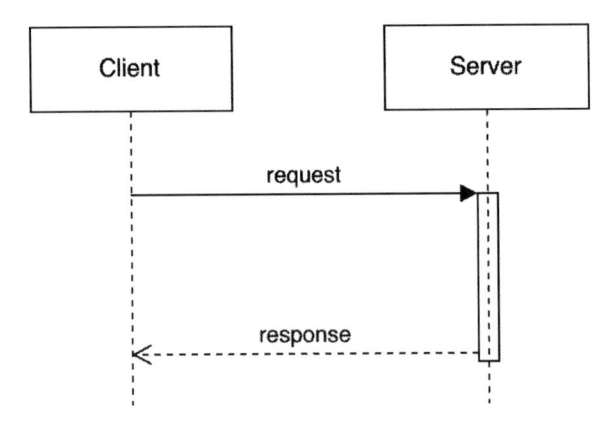

Figure 15.1 – HTTP request and response

Let's investigate the details, starting with the request.

> **Simplified Representation**
>
> In this chapter, I want to focus on the parts of HTTP that are important for the integration of web services with Appian, therefore, I will simplify some things and ignore certain details.

HTTP request

A client sends an HTTP request to a server to initiate a certain function. To specify this function and parameters, a request can have four components:

- **Uniform Resource Locator** (**URL**): The address of the server, such as `https://docs.appian.com/suite/help/21.4/Search_Results.php?q=integration`. The URL consists of four parts:

  - **Protocol**: Always HTTPS

  - **Server**: The address of the server

  - **Path**: A path to a specific resource on the server, similar to folders on your computer

  - **Query parameters**: Additional information after the question mark

- **Method**: This tells the server what to do with the request. While there are many methods defined, we will focus on GET for fetching data, and POST for sending data.

- **Headers**: A list of keys and values, used to send additional information, such as authentication or the language used in the body.

- **Body** (Optional): The actual content of the request. A lot of different formats are used here (a very prominent example is HTML), but we will focus on the **JavaScript Object Notation (JSON)** format, as this is the common format for any modern web service. The request body is only used for POST requests.

Here is a simple example of a GET request:

```
GET /helloworld.html HTTP/1.1
User-Agent: Mozilla/4.0 (compatible; MSIE5.01; Windows NT)
Host: www.server.com
Accept-Language: en-us
Accept-Encoding: gzip, deflate
Connection: Keep-Alive
```

This request could be from a browser asking the server for a web page.

Here is another example, this time a POST request:

```
POST /services/example HTTP/1.1
User-Agent: Appian/22.1
Host: www.tarence.com
Content-Type: text/json; charset=utf-8
Content-Length: length
Accept-Language: en-us
Accept-Encoding: gzip, deflate
Connection: Keep-Alive

{"firstName": "Otto", "lastName": "Lilienthal"}
```

This request sends data in the JSON format to a specific service at Tarence Ltd.

That explains the HTTP request going from the client to the server. Now, let's take a look at the HTTP response.

HTTP response

Quite similar to the HTTP request, the HTTP response consists of three parts:

- **Status line**: This is a numeric status code and a text representation. Codes in the 200 range mean success, the 400 range means an error on the client side, and the 500 range indicates an error on the server side.

- **Headers**: Additional information about the response.

- **Body** (Optional): The data in the format specified in the Content-Type header.

Here is a small example of an HTTP response from a web service serving a request from your browser:

```
HTTP/1.1 200 OK
Date: Mon, 27 Jul 2009 12:28:53 GMT
Server: Apache/2.2.14
Last-Modified: Wed, 22 Jul 2009 19:15:56 GMT
Content-Length: 88
Content-Type: text/html
Connection: Closed

<html>
<body>
<h1>Hello, World!</h1>
</body>
</html>
```

While this is just scratching the surface, it is enough to get a good understanding of how a client and a server communicate using the HTTPS protocol. It is the most commonly used protocol on the web, as it is well structured, flexible, and secure.

The next aspect we need to talk about is security.

Security

When we talk about security on a high level, we have to consider three aspects:

- **Security**: Hiding information from plain sight

- **Authentication**: Proving an identity

- **Authorization**: Access to data and services

This is a further simplification, but sufficient for an introduction to web services with Appian.

HTTPS, the encrypted data transport protocol, covers the security aspect in that data is encrypted on one side and decrypted on the other side. No system in between can read the transferred data.

Authentication is about two things. Firstly, you claim to be someone specific (that's your identity), and then you provide proof. You did that when you logged on to your computer this morning. Your username is the claim, and the password is your proof. The simplest way of authenticating to a server is to provide exactly that: a username and a password. There are more complex authentication schemes, such as **oAuth2**, but the basic idea is always the same.

The third aspect of security is authorization. The server got a secure encrypted message from you and trusts your identity. Now, the server needs to know whether you are permitted to initiate that specific action. In Appian, we do that by assigning groups to objects, and only identities that are a member of those groups may interact with that object.

As you now understand how a client and a server communicate in a secure and trusted way, let me introduce the JSON data format we use for transmitting the actual content.

JSON

The JavaScript Object Notation (JSON: `https://www.json.org`) is a lightweight text-based data-interchange format used by most modern web services. Appian directly supports this format for outgoing and incoming requests and responses.

JSON consists of two basic structures:

- Lists
- Lists of key-value pairs

We indicate lists using square brackets, *[...]*, and we use curly brackets for key-value pairs, *{...}*.

Let's have a look at some examples in Appian:

- A simple list in square brackets, transformed from an Appian list into JSON in **Test Output**.

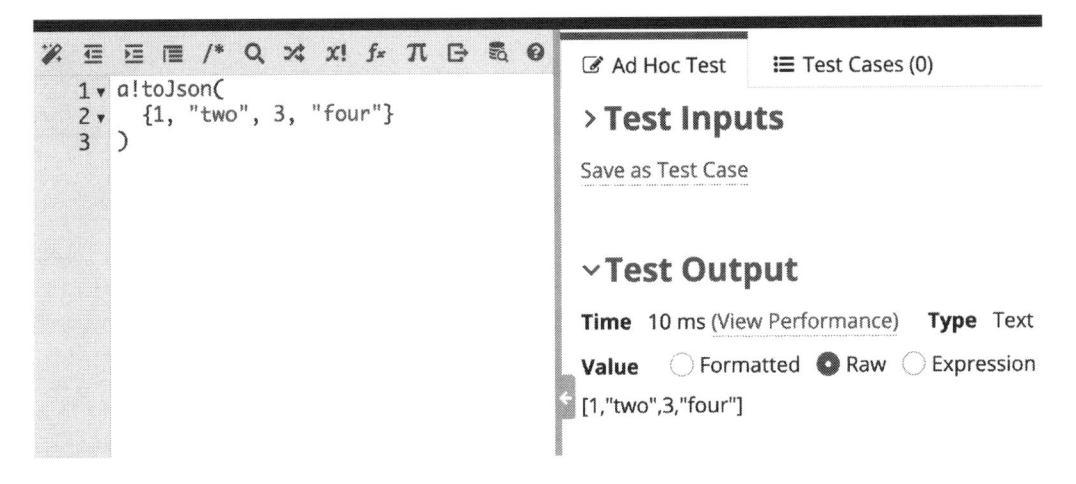

Figure 15.2 – List in JSON

- A map in curly brackets, transformed from an Appian map into JSON in **Test Output**.

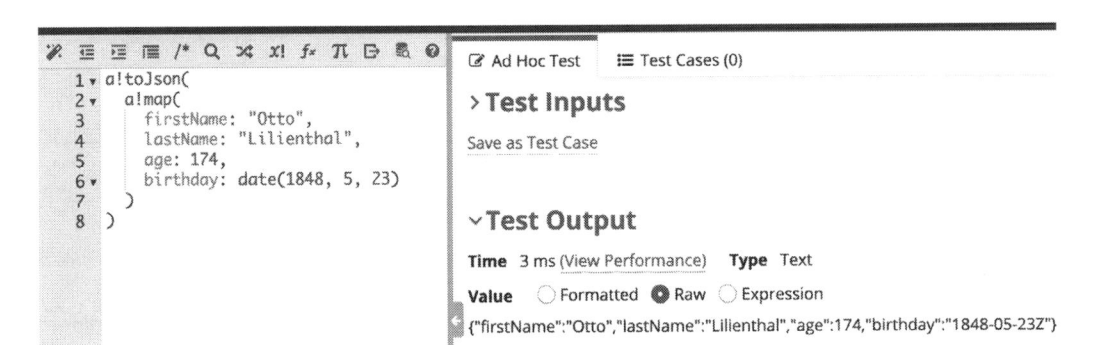

Figure 15.3 – Map in JSON

> **Note**
>
> The field's names and strings are in quotes, while numbers are not. The date becomes a string in the ISO 8601 format.

- A nested data structure, transformed from an Appian map into JSON in **Test Output**.

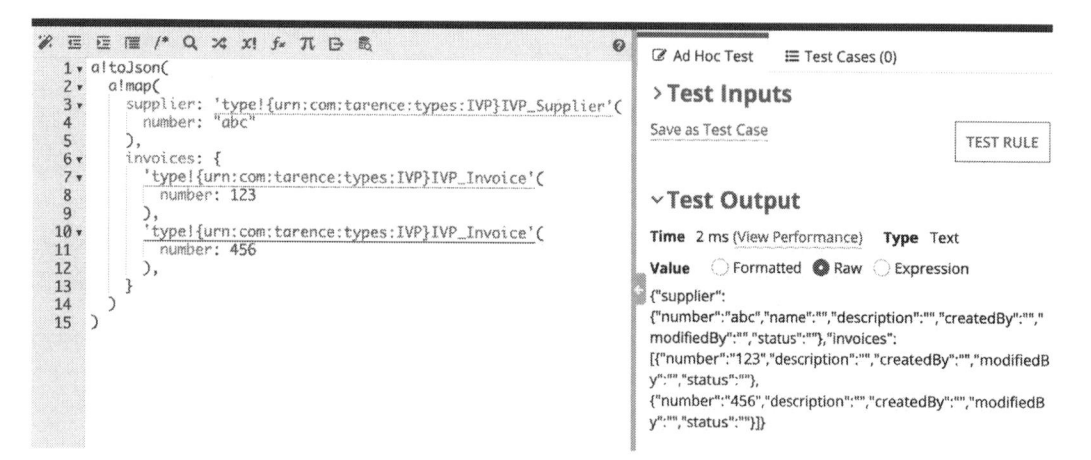

Figure 15.4 – Complex structure in JSON

That output looks a bit confusing. Let's make it more human-readable:

```
{
    "supplier": {
        "number": "abc",
        "name": "",
        "description": "",
        "createdBy": "",
        "modifiedBy": "",
        "status": ""
    },
    "invoices": [
        {
            "number": "123",
            "description": "",
            "createdBy": "",
            "modifiedBy": "",
```

```json
        "status": ""
    },
    {
        "number": "456",
        "description": "",
        "createdBy": "",
        "modifiedBy": "",
        "status": ""
    }
  ]
}
```

It looks complex but still follows the basic principles of lists, and lists of key-value pairs.

Use the two functions, `tojson()` and `fromjson()`, to convert between Appian data structures and text in the JSON format. Keep in mind that the JSON format does not know about any specific data structure in Appian. In the following example, I turned an Appian CDT type into JSON, and back. The actual data type is lost.

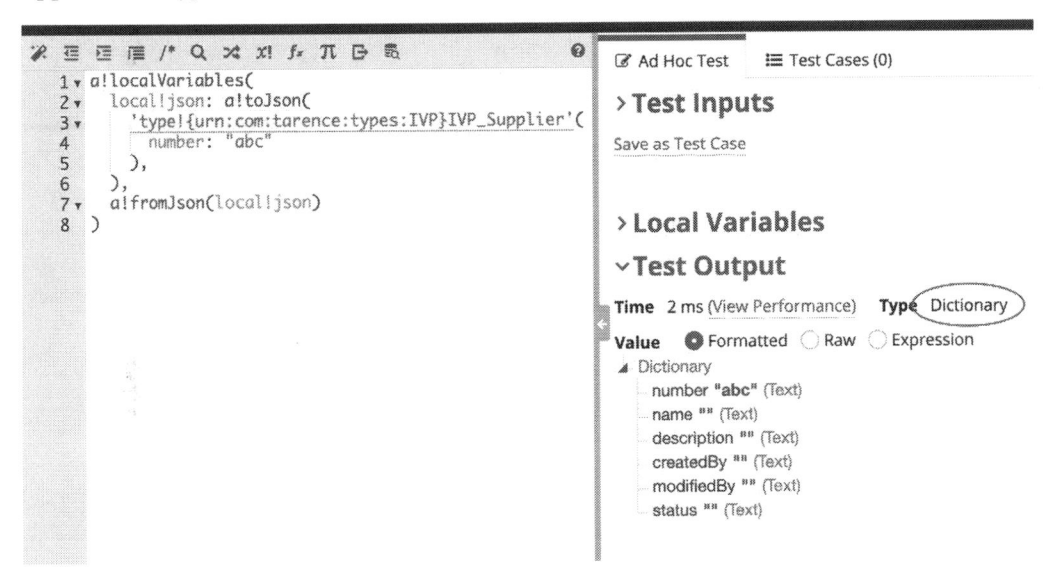

Figure 15.5 – Lost data type in JSON

Use `cast()` to convert the raw data structure into the CDT structure.

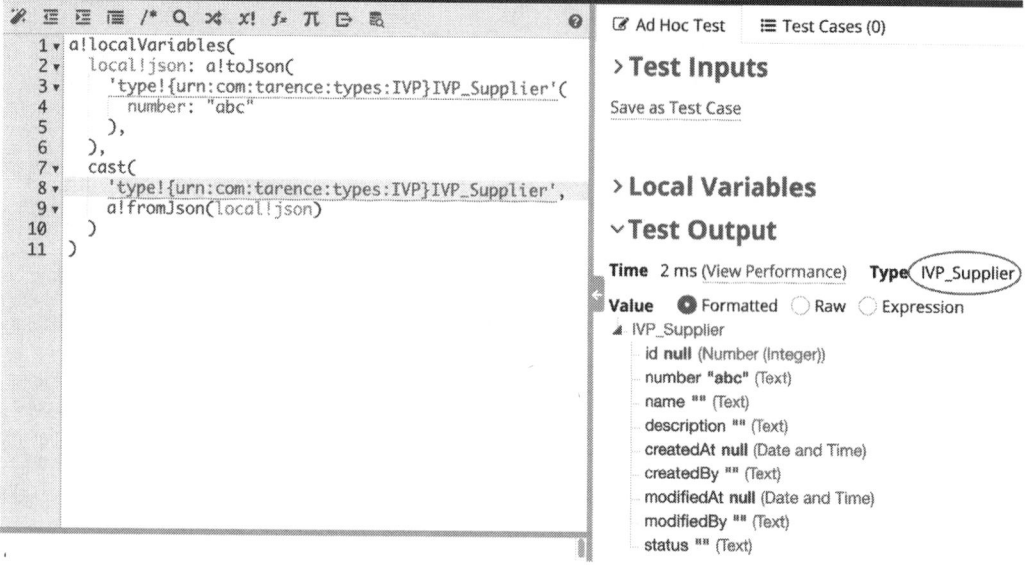

Figure 15.6 – Casting to a CDT type

Let's conclude this section and have a quick look at the OpenAPI specification before we start implementing web services in Appian.

OpenAPI basics

The **OpenAPI Specification (OAS)** gives a technical interface description for HTTP-based web APIs. It describes all the details necessary to understand how to make an HTTP request to that specific web service. Find the full documentation at the following URL: `https://spec.openapis.org/oas/latest.html`.

A basic understanding of the OAS is important when integrating with other systems, as Appian supports OpenAPI directly for outgoing and incoming web service calls. Many of the verbs used in OpenAPI closely resemble the verbs used in HTTP.

When creating a new connected system in Appian, you can select OpenAPI as a type.

Create Connected System

Search Connected Systems...

HTTP

OpenAPI

Amazon Machine Learning

Appian RPA

Figure 15.7 – Connected system types

After uploading the OpenAPI document, Appian will automatically display the required configuration options for the URL and authentication, and when creating the integration objects, Appian lets you select from one of the defined operations. A proper OpenAPI specification document makes consuming a web service much easier. I will show you how to do that in the next section.

Before doing this, let's have a look at the three basic components of an OpenAPI document. In the book's `git` repository, find the document by following this link: `https://github.com/PacktPublishing/Low-Code-Application-Development-with-Appian/blob/main/chapter%2015/Invoice%20Validation%20Process%20-%20OpenAPI.json`.

servers

The `servers` section defines one or more servers on which the specified services are provided:

```
"servers": [
  {
    "url": "https://my_appian_demo.appiancloud.com/suite/
    webapi"
  }
],
```

paths

The `paths` section represents a specific service on a server. Since there can be multiple services on a single server, there can be multiple paths. On each path, there can be one or more operations defined by the HTTP methods, such as `GET` or `POST`:

```
"paths": {
    "/ivp_post_invoice": {
        "post": {
```

Each operation is defined, including its inputs and outputs.

components

This section contains specific definitions reused in other places inside the document. The important part is `securitySchemes`, as it defines the means of authentication supported by the server:

```
"components": {
    "securitySchemes": {
        "api_key": {
            "type": "apiKey",
            "name": "Appian-API-Key",
            "in": "header"
        },
        "basic_auth": {
            "type": "http",
            "scheme": "basic"
        }
    }
}
```

OpenAPI summary

This section is called **OpenAPI basics**. The specification of a real web service can become far more extensive and include many aspects of the described service. For example, a service expects incoming data in a specific structure and has explicit validation rules for each field. These rules are coded as part of the actual service but also put into the interface specification. This way, a consuming system can implement the same rules and validate the data before sending it out.

Now that we have all the preparations behind us, we can finally get into Appian and create a few new objects.

Connected systems and integrations

In Appian, the task of integrating web services is split between two objects: the connected system, which is responsible for the URL and the authentication, and the integration, which implements the actual service call. You create an integration for each path and HTTP method defined in the OAS.

We'll start with creating a web service that we then consume later.

Creating a web service

I will walk you through creating a separate process model and expose that as a web API. Follow these steps:

1. Create the new **IVP_PostInvoiceApi** data type, as shown in the following screenshot:

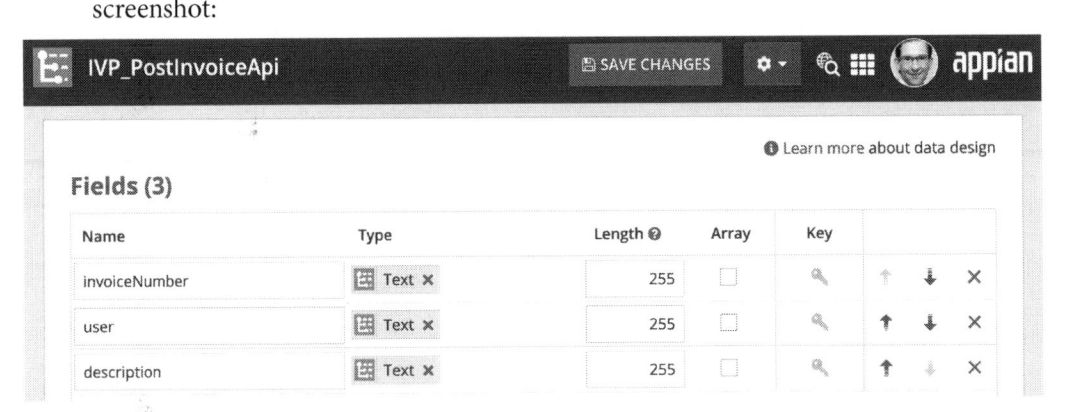

Figure 15.8 – New IVP_PostInvoiceApi data type

2. Create the **IVP Post Invoice API Users** group custom type and add yourself as a member.

3. Create the **IVP Post Invoice** process model and add the **IVP Post Invoice API Users** group in the **Initiator** role.

4. Add the **incomingData** process variable of the **IVP_PostInvoiceApi** type and make it a parameter.

5. Save and publish the model.

6. Create the **IVP_MODEL_POST_INVOICE** constant of the type process model and select the **IVP Post Invoice** model for the value.

7. Create a new Web API and select **START PROCESS** in the **CREATE** section.

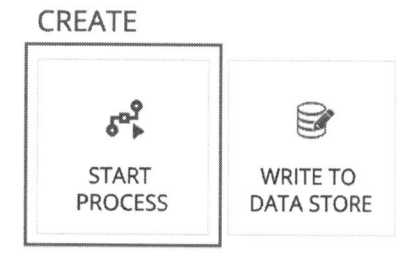

Figure 15.9 – START PROCESS in CREATE

8. Configure the next screen, as shown in the following figure, and click **CREATE** (this will be at the bottom of the page as you scroll):

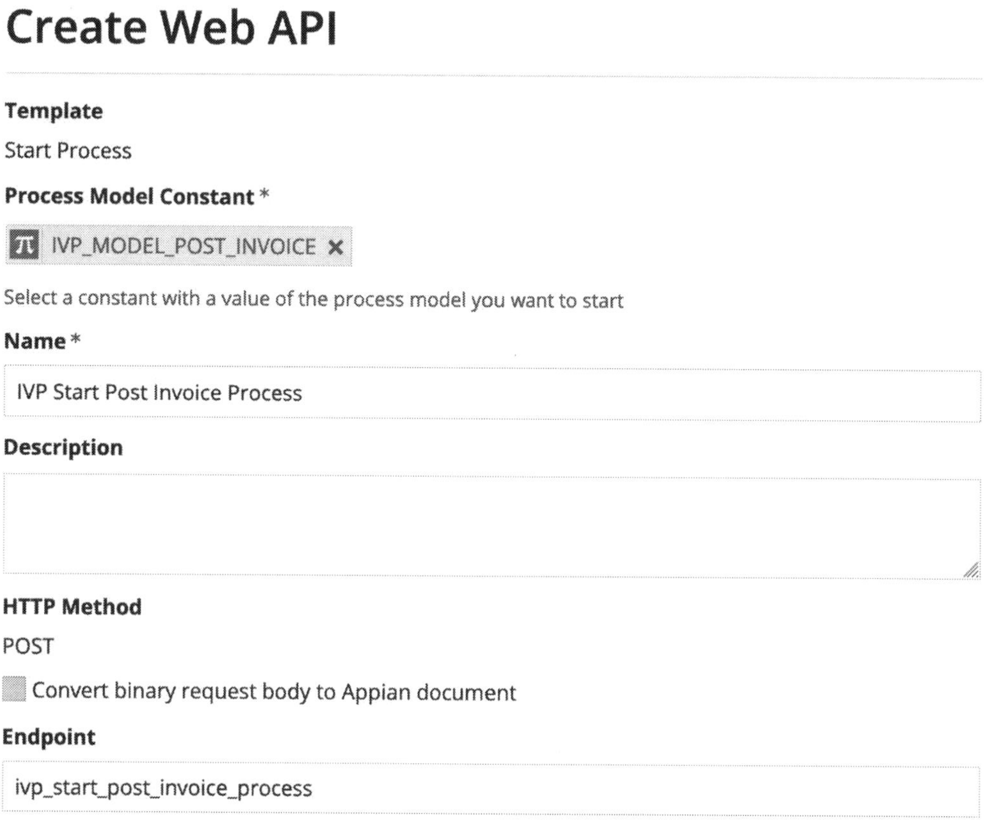

Create Web API

Template

Start Process

Process Model Constant *

π IVP_MODEL_POST_INVOICE ✕

Select a constant with a value of the process model you want to start

Name *

IVP Start Post Invoice Process

Description

HTTP Method

POST

▨ Convert binary request body to Appian document

Endpoint

ivp_start_post_invoice_process

Figure 15.10 – Configuring the Web API

9. Add the **IVP Post Invoice API Users** group as **Viewers**.

10. Modify the Web API code, as shown in the following screenshot:

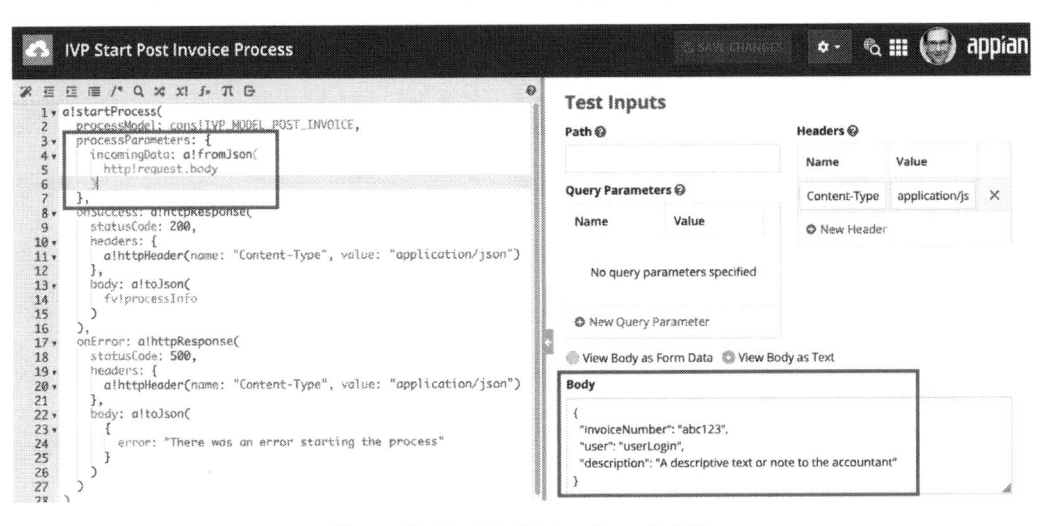

Figure 15.11 – Modifying the web API

This will pass the data from the incoming HTTPS request to the process variable. The value entered in **Body** in **Test Inputs** becomes part of the OpenAPI document we will export later.

11. Click **TEST REQUEST** to do the first test. Look out for the 200 HTTP status code, which means that the call was a success.

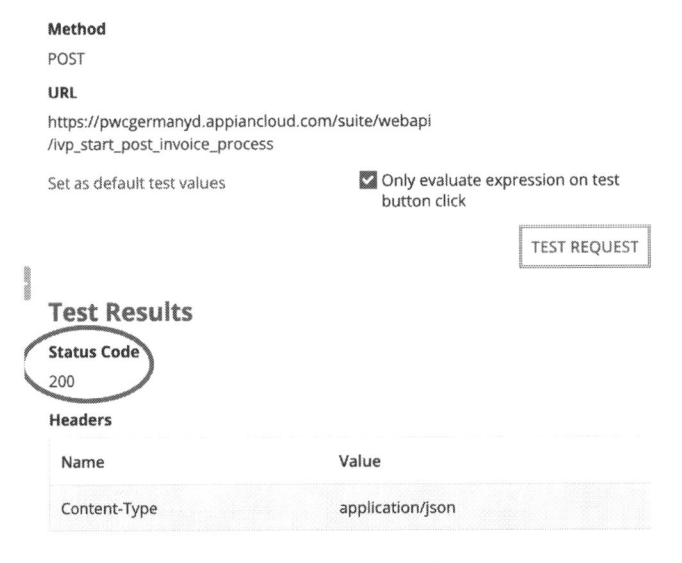

Figure 15.12 – HTTP code 200

Scroll all the way down, and you should see the process variables and the data passed in.

```
"pv" : {
  "incomingData" : {
    "invoiceNumber" : "abc123",
    "user" : "userLogin",
    "description" : "A descriptive text or note to the accountant"
  }
 }
}
```

Figure 15.13 – Process variables in response

12. Save your changes in the web API.

13. In **Appian Designer**, navigate to the list of all applications and tick the checkbox in front of **Invoice Validation Process**.

14. Click **EXPORT**, then **OpenAPI Definition**.

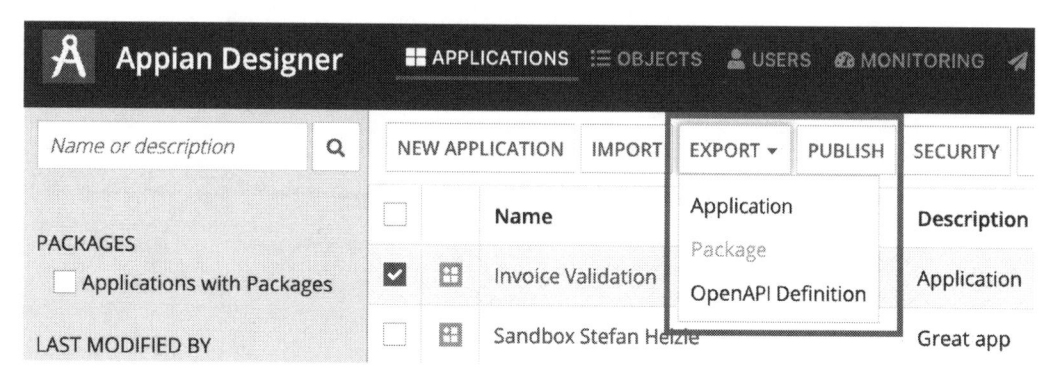

Figure 15.14 – Exporting OpenAPI definition

15. Click **EXPORT**, and **DOWNLOAD OPENAPI DEFINITION**. We will need that document later.

In the next section, I will show you how to utilize the web service you just created.

Integrating the web service

So, we got that Open API document from the system administrator of the ERP system. Let's forget for a while that you plan to call a service you just created yourselves, and that administrator is also you.

That administrator also created a service user for authentication. Using a dedicated service user is important as their passwords do not expire, but typically, these are very restricted and can be used for a specific system only. In our case, the service user is you.

You will now create two objects, a connected system holding the basic configuration of the connection, and an integration that implements the actual web service call. Let's create the first object required to integrate into that web service. Follow these steps to create a new connected system:

1. Select the **OpenAPI** type and enter a name.
2. Upload the Open API document you exported in the last section.

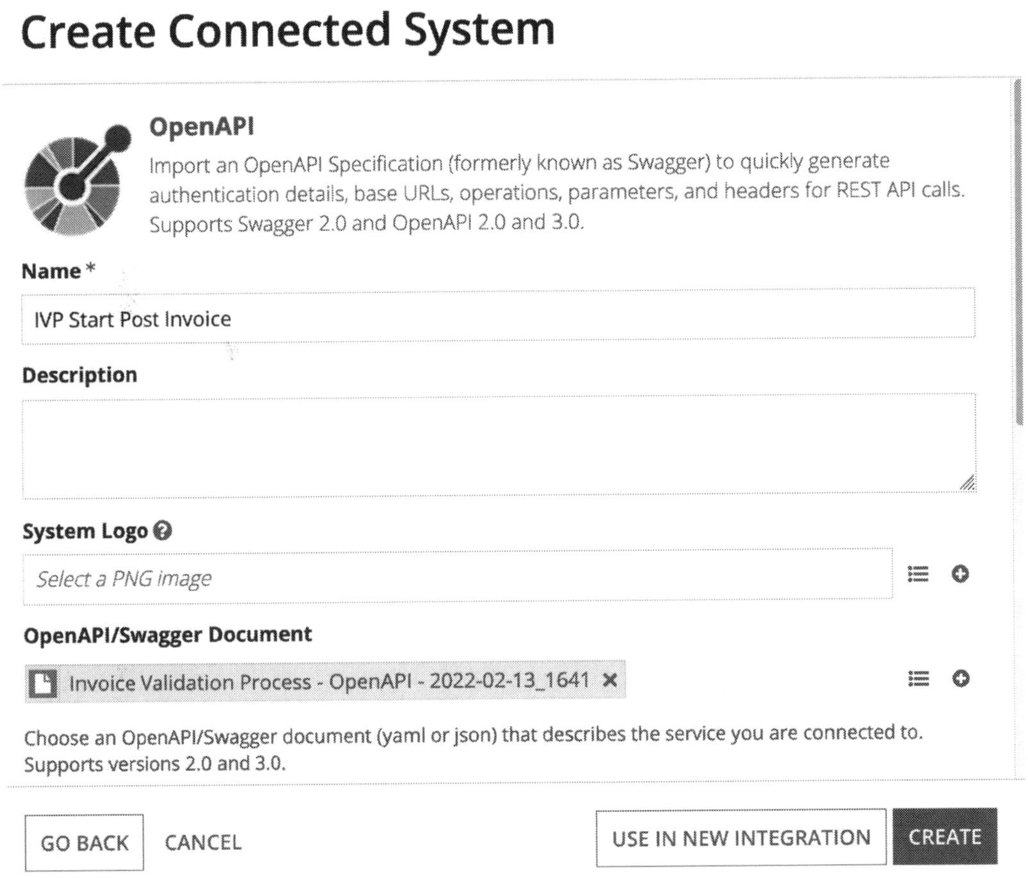

Create Connected System

OpenAPI

Import an OpenAPI Specification (formerly known as Swagger) to quickly generate authentication details, base URLs, operations, parameters, and headers for REST API calls. Supports Swagger 2.0 and OpenAPI 2.0 and 3.0.

Name *

IVP Start Post Invoice

Description

System Logo ❓

Select a PNG image

OpenAPI/Swagger Document

Invoice Validation Process - OpenAPI - 2022-02-13_1641 ✕

Choose an OpenAPI/Swagger document (yaml or json) that describes the service you are connected to. Supports versions 2.0 and 3.0.

GO BACK   CANCEL   USE IN NEW INTEGRATION   CREATE

Figure 15.15 – Creating a connected system – step 1

3.   Select **Basic (basic_auth)** for **Authentication** and enter your credentials.

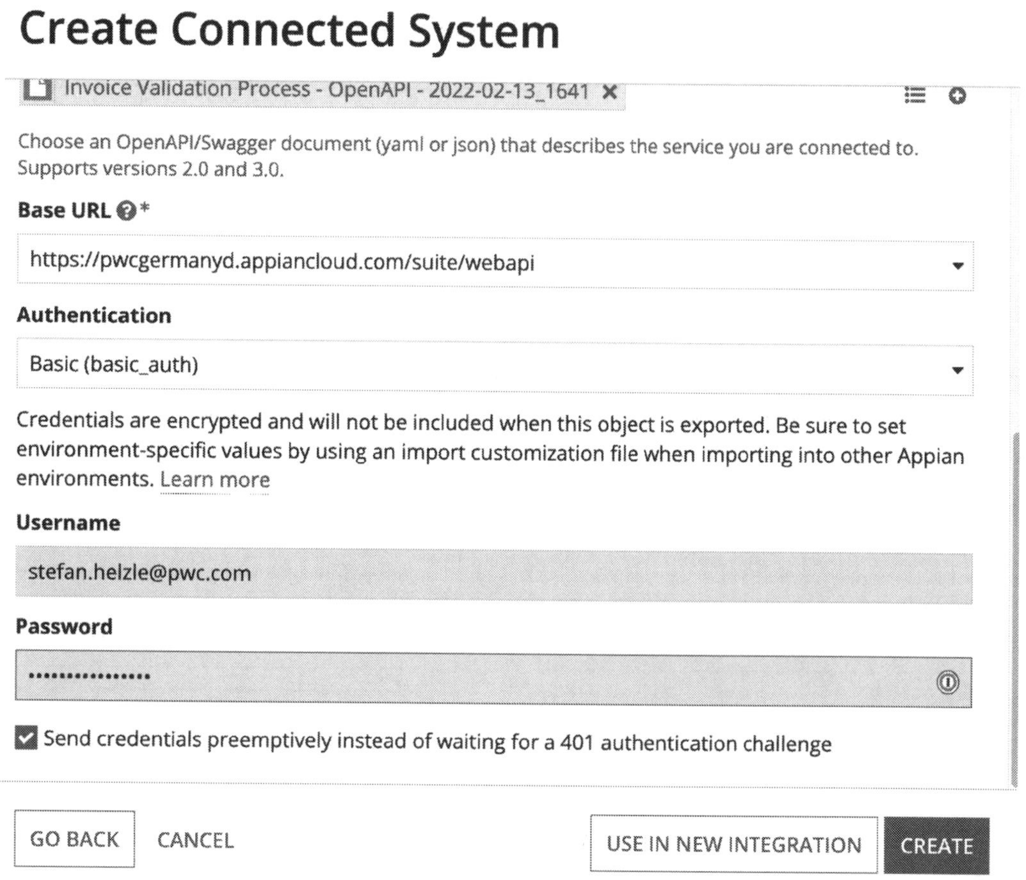

Create Connected System

Invoice Validation Process - OpenAPI - 2022-02-13_1641 ✕

Choose an OpenAPI/Swagger document (yaml or json) that describes the service you are connected to. Supports versions 2.0 and 3.0.

Base URL ❓ *

https://pwcgermanyd.appiancloud.com/suite/webapi

Authentication

Basic (basic_auth)

Credentials are encrypted and will not be included when this object is exported. Be sure to set environment-specific values by using an import customization file when importing into other Appian environments. Learn more

Username

stefan.helzle@pwc.com

Password

················

☑ Send credentials preemptively instead of waiting for a 401 authentication challenge

GO BACK   CANCEL   USE IN NEW INTEGRATION   CREATE

Figure 15.16 – Creating a connected system – step 2

4.   Click **USE IN NEW INTEGRATION** to directly create the second object, and perform integration.

5.   Accept the suggested security for the **Connected System** object.

6. Configure the integration as in the following screenshot and click **CREATE**:

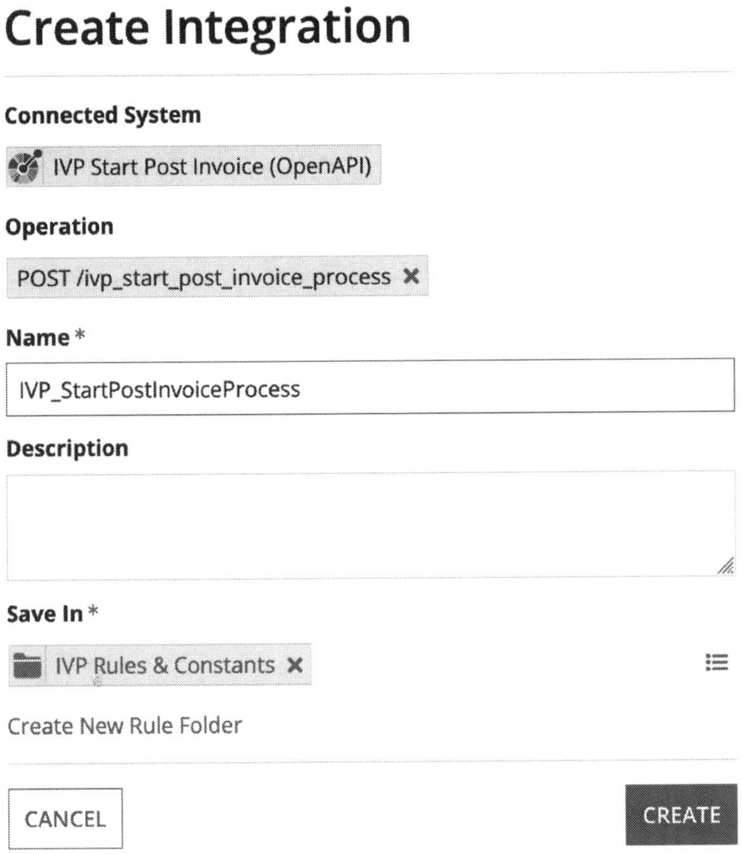

Create Integration

Connected System

IVP Start Post Invoice (OpenAPI)

Operation

POST /ivp_start_post_invoice_process ✕

Name *

IVP_StartPostInvoiceProcess

Description

Save In *

IVP Rules & Constants ✕

Create New Rule Folder

CANCEL   CREATE

Figure 15.17 – Creating an integration object

7. In the **Integration** editor, you will see that all the relevant configuration in the **Connection** section is already done. Scroll down to **Request Body** and enter the following code snippet, as in the next screenshot:

```
'type!{urn:com:tarence:types:IVP}IVP_PostInvoiceApi'()
```

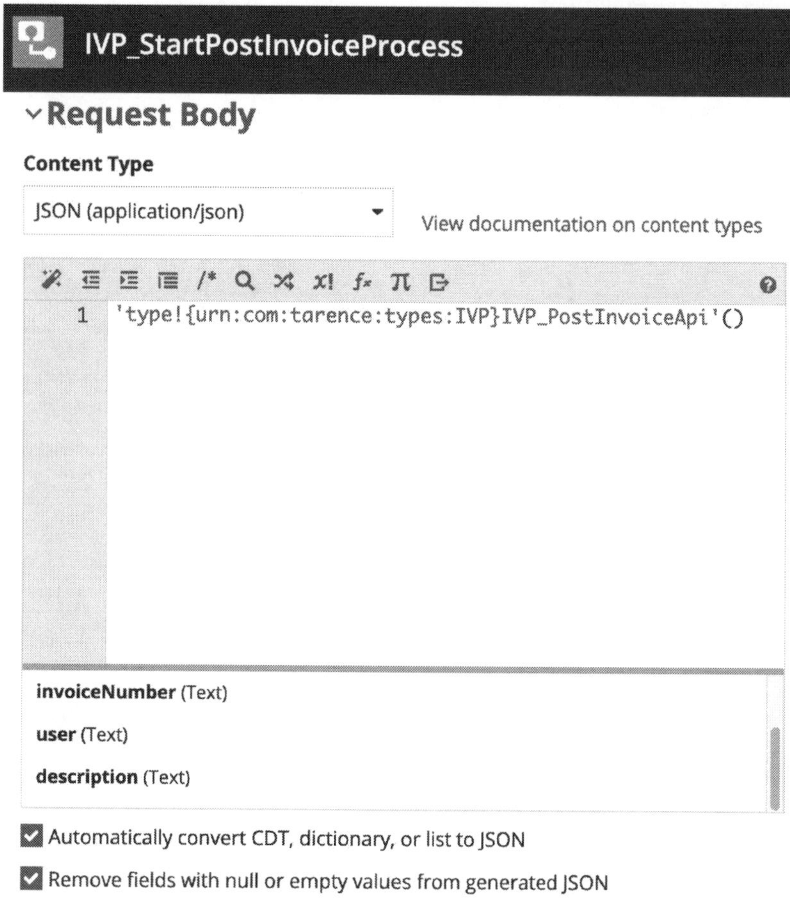

Figure 15.18 – Configuring the request body

8. In the **Response** section, select **Convert JSON to Appian value** in **Response Body Parsing**.

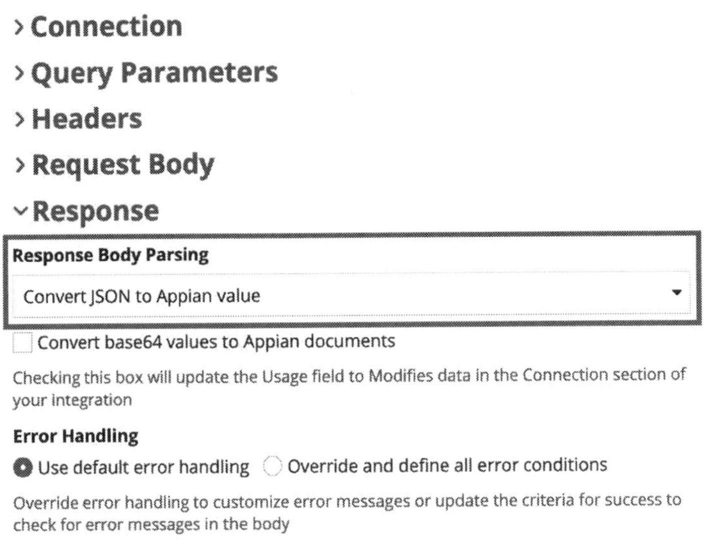

> **Connection**

> **Query Parameters**

> **Headers**

> **Request Body**

∨ **Response**

Response Body Parsing

Convert JSON to Appian value   ▾

☐ Convert base64 values to Appian documents

Checking this box will update the Usage field to Modifies data in the Connection section of your integration

Error Handling

◉ Use default error handling   ◯ Override and define all error conditions

Override error handling to customize error messages or update the criteria for success to check for error messages in the body

Figure 15.19 – Configuring Response Body Parsing

9.   Click **TEST REQUEST**.

You should now see a successful test on the right-hand panel.

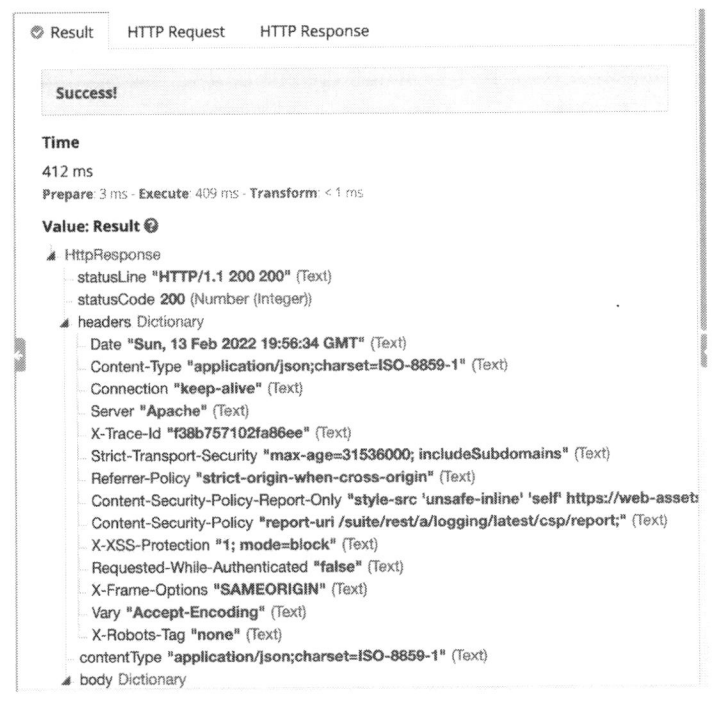

Figure 15.20 – Successful test

I highly recommend having a close look at all sections on the left-hand panel. You will see that all the configurations match what we discussed earlier in this chapter.

You might have noticed that we sent an empty data structure to that service, and the values returned also indicate this.

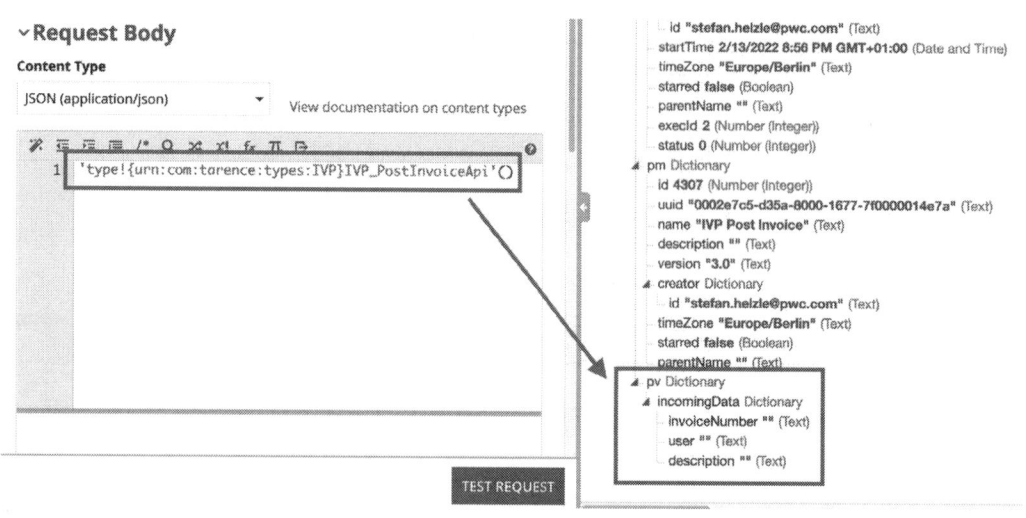

Figure 15.21 – Sending an empty data structure

An integration is similar to an **expression rule** in the sense that it can have **Rule Inputs**. Let's create three of them, as in the following screenshot, to allow passing in the data:

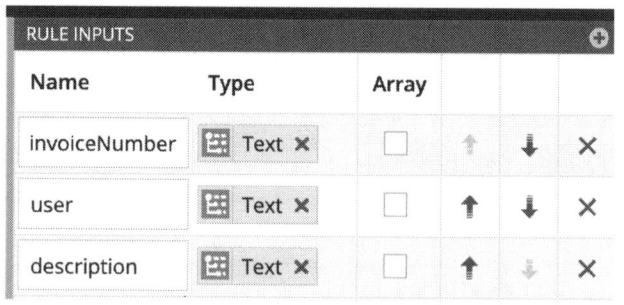

Figure 15.22 – Three rule inputs

Then, change **Request Body** to the following:

```
'type!{urn:com:tarence:types:IVP}IVP_PostInvoiceApi'(
    invoiceNumber: ri!invoiceNumber,
    user: ri!user,
    description: ri!description
)
```

After another test, your screen should look like this:

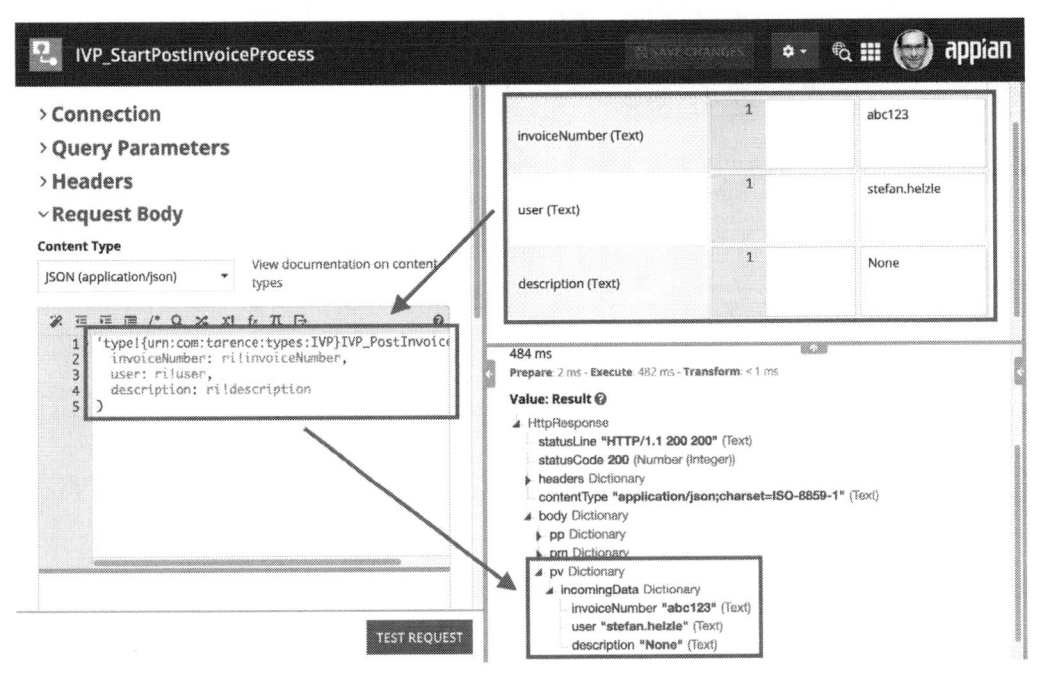

Figure 15.23 – Test with actual data

The data entered in the test inputs are used to create the request body and sent to the other system. That system picked up the data and returned it. You should also see a process instance of the **IVP Post Invoice** model showing that data.

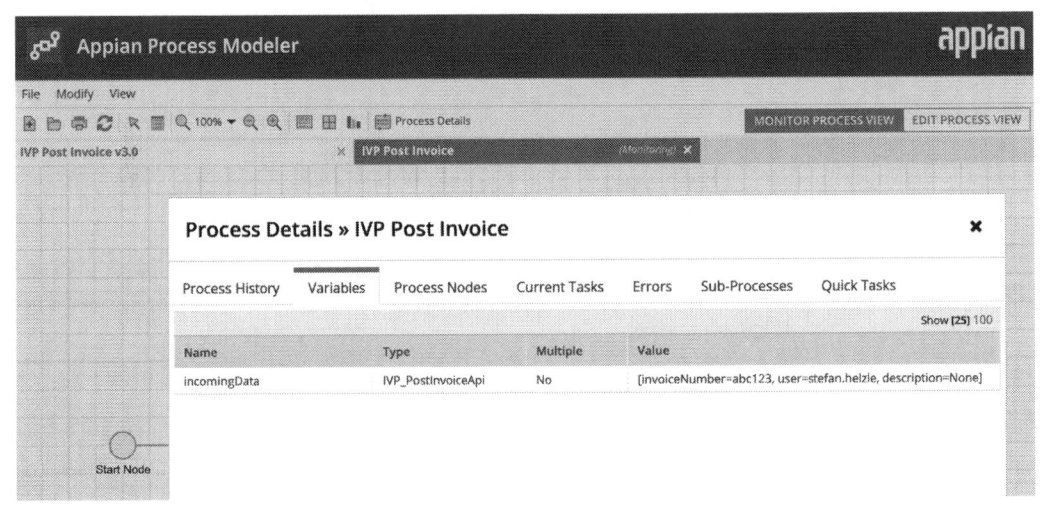

Figure 15.24 – Process instance showing received data

That's it. You now have a fully working integration with that ERP system. In the next section, we will make use of this integration in our invoice validation process.

Using integrations

In general, integration is a type of object similar to expression rules. The **Usage** configuration in the **Connection** section makes a difference in how an integration is used.

There is the **Queries data** option. That integration can be used like any other expression rule because it does not change the state of the other system. Appian might call this integration any number of times.

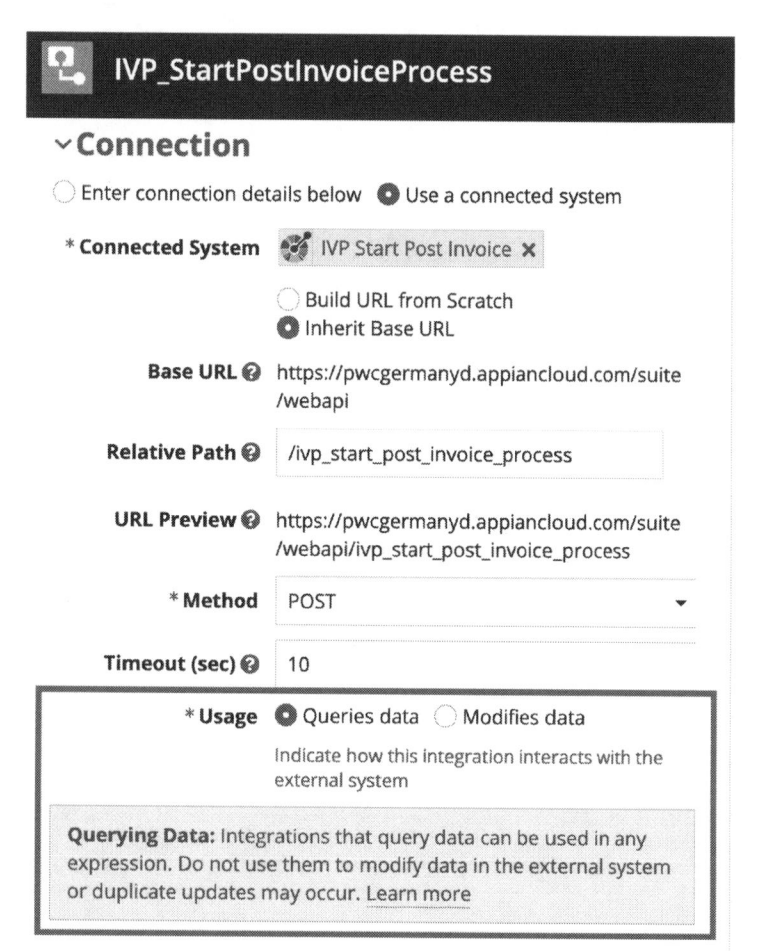

Figure 15.25 – Query type integration

There is also the **Modifies data** option. This integration can only be used in specific places, as it modifies the state of the other system. Appian makes sure that this integration is only called once to prevent any duplicate updates or inserts in the other system.

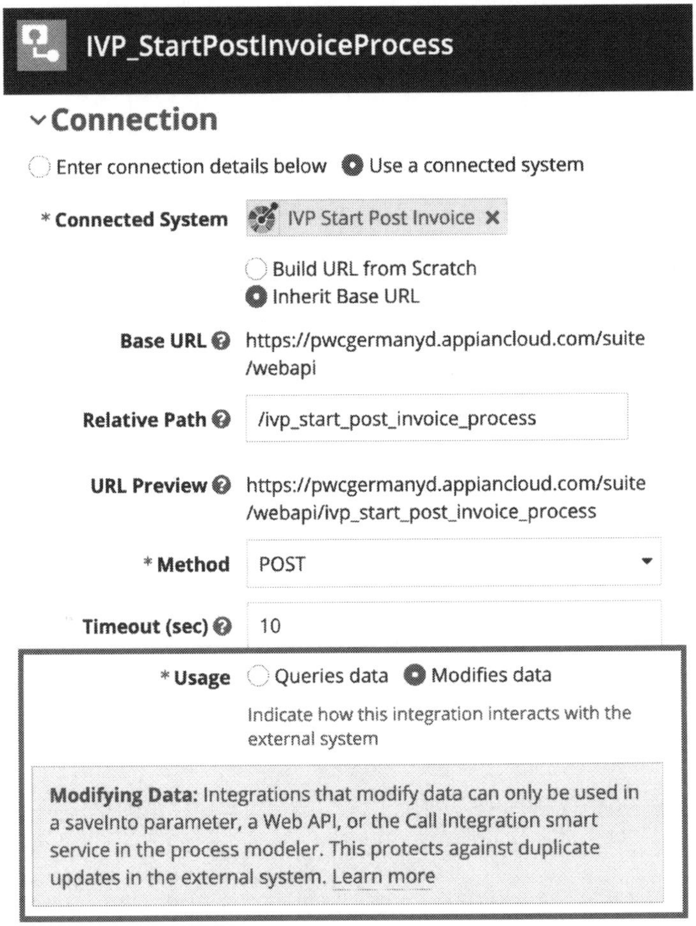

Figure 15.26 – Modify type integration

The integration you created is meant to initiate the invoice posting process. You would not want to start that process twice for the same invoice. Make sure that the **Modifies data** option is selected for **Usage**.

To utilize the integration, open the **IVP Create Case** process and follow the next steps:

1. Add a **Call Integration** node and rename it as in this figure:

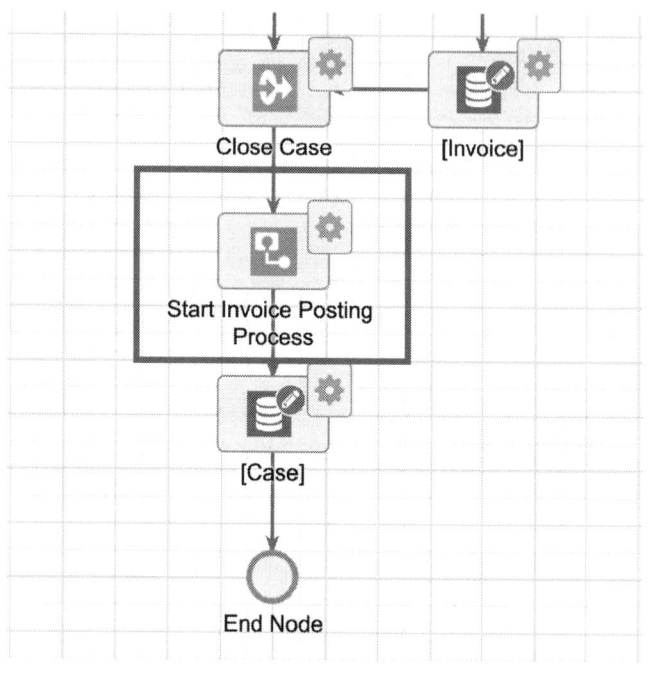

Figure 15.27 – Adding a Call Integration node

2. Open the node's configuration, navigate to the **Setup** tab, and select the **IVP_StartPostInvoiceProcess** integration.

3. On the **Data** tab, on **Inputs**, you will see the three rule inputs you created in the integration. Assign the following values:

```
invoiceNumber: pv!invoice.number
user: pv!taskOwner
```

4. For the **Description** input, we do not have a meaningful value yet. Why don't you try to create your own task that asks a user for a description?

5. On the **Outputs** tab, you have access to the data returned by the integration. Depending on the type of integrated system, you might want to store parts of the result and make the process react to it.

Test your process once again. You will see that the **Create Case** process initiates the **IVP Post Invoice** process automatically. Also, check whether you see the data passed from the case process through the integration with the web API and the posting process.

This was about using an integration that modifies data in the other system. An integration that just fetches data can be called just like any other expression rule. It returns a data structure that includes the status code, headers, and the data itself.

Let's conclude this chapter with some best practices.

Best practices

Best practices with web services are a bit difficult. While the protocols and formats are pretty simple, there are endless variations in implementations. Also, to be honest, implementing a *good* web service is pretty difficult, as it typically needs to deal with all the internal issues and implementation details of the underlying system.

As if that wasn't enough, there's a whole world in between. Slow networks, dropped VPN connections, and errors in all sorts of network components. But, some practices make life a bit easier.

Validate incoming data

Do never trust incoming data!

When receiving data, make sure that any data, text, or number is within the agreed boundaries: the text is not too long, a birthdate is in the future, or the amount of an invoice is negative. Anything that could be wrong, will be wrong!

Create an expression rule that takes the data, validates each field, and returns a map like this:

```
a!map(
   valid: false,
   errors: {
     "The birth date must not be in the future",
     "The invoice amount must be positive",
     "The description must be 255 characters max",
   }
)
```

Return a 400 HTTP code. This means that the data sent by the client is invalid:

```
a!httpResponse(
   statusCode: 400,
   headers: {
```

```
    a!httpHeader(
      name: "Content-Type",
      value: "text/json"
    )
  },
  body: a!toJson(local!validationResult)
)
```

Wrapping integrations

When creating integration querying data, it is a good idea to wrap these into an expression rule. This way, you can extract the required data from the return data structure. Well-designed web services implement server-side search, filtering, and paging. In that expression rule, add the required rule inputs, such as `pagingInfo` or `search`. Then, pass that to the web service, and wrap the returned data in `dataSubset`, similar to the `queryEntity()` function.

See the following example code snippet:

```
a!localVariables(
  local!responseBody: rule!IVP_FetchData(
    startIndex: ri!pagingInfo.startIndex,
    batchSize: ri!pagingInfo.batchSize
  ).result.body,
  a!dataSubset(
    startIndex: ri!pagingInfo.startIndex,
    batchSize: ri!pagingInfo.batchSize,
    sort: ri!pagingInfo.sort,
    totalCount: local!responseBody.totalCount,
    data: cast(
      'type!{urn:com:appian:types}AA_Comment?list',
      index(local!responseBody, "items", {})
    ),
    identifiers: index(
      index(local!responseBody, "items", {}),
      "id",
      {}
    )
```

```
    )
  )
```

This implementation pattern allows you to use this expression rule directly as the data source for a record or in a read-only grid, as it accepts `pagingInfo` as a parameter and returns `dataSubset`.

Security

Create a separate group to manage access to the Web APIs you created. Add this group to the security of the objects used by these Web APIs. This can include *Data Stores*, *Records*, and *Process Models*. Now, add the technical user to that group to give the user all the required permissions when calling your APIs.

Summary

In this chapter, you created web services providing certain functionality to the outside world. You integrated Appian into an existing web service and got a good understanding of the protocols and data formats required to make this work.

Integrating services is always a challenge. Appian makes things comparatively simple, but never underestimate the basic complexity. If you have little experience with system integration, seek support from system administrators or IT architects.

If you want to dig deeper, there's a great tutorial in the Appian documentation that connects to an API of SpaceX and provides data on all their spacecraft and rocket launches:

```
https://docs.appian.com/suite/help/latest/Service-Backed_
Record_Tutorial.html
```

In the next chapter, the last one, I would like to provide you with a selection of implementation patterns in the hope of making your everyday life as an Appian designer easier.

16
Useful Implementation Patterns in Appian

Many requirements can be served with some simple implementation patterns. It's a good idea to learn them to speed up your development even further. Creating your own library of carefully designed reusable components helps you to focus on faster delivery, instead of repeatedly implementing the same components. Furthermore, there are a few additional modules provided by Appian you should know about.

In this chapter, I will cover the following topics:

- **Solution patterns**: Process versus case management, audit trails, and record security

- **Process patterns**: Process chains, sub-processes, multiple node instances, and loops

- **Interface patterns**: Wizards, tabs, and reusable components

- **Expression patterns**: Universal null checks, nested indexing, and IBAN validation

- **Additional Appian modules**: Intelligent Document Processing, Robotic Process Automation, process mining, and Appian Portals

Let's start by looking at solution patterns.

Technical requirements

You will find the code mentioned in this chapter at the following link:

`https://github.com/PacktPublishing/Low-Code-Application-Development-with-Appian/tree/main/chapter%2016`

Solution patterns

Solution patterns describe abstract concepts for implementing specific requirements and have more of a recommendation than a rule. I want to focus on a few patterns that, I think, are especially important. Appian also provides a library of patterns in the Appian Playbook at the following link:

`https://community.appian.com/w/the-appian-playbook/tags/design_2D00_patterns`

Process versus case management

Case management in its most basic form means that a user only reacts with an ad hoc activity on external triggers. The user must know all the possible activities and conditions. We already discussed some aspects of case management in *Chapter 7*, *Understanding Business Processes in Appian Projects*.

On the other hand, there is a fully automated sequential process with just some user interaction for making decisions or approvals.

The reality is somewhere in between. My typical approach is to try to get as much structure as possible into a process, and only add case management aspects if the topic really requires it.

Adding case management capabilities to an Appian application is simple. You can create a process model and add it to a record as a record action. Keep in mind that the record locking capabilities of Appian are weak. You should try to avoid running processes that modify the same data in parallel.

You can separate the process data from the master data by creating an extra case data type holding the values required to track and control the process.

Recording audit trails

While the idea of keeping an audit trail seems very obvious, this is not an out-of-the-box implementation in Appian. Process models log all the user activity, but this information is very detailed and typically discarded soon after process completion.

In my experience, the requirements for an audit trail vary greatly, depending on the type of application. On the one hand, it may be necessary to log every user interaction, and another application only stores which user has granted a release.

I would consider a typical approach to record relevant process status transitions, including the following values:

- Timestamp
- Old status
- New status
- Responsible user
- User comment
- The outcome of the process step or phase

Sometimes it is necessary to also identify field-level data modifications. In that case, I recommend implementing a **copy-on-write** (**COW**) mechanism, which persists all versions of the data. This can be done in the Appian process models for more complex data models, or as a trigger in the database if it is only about a single table.

Record security

Record security is about controlling access to records based on individual users or groups. The latest version of Appian provides built-in access management support. For older versions, or situations not suitable for synchronized records, please check the following link:

```
https://community.appian.com/w/the-appian-playbook/207/record-
level-security-for-entity-backed-records
```

Record security defines several levels of access and permission:

- First, it defines which user generally has access to a particular dataset.

- Second, it defines which activities a particular user is allowed to perform in general, and which of them under the current circumstances.

> **Note**
> **Access** is defined by configuring default rules or record security in the Appian **Records Designer**.

1. Add a field to the CDT holding the ID of an Appian group.

2. Configure security so that only members of that group have access.

3. For very strict access control, create a separate group for each record in the process and store the group's ID in the record.

4. For less strict control, create as many static groups as necessary as part of the application, and store their IDs.

5. Then, add or remove users from these groups when necessary.

The strictest implementation I did was for the management of medical patient data, one group for each record, and that group had no members by default. Whenever a user required access to the patient's data, a process added that user and removed them after a defined period. All permission management activities are logged.

Now, what about controlling access to certain actions once the user has access to a record? As record actions are implemented using Appian processes, you can use groups assigned to the security roles on process models to manage security.

The last aspect, availability, is controlled using a suitable logic in the visibility configuration of record actions. Visibility can depend on case status, thresholds, or group membership. Keep in mind that visibility should not be used as a replacement for proper security settings in process models.

CDT first versus database first

This aspect of solution design with Appian is about how to create and maintain the application tables in the database. There are two opposing approaches:

- Following the approach to create the database first, you would design the complete data model, then write and execute SQL scripts to create the schema, tables, indexes, and constraints. Then, you would create the CDTs, data stores, and records in Appian based on the existing tables. Any change to the data model requires an update to the SQL scripts, CDTs, data stores, and records.

- The other way is to first design the CDTs in Appian and create a data store. Any change to a CDT will update the database automatically, while synchronized records need a manual update. In case of special database requirements, such as stored procedures, views, triggers, or indexing, additional SQL scripts are required to be executed after the initial deployment of the application.

In my experience, the latter approach is a huge benefit when working in a low-code environment such as Appian. Typical applications do not require any additional database configuration, especially not when using the power of low-code data with Appian synchronized records.

In a situation where there are strict guidelines regarding database structures and naming, it may be necessary to build your Appian application on top of an already existing database structure. You can also adjust the database field names by modifying the XSD files downloadable from the **Appian CDT Designer**.

You can find some more details by following these links:

- `https://docs.appian.com/suite/help/latest/Generating_Database_Tables_from_CDTs.html`

- `https://docs.appian.com/suite/help/latest/Mapping_CDTs_to_Pre-defined_Database_Tables.html`

Waiting for external triggers

When designing business processes, we often face the requirement to wait for an external trigger. Think of a contract sent to the client by email. The process now has to wait for the response.

You can design the Appian process model in a way so that it sends the email, persists all necessary data to the database, and then stops. Do not keep an active process instance just waiting for the response. You can create a process model that checks the database for any pending responses. It will then start a process to activate the user and make them decide how to proceed. Once the external trigger arrives, you can check the status of the case and start the appropriate process.

The pattern to persist a process to the database and reactivate it on the incoming trigger or after a defined period is a very successful one and highly recommended.

Process patterns

Patterns for process design are a bit more concrete than solution patterns and describe how to implement common requirements.

Creating process chains

If you think of an end-to-end business process, you might get the idea of implementing it the same way in Appian. So, you create one main process model, which then utilizes multiple sub-processes. This is a great idea when drawing process models for humans, but a bad idea when implementing a process model to be executed in software.

In Appian, this main model would stay active and cannot be updated until it is completed. So, any change in higher-level logic becomes complicated. Instead of this human-oriented pattern, do not implement the main process at all, but create a chain of process phases in which each phase decides about the next phase to be started. This way, there is no long-lived process instance, and updates to the parent logic are much easier.

Keep these individual process models simple and self-contained. If that process needs to set the status of the case to a specific value, it should do that in the first few nodes, instead of relying on the preceding process to do that. Now, each process could be started multiple times if this is necessary.

Using subprocesses

Subprocesses are a good way to isolate and reuse certain parts of the implementation. You should take care to keep the number of passed data fields low. Depending on the concrete use case, it is recommended to pass only the primary key to the subprocess instead of a whole data structure. This loads itself, then the necessary data from the database.

In Appian, there are two ways to start a subprocess: the **subprocess** node and the **Start Process** smart service. While both will start a given process model as a subprocess, there are some substantial differences worth knowing:

- The **subprocess** node can start a specific process either synchronously or asynchronously, passing data using a simple visual configuration. When configured synchronously, it waits for the subprocess to complete, and can pick up data from that completed subprocess.

- The **Start Process** smart service starts processes asynchronously only and lacks the visual configuration. But, it has the capability to define the to-be-started process at runtime by executing business logic implemented in *expression rules* or *decisions*.

There is one more aspect to consider. If you need to start larger volumes of processes, the Start Process smart service will distribute the started instances on all available Appian execution engines. The subprocess node will start all processes on the same engine as the parent process, which could lead to overloading that engine.

Multiple Node Instances

All nodes in Appian have the capability of starting multiple instances, called **Multiple Node Instances** (**MNI**). The following screenshot shows the **Other** tab, which includes the MNI configuration:

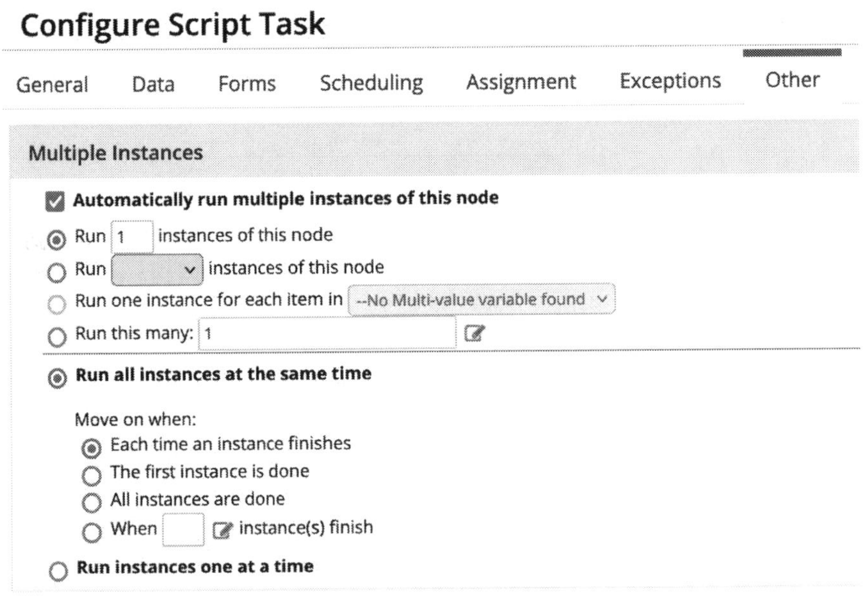

Figure 16.1 – Configuring MNI

You can use MNI in situations that cannot be solved using looping functions in expression rules; for example, uploading multiple records to a web service or deleting a list of temporary documents.

Do not try to process larger data sets using MNI. This will take a long time to process and risks the system's stability.

Building loops in processes

Building loops in Appian process models should generally be avoided. However, for cases that cannot be implemented in expression rules, and for which a single process node is not sufficient, I would like to give you some advice to avoid problems.

All nodes in the loop must be configured to delete previously completed instances. This way, node instances do not accumulate, and the memory consumption of the process stays low. See the following screenshot for how to configure this:

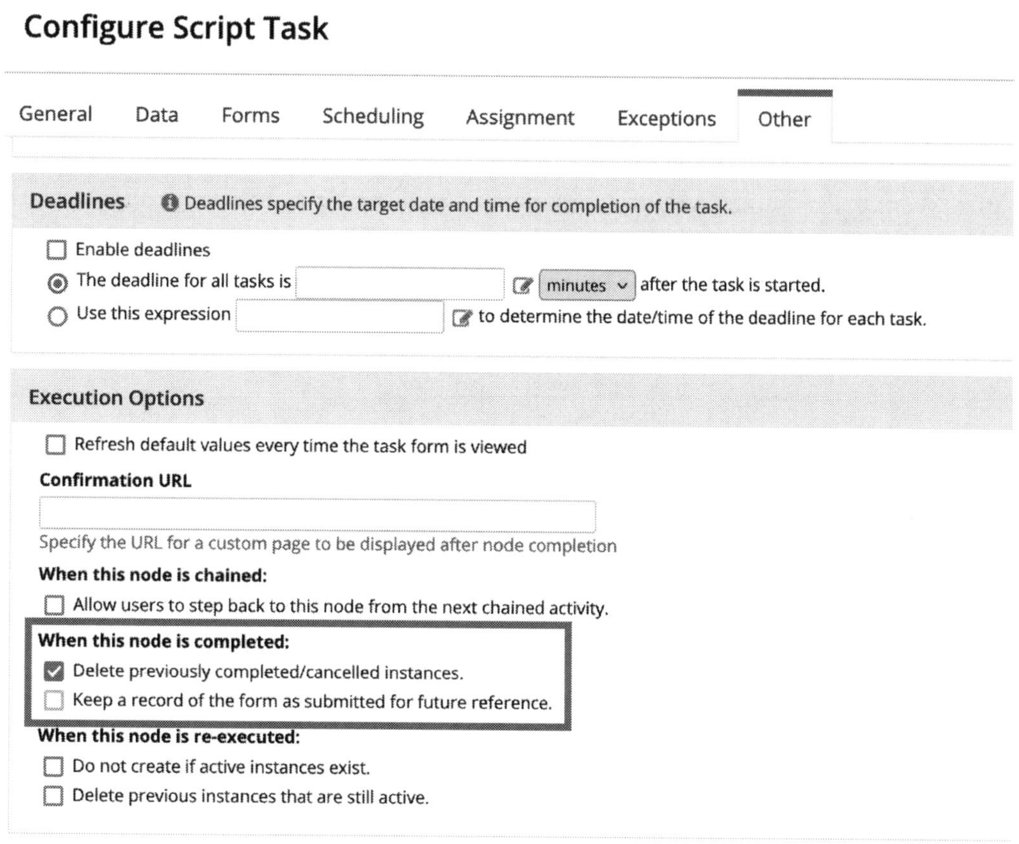

Figure 16.2 – Cleaning up completed node instances

Try to avoid storing larger amounts of text in process variables. This is a general rule, but even more important is a process loop scenario with a higher number of loop iterations. Appian stores all changes to process variables, which can lead to excessive memory consumption in a loop.

As I'm repeating myself here, it is best to avoid loops in processes and, if you can't help it, follow the guidelines mentioned in this section.

Interface patterns

When talking about interface patterns in Appian, I first have to mention the large collection of patterns provided by Appian in the official documentation, and I also want to recommend the Appian UX Design Guide again. Find these links here:

- `https://docs.appian.com/suite/help/latest/SAIL_Recipes.html`
- `https://docs.appian.com/suite/help/latest/ux_getting_started.html`

There are some general design principles that you should know about.

Building wizards

An interface that guides the user through multiple steps is called a **wizard**. With the dynamic features of Appian interfaces, this is easy to implement.

The most important, and obvious, aspect, is to manage the state of the interface:

1. Create a local variable and display individual components based on its value, as shown in the following example:

```
a!localVariables(
  local!step: 1,
  {
    choose(
      local!step,
      rule!IVP_WizardStep1(case: ri!case),
      rule!IVP_WizardStep2(case: ri!case),
      rule!IVP_WizardStep3(case: ri!case),
      rule!IVP_WizardStep4(case: ri!case),
    ),
```

```
a!buttonArrayLayout(
  buttons: {
    a!buttonWidget(
      label: "Next",
      value: local!step + 1,
      saveInto: local!step
    )
  }
)
}
)
```

2. Add common parts of the interface to the main interface to avoid repetitions.

3. Make sure to create rule inputs or local variables for all the data you need.

4. Then, pass the data to the individual components.

Data in Appian interfaces can only be passed top-down, as we discussed in *Chapter 11, Creating User Interfaces in Appian*.

Tabbed interfaces

Tabbed interfaces are very similar to wizard-style interfaces. One difference is that the user can freely select which section to display.

Now, in a scenario in which the user has access to a larger dataset that takes a bit longer to load, you can use tabs to only load a small amount of data on the first screen. Then, as the user switches to other tabs, you can load the data for that tab on demand. This can provide a better user experience as the loading time decreases.

To achieve this, create local variables for all the data to be loaded, but leave them empty. In the save into parameter of the components used to switch tabs, add the code to load the data for that selected tab.

Designing for reusability

In *Chapter 11, Creating User Interfaces in Appian*, we discussed some aspects of creating reusable components. In my experience, it is difficult to design a reusable component in a way that fits into Appian and is robust, beneficial, maintainable, and customizable.

I think the most important requirement for a reusable interface component is that it should not make any assumptions about the environment in which it is used. For example, a component meant to show the username and icon in a card layout should consist of that card layout only, and not add any other layout, divider, or decoration.

Try to keep it simple. It is better to have two components implementing a related but not equal behavior than have one jack-of-all-trades. Both ways have their tradeoffs, but multiple simple components stay simple, while one large complex one will become even more complex over time.

Some good examples of reusable components are the following:

- **Email text field**: Includes an email address validation and a read-only mode showing a clickable email link
- **IBAN field**: Includes the IBAN validation
- **Dropdown field**: Avoids some issues with the default one

The last one, the **Dropdown field**, is a good example of how to add value to the default components provided by Appian. The default component has no nice read-only mode, and it creates an error message in case the data types of the `value` and `ChoiceValues` parameters do not match. I implemented a drop-in replacement for the default component to solve these problems.

Find the code by following this link: `https://github.com/PacktPublishing/Low-Code-Application-Development-with-Appian/blob/main/chapter%2016/IVP_C_DropDownField.txt`.

There is one large reusable interface component I would like to share with you. It is made to display a process report automatically in an Appian interface. It has over 1,500 lines of code and includes some great default functionality, lots of customization options, and implementation help.

You can find the code on GitHub by following this link: `https://github.com/PacktPublishing/Low-Code-Application-Development-with-Appian/blob/main/chapter%2016/IVP_C_DisplayProcessReport.txt`.

Expression rule patterns

You will find the most important information about Appian expression rules in the official Appian documentation, by following these links:

- `https://docs.appian.com/suite/help/latest/Expression_Rules.html`

- `https://docs.appian.com/suite/help/latest/Expressions.html`

- `https://docs.appian.com/suite/help/latest/Appian_Functions.html`

- `https://docs.appian.com/suite/help/latest/Function_Recipes.html`

- `https://docs.appian.com/suite/help/latest/Query_Recipes.html`

Beyond that, there are a few valuable tools from my toolbox that I want to share with you here. These are as follows:

- **Managing collections of constants**

- **Universal null check**

- **Nested indexing**

- **Validating IBANs**

- **Flexible looping predicate**

Managing collections of constants

IVP_Case CDT in our invoice validation application has the **status** field in which we track the current status of processing. That status is updated to reflect a step or a phase in the business process, relevant for reporting or progress display purposes.

My recommendation is to implement this in the following way:

1. Make the **status** field in your CDT a text.

2. Create a constant for each relevant status value:

    A. **Name** and **Values** in upper case and use underscores instead of spaces.

    B. **Status** is not about the start or the end of a step or phase, but about the step or phase itself. When you send a contract to your client and wait for the signature, the status would be `WAITING_FOR_SIGNATURE` instead of `CONTRACT_SENT`.

   C. Create a naming hierarchy to make clear the constants belong together.

   D. Try to make the values in a way a user would understand them, if possible.

   E. Make the last part of the constant name similar to the actual value.

Find some examples here:

```
IVP_CASE_STATUS_CLARIFICATION: CLARIFICATION
IVP_CASE_STATUS_WAITING_FOR_POSTING: WAITING_FOR_POSTING
IVP_INVOICE_STATUS_POSTING_FINAL_APPROVAL: POSTING_FINAL_
APPROVAL
```

3. Create an expression rule that returns a list of all status values belonging together. Make sure to update this expression whenever you add or delete a constant. The code would look like this:

```
{
    cons!IVP_CASE_STATUS_CLARIFICATION,
    cons!IVP_CASE_STATUS_WAITING_FOR_POSTING,
}
```

Now, you have all your values as individual constants and as a list. In case you modify a constant, the expression rule reflects that automatically. You will use it in dropdown fields, for example.

To display these values to the user, I suggest creating a short expression rule with a single **value** rule input of the Text type. Here is the code snippet:

```
if(
  isnull(ri!value),
  ri!value,
  proper(substitute(ri!value, "_", " ")),
)
```

The NULL check makes it handle NULL values gracefully. Then, it takes the passed value, replaces any underscores with spaces, and then proper() turns each first character into uppercase, followed by lowercase for the rest of the characters. So, WAITING_FOR_POSTING becomes Waiting For Posting. Use this expression rule in grids or rich text display fields to display attractively formatted text.

Universal null check

It often happens that you have to check whether a variable actually has a value. The definition of *has no value* can also be a bit more complex than just checking for NULL. What about a list containing only NULL values? Or, a string filled with spaces? Even more curious is a list containing lists, where each list contains only a single null value.

Appian recently introduced a new function called `a!isNullOrEmpty()`, which covers a few more cases than just `isnull()`, but there still is room for improvement. For several years, I have developed and used the `IVP_IsVoid` expression rule in customer projects to answer one question: *Does this variable have a value?* You can find the code by following this link: `https://github.com/PacktPublishing/Low-Code-Application-Development-with-Appian/blob/main/chapter%2016/IVP_IsVoid.txt`.

This expression rule covers the following cases where there is no value:

- NULL

- Lists of NULL

- Lists of lists of NULL

- Lists of the variant, with all items NULL or empty

- Lists of lists of the variant, with all items NULL or empty

- An empty string, not counting any excessive space characters

- A DataSubset with zero items in the data attribute

- Map returned from `a!queryRecordType()` with zero items in the data attribute

The most important case for using this expression rule is that there are some specific edge cases in how Appian stores data in variables. There are situations in which there appears to be a simple list of values. Appian displays it like this in the Expression Editor, but under the hood, it is a list of lists. Now, the answer to *Is there a value?* can become a challenge that you will have a hard time dealing with as a beginner Appian designer.

This is where `IVP_IsVoid` has you covered, and as it first tries to detect a value using `a!isNullOrEmpty()`, there is also no sacrifice in terms of performance.

Nested indexing

When implementing web APIs in particular, you typically have to deal with deeply nested data structures. A best practice is to use the `index()` function instead of the dot notation, as `index()` gracefully handles missing fields. For fields in a nested structure, you would have to nest `index()`, which results in hard-to-read code:

```
index(
  index(
    index(
      index(
        local!response,
        "result",
        null
      ),
      "body",
      null
    ),
    "items",
    null
  )
)
```

Implement an expression rule; I usually call it `IVPDeepIndex` with the following three rule inputs:

- `data` (any)
- `path` (any)
- `default` (any)

Then, type the following code snippet (or copy the code from `https://github.com/PacktPublishing/Low-Code-Application-Development-with-Appian/blob/main/chapter%2016/IVP_DeepIndex.txt`):

```
if(
  isnull(ri!path),
  ri!data,
  reduce(
    index(_,_,ri!default),
    ri!data,
```

```
if(
    runtimetypeof(ri!path) = 'type!{http://www.appian.com/ae/
      types/2009}Text',
    a!forEach(
      items: split(ri!path, "."),
      expression: if(
        exact(tostring(tointeger(fv!item)), fv!item),
        tointeger(fv!item),
        fv!item
      )
    ),
    ri!path
  )
)
)
```

Then, you can write the preceding example in a way that is much easier to read and understand:

```
rule!IVP_DeepIndex(
  data: local!response,
  path: "result.body.items",
  default: null
)
```

This expression rule can also handle numbers in the path. So, if you want the third item in the list of items, then the value of the field named firstName, you write it like this:

```
rule!IVP_DeepIndex(
  data: local!response,
  path: "result.body.items.3.firstName",
  default: null
)
```

Validating IBANs

Validating an **International Bank Account Number** (**IBAN**) is not a trivial task. You can find the details by following this link: `https://en.wikipedia.org/wiki/International_Bank_Account_Number#Validating_the_IBAN`. I will not describe the algorithm here, but I will show you how the implementation works. As Appian does not support 30-digit numbers, we have to implement the piece-wise algorithm as described in the preceding article.

We need two expression rules, as we use the `reduce()` function to realize the piece-wise checksum calculation.

First, create the `IVP_IsIbanValidHelper` helper expression rule with the following rule inputs:

- map (Any): This is a map holding the data used during the calculations.
- count (Integer): The count of the iteration.

Enter the following code snippet:

```
if(
  a!isNullOrEmpty(ri!map.bban),
  ri!map,
  a!map(
    checksum: mod(tostring(ri!map.checksum) & left(ri!map.bban,
      ri!map.num), 97),
    num: 7,
    bban: mid(ri!map.bban, ri!map.num + 1, 100),
  )
)
```

As described in the algorithm, this concatenates the checksum and the next few digits and calculates the modulo of 97. This becomes the new checksum value passed to the next iteration. The bban holds the remaining digits, shortened by the number of digits used in the current iteration.

Next, create the second expression rule, `IVP_IsIbanValid`, with the following rule input: iban (Text)

Then, enter the following code snippet:

```
a!localVariables(
  local!iban: upper(stripwith(ri!iban, " ")),
  local!bban: mid(local!iban, 5, 100) & left(local!iban, 4),
  local!newbban: joinarray(
    a!forEach(
      items: enumerate(len(local!bban)),
      expression: lookup(
        {"0", "1", "2", "3", "4", "5", "6", "7", "8", "9",
          "A", "B", "C", "D", "E", "F", "G", "H", "I", "J", "K",
          "L", "M", "N", "O", "P", "Q", "R", "S", "T", "U", "V",
          "W", "X", "Y", "Z"},
        local!bban[fv!index]
      ) - 1
    )
  ),
  local!result: reduce(
    rule!IVP_IsIbanValidHelper(
      map:_,
      dummy:_
    ),
    a!map(
      checksum: 0,
      num: 9,
      bban: local!newbban
    ),
    enumerate(ceiling(len(local!newbban) / 7))
  ),
  tointeger(local!result.checksum) = 1
)
```

Here, we clean the incoming string and make it uppercase. Next, we move the country code plus the checksum to the end, and replace the individual characters *0-9* and *A-Z* with the numbers 0 to 36. Finally, we iterate piece-wise on these digits using `reduce()`. If the calculated checksum equals `1`, the IBAN is valid.

Flexible looping predicate

In *Chapter 14, Expressing Logic with Appian,* we discussed how to work with lists using the Appian looping functions. For each non-trivial task, you need to create a separate auxiliary expression to implement the logic. You will find an expression rule that allows you to easily implement even complex logic when used together with the Appian looping functions at the following link: `https://github.com/PacktPublishing/Low-Code-Application-Development-with-Appian/blob/main/chapter%2016/IVP_LoopingPredicate.txt`.

Be aware that this expression rule depends on the `IVP_DeepIndex` expression rule described previously. If you want to use `IVP_LoopingPredicate`, create `IVP_DeepIndex` first.

The idea here is to define a list of filters using `a!queryFilter()` to express one or more conditions. These filters work in the same way as when used with `a!queryEntity()` or `a!queryRecordType()`, and they can be combined by the AND or OR operator.

Let's have a look at a simple example. The following snippet creates 100 random numbers between 0 and 1. Then, we use the `filter` function to keep only the values above 0.5. The underscore assigned to the `item` parameter indicates each individual item at execution time. The dot pass to the `field` parameter tells the expression rule that this is just a list of values, and not a list of data structures:

```
filter(
  rule!IVP_LoopingPredicate(
    item:_,
    filters: a!queryFilter(
      field: ".",
      operator: ">",
      value: .5
    )
  ),
  rand(100)
)
```

The next example explains how to filter specific items from a list by a specific value. This returns only the employees working for the IT department:

```
a!localVariables(
  local!data: {
    a!map(
```

```
      id: 1,
      name: "Hans",
      department: "it"
    ),
    a!map(
      id: 2,
      name: "Peter",
      department: "hr"
    ),
  },
  filter(
    rule!SSH_LoopingPredicate(
      item: _,
      filters: a!queryFilter(
        field: "department",
        operator: "=",
        value: "it"
      )
    ),
    local!data
  )
)
```

In the last example, I make the department a nested data structure, and adapt the filter to find items by a substring search:

```
a!localVariables(
  local!data: {
    a!map(
      id: 1,
      name: "Hans",
      department: a!map(
        id: 3,
        name: "hr-tokyo"
      )
    ),
    a!map(
```

```
        id: 2,
      name: "Peter",
      department:  a!map(
        id: 4,
        name: "hr-berlin"
      )
    ),
  },
  filter(
    rule!SSH_LoopingPredicate(
      item:_,
      filters: a!queryFilter(
        field: "department.name",
        operator: "includes",
        value: "berlin"
      )
    ),
    local!data
  )
)
```

Try to understand how `IVP_LoopingPredicate` works, and try it with your own examples. The `filters` parameter is in the plural and takes more than one single filter.

Keep in mind that loading large amounts of data into Appian and trying to filter it using expression rules or process models violates best practices and risks platform stability. Try to make the source system filter the data first, before loading it into Appian.

Additional Appian modules

The Appian platform is an already powerful environment to build business process applications in low code. Furthermore, Appian provides several additional modules; however, these modules have to be licensed separately. Depending on the use case, it can be much cheaper to use them than to purchase separate products and integrate with them, and tightly integrated modules usually speed up development significantly compared to integrating separate products.

Let's have a look at the following modules:

- **Intelligent Document Processing (IDP)**: Classifies documents and extracts data
- **Robotic Process Automation (RPA)**: Automates repetitive manual tasks
- **Process mining**: Identifies and analyzes processes
- **Appian Portals**: Provides an anonymous entrance to business processes

Each of the modules has its own challenges and underlying complexities. In this section, I will give you a brief introduction to each module, example use cases, and usage considerations from my personal experience.

IDP

When there is a business process that incorporates any kind of documents on paper, PDFs, scans, or photos, **IDP** is probably the solution for you.

IDP uses machine learning to automatically classify documents and extract structured data. This includes automatic reconciliation in case of low confidence in the extracted data. Business logic based on document class and extracted data then initiates dedicated Appian processes for further processing.

If you just want to read a barcode or QR code, this is already available with the **Barcode** component in the Appian mobile app. In that app, you can also capture a handwritten signature directly using the file upload component.

When considering using IDP, be aware that automatic classification and extraction will only work for homogeneous and well-structured documents. And, because of its machine learning nature, you will need to invest in a large set of training documents to get a good success rate.

Find out more about Appian IDP by following this link: `https://docs.appian.com/suite/help/21.4/idp-1.7/idp-landing-page.html`.

RPA

RPA helps you to automate simple repetitive tasks conducted by humans. The key here is the words *simple* and *repetitive*. Consider RPA as a bridging technology to get access to data sources or systems not providing any modern technical interfaces.

A robot remotely controls a computer screen to interact with installed software, applications, or websites. This is a complex technical process and not 100% reliable. For example, you need to look up data on a government website or post a new insurance contract in an old mainframe application.

In my experience, there is a significant risk that a complex bot will have an increased need for maintenance. My recommendation is to implement the complex business process, decision-making, and business logic in Appian process models, and add RPA in case you have to integrate a system lacking modern ways of integration such as web services.

Find out more about Appian RPA by following this link: `https://docs.appian.com/suite/help/21.4/rpa-8.0/appian-rpa.html`.

Process mining

Process mining is a method for analyzing protocol data of existing systems to identify and visualize the business processes running in these systems. The aim is to identify existing discrepancies between the specified processes and the actual ones. In addition, process mining is used to identify the performance and quality of the processes.

The huge benefit of adding process mining to the Appian capabilities is to be able to analyze the actual process performance together with the as-is processes and the tools used. The identified processes can be a good starting point to design the to-be process. Special consideration can then be given to the identified weaknesses when designing the new processes. Because of the integration in Appian, the new process can then be directly compared to the replaced one.

Find out more about Appian process mining by following this link: `https://docs.appian.com/suite/help/22.1/pm-5.0/process-mining.html`.

Appian Portals

The Appian platform is designed to be a secure home for all your business process automation needs; but, many use cases would benefit from anonymous and scalable data acquisition capabilities to get a process started. Think of a local government in need of a website to report damages to municipal infrastructure. Or, the insurance company that wants to offer its customers an insurance quote directly after a short questionnaire.

The important aspects of Appian Portals are automatic scalability by using a modern cloud microservices architecture, and the fact that the website itself is built using the powerful capabilities of Appian low-code.

Find out more about Appian Portals by following this link: `https://docs.appian.com/suite/help/22.1/portals-home.html`.

Summary

In this last chapter, I have shared some solutions and design patterns with you in the hope that they will make your future life as an Appian designer easier. You gained a better understanding of how to design and implement certain use cases and requirements in process models, interfaces, and expression rules.

Furthermore, keep the additional Appian modules in mind. RPA, process mining, IDP, and Appian Portals are a great complement for your enterprise low-code strategy using Appian.

You are now ready to successfully transform complex business processes into low-code process models, data, and user interfaces, and to implement fully-fledged, integrated, enterprise-ready, process-driven, and mobile-enabled applications.

I have accompanied you with this book in the development of your first low-code application with Appian and tried to share my experiences with you.

Now, it's up to you to take the next steps. Thank you for being part of this exciting journey.

Index

A

Activity Class (AC) 220
activity node
  configuring 212
advanced task management 67-69
agile development 70
Angular connectors
  versus direct connectors 178
Appian
  about 90
  application object types 40
  best practices 300
  object dependencies 61, 62
  potential 91
  record 131, 132
  report 134
  screens, designing 131
  task 132, 133
Appian CDT Designer 407
Appian Designer
  about 38
  basic principles, exploring 38, 39
  environment 40
  working 38
Appian expression rules 56-61

Appian IDP
  reference link 424
Appian interface designer 222
Appian interfaces
  about 51
  filtering by 52
  interface preview, in fit mode 54
  interface preview, in phone mode 54
  testing 55
Appian looping functions
  reference link 421
Appian, modules
  about 423
  Appian Portals 424, 425
  IDP 424
  process mining 424, 425
  RPA 424
Appian Portals
  about 424, 425
  reference link 425
Appian process mining
  reference link 425
Appian process models
  checking 48, 49
  nodes 50, 51

Appian Quick app
  case data, defining 11-15
  generating 15, 16
  login 4-9
  naming 10
  permissions, settings 15, 16
  testing 17-21
Appian records
  about 40,156
  creating 157-161
  Improvement record type 40-42
Appian RPA
  reference link 425
Appian UX Design Guide
  reference link 411
application configuration
  managing 347
application data
  adding 105
  audit trail 105
  monitoring 105
  process data 105
  reporting 106
application object
  creating 140-144
application programming
      interface (API) 348
application security
  reference link 143
as-is process 114-116
Assign Invoice
  task and interface 297
audit trails
  recording 405

B

best practices
  debugging 258, 259
  expression mode, versus
      design mode 257
  local variables 258
  performance view 257, 258
  reusable components 258
  rule inputs 258
  user experience (UX) 256
  variable flow 258
Billboard cards 323-330
business architecture 86, 87
business entities 97-99
business process 117
Business Process Management 92
Business Process Modeling Notation
      (BPMN) 49, 110, 111

C

Camel casing 148
cancel behavior 196-199
Case 156
case at risk 106
case grid
  adding, to report 322, 323
case management
  about 117
  principles 117
  theses 117-119
  versus process 404
case node
  configuring 211
case ownership 106
case record
  preparing 307

CDT first
  versus database first 407
CDTs, mapping to pre-defined
      database tables
  reference link 407
Clarify Invalid Invoice
  interface 286-291
collections, of constants
  managing 414, 415
conference attendees
  managing 64, 65
connected systems 385
constant logic expressed
  in text 349
constants
  about 347
  data store entities 348
  documents 349
  groups 348
  process models 349
  string literals 347, 348
  summary 349
copy-on-write (COW) mechanism 405
created field 103
Create Invoice interface
  modifying 208-210
current open cases 106
custom data type (CDT)
  about 144, 356
  creating 145-151
  entity fields, creating 148, 149

D

dashboard
  interaction, adding to 330-335

data
  aggregating 313
  case grid, adding to report 322, 323
  cases over time 313
  current case status 313-315
  donut chart, case status 320, 321
  measuring 308-310
  persisting 185-190
  satus over timeline chart 317-320
  visualizing 316, 317
database first
  versus CDT first 407
database tables, generating from CDTs
  reference link 407
data fields
  adding, to entities 101
data store
  about 151, 152
  creating 152, 154
  database, managing 155, 156
  feature 151
data validation
  about 249
  date validation 249
  implementing 249
  range check 250, 251
decision
  about 342, 343
  input configuration 344, 345
  options 342, 343
  output configuration 345-347
  summary 347
Decision object 342
description field 103
diagrams.net
  reference link 98, 128
direct connectors
  versus Angular connectors 178

documents
    managing, in Quick App 31
draft diagram 98
dynamic interfaces
    creating 251-254
dynamic task assignment
    about 265, 266
    using, decision tables 267-271
    using, process variables 266, 267
dynamic types 355

E

elements, for supporting people in tasks
    information 127
    input 127
    orientation 127
    scope 126
enterprise architecture 86
entity relationship model (ERM)
    about 96
    creating 171
escalations tab 271-278
exceptions tab 271-279
expression mode 222
expression rule patterns
    references 414
expression rules
    about 225, 347
    in Appian 56-61
expressions
    about 349
    data types 355-357
    dictionaries 357-360
    inputs 353-355
    locals 353-355
    maps 357-360
    outputs 353-355

paradigms, programming 349-353
    working, with lists 360, 361
expressions, lists
    evaluating 367
    filtering 366
    iterating 362-366
    reducing 368-371
external IDs 102, 103

F

five-whys method 111
flexible looping predicate 421-423
folder security 144
foreign key (FK) 96

H

historic reporting
    best practices 336
HTTP request 375, 376
HTTP response 377
Hypertext Markup Language (HTML) 374
Hypertext Transfer Protocol Secure
        (HTTPS) 374, 375

I

Improvement dashboard, Appian records
    about 42
    List 42, 43
    performance 48
    Precedents screen 61, 62
    Related Actions 46, 47
    Source & Default Filters 42
    Tempo 42
    User Filters 44
    Views 45, 46

information architecture
  about 86-88
  content 88
  context 89
  users 89
initial verification
  modifying 291-297
integrations
  using 396-398
Intelligent Document
    Processing (IDP) 424
interaction
  adding, to dashboard 330-335
Interface Designer
  about 51, 52
  fields 53
interface patterns
  about 411
  reference link 411
interfaces
  about 51
  creating 222
  data validation 249
  process start forms 236, 237
  record views 222
  requirements 237, 238
  site 247
  User Input Task 242
  validation logic, adding 249
International Bank Account
    Number (IBAN)
  about 368
  reference link 419
  validating 419, 420
invoice validation process
  case 298-300
  completing 286, 287

finalizing, logic 298-300
  initial verification, modifying 291-297
  interface, for Clarify Invalid
    Invoice 287-291
  task and interface, for
    Assign Invoice 297
Ishikawa diagram 112
iteration
  of ERM 99
IT landscape
  discovering 86
IVP Create Case
  setting up 210

J

JavaScript Object Notation (JSON)
  about 376-382
  complex structure 380
  lists 379
  map 380
  URL 378

K

key performance indicators (KPIs) 105
key stakeholders, Tarence Limited 82

L

literals configuration
  managing 347
looping functions 366
loops
  building, in processes 410, 411

M

management needs 127, 128
many-to-many relationship
  about 100
  adding 168-171
measurements
  storing 306
Microsoft Visio 98
modified field 103
monitoring 105
Multiple Node Instances (MNI) 409, 410

N

name field 103
naming convention 171
nested indexing 417, 418
nodes, Appian Process Modeler 50, 51

O

oAuth2 378
object dependencies, in Appian 61, 62
objects 143
object security
  reference link 144
object types, Appian application
  expression rules 40
  interfaces 40
  processes 40
  records 40
one-to-many relation 100
one-to-one relation 100
OpenAPI basics 384
OpenAPI Specification (OAS)
  about 382, 383
  components 384
  paths 384
  reference link 382
  servers 383
Open Systems Interconnection
        (OSI) model
  about 374
  URL 374

P

Pareto principle 108
Pascal casing 146
patterns, Appian Playbook
  reference link 404
people, Tarence Limited
  Appian designer 85
  business analyst 85
  business owner, Christine 83
  IT architect, Beth 85
  IT architect, Igor 84
  key stakeholder, Melanie 84
  product owner, Paul 83
  solution designer 85
periodic data measurement 305, 306
primary key (PK) 96
process
  activity, monitoring 304
  loops, building in 410, 411
  versus case management 404
Process Automation 92
process chains
  creating 408
process data 105
process data flow
  best practices 219-220
process mining 424, 425

process model
  about 345
  assigning, to record 191-195
  cancel behavior 196-199
  creating 174-176, 178
  measuring 310-313
  process start form 179-182
  process variable, adding 178, 179
  testing 183, 184
process modeling habits
  best practices 219
process patterns 408
process reports
  about 279
  creating 280-282
  displaying 282-286
Process Start Form
  adding 179-182
Process Start Forms, interfaces
  about 236
  example 237-241
process variable
  adding 178, 179
product backlog
  creating 71-74
project, motivation
  about 90
  cost reduction 90
  scaling up 90
  team upskill 90

Q

queries 347
Query Editor 60
Quick App
  documents, managing 31
  modifying 33-36

record items, managing 24, 25
reference link 74
reporting 32, 33
tasks, managing 25-30
Quick App use cases
  advanced task management 67-69
  conference attendees, managing 64-66
  simple software development process 70

R

RACI matrix
  used, for managing stakeholders 67
record
  deleting 205-207
  updating 200-204
record actions
  adding 200
record, interfaces
  basic layout 226-228
  details, adding to Facts column 229-232
  details, adding to middle
      column 233-235
  list of actions, creating 235, 236
  view, creating 224, 225
  views 222
  views, configuring 223, 224
record items
  managing, in Quick App 24, 25
record security 405, 406
reduce() function 368
related actions
  adding 200
relations
  adding 99
  many-to-many 100
  one-to-many 100
  one-to-one 100

relationships
    about 162-167
    list, defining 167
    many-to-many relationship,
        adding 168-171
report composition
    best practices 336
reporting 304
report interaction
    best practices 336
requirements management
    about 70
    creating 71
reusable components, examples
    Dropdown field 413
    email text field 413
    IBAN field 413
reusable interface components
    creating 254
    IVP_C_AmountField 255, 256
    IVPCThisHappensNext 254
Robotic Process Automation (RPA) 424

S

Salesforce system 66
screens
    designing, in Appian 131
security
    about 377, 378
    authentication 378
    authorization 378
Service Level Agreements (SLAs) 304
simple software development process 70
single sign-on (SSO) 4
SIPOC 87, 112, 113

site
    about 248
    page, configuring 249
    site object, creating 248
software-driven processes 116
solution patterns
    about 404
    audit trails, recording 405
    CDT first, versus database first 407
    process, versus case management 404
    record security 405, 406
    requirement, to wait for external
        triggers 407, 408
Sparx Systems Enterprise Architect 98
stakeholder groups
    best practices 335
Start Process smart service 409
static types 355
status field 103
statusTransition node
    configuring 213-215
subprocesses
    using 408, 409
subprocess node 409

T

tabbed interfaces 412
task-driven processes 116
tasks
    assigning 216-218, 262, 263
    managing, in Quick App 25-30
    process model security 264, 265
    reassignment 264, 265
    reassignment behavior 263
    re-assignment privileges 264
technology architecture 86-90

text
  constant logic expressed 349
to-be process 119-122

U

Uniform Resource Locator (URL) 375
unique identifier (UID) 96, 102
universal null check 416
User Experience (UX)
  about 124
  discovery 124
User Input Task
  about 242
  components, hiding 247
  components, showing 247
  conditional color 246
  conditional style 246
  example 242-244
  related data, loading 244
  requirements 242
  validation results, storing 245, 246
User Interface (UI) 125

V

visual designer
  logic 342, 343

W

web service
  creating 385-388
  integrating 388-396
web service, best practices
  incoming data, validating 399
  integrations, wrapping 400, 401
  security 401

whiteboard 97
wireframes
  about 129, 130
  benefits 130
wireframing tools 128
wizards
  building 411, 412
Write to Data Store Entity (WDSE)
      smart service 241

`Packt.com`

Subscribe to our online digital library for full access to over 7,000 books and videos, as well as industry leading tools to help you plan your personal development and advance your career. For more information, please visit our website.

Why subscribe?

- Spend less time learning and more time coding with practical eBooks and Videos from over 4,000 industry professionals

- Improve your learning with Skill Plans built especially for you

- Get a free eBook or video every month

- Fully searchable for easy access to vital information

- Copy and paste, print, and bookmark content

Did you know that Packt offers eBook versions of every book published, with PDF and ePub files available? You can upgrade to the eBook version at `packt.com` and as a print book customer, you are entitled to a discount on the eBook copy. Get in touch with us at `customercare@packtpub.com` for more details.

At `www.packt.com`, you can also read a collection of free technical articles, sign up for a range of free newsletters, and receive exclusive discounts and offers on Packt books and eBooks.

Other Books You May Enjoy

If you enjoyed this book, you may be interested in these other books by Packt:

Building Low-Code Applications with Mendix

Bryan Kenneweg, Imran Kasam, Micah McMullen

ISBN: 9781800201422

- Gain a clear understanding of what low-code development is and the factors driving its adoption

- Become familiar with the various features of Mendix for rapid application development

- Discover concrete use cases of Studio Pro

- Build a fully functioning web application that meets your business requirements

- Get to grips with Mendix fundamentals to prepare for the Mendix certification exam

- Understand the key concepts of app development such as data management, APIs, troubleshooting, and debugging

Hands-On Low-Code Application Development with Salesforce

Enrico Murru

ISBN: 9781800209770

- Get to grips with the fundamentals of data modeling to enhance data quality
- Deliver dynamic configuration capabilities using custom settings and metadata types
- Secure your data by implementing the Salesforce security model
- Customize Salesforce applications with Lightning App Builder
- Create impressive pages for your community using Experience Builder
- Use Data Loader to import and export data without writing any code
- Embrace the Salesforce Ohana culture to share knowledge and learn from the global Salesforce community

Microsoft Power Apps Cookbook

Eickhel Mendoza

ISBN: 9781800569553

- Build pixel-perfect solutions with canvas apps

- Design model-driven solutions using various features of Microsoft Dataverse

- Automate business processes such as triggered events, status change notifications, and approval systems with Power Automate

- Implement AI Builder's intelligent capabilities in your solutions

- Improve the UX of business apps to make them more appealing

- Find out how to extend Microsoft Teams using Power Apps

- Extend your business applications' capabilities using Power Apps Component Framework

Packt is searching for authors like you

If you're interested in becoming an author for Packt, please visit `authors.packtpub.com` and apply today. We have worked with thousands of developers and tech professionals, just like you, to help them share their insight with the global tech community. You can make a general application, apply for a specific hot topic that we are recruiting an author for, or submit your own idea.

Share Your Thoughts

Now you've finished *Low-Code Application Development with Appian*, we'd love to hear your thoughts! Scan the QR code below to go straight to the Amazon review page for this book and share your feedback or leave a review on the site that you purchased it from.

`https://packt.link/r/1-800-20562-7`

Your review is important to us and the tech community and will help us make sure we're delivering excellent quality content.

Made in the USA
Middletown, DE
27 April 2023

29538161R00256